COMPUTERS AND INFORMATION SYSTEMS

COMPUTERS AND INFORMATION SYSTEMS

Second Edition

Marvin R. Gore
John W. Stubbe

Mount San Antonio College

McGraw-Hill Book Company

New York St. Louis San Francisco Auckland Bogotá Hamburg Johannesburg London
Madrid Mexico Montreal New Delhi Panama Paris São Paulo
Singapore Sydney Tokyo Toronto

COMPUTERS AND iNFORMATION SYSTEMS

Copyright © 1984 by McGraw-Hill, Inc. All rights reserved. Formerly published under the title of *Computers and Data Processing*, copyright © 1979 by McGraw-Hill, Inc. All rights reserved. Printed in the United States of America. Except as permitted under the United States Copyright Act of 1976, no part of this publication may be reproduced or distributed in any form or by any means, or stored in a data base or retrieval system, without the prior written permission of the publisher.

1 2 3 4 5 6 7 8 9 0 HALHAL 8 9 8 7 6 5 4

ISBN 0-07-023807-3

This book was set in Plantin by Ruttle, Shaw & Wetherill, Inc.
The editors were Eric M. Munson and Jonathan Palace;
the designer was Jo Jones;
the production supervisor was Marietta Breitwieser.
The drawings were done by Fine Line Illustrations, Inc.
The photo editor was Lorinda Morris.
The cover photograph was taken by Michel Tcherevkoff.
Halliday Lithograph Corporation was printer and binder.

Library of Congress Cataloging in Publication Data

Gore, Marvin.
    Computers and information systems.

    Previously published as: Computers and data processing.
    Includes index.
    1. Electronic data processing.   2. Electronic digital
computers. I. Stubbe, John. II. Title.
QA76.G598 1984   001.64   83-19922
ISBN   0-07-023807-3

CONTENTS

Preface   xv

UNIT ONE   **INTRODUCTION TO COMPUTER INFORMATION SYSTEMS**   **2**

CHAPTER 1   **DATA PROCESSING CONCEPTS**   **5**

Preview   5
Key Terms to Watch for and Remember   5
Computer Literacy   6
Data Processing and Data Processing Systems   7
Basic Data Processing Operations   9
Data Storage Hierarchy   10
Today, Tomorrow, and the Day After   12
Summary   15
Answers to Feedback Questions   15
For Review and Discussion   16

CHAPTER 2   **THE INFORMATION SOCIETY**   **17**

Preview   17
Key Terms to Watch for and Remember   17
Computer Data Processing   18
    Principles of Computer Data Processing / Advantages of Computer Data Processing
The Postindustrial Society   23
    The Knowledge Industries / The Computer Generations / Classification of Computers / Measures of Change / Employment Opportunities

Information Resource Management   31

    Merging Technologies / The Management Challenge

Summary   34
Answers to Feedback Questions   35
For Review and Discussion   36

CHAPTER 3   COMPUTER INFORMATION SYSTEMS   37

Preview   37
Key Terms to Watch for and Remember   37
Business System Characteristics   38

    Goals and Objectives / The Business: A System of Systems /
    Product Flow and Information Flow / Information Generators /
    Business Levels and Information Uses

Computer-Based Business Systems   44

    Early Problems / Computer Information System—A Definition

The Life-Cycle Method   47

    The Life-Cycle Phases / The Life-Cycle Flowchart /
    Systems Analysis and the Systems Analyst

Summary   51
Answers to Feedback Questions   51
For Review and Discussion   52

CHAPTER 4   COMPUTER SYSTEMS: AN OVERVIEW   55

Preview   55
Key Terms to Watch for and Remember   55
Computer System Architecture   56

    Types of Computers / Functional Units of Digital Computers /
    Hardware, Software, and Firmware

Storage Units   60

    Primary Storage / Data Storage: Bytes and Words / Storage
    Size, K / Instruction Storage / Secondary Storage /
    Control Storage and Local Storage

Central Processing Unit   66

    Control Unit / Arithmetic Logic Unit

Input and Output Units   70

    Input-Output Environment / I/O Interfaces

Multiple Processors   70
Summary   72
Answers to Feedback Questions   73
For Review and Discussion   75

UNIT TWO   COMPUTER SYSTEMS: ELEMENTS AND APPLICATIONS   76

CHAPTER 5   STORAGE AND PROCESSING   79

Preview   79
Key Terms to Watch for and Remember   79
The Business Data Processing Cycle   79
Storage: Components and Criteria   81
    Solid-State Circuits   /   Cost, Capacity, and Access Time
Primary Storage   83
    Magnetic-Core Storage   /   Semiconductor Memory
Electromechanical Secondary Storage   85
    Magnetic Tape   /   Magnetic Disk   /   Magnetic Drum   /
    Mass Storage   /   Optical-Disk Systems
Electronic Secondary Storage   97
    Magnetic Bubble Memory   /   Charge-Coupled Devices   /
    Electron-Beam-Addressed Memory   /   Advanced Memory Systems
Memory Hierarchies   100
Processing Units   100
Summary   103
Answers to Feedback Questions   104
For Review and Discussion   105

CHAPTER 6   INPUT AND OUTPUT   107

Preview   107
Key Terms to Watch for and Remember   107
Using Input-Output Devices   108
I/O Device Speed   108
Magnetic Media Devices   109
    Magnetic Disk, Diskette, and Tape   /   Magnetic Data Recorders
Printers   111
    Characters Printers   /   Line Printers   /   Page Printers
Keyboard Devices   115
    Visual Display Terminals   /   Teleprinter Terminals   /   Point-of-
    Sale Devices
Scanners   119
    Optical Scanners   /   Magnetic Ink Character Recognition
Other Devices   124
    Card Readers   /   Computer Output Microfilm   /   Digitizers   /
    Plotters   /   Voice Recognition and Response Devices
Summary   127
Answers to Feedback Questions   128
For Review and Discussion   130

CHAPTER 7 **COMMUNICATIONS, DISTRIBUTED DATA PROCESSING, AND THE AUTOMATED OFFICE** **131**

Preview 131

Key Terms to Watch for and Remember 131

Elements of Data Communications 133

Data Transmission / Data Communications Services / Trends in Computer-Communications Processing

Distributed Data Processing 139

Distributed Data Processing: A Concept and a Definition / Data Entry Systems / Stand-Alone Systems / Computer Networks / Management Considerations

The Automated Office 144

Data Processing / Data Communications / Word Processing / Electronic Mail / Voice Store-and-Forward Systems / Problems in the Automated Office

Toward the Electronic Office 149

Office Functions / Careers / Administrative Structure

Summary 151

Answers to Feedback Questions 151

For Review and Discussion 153

CHAPTER 8 **PERSONAL COMPUTERS** **155**

Preview 155

Key Terms to Watch for and Remember 155

Everyone's Computer 156

What Is a Personal Computer? / Anatomy of a Personal Computer

Uses for Personal Computers 163

Home and Hobby / Word Processing / Professional / Educational / Small Business / Engineering and Scientific

Trends in Microcomputer Architecture 168

Microcomputer Generations / Software Evolution

Selecting Your Personal Computer 174

Steps in Selecting a Personal Computer / A Personal Computer Selection Checklist

Summary 179

Answers to Feedback Questions 179

For Review and Discussion 181

UNIT THREE **SYSTEMS ANALYSIS** **182**

CHAPTER 9 **SYSTEM STUDY PHASE** **185**

Preview 185

Key Terms to Watch for and Remember 185

System Selection Process: An Overview 186

Problem Identification 186

Problem Statement / Information Service Request

Initial Investigation 190

Data Flow Diagrams / Personal Interviews / Modified
Information Service Request

Performance Definition 193

General Constraints / Specific Objectives / Output
Descriptions

Feasibility Analysis 196

Step 1: Form the Systems Team / Step 2: Describe System Data
Flows / Step 3: Select Candidate Systems / Step 4: Evaluate
Candidate Systems

System Recommendation 204

Project Plan and Cost Schedule 205

Summary 208

Answers to Feedback Questions 209

For Review and Discussion 210

CHAPTER 10   SYSTEM DESIGN AND DEVELOPMENT PHASES   211

Preview 211

Key Terms to Watch for and Remember 211

System Design 211

General System Design / Input Design / Output Design /
File Design / Data Base Management Systems (DBMS) /
Test Requirements / Design-Phase Documentation /
Design-Phase Review

System Development 223

Development Phase Activities: An Overview / Implementation
Plan / Equipment Acquisition / Computer Program
Preparation / Personnel Training and Preparation for Conversion /
Development-Phase Documentation and Acceptance Review

Summary 225

Answers to Feedback Questions 226

For Review and Discussion 227

CHAPTER 11   SYSTEM OPERATION PHASE   229

Preview 229

Key Terms to Watch for and Remember 229

Converting to the New System 229

Conversion of Procedures, Programs, and Files / Changeover to
the New System

Evaluating the System 232

Managing Change   235

    Change Control Procedures / Baseline Documents

Summary   237

Answers to Feedback Questions   238

For Review and Discussion   239

UNIT FOUR   **COMPUTER PROGRAMMING**   **240**

CHAPTER 12   **PLANNING THE COMPUTER PROGRAM**   **243**

Preview   243

Key Terms to Watch for and Remember   243

The Computer Program   244

    The Controlling Function / Computer Instructions /
    Programming a Human

The Purposes of Program Planning   244

    Structuring Program Logic / Documenting the Completed
    Program

Flowcharts   245

    Flowcharting Standards / The IBM Template / The Basic
    Process Loop / Process Loops with Calculations / The Use of
    Connectors / Loops with Multiple Exits / End-Time
    Calculations / Titles and Column Headings

Pseudocode   257

    Why Not Flowchart? / Program Design Language (PDL) /
    Basic Pseudocode Structures

Summary   262

Answers to Feedback Questions   263

For Review and Discussion   264

CHAPTER 13   **PROGRAMMING LANGUAGES**   **265**

Preview   265

Key Terms to Watch for and Remember   265

Writing Program Instructions   265

The Development of Programming Languages   266

    Machine Code / Symbolic Code / Problem-Oriented
    Languages

Common Problem-Oriented Languages   270

    COBOL / FORTRAN IV / PL/I / RPG II / BASIC /
    PASCAL

The Conversion of Symbolic Languages   275

Summary   275

Answers to Feedback Questions   276

For Review and Discussion   277

CHAPTER 14   RUNNING THE COMPUTER PROGRAM   **279**

Preview   279
Key Terms to Watch for and Remember   279
Control Programs   280
    Control Program Functions
Language Processors   283
Service Programs   284
    The Linkage Editor   /   The Librarian   /   Utility Programs   /
    The Sort/Merge Program
Summary   286
Answers to Feedback Questions   287
For Review and Discussion   287

CHAPTER 15   TESTING THE COMPUTER PROGRAM   **289**

Preview   289
Key Terms to Watch for and Remember   289
Types of Program Errors   290
    Coding Errors   /   Logic Errors
Summary   297
Answers to Feedback Questions   298
For Review and Discussion   299

UNIT FIVE   PROGRAMMING IN BASIC   **300**

CHAPTER 16   GETTING STARTED IN BASIC   **303**

Preview   303
Key Terms to Watch for and Remember   303
Standard ANSI BASIC   304
    Averaging Two Numbers   /   An Improved Solution   /
    Compound-Interest Problem   /   A Compound-Interest Solution
    for Multiple Problems   /   Calculation Loops
Basic Library Functions   320
Summary   322
Answers to Feedback Questions   322
For Review and Discussion   323

CHAPTER 17   CONTINUING WITH BASIC   **325**

Preview   325
Key Terms to Watch for and Remember   325

Printed Listings and the Disk Operating System (DOS)   326
    Printed Listings / Disk Commands

Structured Programs in BASIC   329
    The GOSUB and RETURN Instructions / The READ and
    DATA Instructions / The CLS or HOME Statement /
    The TAB Function / The IF-THEN-ELSE Instruction /
    A Program To Calculate Average Sales

Formatting Numeric Output   338
    The PRINT USING Instruction / An Improved Solution to
    Calculate Average Sales

The DO-WHILE Construct   341
    The WHILE and WEND Instructions

Printer Output   345
    The LPRINT Instruction / The LPRINT Using Instruction

Interactive Programs   347
    The INPUT Instruction / The Last Record Test / Program
    to Average a Series of Numbers

Summary   350
Answers to Feedback Questions   350
For Review and Discussion   351

UNIT SIX   COMPUTERS AND SOCIETY   352

CHAPTER 18   PEOPLE IN INFORMATION SYSTEMS   355

Preview   355
Key Terms to Watch for and Remember   355
The Location of Information Services   355
Careers in Information Services   357
    Jobs In Corporate Systems / Jobs in Data Processing
    Operations / Salaries in Information Services

Information Services and the User   366
    The User's View of Information Services / Customer Relations

Summary   368
Answers to Feedback Questions   369
For Review and Discussion   370

CHAPTER 19   TOMORROW AND BEYOND   373

Preview   373
Key Terms to Watch for and Remember   373
The Challenge of Change   374

Ten Socioeconomic Trends   374

The Knowledge Industries   375

Computer Information Systems   377
 Computer System Architecture / Software and Firmware /
 Input, Output, and Communications / Computer Information
 System Development

The High-Tech Home   380

Supercomputers   382

Cybernetics: Robots and Artificial Intelligence   383
 Robots / Artificial Intelligence

Summary   388

Answers to Feedback Questions   388

For Review and Discussion   389

Further Reading   390

SUPPLEMENTS **SPECIAL TOPICS**   392

SUPPLEMENT I **COBOL**   395

Preview   395

Key Terms to Watch for and Remember   395

The COBOL Coding Form   396
 Punching Instructions / COBOL Instructions

COBOL Program Structure   398
 Divisions

A COBOL Example Program   400
 The Problem Statement / COBOL Names / The
 Identification Division / The Environment Division / The
 Data Division / The Procedure Division

Summary   423

Answers to Feedback Questions   423

For Review and Discussion   424

SUPPLEMENT II **RPG II**   425

Preview   425

Key Terms to Watch for and Remember   425

RPG Coding Forms   426

The RPG Cycle   427

An RPG Example Program   427
 Control Card Specifications / File Description Specifications /
 Input Specifications / Calculation Specifications / Output-
 Format Specifications / The Output / Arithmetic Calculations

Summary   435
Answers to Feedback Questions   435
For Review and Discussion   436

SUPPLEMENT III   **NUMBER SYSTEMS**   **437**

Preview   437
Key Terms to Watch for and Remember   437
Basics of Number Systems   438
    Decimal Characteristics / Binary Characteristics / Octal
    Characteristics / Hexadecimal Characteristics
Converting from One Number System to Another   440
    Converting to Base 10 / Converting from Base 10
Shortcut Notations   448
    Octal Notation / Hexadecimal Notation
Arithmetic   452
    Addition / Subtraction
Fixed-Length Fields   463
Summary   463
Answers to Feedback Questions   464
For Review and Discussion   464

SUPPLEMENT IV   **CHARACTER CODES**   **465**

Preview   465
Key Terms to Watch for and Remember   465
Hollerith Code   466
Binary-Coded Decimal Interchange Code (BCDIC)   469
Extended Binary-Coded Decimal Interchange Code (EBCDIC)   470
    Numeric EBCDIC Characters
American Standard Code for Information Interchange (ASCCI)   474
American Standard Code for Information Interchange-8 (ASCII-8)   475
Memory Dumps   476
Summary   478
Answers to Feedback Questions   479
For Review and Discussion   479

Glossary   480
Index   493

PREFACE

In the information society, we have systematized the production of knowledge and amplified our brainpower. To use an industrial metaphor, we now mass produce knowledge and this knowledge is the driving force of our economy.

John Naisbitt, *Megatrends,* 1982

By the middle of the 20th century the United States completed a more than 100-year shift from an agricultural to an industrial economy. Today, it is evident that another major shift occurred within the 25 years that followed. This is the change from an industrial, goods-producing society to a postindustrial, predominantly service-oriented society. At present, over 60 percent of the work force in this nation is engaged in creating, processing, storing, communicating, and otherwise working with information. Computers have become commonplace in homes, offices, stores, schools, and factories. For these reasons the postindustrial society is called the *information society.*

Fueled by a continuing revolution in high technology, information has become our dominant commodity, and the requirements of the workplace are changing at an ever-increasing rate. Through telecommunications, work is being distributed to locations remote from central corporate sites, even moving to the home. Jobs in fields unheard of a few years ago, such as robotics, telemarketing, computer graphics, and artificial intelligence, are providing new career opportunities. Two major challenges of the coming decade are for us to learn to adjust to continuing changes in the nature of work and to acquire the knowledge needed to use computers and the information-related technologies in ways that can improve the quality of life and increase the productivity of business and industry. In order to accomplish these tasks, we must become a computer-literate society. Individuals must develop an understanding of computers and an awareness of what they can and cannot do. A major objective of

Computers and Information Systems is to provide the reader with this understanding and awareness.

Computers and Information Systems is a significant update of the well-received text *Computers and Data Processing*. The term "information" in the title focuses upon the useful output of a data processing system. The systems perspective, which is essential to the effective use of computers as an aid to decision making, was an important characteristic of the predecessor textbook, and this perspective is retained in *Computers and Information Systems*. The textbook is designed to correspond to the systems-oriented, computer information systems curriculum requirements of a growing number of college and university schools of business. Although written to meet the needs of business and information systems majors, the textbook also is suitable for any student who wishes to acquire a basic knowledge of computer systems and components, of their applications in our economy, and of their present and potential impact upon society. No prior knowledge of business methods or of computers is required.

Computers and Information Systems is current and pertinent. Examples of relevant content are:

1. An extensive chapter on personal computers, which describes present and emerging families of popular microcomputers and their many applications. A feature of this chapter is a set of useful guidelines for the selection of a personal computer.

2. Two chapters designed to provide a comprehensive introduction to the BASIC programming language. These chapters allow many opportunities for students to perform meaningful laboratory exercises using popular microcomputers.

3. An integrated coverage of the merging technologies of data processing, communications, and the automated office. Important topics fully described are word processing, distributed data processing, and information resource mangement.

4. An in-depth introduction to the methods of systems analysis, a skill needed not only by programmers and analysts but also by all business majors and other potential users of computer-related business systems. A chapter on computer information systems identifies their principal characteristics and introduces the concept of the system development life cycle. Subsequently, an entire unit reinforces the systems orientation of the text by describing, in sequence, the computer-related information system life-cycle phases: study, design, development, and operation.

5. Four chapters that provide the student with an understandable overview of computer systems; explain the functions performed by their principal elements; and present up-to-date descriptions of the devices used for data input, storage, processing, communications, and output.

6. A unit that introduces students to computer programming. This unit includes chapters that explain computer program planning, flowcharting, structured programming, pseudocode, common programming languages, and running and testing computer programs. These chapters not only present the principles and practices of computer programming but also provide many opportunities for hands-on experiences and laboratory exercises.

7. A unit on computers and society that describes careers in information systems and provides a basis for stimulating discussions of "tomorrow and beyond" topics, such as smart machines, the knowledge industries, the high-tech home, supercomputers, robots, and artificial intelligence.

8. In-text supplements that can easily be integrated into the course to provide additional levels of learning. The supplements are: COBOL, RPG II, number systems, and character codes.

Computers and Information Systems is organized into seven units. As shown in the figure below, there are six units of text and a unit of in-text supplements. The sequence in which major topics are presented parallels the sequence of activities, called the system development life cycle, followed by organizations that have successfully developed computer-related business information systems to solve problems and to assist managers in decision making. Unit One is an overview chapter designed to provide students with important background knowledge about data processing concepts, the information society, computer systems and elements, and computer information systems. Unit Two has two practical purposes. The first of these is to familiarize students with the physical characteristics of the major elements of computer systems. The second is to acquaint students with important, real-world applications of computers. Unit Three presents a comprehensive introduction to systems analysis, including the

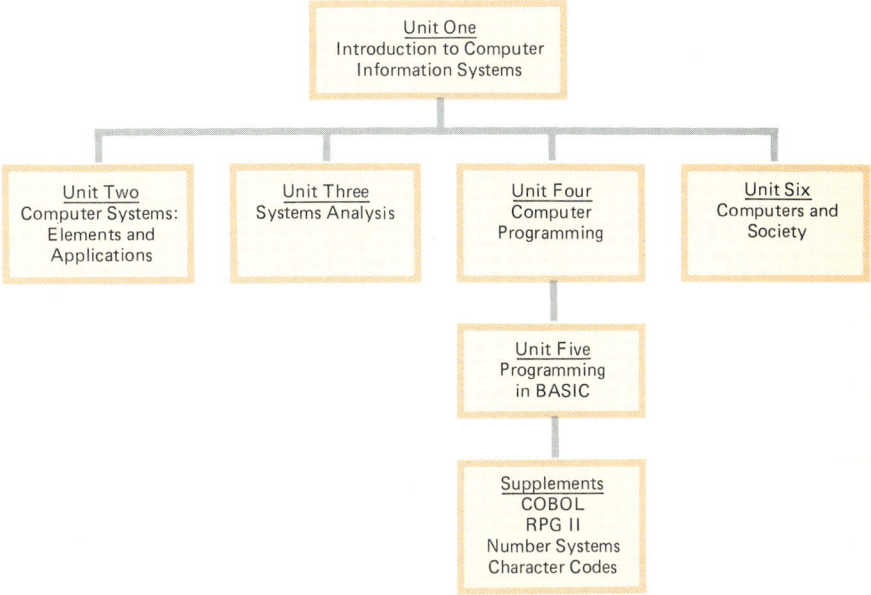

major activities associated with each of the life-cycle phases. Unit Four is designed to familiarize students with important aspects of computer programming. The topics covered range from planning the program to testing it. Unit Five provides those instructors who wish to do so with an opportunity to follow Unit Four with a comprehensive introduction to the BASIC programming languages. Unit Six contains informative discussions of topics related to careers in information systems and to the socioeconomic impact of computers, now and in the future.

The in-text supplements that comprise the seventh unit are complete chapters, all of which are programming-related. However, the organization of the text is such that an instructor has complete flexibility in determining when and to what depth to present the material in these chapters. Indeed, instructional flexibility is an important feature of *Computers and Information Systems*. As the figure on the preceding page shows, Unit Two, Three, Four, or Six could follow Unit One, with the sequence of presentation determined by the emphasis desired by an instructor.

Computers and Information Systems is written to encourage hands-on assignments from the outset of a course and to provide extensive learning reinforcement. Numerous learning aids have been incorporated into the format of the text to assist students in understanding major concepts. Each chapter opens with a capsule preview and a list of key terms to watch for and remember. Each concludes with a concise summary. Major sections of each chapter are followed by feedback quesitons that permit students to test their comprehension as they proceed through the text. Answers to the feedback questions appear at the end of each chapter, where there also are additional questions for review and discussion.

The textbook is one of five components of a complete learning package. The other four are the *Student Study Guide*, the *Instructor's Manual*, the *Test Bank*, and the *Learning Activity Diskette*.

The *Student Study Guide* is designed to assist the student by providing:

1. Study hints, which are suggestions to help the student to master the textbook chapter.

2. Chapter outlines that summarize the main points of each chapter.

3. Vocabulary drills that familiarize the student with the important terms and concepts introduced in each chapter.

4. Test-yourself questions that help the student to prepare for quizzes and examinations. The answers to these questions are contained in the *Student Study Guide*.

5. Additional practice exercises designed to provide students with an opportunity to reinforce their knowledge.

The *Instructor's Manual* identifies unit and chapter goals. For each chapter it includes:

1. Measurable student performance objectives.

2. Key points, indexed to text page and text figure numbers.

3. Transparency masters for all important figures.

4. Answers to the review and discussion questions in the textbook and to the additional practice exercises in the *Student Study Guide*.

5. A chapter quiz and quiz answers.

6. A comprehensive examination for each unit.

The *Test Bank* contains a large selection of matching, true/false, and multiple choice questions for each chapter and the in-text supplements. The diskette is designed to provide instructors with flexibility in selecting questions and preparing examinations.

The *Learning Activity Diskette* is designed to provide demonstrations and "hands on" activities that use the graphics and display capabilities of popular microcomputers to augment in-text explanations of key topics and concepts.

ACKNOWLEDGMENTS   We would like to express our thanks for the many useful comments and suggestions provided by colleagues who reviewed this text during the course of its development, especially to: Jack D. Becker, University of Missouri, St. Louis; E. Allen Eckhard, San Jose State College; Alice Griswold, University of Dubuque; Richard W. Manthei, Joliet Junior College; G. Gary Olson, Jefferson College; and Judith D. Wilson, University of Cincinnati.

Marvin R. Gore

John W. Stubbe

COMPUTERS AND INFORMATION SYSTEMS

UNIT
ONE

INTRODUCTION TO COMPUTER INFORMATION SYSTEMS

The goals of this book are to help you learn about computers and computer-related information systems, apply this knowledge to the world of business, and increase your general awareness of the impact of computers upon individuals and upon the society in which we live. The first unit of this text consists of four introductory chapters. They are designed to provide you with the background knowledge required for the study of computers, data processing, and computer information systems. Chapter 1 of this unit will increase your awareness of the importance of computer literacy, provide you with an understanding of some essential data processing concepts, and familiarize you with the basic data processing operations—whether or not a computer is involved. In Chapter 2, you will learn about computer data processing systems; the emergence of the postindustrial, or information, society; and the importance of information resource management. Chapter 3 will identify the system characteristics of a business, define a computer information system, and introduce you to the concept of the system development life cycle. Chapter 4 will provide you with an overview of the architecture of computer systems and with an understanding of the tasks performed by the major elements of these systems.

CHAPTER 1

DATA PROCESSING CONCEPTS

PREVIEW Informed citizens of our information-dependent society should be computer-literate, which means that they should be able to use computers as everyday problem-solving tools and should be aware of the potential of computers to affect the quality of life. The goal of this chapter is to show you the impact of computers upon our daily lives and to demonstrate the need for computer literacy. It will provide you with a foundation of concepts and vocabulary upon which to build your understanding of data processing systems, whether the data are processed by computers or humans. Also, it will explain the five basic data processing operations and will acquaint you with important terms related to the way data are stored.

In this chapter you will learn:

1. The meaning of and need for computer literacy
2. The definitions of data, data processing, and data processing system
3. The descriptions of the five basic data processing operations
4. The relationship between data elements, records, and files

KEY TERMS TO WATCH FOR AND REMEMBER

computer literacy	transaction
data	record
data processing	file
data processing system	character
inputting	data element
storing	program
outputting	terminal
controlling	word processing system
data base	hierarchy

COMPUTER LITERACY
There was a time when only a privileged few had an opportunity to learn the basics, called the three R's, or reading, writing, and arithmetic. In the United States and in other fortunate countries, this opportunity has long been considered a right of their citizens. Now, as we are rapidly becoming an information-dependent society, it is appropriate to restate this right as the right to learn reading, writing, and *computing*. There is little doubt that computers and their many applications are among the most significant technical developments of the century, bringing with them both economic and social changes. "Computing" is a concept that embraces not only the old third R, arithmetic, but also a new dimension, computer literacy. **Computer literacy** means being able to use a computer as an everyday problem-solving tool and being aware of the potential of computers to affect the quality of life.

In an information society, a person who is computer-literate need not be an expert on the design of computers or even know a great deal about how to prepare **programs,** which are the instructions that direct the operations of computers and enable them to do the remarkable things that they do. A computer-literate citizen is one who, through education and experience, has acquired a general understanding of how computers work and what they can do. An individual who is computer-literate is comfortable in the presence of computers, whether they are encountered in the home, the office, or the store. The computer-literate individual will be as comfortable with a computer as most of us are with an automobile, or, perhaps in the case of small, personal computers, as comfortable as many of us are with bicycles, which we learned to ride after a few experimental tries. All of us are already on the way to becoming computer-literate. Just think about some of your everyday experiences that involve computers busy performing routine but important tasks with great efficiency. If you receive a subscription magazine in the mail, it is probably addressed to you by a computer. If you buy something with a bank credit card or pay a bill by check, computers help process the information about your account number and the amount of money involved in order to complete the transaction. Your account is reduced while the account of the person or business you paid is increased. When you check out at the counter of your grocery store, a computer not only assists the checkout clerk but also helps the store manager to keep track of the produce and groceries that have to be reordered. Perhaps an extension of a computer, called a **terminal,** actually spoke to you, calling out the prices of the items you purchased.

If you happened to read this morning that over 100 million shares of stock changed hands on the New York Stock Exchange yesterday, you know that only computers could keep track of the transaction of tens of thousands of clients of scores of brokerage firms. When you visit your doctor, your schedules and bills for routine and special services, such as laboratory tests, are prepared by computer. Perhaps you also observe that your physician can call up your record from a terminal located nearby and that the vital signs of many patients are being monitored by computers. Near the Christmas season, you notice that yesteryears' ads for a simple computer version of Ping-Pong have long since

THE WONDERS OF THE MAGIC WAND

A magic wand helps preschool children learn to read. Developed by Texas Instruments, the Magic Wand Speaking Reader uses infrared light to read bar stripes printed below lines of normal print in some newly published books.

The bar code is similar to that used on grocery products. In this instance, the bar stripes provide coded vocal instructions, which are translated into human speech sounds by a plastic pen-shaped hand-held wand and a microcomputer. The sounds

are relayed by the wand to the microcomputer, which transforms the information into natural-sounding speech. The human-voice simulation is produced by the electronic circuits on a single chip of silicon. This chip, on which sounds are stored, is called a speech synthesizer chip, and it is multilingual, of course.

As a combination of two technologies, bar-code scanning and speech synthesis, the Magic Wand Speaking Reader will have an impact upon the electronic publishing business. Publishers receiving a special license from Texas Instruments may add a TI-manufactured bar-code stripe to be read by the Magic Wand without having to change their printing techniques or equipment. What's next? The Magic Wand is the first of many learning-aid products. The technique can be used to teach other prereading skills, such as matching, alphabetizing, and solving problems of logic. It will also help youngsters to use their parents' home computer systems.

(Courtesy Texas Instruments, Inc.)

been replaced by glowing descriptions of space-age computerized contests and a bewildering variety of inexpensive home computers.

As a matter of fact, after you registered for this course, a computer helped to sort the information about who was enrolled in order to create this class. Many actions that you have taken or observed fit into a picture similar to these examples, but what do all of these events have in common? Each relates to some aspect of a data processing system.

DATA PROCESSING AND DATA PROCESSING SYSTEMS

In each case facts were processed by a computer to become useful information. In essence, this is the definition of data processing. **Data** are a collection of facts—unorganized but able to be organized into useful information. **Processing** is a series of actions or operations that convert inputs into outputs. When we speak of data processing, the input is data, and the output is useful information. Hence, we can define **data processing** as a series of actions or operations that converts data into useful information. We use the term **data processing system** to include the resources that are used to accomplish the processing of data. As shown in Figure 1-1, which depicts input data being processed to become useful output information, there are four types of resources: people, materials, facilities, and equipment. People provide input to computers, operate them, and use their output. Materials, such as boxes of paper and printer ribbons, are consumed in great quantity. Facilities are required to house the computer equipment, people, and materials.

Throughout this book, we will be focusing on computers and the ways that they can be used to process data. The need for converting facts into useful information is not a phenomenon of modern life. Throughout history, and even prehistory, people have found it necessary to sort data into forms that were easier to understand. For example, the ancient Egyptians recorded the ebb and flow of the Nile River and used this information to predict yearly crop yields. Today, computers convert data about land and water into recommendations to farmers on crop planting. Mechanical aids to computation were developed and improved upon in Europe, Asia, and America throughout the seventeenth, eighteenth, and nineteenth centuries. Modern computers are marvels of an electronics technology that continues to produce smaller, cheaper, and more powerful components.

FIGURE 1-1

A data processing system uses resources such as people, materials, facilities, and equipment to process data into useful information.

Input: Data   Processing: People, Materials, Facilities, Equipment   Output: Useful information

FEEDBACK
1-1 What is computer literacy?
1-2 What is a program?
1-3 What are data? What is useful information?
1-4 Define and distinguish between data processing and a data processing system.

BASIC DATA PROCESSING OPERATIONS

Five basic operations are characteristic of all data processing systems: inputting, storing, processing, outputting, and controlling. They are defined as follows:

1. Inputting: the process of entering data, which are collected facts, into a data processing system

2. Storing: saving data or information so that they are available for initial or for additional processing

3. Processing: performing arithmetic or logical operations on data in order to convert them into useful information

4. Outputting: the process of producing useful information, such as a printed report or visual display

5. Controlling: directing the manner and sequence in which all of the above operations are performed

We can illustrate the five basic operations by describing a data processing scene as it might have occurred in the nineteenth century. As shown in Figure 1-2a, Bob Cratchit is laboriously making booking entries on behalf of his employer, the Scrooge Mortgage Company. Figure 1-2b is a block diagram that

FIGURE 1-2
A manual data processing system. (a) Bob Cratchit at work. (b) The data processing operations that Bob is performing.

(a)

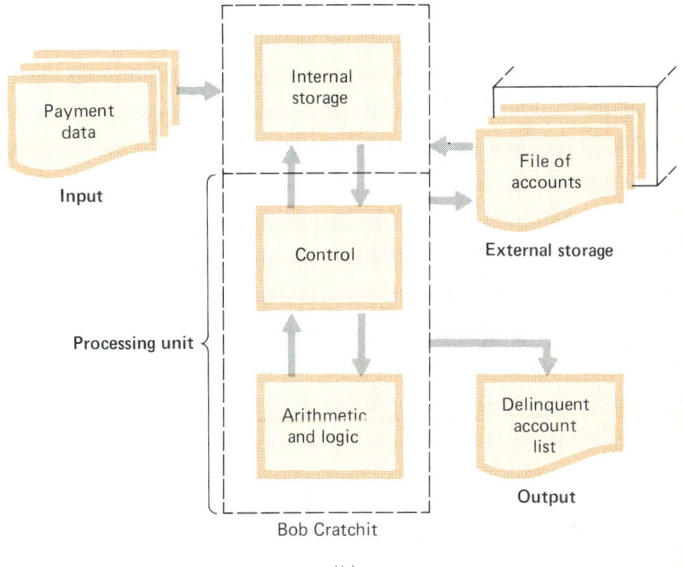

(b)

illustrates the basic data processing operations that he is performing. Notice that the input data to Bob's manual system are facts about payments. These facts result from events, called **transactions,** that cause data to be entered into a data processing system. In this instance, the transactions are the payments made in order to reduce the amount of mortgages. Bob Cratchit's storage areas are both external and internal. Data and procedures that he can recall are in his internal storage area. The file drawer from which he is selecting accounts for processing and to which he is returning them after entering collections is his external storage. Bob, as a human processing unit, controls all arithmetic and logical operations needed to update customer account records.

DATA STORAGE HIERARCHY   The manual data processing system described above also illustrates an important characteristic of data storage. Data, once entered, are organized and stored in successively more comprehensive groupings. Collectively, these groupings are called a data storage **hierarchy.**

The general groupings of any data storage hierarchy, in order of increasing capacity, are illustrated in Figure 1-3.

1. Characters, which are all written language symbols: letters, numbers, and special symbols.
2. Data elements, which are meaningful collections of related characters. Data elements are also called data items or fields.
3. Records, which are collections of related data elements.
4. Files, which are collections of related records. A set of related files is called a **data base.**

Thus, CRATCHIT, BOB27675.3525.00650.35 is a group of characters, but it may not be a meaningful collection. When it is separated into LAST NAME, FIRST NAME, ACCOUNT NUMBER, OLD BALANCE, AMOUNT PAID, and NEW BALANCE, the group becomes meaningful

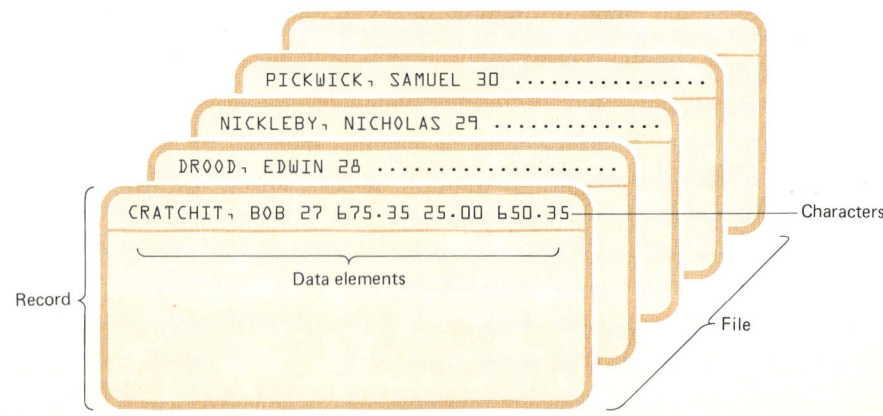

FIGURE 1-3
A data storage hierarchy.

collections of related characters, referred to as data elements, data items, or fields. Collectively, these data elements make up an individual mortgage payment record. The collection of many such records makes up a mortgage payment file. This file, along with other files maintained by the mortgage company—for example, a file of the bills owed to its creditors—would become the company's data base, sometimes referred to as a **data bank.**

Of course, we have developed alternatives to the tedium of nineteenth-century bookkeeping. By the early part of the twentieth century electro-mechanical machines had been developed and were used for business data processing. These machines evolved from the success that Dr. Herman Hollerith, a young statistician employed by the United States Census Bureau, had in tabulating the 1890 census. Typical data to be collected were the number of children in each family and their age and sex. Hollerith devised a means of coding the data by punching holes into cards, which resembled those shown in Figure 1-3. He built one machine to punch the holes and others to tabulate the collected data. Figure 1-4*a* is a picture of the machine that punched the holes in the cards, and Figure 1-4*b* is a picture of the tabulating equipment designed and built by Hollerith. Hollerith subsequently left the Census Bureau

FIGURE 1-4

(*a*) The punch designed by Hollerith to record data on cards. (*b*) Hollerith's machine, which he designed to tabulate the data punched into cards. *(Courtesy IBM.)*

(a)

(b)

and established his own tabulating machine company. Through a series of mergers, this company eventually became the IBM Corporation.

Until the middle of the twentieth century, machines designed to manipulate punched-card data were used for business data processing. These early electro-mechanical data processors were called unit record machines because each punched card contained a unit of data, for example, a record of the hours worked by one employee.

In the mid-1940s electronic computers were developed to perform calculations for military and scientific purposes. By the end of the 1960s commercial models of these computers were in widespread use for both scientific computation and business data processing. Initially these computers accepted their input data from punched cards. By the late 1970s punched cards had been almost universally replaced by keyboard terminals that were able to enter transactions as they occurred. Since that time, advances in science have led to the proliferation of computers throughout our society, and the past is but the prologue that gives us a glimpse of the future.

FEEDBACK   **1-5** What five operations are performed by all data processing systems?
1-6 What is a transaction? Give some examples?
1-7 Describe the data storage hierarchy.

TODAY, TOMORROW, AND THE DAY AFTER   The growth in our society's dependence upon computer-related information systems has been so phenomenal that the future probably is closer than we can imagine. This is illustrated by the following fictional scenario, for which all of the applications of computers exist or are technically feasible today.

It is morning in the home of Len and Dee and their two children, Jeff and Sandy. Near Dee's bedside is a terminal of their home computer. It looks like a small TV set with an attached keyboard. After playing a pleasant tune, the terminal announces that it is 6:30 AM, and the screen displays the following information:

1. The household temperature has been set at 68 degrees by the climate control system.
2. A fellow worker at the studio at which Dee is employed as an animation programmer wishes her to call before leaving for work.
3. A hot cup of coffee has been freshly brewed, and the kitchen computer is awaiting her breakfast order.

Dee types or keys in the symbols for English muffins and arises to face the day. After finishing breakfast in the kitchen, she make the phone call to her coworker and answers a technical question about the computer-created display for the final scene in *Space Wars V*. According to her morning's schedule, the engine of her car is warmed up, and the section of the instrument

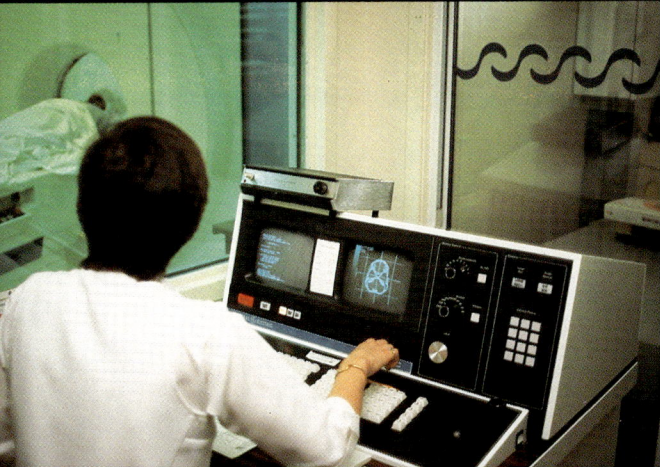

1 Computers have become valuable medical diagnostic tools. This technician is operating a computer axial tomography (CAT) scanner, which combines x-rays with computer technology to give sectional views of the body of the patient in the background. These views are combined into the single image shown on the screen. (© Russ Kinne, 1979/Photo Researchers, Inc.)

2 Space exploration depends on computers for guidance, on-board environment, and research. Astronaut Robert Crippen, pilot of the first Shuttle Orbiter (STS-1), is shown going over an instrumentation checklist in the cabin of the spaceship Columbia during a power-up mission simulation. (NASA)

3 Computer-controlled robots are able to improve the quality of manufactured products and to increase the productivity of industry. Each of these tiroless steel-collar assemblyline workers, busily welding automobiles amid a shower of sparks, is equivalent to six human workers. (© Chuck O'Rear/Woodfin Camp & Associates)

4 Computers can assist in law enforcement. This officer is using a keyboard to enter a license plate number and is receiving information on a display screen that is part of his in-car computer. (Courtesy E-Systems)

5 Computers are used for optical scanning and image processing applications, ranging from pattern recognition to image processing. This computer-created topographic map looks like an unearthly landscape out of some science fiction novel. (© Dr. Melvin L. Prueitt, 1982/Los Alamos National Laboratory)

6 Computers can assist the handicapped. This laser-beam scanner is installed in a public library in New York, where it is scanning a page of text and reading it aloud to a blind person. (Dan McCoy/Rainbow)

7

8

9

10

11

7 Learning on a computer can be fun and cost-effective. Studies have shown that with computer-aided instruction, students spend 88 percent of their instructional time attending to assigned tasks, as compared with 50 percent in the conventional classroom. (Courtesy Apple Computer, Inc.)

8 Banks throughout the nation depend upon computer terminals for millions of daily transactions. Without these terminals, records of deposits and withdrawals would be difficult to maintain, and it would be impossible to make inquiries about the current status of customer accounts. (© Stacy Pick, 1982/Stock, Boston)

9 Forecasters in the National Oceanic and Atmospheric Administration's (NOAA's) National Weather Service provide nearly 2 million predictions per year to public and commercial interests. This meteorologist is operating a new, computerized communications system designed to speed weather data processing. (NOAA)

10 Computer-aided design (CAD) enables engineers to explore a variety of design choices. CAD greatly speeds up the production of drawings and the development of specifications for complex products. (© Alvis Upitis/The Image Bank)

11 Air traffic control is a demanding occupation which depends upon computer-generated information. This air traffic controller is busy monitoring several large CRT screens which display the complex traffic patterns in the vicinity of a busy Boston airport. (© Bryce Flynn/Picture Group)

COMPUTERS ANIMATE TV NEWS

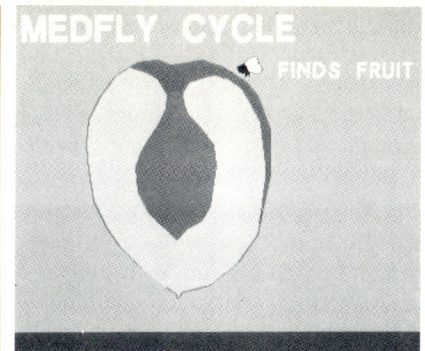

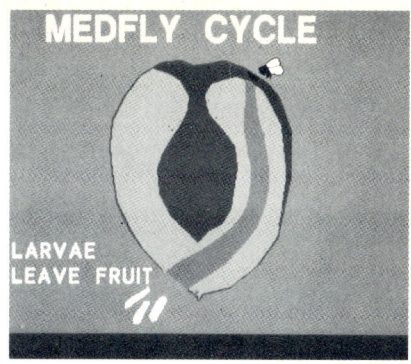

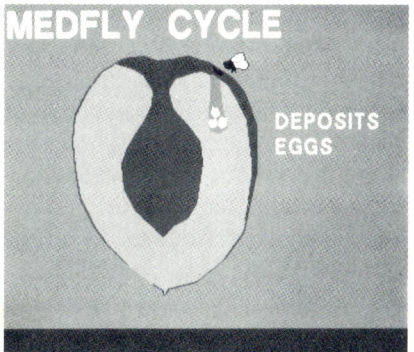

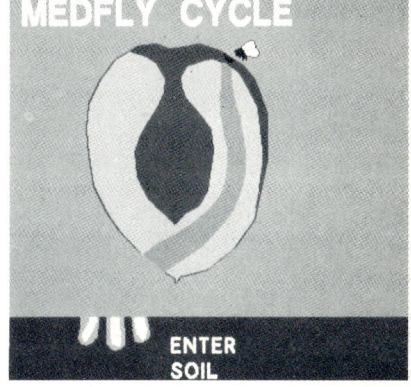

Whenever photographs or live film footage are not available at KRON-TV in San Francisco, imaginative computer-graphic animation is provided to dramatize the text of the announcer. KRON's viewers love the full-color animated sequences, but many are mystified by the ability of the station to produce them on such short notice. The answer is computer animation. The system, designed by Dr. Richard Shoup, has been in use since 1981, offering a virtually unlimited variety of graphic and artistic styles.

One of the most dramatic applications of the animation system was a sequence used to illustrate the medfly infestation in the Bay area. The sequence used a full-color cross section of a peach to show the life cycle of the medfly, from egg to adult fly. The system was also used to depict the effect of the air traffic controllers' strike by illustrating the complex traffic patterns with animated aircraft. Other uses include weather maps, children's programs, sports, and public service announcements.

The process does not require extensive training or prior computer experience. The artist merely uses an electric pen to sketch on a tablet that is designed to provide digitized input to a computer. Creative options are selected from an extensive menu appearing on a monitor. The original image is then altered by the computer to create the desired motion and special effects.

The system has been so very successful that now it is perceived to represent the wave of the future in television journalism. Presently KRON is planning to extend the capabilities of the system to take advantage of the most recent technical advances in the field of digital videographics.

(Computer graphic illustrations by Norman Leong. Courtesy KRON-TV, San Francisco.)

display screen labeled TRAFFIC informs her that she will be delayed if she goes to work by her usual route. This morning Dee prefers to drive herself; otherwise, she would link her automobile control system to the city's traffic management complex. So she requests and receives a recommendation for the best route to take.

Shortly after her departure the rest of the family arises. Len turns on the large TV terminal in the living room and keys in the appropriate code numbers to receive teletext menus from three local grocery stores. After comparing prices and making selections from each and establishing delivery times, he also browses through the catalogs of several department stores. Sandy, who is a fifth-grade student, is already busy at work at her personal computer teminal, communicating with the computer at her school so that she can complete the geography assignment that she started the night before. Later in the morning Len will drive his daughter to school, where many of her courses will be taught in classrooms equipped with computer terminals. Sandy, who had spent two weeks of the previous summer attending computer camp, is excited about the computers that help her with her schoolwork and about the opportunities to experiment with them and use them on special assignments.

Len next goes into his home office, formerly the den. He is a broker-analyst who several years ago made the transition from commuting to work to working at home and communicating electronically with his employers and clients. In this way he is able to combine two professions; stockbroker and financial consultant. Len is employed by two firms, is a consultant to several others, and maintains a group of private clients. His office contains a powerful personal computer that he uses for performing calculations; communicating with data banks, such as the stock exchange; and managing his personal data base. In addition, he is able to use his computer terminal as a **word processing system.** This means that he can create letters and other documents at his terminal, view them on the display screen of his computer, and make any changes he wishes before printing the finished document. The speed at which the final document can be typed is equivalent to that of six well-trained typists working at the same time at high speed.

This morning the stock exchanges are closed. Len is free to complete some financial analyses and make recommendations for several of his clients. He prints these out and, using the graphics capability of his computer, prepares some illustrative charts. He has installed a direct electronic mail link with computers in the homes or offices of most of his clients. While driving Sandy to school, Len will mail reports to those clients who are unable to receive them electronically.

After finishing his task, he has some time to spare, and he decides to use his computer to check this morning's electronic mail. He examines the contents of the electric bill and the communications bill on his screen and decides to pay them, so he enters the codes that send a message to his bank authorizing their payment.

It is now time to drive Sandy to school. Since he is going to be out of the house for several hours attending a computer exhibit, Len awakens Jeff to remind him to turn on the new robo-servo to clean the house before leaving for the nearby university, at which he is an engineering major.

Jeff is the last to leave. He completes a computer-logic design assignment on his computer before leaving for his 11 AM class. He understands why the engineering department requires computing proficiency of all of its first-year students and is pleased that he attended a high school in which emphasis was placed on computer literacy and the acquisition of some programming skills. As a matter of fact, he had actually won a prize for designing a computer game, and this was financing part of his college education.

The above scenario is not unlike one that will take place in the near future in many households as we enter more completely into the information age. Many other uses of computers that we cannot imagine at present willl become commonplace in the transition from an industrial to a postindustrial, or information, society.

SUMMARY

We are constantly encountering examples of how computers are affecting our everyday lives. Informed citizens should be comfortable in the presence of computers. They should be computer-literate to the extent that they have a basic understanding of how computers work and what they can do. They should be able to use a computer as a problem-solving tool and be aware of their potential for affecting the quality of life. Data are a collection of facts—unorganized but able to be organized into useful information—and data processing is a series of operations that converts data into useful information. The term *data processing system* includes the resources needed for data processing to occur. These resources are people, materials, facilities, and equipment.

Whether or not a computer is involved, all data processing systems perform the same five basic operations. These are inputting, storing, processing, outputting, and controlling. Storage may be both internal and external, and we can describe a data storage hierarchy. Within this hierarchy, in order of increasing data capacity are characters, data elements, records, files, and data bases.

Since the beginning of history, humankind has had a need for data processing. Aids to computation developed prior to this century were largely mechanical in nature. At the turn of the century, Dr. Herman Hollerith devised a method for coding census data on punched cards and developed electromechanical machines for tabulating the results of the 1890 census. Thereafter, electromechanical devices, called unit record machines, were widely used in business. However, these machines were supplanted by electronic computers that evolved from military and scientific developments of the 1940s. Today, the use of computers in business and industry is widespread, and home users are increasing rapidly, as are our personal encounters with computers. We have become a postindustrial, or information, society.

ANSWERS TO FEEDBACK QUESTIONS

1-1 Computer literacy means possessing sufficient knowledge of how computers work and what they can do to use them as problem-solving tools and to be aware of their potential to affect the quality of life.

1-2 A program is the set of instructions that direct the operations of computers.

1-3 Data are facts, unorganized but able to be organized. Useful information is the output of a data processing system.

1-4 Data processing is a series of operations that results in the conversion of data into useful information. The term *data processing system* includes the resources required to accomplish the processing of data. These resources are personnel, materials, facilities, and equipment.

1-5 The five operations performed by all data processing systems are inputting, storing, processing, outputting, and controlling.

1-6 A transaction is an event that can generate the facts, called data, that become the inputs to a data processing system. Examples are mortgage payments, registration in classes, and credit card purchases.

1-7 The data storage hierarchy proceeds, in increasing capacity, as follows: characters, data elements, records, files, data bases.

FOR REVIEW AND DISCUSSION

1 Explain the relationship between facts, data, and information.

2 Define and distinguish between data processing and data processing system.

3 What do data element, data item, and field have in common?

4 What is the relationship between Hollerith, punched card, and unit record equipment?

5 Match the following basic data processing operations with their definitions.

1	Inputting	**a**	Performing arithmetic and logical operations
2	Processing	**b**	Directing a sequence of operations
3	Storing	**c**	Producing a visual display
4	Outputting	**d**	Filing data for future reference
5	Controlling	**e**	Recording data transactions

6 Match the elements of the data storage hierarchy with their definitions.

1	Data elements	**a**	All written language symbols
2	Characters	**b**	A set of related files
3	Files	**c**	Meaningful collections of related characters
4	Records	**d**	Meaningful collections of related data elements
5	Data base	**e**	Meaningful collections of related records

CHAPTER 2
THE INFORMATION SOCIETY

PREVIEW   Our society has changed from an industrial to a postindustrial, or information, society because of advances in technology, particularly microelectronics, that have made possible a phenomenal increase in the numbers and uses of computers of all sizes. One goal of this chapter is to acquaint you with the operations performed by computer data processing systems and with the terminology for describing them. Another is to acquaint you with the characteristics of the postindustrial society and with the benefits and challenges of managing information as a resource.

In this chapter, you will learn:

1. The principal elements of computer data processing systems
2. The differences between systems and applications software
3. Four advantages of computer data processing systems
4. The origins and importance of the knowledge industries
5. A method for classifying computer systems and measures of their growth
6. The reasons for the convergence of computer-related technologies and the importance of information resource management

KEY TERMS TO WATCH FOR AND REMEMBER

central processing unit (CPU)
arithmetic logic unit
primary memory
secondary memory
applications software
program
postindustrial society
millisecond
nanosecond
integrated circuit (IC)

binary code
control unit
hardware
software
systems software
programmer
knowledge industry
microsecond
microelectronics
cost-effective

usability   systems analyst
information resource management   computer data processing system
distributed data processing   system development life cycle

COMPUTER DATA PROCESSING
Principles of
Computer Data Processing

In the previous chapter we stated that the electronic computer was made possible by technological developments that occurred during World War II. Actually, the concepts that underlie the modern digital computer were formulated during the early nineteenth century. In 1833, Charles Babbage, a gifted English mathematician, proposed to build a general-purpose problem-solving machine that he called the "analytical engine." As shown in Figure 2-1, the analytical engine was designed to perform all five of the basic data processing operations:

1. Data was to be input on punched cards.

FIGURE 2-1
Babbage's analytical engine. (a) Analytical engine-block diagram. (b) Part of analytical engine as drawn by Babbage.

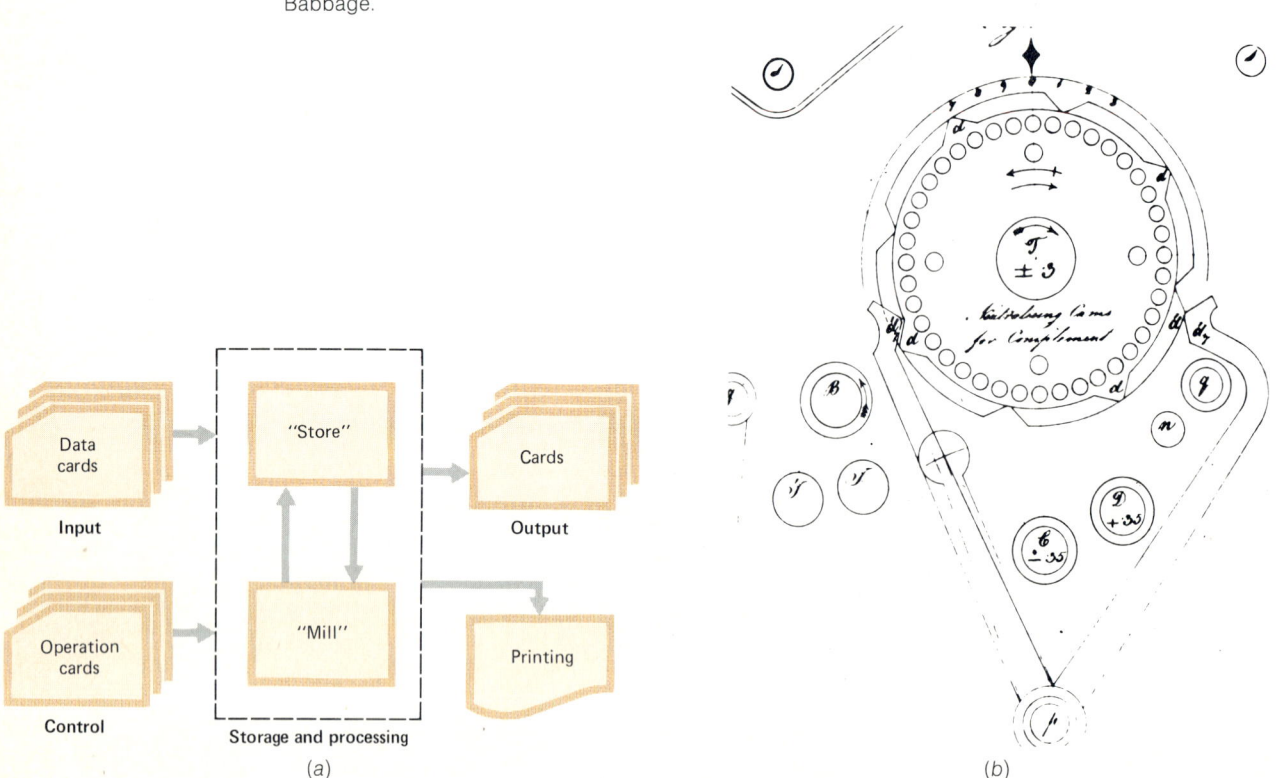

(a)

(b)

2. Processing was to be accomplished by the "mill," which could "grind out" the arithmetic operations of addition, subtraction, multiplication, and division. The mill could also change the computational process on the basis of the sign of computed results.

3. Storage took place in the memory, or "store," in which the variable to be operated on and the result of operations were to be kept.

4. Output was to be on punched cards or by printing.

5. Control of operations was to be by means of instructions that were also punched into cards and entered into the mill in sequence.

Unfortunately, Babbage's undertaking was not successful, because he had to work with the technology of his time. For example, his analytical engine was a totally mechanical machine designed to be driven by steam. The electromechanical and electronic components required to make data processing systems successful and to convert his dream into reality were over a hundred years in the future.

Many technical developments which set the stage for the widespread use of eletronic digital computers in business and industry took place in the 1940s and the 1950s. The contributions of John von Neumann were particularly significant. As contrasted with Babbage's analytical engine, which was designed to store only data, von Neumann's machine, called the Electronic Discrete Variable Computer, or EDVAC, was able to store both data and instructions. This feature was important because it enabled the computer to execute instructions at its internal speed, rather than having to rely upon much slower processes such as wired boards or punched cards for entering instructions.

Von Neumann also contributed to the idea of storing both data and instructions in a **binary code** that uses only ones and zeros instead of in decimal numbers or alphabetic characters. This simplified computer design because devices that represented the electronic equivalent of only two possible conditions, "holes" and "no holes," in punched cards were easier to construct and more reliable than the devices that would have had to have been designed to represent ten different number symbols. Computers thus use two conditions, high voltage and low voltage, to translate the symbols by which we communicate into unique combinations of electrical pulses. We refer to these combinations as codes.

We can use the Scrooge Mortgage Company's manual data processing system, described in Chapter 1, to show the similarity between the operations performed by Bob Cratchit and by a computer data processing system. Figure 2-2*a* is the same as Figure 1-2*b*, the Bob Cratchit Data Processing System. Figure 2-2*b* is a block diagram for a stored-program digital computer system. The similarity between the two diagrams is evident. Both have the same elements. However, an electronic **control unit** has taken over many of the detailed tasks that Bob Cratchit had to perform. It interprets the instructions, which are inputted and stored along with the data, and it controls all of the

The Mark I computer (1937–1944) In 1944, after five years of work, Dr. Howard Aiken of Harvard University completed the Automatic Sequence-Controlled Calculator. Called the Mark I computer, this machine was the largest electromechanical calculator ever built. It used over 3000 electrically actuated switches to control its operations. Although its operations were not controlled electronically, Aiken's machine is often classified as a computer because its instructions, which were entered by means of a punched paper tape, could be altered.

The Atanasoff-Berry computer (1939–1942) Even as the Mark I computer was being constructed, work was underway to introduce electronics into the design of computers. Dr. John Atanasoff, a professor of physics at Iowa State College, developed an electronic machine to solve certain mathematical equations. This machine was called the Atanasoff-Berry Computer, or ABC, after Atanasoff and his assistant, Clifford Berry. It used 45 vacuum tubes for internal logic and capacitors for storage.

The ENIAC (1943–1946) The first all-electronic computer, the Electronic Numerical Integrator and Calculator (ENIAC), was developed at the Moore School of Electrical Engineering of the University of Pennsylvania during the period 1943–1946. It was developed as a result of a military need. The Aberdeen Proving Ground was having difficulty calculating firing tables for new weapons, and J. Presper Eckert and John Mauchly proposed that the ENIAC be developed to solve the problem. Their proposal was accepted and supported strongly by the

Army liaison officer, Dr. Herman Goldstine.

The ENIAC took up the wall space in a 20 × 40 foot room and used 18,000 vacuum tubes. Although it was fully electronic, the ENIAC had two major shortcomings: It could store and manipulate only a very limited amount of information, and its programs were wired on boards. These limitations made it difficult to detect errors and to change the programs. Nonetheless, the project was successful, and the ENIAC was used by the Aberdeen Proving Grounds for many years to solve ballistics problems.[1]

The EDVAC (1946–1952) Dr. John von Neumann, professor of mathematics at the Princeton Institute of Advanced Study, became familiar with the ENIAC project while acting as a consultant to the Aberdeen Proving Grounds. He became acquainted with Goldstine, who helped establish a new project at the Moore School. This project had as its goal the construction of an improved computer, the Electronic Discrete Variable Computer (EDVAC). Project members included Eckert and Mauchly, in addition to Goldstine and von Neumann.

Von Neumann was a major contributor to the project, and he is given a large share of the credit for developing the concept of storing instructions as well as data in the memory of the computer. As a result, it be-

[1] In 1972, as a result of a lawsuit brought against the Honeywell Corporation by Sperry Rand for infringement on the ENIAC patent, that patent was declared invalid, and John Atanasoff was established as the inventor of the automatic electronic digital computer.

came possible to replace the wiring board, which so seriously handicapped the operation of the ENIAC. The stored-program feature is the reason that we now, properly, refer to modern digital computers as stored-program digital computers.

Von Neumann is also given a share of the credit for introducing the idea of storing both instructions and data in a binary code instead of as decimal numbers or human-readable words.

The Univac I (1951) Eckert and Mauchly left the EDVAC project to form their own company. This company, which was purchased by Remington-Rand in 1949, built the UNIVAC I computer. UNIVAC stands for UNIVersal Automatic Computer. The first UNIVAC was installed in the Census Bureau in 1951, and it was used continuously for 10 years. The UNIVAC I was the first digital computer which was not "one of a kind." It was produced in quantity. In 1952 the UNIVAC I predicted the election of Dwight Eisenhower. The first business use of a computer, a UNIVAC I, was by the General Electric Corporation in 1954.

In 1952, IBM introduced the 701 commercial computer. Although slow and limited in storage capacity by modern standards, the 701 could add a column of 10-digit numbers as tall as the Empire State Building in 1 second. In rapid succession improved models of the UNIVAC I and other 700-series machines were introduced. IN 1953, IBM produced the IBM 650 and sold over 1000 of these computers. The IBM 650 used a magnetic drum for storage and was popular with business and science.

operations of the **arithmetic logic unit.** We call the control unit and the arithmetic logic unit combined the **central processing unit** (**CPU**).

Of course, the computer is not as flexible as Bob was, because it can perform only what it is programmed to do. However, it is much faster than Bob, and its components never tire of repetitious calculations. To a much greater degree than its mechanical and electromechanical predecessors, the electronic digital computer has freed the Bob Cratchits of this world from manual computations and has created opportunities for a multitude of enhancements of humanity's computational abilities.

Now we can add to our vocabulary some important terms that are related to computers. Both Bob Cratchit and the computer have internal and external storage. In speaking about a computer data processing system, we often refer to internal storage as **primary memory** (or **main memory**) and to external storage as **secondary memory** (or **auxiliary memory**).[2]

Two other important terms are hardware and software. **Hardware** refers to the physical components of a data processing system. Thus, the input, storage, processing, and control devices are hardware. As contrasted with hardware, **software** refers to the set of computer programs, procedures, and associated documentation related to the effective operation of a data processing system. Software programs are of two types: applications software and systems software.

FIGURE 2-2

Human and computer data processing systems. (a) The Bob Cratchit data processing system. (b) A stored-program digital computer system. Both human and computer data processing systems perform the same basic operations: inputting, storing, processing, outputting, and controlling.

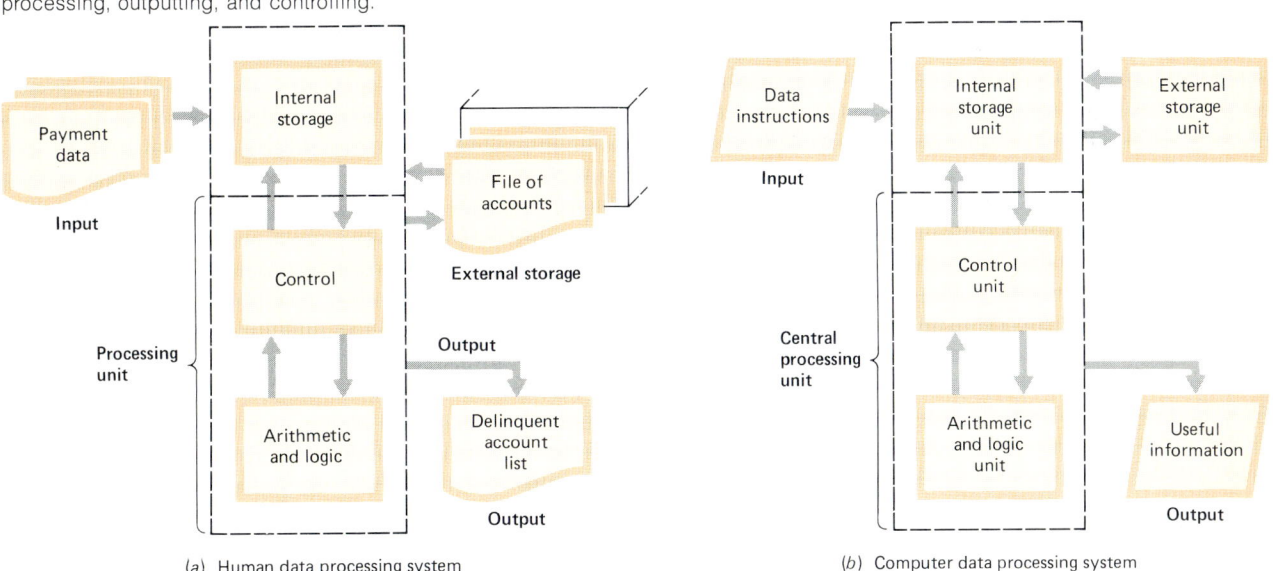

(a) Human data processing system

(b) Computer data processing system

---

[2] The terms memory and storage are interchangeable.

1. Applications software are the programs written to solve specific problems. The word **program** usually refers to an applications program, and the word **programmer** usually refers to the person who prepares applications software.

2. Systems software are the programs designed to control the operation of a computer system. They do not solve specific problems. They are written to assist humans in the use of the computer system by performing tasks, such as controlling all of the operations required to move data into and out of a computer and all of the steps in executing an applications program. The person who prepares systems software is referred to as a **systems programmer.**

Advantages of Computer Data Processing

Although data processing systems that involve computers perform the same functions as those that do not, the differences between the two are extremely significant. Computer-oriented data processing systems, often called **computer data processing systems,** should not be designed to imitate manual systems. They should blend the capabilities of both humans and computers. Computer data processing systems can be designed to take advantage of four capabilities of computers.

1. *Accuracy.* Once data have been entered correctly into the computer component of a data processing system, the need for further manipulation by humans is eliminated, and the possibility of error is reduced. Also, computers, when properly programmed, are unlikely to make computational errors. These are important reasons why we see so many terminals placed at locations where sales occur, such as fast-foods counters and department store sales stations. These terminals, called point-of-sale, or POS, stations, capture data as the transactions that create the data take place. Of course, computer systems remain vulnerable to the entry by humans of invalid data.

2. *Ease of communications.* Data, once captured at a POS station or entered by any other means, can be transmitted wherever needed by communications networks. These may be either earth- or satellite-based systems. A travel reservations system is an example of a data communications network. Reservation clerks throughout the world may make an inquiry about transportation or lodgings and receive an almost instant response. Another example is an office communications system that provides executives with access to a reservoir of data, called a corporate data base, from their personal microcomputer work stations.

3. *Capacity for storage.* Computers are able to store vast amounts of data, to organize it, and to retrieve it in ways that are far beyond the capabilities of humans. The amount of data that can be stored on devices such as magnetic disks is constantly increasing. All the while, the cost per character of data stored is decreasing. Some examples of very large files maintained by computers are those of banks, Congress, and the Internal Revenue Service. Also, data bases and data base management systems will be widely used by corporations in the decades ahead.

4. *Speed*. The speed at which computer data processing systems can respond adds to their value. For example, the travel reservations system mentioned above would not be useful if clients had to wait more than a few seconds for a response. Similarly, the response required of a complex computer-controlled manufacturing process might be a fraction of a second.

Thus, an important objective in the design of computer data processing systems is to allow computers to do what they do best and to free humans from routine, error-prone tasks. The most **cost-effective** computer data processing system is the one that does the job effectively and at the least cost. It is not necessarily the least expensive system. Nor is it necessarily the system with the greatest data processing capability, if that capability is not needed and adds extra cost. By using computers in a cost-effective manner, we will be better able to respond to the challenges and opportunities of our postindustrial, information-dependent society.

FEEDBACK

2-1 Explain binary code.

2-2 Describe the principal parts of a computer data processing system.

2-3 What is the relationship between the arithmetic logic unit, the central processing unit (CPU), and the control unit?

2-4 Define and distinguish between applications software and systems software.

2-5 Describe four important ways in which computer data processing systems differ from manual data processing systems.

THE POSTINDUSTRIAL SOCIETY
The Knowledge Industries

The economy of the United States is changing rapidly from one based upon the production of goods to one based on the provision of services. The predominant services are related to the various aspects of information—its creation, manipulation, transfer, and protection. Figure 2-3 is a projection of the distribution of the workforce in the United States that shows how we have evolved from an agricultural to an industrial to a **postindustrial society.** An important turning point occurred in 1880, by which time the percentage of the labor force engaged in agriculture and related occupations had dropped from over 70 percent in the first part of the century to 50 percent. Another was 1920, when the percentage of the labor force employed in manufacturing, commerce, and industry grew to 50 percent. The rate of increase in the information-related occupations between 1920 and 1976 is the striking change, however, and from the perspective of the present, 1976 appears to be another important turning point of our society. In that year, 50 percent of the jobs in the United States were in information occupations. Not surprisingly, we refer to the industries that provide these occupations as the **knowledge industries.** Also, when we include other services, we observe that in 1976 two-thirds of U.S. employment was in service industries.

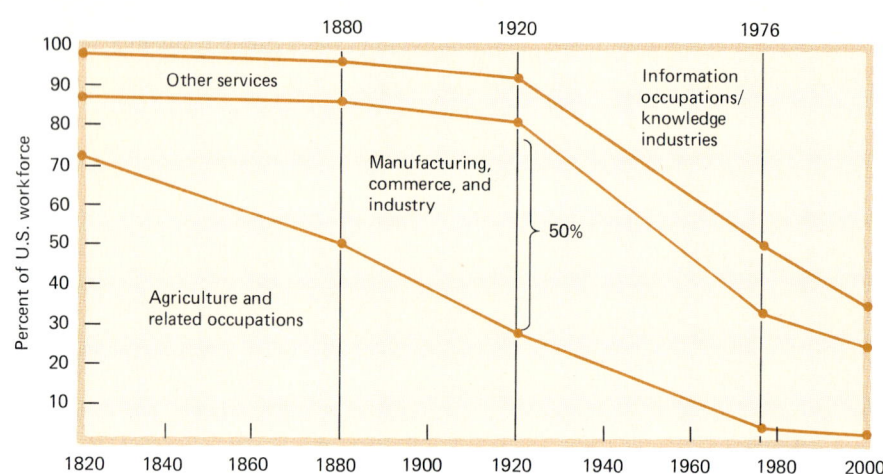

FIGURE 2-3

Postindustrial society workforce distribution. (The Futurist, *April 1981.*)

Just as the industrial revolution created many opportunities for enterprising individuals as capital investment and labor moved from agriculture to the manufacturing industries, similar opportunities for new businesses are being created today as a result of the information revolution. Typical of the knowledge industries spawned by the information revolution is computer services, which encompasses a wide variety of enterprises with activities that include systems and applications software packages, facilities management, and contract programming. Another is computer products, which includes computers, telecommunications systems, automated office machines, peripheral equipment, and electronics components.

The Computer Generations

Several key events contributed to the emergence and dominance of the knowledge industries. These are shown in Figure 2-4, which emphasizes not only the rate of change in technology but also the rate of improvement in information-processing performance per unit cost. We have already mentioned von Neumann's stored program computer. This machine and others of its day were made possible by the invention of the vacuum tube, which was a fragile glass device that could control and amplify electronic signals. Early computers, using vacuum tubes, could perform computations in thousandths of seconds, called **milliseconds,** instead of the seconds required by mechanical devices. These vacuum tube computers are referred to as first-generation computers, and the approximate period of their use was from 1950 to 1959. Not only were they bulky; they were also unreliable. The thousands of vacuum tubes that were needed emitted large amounts of heat and burned out frequently.

The transistor, a smaller and more reliable successor to the vacuum tube, was invented in 1947. However, computers that used transistors were not produced in quantity until over a decade later. So-called second-generation

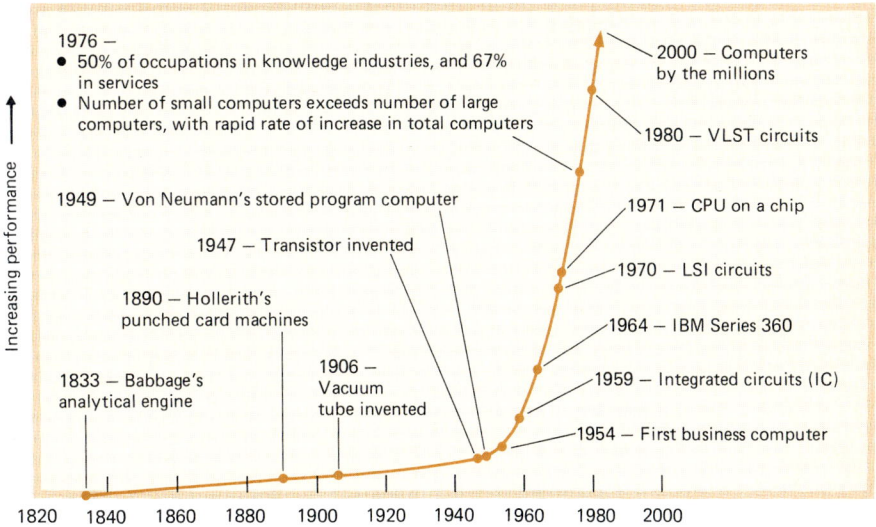

FIGURE 2-4

Milestones in computer technology.

computers, which used large numbers of transistors, dominated the data processing marketplace from 1959 to 1964. These computers were able to reduce computational times from milliseconds to **microseconds,** or millionths of seconds.

A key event was IBM's introduction of a family of general-purpose computers in 1964. These machines were designed to meet the data processing needs of both science and industry, and they were called the System/360 series, which designated a capability to meet the needs of every degree of a user's compass. The System/360 was followed quickly by similar products of other manufacturers.

Advances in electronics technology continued, and **microelectronics** made it possible to reduce the size of transistors and integrate large numbers of circuit elements into very small chips of silicon. The computers that were designed to use **integrated-circuit,** or **IC,** technology were called third-generation computers, and the approximate time span associated with these machines was from 1956 to 1979. They could perform many data processing operations in **nanoseconds,** which are billionths of seconds. Figure 2-5 illustrates the reduction in size that occurred with each generation of computers. Each produced a more-reliable, higher-performance, and less-expensive product. Transistors were smaller than vacuum tubes, and integrated circuits are smaller than transistors. In addition, integrated circuits contain large numbers of miniaturized transistors. We have progressed from small-scale integrated (SSI) circuits, which held a few transistors, through large-scale integration (LSI) into very-large-scale integration (VSLI). VSLI chips contain over 10,000 transistors. Advances in microminiaturization are continuing, and they will continue into the forseeable

Microelectronics is the ability to design and to fabricate large numbers of miniaturized circuit elements. Current microelectronic techniques place thousands of elements on a small silicon *chip*. These techniques also combine these components into complex electronic circuits. These electronic circuits are called *integrated circuits*, or ICs. Because they are low-cost, reliable, and reproducible, ICs are used in digital computers in large quantities.

The element silicon, which has the chemical composition of common sand, is a *semiconductor* that is used to manufacture miniaturized electronic components. Silicon is classified as a semiconductor because it can be made to be either electrically conducting or nonconducting. By adding impurities, a process called *doping*, scientists are able to remove electrons from a small area in a silicon chip. The lack of electrons makes the area electrically positive. This positive area is called a *p-zone*. By adding other impurities, or dopants, they are able to give an adjacent area a surplus of electrons. This addition makes it an electrically negative area, or *n-zone*.

The simplest semiconductor device is the diode, which acts as an electronic on-off switch when the flow of current between the negative and positive areas is controlled. Transistors are the most important semiconductor devices. They are more complex than diodes because they are capable of giving the amplification needed in many electronic circuits. They can also act as switches that turn electrical pulses on and off.

Chip manufacture is a high-technology process. About 250 chips are made from a razor-thin wafer of polished silicon about 3 inches in diameter. These wafers are sliced from crystal cylinders of 99.9 percent pure silicon, which are grown in a laboratory. The large crystals look like rock candy.

The complex circuitry of chips is created one layer at a time on each silicon wafer. First, racks with wafers are placed in long cylindrical ovens at a temperature of about 1000°. Here a hot oxygenated gas "rusts" the wafers, covering the surface with a thin, electrically insulating layer of silicon dioxide.

Then, the wafers are coated with a photographic emulsion called the *photoresist*, which is sensitive to ultraviolet light. Next, a glass mask that contains 250 identical patterns for a single layer of an integrated circuit is placed over the wafer. These tiny circuit patterns have been placed on the mask by means of a photographic system that reduces them by a factor of 10.

When the wafers are exposed to ultraviolet light, the photoresist hardens, but the masked areas remain soft. The next step is an acid bath, which etches away the soft masked areas. The unmasked areas remain hard. These hard areas form the outline of the circuit for that particular layer.

Then the wafers are baked in the oven again in an atmosphere of gas loaded with a dopant such as boron or phosphorus. The dopant sinks into the underlying silicon, creating the miniaturized transistors.

Since wafers usually contain as many as 10 layers, all of these steps—rusting, photomaking, etching, baking, and doping—are repeated for each layer. Then, the entire wafer is coated with aluminum conductor, which must also be masked, rusted, etched, doped, and baked. Finally, after a computerized probe scans it for defective circuitry, the wafer is cut into numerous chips by means of a diamond cutter. These tiny chips, smaller than a postage stamp, have revolutionized the computer industry.

future at such a rate that the concept of computer generations will become a less useful yardstick by which to measure progress in computer performance throughout the 1980s and 1990s.

Classification of Computers

In 1971, an entire central processing unit was placed upon a single chip of silicon. Called a microprocessor, this chip became a principal building block of computers of all sizes, with overlapping capabilities and costs. One method of classifying computers was to identify them as micro-, mini-, midi-, or maxicomputers. We will use two broad classifications: small and large. When we refer to small computers, we will mean micro- or minicomputers. When we

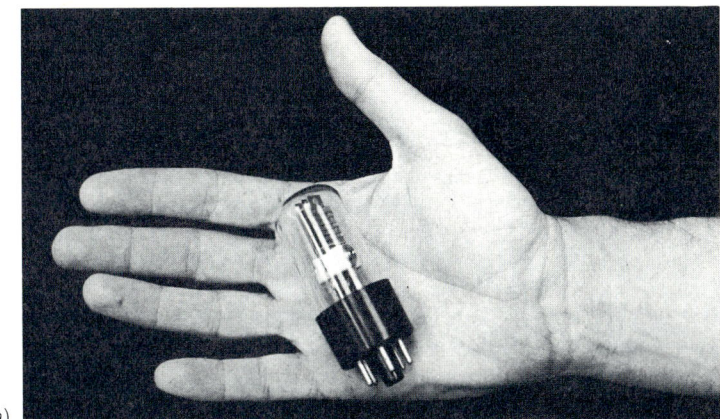

(a)

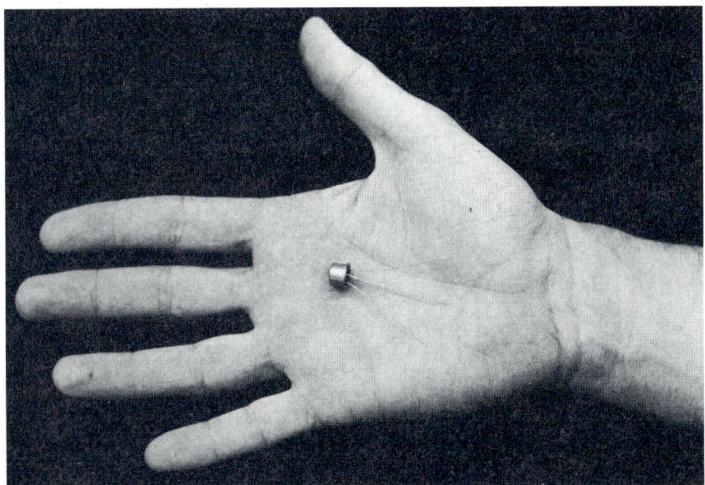

(b)

(c)

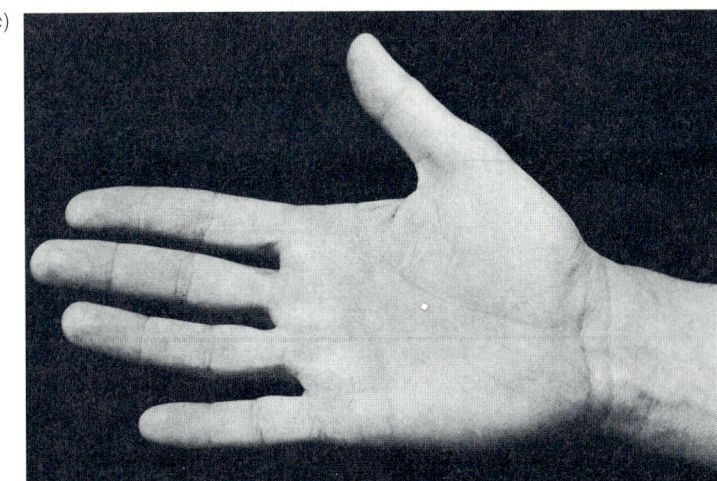

FIGURE 2-5
Size reduction with each generation of computers. (*a*) A vacuum tube. (*b*) Transistors. (*c*) Integrated circuits. *(Courtesy IBM.)*

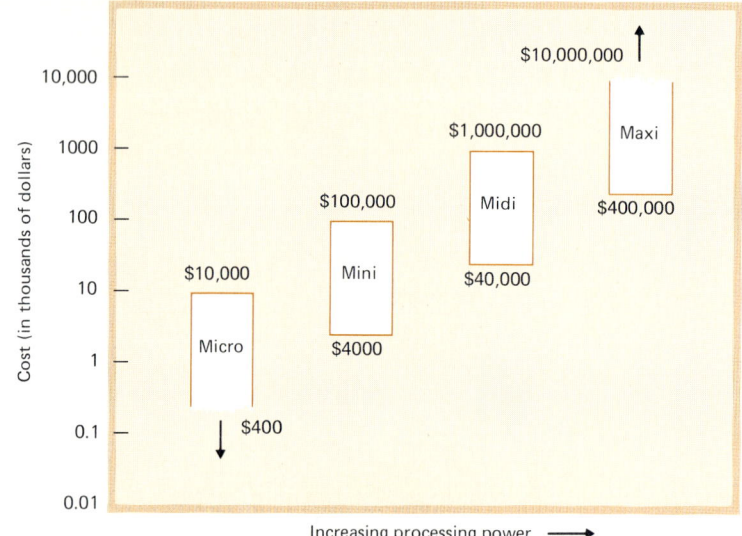

FIGURE 2-6
Cost ranges of micro-, mini-, midi-, and maxicomputer systems. Because performance and costs overlap, computer system users have many options in selecting hardware and software.

refer to large computers, we will mean midi- or maximachines. Figure 2-6 distinguishes between classes of computer systems on the basis of approximate ranges of cost. Each range covers at least a tenfold increase in cost. Also, the ranges overlap. The cost of a microcomputer could range from as little as a few hundred dollars for a no-frills model to $10,000 or more with the addition of the input, output, and storage capability required to process data for a small business. At the other end of the cost spectrum, a maxicomputer system could range in cost from several hundred thousand dollars to many millions of dollars.

Because each data processing transaction costs less on larger computers, they often appear to be more cost-effective than smaller computers. However, the effectiveness of the entire system must be considered. The apparent savings of a large, centralized computer system may be more than offset by the advantages of **distributed data processing.** This involves distributing computing resources to several locations, which could result in improved performance by reducing the cost of communications, increasing user involvement and acceptance, and distributing a share of the responsibility to users.

Measures of Change   The rate at which we are becoming a postindustrial society can be measured in several ways. Three significant measures of change are: expenditures for computer data processing, the number of computers in use, and opportunities for employment. The trend in estimated annual spending for large and small computer systems is shown in Figure 2-7. It is estimated that by 1990 the amount spent annually in the United States on computers by businesses and individuals will approach $55 billion for small systems and $40 billion for large systems, or a total of $95 billion. This does not include personnel costs, which could exceed $25 billion.

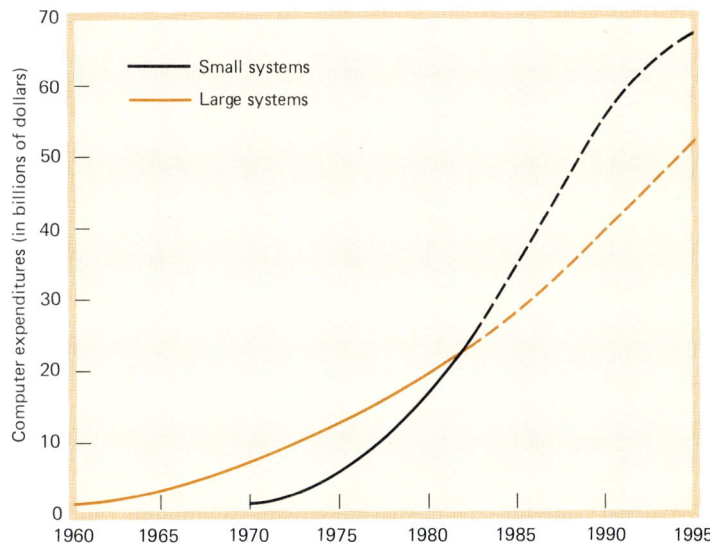

FIGURE 2-7
Computer expenditures, 1960–1990. Expenditures for both large and small systems will increase dramatically in the future, with the expenditures for small systems greatly exceeding those for large systems.

Note that 1976 marks the time at which a significant increase in the rate of expenditures for small computers began. We are all aware of the phenomenal growth in the number of small computers, so it is not surprising to find that in the future, in spite of the large differences in costs between small and large systems, expenditures for small systems will far exceed those for large systems. Figure 2-8, which shows the increase in the total number of small and large computer systems, indicates that the number of small systems exceeded the

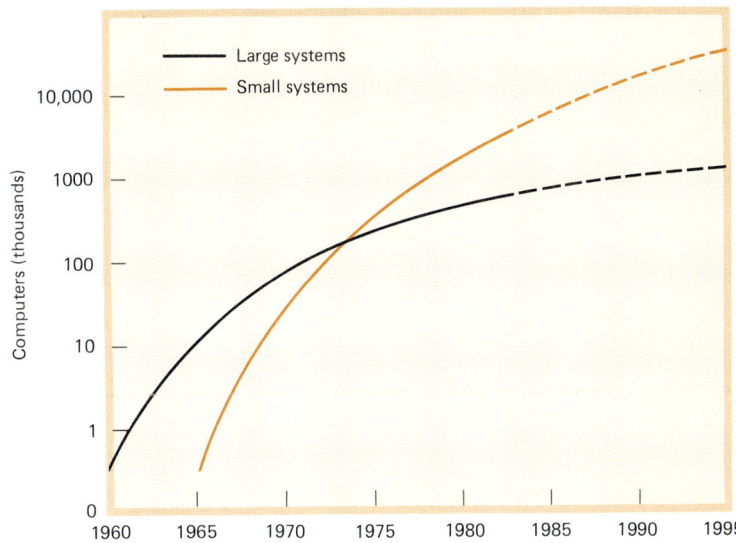

FIGURE 2-8
Number of computer systems, 1960–1990. In the early 1970s the number of small computer systems exceeded the number of large systems—a trend that is expected to continue in the future.

number of larger ones by the mid-1970s. As a forecast of the future, this figure is actually an *under*estimate because it does not take into account the multitude of specialized applications of the "computer on a chip" in automobiles, household appliances, entertainment, and so forth.

Employment Opportunities

The question often asked of a child, What do you want to be when you grow up? will soon have more possible answers than ever before. New careers will exist, for example, in artificial intelligence and robotics; personal computer sales, software, and repair; and data entry and word processing. And a multitude of as-yet-unidentified careers will emerge to affect the education and employment of future citizens of our information society.

The occupation most often associated with computers is programming. Let us take a brief look at employment opportunities in this area. (In Chapter 18, "People in Information Systems," we will describe other information-related careers.)

It is not unusual to hear a concern expressed that the job opportunities for programmers will decrease in the near future. One often stated reason is that computer programs are becoming increasingly general purpose and "user-friendly," making it easier for people without special training to use them. For example, many corporations could purchase programs to meet major applications needs, such as data base management, accounting, and inventory control. Although most purchased programs will have to be tailored to meet the specific information needs of an organization and although changes will have to be made from time to time, it is true that the number of programmers per general-purpose computer will decrease. The last column of Table 2-1 is a projection of the decrease in the number of programmers employed per installed large (midi- or maxi-) general-purpose computer. However, as was shown in Figure 2-8, from which the data in column 2 was taken, the number of such computer systems is increasing. If we combine the data in these two columns of Table 2-1, we obtain the information shown in the third column of the table, which forecasts an increasing demand for programmers. Also, this forecast does not take into account the needs of the microcomputer software market, which will

TABLE 2-1   **U.S. PROGRAMMER EMPLOYMENT, GENERAL-PURPOSE COMPUTERS**

Year	Computers (thousands)	Programmers (thousands)	Programmers per computer
1960	0.5	3	6.0
1965	10	40	4.0
1970	100	340	3.4
1975	150	450	3.0
1980	600	1440	2.4
1985	900	1710	1.9
1990	1000	1800	1.8

continue to expand. The job skills required of programmers may be different and more demanding in the future because of the variety and complexity of the information resources that will be available.

INFORMATION RESOURCE MANAGEMENT
Merging Technologies

The growth in the number of computers and in their capacity for higher performance that led us into the information age is but the forerunner to more extensive changes that will take place throughout the remainder of this century. During the industrial era increases in productivity were achieved by investing large amounts of capital in physical-plant facilities. The investment in the office and in business information systems was relatively small. Toward the end of this era the investment in computers increased, particularly as the transition from manual data processing systems to computer data processing systems took place. This investment trend is continuing; it is significant because the costs for labor, including office workers, are rising more rapidly than are the costs for data processing facilities and equipment. Table 2-2 shows the reductions that have taken place in the cost of computer components; the trend in cost reduction will continue.

Today, an additional transition is evident. Computers now affect all the information resources used by businesses and are responsible for the convergence of three "islands of technology"—data processing, the automated office, and communications—into an "information archipelago." Table 2-3 shows how the merging of these technologies has taken place as a result of increasing use of computers. The automated office provides an excellent example of the merger and of the opportunity for a high return upon capital investment. Figure 2-9 depicts an office information network that could be typical of the early 1990s. Small computers with extensive capabilities to edit text will perform word processing operations. Input will be provided by keyboards, by optical devices that can recognize characters, and increasingly, by voice. Output, called reprographics, will include all the equipment, such as printers and photocopiers,

TABLE 2-2   **COMPUTER COMPONENT COST AND PERFORMANCE TRENDS**

Year	Technology	Cost per circuit element	Cost per logic circuit	Operation time
1958	Vacuum tube	$6.00	$160.00	16 milliseconds
1965	Transistor	0.25	12.00	4 micro-seconds
1972	Integrated circuit	0.02	200.00	40 nanoseconds
1980	Large-scale integrated circuit	0.001	0.05	0.2 nanoseconds

Source: James L. McKenney and F. Warren McFarlan, "The Information Archipelago—Maps and Bridges," *Harvard Business Review,* September-October, 1982, pp. 109–119.

TABLE 2-3   **MERGING ISLANDS OF TECHNOLOGY**

Functions of technology	Islands of technology		
	Office automation	Data processing	Communication
1920			
Human-to-machine translation	Shorthand, dictaphone	Form, keypunch	Phone
Manipulation of data	Typewriter	Card sorting	Switch
Memory	File cabinet	Cards	None
Links	Secretary	Operator	Operator
1965			
Human-to-machine translation	Shorthand, dictaphone	Form, keypunch	Phone
Manipulation of data	Typewriter	Computer	Computer
Memory	File cabinet	Computer	None
Links	Secretary	Computer	Computer
1980			
Human-to-machine translation	Shorthand, dictaphone, keyboard	Keyboard	Phone, keyboard
Manipulation of data	Computer	Computer	Computer
Memory	Computer	Computer	Computer
Links	Computer	Computer	Computer

Source: James L. McKenney and F. Warren McFarlan, "The Information Archipelago—Maps and Bridges," *Harvard Business Review,* September-October, 1982, pp. 109–119.

used to prepare documents. Methods for distributing output to users will include telecommunications, facsimile transmission, and electronic mail.

The Management Challenge

Throughout the postindustrial era, corporations will have opportunities to enhance their productivity in many areas where the costs of labor and management are now high by consolidating their information resources. Corporations have come to realize that information, like any other important resource, such as capital or labor, requires management. Management of the data processing, communications, and automated office resources is called **information resource management.** Three important considerations in information resource management are acceptance of computer systems by their users, location of responsibility for information resources, and methods for system life-cycle management.

Productivity can only be enhanced if the information systems are accepted

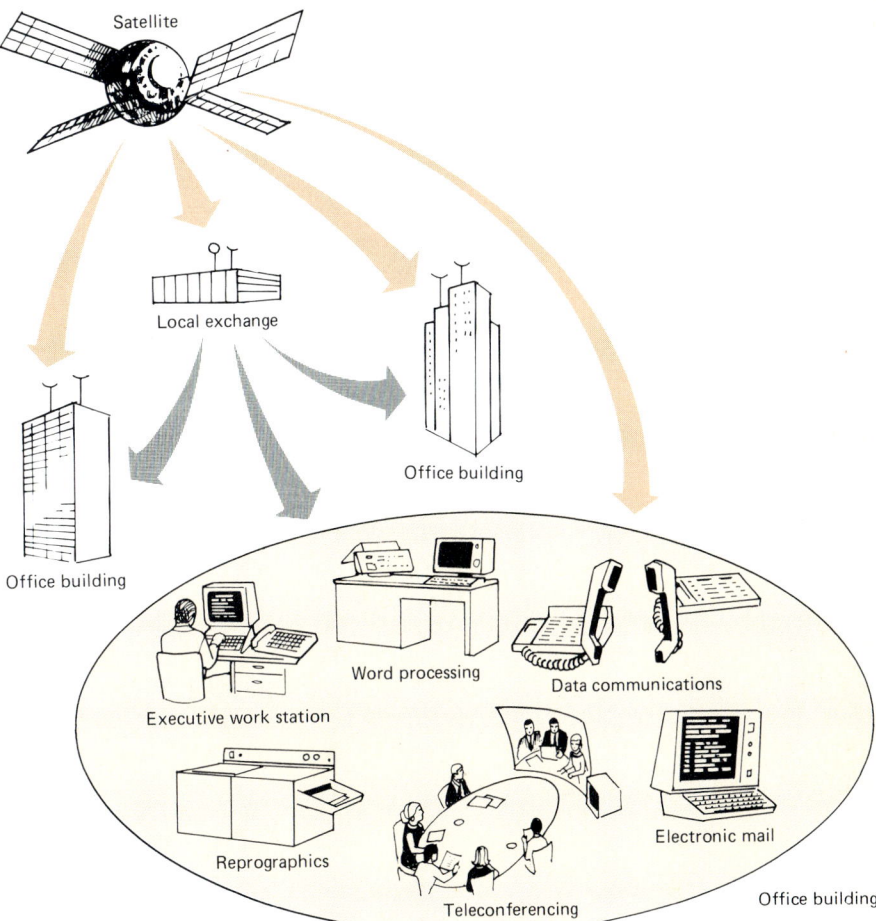

Satellite

Local exchange

Office building

Office building

Executive work station

Word processing

Data communications

Reprographics

Teleconferencing

Electronic mail

Office building

FIGURE 2-9

Communications services for future business information systems. Data collected from many sources will be communicated to on-site locations within offices; between office buildings and special facilities, such as hospitals, warehouses, and banks within a city; and between offices and special facilities in different cities.

by their users. This means that users must be involved in the development of those systems. They must have a role in deciding how their needs for information will be met. In the final analysis, **usability,** which is the value of an information system as perceived by its principal users, will determine the success of failure of the system. Usable information systems must be designed to meet the needs of persons in all levels in a corporation, including top management. We have only begun to take advantage of the use of computers to assist decision makers. Computer-literate business school graduates will make greater and greater use of computer-generated information to support their decisions.

Responsibility for information resources must be placed at a high corporate level to be sure that they benefit the whole firm. With increasing frequency this responsibility will be assigned to an individual who reports directly to the president of the corporation.

Step-by-step methods have been developed for managing the design and development of computer-related business information systems. These structured methods are based upon the concept of the system as an entity that passes through several phases throughout its lifetime, or life cycle. The phases that make up the life cycle of business information systems are study, design, development, and operation. Collectively, these phases often are referred to as the **system development life-cycle.** In the study phase an existing business information system problem is defined with the assistance of those who will use the new system, and a solution is proposed. In the design phase the new or modified information system is designed. In the development phase it is constructed, and in the operation phase the system is operated by its users.

Special skills and training are required for successful life-cycle management of a business information system. The persons who are qualified by education and experience to manage the life-cycle phases are called **systems analysts.** Systems analysts are trained to bridge the communications gap between managers, users, and programmers. In the information society, career opportunities for systems analysts will increase as we progress toward the effective management of our information resources.

FEEDBACK

2-6   What are the knowledge industries?

2-7   Distinguish between millisecond, nanosecond, and microsecond.

2-8   Identify the merging information technologies.

2-9   What is information resource management?

2-10 What is the meaning of the terms *cost-effective* and *usability?*

SUMMARY   Computer data processing systems perform the same basic operations as manual systems: inputting, storing, processing, outputting, and controlling. Storage is both internal and external, and processing is performed by the central processing unit, which contains a control unit and an arithmetic logic unit. Data processing systems that are designed to take advantage of the characteristics of computers are superior to manual systems because of their potential for accuracy, communications, storage, and speed of response. Hardware refers to the physical components of a data processing system, and software refers to the set of computer programs, procedures, and associated documentation related to the effective operation of a data processing system. The two types of software programs are applications software and systems software. The former consist of programs written to solve specific problems; the latter consists of programs designed to control the operation of a computer system.

There has been a change in the economy of the United States from one based upon industrial production to one based upon services. The year 1976 marks the time of transition from an industrial society to a postindustrial society. In that year 50 percent of the jobs in the United States were in information-related occupations, called the knowledge industries. Other characteristics of the postindustrial, or information, society include (1) reductions in size and improvements in performance of computers owing to advances in microelectronics; (2) rapid increases in expenditures for computers and in the number of computer systems of all sizes, with an increasing proliferation of small computers; and (3) increasing opportunities for employment in existing and emerging information-related professions.

As a result of the widespread uses of computers, three islands of technology—data processing, word processing, and communications—are merging. This merger provides corporations with opportunities to improve productivity through information resource management. Important information resource management considerations are user acceptance, information resource responsibility, and system life-cycle management.

ANSWERS TO FEEDBACK QUESTIONS

2-1 A binary code is a code based upon two conditions, such as high voltage or low voltage; it uses a unique combination of these conditions to represent each of the symbols by which we communicate.

2-2 The principal parts of a computer system are the input and output units; storage, which may be internal and external; and the central processing unit.

2-3 The control unit interprets instructions and controls all of the operations of the arithmetic and logic unit. The central processing unit, or CPU, contains the control unit and the arithmetic logic unit.

2-4 Applications software consists of the programs written to solve specific problems. Systems software is not written to solve specific problems; it consists of the programs that control the operations of a computer system.

2-5 Four important ways in which computer data processing systems differ from manual systems are potential for accuracy, communications capability, storage capacity, and speed of response.

2-6 The knowledge industries are those industries that provide information-related occupations.

2-7 A millisecond is a thousandth of a second, a nanosecond is a billionth of a second, and a microsecond is a millionth of a second.

2-8 The merging information technologies, all computer-oriented, are data processing, the automated office, and communications.

2-9 Information resource management refers to the management of all of the information resources of a corporation, particularly the merging, computer-oriented technologies.

2-10 *Cost-effective* refers to the least costly system that is effective in performing the job that needs to be done. The most cost-effective system is not necessarily the least expensive one. *Usability* is the value of an information system as perceived by its principal users, and it determines the success or failure of the system.

**FOR REVIEW
AND DISCUSSION**

1 Define and distinguish between the following pairs of terms:
  a Hardware and software
  b Applications software and systems software
  c Memory and storage
  d Internal storage and external storage
  e Industrial and postindustrial society
  f Traditional and nontraditional society
2 What are the principal elements of both a manual data processing system and a computer data processing system?
3 What are the two parts of the control unit, and what is the function of each?
4 Under what conditions would you use a computer data processing system instead of a manual one?
5 What are the advantages and disadvantages of using binary codes to store data and instructions?
6 Why is 1976 identified as time that marks the transistion from an industrial society to a postindustrial society?
7 What are the principal characteristics of the postindustrial society that will affect how we live and where and how we work?
8 What are the "islands of technology," and what has caused them to merge?
9 What are the opportunities and challenges associated with information resource management?
10 Discuss usability, placement of responsibility, and life-cycle management as they relate to information resource management.

CHAPTER 3
COMPUTER INFORMATION SYSTEMS

PREVIEW   The computer is a marvelous tool. However, it is only a tool and not an end in itself. In the world of business, computers and computer systems are parts of an even larger system—the business system. The goals of this chapter are to acquaint you with the system characteristics of businesses and to familiarize you with a structured procedure, called the life-cycle method, which many businesses are following in order to make effective use of computers to solve problems and to support managers in decision making. You will then be able to study computers and information systems from an overall system viewpoint.

In this chapter you will learn:

1. Why a business is a "system of systems"
2. The difference between product flow and information flow
3. The four levels of information systems and their uses
4. The four life-cycle phases of computerized business systems
5. The role of the systems analyst in developing effective computer data processing systems

KEY TERMS TO WATCH FOR AND REMEMBER

business	operation phase
product flow	performance specification
information flow	design specification
life-cycle method	system specification
study phase	systems analysis
design phase	principal user
development phase	subsystems
data carrier	hard copy
goal	soft copy
objective	computer information
baseline specifications	system
user	

In the preceding chapter we described the increases in the number and uses of computers of all sizes. We emphasized the importance of information resource management in assisting modern businesses to increase productivity. The need to develop methods for managing the design and development of computer-related business information systems was identified as a key element for successful information resource management. We stated that successful management methods were based upon the identification of phases that made up the life cycle of all business information systems.

You will learn more about the life-cycle method and its importance in this chapter. First, however, let us become familiar with some important general characteristics of business systems.

BUSINESS SYSTEM CHARACTERISTICS

Goals and Objectives

A business is a system. It receives inputs, processes them, and converts them into outputs. Figure 3-1 shows this activity graphically. Every business, whether it is a service enterprise or a manufacturing company, exhibits input, processing, and output. For example, if you ran a small word-processing service while in school, the input would be your client's handwritten copy and the output could be a finished term paper.

Like all systems, your business would use resources in order to accomplish

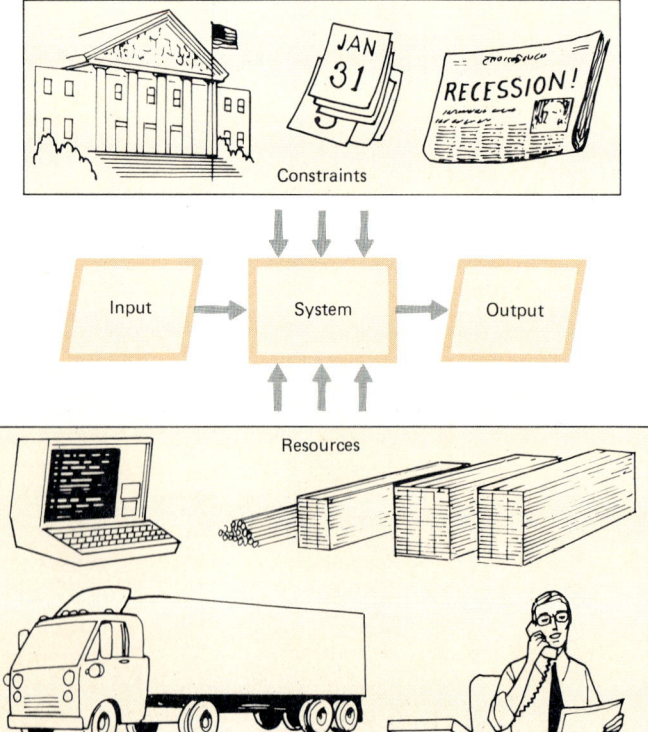

FIGURE 3-1

Business system environment. A business is a system that receives inputs, processes them, and produces useful outputs. Businesses use resources, such as people, facilities, material, and equipment. Also, they are subject to environmental limitations or constraints.

its objectives. Resources used by systems are personnel, materials, facilities, and equipment. In the case of your word processing service, the resources would be you, the paper, ribbon, and other supplies that were consumed, the room in which you worked, and your word processor. Similarly, a manufacturing company would use resources such as labor, steel, buildings, and tools to convert an engineering concept into a useful product like an automobile.

All systems, including businesses, are affected by the limitations that they must observe. Examples of constraints upon business enterprises are federal regulations, limited quantities of natural resources, time, and the laws of science.

When we define a business as a system, we mean that it is more than a series of parts connected together in a haphazard manner. A true system must have a purpose that unifies its parts. For a business system, this purpose is to accomplish meaningful goals and objectives. A **goal** is a broadly stated purpose of the business. As an example, the goal of an automobile manufacturing company is to make money for its owners. As another example, the goal of a college is to educate its students. **Objectives,** as contrasted with goals, are short-term, specific accomplishments necessary to the achievement of goals. One objective of an automobile manufacturer is the production of a competitive car. An objective of a college is to teach useful courses. Of course, major objectives may be made up of lower-order objectives.

From a systems point of view, we can define a **business** as a combination of personnel, facilities, materials, and equipment that accomplishes specific objectives in order to achieve defined goals. These goals and objectives may be considered to be the outputs of a business system.

The Business: A System of Systems

A business is a major system that is made up of smaller systems, sometimes called **subsystems.** In most corporations, a board of directors elected by the owners selects a president and other operating officers. The president decides upon the type of organization that will best meet the goals and objectives of the company. For example, a company that manufactures automobiles would

FIGURE 3-2

A top-level organization chart shows the upper-level units of a company.

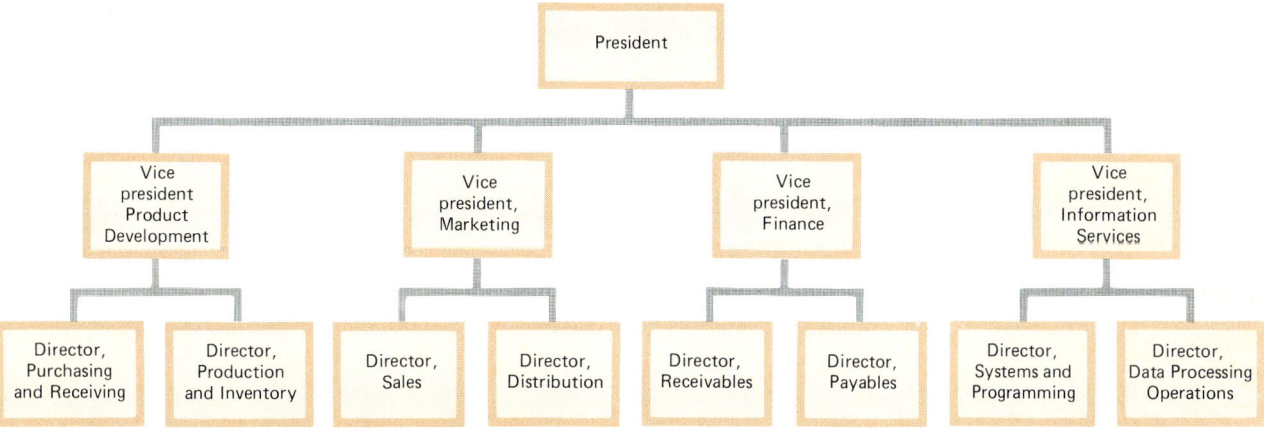

be organized differently than a college, which has education of students as a goal. Figure 3-2 is an example of a top-level organization chart for a manufacturing company. The company is divided into four major divisions: product development, marketing, finance, and information services. Each division, in turn, is divided into lower-level units, such as departments. If we look beyond the organization chart by examining product flow and information flow, we will be able to identify the actual systems that make the company operate.

Product Flow and Information Flow

Many of the subsystems that make up the business organization are related by the flow of activities between them. These activities may be either product-related or information-related. Figure 3-3, which identifies nine processes that are common to most manufacturing businesses, distinguishes beween product flow and information flow. The color lines represent product flow, and the black lines represent information flow. **Product flow,** which usually is highly visible, is the flow of raw materials into finished goods. **Information flow,** also called data flow, is the creation and movement of information within and beween the departments in a company. Information flow accompanies product flow and also meets other communications needs. The movement of information is accomplished by means of **data carriers,** which are printed reports or their electronic equivalent, such as a display screen. Printed reports are called **hard-copy** output because they are relatively permanent. Displays are called **soft-copy** output because, although they can be retrieved, they disappear when the display screen is changed or turned off. Figure 3-4 is an expansion of Figure 3-3; it identifies the principal information flows in a typical manufacturing business. For purposes of illustration, all the data carriers are shown as hard-

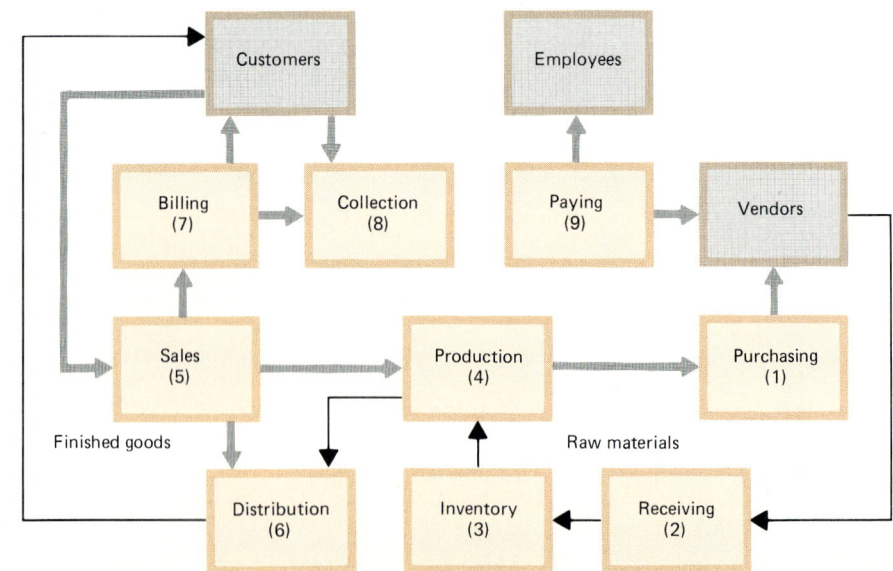

FIGURE 3-3
Product flow and information flow. The color lines show the path taken by materials as they are developed into products. The black lines show the paths along which information needed for the operation of the business must flow. The nine numbered rectangles identify the processes that are characteristic of manufacturing businesses.

FIGURE 3-4

Principal information flow documents. This figure identifies some of the more important documents that are created to meet information needs of a business.

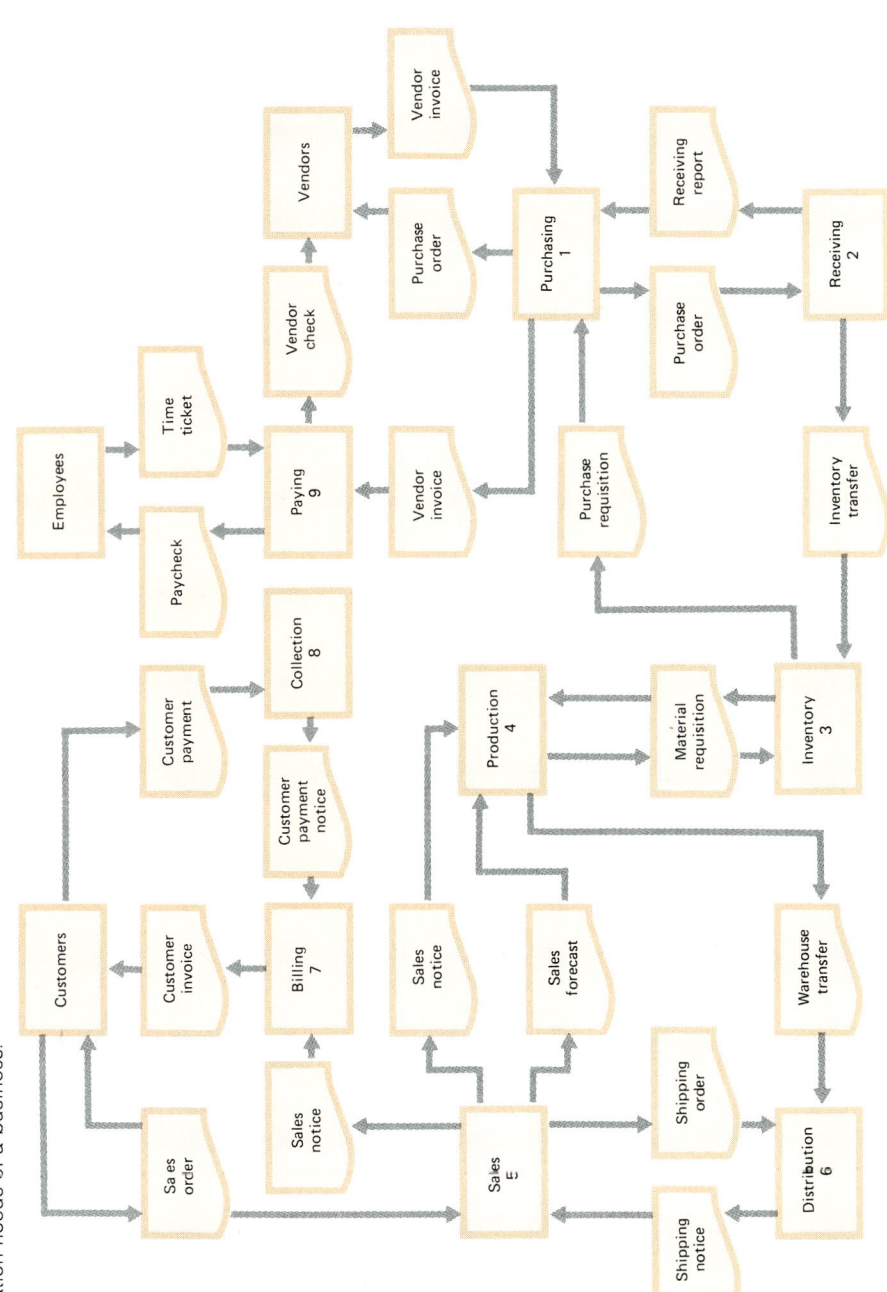

copy documents. However, often the same information is also available as a screen display.

We can define these documents by referring to the numbers in Figure 3-4, as follows:

1. The purchase order is prepared by Purchasing, which sends the original to the vendor, retains a copy, and sends a copy to Receiving.

2. When the material ordered arrives, Receiving verifies the order against its copy of the purchase order, inspects the material, and informs Purchasing of its arrival and acceptance by means of a receiving report. The material is transferred to Inventory accompanied by an inventory transfer.

3. By means of a purchase requisition, Inventory requests Purchasing to order those materials that are not on hand in sufficient quantity.

4. Production designs and develops the product. Production uses a material requisition to request needed materials from Inventory. Inventory notifies Production of the availability of the requisitioned materials by returning a copy of the material requisition.

5. Sales contacts the customer, sells the product, and prepares the sales order. The customer is provided with a copy of the sales order. Other copies of the sales order, entitled sales notices, are sent to Billing and Production. An additional copy, the shipping order, is sent to Distribution.

6. Distribution receives the finished goods from Production, accompanied by a warehouse transfer. Distribution ships the product to the customer and informs Sales by means of a shipping notice.

7. Billing prepares and mails the customer invoices.

8. Collection receives customer payments from the customer and sends updated information to Billing by means of a customer payment notice.

9. Paying makes payments to vendors (sellers to the company) by means of a vendor check. This check is prepared after the vendor has submitted a vendor invoice and after that invoice has been verified and forwarded by Purchasing. Paying also distributes paychecks to employees. The amounts of the paychecks are based upon time tickets submitted by employees.

As complicated as the information network shown in Figure 3-4 may appear, it is an oversimplification of the real volume of data flow in a typical corporation. Every major business system is composed of complex subsystems, each of which has its information needs. Two other factors add to the complexity of the information network: First, there are external as well as internal generators of information; and second, information must be reported with different emphasis and formats according to the needs of different levels of management.

Information Generators   Business system information needs are generated by both external and internal sources. As shown in Figure 3-5, the departments within the company are the internal information generators, and the general business environment provides

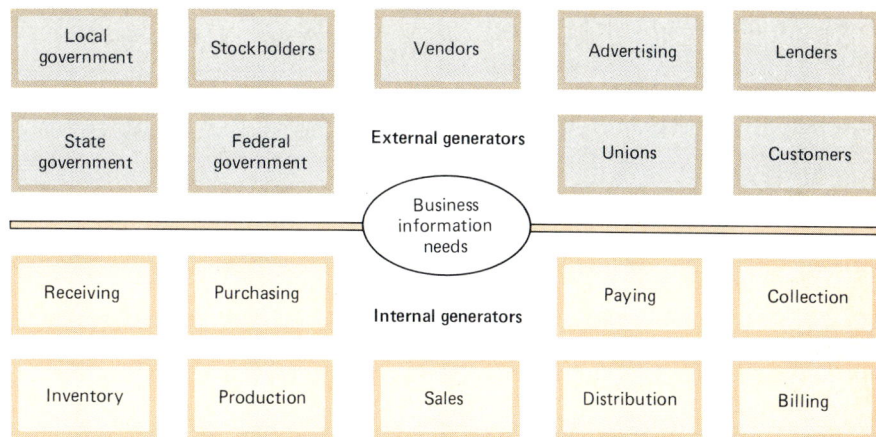

FIGURE 3-5

Business information needs are generated by both external and internal sources.

the external generators. Examples of external information generators are the needs of the owners of the company for information about its activities and reports required by vendors, lenders, customers, and state, federal, and local government agencies.

Business Levels and Information Uses

As shown in Figure 3-6, there are four levels in a typical business. These levels are: operational, lower management, middle management, and top management. As this figure also indicates, different uses are made of information at each level.

At the operational level, workers perform routine production and clerical tasks. Their information needs also are routine. Usually, they require only the information needed to perform their assigned jobs. They seldom use this information to modify their activities or to control the actions of others. For example, a materials clerk receives a requisition for material, fills the requisition, and makes a record of the transaction. A supervisor checks the performance of the clerk. However, the same information that is routine at the operational level, or summary information derived from it, often is the basis for decisions and actions at higher levels of management.

Lower management supervises the tasks and clerical functions performed by operational-level employees. These managers deal with day-to-day problems like job scheduling, checking the results of tasks performed, and taking the actions needed to correct problems as they arise.

Middle managers are responsible for controlling the resources that contribute to the goals of the company. For example, the director of sales in Figure 3-2 would give assignments to the sales staff and evaluate their performance. As a middle manager, the director of sales develops short-range plans, or tactics, for increasing sales. Advertising campaigns, contests, and sales-staff bonuses are examples of the tactics that this manager might use. Middle managers supervise lower managers. In our example, lower managers could be district

FIGURE 3-6

In a typical business, there are three management levels, in addition to an operational level. Each level has its own use for information.

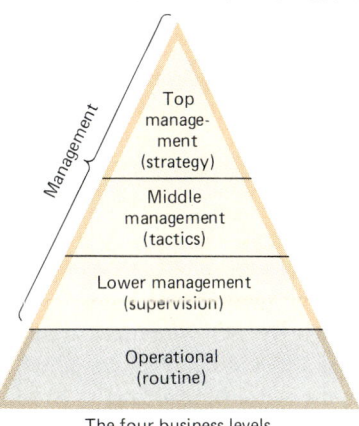

The four business levels

WHAT IS A DECISION SUPPORT SYSTEM?

In the 1970s, much attention was focused upon management information system (MIS) development. These systems further processed and refined information developed to meet operational needs. Their purpose was to provide managers with information for effective planning, control, and decision making. In the 1980s and 1990s the emphasis on information systems for managers will continue in order to improve their productivity. These systems will be called decision support systems (DSS).

As contrasted with an MIS, a DSS identifies an outcome, that is, a decision, and emphasizes that the purpose of computer-generated information is to support, and not replace, the manager in the decision-making process. A full-scale DSS is identified by five basic capabilities:

1. Critical information is obtained from a variety of sources and is available from an integrated and accessible data base.

2. The information is useful for the analysis of unexpected situations that come up suddenly.

3. The system can be used for modeling. This means that it provides the ability to supply answers to questions such as "What sales did we lose in Los Angeles when our competitor introduced a new product last quarter?"

4. A global-analysis capability is available. This means that information, for example, for marketing, finance, and production, can be communicated across the corporate organization chart.

5. The system is user-friendly. The user of the DSS is a manager, not a computer programmer. Therefore, the DSS should be English-based as opposed to being based on a programming language and suitable for an executive terminal, typically a personal computer.

Sources: M. R. Gore and J. W. Stubbe, *Elements of Systems Analysis,* Wm. C. Brown Co., Dubuque, Iowa, 1983; "The Changing Software Environment," *Computerworld Extra,* Sept. 1, 1982, pp. 7, 11.

sales managers who would receive their sales goals from and be evaluated by the director of sales.

Top management's prime function is to establish goals for the company and to develop long-range plans, or strategies, for meeting these goals. For example, the vice president of marketing shown in Figure 3-2 might be exploring new markets for the products of the company or identifying needs for new products that the company might sell at a profit. Top managers direct and evaluate middle managers. Thus, the vice president of marketing would set sales goals for the director of sales.

Expanding information needs at the operational and managerial levels of business have made the computer an indispensable tool of our industrialized society. The computer not only meets business information needs by storing and manipulating large volumes of data but also, through its presence, tends to create additional needs for information by stimulating people to think of new ways in which it can be used.

COMPUTER-BASED BUSINESS SYSTEMS
Early Problems

Throughout the 1960s and much of the 1970s computers were often used to solve problems in an undisciplined manner. Business people were aware of the potential of computers, but often the methods for applying them to specific problems were not thought out. As a result, computers sometimes caused problems which were more severe than those which they intended to solve. Even now, headlines that publicize computer failures are not uncommon.

Three of the real reasons for early computer-based information system failures were:

12

14

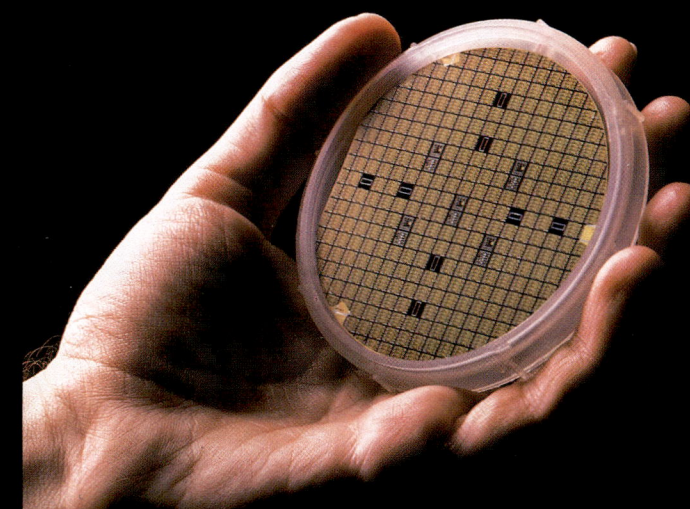

15

13

12 The production of integrated circuits (ICs) begins with a large-scale drawing of the complex electronic circuits that are to be placed on a tiny chip of silicon. A photo-reduced mask, greatly reduced in size, is used in the chip fabrication process. (© Chuck O'Rear)

13 Silicon, one of the earth's most common elements, is extracted from rock quartz. Shown here are pieces of purified crystals of silicon. (© Chuck O'Rear).

14 Thin slices of silicon crystals, called "wafers," are coated with a mask of hardened photo-resist and baked in an oven containing super-hot gases loaded with impurities. These impurities, or "dopants," create the miniaturized circuit elements. (© Chuck O'Rear / Woodfin Camp & Associates)

15 Each wafer is made up of as many as 10 layers of circuitry. A finished wafer can contain 200 or more individual chips. After they have been tested with a computerized probe, these chips are separated by a computer-controlled diamond cutter. (© Joel Gordon, 1982 / DPI)

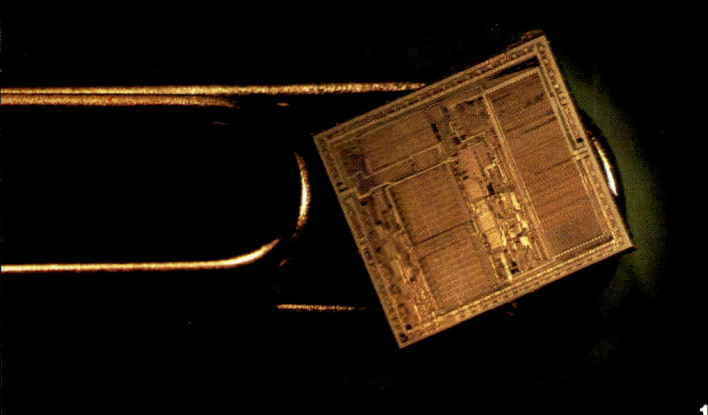

16

17

19

18

16 An individual chip, which may contain all the circuitry needed to store and process data, is smaller in size than a paper clip. Computers on a chip will become commonplace for many scientific and commercial uses. (© Chuck Gordon)

17 Minicomputers are frequently used in small businesses and offices, where they perform accounting and other data processing tasks, such as sales analysis and word processing. Shown is the IBM System 34. (Courtesy IBM)

18 This businessman is using a hand-held computer while enroute to his destination. Inexpensive microcomputers of this type have the processing capability possessed by much larger computers only a few years ago. (Courtesy Hewlett-Packard)

19 The Cray 1S is a supercomputer. It can store several million characters of data in main memory and can execute approximately 100 million instructions per second. This type of computer is fast enough to perform very complex scientific calculations. (Courtesy Cray Research, Inc.)

20

20 From the air, Silicon Valley, the world's largest semiconductor center, appears to look like an integrated circuit itself. Located between Palo Alto and San Jose, California, an hour's drive south from San Francisco, this former fruit grove hosts more than 80 silicon chip manufacturing plants. Named in 1980 as the fastest-growing area in America, Silicon Valley has a population of 1.2 million, and the average annual income of its residents is over $24,000, the nation's highest. (© Chuck O'Rear/Woodfin Camp & Associates)

21 An Apple II microcomputer is busy at work on a Missouri ranch, keeping accurate records on 350 head of cattle. The computer is helping to improve the quality of livestock by recording weight, immunization records, and other data related to cattle breeding. (© David Burnett, 1982/Contact Press Images)

21

22   This design engineer is using a hand-held stylus to trace images on a sensitized tablet. The images are translated into digital data which are stored in the computer and shown on a visual display terminal. (© Alvis Upitis/The Image Bank)

23   Renowned jazz musician Herbie Hancock uses a Fairlight computer and an Apple II in his experiments with multiple-keyboard instruments. Hancock connects the computers to his array of keyboards in his studio at his Hollywood, California, home. By matching different melodies and instruments, Hancock hopes to be the ultimate one-man band, creating a music never before heard. (© David Burnett, 1982/Contact Press Images)

22

23

1. Business people became overenthusiastic about computers and failed to evaluate correctly the complexity of the systems that they wanted to establish.

2. Because of the differences between business language and computer languages and jargon, users and computer professionals often failed to communicate.

3. Computer hardware and software continued to change, and systems were often obsolete before they were installed or were incompatible with older or newer systems.

Early efforts to use computers in business proved most successful when they were at the operational level and were limited to single functions, such as payroll, billing, and inventory control. Often, though, with too little planning and too much enthusiasm, people applied computers to the solution of complex problems, such as combining the special information needs of the three management levels.

Complex systems often proved to be costly and difficult to develop. They required the participation of many different types of users. Communication between users and computer personnel was limited at best; hence, requirements were difficult to define. As a result, many computer-based business information systems, although perhaps successful from the viewpoint of the data processing department, in reality lacked usability because they did not meet the real needs of the persons who would have to use them.

Computer Information System— A Definition

Nonetheless, the use of the computer as an aid to management decision making remained an important objective. As shown in Figure 3-7, the output of a data processing system is information, which becomes an input to management. Management, in turn, has as its output decisions for planning and controlling. However, management decision support systems proved to be difficult to design—not because they required that large volumes of data be processed, but because managers required selective "exception" information, such as the number of customer accounts delinquent by more than 60 days.

Table 3-1 lists the information requirements at each management level. The possibility of using the computer to study the effect of alternative, or "what if," actions increases its value to middle and top management. The term

FIGURE 3-7

Data processing and management decisions. Data processing systems can provide managers with information that assists them in making decisions for planning and controlling.

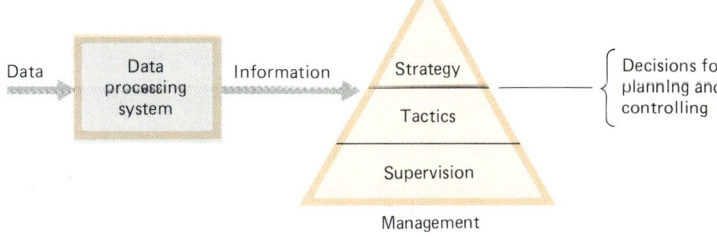

TABLE 3-1   **MANAGEMENT LEVELS AND INFORMATION REQUIREMENTS**

Management Level	Information use	Information requirement

Top management	1 Setting goals
	2 Long-range plans
	3 Strategy
		1 External information
		  (a) Competitor actions
		  (b) Government actions
		  (c) New markets
		  (d) Resource availability
		2 Internal information
		  (a) Financial reports
		  (b) Key exception trends
		3 Long-term trends
		4 "What if" information

Middle management	1 Defining objectives
	2 Medium-range plans
	3 Tactics
		1 Internal information
		  (a) Financial reports
		  (b) Exception reports
		2 Short-term trends
		3 Some "what if" information

Lower management	1 Achieving objectives
	2 Short-range plans
	3 Supervision
		Internal information
		  (a) Recent historical information
		  (b) Detailed operational reports
		  (c) Appropriate exception reports

computer information system frequently is used instead of **computer data processing system** to refer to computer-based business systems because it is a phrase that:

1. Focuses upon information, which is the useful output of the system

2. Emphasizes the three management-level uses of information, as contrasted with the operational-level use of processed data

A computer information system includes not only the computer component but also all the other necessary system resources: people, materials, facilities, and equipment.

Although finding more effective ways to manage computer applications projects will continue as one of the greatest challenges of the 1980s and beyond, much progress has been made and will continue to be made. An orderly procedure for managing the development of computer information systems has emerged. This procedure is called the life-cycle method.

FEEDBACK   **3-1** What is the difference between the goals and the objectives of a business?

3-2 What is the difference between product flow and information flow? Give an example of each.

3-3 What are the two types of information generators? Explain and give an example of each.

3-4 How many levels are there in a typical business? How many managements levels?

3-5 Describe the difference in information use at each management level.

3-6 Identify and discuss three reasons for failures of early computer-based business information systems.

THE LIFE-CYCLE METHOD

The **life-cycle method** is a structured, step-by-step approach to the development of complex systems. As applied to computer information systems, the life-cycle method is based upon the four distinct phases through which a business system must pass. Figure 3-8 identifies the four phases of a systems' life-cycle as:

1. The study phase
2. The design phase
3. The development phase
4. The operation phase

This figure lists the major activities that take place during each phase. At this time, we will introduce you to each phase with a brief overview. We will examine most of the listed activities in more detail in later chapters.

The Life-Cycle Phases

The study phase   The **study phase** is the phase during which a problem is identified, alternative solutions are studied, and recommendations are made about committing the personnel, money, and other resources required to design this system.

Study phase activities include the investigation of the problem, the determination of the desired system performance, the identification and evaluation of potential system solutions, and the analysis of alternative solutions. The reason for these activities is to pick the most *cost-effective* system—one that meets the desired system performance requirements at the lowest cost. A study phase report is prepared, and this system is recommended to the user, or users, of the system as the most feasible solution to the problem. The report and recommendations are in the language of the user and not filled with computer jargon. The user is the manager who will accept or reject the solution. The greater the participation of the user in the study phase, the more likely the success of subsequent phases.

FIGURE 3-8
The life-cycle phases

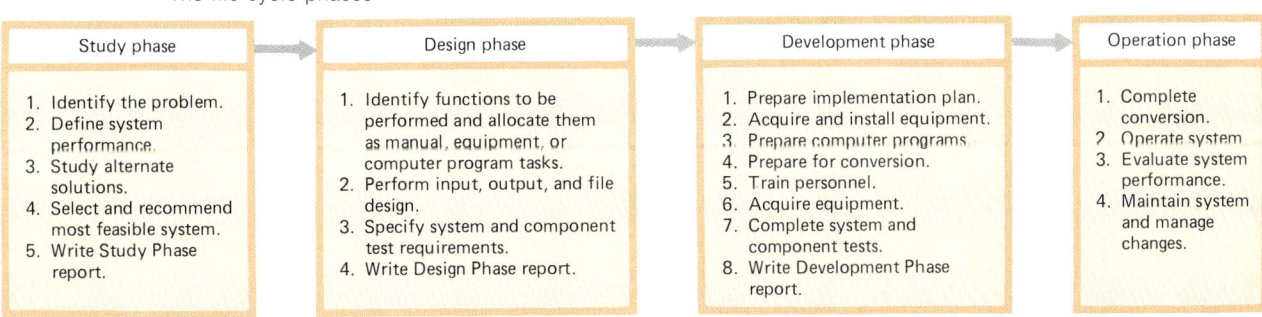

Study phase	Design phase	Development phase	Operation phase
1. Identify the problem. 2. Define system performance. 3. Study alternate solutions. 4. Select and recommend most feasible system. 5. Write Study Phase report.	1. Identify functions to be performed and allocate them as manual, equipment, or computer program tasks. 2. Perform input, output, and file design. 3. Specify system and component test requirements. 4. Write Design Phase report.	1. Prepare implementation plan. 2. Acquire and install equipment. 3. Prepare computer programs. 4. Prepare for conversion. 5. Train personnel. 6. Acquire equipment. 7. Complete system and component tests. 8. Write Development Phase report.	1. Complete conversion. 2. Operate system. 3. Evaluate system performance. 4. Maintain system and manage changes.

The design phase   The detailed design of the system selected in the study takes place during the **design phase.** System design is started by reviewing the study phase activities and making final decisions about which functions are to be performed by hardware, software, or humans. These decisions make it possible to establish requirements for equipment, for computer programs, and for personnel and their training. In this phase, the output, input, and data storage designs are completed for each of the computer programs. The design phase recommendations are presented to the user in a report that is oriented to the needs of programmers and other technical personnel who will be involved in developing the system.

The development phase   In the **development phase,** the system is constructed to fulfill the requirements outlined in the design phase. Development phase activities include preparing manuals and training employees, writing and testing computer programs, and testing the entire system, of which the computer programs are a part. At the conclusion of the development phase, the system is ready to be put into use. The last step of this phase is to present the completed system for acceptance by the user at a management review meeting.

The operation phase   The **operation phase** is the period during which the system is used. Activities include changing over the new system, monitoring the system's performance, and establishing procedures for making modifications or changes in the system. This phase continues for the rest of the system's useful life.

The Life-Cycle Flowchart

Figure 3-8 listed activities performed in each life-cycle phase. Figure 3-9 is a flowchart of the life cycle of a computer-based business system that includes the equally important functions of management review by the user and continuous documentation.

Management review of the life-cycle activities   Management review of the life-cycle activities may occur at any time. However, the conclusion of each phase is a natural time for a major review by the user. The major management reviews are shown by the process symbols at the top of Figure 3-9. These are formal scheduled reviews that must occur before a phase can be considered complete. They are essential because they ensure user involvement at critical decision points. Any of three decisions can be forthcoming at each review:

1. Proceed to the next phase.
2. Cancel the project.
3. Redo certain parts of a previous phase.

The "redo" activities are performed and reviewed before the project can proceed to the next phase. As shown in Figure 3-9, management review often triggers "cycling back," or feedback, to an earlier state in the life cycle of the system in order to remedy performance deficiencies or to respond to changes in requirements. Each successful review is a renewal of management commitment to the project.

Documentation of the computer information system   Documentation of the tasks completed in each phase parallels the life-cycle performance and management review activities. Documentation is not a task to be accomplished as a "wind-up" activity. It is the evidence that progress is being made; it is continuous and cumulative. Cumulative documentation is indicated by the heavy black lines and arrowheads of Figure 3-9. The most essential documents are called **baseline specifications,** which are documents that are used as references when the system is changed. There are three baseline specifications:

1. **Performance specification** is completed at the conclusion of the study phase. It describes in the language of the user exactly what the system is to do.

2. **Design specification** is completed at the conclusion of the design phase. It describes in the language of the programmer (and others employed in actually constructing the system) how to develop the system.

3. **System specification** is completed at the conclusion of the development phase. It contains all of the critical system documentation and is the basis for all manuals, procedures, and changes.

The design specification grows from the performance specification, and the system specification grows from the design specification. Each of these specifications is included in the written report prepared at the end of the corresponding phase. The key to the successful management of the life cycle of computer-based business information systems is to complete these critical baseline specifications at the end of each phase.

FIGURE 3-9

The life-cycle flowchart illustrates the relationships between performance, documentation, and user review throughout the life cycle of a computer-based business system.

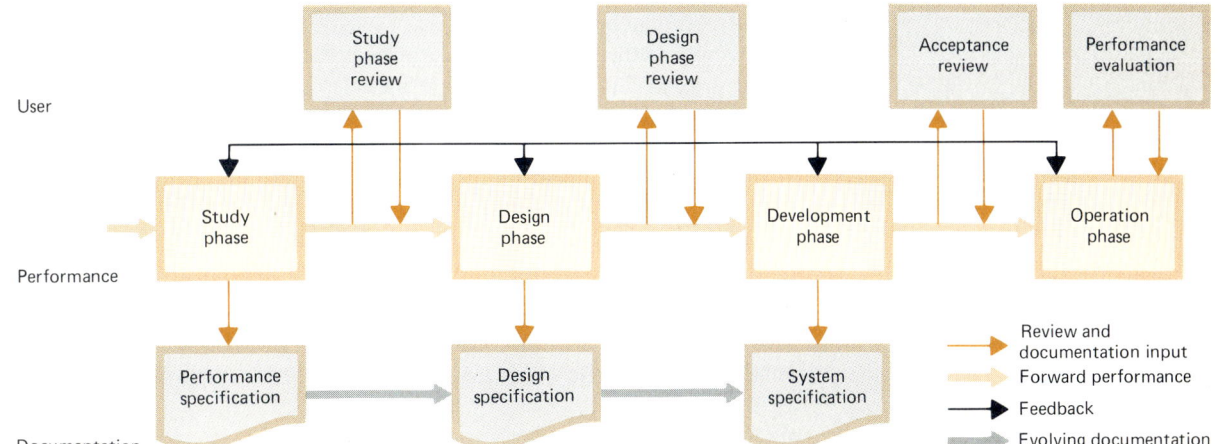

Systems Analysis and the Systems Analyst

Systems analysis is a general term for problem-solving techniques, that follow the life-cycle sequence that we have just described. Generally, the study phase activities are emphasized. Within the context of the life-cycle flowchart of Figure 3-9, we define **systems analysis** as the performance, documentation, and management of the activities associated with the four phases of the life cycle of a business information system. This is an important definition because the application of the life-cycle method has led to the emergence of a new professional, trained to perform systems analysis, called the systems analyst. The systems analyst is an individual who is qualified by education and work experience to bridge the communication gap between the user and the computer programmer. Often a member of the information services department, the systems analyst is experienced in data processing, in several applications areas, and in the application of the life-cycle procedures. In terms of Figure 3-9, the systems analyst is the person responsible for the performance of systems analysis tasks throughout the life cycle of a business system.

The systems analyst is the key individual in the successful application of the life-cycle method. However, the experienced analyst never forgets that the success of a system depends upon the satisfaction of the user. There are many users of a data processing system. A **user** is any individual who, in the course of the performance of his or her job, must provide input data to, or use information generated by, a computer-based business system. Effective systems cannot be designed by the data processing department alone. The user is the source of information, and the user pays the bills. Therefore, the analyst must:

1. Understand the user, the user's problem, and the user's language

2. Obtain and retain the user's participation throughout the life of the project

3. Represent the user's interests in dealing with data processing personnel

In reality, any individual who is affected to a significant degree by a computer-based business system is a user. However, there is usually one user whose needs the analyst must be particularly sensitive to. This is the **principal user,** the person who in practice will accept or reject the computer-based business information system. The principal user usually is the lowest-level manager to whom all of the organizations using the system report.

FEEDBACK   **3-7** What is the life-cycle method?

3-8 How many life-cycle phases are there? What are they? What is the purpose of each?

3-9 What baseline documents are produced when a life-cycle approach is taken toward the design of computer data processing systems.

3-10 Distinguish between systems analysis and systems analyst in terms of the life-cycle concept.

3-11 What does the term *principal user* mean?

Almost certainly, you, the user of this text, will become a user—perhaps the principal user—of one or more computer information systems in the course of your professional career.

SUMMARY

A business is a system that accomplishes specific objectives in order to achieve defined goals. A business is divided into smaller systems, called subsystems, that vary according to the organization of the business. The flow of activities between these systems may be product-related or information-related.

Information flow consists of the creation and movement of information within and between the departments of a company, and it is caused by internal and external information generators. There are three levels of information requirements for managers, which correspond to the needs of lower management, middle management, and top management.

The computer offers great potential as an information tool at all levels. In the past, because of overenthusiasm, language barriers between users and computer professionals, and continual changes in hardware and software, many problems were encountered by businesses that tried to use computers effectively.

Much recent progress has been made in developing a step-by-step procedure for the successful development of computer-based business systems, often referred to as computer information systems. This procedure, called the life-cycle method, is based upon the concept of a business information system life cycle that has four distinct phases: study, design, development, and operation.

Systems analysis is the performance, management, and documentation of all the activities associated with the four phases of the life cycle of a business information system. The person who performs systems analysis is called a systems analyst. The systems analyst is equipped by education and experience to bridge the communication gap between the user and the data processing staff and will play a key role in the management of information resources. He or she is sensitive to the needs of the principal user and is aware that the success of computer applications depends upon their being accepted by users.

ANSWERS TO FEEDBACK QUESTIONS

3-1   A goal is a broadly stated purpose of a business. An objective is a short-term, specific accomplishment needed to achieve goals.

3-2   **a** Product flow is the flow of raw materials into finished goods. The movement of raw materials from a receiving area into an inventory of materials in a warehouse is an example.

b Information flow is the creation and movement of documents that support product flow and meet the other information needs of a business. A receiving report and an inventory transfer document are examples.

3-3   Internal and external. A receiving report is an example of an internal information generator. A report to stockholders is an example of an external information generator.

3-4   **a** Four.
b Three.

3-5   Lower management uses information to supervise operational-level activities. Middle management uses it to control the resources needed to achieve the goals of the company. Top management uses it to establish goals and develop long-range plans. Each level directs the one below it.

3-6   **a** Overenthusiasm for computer systems without understanding of their complexity.
b Communications problems caused by computer jargon.
c Continual changes in computer hardware and software.

3-7   A structured approach to the development of complex systems, such as computer information systems.

3-8   Four. In the study phase, a problem is identified, alternative solutions are studied, and a system recommendation is made; in the design phase, the detailed design of the system takes place; in the development phase, the system is constructed from design phase requirements; and in the operation phase, the system is used and modified, as necessary.

3-9   **a** The performance specification.
b The design specification.
c The system specification.

3-10 Systems analysis is the general term for problem-solving techniques that follow the life-cycle sequence. It is the performance, documentation, and management of the activities associated with the four phases of the life cycle of a business information system. The systems analyst is the individual who performs systems analysis.

3-11 The principal user is the person who will accept or reject a computer-based business system.

FOR REVIEW AND DISCUSSION

1 Why can we call a business a "system of systems"?

2 For a typical manufacturing business, give an example of each of the following:
a Goal
b Objective
c Product flow
d Information flow
e Internal information generator
f External information generator
g Study phase activity
h Design phase activity
i Development phase activity
j Principal user

3 In the life-cycle method:
  a What is the importance of user reviews?
  b What is meant by the term *cumulative documentation*?
4 Describe the life-cycle approach to the design and development of computer data processing systems. How does feedback relate to this approach?
5 Why is it more difficult to design information systems for higher-level managers than for lower-level managers?
6 What is a data carrier? Give some examples of hard-copy and soft-copy data carriers?
7 The text identified several reasons for difficulties with early computer-based business information systems. Are we still encountering difficulties? Explain your answer.
8 Discuss the differences and similarities between the terms *computer information system* and *computer data processing system.*
9 What is the relationship beween the *principal user* and *usability?*
10 Why is it important for users of this text to become familiar with the life-cycle method and with computer system elements and applications?

CHAPTER 4

COMPUTER SYSTEMS: AN OVERVIEW

PREVIEW   All computer systems perform the functions of inputting, storing, processing, controlling, style, and outputting. The goal of this chapter is to familiarize you with the computer system units that perform these functions. We will accomplish this by examining computer systems from the perspective of the system designer, or architect. You will be introduced to the architecture of the primary and secondary storage units, the central processing unit, and the input and output units.

In this chapter you will learn:

1. The three different types of computers
2. The relationship between hardware, software, and firmware
3. How data and instructions are stored in primary and secondary storage
4. The major functions performed by the control unit, the arithmetic logic unit, and the input and output units

KEY TERMS TO WATCH FOR AND REMEMBER

computer system architecture	E-time
analog computer	multiprocessing
digital computer	binary code
hybrid computer	byte
firmware	word
read-only memory (ROM)	K
branch	accumulator
bit	I/O interfaces
memory	microprogram
variable field length	secondary storage
binary number system	channels
I-time	bus

COMPUTER SYSTEM ARCHITECTURE

In our discussion of computers and business systems in Chapter 3, we emphasized the importance of the computer as a problem-solving tool for businesses. We also identified the systems analyst as the person qualified to make effective use of this tool. Although the analyst must be able to specify the tasks that a computer must perform and to select the most appropriate computer, the analyst does not design the computer itself. Computers and their accessory equipment are designed by a *computer system architect*, who usually has a strong engineering background. As contrasted with the analyst, who uses a computer to solve specific problems within a certain business, the computer system architect usually designs computer that can be used for many different applications in many different businesses. For example, the product lines of major computer manufacturers such as IBM, Burroughs, Honeywell, Control Data, and Digital Equipment Corporation are the result of the efforts of teams of computer system architects.

Unless you are studying engineering, you are not likely to become a computer system architect. However, it is important that as a potential user, applications programmer, or systems analyst you understand the functions of the major units of a computer system and how they work together. This unit will help you to acquire that understanding. This chapter will provide you with an overview of computer systems as they are viewed by computer system architects. It is an introduction to Chapters 5 and 6, which describe the major units and their functions in more detail.

The only architecture that we will emphasize is that of digital computers, which are the most common computers and which are the subject of this text. However, there are other types of computers, and we will first describe these briefly.

Types of Computers

The two basic types of computers are analog and digital. **Analog computers** simulate physical systems. They operate on the basis of an analogy to the process that is being studied. For example, a voltage may be used to represent other physical quantities such as speed, temperature, or pressure. The response of an analog computer is based upon the measurement of signals that vary continuously with time. Hence, analog computers are used often in applications that require continuous measurement and control.

Digital computers, as contrasted with analog computers, deal with discrete rather than continuous quantities. They count rather than measure. They use numbers instead of analogous physical quantities to simulate on-going, or real-time, processes. Because they are discrete events, commercial transactions are in a natural form for digital computation. This is one reason that digital computers are so widely used in business data processing.

Machines that combine both analog and digital capabilities are called **hybrid computers.** Many business, scientific, and industrial computer applications rely on the combination of analog and digital devices. The ultrasonic diagnostic system shown in Figure 4-1 is an example of a hybrid computer system. Analog signals generated by the scanner as continuous voltages are

COMING HOME TO ROBIE

A personal robot, called Hero I, is being sold as a computerized "pet," by the Zenith Radio Corporation's Heath Company. Heath and several other companies are marketing programmable robots which can speak, respond to verbal commands, move around obstacles, and lift several pounds with one "hand."

Manufacturers of home robots agree that the initial models are relatively crude, but they feel that the capabilities of the home robots will increase quickly because the initial buyers will tend to be technically sophisticated, and they will create software to make the hardware more useful. Heath feels that the home robots constitute a whole new field for programmers and that the only limit is the collective imagination of the users.

Heath's 20-inch-tall Hero I robots come with a clawed arm capable of lifting 1 pound, a semiconductor chip that permits computer-synthesized speech, a microphone that lets it hear, and an internal clock for scheduling its chores. The rechargeable robot contains ultrasonic sensors to detect movement and to avoid obstacles.

Topo, a robot product of Androbot Inc., is designed to be controlled by a radio link to a home computer. Topo has two slanted wheels that enable it to make quick turns and charge in any direction over flat surfaces. It will give home computer owners an opportunity to learn and apply programming. A more advanced version will contain a microcomputer "brain" and will be able to navigate by making decisions about its movements.

Genus I, a robot made by Robotics International, can lift 5 pounds, has a video display, can store 48,000 bits of data, and carries a built-in vacuum cleaner. With the help of ultrasonic sensors, Genus I is intended to be able to "learn" the layout of a home well enough to clean all of the dirty corners. A security package that includes infrared and microwave sensors is designed to detect smoke, fires, and intruders.

The present personal robot market seems to be of interest primarily to well-to-do hobbyists and to the educational institutions, particularly schools that teach robotics. However, with 1983 sales estimated at 25,000 units, home robot manufacturers anticipate that in the future, when the technology is fully developed, home robots may rival home computers.

Source: Business Week, Dec. 13, 1982, p. 962.

"digitized" (periodically measured and converted to numbers) and supplied to a small digital computer that monitors the patient's condition.

The use of combination analog and digital devices will continue to increase with the growth in applications of microprocessors and microcomputers. An example of this growth is the trend toward installing control systems in household appliances such as microwave ovens and sewing machines. In the future, we will have complete indoor climate control systems and robots to do our

FIGURE 4-1

Ultrasonic diagnostic scanner. Ultrasonic scanners are used in medicine for clinical examinations of the human body. The system shown is controlled by the computer, which receives its input from the ultrasonic scanner. A typical output is the functioning of the heart. This output is displayed on a screen, which can be scanned by a television camera that creates a permanent record.

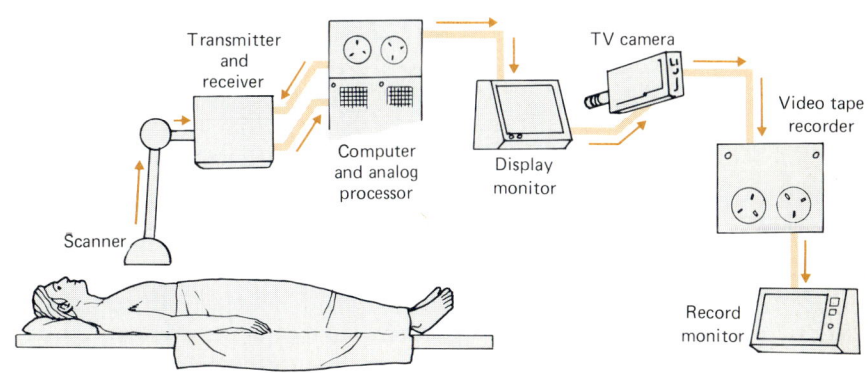

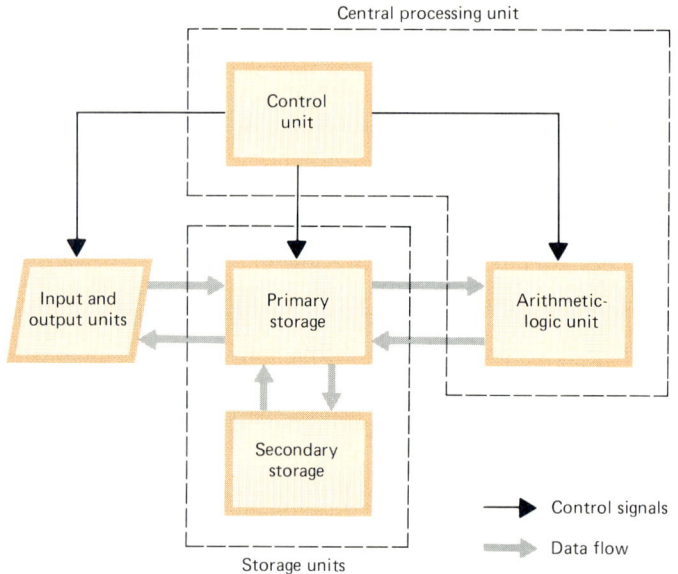

FIGURE 4-2

Computer system organization. The control unit issues signals which control the flow of data between the other units of a digital computer.

housecleaning. Analog sensors will provide inputs to the control centers of these systems, which will be small digital computers.

Functional Units of Digital Computers

As it applies to digital computers, we can define **computer system architecture** as the purposeful combination of hardware and software into an effective, user-oriented computer system. Now we can examine the building blocks, or functional units, of a digital computer system with which the architect works.

Figure 4-2 is a sketch that displays the major functional units of a digital computer system. These are: the input and output units; the storage units; and the control and arithmetic and logic units, which make up the central processing unit.

If you compare Figure 4-2 with Figure 2-2b, you will observe that the five basic data processing operations with which we are familiar are represented in both. Figure 4-2 is more suitable for describing the relationships between the functional units that are present in all digital computers. In this figure the gold lines indicate data flow, and the black lines represent the control exercised by the control unit.

A typical commercial digital computer system is shown in Figure 4-3.

Hardware, Software, and Firmware

The units that are visible in Figure 4-3 are the physical components, or hardware of the system. Not visible is the software—the computer programs, procedures, and associated documentation that make possible the effective operation of the computer system. As we learned in Chapter 2, there are two types of software programs: *systems software,* which comprises the programs that perform routine tasks for all users, and *applications software,* which com-

FIGURE 4-3
A typical small computer system.
(Courtesy Burroughs Corp.)

prises the programs that are written for specific computer applications such as payroll, inventory control, and investment analysis. Computer system architects are concerned more with computer hardware and systems software than with applications software. Systems programmers, who prepare systems software, are highly trained specialists and important members of the architectural team.

Often programs, particularly systems software, are stored in an area of memory not used for applications software. These protected programs are stored in an area of memory called **read-only memory (ROM),** which can be read from but not written on. **Firmware** is a term that is commonly used to describe certain programs that are stored in ROM; firmware often refers to a sequence of instructions (software) that is substituted for hardware. For example, in an instance where cost is more important than performance, the computer system architect might decide not to use special electronic circuits (hardware) to multiply two numbers, but instead write instructions (software) to cause the machine to accomplish the same function by repeated use of circuits already designed to perform addition. However, because improvements in memory technology are occurring continuously, firmware is frequently a cost-effective alternative to wired electronic circuits, and its use in computer design will increase.

Computer system architecture is organized around the primary storage unit because all data and instructions used by the computer system must pass through primary storage. Our discussion of computer system units will begin with the functions of the primary and secondary storage units. This leads to the examination of the central processing unit and from there to consideration of the input and output units. Therefore, the sequence in which we will describe the functional units of a digital computer is:

1. Storage units, primary and secondary
2. Central processing unit
3. Input and output units

In this chapter we will describe the functions that these units perform. In Chapters 5 and 6 we will learn about the actual devices (hardware) that perform these functions.

FEEDBACK **4-1** What does a computer system architect do?
4-2 What are the three types of computers? How do they differ?
4-3 What are functional units of a digital computer?
4-4 What are the differences between hardware, software, and firmware?
4-5 What is a systems programmer?

STORAGE UNITS Figure 4-2 showed both primary and secondary storage units. Both contain data and the instructions for processing the data. Notice again how (under the management of the control unit) all data that are contained in the other units must flow into and out of primary storage. Instructions must also flow into and out of primary storage. Important concepts that are essential to your understanding of how digital computers function are described in this section.

Primary Storage Primary storage is also called main storage or internal storage. *Internal storage* is an appropriate term, because primary storage usually occupies the same physical enclosure, called the computer *mainframe,* as does the central processing unit. The specific functions of internal storage are to hold (store):

1. All data to be processed
2. Intermediate results or processing
3. Final results of processing (prior to their release to an output device)
4. All the instructions required for ongoing processing

Another name for primary storage is **memory,** because of its similarity to a function of the human brain. However, computer storage differs from human memory in important respects. Computer memory must be able to retain very large numbers of symbol combinations indefinitely, without forgetting or changing any details. It must be able to locate all its contents quickly upon demand. Another analogy for computer memory is an array of post office letter boxes, as shown in Figure 4-4. As this figure illustrates, the letter boxes are numbered in sequence and are of the same size. The letter-box analogy illustrates a concept that is essential to understanding the operation of a digital computer. It is this:

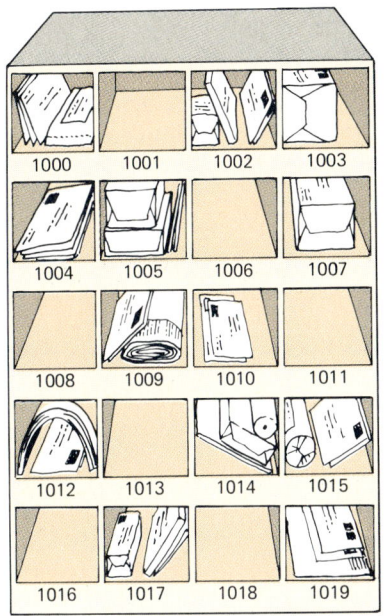

FIGURE 4-4

Letter-box analogy for computer storage. Each box is one storage location. The address of a location does not change. The contents of a location may change.

Data Storage: Bytes and Words

FIGURE 4-5

Examples of binary hardware devices. Binary devices can only represent two conditions: on or off. These conditions can represent either a 1 or a 0 or a yes or a no.

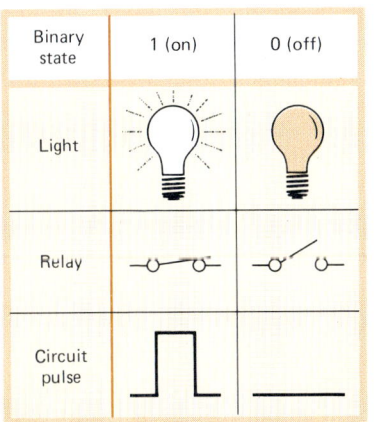

Binary state	1 (on)	0 (off)
Light		
Relay		
Circuit pulse		

The address of each storage location (letter box) does not change; however, the contents of the address may change.

Unlike a letter box, the contents of an address in primary storage are not in a format that is easily read by humans. The combinations of *characters*, that is, the letters, numbers, and special symbols by which we normally communicate, are coded. The codes used by computer designers are based upon a number system that has only two possible values, 0 and 1. A number system with only two digits, 0 and 1, is called a **binary number system,** as contrasted with the decimal number system, which has 10 digits, 0 through 9. Each binary digit is called a **bit,** from BInary digiT. Computer architects use binary codes because hardware components that represent only two possible conditions are less expensive and more reliable to work with than those that have to represent many possible conditions. These components act as high-speed switches that are either on or off, corresponding to the binary values of 1 or 0. The concept of binary components is illustrated in Figure 4-5. Modern microelectronics technology makes it cost-effective to place many thousands of tiny binary switches on a small silicon chip, each able to provide electronic on or off signals.

Because the information capacity of a single bit is limited to 2^1, or two alternatives, codes used by computer designers are based upon combinations of bits. These combinations are called **binary codes.** The most common binary codes are 8-bit codes because an 8-bit code provides for 2^8, or 256 unique combinations of 1's and 0's, and this is more than adequate to represent all of the characters by which we communicate.[1]

Data in the form of coded characters is stored in adjacent storage locations in main memory in two principal ways:

1. As "strings" of characters
2. Within fixed-size "boxes"

Important terms which are used to describe these methods of data storage are byte and word.

Byte   A fixed number of consecutive bits that represent a character is called a **byte.** Because the most common byte size is 8 bits, we will use byte to mean the 8-bit byte. Figure 4-6a shows primary storage organized into 8-bit bytes that have not been coded to contain data. The smallest addressable unit of storage is the byte. When a computer program causes a character to be read into primary storage, the program also causes an address to be assigned to the location of that character. In terms of our letter-box analogy, each 8-bit box would have the capacity to store one character of data.

---

[1] The notation 2^1 means 2 to the first power, or 2×1; similarly 2^2 means 2 to the second power, or 2×2, and 2^8 means 2 to the eighth power, or $2 \times 2 \times 2 \times 2 \times 2 \times 2 \times 2 \times 2$, which is 256.

PRIMARY STORAGE

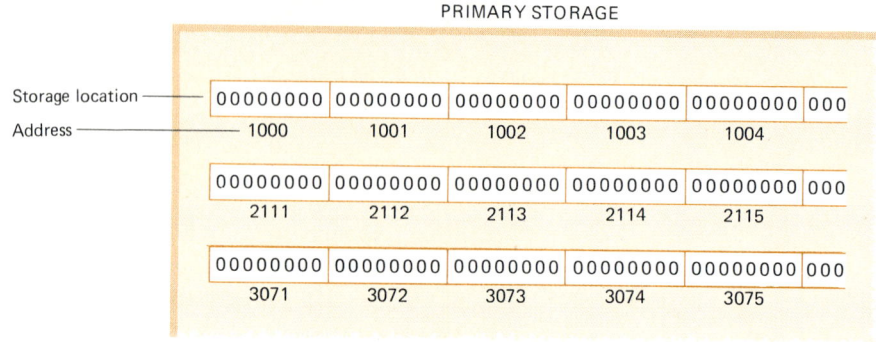

(a)

PRIMARY STORAGE

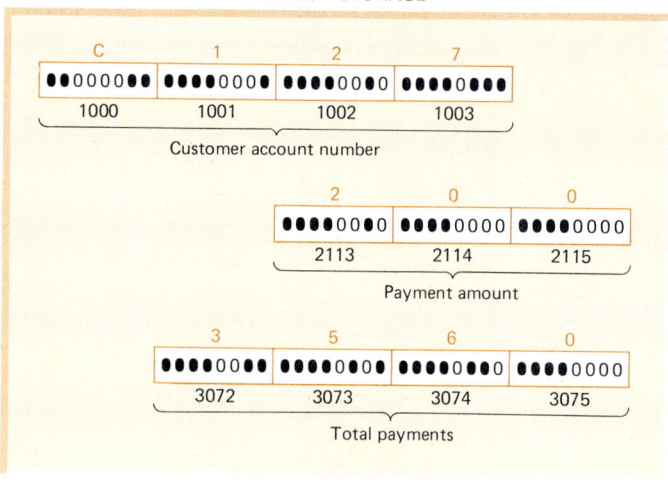

(b)

FIGURE 4-6

(a) Empty sets of consecutive storage locations are shown in this illustration. When coded, each location is able to contain 1 byte, that is, 1 character, of data. The addresses (in decimal) assigned to each byte of storage are also indicated. (b) The three coded strings of characters shown in this illustration are examples of variable-field-length storage. The Payment Amount field is 3 bytes long. The other two fields, Customer Account Number and Total Payments, are 4 bytes long.

Data elements, also called fields, may vary in size. For example, in a system that processed mortgage payments a customer-name field might be 20 or more characters (bytes) in length, and a payment-amount field might be as few as 3 or 4 characters in length. Figure 4-6b illustrates how the data elements representing Customer Account Number, Payment Amount, and Total Payments might appear in a common 8-bit computer code called EBCDIC. [You will learn more about EBCDIC (extended binary-coded decimal interchange code) and other computer codes in later chapters when we discuss computer programming.]

Notice that Customer Account Number and Total Payments are strings of characters 4 bytes in length and that Payment Amount is a 3-byte string. When a field is processed, the instruction specifies not only the address of the first byte but also the number of bytes in the field. As the above example illustrates, commercial applications of computers often require flexibility in manipulating strings of characters. Computers designed to provide this flexibility are known as **variable-field-length** computers.

Word   Although variable-field-length computers make efficient use of storage, they are less effective in performing arithmetic operations than in moving characters. Eight bits are required to store each digit of a number, and an arithmetic operation such as addition requires that the numbers be added serially, binary-coded digit by binary-coded digit.

An alternate approach for performing arithmetic operations is to store decimal numbers as their true binary equivalents. Although the number of digit positions in the binary equivalent of a decimal number usually is greater than the number of digit positions in the decimal number, the potential improvement in storage efficiency is illustrated by a simple example. The decimal number 15 would be stored in EBCDIC as 2 bytes, 11110001 and 11110101. The pure binary equivalent of a decimal 15 is 1111 (that is, $8 + 4 + 2 + 1$).

The reduction in storage bits is significant. Since many scientific applications require lengthy calculations involving large numbers, computers were designed to work with the binary equivalents of decimal numbers. These "scientific" computers used high-speed arithmetic circuits that, as contrasted with the serial, or digit by digit, arithmetic performed by variable field-length machines, operated upon all of the digits in a number at the same time. This type of arithmetic is called parallel arithmetic.

In order for parallel circuits to be efficient, the binary equivalents of decimal numbers had to be placed in fixed-size storage boxes, called **words.** Typically, words are 1 or more bytes in length.

Word size is fixed within a machine. Therefore, word size is an important architectural factor. Small machines have word sizes of 1 or 2 bytes; large machine word sizes are 4 or more bytes.

Data and instructions are moved to and from memory in word-sized bunches. Therefore, even if the electronic circuits used are comparable in speed, small machines are slower than big machines. This difference is analogous to providing the user of a small machine with a small data shovel and the user of a large machine with a large data shovel. Even though they both may be shoveling at comparable speeds, the user with the small shovel will be slower because more shovelfuls are needed to move the same amount of data.

Machines designed to store data in fixed word lengths are called *fixed-word-length* computers. These include some of the largest scientific computers because they need the speed of calculation that accompanies fixed word-length architecture. However, most business and scientific processing is performed by flexible computers, called *general-purpose computers*. General-purpose computers can employ either a fixed-word-length or a variable-field-length storage organization. The latter is often referred to as *variable-word-length* storage.

Storage Size, K

Large computer systems have more internal storage capacity than small systems. This capacity is stated in bytes or words. A symbol commonly associated with storage size is the letter K, which stands for the decimal value of the power of 2 that is closest to 1000. Thus, **K** is equal to 2^{10}, or 1024. Memory sizes range from a few K bytes or words in small machines to several thousand K bytes or words in large machines. *Remember,* if memory is stated in words, it is necessary to know the word size in bytes in order to determine the actual storage capacity of the computer.

Instruction Storage

The sequence of instructions that makes up the computer program is stored in primary storage along with data. Each instruction is designed to occupy a fixed number of storage locations, and instruction sizes are stated in bits, bytes, or words. The size of an instruction depends upon the complexity of the operation to be performed. Large computers have large, powerful instruction sets. Small computers have fewer and less-versatile instructions; these are usually subsets of instructions available on larger machines. A subset of instructions is a set that includes all of the basic instructions needed to perform the arithmetic and logical operations required of computers. However, it may not include additional powerful instructions that increase the versatility and speed of the computer. For example, a programmer working with a large machine might use a single instruction to add two data fields and to place the result of the addition into one of those fields. A programmer working with a smaller machine might have to write several instructions to achieve the same result.

Figure 4-7*a* shows the format of an instruction, used by several families of large IBM computers, to add the contents of two primary-storage locations. The contents of a storage location are called an *operand*, and this particular instruction directs the central processing unit of the computer to add both operands and to replace the first operand with the resulting sum. The computer system architects who developed the instruction set, of which this instruction is an example, used a base-displacement addressing scheme. The first four bits of byte-3 and byte-5 identify reserved storage locations, called *registers*. The contents of the registers specified in the instruction are base values used to determine the addresses of operands. The remaining bits in the second and third half-words specify displacements with respect to the base values. Thus, the address of a data element is the sum of the contents of a base register and a displacement. Figure 4-7*b* illustrates the base-displacement addressing scheme for the instruction shown in Figure 4-7*a*. Instruction formats vary from computer to computer. A complex machine, such as a large, general-purpose computer, may employ several different instruction formats.

Secondary Storage

Primary storage is expensive because each bit is represented by a high-speed device, such as a semiconductor. A million bytes (that is, 8 million bits) is a large amount of primary storage. Often, it is necesary to store many millions, sometimes billions, of bytes of data. Therefore, slower, less expensive storage units are available for computer systems. These units are called **secondary**

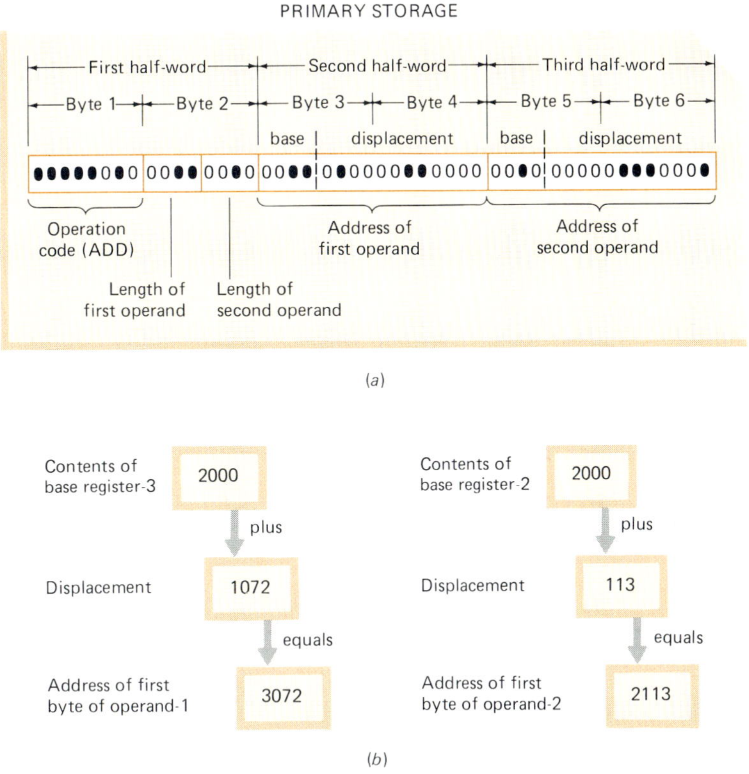

FIGURE 4-7

FIGURE 4-7

(*a*) The format of an instruction that adds the contents, called operands, of two primary storage locations. This instruction is for a machine with a word size of 32 bits, and the instruction is organized into 3 half-words, or 6 bytes. The first byte indicates the operation to be performed. The second byte indicates the lengths, in bytes, of the storage locations in which the fields of data are to be found. The second and third half-words, respectively, identify the address of the first byte of each operand. (*b*) The base-displacement addressing scheme associated with the instruction shown in Figure 4-7(*a*). If the contents of both base-value registers is 2000 (in decimal) and the values of the remainders of the second and third half-words, respectively, are 1072 and 113, the address of the first byte of the first operand is 3072, and the address of the second operand is 2113. Notice that the lengths of the operands are identified by the bit patterns in byte-2 of the instruction. The lengths of the data fields, in decimal, are interpreted as being equal to the binary values plus 1. In this example, the length of the first operand is 4 bytes, and the length of the second operand is 3 bytes.

PRIMARY STORAGE

(*a*)

(*b*)

storage. Data are stored in them in the same binary codes as in main storage and are made available to main storage as needed. A wide range of secondary storage devices is available. Typical hardware devices are magnetic tape and magnetic disk. We shall learn about many different types of secondary-storage devices in the next chapter.

Control Storage and Local Storage

Some storage areas, usually located in main memory, cannot be used by programmers. They are reserved for the use of the computer system. Typical of this type of storage are control storage and local storage.

Control storage   Control storage is read-only memory that contains special firmware programs called **microprograms,** or *microcode,* written to aid the control unit in directing all of the operations of the computer system. These microprograms are cost-effective because they make it possible to re-use a few hardware components to implement many different control functions.

Local storage   Local storage areas are registers that help the central processing unit to interpret instructions and to perform arithmetic and logic operations. Two important registers are the storage register and the address register. They

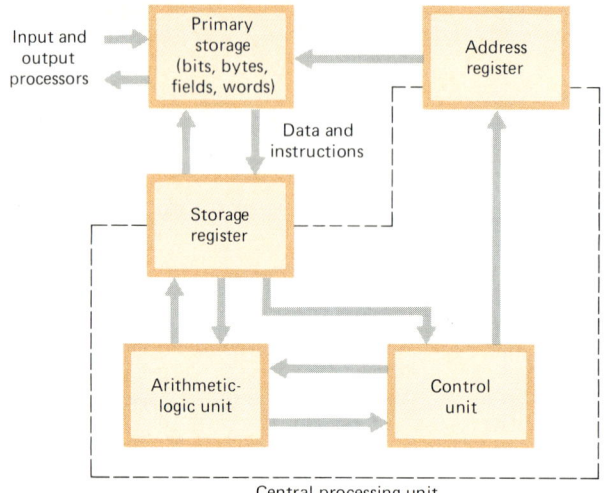

Input and
output
processors

Primary
storage
(bits, bytes,
fields, words)

Address
register

Data and
instructions

Storage
register

Arithmetic-
logic unit

Control
unit

Central processing unit

FIGURE 4-8

Communication between the primary
storage unit and the arithmetic logic
and control units.

are shown in Figure 4-8 which illustrates how the primary storage unit communicates with other units.

All data and instructions enter and leave primary storage through the storage register. The sequence of instructions is maintained by the address register, which contains the address of the next instruction to be executed. The capacity and speed of these registers are important architectural design considerations because they affect the cost and performance of the central processing unit.

FEEDBACK

4-6   What does address mean?

4-7   Use the terms *byte, field,* and *word* to describe how data and instructions are stored.

4-8   How many bytes can be stored in the primary storage unit of a 1000K computer?

4-9   What are control storage and local storage?

4-10 What is an operand?

CENTRAL PROCESSING UNIT

As Figure 4-8 shows, the central processing unit (CPU) consists of the control unit and the arithmetic logic unit. Each of these units makes extensive use of registers.

Control Unit

The control unit manages and coordinates the entire computer system. It obtains instructions from the program stored in main memory, interprets the instructions, and issues signals that cause other units of the system to execute them. Instructions obtained by the control unit identify the operation to be

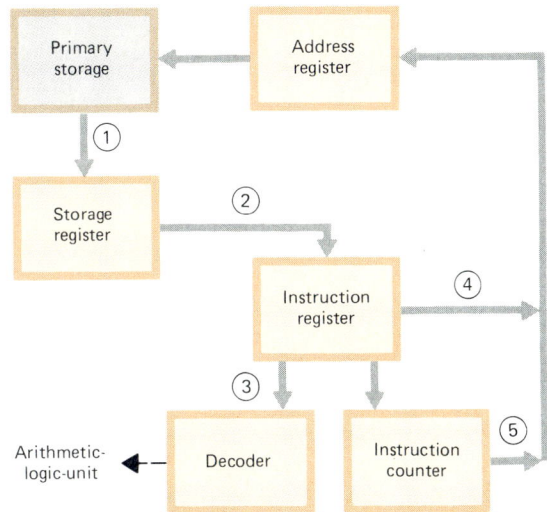

FIGURE 4-9
Control unit functional diagram.

performed and the address of the operand (that is, the address of data required by the operation specified in the instruction).

Sequence of control unit operations   Figure 4-9 shows the major registers used by the control unit. The sequence of control unit operations shown in this figure is as follows:

1. The next instruction to be executed is read-out (copied electronically) from primary storage into the storage register.

2. The instruction is passed from the storage register to the instruction register.

3. The operation part of the instruction is decoded so that the proper arithmetic or logical operation can be performed.

4. The address of the operand is sent from the instruction register to the address register.

5. The instruction counter register provides the address register with the address of the next instruction to be executed.

Change in instruction sequence   A remarkable feature that is responsible for the versatility of the digital computer is its ability, under program control, to change the sequence in which instuctions are executed. Instructions are executed sequentially until an instruction calls for a **branch** (that is, a jump) to a different point in the program. This branch causes the contents of the instruction counter register to be modified so that an instruction that is not the next in sequence is obtained. And unless there is another branch, instructions are executed in sequence from the point to which the jump was made. As an example of branching, consider a program that is processing customer credit orders and is checking each order to determine whether or not the customer's credit limit has been exceeded. Each order is compared with the remaining credit balance. If the credit balance is greater than the amount of the order, the program proceeds to the next instruction in sequence. If the credit balance is less than the amount of the order, the sequence is modified by a branch to a different sequence of instructions. These may call for some special action, such as printing an overcredit notice.

I-time and E-time   The time required to move an instruction from main storage to the control unit and to decode it is called the instruction time, or **I-time.** Each I-time is followed by an execution time, called **E-time.** During E-time, the operation that is decoded by the control unit is carried out by the arithmetic-logic unit. I-times and E-times alternate until the complete instruction sequence has been executed.

Arithmetic Logic Unit

The arithmetic logic unit (ALU) executes the processing operations called for by the instructions brought from main memory by the control unit. As shown in Figure 4-10, data enter the ALU and return to main storage through the storage register.

The **accumulator** shown in this figure is a register that holds the results of processing operations. Both the storage register and the accumulator can make their contents available to the adder so that arithmetic and logical operations can be performed.[2] Larger computers have many registers that can serve as accumulators or perform other special functions. Smaller computers have fewer registers.

The results of arithmetic operations are returned to the accumulator for transfer to main storage through the storage register.

The comparer performs logical comparisons of the contents of the storage register and the accumulator. Typically, the comparer tests for conditions such as "less than," "equal to," or "greater than." Thus, in the preceeding example of branching to a different sequence of instructions, the comparer would compare order amount with credit balance to determine whether or not order amount was greater than credit balance. If so, a branch would occur.

Figure 4-11 uses an "add" instruction to demonstrate the operation of the arithmetic logic unit. The example also summarizes our previous discussions of storage and the control unit by showing major steps in the flow instructions and data between the primary storage unit and the central processing unit. The flow of instructions is shown by the black lines and the flow of data by the colored lines. The sequence illustrated in Figure 4-11 is as follows:

1. The instruction is moved from primary storage into the instruction register, where the operation code is interpreted and the addresses of the operands determined.

FIGURE 4-10
Arithmetic logic unit functional diagram.

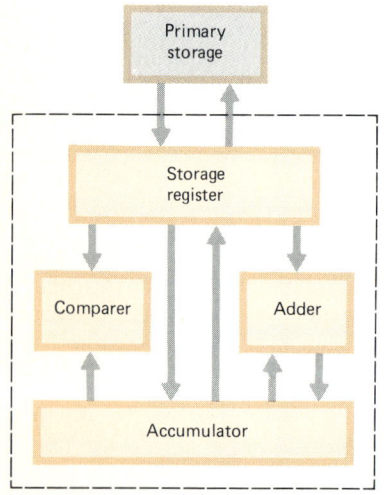

Primary storage

Storage register

Comparer   Adder

Accumulator

ALU

2 Directly or indirectly, digital computers base all arithmetic operations upon addition.

2. The first operand is moved into the accumulator in the arithmetic logic unit, replacing its previous contents.

3. The second operand is moved into an internal register in the arithmetic logic unit.

4. The adder adds the contents of the storage register to the contents of the accumulator and places the total in the accumulator.

5. The contents of the accumulator are moved to the location of operand 1 in primary storage, replacing its previous contents.

As the above example illustrates, the letter-box analogy that we introduced earlier in this chapter is useful, but primary storage in a digital computer differs from a letter box in several important ways. Unlike a letter box, an address in primary storage can hold only one item at a time. When the contents of a letter box are removed, the box is empty. When the contents of an address in storage are read, they are not removed but are duplicated electronically and reproduced elsewhere. Also, unlike a letter box, when a new item is placed in primary storage, the previous contents are erased.

FIGURE 4-11

This figure illustrates the operation of the control unit and the arithmetic logic unit. The control unit obtains an instruction from primary storage and determines it to be an ADD instruction (step 1). It also obtains the data, called operands, required to execute the instruction and places them in special storage areas in the arithmetic logic unit (steps 2 and 3). The arithmetic logic unit then executes the instruction. Notice that the initial value of operand-1, which is 3560, is replaced in the accumulator by the result of the addition, which is 200 + 3560 = 3760 (step 4). The control unit then moves the sum to primary storage, which changes the value of operand-1 from 3560 to 3760 (step 5). Thus, if operand-1 is Total Payments and operand-2 is a monthly Payment Amount, this instruction would be suitable for keeping a current record of cumulative payments.

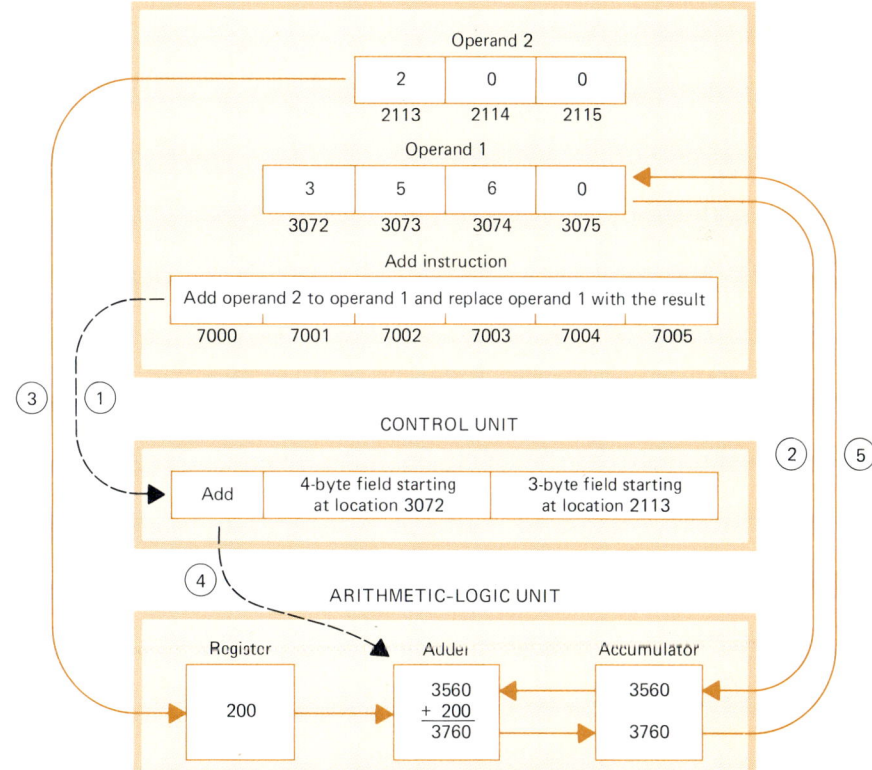

INPUT AND OUTPUT UNITS

Data and instructions must enter the data processing system, and information must leave it. These operations are performed by input and output (I/O) units that link the computer to its external environment.

Input-Output Environment

The I/O environment may be human-related or human-independent. A remote banking terminal is an example of a human-related input environment, and a printer is an example of a device that produces output in a human-readable format. An example of a human-independent input environment is a device that measures traffic flow. A reel of magnetic tape upon which the collected data are stored in binary format is an example of a human-independent output environment.

I/O Interfaces

Data enter input units in forms that depend upon the particular device used. For example, data are entered from a keyboard in a manner similar to typing, and this differs from the way that data are entered by a bar-code scanner. However, regardless of the forms in which they receive their inputs, all input devices must provide a computer with data that are transformed into the binary codes that the primary memory of the computer is designed to accept. This transformation is accomplished by units called **I/O interfaces.** Input interfaces are designed to match the unique physical or electrical characteristics of input devices to the requirements of the computer system. Similarly, when output is available, output interfaces must be designed to reverse the process and to adapt the output to the external environment.

MULTIPLE PROCESSORS

Up to this point we have considered a single processor, the central processing unit. The performance of a computer system can be improved if the processing tasks are shared by more than one processor. These I/O processors that share main memory with the central processing unit and control the formatting and movement of data and instructions between main storage and peripheral I/O devices are called **channels.** I/O processors improve the efficiency of the computer system by making possible concurrent input, processing, and output operations. The central processing unit can perform arithmetic and logical operations on parts of one or more programs while input and output operations take place concurrently on other parts of programs. Figure 4-12*a* illustrates the I/O multiple processor design concept.

Systems have also been developed to make use of more than one central processing unit. Such systems are called **multiprocessing** systems. Figure 4-12*b* shows the architecture of a typical multiprocessing system.

Current advances in integrated-circuit technologies have made the distribution of processing functions among multiple processors a standard design technique. Typical tasks assigned to processors are I/O processing, communications processing, and processing of selected instruction sets. Figure 4-12*c* displays the multiple-processor architecture of a minicomputer. In this figure, a central processor, a communications processor, a scientific instruction processor, and high- and low-speed peripheral processors are connected to a group of circuits called a **bus,** which provides an electronic communication path between the elements of the computer system.

In the future, all large computer systems will use multiple, parallel processors to share high-speed or complex operations and to enhance processing throughout. There will be computers within computers, because some of these processors will be complete microcomputers. The entire system will be under the control of a complex, powerful operating system.

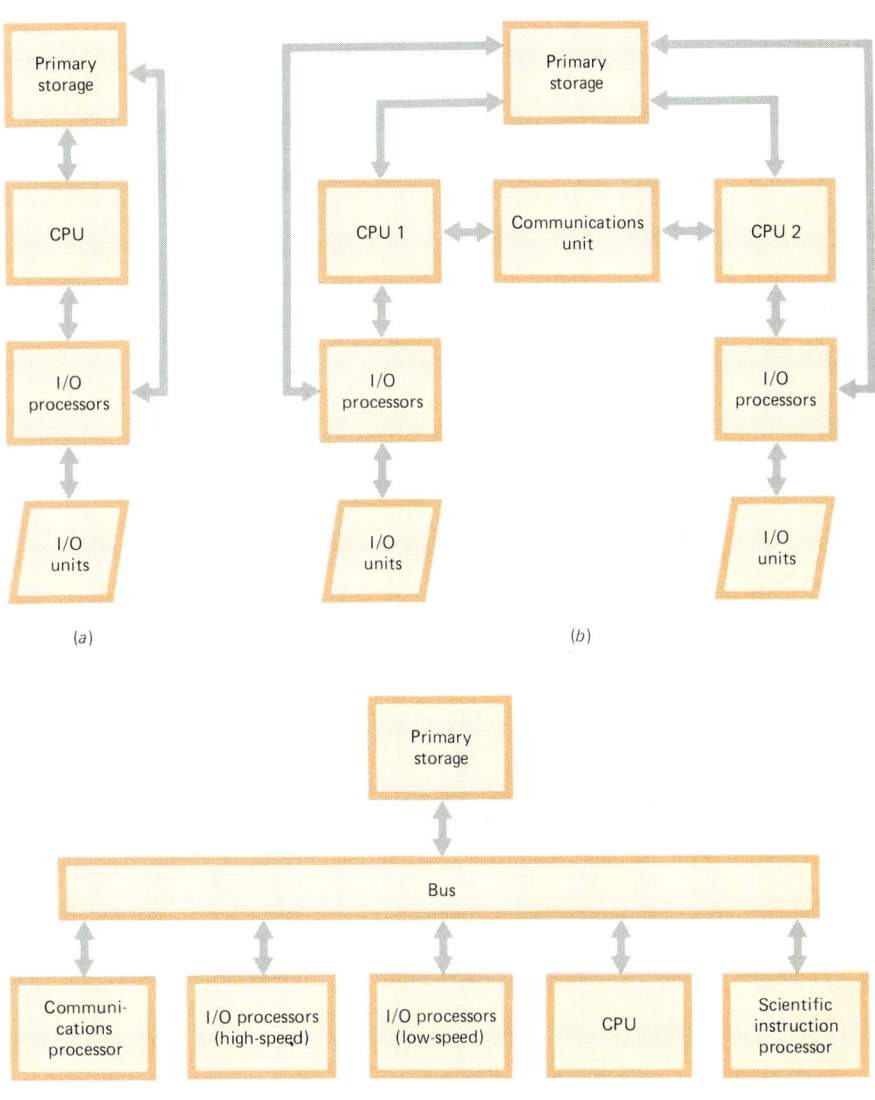

FIGURE 4-12

Multiple processor architecture. (*a*) I/O processor. (*b*) Multiprocessors. (*c*) Minicomputer with multiple processors.

Computer systems of all sizes perform the same five basic data processing operations. The major differences are in speed and cost, and these depend upon the design decisions made by the computer system architects. Computer application needs vary from those of the home hobbyist to those of large industrial enterprises. Once these needs have been identified, the task of the computer system architects is to meet them with a computer system composed of functional units that are balanced in performance and cost. In Chapter 5 we will describe many storage and processing devices, and in Chapter 6 we will describe input and output devices.

FEEDBACK

4-11 Name the two units that make up the central processing unit. What are the principal functions of each?

4-12 What is an accumulator?

4-13 What are I-time and E-time?

4-14 What is the function of an I/O interface.

4-15 What does *multiprocessing* mean?

4-16 What is a bus?

SUMMARY

Computer system architecture is the purposeful combination of hardware and software into an effective, user-oriented system. The two basic types of computers are analog computers, which measure, and digital computers, which count. Hybrid computers are a combination of both types.

The major functional units of a digital computer are the storage units, the central processing unit, and the input and output units. The computer system architect implements specific functions as hardware, software, or firmware. Firmware is a program that is stored in read-only memory (ROM). The principal storage units are primary storage, secondary storage, and local storage. Primary storage contains all data to be processed, intermediate processing results, final processing results, and instructions.

Storage locations are assigned addresses, and data are stored at these addresses in binary codes. A fixed number of consecutive bits, representing a meaningful written symbol, is called a byte. The most commonly used byte is the 8-bit byte, and it is able to contain a single binary-coded character. The byte is the smallest addressable unit of storage.

Computers designed to store strings of characters in consecutive byte locations are called variable field-length or variable word-length computers. Computers designed to store data in fixed-size boxes are called fixed word-length computers. Words are one or more bytes in length. Variable field-length machines are best for character manipulation, and fixed word-length machines are best for high-speed arithmetic. General-purpose computers combine the capabilities of both types of machines.

Instructions are stored in main memory, and their sizes are stated in bits, bytes, or words. Control storage is read-only memory that contains microprograms used by the control unit. Local storage areas, called registers, help the central processing unit to interpret and to execute instructions. The central processing unit is made up of the control unit and the arithmetic logic unit. The control unit obtains instructions during I-time, and the arithmetic logic unit executes them during E-time.

Input and output (I/O) units enable the computer system to communicate with its environment, which may be human-related or human-independent. The characteristics of input and output devices of different types are matched to those of the computer by I/O interface units.

Multiple processors can improve the performance of computer systems by allowing parallel processing of segments of programs. The incorporation of multiple processors into the design of larger computer systems will become commonplace in the future.

Small computer systems are less efficient than large computer systems. They are also less expensive. Therefore, they may be more cost-effective for some applications. The computer system architects must design systems that are balanced in performance and cost to meet a broad range of application needs.

ANSWERS TO FEEDBACK QUESTIONS

4-1   A computer system architect designs computers and their accessory equipment.

4-2   Analog, digital and hybrid. Analog computers simulate continuous, physical processes by measuring analogous electrical signals. Digital computers deal with discrete, instead of continuous, quantities. They count instead of measure. Hybrid computers combine the characteristics of analog and digital computers.

4-3   The input unit, the storage units, the arithmetic logic unit, the control unit, and the output unit.

4-4   Hardware is the physical components of a computer system. Software is the computer programs, procedures, and associated documentation that make possible the effective operation of the computer system. Firmware is a program that is stored in read-only memory.

4-5   A systems programmer is a specialist who prepares systems software, which is designed to perform routine tasks for all computer users.

4-6   *Address* refers to a storage location. The contents of a storage location may change, but its address does not.

4-7   A byte is a fixed number of adjacent bits that represent a meaningful written symbol. A field of data is a meaningful collection of related characters, each of which could be represented by a byte. Words are fixed-size storage boxes that are 1 or more bytes in length.

4-8 $1000K = 1000 \times 1024 = 1,024,000$ bytes

4-9   Control storage is read-only memory that contains small firmware programs used by the control unit to direct operations of the computer system. Local storage areas, or registers, are used by the central processing unit to interpret instructions and to perform arithmetic and logic operations.

4-10 An operand is the contents of a storage location.

4-11 The control unit and the arithmetic logic unit. The control unit manages and coordinates the operation of entire computer system. The arithmetic logic unit performs the processing called for by instructions obtained from memory by the control unit.

4-12 An accumulator is a register that holds the results of processing operations.

4-13 I-time, or instruction time, is the time needed to move an instruction from main storage to the control unit and to decode it. E-time, or execution time, is the time required for the arithmetic logic unit to perform the instruction.

4-14 The I/O interface transforms input data into a binary format that the computer can accept and performs the reverse operation for outputs.

4-15 Multiprocessing refers to the use of more than one processor to share the processing functions required of a computer.

4-16 A bus is a group of circuits that provides an electronic communication path between the elements of a computer system.

1 What is a hybrid computer? Can you give some examples of hybrid devices?

2 What is firmware and what is its importance to the computer system architect?

3 What is the difference between an applications programmer and a systems programmer?

4 How is read-only memory used?

5 Explain the difference between an address and the contents of an address?

6 What is the difference between a bit, a byte, and a word?

7 What is the importance of the difference in word sizes between small and large computers?

8 What is a subset of instructions?

9 Why is the ability to branch an important feature of a digital computer?

10 How can multiple processors improve the performance of computer systems?

UNIT
TWO

COMPUTER SYSTEMS: ELEMENTS AND APPLICATIONS

In Unit One, you began the study of computers and information systems by learning general concepts common to all data processing systems and by relating these to computer data processing systems. You studied the characteristics of business systems and became acquainted with the life-cycle method for managing the development of computer-related information systems. The first unit concluded with an overview of computer systems, which identified their principal components and the tasks performed by each.

In this unit, you will add to the knowledge that you acquired in Unit One through the examination of the devices that actually are the elements of computer systems and by learning about important real-world applications of computers. In Chapter 5, you will learn about several types of storage devices and about the operation of processing units. Chapter 6 will acquaint you with many different types of input and output devices. Chapter 7 extends the previous discussions of computer systems to the merging technologies of computers, communications, and the automated office. Chapter 8 is designed to introduce you to personal computers and their varied uses. It will provide you with some guidelines for selecting your own computer.

CHAPTER 5

STORAGE AND PROCESSING

PREVIEW   Many different media are available for storing and for processing data. The goal of this chapter is to describe the principal devices that perform the storing and processing functions described in Chapter 4. This will help you to relate these devices to small and large computer systems and to applications of these systems.

In this chapter you will learn:

1. The business data processing cycle
2. How storage media are classified by cost and access time
3. The characteristics of primary storage media
4. The characteristics of electromechanical storage media
5. Uses for emerging new electronic storage media
6. How electronic circuit cost and performance trends are affecting the design of processing units

KEY TERMS TO WATCH FOR AND REMEMBER

master file	random access
access time	magnetic disk
semiconductor	floppy disk
magnetic tape	archival storage
data transfer rate	magnetic bubble memory (MBM)
mass storage	transaction-driven processing
key field	optical-disk storage systems
transaction file	batch processing
sequential access	random-access memory (RAM)

THE BUSINESS DATA PROCESSING CYCLE   All data processing systems store and process data. However, many business information systems tend to repeat a cycle of processing operations because of the periodic availability of inputs and because of daily, weekly, and monthly

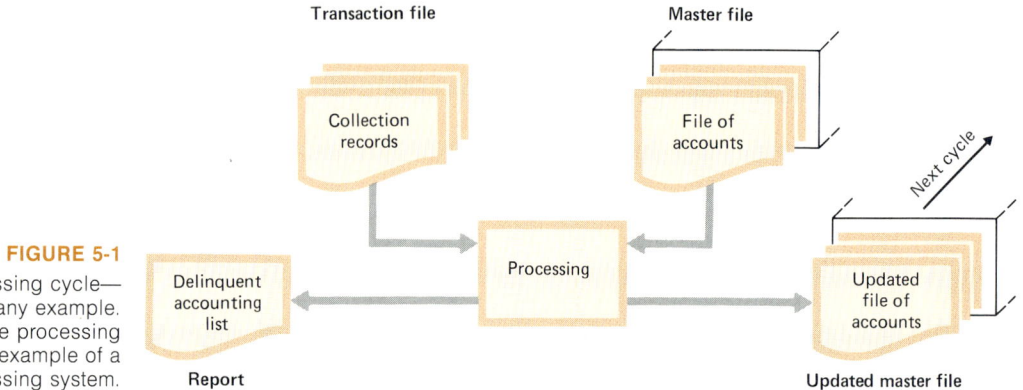

FIGURE 5-1

Typical data processing cycle—
Scrooge Mortgage Company example.
The master-transaction file processing
cycle is illustrated in this example of a
data processing system.

schedules for producing outputs. The basic business data processing cycle
requires the use of both primary and secondary storage media. Before discussing
the various types of storage devices, we should be familiar with this cycle. We
can use the example of the Scrooge Mortgage Company, introduced in Chapter
1, to illustrate a typical bussiness data processing cycle. Let us assume that
one of the important data processing functions of the Scrooge Mortgage Company is to prepare a monthly record of delinquent accounts, that is, a list of
persons who did not make their payments on time.

The data processing cycle for producing this information is shown in
Figure 5-1. A **master file** is one in which records that are to be preserved are
stored. A **transaction file** is one in which current data are stored for subsequent
processing. Because they contain details that change frequently, transaction
files are also called *detail files*. The cycle is called the master-transaction-file (or
master-detail-file) processing cycle because the file can be either a master file
or a transaction file. In a mortgage system, the transaction file would contain
data elements such as payment amount, date of payment, and late-payment
charges. As contrasted with a transaction file, a master file would contain
relatively permanent data, such as the interest rate, and information required
to be kept up to date, such as year-to-date interest paid and balance due.

Both files must contain a common field, called a **key field,** which is an
identifying field that is used to distinguish each account from all others. Typically, a key field might be an assigned account number. The basic business
data processing cycle depends upon the matching of detail and transaction
records by key field. Individual records are entered into primary storage from
both the transaction and master files after being sorted into a meaningful
sequence, such as ascending account number. The contents of the master file
are updated whenever there is a match between keys. The entry of a detail
record with a key field for which there was no matching master record could
mean that that a new account had been opened and that a new master record

would have to be created. The entry of a master-file record with a key field for which there was no matching detail record could mean that an account was delinquent. As shown in the example of Figure 5-1, the outputs at the end of a cycle could be a list of delinquent accounts and an updated master file. The entire process, then, would be repeated during the next processing cycle. The periodic updating of a master file is often referred to as **batch processing.** This means that records are collected into batches for processing at a later time. An example is the periodic printing of paychecks. In many instances it is important to process transactions as they occur. In this case, the master file is updated continuously, and this type of processing is called **transaction-driven.** Examples are student enrollments in classes and inventory management. In many modern computer centers there is a balance between batch and transaction-driven processing. Also, much of the output information is available as a screen display, which reduces the requirement for printed reports.

STORAGE: COMPONENTS AND CRITERIA
Solid-State Circuits

In Chapter 4 we described the functions performed by the units of a computer system. We learned that the function of primary storage is to hold the data and instructions that are being processed. Primary storage is expensive because each bit requires a high-speed element that can be switched on or off. Fast-access primary storage is necessary in order for a computer system to process large amounts of data efficiently. However, because of cost, not all of the data that must be processed can be placed in primary storage. Instead, secondary storage units, which are slower and less expensive, are used to store data until it is needed for processing in primary storage.

Computer storage has undergone many changes over the past two decades. Most recent improvements in storage are based on the development of solid-state circuits. A *solid-state circuit* is a component whose operation depends on the control of the electric or magnetic properties of a solid, such as the transistors that are miniaturized elements of integrated circuits. Solid-state electronic circuits have reduced the cost and improved the reliability of computer systems. Users of both small and large computer systems have benefited from these developments because they are able to select from a wide range of storage devices on the basis of cost, speed, and capacity.

Many of the devices that we will examine in this chapter are based upon advances in solid-state circuit components, and there are likely to be even greater changes in the coming decade. We will begin by presenting an overview of the media that are available for primary and secondary storage. This will enable us to define some important terms that are used to describe the performance of all storage, or memory, devices. Then, we will describe media that are available for primary storage, electromechanical secondary storage devices, and the newer electronic memory media. We will also describe briefly the application of solid-state circuits to the components of the central processing unit.

Cost, Capacity, and Access Time

The cost of storage devices is expressed as the cost per bit of data stored. The most common units of cost are cents, millicents (10^{-3} cents, or 0.001 cents), and microcents (10^{-6} cents, or 0.000001 cents). The time required for the computer to locate and transfer data to or from a storage medium is called the **access time** for that medium. The relationship between cost per bit of storage capacity and access time for the media that we will consider in this chapter is shown in Figure 5-2.

As Figure 5-2 also indicates, storage capacity increases as cost and access time decrease. Capacities range from a few hundred bytes of primary storage for very small computers to many billions of bytes of archival storage for very large computer systems. Memories may be classified as electronic or electromechanical. Electronic memories have no moving mechanical parts, and data can be transferred into and out of them at very high speeds. Electromechanical memories depend upon moving mechanical parts for their operation, such as mechanisms for rotating magnetic tapes and disks. Their data access times are longer than are those of electronic memories; however, they do cost less per bit stored and have larger capacities for data storage. For these reasons most computer systems use electronic memory for primary storage and electromechanical memory for secondary storage. Newer electronic memories, such as magnetic bubble memory, were developed to fill the cost and access time gap

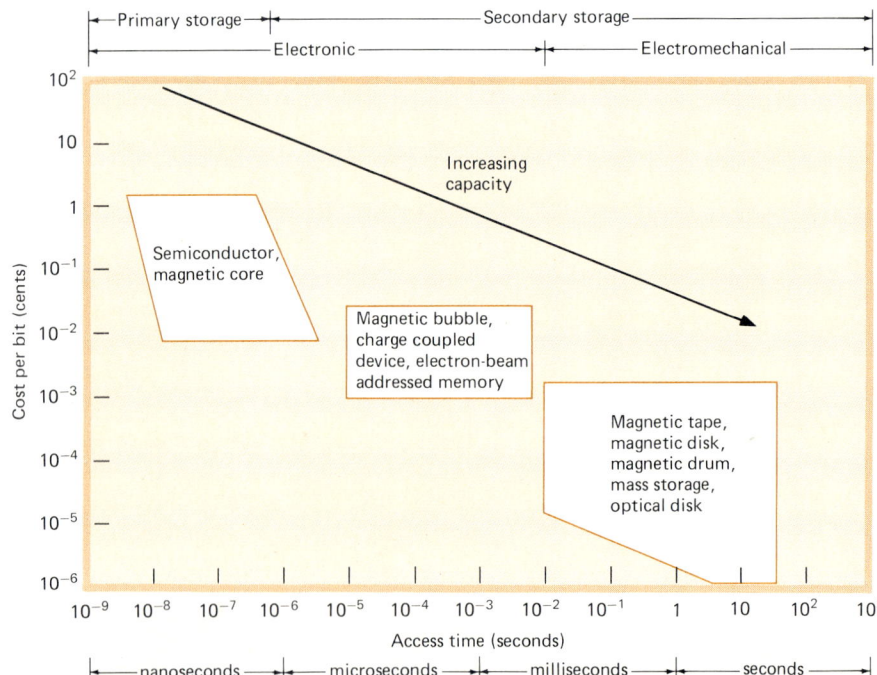

FIGURE 5-2

Storage media: cost, capacity, and access time.

between electronic primary memory and electromechanical secondary memory. These offer potential for the future, but at present are limited to special applications such as small, portable computer terminals.

PRIMARY STORAGE
Magnetic-Core Storage

The two primary storage media identifed in Figure 5-1 are solid-state devices: magnetic cores and semiconductors. For many years magnetic cores were the principal elements used in digital computers for primary storage. A *magnetic core* is a tiny doughnut-shaped iron ring a few thousandths of an inch in diameter. It is a solid-state medium that can be magnetized by means of an electric current sent through its center (see Figure 5-3). The direction of current flow determines the polarity of the core; hence, a single core can be magnetized to represent a binary 1 or 0. Presently, core memory has been largely displaced by semiconductor memories, which now provide faster access times at an equivalent or lower cost. However, unlike semiconductor memories, which are volatile and lose stored data when power is lost, core memory retains its binary-coded data, and it is still used in special applications, such as automatic control systems, where nonvolatility is important.

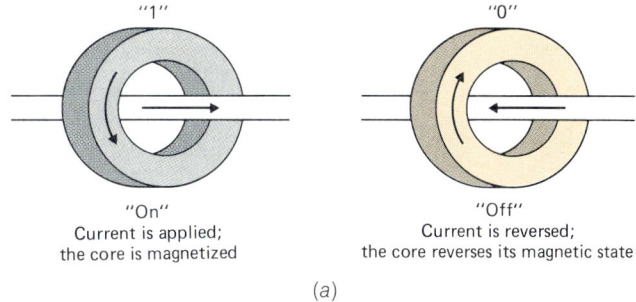

"1"

"0"

"On"
Current is applied;
the core is magnetized

"Off"
Current is reversed;
the core reverses its magnetic state

(a)

FIGURE 5-3

Magnetic core polarity and selection. (a) Magnetic core polarity. A core remains polarized until the direction of a current is reversed. (b) A magnetic core plane.

(b)

Semiconductor Memory

A substance that permits electricity to pass through it easily is called a *conductor.* An example is the copper wire in a household extension cord. A substance through which electricity cannot pass is called a *nonconductor.* The insulation around the wire in an extension cord is a nonconductor. In between conductors and nonconductors are solid-state materials called **semiconductors.** When semiconductors are used as circuit elements in a computer, they can be made to conduct or not to conduct. Therefore, semiconductors can be used as primary storage media in a manner analogous to the way magnetic cores are used. Electronic circuits that contain semiconductors are often called "gates" because they represent a 1 when current is permitted to flow and a 0 when it is not.

The two principal types of semiconductors used for memory are bipolar and metal-oxide semiconductors (MOS). The former is faster; however, because of cost, the latter is more commonly used at present. Both technologies will be used extensively in future systems. As noted, semiconductor memories are volatile, losing stored data when power is turned off. Because data can be accessed randomly, semiconductor memories are referred to as **random-access memory,** or RAM.

Figure 5-4 illustrates the size of a typical semiconductor memory chip. Chips able to store 256K bits of RAM on a silicon chip the size of a fish scale and with access times of less than 50 nanoseconds are anticipated to be in production in the 1980s. Semiconductor primary storage costs will then be between $0.001 and $0.01 per bit.

Main memories of small machines will become comparable in speed to those of large machine because they will use the same technology. Also, larger-capacity memories will become available for small machines at reduced cost.

FIGURE 5-4
Semiconductor memory chip. This photograph compares a memory chip with a paper clip to illustrate its size.

However, main memory will remain relatively expensive, compared to other computer components, regardless of the technologies used. Therefore, primary storage size will continue to be a distinction between small and large machine architectures.

FEEDBACK

5-1 What is a transaction file? A master file?

5-2 Distinguish between batch processing and transaction-driven processing.

5-3 What is access time?

5-4 Distinguish between *conductor, nonconductor,* and *semiconductor.*

5-5 Why are semiconductors used for primary memory and not for secondary storage?

ELECTROMECHANICAL SECONDARY STORAGE

Electromechanical media that use magnetic recording methods have been the most common secondary storage units for many years. In particular, magnetic tapes, disks, and drums are the secondary storage hardware most often used in computer systems. Other electromechanical devices with extremely large capacities for storage are also available.

Magnetic Tape

Magnetic tape, which was invented by the Germans during World War II for sound recording, is the oldest secondary storage medium in common use. Data are recorded on tape in the form of small magnetized "dots" that can be arranged to represent coded patterns of bits. Data recorded on tape are stored on reels, cassettes, or cartridges.

Magnetic tape reels As Figure 5-5a illustrates, a typical reel that stores magnetic tape data is 10½ inches in diameter and holds up to 2400 feet of ½-inch-wide tape.

Data recording on tape Data on magnetic tape are recorded on frames and stored along tracks or channels. As shown in Figure 5-5b, tracks are recording surfaces that run the full length of the tape. Tapes that use the most common data recording code, EBCDIC, require nine tracks. Eight are required by the

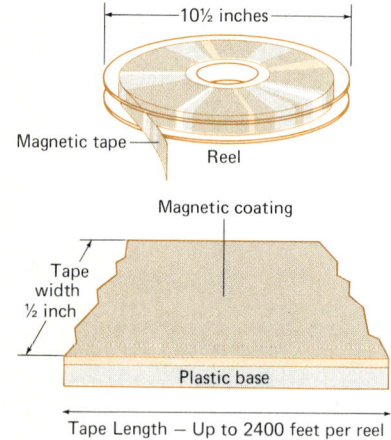

Tape Length — Up to 2400 feet per reel

(a)

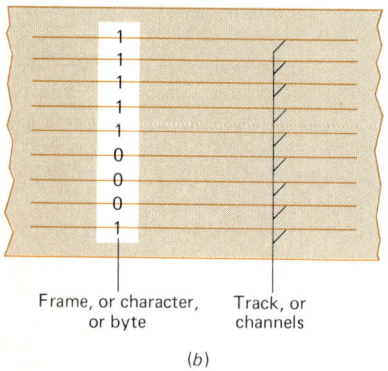

Frame, or character, or byte

Track, or channels

(b)

FIGURE 5-5

Magnetic tape data recording. (a) Characteristics of a tape reel. (b) A 9-track tape. The frame illustrates 8 EBCDIC bits, plus a check bit.

8-bit EBCDIC, and the ninth is a check bit. (The EBCDIC code is discussed in Supplement IV, Character Codes.)

Frames on a magnetic tape are narrow, vertical strips that are at right angles to the tracks. The bit patterns on these strips represent binary-coded characters.

Data transfer rate   Because of their slower access times, secondary storage devices are not able to transfer data to main storage at as rapid a rate as the data can be accepted. Nevertheless, this rate, called the **data transfer rate** or data rate, is one measure of the quality of a secondary storage device. The data transfer rate for magnetic tape is the product of tape speed and tape density. Tape speed is measured in inches per second, and high-performance tapes have speeds in excess of 200 inches per second.

Tape density is the number of frames that can be compressed into 1 inch of tape. Because a frame contains a character, or a byte, tape densities are expressed in characters per inch (CPI) or bytes per inch (BPI). High-performance tape units have densities of 6000 BPI or more and data transfer rates in excess of 1 million bytes per second.

Tape cassettes and cartridges   Micro- and minicomputer systems can be designed to use the same magnetic tapes as midi- and maxicomputer systems. However, because the cost of these secondary storage media might easily exceed the cost of all of the other units of the system, less costly units are usually used. This means that relatively low data-transfer-rate devices such as miniature tape units, tape cassettes, and tape cartridges are often used with small computer systems. Figure 5-6 shows a tape cartridge unit. The data transfer rate of small-system tape units is typically less than 10,000 bytes per second.

Blocking factor   As illustrated in Figure 5-7a, reels of tape are mounted in units called *tape drives* or *tape transports*. The tape transport mechanism is shown in Figure 5-7b. Writing (recording) on tape or reading (playing back) from tape can occur only if the reel of tape is rotating at a constant speed. The tape drive must accelerate the tape reel to its operating speed before the frames (bytes) that make up a record can be written on or read from the tape, and the drive must decelerate the tape afterward. The space on the tape that corresponds to the distance that the reel moves during acceleration or deceleration is not available for reading or writing data. This unavailable, or lost, space is called the *interrecord gap*. Typically, a gap is approximately 0.5 inches long. Unless the *logical record*, which is the data record operated upon by the computer, is long compared to the gap, unused space could exceed the data space on tape. For example, consider a tape with a density of 1600 BPI, a gap of 0.5 inches, and a logical record length of 100 bytes.

$$\text{Logical records/gap} = \frac{1600 \text{ bytes/inch} \times 0.5 \text{ inches}}{100 \text{ bytes/record}}$$

$$= 8 \text{ records}$$

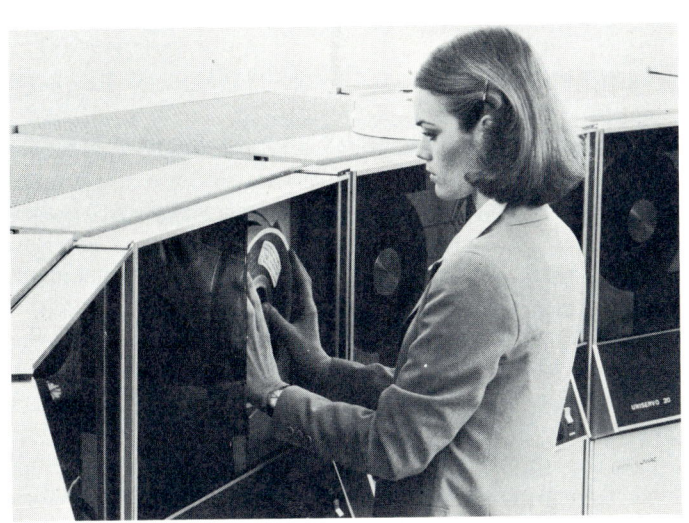

(a)

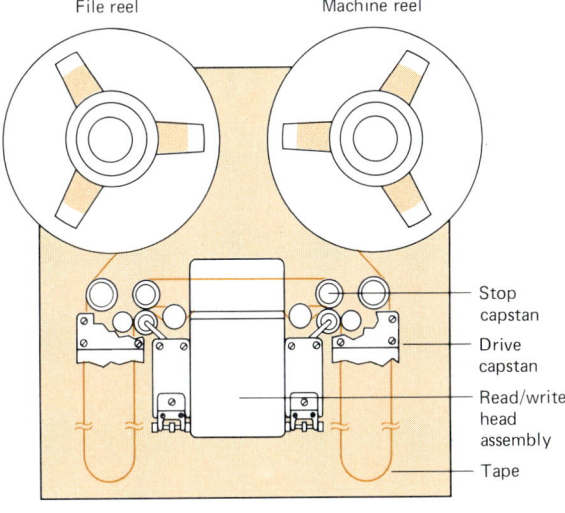

File reel

Machine reel

Stop capstan

Drive capstan

Read/write head assembly

Tape

(b)

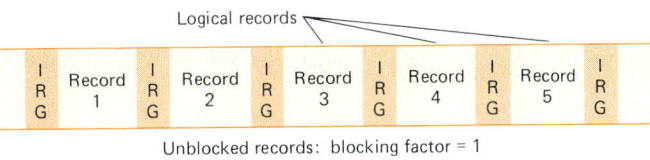

Logical records

| I R G | Record 1 | I R G | Record 2 | I R G | Record 3 | I R G | Record 4 | I R G | Record 5 | I R G |

Unblocked records: blocking factor = 1

|←——Physical record——→|

| I B G | Record 1 | Record 2 | Record 3 | I B G | Record 4 | Record 5 | Record 6 | I B G |

Blocked records: blocking factor = 3

(c)

Thus, in this example the unused space on the tape would be 8 times as large as the data space.

The data that are transferred to and from main storage are recorded on the physical area between the gaps. Therefore, a technique to minimize the inter-record-gap problem is to "block" (that is, combine) several logical records into a single physical area. These combined logical records are called a *physical record*. The physical record is usually long compared to the gap. The number of logical records contained in a physical record is called the blocking factor. If records are not blocked, the logical and physical records are equal in size, and the blocking factor is 1. When records are blocked, the interrecord gap becomes the interblock gap. The effect of blocking records is shown in Figure 5-7c. If we consider the previous example, using a blocking factor of 100, we find that:

$$\text{Physical records/gap} = \frac{1600 \text{ bytes inch} \times 0.5 \text{ inches}}{100 \times 100 \text{ bytes/record}}$$

$$= 0.08$$

And the unused tape space is less than 10 percent of the data space.

Tape file access and organization   A file is a collection of related records, and there are two general methods for accessing data on files. These are **sequential access** and **random access.** Sequential access means that records can only be written or read one after the other. Random access means that any record can be accessed directly whenever it is needed. The records on magnetic tape can be read or written only when the tape is passing through a read/write head assembly, such as is shown in Figure 5-7b. Therefore, the only feasible access method for tape is sequential.

The basic business data processing cycle described in this chapter involves the comparison of key fields for records stored on transaction and master files. Because records on tape can only be accessed sequentially, efficiency in processing transaction files against master files requires that the records on both files be organized in the same sequence according to a selected key field, such as part number, social security number, or account number.

Magnetic tape is effective for processing sequentially organized files when there are transactions for most of the stored records during each processing cycle. This type of file is called an *active file*. Examples of active files are payroll files and student grade-reporting files. If the transactions do not involve most of the records in the file, the file is said to be *inactive*. An example of an inactive file is a student information file, which might be used to examine randomly a small number of student records. Other types of organization are superior to sequential organization for dealing with inactive files. These, however, require the use of media such as magnetic disks and drums, which permit direct access to records.

FEEDBACK 5-6 Why are electromechanical storage media slower than electronic media?

5-7 Define data transfer rate.

5-8 What is the data rate for a magnetic tape drive for which the tape density is 1600 BPI and the tape speed is 200 inches per second?

5-9 What is the difference between a physical record and a logical record?

5-10 If a logical record is 100 bytes long and the blocking factor is 10, how large is the physical record on a magnetic tape?

Magnetic Disk Magnetic disk storage, introduced in the early 1960s, has replaced magnetic tape as the main method of secondary storage. As contrasted with magnetic tapes, magnetic disks can access records either in sequence or at random.

Data recording on magnetic disks Magnetic disks are thin, circular metal plates coated on both sides with a recording material similar to that used on tapes. Data are recorded as coded patterns of bits; a 1 bit is represented by a magnetized spot and a 0 is represented by the absence of a spot. As shown in Figure 5-8a, bits are aligned along tracks that form concentric circles on a disk surface. In some systems tracks are divided into sectors. Like blocking on tape, blocking of records on disks makes them more efficient. Records are usually processed most effectively if logical records are blocked into physical records.

Disks rotate at high speeds, and data are accessed or stored as the spot areas pass under read-write heads. There are three basic types of magnetic disk units:

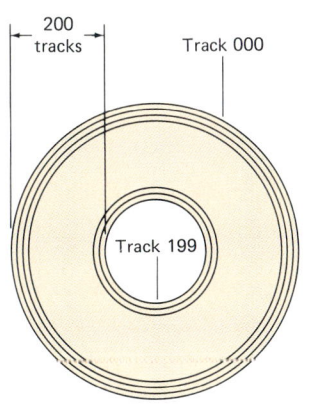

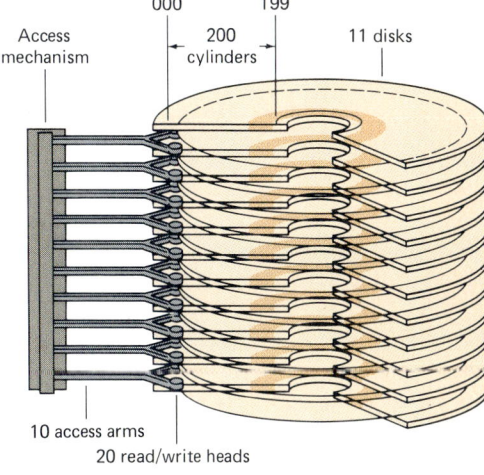

FIGURE 5-8
Moving-head magnetic disk. (a) Tracks on a disk. (b) Moving-head magnetic disk access mechanism.

(a)

(b)

1. Moving-head disks
2. Fixed-head disks
3. Combined moving-head and fixed-head disks

Moving-head magnetic disks   The principles of operation of a moving-head disk system are illustrated in Figure 5-8*b*. The unit sketched has 20 read-write heads, all of which are attached to a single movable-access-arm mechanism. Magnetic disks are direct-access devices. This means that the access arm is able to move a read-write head directly to a record address supplied by the computer system. An address includes cylinder number, head number, and record number. A cylinder is defined as the area covered by all of the read-write heads for one position of the access mechanism. The device sketched in Figure 5-8*b* has 200 cylinders, one for each of the tracks on a disk surface. Data are not recorded on the top or bottom surfaces of the disk "pack." Moving-head magnetic disk drives with much greater capacities than the unit sketched in Figure 5-8*b* are available, and the principles of operation are the same.

Unlike tapes, disks may be employed with other than sequential-file organizations. Two of the most common of these are direct and indexed-sequential. Direct files are those that the computer, using software that is part of the operating system, creates from the contents of key fields on data records. The data records are stored on magnetic disks at addresses calculated by the computer system. Records within a direct file can be accessed whenever needed (that is, at random) by recalculation of the appropriate addresses. Indexed-sequential files are created in sequential order, just as are tape files. However, in addition to the file itself, a set of address indexes is also created. These indexes are used by the system to look up the addresses of required records so that they may be accessed whenever needed.

Moving-head disks can have large capacities and fast data transfer rates. However, their access time, which is essentially the time for the read-write head to locate a record, is long, relative to other types of magnetic disks. Disk access time has two components: seek time and rotational delay. Seek time is the time required to position the access arm, and rotational delay is the time required for the selected record to pass under the read-write head. The rotational delay depends upon where the data are located with respect to the read-write head and upon how fast the disk is rotating. The speed of rotation and the bit density along a track determine the data transfer rate. Figure 5-9 shows a typical moving-head disk drive. In this system the rotating disks are enclosed in a protective cover, and the disks and cover together are called a disk pack. A disk pack is shown in Figure 5-9. In smaller systems, which have only one platter, the disk and cover are called a disk cartridge.

Fixed-head magnetic disks   Fixed-head magnetic disks were developed to reduce the access time by eliminating seek time. These devices do not have a

FIGURE 5-9
Moving-head magnetic disk drive and disk pack. *(Courtesy Sperry Corp.)*

moving access arm. Instead, a large number of read-write heads are distributed over the disk surfaces, one head for each track. The head-per-track disks used with this type of storage unit are not removable. Because of the space required for the additional read-write heads, fixed-head disks have less capacity and cost more per byte of data stored than moving-head disks.

Combined moving-head and fixed-head magnetic disks One method of utilizing the high capacity of a moving-head disk and the rapid access of a fixed-head disk is to combine the characteristics of each in a single unit. The Direct Access Storage Facility shown in Figure 5-10*a*, is an example of this type of unit. Systems using multiple storage units have capacities in excess of 3 billion bytes of storage. The disks used in this particular system are not removable. Other systems use data modules, which are removable. Data modules, as contrasted with disk packs, contain not only the magnetic disks but also the associated access arms and read-write heads. A data module is shown in Figure 5-10*b*.

FIGURE 5-10
(a) Direct-access storage facility: combined moving-head and fixed-head disk. (b) Data module. *(Courtesy IBM.)*

(a)

(b)

FIGURE 5-11
Diskette I/O unit. *(Courtesy Sperry Corp.)*

Floppy disks   The disk storage media that we described above often are too expensive for small computer systems. Small- and medium-sized disks are available. An increasingly popular storage medium for micro- and minicomputer systems is the flexible, or floppy, disk. Called diskettes, the "floppies" were introduced by IBM in 1972 and are now produced by many manufacturers to meet the growing demands of the microcomputer market. Figure 5-11 is a picture of a typical floppy disk. Diskettes greatly enhance the on-line storage capacity of small systems at an affordable price. They are also convenient off-line storage medium for the small system user. *On-line* means connected to a computer system and under the control of the central processing unit. *Off-line* means not connected to a computer system.

Floppy disks are typically 3, 5¼, or 8 inches in diameter. They range in design from single-sided, single-density to dual-sided, double-density, with typical capacities ranging from 100,000 to 1 million bytes of storage. They are an inexpensive storage medium and are sold in great numbers to users of microcomputers.

Comparison between magnetic tape and magnetic disk storage   Both magnetic tapes and magnetic disks can be used for sequential processing. Magnetic tape is a reliable and inexpensive medium for storing large amounts of data off-line. It is effective in processing large, active files.

Magnetic disks can be used for both sequential and random processing applications. They are less vulnerable to damage from dust or careless handling than magnetic tape. However, they are more expensive for off-line storage. Disks are available over a broad range of speed and capacities. Most computer systems in use today are disk-, rather than tape-oriented.

FEEDBACK

5-11 What are the three types of magnetic disk units?

5-12 What are the advantages and disadvantages of each of the three types of magnetic disk units?

5-13 What is a sequential file? A direct file? An indexed-sequential file?

5-14 What is the access time for a magnetic disk unit that has a seek time of 20 milliseconds and a rotational delay of 7 milliseconds?

5-15 What is a floppy disk?

Magnetic Drum

Magnetic drums are rotating cylinders coated with a magnetizable material. As illustrated schematically in Figure 5-12, the surface of the drum is divided into tracks upon which data are stored as magnetized spots in the same manner as on the surface of a disk. Data are recorded and read as records pass beneath sets of stationary read-write heads. Like the magnetic disk, the drum is a direct-access device that can be used for both sequential and random processing. Magnetic drums have fast data transfer rates but are more limited in capacity than magnetic disks. Although drums are available as components for some computer systems, they have largely been replaced by fixed-head disks that also have high data transfer rates.

FIGURE 5-12
Magnetic drum storage. (*a*) Drum storage unit. (*Courtesy IBM.*) (*b*) Character storage on a magnetic drum.

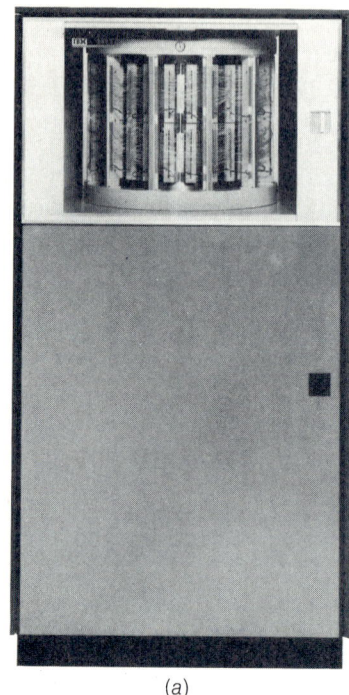

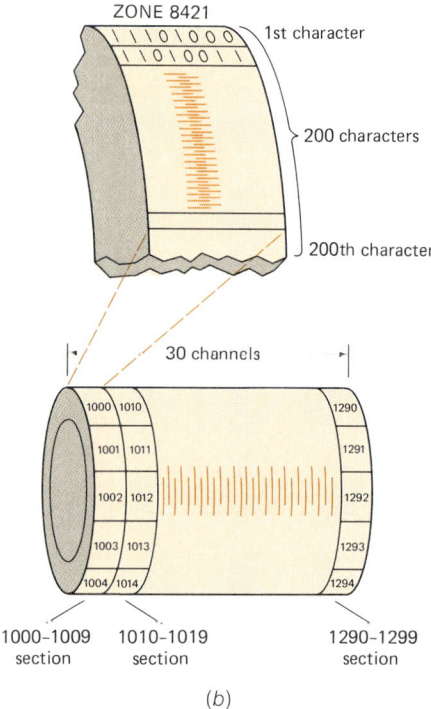

(*b*)

FIGURE 5-13
(*a*) Mass storage facility. *(Courtesy IBM.)* (*b*) IBM 3850 Mass Storage. The IBM 3850 Mass Storage Unit is a beehive of electronic activity. It can store up to 472 billion characters of information. This is accomplished by cartridges in each honeycomb cell that contain data on tape. This data can be transferred to main memory as it is needed. *(Courtesy IBM.)*

(*a*)

(*a*)   (*b*)

Mass Storage

Mass storage systems are storage systems that provide access to hundreds of billions of bytes of stored data. Some of these systems combine both tape and disk technologies. The IBM 3850 Mass Storage Facility (Figure 5-13a) is able to store 472 billion charaters of data; the storage mechanism is shown in Figure 5-13b. The access times of mass storage systems are measured in seconds instead of milliseconds because a transport mechanism must move to retrieve the cartridge upon which the designed data is stored. Relatively slow access times limit the use of mass storage systems for some applicants.

However, in many large-file processing applications rapid access to data is not essential. In these instances, mass storage systems can be a cost-effective alternative to on-line magnetic tape or disk storage. When used for off-line storage, mass storage systems are often referred to as **archival storage** because of the very large volumes of historical or backup data that they can store.

Optical-Disk Systems

The need to store and retrieve very large amounts of data has also lent impetus to the development of **optical-disk storage systems.** An optical-disk storage system is similar in principal to the laser-optical video disks sold for home use. As applied to computer-related information systems, optical disks store digitized data instead of the digitized elements of a picture.

Figure 5-14 is a sketch of the elements of an optical-disk recording system. An intense laser light source is focused on a rotating disk, which is coated with a reflective surface. Data recording is accomplished by turning the laser beam

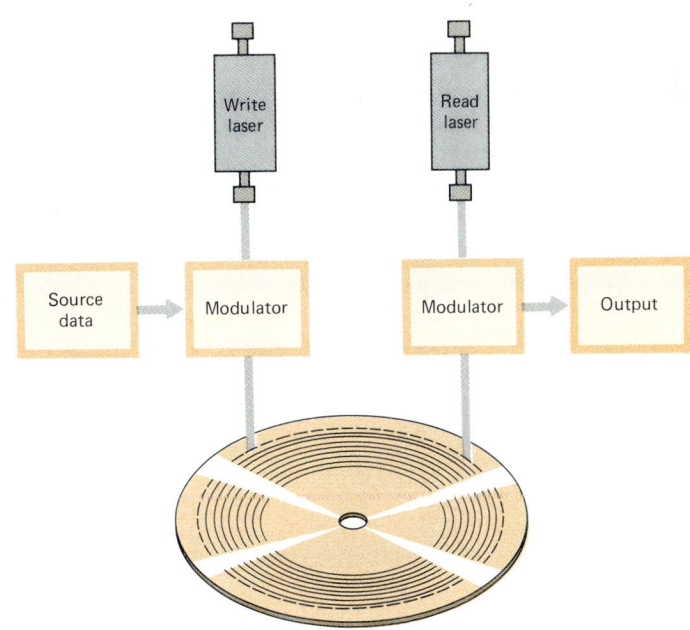

FIGURE 5-14

Digital data is used to modulate a high-powered laser beam, etching pits on the surface of a rotating disk. During playback these pit marks alter the amplitude of the reflected beam, producing an output signal that can be decoded. Data, once recorded, cannot be erased.

THE ERASABLE OPTICAL DISK

Computers never seem to have enough memory. The more memory a computer has, the larger are the applications that are undertaken. Larger applications, in turn, create a demand for more memory capacity. Because optical disk systems can store as much as 100 times the contents of current magnetic disk drives, they seem to afford a promising solution to the storage problem. However, a serious-shortcoming of currently available optical memories is the fact that they are permanent storage devices. The laser beam that is used to encode data on the optical disk does so by etching permanent pits on the surface of the recording media.

Because of the size of the market for optical disk memories, estimated to be a $10 billion-a-year market within a decade, several manufacturers are competing to develop erasable optical memories. In April 1983, the Matsushita Electric Industrial Company, a giant Japanese consumer electronics corporation, displayed a developmental model of the world's first erasable optical disk. Matsushita's erasable disk technology differs from that used to make regular optical disks for data storage. Instead of using a laser to burn permanent pits in the metallic recording layer buried inside a video disk platter, the erasable technique melts tiny pools of metal on the surface of the recording medium. Each time that happens, the metal changes state from crystalline to noncrystalline, or the reverse. A laser beam detects the digital code by distinguishing the difference between the reflectivity of the two metal states. As yet, this product does not satisfy the extreme accuracy required for use as computer memory, which demands no more than a single error in a trillion bits of data.

In Japan, Toshiba, Nippon Electric Company, and others are in competition with Matsushita to market an erasable optical disk that will meet the levels of precision required by the computer industry. In the United States, corporations such as Storage Technology and Shugart, a subsidiary of Xerox, expect to market high-precision optical disks in the near future. Most experts agree that the combination of precision and erasability will be achieved within this decade and that optical disks no longer will be limited to archival storage applications. Instead, they will prove to be competitors in many applications now served by magnetic disk drives.

Source: Business Week, May 2, 1983, p. 56.

FIGURE 5-15
Toshiba DF-2000 Document Filing System. The laser file, marketed as the DF-2000 Document Filing System, has a capacity of 10,000 document pages per disk. Documents are retrieved by entering an address code on the keyboard; they may then be displayed on a CRT screen or printed. *(Courtesy Toshiba Corp.)*

on and off at a varying rate. This process creates pits of varying length along tracks on the disk. A less intense laser beam is focused on the disk in order to read the stored data. The beam is strongly reflected by the coated surface and weakly reflected by the pits, producing patterns of on-off reflections that can be converted into electronic signals.

The optical disk is particularly well suited for the archival storage of vast amounts of data. Typical applications are image processing, geological survey data, medical publishing indexes, historical information files, and very large business data bases. For example, the Laserfile, shown in Figure 5-15, is able to store approximately 2000 documents on each side of an optical disk. A disadvantage of optical disks is that at present they are an unalterable storage medium, which means that data, once entered, cannot be erased.

ELECTRONIC SECONDARY STORAGE

The region in Figure 5-2 between 1 microsecond and 10 milliseconds is often referred to as the *access gap*. This gap stimulated research to develop electronic alternatives to rotating electromechanical storage systems that have low cost per bit and fast access times. Three memory media developed to fill this gap have emerged and have the potential to meet some of the future demands for storage. These media are the **magnetic bubble memory** (MBM), the *charge-coupled device* (CCD), and the *electron-beam-addressed memory* (EBAM).

Magnetic Bubble Memory

Magnetic bubble memory (MBM) can be placed on very small integrated-circuit memory chips. Magnetic bubbles are cylindrical regions formed by applying magnetic fields to thin sheets of certain magnetic materials, such as garnet crystal. The magnetic fields strengthen some regions in the material and weaken others. The strengthened regions break into isolated cylinders that resemble small islands surrounded by a sea of charges of opposite polarity. Figure 5-16a shows a bubble region before and after the application of the external magnetic field that causes the cylindrical bubbles to rise. When viewed under a microscope, these cylindrical islands appear as black specks, or bubbles—hence, the name of this type of memory. The presence or absence of a bubble corresponds to a 1 or 0 in the binary code. Bubbles can be moved around electronically to store and provide access to coded data.

Figure 5-16b is a magnified view of a magnetic bubble memory. In the future, MBM chip densities are expected to achieve densities in excess of 10 million bits per square inch. At a low cost of only a few hundred dollars, including connection to a computer system, MBMs fit well into the architecture of microcomputer systems and are used as main memory in custom commercial microprocessor applications, where fast access time is not at a premium, or in a memory hierarchy as a low-cost alternative to moving- or fixed-head magnetic disks. Typical applications are portable terminals, telephone systems that redirect improperly dialed numbers, and robots.

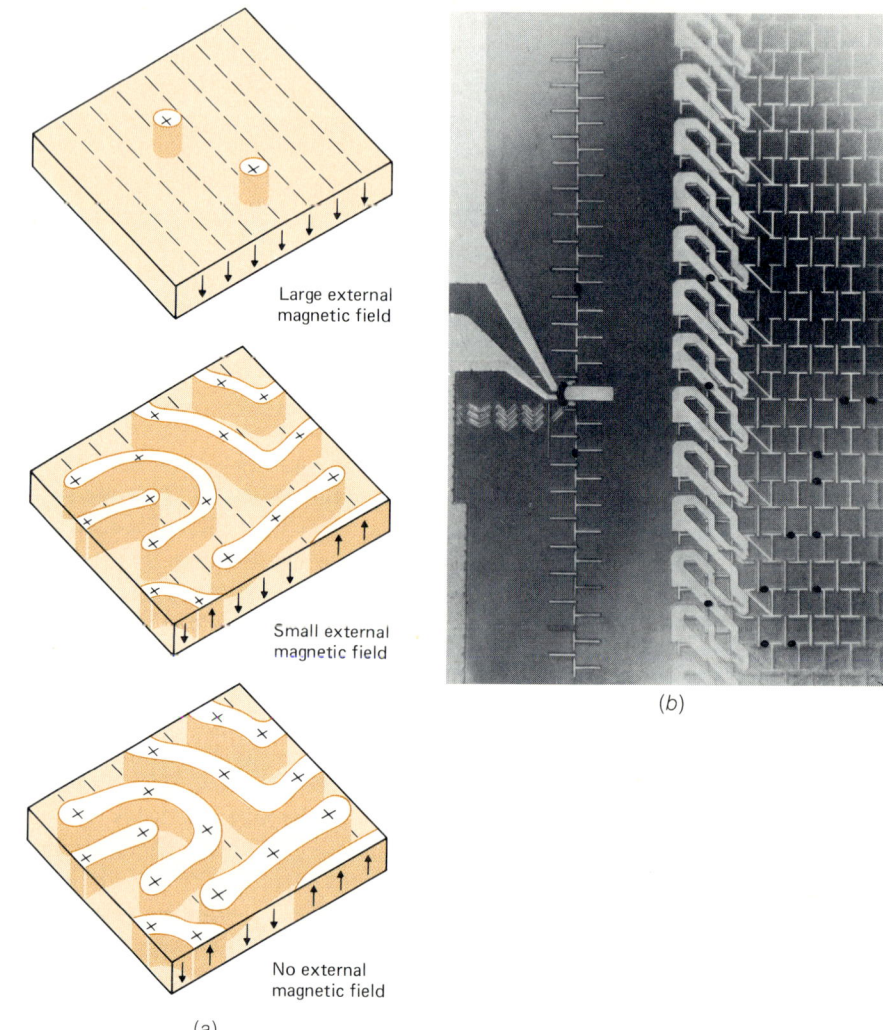

FIGURE 5-16

(a) The process of bubble formation. The regions in an increasing external field shrink in size until they form cylindrical domains, or bubbles. The domains are mobbile. (b) A magnified view of a magnetic bubble memory.

Large external magnetic field

Small external magnetic field

No external magnetic field

(b)

(a)

Charge-Coupled Devices

A charge-coupled device (CCD) is a semiconductor that uses the electrons within a metal-oxide semiconductor (MOS) crystal to store data. Techniques for the large-scale manufacture of CCDs are lagging behind those for MBMs. However, the two media are complementary rather than competitive. CCDs have faster access times than MBM; they have potential as secondary storage and even as extended main memory as manufacturing techniques evolve.

Electron-Beam-Addressed Memory

Electron-beam-addressed memory (EBAM), also called beam-addressed MOS (BEAMOS), uses electrical circuits to control an electron beam that reads from or writes on an MOS surface. Data is stored in the target in the form of the presence or absence of positive charges. The use of an electron beam, which can be less than a millionth of a meter in diameter, makes possible large data storage capacities and fast access times. The cost of EBAM is relatively high at present; however, the potential exists for developing low-cost EBAM systems.

Advanced Memory Systems

Figure 5-17 is Figure 5-2 redrawn to pinpoint the storage media that we have discussed in the cost-per-bit versus access-time spectrum.

Other advanced methods for storing data are undergoing research and development. Among the most promising of these are holography and Josephson-junctions. Holography is a method of recording images on a film without a lens. Holographic systems have a potential for storing a trillion bits of data. Experimental memory systems using supercold circuits, known as Josephson junctions, have shown a potential for high-performance memory. Storage access times of less than a nanosecond have been obtained in the laboratory.

These are examples of advanced memory technologies which, by the end of the century, could lead to the ability to pack memory circuits within a few molecules. However, in the immediate future, the secondary storage media will continue to be either electromechanical or electronic. In particular, the capabilities of disk systems will continue to improve, and they will remain cost-effective for most applications.

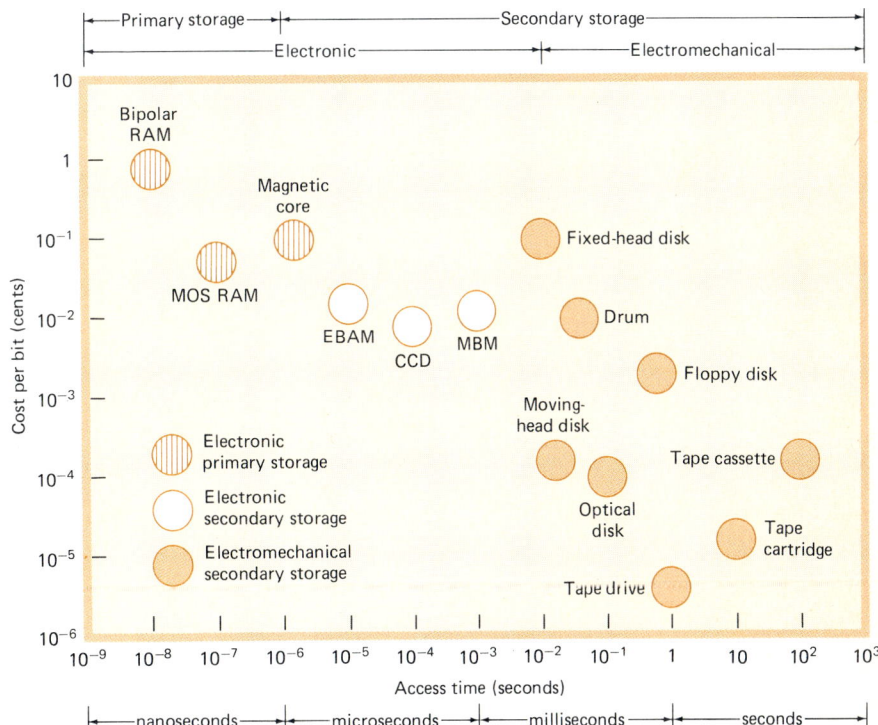

FIGURE 5-17
Storage devices: cost per bit versus access time.

MEMORY HIERARCHIES

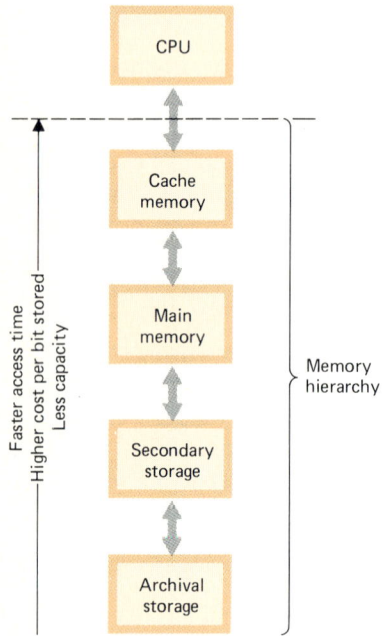

FIGURE 5-18

Memory hierarchy. Mixed memory technologies provide the computer system architect with a means of achieving both performance and economy. Combinations are made upon the basis of capacity, cost per bit stored, and access time.

Most of the technologies involved in producing the existing spectrum of memories will continue to improve and to reduce the cost-per-bit of various storage media at similar rates. This fact, coupled with the expense of developing sophisticated advanced memory systems, means that the classifications of primary and secondary storage shown in Figures 5-2 and 5-17 will continue to coexist throughout the 1980s and 1990s, each meeting specific memory needs.

A cost-effective technique for the design of large computer systems is the use of a hierarchy of memory technologies. Figure 5-18 shows a typical memory hierarchy. It includes cache memory, main memory, secondary storage, and archival storage. Typically, main memory is high-speed semiconductor memory. *Cache memory* is very high speed semiconductor memory used to enhance the speed of main memory. Cache memory is inserted between the CPU and main memory, and it is not addressable by the user of the computer system. Its purpose is to look ahead and to provide main memory with currently needed information. The design of an efficient cache memory is a major task for the systems architect. However, for many applications, cache memory makes main memory appear to be larger than it really is because it is operating at a speed close to that of cache memory. Since main memory is less expensive than cache memory, the potential cost savings is considerable.

As shown in Figure 5-18, secondary storage media such as magnetic disk memories make up the level of the hierarchy just below main memory. Slower secondary storage devices, often referred to as archival storage, are at the bottom of the memory hierarchy. They are cost-effective for the storage of very large quantities of data when fast access time is not necessary.

Another significant near-term trend in the design of memory devices is so-called *intelligent memory*. With intelligent memory the tasks related to the control of peripheral devices are shifted from the CPU to the devices. An example is the task of locating data stored on a magnetic disk. A microprocessor assigned to the device can perform this function and other I/O operations. Intelligent memories are becoming important elements of hierarchical memory systems.

PROCESSING UNITS

Processors (for example, the central processing unit of a computer) contain many electronic components, such as transistors. These components perform control, arithmetic, and logical operations. Our discussion of storage media has shown that the microminiaturization of memory elements is taking place at an astonishing rate. The same observation applies to the electronic circuits in the CPU. Cost, performance, and reliability of of microprocessor units (MPUs), which are miniaturized CPUs found in microcomputers, improve as these components become smaller and are more densely packed on silicon chips.[1] The trends in components-per-integrated-circuit (IC) chip, in chip size, and in cost per circuit are illustrated by the graphs of Figure 5-19. Figure 5-19*a* shows the trend in circuit complexity as measured by the number of components per

---

[1] One micron is equal to 0.001 millimeter, or approximately 0.00004 inch.

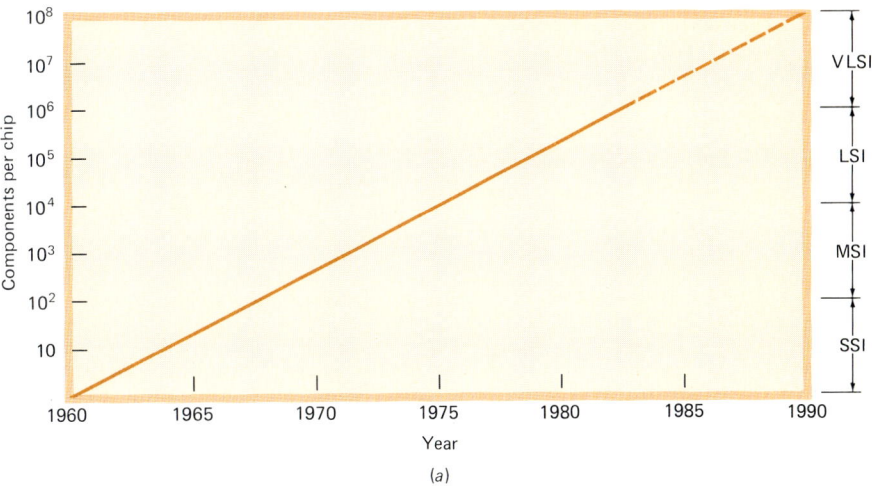

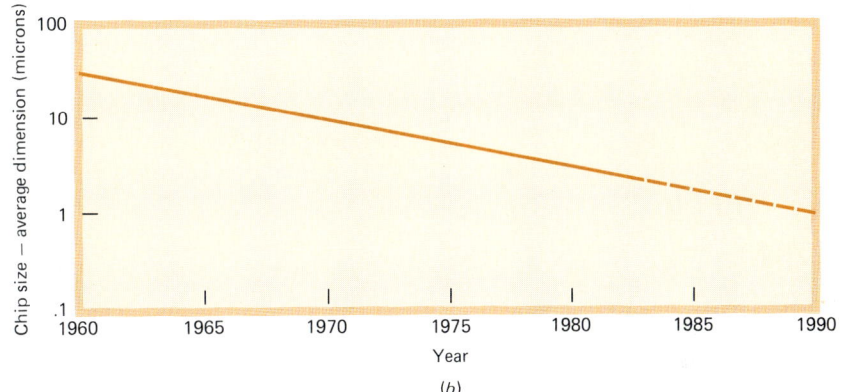

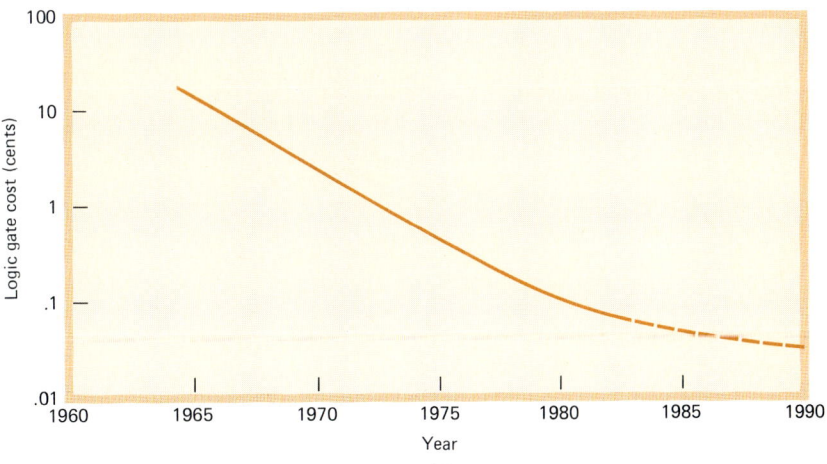

FIGURE 5-19

Trends in circuit components. (a)
Circuit complexity trend. (b) Chip size
trend. (c) Logic gate cost trend. (M. L.
Dertouzous and J. Moses, The
Computer Age, *MIT Press, Cambridge,*
1980, pp. 321–332.)

integrated-circuit chip. As this graph indicates, component density is increasing logarithmically (that is, by factors of 10) and will continue to do so until 1990 at least. Component densities are identified as small-scale integration (SSI), medium-scale integration (MSI), large-scale integration (LSI), and very-large-scale integration (VLSI). According to this graph, we can anticipate the ICs that will contain several million components per chip will be available.

Figure 5-19*b* shows the decrease in chip size, as measured by the minimum average chip dimension in microns. Photographic etching techniques are used to produce the chips. Quantity production of chips as small as 4 microns is now possible. A physical limit for this technique of manufacturing chips is approximately 1 micron.

Figure 5-19*c* is a graph that displays the cost trend for a logic-gate circuit (a circuit that can represent a binary 1 or 0). These gates are the building blocks of the central processing unit, and the cost per circuit, which is already less than 0.001 cents, will decrease substantially in the future.

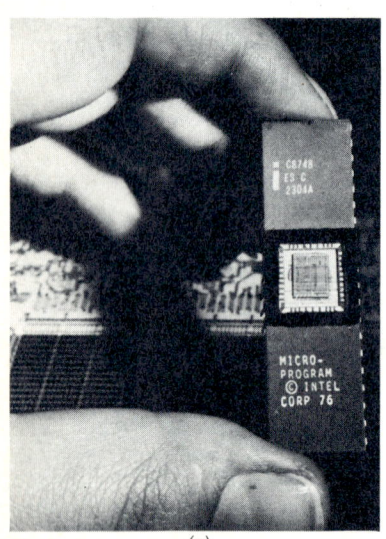

(a)

FIGURE 5-20

CPU on a single chip. (a) 8748 chip in package form. (b) Close-up of 8748 chip. (*Courtesy Intel Corp.*)

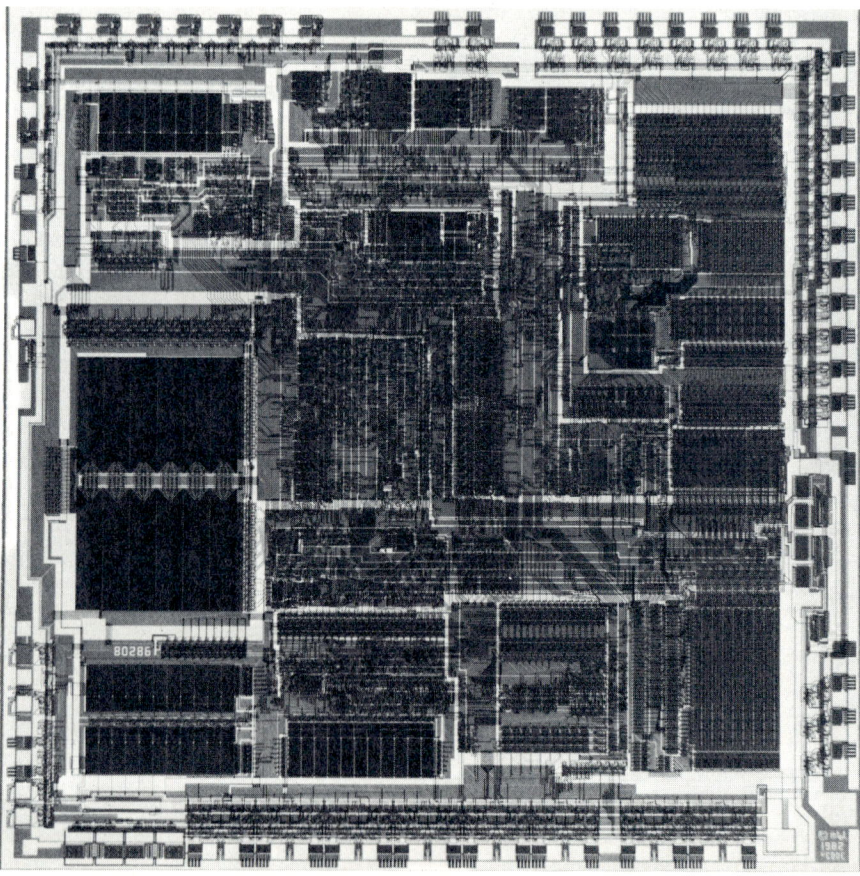

(b)

The effect of VLSI upon processor design will have considerable impact on the architecture of computer systems of all sizes. It will be possible to develop microcomputers with performance equal to that of many of today's large computers and to manufacture them at a fraction of the cost. The ability of large systems to process large volumes of data will increase greatly. This performance increase will be achieved largely by the incorporation of both hierarchies of memory and multiple microprocessors into large-systems archi- tecture. As we discussed in Chapter 4 and illustrated in Figure 4-12 multiple processors will enable computers of the future to perform like many small computers operating in parallel.

Figure 5-20 shows a single chip containing a complete central processing unit. Complete computers on a chip will become commonplace in the future.

FEEDBACK
5-16 What is mass storage? Archival storage?
5-17 What is an advantage of optical-disk storage? A disadvantage?
5-18 Why are magnetic bubble memory and charge-coupled devices con- sidered to be access-gap fillers?
5-19 What is a memory hierarchy? Intelligent memory?
5-20 What is a microprocessor unit (MPU)?

SUMMARY
Most business data processing systems repeat a cycle of operations in order to produce output information. The basic business data processing cycle involves the use of master files, which contain relatively permanent data and transaction files, which in turn contain current data to be processed. As a result of master- transaction file processing, outputs are produced, and the master file is updated.

Storage media are classified as primary storage or secondary storage on the basis of combinations of cost, capacity, and access time. Primary storage has the least capacity and is the most expensive; however, it has the fastest access time. The principal primary storage circuit elements are solid-state components called semiconductors. Semiconductor circuits act as "gates" that permit cur- rent to flow or not to flow, providing the 1's and 0's used to make up binary codes. Except for special applications, semiconductors have replaced magnetic cores, an earlier technology, as primary memory because they are faster and cost less.

The principal secondary storage media are rotating electromechanical de- vices. Magnetic tapes are used for sequential processing. Tape devices range from large-capacity, high-data-rate units used with large data processing systems to cassettes and cartridges used with small systems. Magnetic disks can perform both sequential and random processing. They are classified as moving-head, fixed-head, or combination moving-head and fixed-head devices. Magnetic disks are the predominant secondary storage media. They include floppy disks, or diskettes, which are widely used with small computer systems.

Mass storage systems provide access to large files, with capacities of hun- dreds of billions of bytes. They have longer access times than magnetic disk systems, and this limits their use for some applications. However, they are often used for archival storage. Optical-disk storage systems are a type of archival storage that provides access to very large amounts of data; however, at present these systems do not permit stored data to be altered.

Nonrotating electronic memories have been developed to fill the cost and access-time gap between electronic primary storage and electromechanical secondary storage units. These include magnetic bubble memory (MBM) and the charge-coupled device (CCD). Although they have potential, at present these systems are used primarily for special applications. Other types of advanced memory systems are being developed, and they will be introduced in the future.

Most of the existing memory technologies will continue to improve at similar rates and will provide computer systems architects with a variety of choices. Many computer systems will employ more than one type of memory. They will use a hierarchy of memory technologies, including very high speed cache memory, main memory, secondary storage, and archival storage.

The electronic circuits used in the central processing unit will continue to improve in performance and reliability. Integrated circuits will continue to become smaller and to cost less. Small computers will become more powerful, and large computer systems will improve their performance by incorporating hierarchies of memory and multiple processors into their architecture.

ANSWERS TO FEEDBACK QUESTIONS

5-1 A transaction file is one that contains data that change frequently. A master file contains relatively permanent data.

5-2 Batch processing means the collection of data for processing at a future time. Transaction-driven means that processing takes place as input transactions occur.

5-3 Access time is the time required for the computer to locate and transfer data to or from a storage medium.

5-4 A conductor is a substance that permits electricity to pass through it easily. A nonconductor does not permit electricity to pass through it. A semiconductor has the properties of both and can represent binary 1's and 0's.

5-5 Semiconductors are used for primary storage because of their fast access times. They are not used for secondary storage because of the need for high capacity and the cost per bit stored.

5-6 Electromechanical storage media are slower than electronic media because they use rotating mechanical components.

5-7 The date transfer rate is the rate at which data can be transferred from a secondary storage device to main memory.

5-8 Data rate = speed × density
= 200 inches/second × 1600 bytes/inch
= 320,000 bytes/second

5-9 A physical record is a physical area on a storage medium. It contains one or more logical records.

5-10 Physical record size = logical record size × blocking factor
$$= 100 \text{ bytes} \times 10$$
$$= 1000 \text{ bytes}$$

5-11 Moving-head, fixed-head, and combined moving-head and fixed-head.

5-12 Moving-head disk systems have large storage capacities (per dollar) and slow access times. Fixed-head systems have small storage capacities (per dollar) and fast access times. Combination systems provide the capabilities of both moving-head and fixed-head devices at an in-between cost.

5-13 A sequential file is one on which records are written or read, one after the other. A direct file is created and accessed from the contents of key fields on records. An indexed-sequential file is created like a sequential file, but records can be accessed at random, using a set of indexes created by the computer system.

5-14 Access time = seek time + rotational delay
$$= 20 \text{ milliseconds} + 7 \text{ milliseconds}$$
$$= 27 \text{ milliseconds}$$

5-15 A small flexible disk used as a storage medium for small computer systems.

5-16 Mass storage is high capacity and relatively slow access-time storage used for both online and offline storage. Archival storage is inexpensive, high capacity, and slow access-time storage that is used for offline applications such as maintenance of historical files.

5-17 An advantage of optical disks is large-capacity storage. A disadvantage of present systems is that storage is unalterable.

5-18 Magnetic bubble memory and charge-coupled devices are considered to be access gap fillers because they are between primary memory and electromechanical secondary storage in cost per bit stored and access time.

5-19 A memory hierarchy is a combination of memory technologies, ranging from high-speed cache memory to archival storage. Intelligent memory is control memory located in a peripheral device.

5-20 A microprocessor unit, or MPU, is the central processing unit of a microcomputer.

FOR REVIEW AND DISCUSSION

1 Describe the typical business data processing cycle using the terms master file, transaction file, and key field.

2 Distinguish between primary storage, electronic secondary storage, and electromechanical secondary storage in terms of cost per bit stored and access time.

3 Discuss the relative advantages and disadvantages of magnetic tape and magnetic disk storage for processing active and inactive files.

4 Name the general classes of storage media that might make up a memory hierarchy, and briefly describe their uses.

5 Why are semiconductor memories widely used for primary storage?

6 Identify and distinguish between the various types of magnetic disk memory.

7 For what type of application would you select magnetic tape? Magnetic disk? Archival storage?

8 What is the relationship between a logical record, a physical record, and the blocking factor?

9 Define seek time and data transfer rate. How might they affect the selection of a secondary storage device?

10 What are the trends in central processing unit performance, and how will they affect the design of future computer data processing systems?

CHAPTER 6

INPUT AND OUTPUT

PREVIEW   Computers must be able to communicate with their environments. Input devices are used to enter data into primary storage. Output units accept data from primary storage to provide users with information or to record the data on a secondary storage device. Some devices are used for both the input and output functions. The goal of this chapter is to describe the input and output device choices available for computer systems. You will study the characteristics of several I/O devices and will become familiar with those that you are likely to encounter.

In this chapter you will learn:

1. The choices in magnetic I/O media and data recorders
2. The characteristics of the three types of printers
3. The most common types of keyboard devices
4. The characteristics of the most common types of scanners

KEY TERMS TO WATCH FOR AND REMEMBER

I/O interface
magnetic disk
magnetic diskette
magnetic tape
character printer
line printer
page printer
visual display terminal (VDT)
teleprinter terminal
point-of-sale device (POS)

optical character reader (OCR)
optical mark reader (OMR)
bar-code scanner
magnetic-ink character
  recognition (MICR)
card reader
computer output microfilm (COM)
digitizer
plotter
voice recognition and response devices

USING INPUT-OUTPUT DEVICES

A computer cannot perform or complete any useful work unless it is able to communicate with its external environment. All data and instructions enter and leave the central processing unit through primary storage. Input-output (I/O) devices are needed to link primary storage to the environment, which is external to the computer system. The data with which these devices work may or may not be in a form that humans can understand. For example, the data that a data entry operator keys into the memory of a computer by typing on a keyboard are readable by humans. However, the data that tell a computer about the performance of an automobile engine are not in a form that humans can read. They are electrical signals from an analog sensor. Similarly, output may be on a printed page, which humans can read easily, or upon some other medium where the data are not visible, such as on magnetic tape or disk.

As we learned in previous chapters, all of the data flow, from input to final output, is managed by the control unit in the CPU. Regardless of the nature of the I/O devices, special processors called **I/O interfaces** are required to convert the input data to the internal codes used by the computer and to convert internal codes to a format which is usable by the output device. These I/O interfaces are also called channels or input-output processors (IOP).

The major differences between devices are the media that they use and the speed with which they are able to transfer data to or from primary storage.

FEEDBACK

6-1 What is the purpose of input and output devices?
6-2 What is an I/O interface?
6-3 What are the major differences between the various I/O devices?

I/O DEVICE SPEED

Input-output devices can be classified as high-speed, medium-speed, and low-speed. Table 6-1 lists the principal I/O devices that will be described in this chapter. The devices in this table are grouped according to their speed. It should be noted that the high-speed devices are either entirely electronic in their operation or magnetic media that can be moved at high-speed. Those high-speed devices are both input and output devices and are used as secondary storage. The low-speed devices are those with complex mechanical motion or operate at the speed of a human operator. The medium-speed devices are those that fall between—they tend to have mechanical moving parts which are more complex than the high-speed devices but not as complex as the low-speed. It should be noted that the terms high-speed, medium-speed, and low-speed are relative terms for speed as compared to other input or output devices—even the fastest of the I/O devices is very slow when compared to the speed of primary storage.

TABLE 6-1   **INPUT-OUTPUT DEVICES**

High-speed devices
Magnetic disk
Magnetic tape

Medium-speed devices
Card readers
Computer output microfilm (COM)
Line printers
Magnetic diskette
Magnetic-ink character recognition (MICR)
Optical character readers (OCR)
Optical mark readers (OMR)
Page printers
Visual displays

Low-speed devices
Bar-code readers
Character printers
Digitizers
Keyboard input devices (all types)
Plotters
Voice recognition and response units

FEEDBACK

6-4 What types of I/O devices tend to be high-speed devices?

6-5 What types of devices tend to be low-speed devices?

6-6 How do high-speed input-output devices compare to primary storage in speed?

MAGNETIC MEDIA DEVICES

Some of the devices listed in Table 6-1 can perform both the input and output functions. **Magnetic disk, magnetic diskette,** and **magnetic tape** are examples of such devices.

Magnetic Disk, Diskette, and Tape

Magnetic disks, diskettes, and tapes can record data as output from primary storage and can also serve as input devices returning the data to primary storage. All of the secondary storage devices discussed in Chapter 5—magnetic bubble, magnetic disk, magnetic tape, and the electronic memories—are both input and output devices.

Because we described magnetic media devices in detail in the previous chapter, we will not discuss them here beyond identifying their additional use as input-output devices.

Magnetic Data Recorders   Data are recorded on magnetic disks and magnetic tapes either by outputting the data from primary storage or by using a data recorder. Data recorders are not input devices, and they are not connected to the computer system. Instead, they are offline recorders. The magnetic media recording devices are key-to-disk, key-to-diskette, and key-to-tape machines.

Key-to-disk   Key-to-disk devices are used as data recording stations in multi-station shared-processor systems. Typically, from 8 to 64 keyboard stations are linked to a small special-purpose computer to record source data. These key-to-disk data entry systems are able to validate and edit input data, tasks usually performed by the main computer. Thus, they are able to correct data before storing it on a magnetic disk and before its entry into the main computer system. Figure 6-1 shows a key-to-disk shared-processor system.

Key-to-diskette   Key-to-diskette systems have been introduced as low-cost data recording systems. These systems store data on flexible disks, called diskettes. Diskettes are inexpensive (approximately $5 each) and reusable.

Key-to-tape   Various key-to-tape devices are available. They can record data magnetically on reels, on cassettes, and on tape cartridges. The magnetic tape reels produced by key-to-tape systems are in a computer-compatible format for subsequent direct data input into a computer. However, data on cartridges and cassettes often are transferred to higher-speed media, such as a full-sized reel of magnetic tape or magnetic disk, for efficient data transfer to the computer.

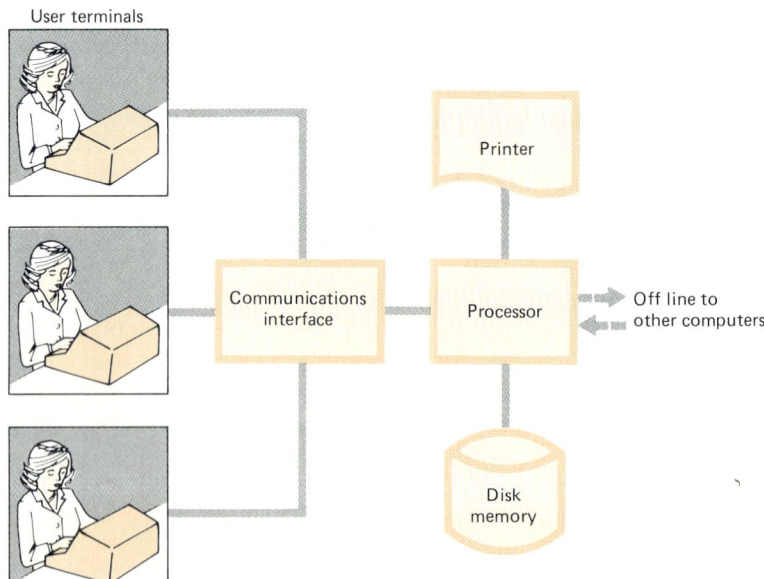

FIGURE 6-1
Key-to-disk shared-processor system.

FEEDBACK **6-7** Why are the devices that are both input and output called secondary storage devices?

6-8 What is the difference between an input device and a data recorder?

6-9 What are the common magnetic media data recorders?

PRINTERS Printers provide information in a permanent, human-readable form. They are the most commonly used output devices and are components of almost all computer systems. Printers vary greatly in performance and design. We will classify printers as **character printers, line printers,** and **page printers** in order to identify three different approaches to printing, each with a different speed range. In addition, printers will be described as either impact or nonimpact. Printers that use electromechanical mechanisms that cause hammers to strike against a ribbon and the paper are called impact printers. Nonimpact printers do not hit or impact a ribbon to print.

Character Printers Character printers print only one character at a time. A typewriter is an example of a character printer. Character printers are the type used with literally all microcomputers, but they are also used on computers of all sizes whenever the printing requirements are not large.

Letter-quality printers Figure 6-2 illustrates a printwheel font, called a daisy wheel, common to many character printers. The font characters are around the outside of the wheel, which spins to position the character to be typed in the correct position. These printers are impact printers and produce output that looks like it has been typed. These letter-quality printers typically have speeds

FIGURE 6-2
Daisy wheel. (Courtesy Dataproducts Corp.)

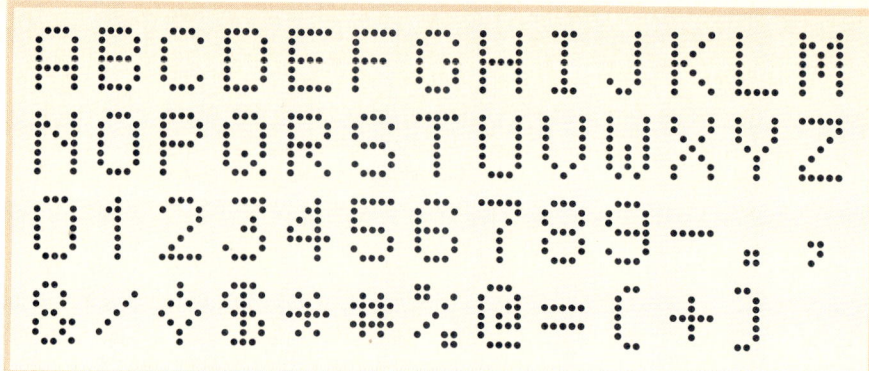

ranging from 10 to 50 characters per second. If you are a typist, that translates to a speed range of 120 to 600 words per minute.

Dot-matrix printers   Other character printers form each character as a pattern of dots. Figure 6-3 shows the dot pattern used to produce the characters. These printers have a lower quality of type but are generally faster printers than the letter-quality printers—in the range of 50 to 200 characters per second. The dot matrix has two additional advantages over the letter-quality printers. First, they do not have a fixed character font, so they can print any shape of a character that a programmer can describe. This allows for many special characters, different sizes of print, and the ability to print graphics such as charts and graphs. Second, dot-matrix printers tend to be less expensive than letter-quality printers. If the print quality of a letter-quality printer is not needed, the dot-matrix printer can be a very flexible tool.

Ink-jet printers   One of the newest types of character printer is the ink-jet printer. It sprays small drops of ink onto paper to form printed characters. The ink has a high iron content, which is affected by magnetic fields of the printer. These magnetic fields cause the ink to take the shape of a character as the ink approaches the paper. Advantages of this type of printer are that it is quiet (nonimpact), produces a high-quality output, and can form any kind of character. The documents printed may contain multiple character styles and a variety of type sizes. Some models allow for different colors of ink for multiple color printing.

Line Printers   Line printers are electromechanical machines used for high-volume paper output on most computer systems. Their printing speeds are such that to an observer they appear to be printing a line at a time. They are impact printers. The speeds of line printers vary from 100 to 2500 lines per minute. Output is on computer printer paper, for which the typical line length is 132 characters. Some line printers have a line length of 120 characters and a few have a line length of 144 characters. Line printer output efficiency can be increased by use of multiple-part forms (pages with carbon paper inserts). Line printers have been designed to use many different types of printing mechanisms. Two of the most common print mechanisms are the drum and the chain.

Drum printers As shown in Figure 6-4*a*, drum printers use a solid, cylindrical drum, which rotates at a rapid speed. Raised characters are in bands around the drum, with each band containing all of the possible printed characters. The number of bands is equal to the number of print positions on a line. A print hammer for each possible print position is located behind the paper. These hammers strike the paper (and an inked ribbon) against the appropriate character on the drum as the correct character is rotated into position. The entire line can be printed in one revolution of the drum. This means that all characters on the line are not printed at exactly the same time, but the time to print the line is fast enough to call them line printers. Speeds of drum printers vary from 200 to over 2000 lines per minute.

Chain printers Chain printers have their character set on a rapidly rotating chain called a *print chain*. Each link in the chain is a character font. A typical print chain is shown in Figure 6-4*b*. The character set is repeated several times on the chain. As the chain rotates, print hammers (done for each print position) strike the paper (and a ribbon) against the selected character on the chain. As

FIGURE 6-4

(*a*) Drum from drum printer. (*b*) Chain from chain printer. (*c*) Chain printer. (Courtesy IBM Corp.)

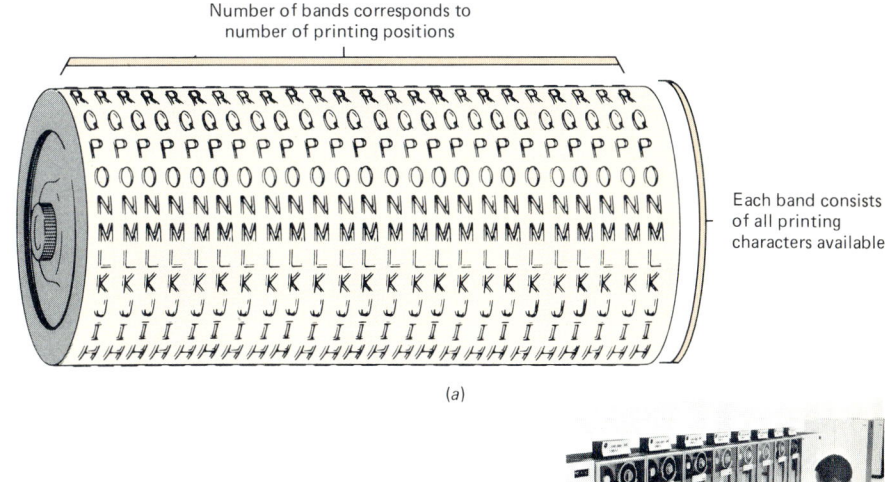

Number of bands corresponds to number of printing positions

Each band consists of all printing characters available

(*a*)

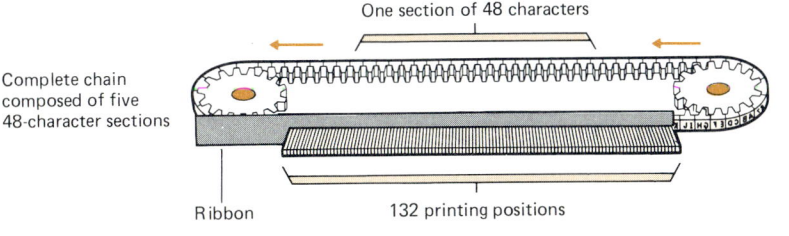

One section of 48 characters

Complete chain composed of five 48-character sections

Ribbon   132 printing positions

(*b*)

(*c*)

in the case of the drum printer, the chain printer does not truly print the letters. A standard character set is 48 characters, but larger and smaller character sets are available. Because the character set is repeated around the chain, it is not necessary to wait for the chain to make a complete revolution to position the desired character in the correct print position. Character sets larger than 48 repeat the characters fewer times than the standard set. This lengthens the time to position the desired character and therefore reduces the effective print speed of the printer. Figure 6-4c is a picture of a high-performance chain printer. Speeds of chain printers range from 400 to 2400 lines per minute.

Some models of printers use a metal band instead of a chain. The band has the raised print characters on it, and it is rotated in the same way as a chain.

Page Printers Page printers are high-speed nonimpact printers. Their printing rates are so high that output appears to emerge from the printer a page at a time. A variety of techniques are used in the design of page printers. These techniques, called *electrophotographic techniques*, have developed from the paper copier technology. Page printers can produce pages of output at a rate equal to a paper copier. *Laser-beam printers* use a combination of laser beam and electrophotographic techniques to create printer output at a rate equal to 18,000 lines per minute. Figure 6-5 shows a laser-beam printer.

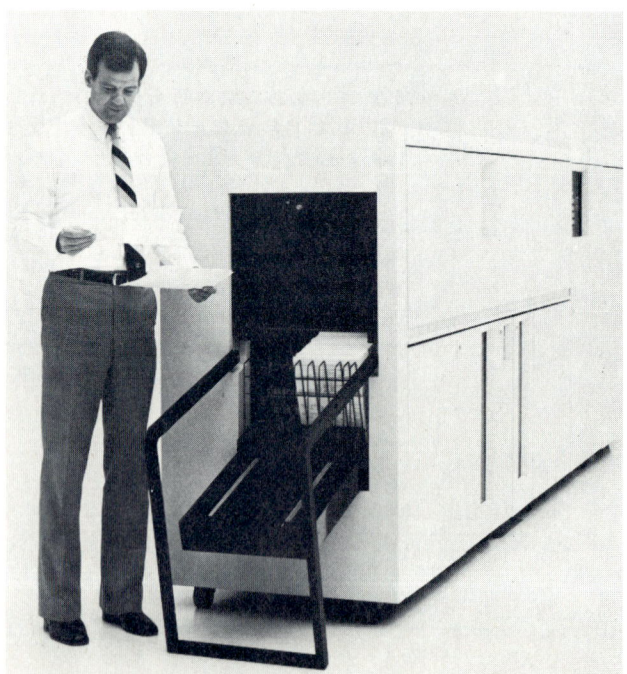

FIGURE 6-5
Laser beam printer. Shown is the IBM 3800 Printing Subsystem Model 3, which prints at speeds of up to 20,040 lines per minute. (Courtesy IBM Corp.)

One of the original limitations of nonimpact printers was that the technique limited the output to single copies. As a solution to this problem and to the general multiple-copy problem, manufacturers have designed printers that can be used as offline devices to produce additional copies of computer-prepared output, reduced to a regular paper size of 8 1/2 × 11 inches if desired. The printer accepts data from magnetic tapes and produces printed output at rates of up to 20,000 lines per minute.

FEEDBACK

6-10 What are the three types of printers?

6-11 What is a letter-quality printer? A dot-matrix printer?

6-12 What type printer is the most common with microcomputer systems? On larger computer systems?

6-13 What is an impact printer? A nonimpact printer?

KEYBOARD DEVICES

There is a wide variety of keyboard devices, or terminals, available for use in entering data directly into a computer. As the cost of terminals continues to decline, data recorders such as card punch equipment and key-to-tape are being replaced. Since these devices are online to the computer, data entered through them are available to users in less time than through the use of offline data recorders. The keyboard devices discussed here are **visual display terminals (VDT), teleprinter terminals,** and **point-of-sale devices (POS).**

Visual Display Terminals

The most popular type of I/O device in use today is the visual display terminal (VDT). It consists of a typewriterlike keyboard for inputting and a cathode ray tube (CRT) for displaying output data. Each character entered through the keyboard is also displayed on the CRT. As data are keyed, they are held in a small memory, called a buffer, within the terminal itself. The data are not sent on to the computer until the operator presses an enter key on the keyboard. This allows the operator the opportunity to proofread or verify the data being entered by reading the data displayed on the screen. A small square or underscore character, called a cursor, shows the operator where the next character to be keyed will be displayed on the screen. Keystroke errors can be easily corrected by moving the cursor to the data in error and rekeying the data. As long as this is done prior to pressing the enter key, error correction is very easy. There are three major uses of VDTs: alphanumeric displays, graphic displays, and input through a light pen.

Alphanumeric displays The most common use of the visual display terminal is to display alphanumeric data, that is, character data. Because of their relatively fast output rates and their ability to provide a viewer with an "instant" output, video displays have replaced printers for many applications. Users have

FIGURE 6-6

Visual display terminal with alphanumeric display. (Courtesy NCR Corp.)

recognized that printed copies of the outputs are not really needed. Figure 6-6 shows a typical VDT with an alphanumeric display.

Graphic displays   Visual display terminals with a graphic display capability provide a very powerful and versatile tool for many users. Graphic-display devices provide not only a means of displaying high-resolution drawings but also the capability of manipulating and modifying the graphic display. As an example, a graphic display can provide an engineer with a succession of different views of a design, such as a building or aircraft. The scale of the presentation can be altered so that either an entire assembly or a small section of that assembly can be examined. Many graphic terminals can display in color to highlight particular portions of the display. The businessperson can use the graphic display to present data in the form of line charts, bar charts, or pie charts. These charts can be developed easily and quickly to help summarize trends and relationships in the data. Graphic displays can be very effective in information systems for business managers. Figure 6-7 is a typical graphic display.

Light pens   A light pen is a photosensitve penlike instrument which can sense a position on the CRT when the end of the pen is held against the screen. The light pen is an input device. By sensing the position on the screen being touched

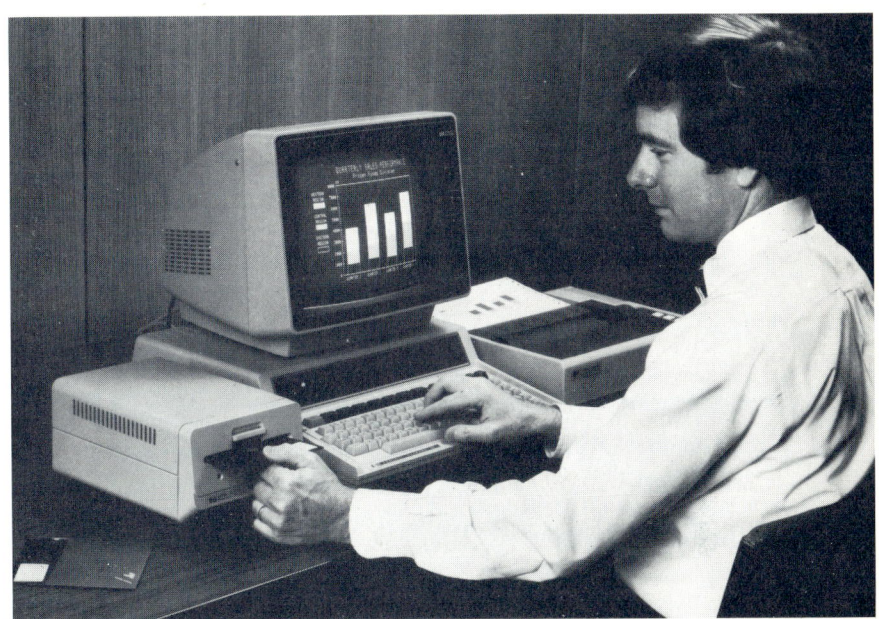

FIGURE 6-7
Visual display terminal with graphic display. (Courtesy Hewlett-Packard)

by the light pen, you are inputting data to the program (in main storage). As an example, the screen display might have a list of inventory system choices such as DISPLAY INVENTORY ITEM DATA, ENTER NEW INVENTORY ITEM, MODIFY INVENTORY ITEM DATA, PRINT INVENTORY ITEM DATA. By touching the light pen against the description of the desired function, you are inputting your choice. This approach may also be used with graphic displays. An electrical distribution system diagram can be displayed using graphics. The diagram could show the various relays and switches used to control the routing of the electrical power. By touching a relay or switch symbol on the display with the light pen, you can input your desire to change the switch setting. Thus, if the switch represented on the screen diagram was open and you touched that symbol, the switch would close. If the switch was already closed, it would open. The light pen is commonly used by engineers to modify designs which are displayed on a CRT during the design development process. This is part of an activity called computer-aided design (CAD). A light pen is being used in Figure 6-8.

Teleprinter Terminals   There are situations where it is desirable to have a printed copy of data outputted to a terminal. If a user finds that a printed copy, or "hard copy," is usually required, the solution could be a teleprinter terminal. A teleprinter terminal has a keyboard for input and a typewriterlike printer for output, as shown in Figure 6-9. These printers are character printers and are therefore slower output devices than CRT displays.

FIGURE 6-8
Visual display terminal with light pen
in use. (Courtesy IBM Corp.)

FIGURE 6-9
Teleprinter terminal. (Courtesy Radio
Shack, A Tandy Corp.)

Point-of-Sale Devices   A point-of-sale (POS) device is essentially the electronic equivalent of a cash register in that it can perform all the functions of a cash register. A POS device, however, is capable of capturing more data than a cash register. Some POS devices are offline, stand-alone machines that record transaction data on a cassette tape contained in the register. This cassette tape data is collected and processed at a later time. This approach does not take advantage of the power of a computer. Most point-of-sale devices are online terminals attached to a computer for processing the transaction while the customer is making the purchase. Examples of the processing that may take place during the recording of the transaction are the checking of a customer's credit, maintaining perpetual inventory records, updating sales accounting records, and the printing of detailed sales receipts.

The significant features of most of the current electronic POS devices include: the capability of entering extensive information about the sale, the guiding of the operator through the possible transactions by a series of lighted indicators or messages, a provision for transmission of the data to a central computer, and the provision for a local computational capability such as price extensions and tax calculations.

FEEDBACK   **6-14** What is the most popular I/O device in use today?

6-15 What is an alphanumeric display? A graphic display?

6-16 How is a light pen used? Is it an input or output device?

6-17 What is a POS device?

SCANNERS   Scanners provide a capability for direct data entry into the computer system. The major advantage of this direct data entry is that humans do not have to key the data. This leads to faster and more accurate data entry. The two major types of scanners are optical scanners and magnetic-ink character recognition devices.

Optical Scanners   Optical scanners are input devices that can "read" data recorded on paper. The scanning techniques used involve a light source and light sensors; thus, they are called optical devices. The data to be scanned may be typewritten or handwritten characters, data-coded as pencil marks, or data-coded as bars. The common optical scanner devices are called **optical character readers (OCR), optical mark readers (OMR),** and **bar-code readers.**

Optical character readers   An optical character reader (OCR) inputs data by using optical scanning mechanisms that can detect or scan alphabetic and numeric characters printed on paper. Figure 6-10 shows a typical optical character reader. The characters that can be read may be either typewritten or handwritten. If the data are typewritten, they must be typed using a special type font (called an OCR font), as shown in Figure 6-11. Most brands of typewriters are available with an OCR character set.

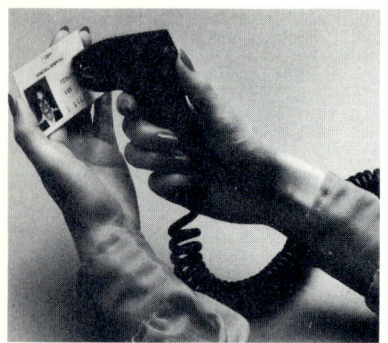

FIGURE 6-10
Optical character reader. (Courtesy
NCR Corp.)

Examples of the use of OCR devices include the scanners used by the U.S. Postal Service to aid in sorting bulk mail, and as first-draft input for word processing systems. Word processing systems are computer programs which are used to manipulate words in letters and reports. They are an important component in the automated office, discussed in detail in Chapter 7. The advantage of using OCR devices to input the first rough draft for word processing systems is that any typewriter with an OCR font may be used to keystroke the draft data. Since typewriters are less expensive than terminals, typewriter-OCR systems can be very cost-effective.

If the characters to be scanned are handwritten, they must be written following some fairly rigid rules—the characters must be a standard size, all lines making up the characters must be connected, and no stylish loops may be used. Because of the relative difficulty of strictly following the rules for handwritten data, most OCR devices are used for the scanning of typewritten data.

Optical mark readers   Optical mark readers are able to detect pencil marks made on special paper forms. Many students are very familiar with exam answer sheets where answer choices are made by filling in a bubble with a soft lead pencil. These answer sheet data are inputted to a computer for grading with the use of an optical mark reader. The use of OMR is not limited to the recording of student responses on exams. Any input data that is of a choice or selection nature can be recorded for OMR input.

Examples of effective uses of OMR include the selection of merchandise on an order form or the recording of an employee's hours for the day or project. Data recording for OMR is most effective when the number of choices is limited. For this reason, the most common form of data to be recorded is a single digit of numeric data. Alphabetic data can also be recorded, but it requires 26 choices for each character in the field.

The actual inputting of data through an OMR device involves shining a light on the page being scanned and detecting the reflections from the pencil

0123456789 |ч♪ᐧ-

0123456789 < >+-/

0123456789

0123456789 ./-+H

0123456789|+$.-/

FIGURE 6-11
OCR character set.   0 1 2 3 4 5 6 7 8 9 ⣀⡀⠂⡇⠀

marks. Pencil marks made with a soft lead pencil (high graphite content) will reflect the light. It is this reflection that the OMR device detects.

Bar-code readers Optical bar-code readers detect combinations of marks or printed bars that represent the data. Bar codes have been used for a number of years for some types of credit card processing and by the post office for mail sorting. It is very common to use bar code readers in conjunction with point-of-sale devices. The most widely known bar code is the universal product code (UPC), which now appears on almost all retail packages. The UPC is designed to simplify customer checkout and retail store inventory management. Figure 6-12 shows a supermarket checkout system in operation. The universal product code on each item is read by a laser-beam scanner as the clerk passes the package over the scanning window.

The UPC code consists of a series of vertical bars of varying widths. These bars are read as 10 digits. The first five of these digits identify the manufacturer or supplier of the product. The second five digits identify a specific product of

FIGURE 6-12

Supermarket checkout bar code reader. (Courtesy NCR Corp.)

Number System Character
0 = grocery products
3 = drugs and health-
        related products etc.

0

16000   66210

Product/Part Code Number
66210 = 18-ounce box of Wheaties
67670 = 10-ounce box of Buc Wheats etc.

Manufacturer's Identification Number
16000 = General Mills
21000 = Kraft Foods, etc.

FIGURE 6-13
UPC bar code.

the manufacturer. (See Figure 6-13.) With this product identification information, the name of the product and the product price can be looked up by the computer for output on the sales receipt.

Magnetic-Ink Character Recognition

Magnetic-ink character recognition (MICR) devices were developed to assist the banking industry. MICR devices speed up data input for the banking industry by reading characters imprinted on paper documents using a magnetic ink (that is, an ink that contains iron oxide particles). Check and deposit form processing is the largest application of MICR. Currently, approximately 30 billion checks are processed each year. Data processing centers for large banks often process over 1 million checks and deposits every day. Figure 6-14a is a picture of a magnetic-ink character reader.

Figure 6-14b shows how these characters appear on a check. The characters on the lower left of the check are imprinted before the checks are given to the user. The characters on the lower right, which are the amount of the check, are printed after the check has been written and presented for payment. Figure 6-14c shows a check moving through the MICR unit.

Data are transferred from checks to the computer by an MICR reader-sorter. The special ink is magnetized by the reader during the input process. It is the magnetic pattern of the character that can be detected by the MICR device. The individual characters are identified by comparing them with a special pattern—called a matrix—in the reader storage unit. The sorter function is used to sort the checks by account number so that they can be returned to the appropriate bank customer.

FEEDBACK

6-18 What is an optical scanner?

6-19 What are the three most common types of optical scanners? What type of data does each scan?

6-20 What is MICR? What industry is the primary user of MICR?

(a)

(b)

FIGURE 6-14
Magnetic-ink character reader. (a) Magnetic-ink character recognition unit. (b) MICR character set. (c) Check moving through MICR unit. (Courtesy Irving Trust Co.)

(c)

OTHER DEVICES

The variety of input and output devices continues to grow. The devices covered so far are the most common ones found in computer information systems. The devices in this section are either older devices that are still found in data processing centers, such as card readers, or more specialized devices.

Card Readers

Units that input the data coded on punched cards into primary storage are called **card readers.** Figure 6-15a is a typical card reader. The movement of a card through the reading mechanism of a card reader is shown in Figure 6-15b. As the card moves from the hopper to the stacker, it passes a sensing station. At this sensing station either wire brushes or photoelectric cells detect the presence of holes. After the data are read at this first station, the card passes a second sensing station where it is read again. The read results of the two stations are then compared to verify the accuracy of the input operation. If the two reads do not match, the card reader is stopped and an error message is given to the operator.

Card reader speeds range from 300 to 2000 cards per minute. The simple calculation of multiplying 2000 cards per minute times 80 characters per card (maximum) gives a data transfer rate of 160,000 characters per minute. This data transfer rate is not even 1 percent of the data transfer rates of the magnetic media such as magnetic disk and tape. As such, card readers are medium-speed devices.

Computer Output Microfilm

Computer output microfilm (COM) devices use combinations of electronic, photo-optical, and electromechanical techniques to convert digital computer output to human-readable records that can be stored either as rolls of microfilm or as microfilm frames stored on cards called *microfiche*. Microfiche cards measure 4 × 6 inches and hold 270 frames (pages) each. COM is a low-cost,

FIGURE 6-15
Card reader. (a) Typical card reader. (Courtesy IBM Corp.) (b) Card movement in card reader.

(a)

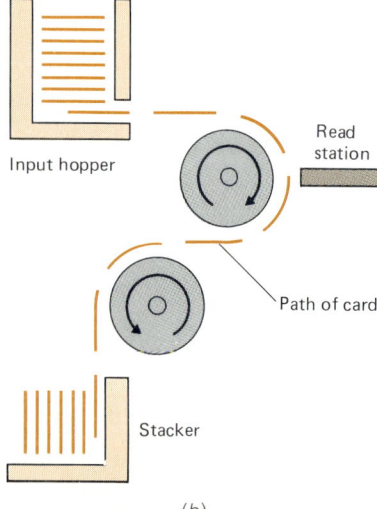

Input hopper

Read station

Path of card

Stacker

(b)

FIGURE 6-16
Microfiche reader. (Courtesy
Datragraphix)

fast alternative to printed-paper output. The COM recording process produces characters that can be 48 times smaller than those produced by conventional printers. This reduction means that a single microfiche can hold approximately 300 times as much information as a standard computer printed page. Microfiche data may be retrieved by means of manually or automatically operated viewers called microfiche readers. Figure 6-16 is a picture of a microfiche reader. Many businesses use microfiche to store large volumes of data that are relatively unchanging. Examples of relatively stable data are item locations for a large inventory, catalog data, and repair instruction manuals for complex mechanical devices.

COM devices are not new. They have been available for more than 20 years. However, because of factors such as high initial investment, retrieval delays, and the reluctance of many people to give up paper listings, growth of the micrographics industry has been slow. Growth of COM equipment will continue steadily because the volume of output reports of a typical business is increasing along with the costs of paper and record storage.

Digitizers

Digital input devices, or **digitizers,** convert graphic and pictorial data into binary, numeric inputs to digital computers. These digitizers are of two types: rectangular-coordinate and image-scan. A typical rectangular-coordinate digitizer, also called a flatbed digitizer, functions as follows: the drawing that is to be digitized is placed on a rectangular flatbed table, and a mechanism is moved over the surface of the drawing to produce signals related to the X and Y coordinates of the table. Figure 6-17 shows a rectangular-coordinate digitizer.

Image-screen digitizers scan and reproduce entire drawings or photographs automatically. Not only can they detect the presence of filled or empty areas; they can also distinguish intensities on a gray-to-black scale. Figure 6-18 is an example of an image-scan processing system.

FIGURE 6-18
Image-scan processing system.
(Courtesy Optronics International, Inc.)

FIGURE 6-17
Rectangular-coordinate digitizer with
floating keyboard and magnetic tape
recorder. (Courtesy Altek Corp.)

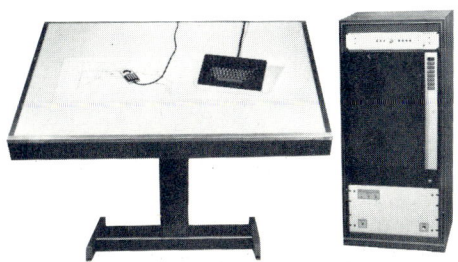

FIGURE 6-19
Flatbed plotter. (Courtesy Versatec, A
Xerox Company)

Plotters   The computer printer, with its limited character set, is not suitable for precise graphic presentations such as graphs and precise design plans. Digital plotters and graphic display devices are more suited to this purpose. Digital plotters are rectangular-coordinate "drafting" tables that are able to produce complex line drawings without the aid of a human drafter. Instead, the plotter is under computer control. Because of the value of graphs to mathematicians, engineers, and scientists, there is an important marketplace for plotters. A large flatbed plotter is shown in Figure 6-19, and an output that demonstrates the versatility of this type of plotter is shown in Figure 6-20.

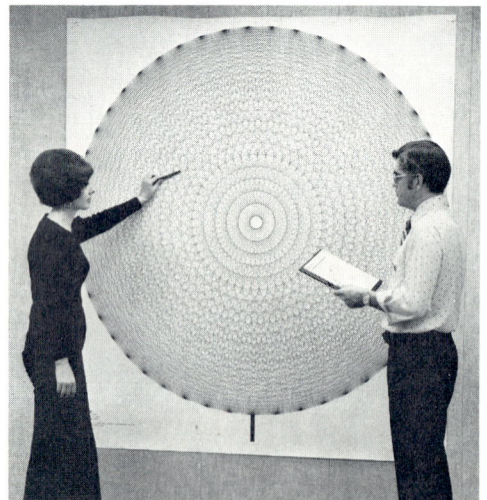

FIGURE 6-20
Plotter output example. (Courtesy
Versatec, A Xerox Company)

Voice Recognition and Response Devices

Voice recognition and response devices are attempts at getting the computer to listen to us and talk to us. Of the two applications, the voice response (output) have been far more successful then the voice recognition. The reason, of course, is that the rules for generating a voice through a speaker or over a telephone are easier to define than the rules for interpreting what a human says. If humans all spoke with the same tone of voice, with the same speed, with the same accent, and pronounced the words exactly the same way voice recognition would be a lot easier.

The primary business uses of voice response devices are to instruct a person in how to enter data and to output very low volume answers to requests. The banking industry is the largest user of voice response techniques. Some banks allow customers to call the bank's computer on a Touch-Tone telephone. The computer will answer the telephone and instruct the customer on how to request information by keying numbers on the Touch-Tone pad. Voice response should only be considered for those applications where there is a low-speed human-machine interaction. The most common banking applications include responding to bank account status inquiries over tellers' telephones and credit authorization for over-limit credit card transactions.

Voice recognition equipment has been available since the early 1970s, but its cost-effectiveness has slowed user acceptance. As an input device, it is slower and more costly than a keyboard device. In addition, a typical voice recognition device recognizes fewer than 50 words. Some industry analysts predict that technological advancements in the semiconductor chip industry will lower the price and increase the capabilities of voice recognition equipment. These same analysts foresee the day when computers will be programmed by voiced statements and speech will be directly converted into written copy.

While voice recognition devices currently have limited vocabularies, they do have the capability of evaluating the characteristics of a human voice. The characteristics of a person's voice are unique, that is, different from any other voice. The pattern of a voice is called a voice print. This voice analysis capability has been used in security systems where the computer controls access to restricted areas. The voice print must match an authorized person's voice as stored with the computer before doors are unlocked.

FEEDBACK

6-21 Why are card readers designed to read each card twice?

6-22 What is COM? When might it be used?

6-23 What is a digitizer?

6-24 What is the principal use of the plotter?

6-25 Under what conditions should a voice response unit be considered?

SUMMARY

In order to perform useful work, a computer system must be able to communicate with its environment. The devices by which this communication is accomplished are called input-output (I/O) devices.

These I/O devices may be described as high-, medium-, and low-speed devices. The high-speed I/O devices are those that are entirely electronic or those that use a magnetic media such as magnetic tape and magnetic disk. These high-speed devices perform both input and output functions and are used as secondary storage devices. The low-speed devices are those with complex mechanical motion and those that require human interaction. All other I/O devices are described as medium-speed.

Printers provide output in a permanent, human-readable form. The three types of printer are described as character, line, and page printers. Character printers print one character at a time, much like a typewriter. Line printers effectively print an entire line at a time. Page printers use the copier-related technologies to output entire pages of output at a time.

The most common types of keyboard devices are visual display terminals (VDT), teleprinter terminals, and point-of-sale devices. The most popular input-output device is the VDT. It consists of a keyboard for input and a cathode ray tube (CRT) screen for displayed output. Teleprinter terminals have a printed output rather than a display. Point-of-sale devices are electronic cash registers attached to a computer. These POS devices can capture a large amount of transaction data while the transaction takes place.

The main types of scanners are optical scanners and magnetic-ink character recognition (MICR) devices. Optical scanners detect input data using light sensors. The three types of optical scanner are the optical character reader (OCR), the optical mark reader (OMR), and bar-code readers. Magnetic-ink character readers detect data by sensing a magnetic field formed in characters printed with an ink with a high iron content. The banking industry is the major user of MICR.

Other devices which may be found in data centers are: card readers, computer output microfilm (COM), digitizers, plotters, and voice recognition and response units.

ANSWERS TO FEEDBACK QUESTIONS

6-1 Input-output devices allow the computer to communicate with its external environment.

6-2 An I/O interface is a special processor that converts input data to the internal codes used by the computer and the internal codes to a format which is usable by the output device.

6-3 The major differences between devices are the media that they use and the speed with which they are able to transfer data to or from primary storage.

6-4 The high-speed devices are those that are entirely electronic in their operation or are magnetic media that can be moved at high-speed.

6-5 The low-speed devices are those with complex mechanical motion or those that operate at the speed of a human operator.

6-6   Even the highest-speed input-output devices are only a fraction of the speed of primary storage.

6-7   Any device that outputs data in a form that can be inputted again at a later time can be used as a secondary storage device. Devices which are both input and output devices, such as magnetic disk and magnetic tape, can input data previously outputted.

6-8   An input device is attached to a computer system and inputs data into primary storage. A data recorder is an offline device which records the data on a medium that can be read by an input device. A key-to-diskette device is a data recorder. The data recorded on the diskette can be inputted into a computer system using a diskette drive, an input device.

6-9   The common magnetic media data recorders are key-to-disk, key-to-diskette, and key-to-tape.

6-10   The three types of printers are character printers, line printers, and page printers.

6-11   A letter-quality printer is a character printer which produces output of typewriter quality. A dot-matrix printer forms its characters as a series of dots.

6-12   The most common printer used with microcomputers is the character printer. The most common printer type used on larger systems is the line printer. This is a reflection of the typical quantity of printing produced on microcomputers compared to larger systems.

6-13   An impact printer produces a printed character by hitting or impacting a character font against the paper. A nonimpact printer does not use a character font or a ribbon to produce printed copy.

6-14   The most popular I/O device in use is the visual display terminal (VDT).

6-15   An alphanumeric display is one which can display character data. A graphic display can display high-resolution drawings. In addition, graphic displays have the capability of manipulating and modifying the graphics.

6-16   A light pen is used in conjunction with a VDT. It is an input device that can detect a position on the screen.

6-17   A POS is a point-of-sale device. It is an electronic cash register that also serves as an online terminal to a computer.

6-18   An optical scanner is an input device that uses light-sensing devices, optics, to detect data recorded on paper.

6-19   The three most common types of optical scanners are optical character readers (OCR), optical mark readers (OMR), and bar-code readers.

6-20   MICR is magnetic-ink character recognition, a magnetic scanning input device. The banking industry is the biggest user of MICR.

6-21   Card readers read the cards twice as a check for reading errors.

6-22 COM is computer output microfilm. It allows output data to be recorded on microfilm rather than printing the data on paper. It is used in those applications where the data are not frequently changed or updated.

6-23 A digitizer is a device that inputs graphic and pictorial data into main storage as binary numbers.

6-24 The principal use of the plotter is to output precise graphical presentations such as graphs and design plans.

6-25 A voice response unit would be considered for those applications where there is low-speed human-machine interaction.

FOR REVIEW AND DISCUSSION

1 How do data get into and out of primary storage?
2 Why are all keyboard devices classified as low-speed devices?
3 Match the following:

1	Bar code	**a**	Data recorder
2	Page printer	**b**	Impact printer
3	MICR	**c**	Unit used in banking industry
4	Key-to-disk	**d**	Universal product code
5	OCR	**e**	Microfiche
6	Digitizer	**f**	High-speed nonimpact printer
7	Line printer	**g**	Scans characters
8	COM	**h**	Scans graphs

CHAPTER 7

COMMUNICATIONS, DISTRIBUTED DATA PROCESSING, AND THE AUTOMATED OFFICE

PREVIEW Improvements in small computers and in data communications have increased the usability of remote computing systems and have led to their consideration as alternatives to centralized data processing. The goal of this chapter is to extend the discussion of input-output devices in the previous chapter to remote data entry systems. You will become familiar with computer-communication systems of the type that have become a multibillion dollar market and are changing many business office occupations.

In this chapter you will learn:

1. The four elements of data communications
2. The three data transmission modes
3. The concept and definition of distributed data processing
4. The three major classes of distributed data processing systems
5. How communication systems and distributed data processing are leading us toward the automated office

KEY TERMS TO WATCH FOR AND REMEMBER

data communications	distributed data processing (DDP)
modem	star network
simplex	ring network
half-duplex	local-area network (LAN)
full-duplex	word processing
baud	electronic mail
	voice store-and-forward system

Computers have come a long way from the large and bulky machines that were in use in the 1950s and 1960s. As you have read through the chapters in this book, you have seen several important trends described: (1) the size of computers has been reduced by changes in electronics; (2) the cost-effectiveness of computer systems has been increased because more data can be processed at lower cost; and (3) computer applications are serving the needs of more users in all areas of science and industry.

These trends will continue for at least the rest of this century. In the 1980s we are seeing large numbers of small computer systems made available to all businesses, particularly smaller firms or departments of larger companies. Indeed, this is the age of the personal computer. The distribution of computing capability to users is the result of improvements in both data processing and data communications.

In Chapters 5 and 6 we learned about the units that are the building blocks of computer systems. In those chapters we emphasized computer systems with all of their units in a centralized location. This was the common arrangement for computer systems through the 1960s. Users had to transport their data to large centralized data processing centers for batch processing.

Toward the end of the 1960s, changes began to occur. The use of telephone lines to communicate data from remote terminals to a central data processing location was introduced. This kind of data processing was called *teleprocessing*. The terminals used in teleprocessing systems usually were "dumb" terminals. They acted only as input or output units and had no data storage or processing capabilities of their own. Refinements introduced in the 1970s extended the usability of these terminals, increasing their "intelligence" by adding the capability for storage and processing at user locations. In effect, remote terminals became small computers that could communicate with a centralized computer system or perform independent (called *stand-alone*) data processing. It is this aspect of modern data processing that we will emphasize in this chapter.

In Chapter 3 we stressed the worth of a data processing system to the end user and called this worth the *usability* of the computer system. Usability depends not only upon the technical capability of a data processing system but also upon the ease with which users can communicate their needs to the system and the ability of the system to respond to those needs. In our discussions in this chapter, we should bear in mind the concept of usability. It is the criterion by which users should make their choices of computer data processing systems.

In some instances, large computer systems are needed to solve problems in business and science. In other cases, computer power and the responsibility for business system development and control cannot be dispersed throughout a company. However, we are seeing an increase in the situations in which usability can be enhanced by placing the data processing capability where the results are needed. This is bringing about a blending of computer and communications capabilities. This blending is shown as the overlap area in Figure 7-1.

In Figure 7-1, computing means the processing of data. *Communication* means the transmission of data to and from the computer. The overlap area

FIGURE 7-1

Overlap of data processing and communications.

Overlap is area of computer-communications processing

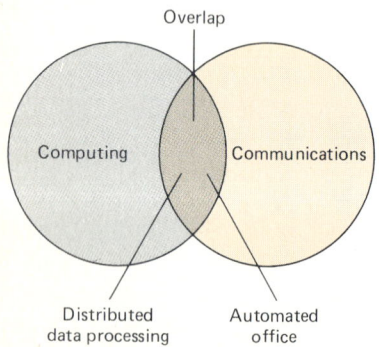

Overlap

Computing   Communications

Distributed   Automated
data processing   office

indicates applications that include data processing and the use of communications to transmit data to and from remote I/O stations. These stations may have a significant stand-alone data processing capability. We will explain some of the elements of data communications. Then we will examine two computer-communications applications in the overlap area: distributed processing and the automated office.

ELEMENTS OF DATA COMMUNICATIONS

Communications is the process of transferring messages from one point to another. Figure 7-2 identifies the four elements of any communications process as:

1. The *sender* which creates the message
2. The *medium,* which carries the message
3. The *receiver,* which receives the message
4. *Feedback,* which verifies the message

When you speak to a friend on the telephone, you are the sender. The medium is the telephone line. Your friend is the receiver, and your friend's responses are feedback. In this chapter, the senders and receivers are computers and terminals. The medium usually is the same as that used for telephone conversations. However, the messages that we will be concerned with are data, not voice conversations. Feedback is a response or action that verifies receipt of the message. An example is the use of a financial communications system such as the one in Figure 7-3. In this instance, the sender is the clerk, who is using a remote terminal to communicate with the receiver, a distant computer.

FIGURE 7-2
The communication process.

FIGURE 7-3
Financial communication system.

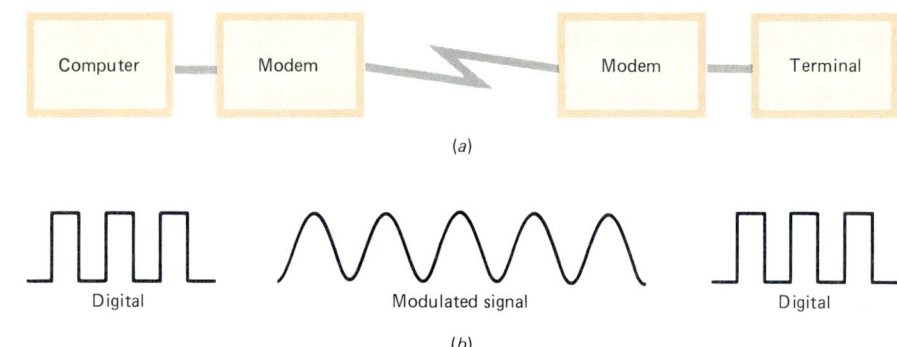

FIGURE 7-4

Digital data transmission. (a) Data
transmission system elements. (b)
Digital signal modulation.

The medium is a telephone line. Feedback is in the form of an updated deposit book, and the customer's ability to verify the accuracy of the transaction.

The electronic systems that transfer data from one point to another are called *data communications* systems. Unlike computers that process and rearrange data, data communications systems transmit data from one point to another and cause them to arrive without alteration. Knowledge of data communications is important to the study of computer data processing because over 90 percent of the data processing systems employed by the end of the 1980s will use some form of data communications. The features of data communications of importance to us are (1) how data are transmitted; (2) what data communications services are available; and (3) what the trends are in data communications applications.

Data Transmission

Figure 7-4a shows the elements of a typical data communications system. In this instance communication is between a computer and a terminal (it may be in either direction). The medium is an electronic link, such as a telephone line or a microwave transmission system (which is similar to the way TV is transmitted). Fortunately, the same lines that are used for voice conversations can transmit data. However, when a voice message is sent over a telephone line, it looks like a wavy line. Binary data coming out of a terminal or a computer look more like a square wave. This square wave has to be turned into a wavy voicelike wave for data to be transmitted through the telephone system from one point to another. This is accomplished by the boxes labeled *modem* in Figure 7-4a. **Modem** stands for modulator-demodulator, and it means that the boxes can turn square waves into voicelike waves—and vice versa. The demodulation and recovery of a digital signal—that is, a square data wave—is also shown in Figure 7-4b.

Data Communications Services

Data transmission modes   There are three ways, or modes, for transmitting data. As shown in Figure 7-5, these are simplex, half-duplex, and full-duplex. If transmission is *simplex*, communication can take place in only one direction. The simplex mode can be used to transmit data to a computer from a remote source.

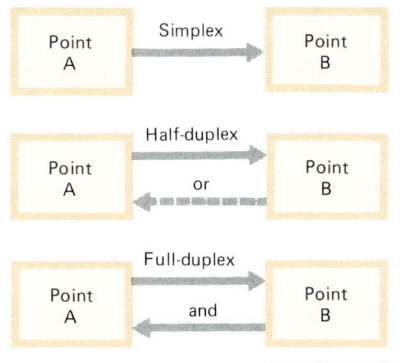

FIGURE 7-5
Transmission modes.

A *half-duplex* system can transmit data in both directions, but only in one direction at a time. This is the most common type of transmission for voice communications. The financial communication system of Figure 7-3 is an example of a half-duplex system used for data communications. This type of system enables the terminal and computer to exchange data.

Sometimes, because of the volume of data that has to be exchanged, transmission must be in both directions at the same time. This type of transmission is called *full-duplex*.

Types of communications services   A term used to describe the data-handling capacity of a communications service is bandwidth. *Bandwidth* is the range of frequencies that is available for the transmission of data. A narrow range of frequencies in a communications system is analogous to a garden hose with a small diameter. The flow of information in such a system—its data rate—is restricted, just as is the flow of water in the narrow hose. Wider bandwidths permit more rapid information flow. The communication data transfer rate is measured in a unit called *baud*. **Baud** is identical to bits per second. Therefore, a rate of 300 baud is 300 bits per second.

Communications companies such as American Telephone and Telegraph (AT&T) and Western Union are called *common carriers*, and they provide three general classes of service for both voice and data communication:

1. *Narrowband* handles low data volumes. Data transmission rates are from 45 to 300 baud. The low-speed devices might use narrowband communications.

2. *Voiceband* handles moderate data transmission volumes between 300 and 9600 baud. They are used for applications ranging from operating a CRT to running a line printer. Their major application is for telephone voice communication—hence, the term *voiceband*.

3. *Broadband* handles very large volumes of data. These systems provide data transmission rates of 1 million baud or more. High-speed data analysis and satellite communications are examples of broadband communications systems.

Some of the major common carrier communications services that are available to the computer industry are listed in Table 7-1.

Trends in Computer-Communications Processing

The common carriers are continuing to expand their capabilities. Also, the Federal Communications Commission, the agency that regulates the communications companies, has made decisions that provide computer users with some alternatives to the use of the common carriers. In 1968 the FCC granted non-Bell System companies permission to sell equipment that interfaced (that is, connected electrically) with the common carrier communication networks. In 1970 the FCC further opened up the computer-communications business to competition by allowing companies, known as *specialized common carriers*, to sell broadband, point-to-point communications services in selected high-density areas. As an example, Microwave Communications, Inc. (MCI) provides voice,

TABLE 7-1   **COMMON CARRIER COMMUNICATION SERVICES**

Type of service	Name and description of service
Narrowband	*Teletypewriter exchange service* (*TWX*): a dial-up system using leased telephone lines. *Telex:* Western Union's teletypewriter service.
Voiceband	*Direct distance dialing* (*DDD*): direct long-distance dialing by consumer. Charges are by time and distance.
	Dataphone digital service (*DDS*): Bell Telephone Company system that transmits data between large cities, using modems and voice lines.
	Wide-area telephone service (*WATS*): AT&T provides a user with a communications service at a flat monthly rate for selected national areas.
	Private lines: lines leased from AT&T for communications between user locations.
Broadband	*Telpak:* Full-duplex service leased from AT&T. Services available in several bandwidth packages.
	Dataphone-50: dial-up AT&T service.
	Broadband exchange service: dial-up Western Union service.

data, and image facsimile transmission services. There also are companies, called *value-added carriers*, which lease networks from common carriers and combine messages from customers into packets for transmission. The customer pays only for actual data transmitted, and this can be much cheaper than paying for idle time on a private line. Telenet, Tymeshare, and Graphnet are examples of value-added services that make use of the common carrier lines. Telenet and Tymeshare transmit data, and Graphnet specializes in image facsimile transmission.

One of the newer developments in computer communications has been the *information utility*. These companies assemble a data base from information providers and make it available to their customers. The access to the information utility computers is most often through one of the value-added carriers. Some of the utility companies provide very specialized information—such as aviation weather for flight planning and stock market quotations—while most provide general information services. One such utility is Source Telecomputing Corporation. They have approximately 800 information and communication services available to their subscribers. To gain access to the system subscribers must have a computer (or word processing equipment) and a modem. Subscribers call a local telephone number to connect to either Telenet or Tymeshare. These value-added carriers in turn connect you through to a bank of computers located in McLean, Virginia. Customers are billed on an hourly basis for the time their computer is connected to the system.

At present, the most promising computer-communications advance is satellite communications. The Communications Satellite Corporation (COMSAT) was chartered by the U.S. Congress in 1962 as a privately owned company for voice and television telecommunications. COMSAT, in turn, is a member of the International Telecommunications Satellite Consortium (INTELSAT). In 1974, Western Union launched the Westars as domestic satellite operations.

THE INFORMATION UTILITY

There are now several companies in the business of providing subscribers with access to information. One such company is Source Telecomputing Corporation located in McLean, Virginia. More commonly referred to as The Source, it is a subsidiary of The Reader's Digest Association, Inc.

Subscribers to The Source must have either a standard data terminal with a modem or word processing equipment with communications software and a modem. Your hardware system must be set up to communicate at either 300 or 1200 baud, use full-duplex, have no parity, and use the 8-bit ASCII code. To become a subscriber, you must pay a one-time registration fee to cover the set-up of your account, your user ID and password assignment, a user's manual, and a command guide. The registration fee is listed as $100, but you can get a discount at many computer stores. In addition, there are monthly fees based on amount of time you are connected to The Source and the amount of their disk storage you use for your files.

As a subscriber to The Source, you have access to approximately 800 information and communication services. The major categories of service are communications, news and information, business services, consumer services, entertainment, publishing, travel, education, and computations.

To gain access to the system, you must first dial the local telephone number of the Telenet or Tymeshare value-added network. The telephone can be dialed using your telephone or the keyboard of your terminal, or it can be done for you by the communications software for your terminal. When the computer "answers" the telephone, you will be asked to enter a code to identify the type of terminal you are using, and the network's code for the Source Telecommunications Corporation. You will then be asked to enter your user identification and password. Assuming that you have entered your identification and password correctly, you will be connected to The Source and will see a menu of choices. You may now choose a specific information source or service.

The communications services include Electronic Mail, Chat (for communication to any other subscriber currently on the system), Teleconferencing, Bulletin Boards (for posting and reading notices), the User Directory (where subscribers may list their special interests for others to see), and Mailgram Message Service (Western Union Telegraph Company).

If the subscriber wants to get the latest news, the news and information services include the United Press International (UPI) news service, Business Update, U.S. News Washington Letter, Raylux Financial Reports, Commodity News, United Media Features Syndicate articles, sports news from UPI, and Reference. The reference service provides a direct link to a major reference research organization, Information on Demand (IOD). IOD can search hundreds of data bases of specific or generic orientation to answer your requests.

These are only a sample of the services and information sources available to subscribers to The Source.

Initially used for voice transmission, these satellites are also capable of data transmission. These satellites are positioned in a geosynchronous orbit, that is, an orbit where one revolution around the earth equals 24 hours. Since the earth also turns once every 24 hours, the satellite always stays over the same point on the ground. This allows a ground station to aim its antenna at a fixed point in the sky. A major drawback of satellite communications has been the high cost of placing the satellite into this orbit.

The complexity and cost of this operation is being reduced by the success of the NASA shuttle program. The satellite is launched as part of the shuttle's cargo. Once the shuttle is in its low orbit, the satellite is launched toward its higher geosynchronous orbit. With the continuing reduction in satellite communication costs, new information utility companies can provide both businesses and individuals with greater amounts of information at reasonable cost. Figure 7-6 illustrates a communications satellite and some of its potential applications.

THE GEOSTAR SATELLITE SYSTEM

Geostar is a satellite-based system designed to provide users with accurate position information (within a fraction of a meter) and a high-speed message capability.

The position information can be used by aircraft and ships for navigation, the railroads for keeping track of their train cars, and police departments for locating emergency calls. Geostar provides position information in all three coordinates, that is, by latitude, longitude, and elevation. The message capability allows near-instantaneous communication between any two locations in the United States, Canada, and Mexico.

The initial Geostar system configuration consists of three satellites, a ground station, and users with transceivers (transmitter receivers). The three-satellite system provides coverage of North America. World-

wide coverage will require 10 satellites. The user-carried transceivers are inexpensive (estimated at approximately $400) and compact. They can be battery-operated and hand-carried. When a position request is made through a user transceiver, the signal is received by the satellites. The satellites transmit identification and timing information to the ground station, which calculates the position of the user. The position information is beamed up to a satellite and down to the user's transceiver. The delay time from sending a position request to receiving the position information is a fraction of a second. The system design requires that each user transceiver have a unique identification. The capacity of the first-generation Geostar system is sufficient to accommodate a number of users equal to the population of North America.

The potential customers for Geostar services include car, truck, boat, and aircraft owners; operators of truck, taxi, and freight-car fleets; police and fire departments; and operators of ambulances and rescue vehicles.

Potential Geostar customers also include homeowners and businesses wishing security protection and a message-exchange capability that is independent of telephone wires. Geostar services could also implement near-instantaneous verification of credit limits and electronic funds transfers to retail stores.

Testing of the Geostar system began in August 1983. The satellites are scheduled to be placed into geosynchronous orbit by the space shuttle. The Geostar system is expected to be operational by 1987.

FIGURE 7-6
Satellite communications.

Potential uses:

Disaster relief services
(forest fires, floods, earthquakes)

Teleconferencing

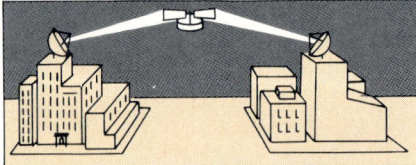

Transmission of bulk data

A potential cost-effective earth alternative to satellite communications for the future will be the use of optical fibers. The Bell System has tested small half-inch-diameter cables that could transmit as many as 50,000 voice messages simultaneously by means of advanced optical techniques based upon laser technology.

Much of the growth in business applications for computer-communications processing will come from two factors—the continuing reduction in cost per bit of data handled and the increasing number of small computer systems.

The combination of the computer and the communications technologies will lead to many new distributed data processing applications and to advances in office automation that could culminate in the "automated office" before the end of the 1980s.

We will now consider some of the computer-communications applications that are illustrated by the overlap area in Figure 7-1. The general classes of applications that we will describe are distributed data processing and the automated office.

FEEDBACK

7-1 What is the meaning of the term computer-communications?

7-2 Identify the four elements of the communications process and the purpose of each.

7-3 Why are modems used in data communication systems?

7-4 What are the meanings of simplex, half-duplex, and full-duplex?

DISTRIBUTED DATA PROCESSING
Distributed Data Processing: A Concept and a Definition

The concept Computers are a business tool, and the developments in small computers have made them increasingly cost-effective. Distributed data processing is a management concept that tries to increase the usability of computers by bringing them closer to the end user and by integrating them into daily business activities at the locations at which these activities take place. Advances in both computer and communications hardware and software are increasing the feasibility of placing data processing power throughout all of the departments or locations of a business firm. The decision to decentralize computing resources will be one that fits in with the top-management philosophy for the entire company.

The definition We define **distributed data processing (DDP)** as any arrangement of computers and/or communications systems that—as an alternative to wholly central-site data processing—places data processing capabilities at the location of the end user. Within this broad definition of DDP we can identify three major classes of distributed data processing: (1) data entry systems, (2) stand-alone systems, and (3) computer networks. There are many variations within and between these classes. We will examine some examples of each class of DDP, and then we will summarize with some management considerations.

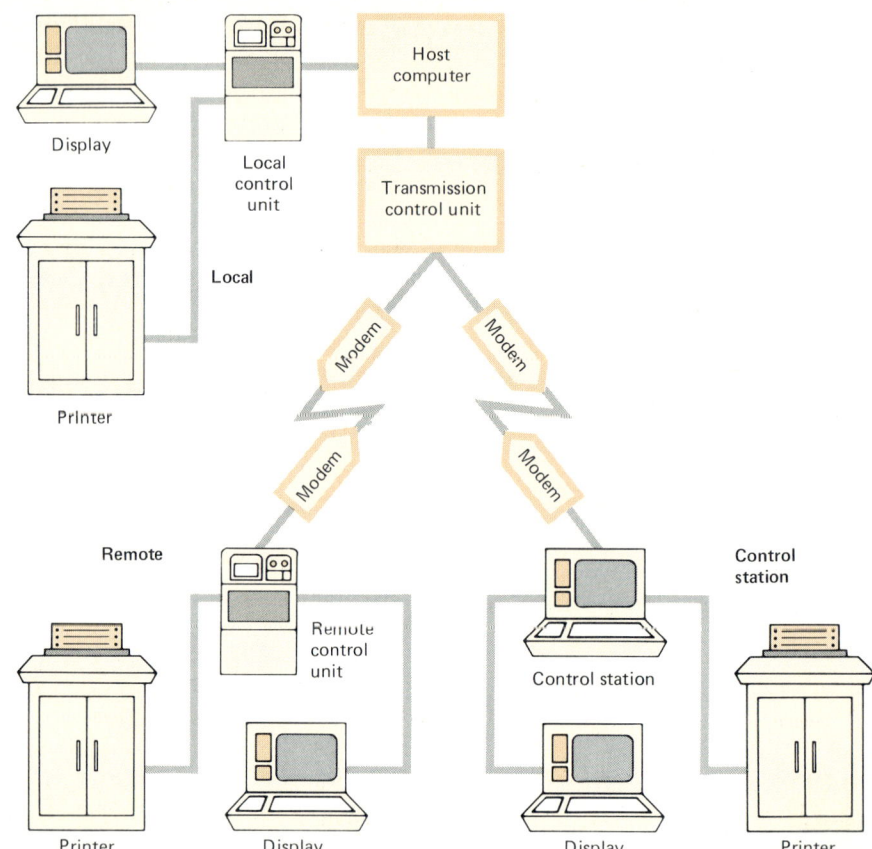

FIGURE 7-7
Information display system.

Data Entry Systems   Earlier we identified the introduction of terminals for use at locations remote from a central-site computer as an important development. We classified these terminals as dumb, intelligent, and programmable.

Typically, data entry stations have both a softcopy (temporary, visual-display) and a hardcopy (permanent, printed) output capability. System configurations that can support multiple data entry stations are available from several different vendors. Figure 7-7 is a sample configuration. The control units control communication between the host, central-site computer and the data entry stations.

Dumb terminals need not appear dumb to the user. Because of the rapidity with which the central-site computer can communicate back to the data entry station, many applications are not affected if no actual processing is done locally. However, there are circumstances under which it is advantageous to have some local data processing capability, and intelligent terminals can provide this. For example, dumb terminals transmit all data directly to the central-site computer.

24 These persons are busy at work inputting invoice data from data entry terminals. These terminals are connected to a dedicated minicomputer by communication lines and are part of a local area network (LAN). (© Eli Heller/Picture Group)

25 Teleconferencing can be a cost-effective substitute for travel. Verbal and visual communication are faster and less expensive than travel. Also, teleconferences often can be scheduled with less interruption of the work schedules of the individuals who need to be involved. (Reproduced with permission of AT&T)

24

26

26 The distribution of desk-top work stations to office staff can increase productivity. For example, word processing programs make it possible to type letters rapidly in rough-draft form and to quickly review or revise them. (© Bill Gallery, 1982/Stock, Boston)

27 The Tracking and Data Relay Satellite System (TDRSS) will consist of specialized relay satellites in synchronous earth orbits and a ground terminal located at White Sands, New Mexico. These satellites will relay data, commands, video, and voice to and from spacecraft and the ground terminal. The TDRSS spacecraft and ground station facilities will support NASA earth-orbital scientific applications and manned spacecraft missions, including the automated spacecraft to be placed in orbit by the space shuttle in the 1980s. (NASA)

27

28

28 An increasing number of persons are communicating by means of electronic bulletin boards, which enable persons at distant locations to share messages. These are transmitted by use of modems and telephone lines and are shown on visual display terminals. (Reproduced with permission of AT&T)

29 Small business owners are finding many uses for computers. For example, counter-top computers can be used not only as cash registers but also as point-of-sales terminals in order to assist in keeping track of inventory information. (© Eli Heller/Picture Group)

30 An automated teller machine (ATM) increases convenience for bank customers by providing access to a computer system which can perform many banking services on a 24-hour basis. (© Miriam Caravella/The Image Bank)

31 Mail can be sent or received electronically by means of communication networks. The menu shown on the screen allows this user to send a brief message, to read a document, to request mail delivery, or to call for other functions. (© John Blaustein, 1981/Courtesy Four-Phase Systems, Inc.)

30

31

This type of data is called "dirty" data because errors are transmitted along with good data. The errors must then be identified at the central site, and processing could be delayed until "clean" data are obtained from remote users. This type of delay, accompanied by the need to process the data over again, can be expensive.

Intelligent terminals have a limited local-processing capability. This means that preliminary processing of input data can take place locally and that the data can be cleaned up before it is transmitted to the central-site computer. Intelligent terminals have some local processing power (a CPU) and storage capacity in addition to I/O capabilities.

Some advantages of intelligent terminals as data entry stations are increased processing efficiency at the host computer center, reduction of the overall time for results to reach the end users, and involvement and motivation of the users to assume the responsibility for making their part of the computer-communications system work well.

Programmable terminals are distributed data processing systems with extensive local data processing power. Large working files can be maintained locally. Only the data that are needed at the central site have to be transmitted, and transmission can take place when it is convenient to schedule it.

As shown n Figure 7-8a, some data entry stations use individual lines to communicate with the central-site computer. Others cluster around a shared remote processor that handles all communication with the host computer. This concept is illustrated in Figure 7-8b. Still other data entry stations, as illustrated by the configuration of Figure 7-8c, use a fully programmable local computer to handle many remote user applications and to manage all communications with a central-site computer.

Stand-Alone Systems

Distributed data processing usually implies communication between a host computer and remote stations. However, a communications link is not essential. The responsibility for performing entire functions may be distributed. In these instances independent, or stand-alone, computer systems may be able to meet the needs of separate departments or branches of large corporations.

Implicit in the pure stand-alone type of DDP is a management decision not to monitor all of the details of an operation and to permit remote locations to function as small businesses. Stand-alone DDP can improve the effectiveness of local operations, especially if files are maintained and managed locally. However, this decision also means that each location needs people who are knowledgable about computer data processing. Of course, summary data can be sent to corporate headquarters as printouts or in computer-processable format on tape or disk.

Stand-alone systems may be general-purpose computers or specialized, programmable data entry systems with a secondary emphasis upon communications. In recent years, there has been a tremendous growth in the use of microcomputers as stand-alone systems.

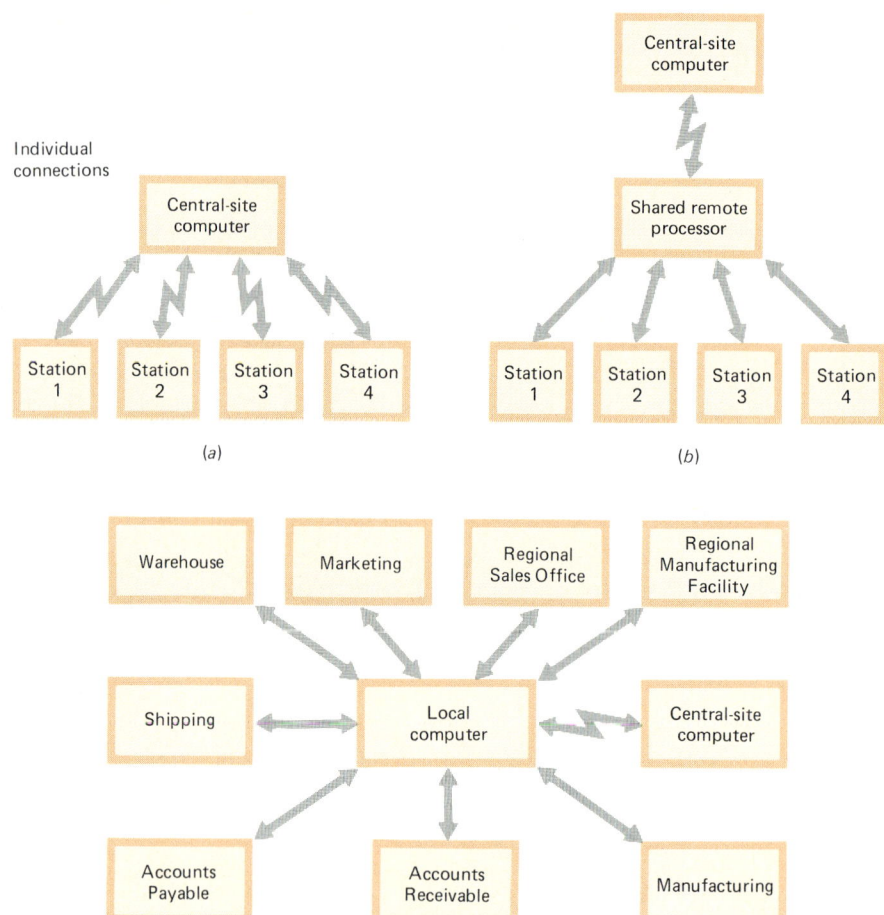

FIGURE 7-8
Communications for data entry.

Computer Networks

The most complex form of distributing the data processing function is the computer network. A network attaches multiple computers together for the purpose of communicating data and sharing resources. The major complication of the computer network is the software required to allow the computers to "talk" to each other. There are two general configurations of computer networks: the star and the ring. In addition, if the network is entirely within a business, it is called a local-area network (LAN).

The star network   In a **star network** there is a host computer which is attached to local computers through multiple communication lines. As shown in Figure 7-9a, the local computers are not attached directly to each other but communicate through the host computer. An advantage of the star network configuration is that if any of the local computers fail, the remaining portion of the network is unaffected. Of course, if the host computer fails, the entire network fails.

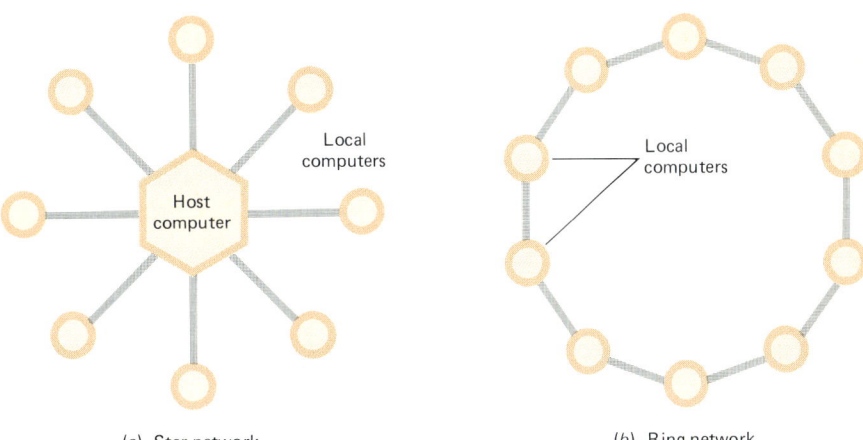

FIGURE 7-9

Star and ring networks.

(a) Star network

(b) Ring network

The ring network   The **ring network** is a no-host network. That is, there is no main or controlling computer in the network. Figure 7-9*b* illustrates the circular or ring arrangement of the attached computers. The ring network works well where there is no central-site computer system. It is a truly distributed data processing system. One disadvantage of the ring network is that unless bypass circuitry has been installed at each local computer, the failure of any one computer in the network causes the entire network to fail. The ring network is not as popular as the star network because of its more complicated control software. Sophisticated distributed data processing systems of the future will have elements of both star and ring architectures.

The local-area network   The **local-area network** (**LAN**) is an intracompany, privately owned, user-administered network. In addition, it covers a limited geographic area, normally no more than a distance of a few miles. The configuration of the LAN can be a star, a ring, or simply devices attached along a length of cable.

The typical local-area network connects computers located within half a mile of each other. The attached computers may be of different types and be performing a variety of functions such as data processing, word processing, and electronic mail. The two main purposes of the local-area network are to link workstations within a facility so that they may share peripherals (such as magnetic disks holding the data base) and to allow workstations to communicate with each other.

It is not unusual to connect a local-area network to an intercity network or a value-added network. This allows all devices attached to the LAN to have access to outside sources of data.

Management Considerations   It is clear that DDP options range from a few simple terminals to complex computer networks. As we have already mentioned, the elements of the DDP decision are hardware, software, and management philosophy. Hardware is the least complex element because it is the area of the greatest technical achievement and ongoing progress. Software is lagging behind hardware, and for this reason, complex networks tend to be pioneering projects. However, major software improvements are being made. The critical factor is management attitudes toward the usability of DDP. On the one hand, there is a reluctance to give up control by allowing too much local authority. On the other hand, there is the opportunity to provide regional offices with extensive on-site data processing capability and to use the same technology to provide useful summary and exception information to corporate headquarters, thus improving control over dispersed operations.

DDP is not a solution for all companies, but many industries are moving in that direction, and others will join them. A technically sound DDP capability, coupled with well-designed feedback for management control, might provide the best of both worlds—centralized and decentralized processing.

FEEDBACK

7-5 Define distributed data processing.

7-6 Identify and distinguish between the three types of distributed data processing.

7-7 What are the differences between dumb terminals and intelligent terminals?

7-8 Distinguish between a star network and a ring network.

7-9 What is a local-area network?

THE AUTOMATED OFFICE

The goal of automating an office is to make the office more efficient and effective. In implementing office automation we must look for ways to eliminate time-wasting activities and avoid duplication of effort. To achieve this goal, data must never be entered into the system more than once, and we must be able to communicate the data to the appropriate person or location. The modern office may be automated through the use of data processing, data communications, word processing, electronic mail, and voice store-and-forward systems.

Data Processing

Many offices have been highly automated in the processing of business data for several years. With the declining costs of computers and the development of the microcomputer, businesses of all sizes can afford to automate their data processing functions. When the costs of manually maintaining accounting records is compared to the cost of using a microcomputer, it is obvious that most businesses cannot afford to process data by hand. The accounting, material control, and sales management records are the major data processing areas affecting the office. We have attempted to improve the accuracy of the data through point-of-sale devices, scanners, and other devices designed to eliminate potential errors arising from the manual keying process. The transaction data is entered only once and then is manipulated by the computer for all uses of the data.

Data Communications

Once entered into a computer, data can be transmitted to any other computer or output device through a computer network. If the data is used only at one location, it can be communicated to all users through a local-area network. There is no need to print reports on paper and then deliver or mail them to the user.

Data communications is not limited to the sending of words and numbers. Image transmission systems allow printed pages, pictures, graphs, charts, and tables to be transmitted as well. As discussed earlier in this chapter, teleconferencing is a two-way communication of a combination of audio, visual, and image information.

Word Processing

Word processing is one of the most important components of the automated office. It is the processing or manipulation of words that allows us to produce text material in a cost-effective, timely manner. A word processing system is a highly automated typewriter. The typical system consists of a keyboard, a CRT screen, and secondary storage in the form of magnetic disk or diskette.

The operator of a word processing system uses the keyboard exactly as a typist uses the keyboard of a typewriter. As the characters are entered with the keyboard, they are displayed on the screen. The word processing operator can set up the format of the document to be entered by specifying the margins, spacing (single, double, etc.), number of lines per page, and tab stops. These are equivalent options to those of a typist using a conventional typewriter. As the operator enters the data, the lines will show on the screen exactly as they will appear on paper when they are printed. The first major difference between a word processor and a typewriter that you will notice is that you do not press the return key at the end of each line, only at the end of a paragraph. When the word processor gets to the end of a line, it automatically drops down to the next line on the screen. If you were keying in the middle of a word when the end of the line was reached, the word processor will move the entire word to the beginning of the next line. If you change your mind about the spacing or margins, you may change them and the word processor will reformat the lines. Another common function is to justify the lines on both right and left margins. This is a difficult and time-consuming task with a typewriter, but it takes no time at all with a word processor.

The real power of the word processor is made evident with its editing functions. Text entered through a word processor can be stored on magnetic disk or diskette. It is, therefore, available at any time by inputting the text back into the memory of the word processor from the secondary storage device. If any changes or modifications must be made to the text, only the changes must be keyed. All text material that is unchanged remains in memory. The common editing functions of a word processor are inserting the deleting characters or words, inserting and deleting lines or paragraphs, and moving text around in the document. If you decide that two paragraphs are reversed, you can change their order with a few keystrokes.

Growth in word processing   What is a word processing system? A word processing system is a computer with software to perform the logical functions required to manipulate characters and words. Any general purpose computer can be used for word processing if it has the appropriate software.

The automation of word processing began in 1964 when IBM introduced the Magnetic Tape Selectric Typewriter (MT/ST). This device was based on the IBM Selectric typewriter. It had a limited processing capability and could output to and input from a magnetic tape. It was a great improvement over the typewriter when producing form letters. The MT/ST was very limited as compared to a modern word processing system, but it was developed 10 years before we had the microcomputer. Today's microcomputers and intelligent terminals have visual displays, magnetic disks or diskettes, powerful processors, and large amounts of primary storage that were not feasible 20 years ago.

Today, almost all computers have word processing software available for them. The most common business use of microcomputers in the office and in the home is word prosessing.

Types of word processing systems   There are three basic types of word processing systems: stand-alone systems, shared-logic systems, and time-shared services.

Stand-alone word processing systems are those that are not connected to another computer. They perform all of their own word processing functions and have no access to the data files of other computers. The personal computer used as a word processor is a stand-alone system if it is not attached to a network. Many of the stand-alone word processing systems are dedicated word processor systems; that is, they are computers that are dedicated to that one function rather than being general purpose. IBM, NBI, Wang, and many others make dedicated word processing systems. One advantage of dedicated systems is that the keyboards can be customized to word processing functions for easier use.

Shared-logic word processing systems share the processing and storage capabilities of a business computer among several terminals. These terminals perform word processing functions in a manner analogous to the entry of data by terminals in a distributed data processing system. A closeup of a word processor display is shown in Figure 7-10. The operator can work with a displayed page while the printer is producing copies of documents previously stored in memory. Systems of this type can also be used as computers for performing many pure data processing applications.

Many organizations are finding that the most efficient way to implement word processing is to establish work areas, each with its own cluster of stations. Shared-logic systems are designed for this purpose. Equipped with communications options, shared-logic systems are able to tie into central-site data bases and to share data with other stations.

The line between distributed data processing and word processing is becoming blurred. Some shared-logic processors can be used for word processing

FIGURE 7-10
Word processing on screen.

part of the time and for local data processing the remainder of the time. A typical example is for the law firm that uses word processing to create customized contracts to use the same computer system for keeping track of time charged by attorneys to the accounts of clients.

The line will become even further blurred as more intelligence is moved from the shared-logic processor to workstations in order to increase their versatility. An example of this blending is the introduction of portable intelligent terminals. Portable terminals, with their own microprocessors and memory, can operate as independent workstations or connected online to a host computer. Figure 7-11 is a picture of the Texas Instrument Portable Memory Terminal. This terminal has a magnetic bubble memory that can store up to

FIGURE 7-11
Portable terminal.

80K bytes of data, which is the equivalent of 20 typed pages. The software includes a file management system with extensive data editing capability. A typical application is in sales. A salesperson can enter sales data throughout the day. These data are stored in the memory of the terminal. At a later time, the salesperson can have complete sales records printed out and can make changes to the record before transmitting the data to the home-office computer. Sales and other data are transmitted at a rate of 30 characters per second over a dial-up telephone line. Shortly thereafter, the processing of customers' orders can take place.

Time-shared word processing systems use the resources of a remote, central-site computer for processing and storage. A terminal, similar to those of share-logic systems, is attached to the central-site computer directly or through a network.

Electronic Mail

Electronic mail systems are a combination of data communication systems and word processing systems. All office personnel, at all levels, have one common need—they need to communicate. Word processing systems allow us to prepare written communications quickly and easily, but there is often a considerable delay in getting the communication to its recipient. Electronic mail systems can be the answer to this communication delay. The system functions by creating the communication using word processing techniques. The data are then transmitted through a network to the terminal of the recipient. If the person to receive the communication is not "signed on" to a terminal, the data are stored on magnetic disk. In electronic mail systems, the first thing you would normally do after signing on to a terminal is to inquire about your "mail." If you have mail waiting for you, you may scan it (see who sent the mail and what the subject of the mail is), read it, or print it. When you are finished with your mail, you may either leave it stored on the magnetic disk or delete it.

If you are sending mail though the system, you may send it to one individual or to an entire list of people. Systems attached to a local-area network allow you to send mail to anyone with a user ID on the network. If the system is connected to an outside or value-added network, you may send mail to anyone anywhere in the world that has access to the network.

Voice Store-and-Forward Systems

One of the latest additions to the automated office is the **voice store-and-forward system.** As the name implies, this system has the capability of storing verbal data and/or communicating it to another location. These systems are also referred to as voice mail or structured verbal inquiry-response exchanges. The first commercial system for voice mail was installed in 1980.

Problems in the Automated Office

The biggest problem in any office is poor communication. The automated-office approach attempts to solve this communication problem through the use of data processing, data communication systems, word processing, electronic mail, and voice store-and-forward systems. One of the drawbacks of much of the office automation hardware available today is that it can be difficult (or threatening) to use for many office workers. It appears that the reason for much of the difficulty is that the systems tend to be stand-alone, incompatible products. Each system has its own operational keystrokes and commands that are different from all other systems. This means that there may be several systems that must be mastered by each person in the office. As the automated office matures, we should see more integrated, friendly systems—those that are both easy to use and that communicate with each other.

TOWARD THE ELECTRONIC OFFICE

As word processing and data processing continue to merge, office functions, secretarial and administrative careers, and the structure of the office as we understand them today will change dramatically.

Office Functions

Office functions, such as document preparation, storage, retrieval, reproduction, and distribution, are being altered by advances in computers, word processing, and communications. Comprehensive text manipulation features, including visual display, can be used for document preparation. Documents can be kept in electronic storage. This is less expensive than storing printed materials in scattered collections of file cabinets. It is possible to store and retrieve documents electronically, reproduce them by image facsimile techniques, and then transmit them by electronic mail to persons in the office building or at geographically dispersed branch offices.

Careers

Careers of clerks, secretaries, and office administrators are affected. Some knowledge of data processing and training in word processing systems are essential parts of their education and work experience. This is introducing many changes into the curriculum of schools throughout the nation.

It has been predicted that the job that we call "secretary" will disappear by the end of the century. One contributing factor may be the development of voice recognition data entry systems. Most certainly, jobs and job titles will change. As examples, the administrative secretary is becoming the executive link between administrators and computers. Corresponding secretaries should be skilled in the use of all types of word processing equipment. Basic typing skills still are needed, but additional training is required to make effective use of all of the features of automated office machines. Work assignments in a modern office have features of both word and data processing. The secretarial supervisor performs many functions closely related to those performed by data processing managers. These include informing users of the capabilities of electronic office systems and recommending appropriate services. This person should have a background of knowledge about computers and communications equipment.

Administrators and managers will have to learn how to work in an office environment that may be largely paperless. Data transmission and image facsimile systems are changing the manner in which managers are accustomed to receiving, reading, and utilizing documents. Management workstations are an example of the trend toward the automated, paperless office. These workstations are minicomputer-based and enable a manager and a secretary to create, transmit, and receive information through intelligent terminals and to file documents on floppy disks. Many companies are moving toward the completely electronic office.

Administrative Structure

The administrative functions in most businesses are centralized by the type of activity, such as sales, accounting, and personnel. This enables individuals within a group to communicate with each other and establishes channels of communication between groups. As organizations move into the automated office, decentralization of functions is likely to occur. This decentralization process will go through three phases:

1. *Fragmentation:* linking separated elements of an administrative group through distributed data processing
2. *Dispersion:* assigning an employee to a work site because it is near home, instead of by the nature of the particular type of work performed at the site
3. *Diffusion:* permitting individuals to work at home (possibly for more than one employer) with all-electronic communications

These projections may seem remote to us. However, a sense of reality is imparted if we stop to realize that people and travel costs are continuing to increase while computer-communication costs are decreasing. As a specific example, we already have the technology to substitute electronic communications for travel. A teleconference—in which persons sitting at CRT screens see and talk to each other via a computer-communications network—is only a fraction of the cost of travel, to say nothing of the executive time that would be lost en route. Even greater savings are realized if groups of people are involved in the conference.

FEEDBACK

7-10 What are the electronic techniques being used in the automated office?

7-11 Identify and describe the three basic types of word processing systems.

7-12 What is electronic mail?

7-13 How will the "automated office" affect secretarial careers?

7-14 Describe some ways in which word processing and data processing are blending.

SUMMARY

The usability of many data processing applications can often be increased by placing the computer power at the location at which results are needed. Many remote computing options have become available because of advances in computer-communications processing, which is the blending of both the computer and the electronic communications technologies. Examples of rapidly growing computer-communications applications are distributed data processing and the automated office.

Communications is the process of transferring messages from one point to another. The four elements of communications are: the sender, the medium, the receiver, and feedback. Data transmission is by electronic media, and services are available that provide three different transmission modes—simplex, half-duplex, and full-duplex. Simplex is a communication service for transmitting data in one direction only. Half-duplex systems can transmit information in both directions, but in only one direction at a time, and full-duplex systems can transmit data in both directions at the same time. High-data-rate satellite communication systems have been developed and are finding widespread use in data communications. In the future, high-data-rate earth communications systems will be developed, using new optical technologies.

Distributed data processing (DDP) is any arrangement of computers and/or communications systems that, as an alternative to central-site processing, places processing capabilities at the location of the end user. The three major classes of distributed data processing systems are data entry systems, stand-alone systems, and computer networks. The capabilities of remote DDP terminals range from dumb terminals through intelligent terminals, to computers.

Office automation systems perform operations on data for the efficient transfer of ideas from one person to another. Word processing systems have extensive text editing and formatting capabilities. Word processing devices may either stand alone or share the logic of a computer. Word processing, combined with distributed data processing, is leading us toward the electronic office and a business environment in which the jobs of clerks, secretaries, and office administrators will be changed greatly by the automation of functions ranging from the statement of ideas to the delivery of documents by electronic mail.

ANSWERS TO FEEDBACK QUESTIONS

7-1   Data processing applications that require a blending of computer and communications capabilities.

7-2   a   The sender creates the message.
   b   The medium carries the message.
   c   The receiver receives the message.
   d   Feedback verifies the message.

7-3   They modulate binary data for voice-line transmission and demodulate the transmitted data for computer processing.

7-4 Simplex is a data transmission mode that allows communication in only one direction. Half-duplex allows two-way communication, but only in one direction at a time. Full-duplex permits simultaneous transmission of data in two directions.

7-5 Any arrangement of computers and/or communication systems that places data processing capabilities at the location of the end user.

7-6 a Data entry systems that use dumb or intelligent terminals to transmit data to a central-site computer.

    b Stand-alone systems that have an independent data processing capability. These systems may or may not communicate with a central-site computer.

    c Computer networks used to link multiple processing sites. These sites may vary in capability from simple terminals to complete computer systems.

7-7 Dumb terminals have no local data processing capabilities. Intelligent terminals have a limited local data processing capability.

7-8 A star network is a computer network in which there is a host (a star) that communicates with and controls satellite systems. A ring network is a "no-host" network.

7-9 A local area network (LAN) is a network that is within one company. In addition, it is geographically limited to within a few miles.

7-10 The electronic techniques used in the automated office include: data processing, data communications, word processing, electronic mail, and voice store-and-forward systems.

7-11 a Stand-alone systems that are independent minicomputers.

    b Shared-logic systems that share the processing and storage capabilities of a small business computer among several workstations.

    c Time-shared services that are word processing systems communicating with a remote computer via a data transmission link.

7-12 Electronic mail is a data communication and word processing system for the electronic creation, sending, and receiving of messages.

7-13 a Documents will be kept in electronic storage, text will be manipulated electronically, and images will be communicated by electronic mail.

    b Administrative secretaries will become executives who provide managers with a link to the computer.

    c Corresponding secretaries will be skilled operators of word processing equipment.

7-14 a The use of computer-communication systems to create, manipulate, and transmit documents electronically.

    b The replacement of the secretary by computer-oriented executives and word processing equipment operators.

    c The impact of data processing upon the training of all types of office administrators.

FOR REVIEW AND DISCUSSION   **1** Match the following:

1	Modern	**a**	Western Union
2	Communications	**b**	An arrangement of computers and/or communications systems that places data processing capability with a user
3	Star network		
4	Dumb terminal	**c**	Used to transmit data over voice lines
5	DDP	**d**	May transmit "dirty" data
6	Common carrier	**e**	Network of clustered terminals
7	Half-duplex	**f**	A system that can transmit data in both directions, but only in one direction at a time
		g	The process of transferring messages from one point to another

2 Describe the four elements of any communications process.

3 Discuss the distributed data concept.

4 Discuss management considerations related to DDP.

5 What is the difference between a programmable terminal and a stand-alone terminal?

6 What do you think the office of 1990 will be like?

7 Why do you think that the authors state that DDP and word processing are blending?

CHAPTER 8

PERSONAL COMPUTERS

PREVIEW   In less than a decade the microcomputer has been transformed from a calculator and a hobbyist's toy into a personal computer for almost everyone. The goals of this chapter are to describe this transformation and to increase your microcomputer literacy. In particular, it will provide you with knowledge about the parts of a personal computer and what they do, the principal uses of personal computers, and a method for selecting one to meet your needs.

In this chapter you will learn:

1. The identifying features of personal computers
2. A useful microcomputer vocabulary
3. How to distinguish among microcomputer systems
4. Six major categories of applications of personal computers
5. A three-step procedure for selecting a personal computer

KEY TERMS TO WATCH FOR AND REMEMBER

personal computer	peripheral device
MPU	floppy disk
RAM	diskette
mass storage	hard disk
ROM	DOS
cursor	bootstrapping
monitor	keyboard
joystick	CAI
bus	user friendly
menu	CMI
modem	electronic worksheet
courseware	CP/M
supermicro	environmental software

EVERYONE'S COMPUTER

What is a Personal Computer?

Time magazine's selection of Man of the Year for 1982 was not a human at all, but a machine: the computer. In particular, the personal computer. The "technological upheaval that is bringing computers to the millions" was the reason given for *Time's* selection. The publisher further wrote: "Computers were once regarded as distant, ominous abstractions, like Big Brother. In 1982 they truly became personalized, brought down to scale so that people could hold, prod, and play with them."[1]

Yet, in spite of the presence of personal computers everywhere—in the office, in school, in government, and in the home—a question often asked and still difficult to answer is, Just what is a personal computer? Probably there is no single characteristic that identifies a personal computer. However, there are several attributes that, collectively, do tend to characterize personal computers. Typically, a **personal computer:**

1. Is microprocessor-based; that is, its central processing unit, called a microprocessor unit, or **MPU,** is concentrated on a single silicon chip.

2. Costs less than $10,000, with start-up systems available for only a few hundred dollars.

3. Has a memory and word size that are smaller than those of minicomputers and large computers. Typical word sizes are 8 or 16 bits, and main memories range in size from 16K to 512K.

4. Uses smaller, less expensive, and less powerful input, output and storage components than do large computer systems. Most often, input is by means of a keyboard, and soft-copy output is displayed on a CRT screen. Hard-copy output is produced on a low-speed character printer.

5. Employs floppy disks as the principal online and offline storage devices and also as input and output media.

6. Is a general-purpose, stand-alone system that can begin to work when plugged in and be moved from place to place.

Not all personal computer systems exhibit all of the above characteristics. Microcomputer kits and introductory computers may have less than 16K of memory and sell for less than $100. A high-performance system may have multiple microprocessors, very large main memory, hard-disk storage, and multiple input and output stations. As reductions in cost and improvements in performance continue for computer systems of all sizes, the microcomputers of tomorrow will have many of the capabilities of the large computers of today.

Probably the most distinguishing feature of a personal computer is that it is used by an individual, usually in an interactive mode. Regardless of the purpose for which it is used, whether for leisure activities in the home or for business applications in the office, as long as a microcomputer is perceived as belonging to or assignable to an individual, we can consider it to be a personal computer.

---

[1] *Time,* January 3, 1983, p. 3.

NEW PERSONAL COMPUTERS: SMALLER AND SMARTER

The estimated 300 new computers scheduled to enter the market in 1984 and 1985 "will be as different from today's computers as the Porsche is from the Model T," predicts software consultant David L. Ferris. Home computers will cost as little as $50. Future models will include a 5-pound, book-size, battery-operated portable unit; briefcase units with flat panelled screens; and units which will respond to spoken directions. These innovations will be partly responsible for increasing the sales of home computers from 2.8 million units in 1982 to an anticipated 10.5 million in 1985, at a 50 percent annual growth rate.

Future shoppers will notice that computer prices drop approximately 25 percent a year and will continue to do so. In part, the price decrease will be due to increased competition with Japanese models. Technical innovations will also be responsible for lower prices. They will account for the reduced size and increased power of home computers and enable manufacturers to design compact parts specifically for personal computers. Because of the use of very-large-scale integration (VLSI) techniques, microprocessor units will have more circuits and will need fewer chips. These advances will result in a 90 percent reduction in manufacturing costs. Production plans are underway for 32-bit machines, designed to replace today's 8- and 16-bit models. The more powerful personal computers are needed to run the sophisticated, user-friendly software now under development. The 1985 desktop models will respond to certain frequently used verbal commands, such as "save" and "delete." Some models will permit several projects to be worked on simultaneously, moving information from program to program, using techniques introduced in Apple's LISA.

Some experts predict that 80 percent of the personal computers sold in 1985 will be portable. For example, the PC-8200 computer, marketed by Nippon Electric Co., is the size of a loose-leaf binder. Selling for $550, it has a flat panel display and the computing power of a desktop Apple II with a full-size keyboard. The PC-8200 will operate for 18 hours on one set of batteries.

While we are awaiting the many innovations of the near future, we can also expect to see new machines modeled after existing best sellers, utilizing the software specifically designed for the originals. In addition, these models will be easy to update with higher capacity memory or increased word size. The second decade of microcomputers will be as exciting as the first.

Source: Business Week, Mar. 28, 1983, p. 134.

Anatomy of a Personal Computer

Figure 8-1 displays the functional units of a microcomputer system. This figure emphasizes the fact that microcomputer systems perform the same basic operations as do larger systems. Although the components of a microcomputer system are less expensive and less powerful than those of larger computer systems, the vocabulary that we have learned to use to describe computer systems applies equally well to microcomputers. In practice, though, some terms are used more often than others and have become part of what might be called a microcomputer dialect. For example, primary storage is usually referred to as **RAM,** which means random access memory. Secondary storage, usually on a floppy disk, is called **mass storage.** Also, a cryptic phrase such as "16 bit, 256K" is a frequently encountered shorthand way of describing word size and main memory. These are two important architectural features that relate to the performance potential of a microcomputer. Thus, "16 bit" refers to the word size of the MPU, and "256K" refers to the amount of RAM. We will use these terms and others as we continue, and you will become increasingly familiar with the microcomputer dialect.

As Figure 8-1 shows, the microcomputer box contains the MPU and internal memory, which is made up of both random access memory, RAM, and

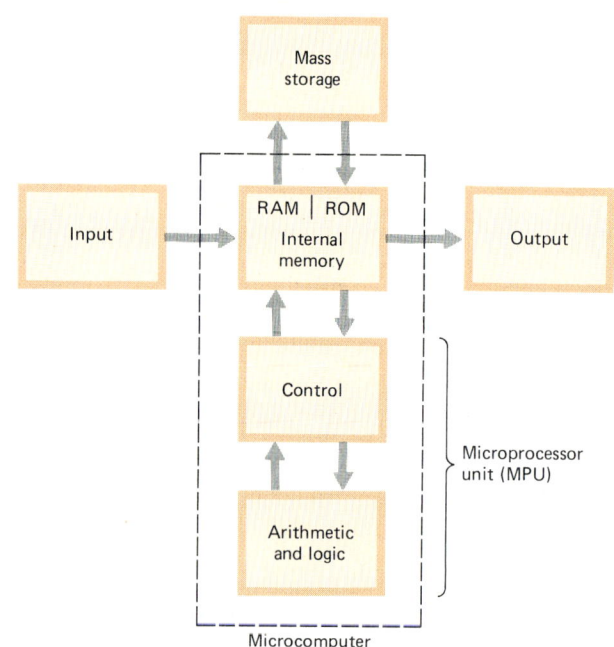

FIGURE 8-1

Microcomputer system organization. The organization of a microcomputer system is the same as that of a larger computer system. The microprocessor unit (MPU), usually concentrated in a single chip, consists of the control unit and the arithmetic logic unit. Internal memory is made up of random access memory (RAM) and read-only memory (ROM). A microcomputer includes both an MPU and internal memory. The MPU and memory are housed in a common enclosure that also contains the power supply and electronic circuits essential to the operation of the microcomputer. When input, mass storage, and output units are added to the microcomputer, the result is a microcomputer system. Microcomputer systems are commonly referred to as "microcomputers."

read-only memory, **ROM.** Because RAM is only temporary storage, all microcomputers require some instructions to get started after they are turned on, and these are contained in ROM. The portion of the system software that is in ROM brings into RAM the additional instructions required to operate the microcomputer. Typically these instructions are stored on a magnetic disk; hence, they are called a disk operating system, or **DOS.** This start-up process is called **bootstrapping.** ROM also contains other programs that help to make personal computers easy to use, such as a programming language. Computer games are often stored in ROM cartridges.

Figure 8-2 shows the parts of a typical personal computer system. In addition to the MPU, RAM, ROM, and associated control circuits that reside in the microcomputer itself, other components, called **peripheral devices,** are needed to make a complete microcomputer system. The principal peripheral units are: input devices, output devices, mass storage units, and communications components. Like a DOS, the programs that control the flow of data between a microcomputer and its peripheral devices are a part of systems software.

The most common input device used with personal computers is the **keyboard,** which resembles that of a typewriter. As shown in Figure 8-3, most personal computer keyboards have extra keys that perform special functions and that can be used to control the movement of a position indicator, called a **cursor,** on a CRT display screen. A leverlike device, called a **joystick,** is

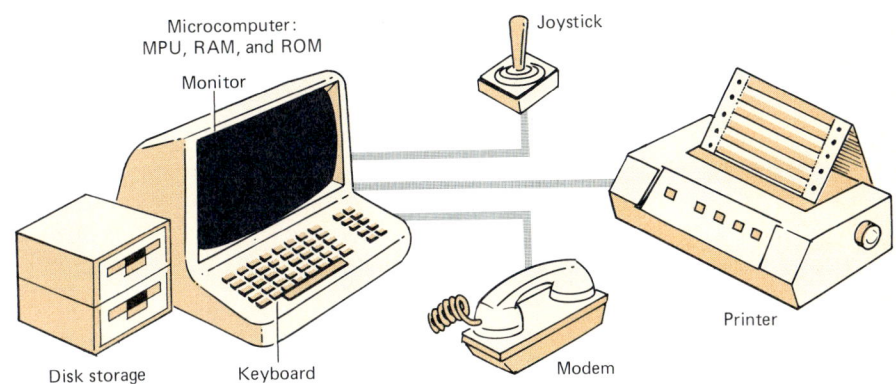

Microcomputer:
MPU, RAM, and ROM

Joystick

Monitor

Printer

FIGURE 8-2

Parts of a typical personal computer
system.

Disk storage   Keyboard   Modem

also used as an input device, commonly for playing video games. Voice input will become increasingly available, first for special commands and then for applications.

The CRT screen used with personal computers is called a **monitor.** The least expensive monitors are usually white or green phosphor on a black background. Color displays are also available. Inexpensive systems often use a home television receiver as a monitor, although the resolution is less than that of monitors designed for use with personal computer systems. Typical screen sizes, measured diagonally, are 12 or 13 inches, with the capability to display 24 lines of 80 characters each. As shown in Figure 8-4, keyboards and monitors may be part of a single unit that also contains the microcomputer and the disk drives, or they may be separate units.

FIGURE 8-3

Personal computer keyboard. The
keyboard shown is for the Apple IIe
Microcomputer. It is similar to the
keyboard of a standard typewriter;
however, there are additional, special
purpose keys. The control, escape,
and reset keys are examples of special
purpose keys that are provided to
assist in the operation of the
microcomputer system. The up, down,
right, and left arrow keys are used to
control the movement of the cursor.
The "apple" keys can be assigned
special functions, such as performing
diagnostic tests of the computer.
(Courtesy Apple Computer, Inc.)

Besides the monitor, the most common output units are dot-matrix and letter-quality printers. The contrast between dot-matrix and letter-quality printing is shown in Figure 8-5. Dot-matrix printers are not as expensive as letter-quality printers. They cost less than $1000, with inexpensive models available for a few hundred dollars. Dot-matrix printers are suitable for most microcomputer applications. Letter-quality printers usually cost more than $1000, and they are used for high-quality office correspondence. Both types of printers are considered to be low-speed character printers because typical print speeds range from 25 to 150 characters per second. Although these speeds are slow compared to those of the line or page printers used with larger computer systems, they provide the individual with a capability that far exceeds that of ordinary typing. For example, a printer similar to those shown in Figure 8-5, operating at a speed of 60 characters per second, is equivalent in performance to six humans typing at a rate in excess of 100 words per minute—without any errors.

Mass storage units are available over a range of capacities and access times.

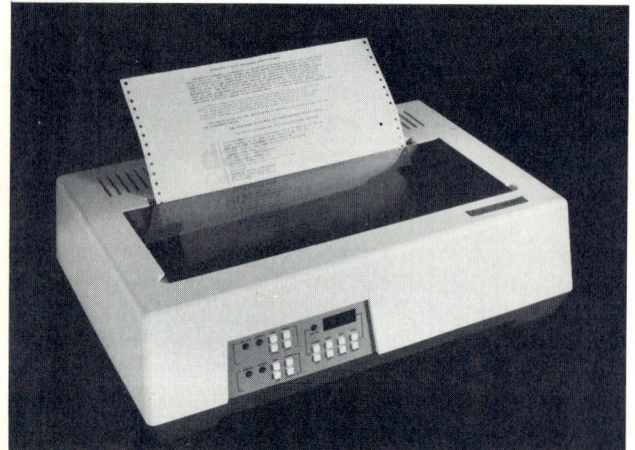

(a) **Dot matrix**

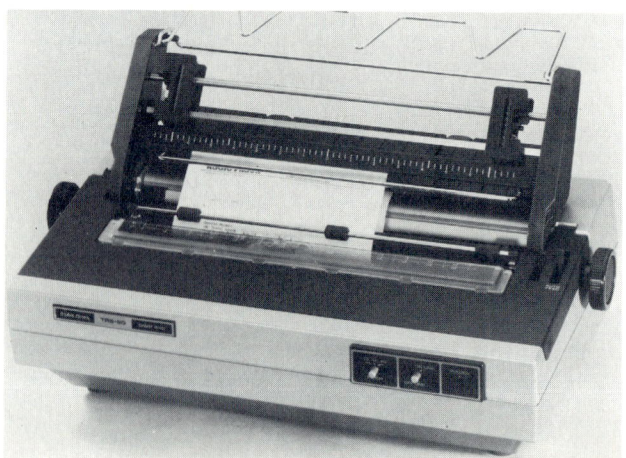

(b) Letter quality

FIGURE 8-6
5¼-inch floppy disk platter. (Courtesy IBM Corp.)

Initially tape cassettes were used extensively, but these are now limited to inexpensive introductory systems. **Floppy disks,** or **diskettes,** are the most common mass storage media. They store patterns of bits on magnetically coated, flexible plastic platters. As shown in Figure 8-6, a floppy disk platter is sealed permanently in a paper jacket with a small window for reading and writing. Most commonly, floppy disks are 5¼ or 8 inches in diameter, although some units, called *microfloppies*, are only 3½ inches in diameter. Floppy disk capacities range from approximately 100K bytes to over 1 million (mega-) bytes of storage. **Hard disk** storage systems are also available. They are more expensive than floppy disk systems, and the disks may be fixed or removable. Standard capacities of hard disks are 5, 10, and 20 million bytes. As shown in Figure 8-7, some mass storage units contain both floppy and hard disk drives.

Low-cost modulator-demodulator devices, called **modems,** that allow microcomputer systems to communicate over telephone lines have become increasingly popular. Modems permit networks of personal computer owners to exchange information or to access large data banks. These data banks may be dedicated to special applications, such as law or medicine, or they may provide

(a)

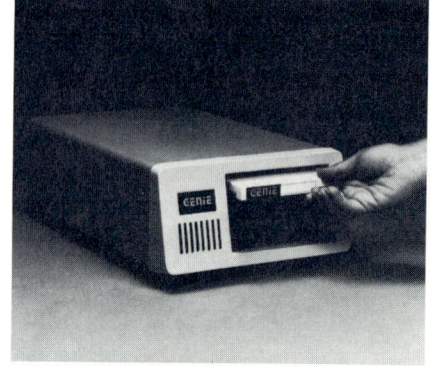

(b)

(c)

FIGURE 8-7

Mass storage systems. (a) Apple II 5¼-inch floppy disk drive. Each removable platter has a capacity of 140K bytes. (Courtesy Apple Computer, Inc.) (b) Removable hard disk cartridges provide high-capacity on-line and off-line storage. A typical removable cartridge is equivalent in storage capacity to over 30 floppy disks. (Courtesy Genie Computer Corp.) (c) The Hewlett-Packard 9133 Mass Storage System combines two disk drives in a single unit. They are a permanently enclosed hard disk storage system, called a Winchester, and a removable 3½-inch microfloppy disk system. The capacity of the hard disk system is 10 megabytes; that of the microfloppy is 270 K bytes. (Courtesy Hewlett-Packard)

a variety of consumer services. These services include electronic mail, community bulletin boards, stock exchange quotes, and videotext information for shopping at home. These are just a few examples of the uses of networks that, truly, soon will put the world at the fingertips of personal computer owners.

FEEDBACK

8-1 Describe six identifying characteristics of personal computers.

8-2 What do the terms mass storage, RAM, and ROM mean with reference to microcomputers?

8-3 What does the expression "16 bit, 512K" mean?

8-4 What is bootstrapping? How does it relate to DOS, and why is it necessary?

8-5 Distinguish between dot-matrix and letter-quality printers.

USES FOR PERSONAL COMPUTERS

Personal computers often appear to have increased in numbers like generations of rabbits, and almost daily we seem to be barraged by new suggestions for their use. The uses of microcomputers are so diverse that they cannot easily be classified. Nonetheless, it is possible to identify six major categories of applications of personal computers: home and hobby, word processing, professional, educational, small business, and engineering and scientific. Of course, many applications overlap, and often owners of personal computers purchase them for use in more than one category. Word processing, for example, is so popular that it appears on almost everyone's list of uses for personal computers; this is why we present word processing as a separate category. It is helpful, though, to examine the variety of applications within each major category to provide you, as a potential user, with some insights about how a personal computer might improve your personal life or increase the profitability of your business.

Home and Hobby

In the mid- to late-1970s many of the personal computers introduced by Tandy Radio Shack, Commodore, and Apple were sold because of their popularity among experimenters and hobbyists. And personal computers still are an exciting hobby. Many people prefer to build their own computers from kits or modify systems that they have purchased. This can provide a sense of personal accomplishment and lead to new and rewarding innovations in technology. For example, the successful Apple I computer was the direct result of the activities of an individual involved with a group called the Homebrew Computer Club. This person, Steve Wozniak, became a cofounder of Apple Computer, Inc. Today it is expected that much of the progress that will occur in developing home robots will be the result of the hardware and software efforts of experimenters.

All hobbyists need not be engineers or programmers. Relaxation is an excellent reason for acquiring a home computer. Versions of almost all of the popular games played in the video arcades are available to the personal computer owner. Also, there are many other games that use the full capabilities of a computer to provide many hours of challenging and exciting leisure-time adventure.

The list of other home and hobby applications of personal computers is almost endless, including: checking account management, budgeting, personal finance, planning, nutrition analysis and dieting, biorhythm charting, personal income tax preparation, investment analysis, telephone answering and dialing, home security, home environment and climate control, appliance control, calendar management, and maintenance of address and mailing lists.

**Word
Processing**

A word processing system is as much an advance over a typewriter as a microcomputer is over a hand-held calculator. At home or at work, applications software, called a word processing program, enables you to type any document at rough-draft speed and then to correct or modify it in any manner you wish before printing it. Using the CRT monitor as a display screen, you are able to view what you have "typed" to correct mistakes in spelling or grammer, add or delete sentences, move paragraphs around, and search for and replace words. The computer quickly modifies the document to accommodate all of the changes. It can then be printed, error-free, by a dot-matrix or letter-quality printer.

The letter or document can be stored on a diskette for future use. Diskettes are inexpensive. The manuscript for this textbook was prepared on a word processing system, and it required approximately twenty 5¼-in floppy diskettes—at a total cost of approximately fifty dollars. This cost was saved many times over because it was not necessary to pay for secretarial services or to perform extensive retyping of large segments of the manuscript.

The opportunities for cost-effective uses of word processing in industry are many, whether performed by individuals or by word processing specialists. Word processing can be combined with other applications programs or features. For example, a program called *mailmerge* may be used to send customized letters to large groups of customers, with each letter and envelope individually addressed. Microcomputers have brought an inexpensive word processing capability to the home, to self-employed professionals, and to small businesses. Therefore, it is not surprising to find that word processing programs are the best sellers among all of the personal computer applications software.

Professional

The category of professional includes persons whose occupations are particularly suited to the desk-top use of personal computers. As already indicated, authors are professionals who make extensive use of word processing. Examples of other occupations are accountants, financial advisors, stock brokers, tax consultants, lawyers, architects, engineers, educators, and all levels of managers. Applications programs that are popular with persons in these occupations include accounting, income tax preparation, statistical analysis, graphics, stock market forecasting, and computer modeling.

The **electronic worksheet** is, by far, the computer modeling program most widely used by professionals. An electronic work sheet is a program that displays the equivalent of a work sheet made up of rows and columns. Figure 8-8 is an example of an electronic work sheet, called VisiCalc, developed by VisiCorp. Although a CRT screen is limited in the number of rows and columns that it can display at one time, the work sheet may, in fact, consist of a very large number of rows and columns. It may be used for anything that a person would compute or display in tabular form. The power of the spreadsheet is derived from its use to simulate "what if" situations. When one quantity is changed, the effect upon all other quantities becomes immediately visible. Thus, it is possible to analyze the impact of decisions before they are made.

FIGURE 8-8
An electronic worksheet. One of the best-known electronic worksheets is VisiCalc, a product of VisiCorp. The monitor of a personal computer becomes a window through which any part of a worksheet that is 63 columns wide and 254 rows deep can be viewed. Words, numbers, and formulas can be entered on the worksheet by means of the computer keyboard, and the results of calculations can be displayed. For example, a budget could be created and updated with new data. Every time new data is entered, all the related entries and totals affected by the changes are recalculated and displayed in a matter of seconds. The worksheet displays the effect of changes almost instantly, making it an invaluable tool in exploring answers to "what if" questions. (Courtesy Radio Shack, a division of Tandy Corp.)

Typical applications of electronic work sheets are scheduling, cost estimating, and financial planning.

Educational

Personal computers are having and will continue to have a profound influence upon the classroom, affecting both the learner and the teacher. Microcomputers are making their way into classrooms to an ever-increasing extent, giving impetus to the design of programmed learning materials that can be tailored to the needs of student and teacher.

Two important types of uses for personal computers in education are computer-managed instruction, **CMI,** and computer-assisted instruction, **CAI.** CMI software is used to assist the instructor in the management of all classroom-related activities, such as record keeping, work assignments, testing, and grading. Computer-assisted software actually instructs students. Applications of CAI include mathematics, reading, typing, computer literacy, programming languages, and simulations of real-world situations, such as the operation of a small business or a problem in rocket flight. Typically, the computer provides the student with some information and then with an exercise. The purpose of the exercise is to provide instant feedback to students and to the instructor about progress in learning. The CAI program evaluates the responses of students and adjusts the learning levels to their needs. Students can be allowed to proceed, or they can be provided with additional exercises at appropriate skill levels.

The purpose of computers in the classroom is not to replace the instructor but to increase the effectiveness of the instruction process and to tailor instruction to the needs of the individual. Computers can combine text, sound, and graphics, making possible a multidimensional presentation of subject matter. For example, keyboarding, an important information-age skill, can be taught effectively using the graphics capability of a microcomputer to display basic character combinations. The program provides learning exercises in these character combinations and permits the student to proceed after achieving a satisfactory score. Many of the aspects of videogame playing carry over into the lesson, and students generally respond positively when the computer asks, "Would you like to try for a better score?" Compare this with the response you would have given in a conventional classroom if you were asked whether or not you wanted to take another test.

A general term for software used for educational purposes is **courseware.** Courseware can include aspects of both CAI and CMI. To the extent that the keyboarding program described above was aiding in teaching the student, it was CAI. To the extent that it also provided the instructor with records of individual and class performance, it was CMI. Because of the rate at which microcomputers are appearing in classrooms, the market for courseware is increasing. Also, the process is regenerative because the increasing availability of courseware is creating an increase in the demand for classrooms of microcomputers. For these reasons publishers are becoming a primary source of software, either through arrangements with firms that specialize in courseware or by establishing their own courseware capabilities. This means that throughout the decade of the 1980s, we will see increasing evidence of a transition from written texts to courseware as the primary teaching resource.

A very important aspect of the relationship between computer, teacher, and student is that using a computer is an education in itself. Probably the most effective way to acquire a basic knowledge about computers is to use one in a productive way. Through educational software programs, students can acquire a familiarity with computers and what they can do at an early age. For example, LOGO, a language for computers developed at the Massachusetts Institute of Technology, encourages young children to develop problem-solving and programming skills by working with simple commands that can create ordinarily complex graphics. Thus, computer literacy for both students and teachers will become a normal part of our educational process, and it will be achieved through teaching about and teaching with computers.

Small Business Personal computers make affordable to the owners of small businesses many of the data processing services and capabilities previously available only to large corporations. Although in some instances microcomputers will be dedicated to a major application such as inventory management, in general, owners of small businesses will benefit from more than one applications program. In addition to word processing and many of the professional programs that we have mentioned, small businesses will make extensive use of accounting packages such as general ledger, payroll, accounts receivable, accounts payable, and customer billing. Small-business accounting packages were among the first programs to become available as the size of the personal computer market became evident. At present there are a large number of reliable, easy-to-learn and easy-to-use accounting packages from which small-business owners can choose.

Small-business applications of microcomputers will tend to differ from other applications that we have discussed in terms of the number of records that must be stored. Large amounts of data will be stored electronically, using data base management systems. In many instances small businesses or departments of larger businesses will communicate directly with centralized data banks by means of modems and communications networks. Small-business applications will also have relatively large requirements for inputting data and for producing multiple hard-copy and soft-copy outputs.

Application programs will be relatively complex, and processing times will be significant. The microcomputer systems used by small businesses will tend to be heavy-duty systems, operating continuously many hours a day. Often there will be requirements for multiple input and output stations, some local and some remote. Thus, small businesses will tend to require more expensive microcomputer systems than most of the other personal computer applications that we have identified. However, powerful microcomputers capable of delivering high performance at reasonable cost are available, and many of these systems have capabilities equivalent to those of large mainframe computers of a few years ago. Therefore, small businesses will be a major market for microcomputer systems.

Engineering and Scientific

Students who enroll in technical programs in many major universities now are required to come to class prepared to "plug in" their personal computers. Thus, it is not surprising to learn that the distribution of personal computers among the engineering and scientific staffs of large and small corporations has become almost commonplace. Microcomputers are used not only as personal computers but also as intelligent terminals that can access large scientific data bases. Typical applications of personal computers are the performance of both routine and complex calculations in fields such as chemistry, engineering, physics, and aerodynamics. They are used to design and test new products, such as missiles, aircraft, home appliances, computers, and communications equipment.

The use of personal computers is increasing in two fields in which extensive use is made of computers to improve productivity. These are computer-assisted design, **CAD,** and computer-assisted manufacturing, **CAM.** In CAD, computers are used to assist engineers and drafters in preparing complex drawings in a fraction of the time that would be required if the task were performed only by humans. Examples are the design of complex structures, detailed maps, and circuit boards for microcomputers.

Computer-assisted manufacturing led to major improvements in the quality of end products such as automobiles. CAM requires the development of applications programs that control the operation of lathes, milling machines, and other special tools, such as robots working on an assembly line. Microcomputers can be used to develop the required control programs.

FEEDBACK

8-6 Name the six major catagories of microcomputer applications and give an example of each.

8-7 Distinguish between CAI, CMI, CAD, and CAM.

8-8 What is an electronic work sheet? What are some of its uses?

8-9 Why are small-business applications of personal computers likely to require high-performance systems?

8-10 What is courseware? Give an example of its use.

TRENDS IN MICROCOMPUTER ARCHITECTURE

Personal computers have been so heavily promoted that many people are investing in them without considering how they might really be used—often for no other reason than as a status symbol. The serious would-be user often finds it exceedingly difficult to select from a seemingly unending list of heavily advertised microcomputers and applications packages. Fortunately, those who are equipped with a measure of computer literacy are aware of significant events that have taken place in microcomputer technology and are able to identify and evaluate new events as they occur. Furthermore, armed with a step-by-step procedure for selecting a personal computer, these people can be assured that their needs can be reasonably well matched with available hardware and software. Before describing this procedure, we will briefly explore the significant changes that have occurred in the architecture of microcomputers and in supporting software.

Microcomputer Generations

Few could have guessed that in the decade between 1972 and 1982 advances in microelectronics would lead us from calculators through three generations of microcomputers and into a fourth. The most significant measures of the power of a computer system are its word size and internal memory capacity. Power is related to processing speed, which depends upon word size, and to main memory storage capacity, which determines the amount of data and instructions available to the MPU with the quickest access time. Figure 8-9 is a diagram of a microcomputer system that identifies the principal circuits, called **buses,** along which electronic signals travel. The buses shown in Figure 8-9 are the control bus, the address bus, and the data bus. Word size refers to the internal bus design of the MPU, in particular the path width of the data bus.

Figure 8-10 shows the significant increase in the speed and storage capabilities of microprocessors. Several trend-setting microprocessors are identified, along with the standard RAM for each. In most instances additional RAM is available or can be made available. Not surprisingly, RAM has increased along with word size because comprehensive systems software packages

FIGURE 8-9

Microcomputer system bus structure. The three principal circuit paths along which electronic signals flow are the address bus, the data bus, and the control bus. The address bus provides the microcomputer system with the information needed to locate data in memory, and the data bus moves data into and out of the MPU. Since data must enter and leave the microcomputer, there is also an external extension of the data bus, called an I/O bus, that allows peripheral devices to interface with the microcomputer. The electronic signals needed to manage all of the operations of the microcomputer system are carried by the control bus.

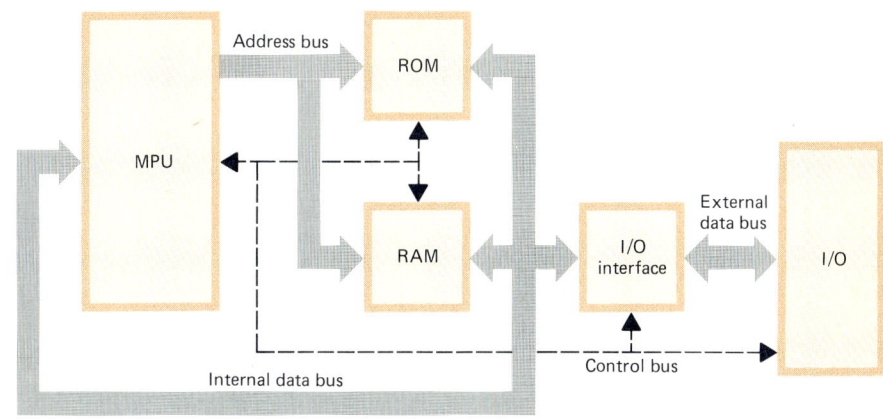

are required for efficient use of powerful computers and because increasingly complex applications have been developed as computer capability has increased. Of course, the need for these programs also has given impetus to the design and development of advanced microcomputer systems. Consequently, in the brief period between 1978 and 1982 we witnessed at least a 20-fold increase in the power of microcomputer systems.

FIGURE 8-10

Trends in microprocessor performance. The performance of several historically significant MPUs is displayed in order to show the trends in wordsize and RAM, two factors which affect the power of a microcomputer system. As we have progressed from MPU wordsizes of 4 bits to 32 bits, the increase in RAM has been so great that we have used a logarithmic (factor of ten) scale to indicate the amount of addressable RAM. In some current microcomputer systems, RAM can be extended far beyond the amounts shown, 16 megabytes or more not uncommon.

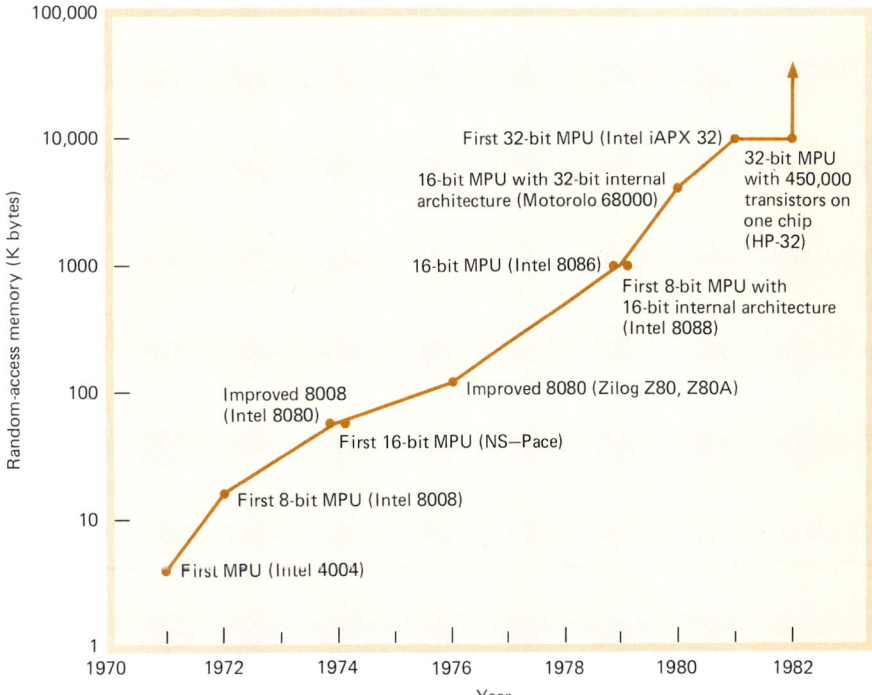

Personal computers have become so much a part of the American way of life that it is estimated that 75 percent of the households in the United States will have one by the end of the 1980s. Yet in 1971, few could have guessed that in approximately one decade advances in the miniaturization of electronic circuits would lead us from hand-held calculators through three generations of microcomputers and into a fourth.

A major milestone in the development of microcomputers occurred when Dr. Marcian E. "Ted" Hoff, Jr., a young engineer from Stanford and the twelfth employee to join the newly formed Intel Corporation, was assigned the task of designing a set of twelve chips for a planned family of high-performance, programmable calculators for Busicom, a now defunct Japanese manufacturer of calculators. Ted Hoff's architectural concept for solving an extremely complex design problem was to place the entire central processing unit of a computer on a single chip of silicon; to use read-only memory (ROM), placed upon a second chip of silicon, to store the fixed program; and to use a third chip for random access memory (RAM) to store data. The number of RAM and ROM chips could be varied to accommodate the needs of different families of calculators. Hoff's design approach proved successful, and in 1971 an engineering team produced a viable product. This was the Intel 4004 microprocessor, which had a word size of 4 bits.

In 1972, Intel introduced an 8-bit microprocessor, the 8008, which was able to address 16K of memory and was the first integrated circuit chip with the speed and power to support a true microcomputer. The Intel 8080,

an improved model of the 8008, was very popular among computer hobbyists who, during the period 1973 to 1975, were active in designing and building so-called home-brew microcomputers.

The home-hobby computer era was established when MITs, a company based in Albuquerque, New Mexico, introduced the Altair microcomputer. Based upon the 8-bit Intel 8080 microprocessor, the Altair sold by the thousands in kit form for $395. It was sold primarily to hobbyists and experimenters with electronics and programming experience. Computer clubs sprang up, and computer enthusiasts gathered by the hundreds at personal computer trade shows. In 1975 the retail computer store appeared, serving as a meeting place for hobbyists and as a source of information.

By 1977 other widely used 8-bit chips were being marketed. Among them were the Zilog Z80, an improvement of the Intel 8080 and the MOS Technology 6502. The latter was used in the Commodore PET. The former was used in the Apple I, from which the popular Apple II and Apple IIe personal computers evolved.

The first 16-bit microprocessor appeared in 1974, when National Semiconductor announced its Pace unit. However, the 16-bit generation did not begin in earnest until 1978, when Intel introduced its high-performance processor, the 8086. The 8086 and other 16-bit MPUs offered increases in memory capacity over their 8-bit predecessors and much faster operating speeds. The memory size for most 8-bit microcomputers was 64K or less, and they had difficulty in running complex programs. The 16-bit microprocessors had 128K

of RAM or more. The best selling 16-bit chip was the Intel 8088. This chip was used in the popular IBM Personal Computer and its many clones. Actually, the 8088 is not a true 16-bit chip. It is a hybrid 8/16 bit MPU because it uses an 8-bit external data bus but does its internal processing 16 bits at a time. This dual word size proved to be a cost-effective architectural compromise. Many applications could afford low-cost 8-bit peripheral devices and could benefit from fast internal processing speeds. Other popular personal computers, such as the NEC Advanced Personal Computer and the Eagle 1600, were designed to use the Intel 8086, which was introduced a year after the 8088 and which is a true 16-bit MPU. The 8086 can run 8088 instructions and is faster. Both the 8086 and the 8088 are able to address 1 million bytes of RAM.

The 16-bit chips were followed by hybrid 16/32-bit chips, among which were the Motorola 68000 and the Zilog 8000. These chips have 16-bit external data paths and 32-bit internal data buses. LISA, the powerful business microcomputer introduced by Apple in 1983, uses the Motorola 68000 MPU. The first true 32-bit microprocessor chip was the iAPX 432, developed by Intel and introduced in 1981. Since then other semiconductor companies have announced 32-bit chips. Among them are NCR, Texas Instruments, and Motorola. The microcomputer systems designed around 32-bit MPUs often use additional chips to perform memory management and to act as input and output units. Microcomputers designed to use 32-bit MPUs are known as supermicros. They are able to handle relatively large scientific calculations and business data processing applications. Possessing most of the capabilities of present-day medium-size computers, the supermicros will be able to run complex programs and handle multiple input and output units.

The increase in chip complexity and in the magnitude of MPU design effort that has occurred is difficult to comprehend. The 4-bit Intel 4004 chip was designed by one man in 4 months. The iAPX432 required 100 "man-years" of engineering time and was the result of a design effort the cost over $100 million. The microcomputer industry went from 4-bit chips to 32-bit chips in just over 11 years. Reassuringly, though, in spite of this extremely rapid rate of technical development, MPU word size probably will not increase beyond 32 bits. This word size is the standard for large computers, and it probably will become the microcomputer standard as well.

Sources: J. Raskin and T. Whitney, "Perspectives on Personal Computing," *Computer,* January 1981, pp. 62–73; R. N. Noyce and M. E. Hoff, Jr., "A History of Microcomputer Development at Intel," *IEEE Micro,* February 1981, pp. 8–21; A. Gupta and H. D. Toong, "An Architectural Comparison of 32-bit Microprocessors," *IEEE Micro,* February 1983, pp. 9–22.

The first generation of microcomputers was that of the programmable calculator, which made use of three microelectronics chips: a 4-bit MPU, a ROM for program memory, and a RAM for data memory. The second generation of microcomputers featured the 8-bit MPU, which lead to the introduction of many of models of popular personal computers such as those produced by Apple, Tandy Radio Shack, and Commodore in the mid- to late-1970s. The popular Apple IIe is an example of a second-generation microcomputer.

The third generation is known as the 16-bit era, and many powerful personal computers, such as IBM's Personal Computer, NEC's Advanced Personal Computer, Tandy Corporation's TRS 80 Model 16, and Apple's LISA, were introduced. LISA is an acronym for *L*ocal *I*ntegrated *S*ystem *A*rchitecture, and this personal computer, shown in Figure 8-11, featured a major advance in the development of software. The systems software provides a desktop work space and allows the user to switch easily between six different types of jobs. Actually, the IBM Personal Computer is a hybrid 8/16-bit computer because it has an 8-bit external data path and an internal word size of 16 bits. Similarly, the TRS 80 Model 16 and the LISA are hybrid 16/32-bit machines.

The development of 32-bit MPUs and 256K bits of RAM on a single chip became architectural objectives for the fourth generation of microcomputers. The former could provide processing power equivalent to that of many large systems, and the latter could make possible microcomputer systems with multimillion bytes of reliable, high-density memory. These objectives have been achieved. For example, even with a significantly reduced chip size, a 32-bit microprocessor produced by Hewlett-Packard contains 450,000 transistors. These high-performance, 32-bit microprocessor systems have been aptly called **supermicros**.

An important characteristic of the supermicros is the use of multiple processors to relieve the MPU of the need to handle the transfer of data to and from main memory, to move data to and from input and output units, and to perform special, complex calculations. With their ability to handle multiple

FIGURE 8-11

The LISA, or *local* *i*ntegrated *s*ystem *a*rchitecture, microcomputer provides users with six key applications packages that are linked together to provide a complete office-desk work environment. These are: word processing, electronic worksheet, business graphics, a personal data base, a graphics capability, and a planning and scheduling program. LISA also provides an advanced, user-friendly method for users to relate to the computer. (Courtesy Apple Computer, Inc.)

input and output devices, these systems will have many of the capabilities of large present-day computers.

FEEDBACK

8-11 Distinguish between the four microcomputer generations.

8-12 What is a bus?

8-13 What generation is the Apple IIe? The LISA?

8-14 Describe the characteristics of a supermicro.

8-15 Why has RAM increased along with word size?

Software Evolution

The importance of effective software cannot be overstated. As our discussion of the microcomputer generations has shown, the hardware for personal computers has become increasingly cost-effective. Hardware advances have been revolutionary in nature and will continue to be so as we move into the era of supermicros. However, without adequate systems software and applications software, the power of the hardware is wasted.

As has been typical of the history of computers, progress in microcomputer software tends to lag behind advances in hardware. Progress tends to be more evolutionary than revolutionary. There are many reasons for this. For example, each of the popular microprocessor chips was different in internal design, and there was little standardization among their operating systems. Consequently, applications programs written for one microcomputer system usually did not

32 Personal computers have many applications in the home. These include menu planning and storage and retrieval of recipes for nutritional meals. (© David Burnett, 1982/Contact Press Images)

33 Personal computers provide endless hours of entertainment and education for players of all ages. They will become as commonplace in the home as television sets are today. (© Chuck Fishman, 1982/Contact Press Images)

32

33

34 Personal work stations enable executives to retrieve information needed for timely responses to telephone inquiries. Computer literacy will become a necessity for managers at all levels as microcomputers become an indispensable executive tool. (© Bryce Flynn/Picture Group)

35 Desk-top terminals are becoming standard equipment in large corporations as well as in the single-person business office. Often word and data processing terminals are connected with a local area business communication network. Before long, every member of an office will have some computer exposure. (© Brad Bower/Picture Group)

34

35

36

36 Microcomputers are becoming common sights in our schools. During 1982 and 1983, legislation was passed that gave significant tax credits to computer manufacturers who donated computers to elementary and secondary schools. This impetus has helped to increase the availability of microcomputers, and some states require computer literacy as a prerequisite for graduation from high school. (© David Burnett, 1982/Contact Press Images)

37 The device held in the left hand of this person is called a "mouse," and it is used to move the cursor to point at objects on the screen. The button is used to select a particular applications program. (Courtesy Xerox Corp.)

39

38 Microcomputers can improve productivity in many ways, even in an informal setting such as a home workshop. This enterprising businessman uses his personal computer to write and edit a newsletter, handle his mailing lists, and keep track of customer services. (© David Burnett, 1982/Contact Press Images)

39 The IBM Personal Computer has quickly become one of the most popular microcomputers and has spawned an industry making compatible products. It has 40K bytes of ROM, up to 640K bytes of RAM, 4-color graphics capability, and simultaneous text and graphics capability. Shown is the IBM Personal Computer XT, which uses a 10-megabyte hard (''fixed'') disk instead of a second disk drive. (Courtesy IBM)

run on another. Also, there appears to be an almost insatiable market for applications software packages of all kinds, with new products appearing continuously and old products disappearing from the market.

Fortunately for purchasers of personal computers, competition has given rise to a thriving software industry that is producing versions of high-quality systems software and popular applications programs for sale to owners of most personal computers. The size of the current market for personal computers and projections of its continued growth demonstrate that successful software products can be very profitable for their authors.

Some major manufactures of personal computers, such as Apple and Tandy Radio Shack, have developed their own disk operating systems (DOS). Disk operating systems are large collections of programs, and all of a DOS is not stored in main memory at the same time. To do so could severely limit the amount of RAM available for applications programs and data. Instead, the DOS brings into RAM additional software routines as they are needed. An example is a general purpose, or utility, program that can be used to copy files of information from one disk to another for back-up purposes. A very large number of applications programs are available to run under the operating systems provided by the manufacturers of popular personal computers, such as the Apple IIe and the IBM Personal Computer.

Fortunately, there are not as many operating systems as there are personal computers, and there is a trend toward some standardization. Many vendors design their microcomputer systems to run the same programs as the market leaders so that there is a ready-made software base for their products. It is not uncommon to find personal computers designed with more than one MPU in order to increase the amount of usable software. The trend toward industry standardization is also helped by the fact that some disk operating systems developed by software specialty firms have found widespread acceptance, and many manufacturers of lesser-known or newly introduced personal computer systems have designed their products to use them. An example of a widely used DOS is the **CP/M** operating system. CP/M, which stands for control program/microprocessor, is a product of Digital Research Corporation, and it has become a standard for many 8-bit personal computers.

Similarly, CP/M 86, another product of Digital Research Corporation, and MS-DOS, developed by the Microsoft Corporation, have tended to become industry standards for many 16-bit personal computers. Both are designed to work with the IBM Personal Computer and with other microcomputers that use the popular Intel 8088 or the Intel 8086 microprocessor chip.

Software packages are becoming increasingly **user friendly.** This means that they appear to be written in the language of the user instead of that of the machine. The use of **menus,** which provide the user with clearly labeled options, is a technique for enhancing user friendliness. As an example, a program designed to assist an instructor in keeping records of class grades might start out by displaying the following master menu on a CRT screen:

MAKE A SELECTION FROM THE MASTER MENU
1. CREATE A CLASS FILE
2. CHANGE A CLASS FILE
3. ENTER GRADES
4. COMPUTE GRADES AND STATISTICS
5. PRINT A REPORT
6. EXIT GRADE PROGRAM
ENTER THE NUMBER OF YOUR SELECTION:

Successively more detailed menus would guide the instructor through all of the features of each selection.

Because users often have to learn the unique features of many applications packages and because it often is difficult to share data or switch from one application to another, the next step in user friendliness was to provide a software umbrella (called **environmental software**) that would permit users to move easily from one application to another and to share data among them. Apple Corporation's LISA computer, which was previously mentioned as a 16-bit microcomputer, introduced this feature among microcomputers.

FEEDBACK

8-16 How is software standardization occurring?

8-17 What is user-friendly software? What is a menu?

8-18 What docs CP/M stand for?

SELECTING YOUR PERSONAL COMPUTER

Steps in Selecting a Personal Computer

An individual who wishes to select a personal computer is faced with a bewildering array of choices. The life-cycle method for the study, design, development, and operation of business information systems, which was introduced in Chapter 3, can be helpful. This method, particularly the study phase, applies to the selection of a personal computer system as well as to the design and development of large systems. The study phase is the life-cycle phase during which a problem is identified and alternative solutions analyzed and evaluated. These are the most important tasks for you to perform before selecting a personal computer. In most instances, you will purchase the software and hardware that best meet your needs. This means that for most personal computer applications you will not be involved in detailed design phase and development phase activities such as are described in Chapters 9, 10, and 11 of this text. However, in the case of complex needs, such as those of an expanding small business, these chapters provide some useful guidelines.

As you set out to identify your needs and to select a personal computer to meet them, your study phase should include these three important steps:

1. Define your requirements.
2. Evaluate available software.
3. Select the hardware.

TABLE 8-1   **COMPARISON OF TWO PERSONAL COMPUTER SYSTEMS**

List of Needs	
System A	**System B**
Short educational programs	Electronic work sheet
Games	Word processing
Budgeting	Graphics
Word processing	Small-business accounting
Printed output	Quality printed output

Requirements	
System A	**System B**
32–48K RAM	64–128K RAM
8-bit word size	8–16-bit word size
Dot-matrix printer	Letter-quality printer
One disk drive	Two disk drives, possibly one a hard disk
Keyboard	Keyboard

Requirements definition   Your definition of requirements should begin with a statement of needs and conclude with a description of the performance that you expect of your personal computer system. Table 8-1 (top) shows two lists of system needs. Clearly, the second list establishes different software requirements and implies more powerful and more expensive hardware. As you prepare your list of needs, you should be realistic about your objectives and constraints, such as the amount of money that you can afford to spend.

The definition of system performance includes descriptions of output, input, processing, and internal and external storage requirements. Table 8-1 (bottom) shows two sets of requirements as they might be described for systems meeting the needs lists of Table 8-1 (top). In some instances, considerable analysis is required to adequately define system performance requirements. However, the results are well worth the effort. One of the most important and costly lessons that we have learned in the short history of computers is the importance of making a front-end investment in study and analysis before making a commitment to expensive investments in software and hardware.

As you define your requirements, you should not hesitate to talk to users of personal computer systems or to visit computer stores. Certainly, you should take advantage of the abundance of information available at trade shows and in personal computer magazines. The more informed you can become, the better will be the quality of your decision. Just remember that your needs probably will be somewhat different than those of others, and remember that the computer salesperson, who has only a limited amount of time to spend with you, may have objectives different from yours. So do not fail to complete all three study-phase steps. If you are considering a considerable investment or if the decision is critical to the success of your business, you may wish to employ an independent consultant to assist you.

Evaluation of available software   As we have learned, a wealth of software has been developed for personal computers, and more is arriving daily. Often the question is, Which package should I select? and not Is there any program to do the job? For example, there are at least two dozen word processing programs and many versions of electronic work sheets. If you did your homework in step 1 and succeeded in defining your requirements, you should be able to make suitable choices of both systems software and applications software.

A guideline for the selection of systems software is to limit your choices to the popular operating systems, such as CP/M for 8-bit systems or MS-DOS for 16-bit systems, or to a well-supported and widely used system developed by a strong, established personal computer manufacturer. This type of choice would enable you to select from a wide array of existing applications programs and to anticipate future enhancements, such as user-friendly environmental software that integrates many applications.

Before selecting applications software, you should insist upon demonstrations that meet the needs established by your analysis of requirements. Most of the popular products, such as word processors and electronic work sheets, have good and bad features. You should experiment with them and select the one that you are most comfortable with. Usually, vendors will allow you time to do this, often offering classes to familiarize potential customers with software packages.

When considering a business program, such as an accounting package, you should test the program by providing samples of input data or records to make certain that the program is able to produce the outputs in a format that is useful to you. You should understand the manner in which data is stored and how the data files are maintained and accessed. It also is wise to enter some bad data to see how the system copes with errors, because there will surely be some.

The quality of software documentation is a very important consideration. A user's manual should be part of the software package. This manual should give you additional information about the package and its capabilities. If you find the documentation confusing and difficult to read, you probably will have the same problem when you try to use the program, and you would be well-advised to look elsewhere. If possible you should talk to other users of the program and solicit their opinions on the quality of the documentation.

Select the hardware   The third step in picking a personal computer is to select the hardware. Most microcomputers use similar components; nonetheless, some important hardware considerations come into focus after requirements definition and software evaluation have taken place. You should know the performance expected of your computer system and its price range. Certainly, price is an important consideration, and your budget may limit your choices. However, support and service are even more important. Therefore, the resources and reputation of the dealer from whom you make your purchase are important. Sooner or later your system will require repair, and service should be readily available.

A Personal Computer Selection Checklist   Table 8-2 is an example of a microcomputer selection checklist. It is compatible with a standard systems analysis procedure for evaluating candidate systems, which is explained in detail in Chapter 9. The personal computer selection checklist will enable you to compare personal computer systems as they relate to your specific needs. You should note the decision factors important to you in the first column of the checklist. In most cases, these will be factors that have been discussed in this chapter. The second column indicates the relative importance of each factor. This is accomplished by assigning a weight to each, typically on a scale of 1 to 5, with 5 assigned to the most important factors. Similarly, a rating for each factor is assigned to each candidate system, typically on a scale of 1 to 10. The score for each factor is the product of its weight and rating. By this means total scores can be computed for as many candidates as are considered.

Some helpful guidelines   Some general guidelines are of value in the selection of personal computer systems. These are related to the six categories of applications that we discussed in this chapter and to experience with typical microcomputer systems used within each category, These guidelines are summarized

TABLE 8-2
MICROCOMPUTER SELECTION CHECKLIST

Decision factors	Factor weight	Candidate A Rating	Candidate A Score	Candidate B Rating	Candidate B Score
Applications software	5	8	40	9	45
System software	4	7	28	7	28
Hardware:					
Speed	3	5	15	4	12
Storage	3	5	15	4	12
Monitor	2	4	8	5	10
Printer	3	6	18	6	18
Keyboard	2	4	8	10	20
Documentation	5	2	10	8	40
Ease of use	4	1	4	7	28
Vendor support	5	1	5	9	45
Cost:					
Acquisition	3	10	30	4	12
Maintenance	3	2	5	3	9
Special features					
Graphics	4	7	28	6	24
Communications	2	4	8	4	8
Growth	3	3	9	3	9
Total score			231		320

in Table 8-3. Thus, a hobby personal computer might be an 8-bit system with 16K of RAM and a single disk drive. With this system a programming language could be learned, games could be enjoyed, and some simple programs could be run. With an additional 16K of RAM, more extensive home applications software could be used. Most applications packages designed for professional use, such as statistical packages and simulation programs, require a minimum of 48K of RAM and work best with two disk drives. Similar configurations are desirable for some educational courseware packages, and many word processing programs require 64K of RAM. Much small-business software and some engineering and scientific programs require large amounts of RAM and mass storage. For these types of applications, the use of hard disk drives is increasing.

Information such as that contained in Table 8-3 must be used carefully because the table is only a general guide. It is not a substitute for following the three steps for selecting a personal computer that we have emphasized in this chapter: requirements definition, software evaluation, and, *finally*, hardware selection.

FEEDBACK   **8-19** What are the three steps in selecting a personal computer?
8-20 What does the definition of system performance include?
8-21 What is the guideline for selecting systems software?
8-22 What is the importance of software documentation?
8-23 What is a personal computer selection checklist.?

TABLE 8-3
PERSONAL COMPUTER SELECTION GUIDELINES

Application	System			
	Micro I $ (8-bit word, 16–32K RAM, one floppy disk, slow I/O, single user stations, serial processing)	Micro II $$ (8–16-bit word, 48–64K RAM, two floppy disks, slow–medium I/O, single user station, serial processing)	Micro III $$$ (16–32-bit word, 128–512K RAM, hard disk, medium I/O, multiple user stations, overlapped processing)	Supermicro $$$$ (32-bit word, large memory and disk storage, fast I/O, multiple user stations, parallel processing)
Home and hobby	✔	✔		
Word processing		✔	✔	
Professional		✔	✔	
Educational	✔	✔	✔	
Small business		✔	✔	✔
Engineering and scientific	✔	✔	✔	✔

SUMMARY   The most distinguishing characteristic of a personal computer is that it is a small computer used by an individual, usually in an interactive mode. Personal computers have the same parts as larger computers and perform similar functions. However, the central processing unit of a personal computer—called a microprocessor unit, or MPU—is concentrated in a single silicon chip. Also, personal computers are less expensive than larger machines because they have smaller internal memories, called RAM, and use less powerful peripheral devices. Floppy disks or hard disks are used for mass storage, and input usually is by means of a keyboard. Soft-copy output is displayed on a CRT screen, and hard copy is produced by low-speed character or dot-matrix printers.

Personal computers have a wealth of applications, and because new uses are being introduced almost daily it is difficult to classify all of them. However, there are six major categories of applications:

1. Home and hobby
2. Word processing
3. Professional
4. Educational
5. Small business
6. Engineering and scientific

Each application category has a range of microcomputer performance requirements; however, the small-business and the engineering and scientific applications tend to be the most demanding in terms of speed and storage.

In the decade between 1971 and 1982 advances in microelectronics led us from calculators to supermicros. Four generations of microcomputers can be identified with this transition. Classified by word size, these generations are the 4-bit, 8-bit, 16-bit, and 32-bit MPU. With each successive generation additional RAM has become available, and more powerful systems and applications software have been introduced. The trend in systems software is toward more powerful, standardized operating systems, and the trend in applications software is toward enhanced ease of use, called user friendliness.

An individual who wishes to select a personal computer is confronted by a bewildering array of choices. A three-step method for making an appropriate choice is:

1. Define your requirements.
2. Evaluate available software.
3. Select the hardware.

**ANSWERS TO FEEDBACK
QUESTIONS**   **8-1** Six identifying characteristics of personal computers, as compared to larger computers, are: microprocessor-based, low cost, small internal memory and word size, less powerful peripheral components,

use of floppy disks for mass storage, and a plug-in system that can be assigned to an individual.

8-2 Mass storage refers to floppy or hard disk external storage systems. Internal storage is called random access memory, or RAM. ROM stands for read-only memory, and it is used to store important systems software instructions.

8-3 "16-bit, 512K" refers to a personal computer with a 16-bit word size and 512K of RAM.

8-4 Bootstrapping refers to the process by which instructions contained in ROM are used to bring additional instructions into RAM when a personal computer is turned on. The additional instructions are part of the disk operating system, DOS, and they are needed to start up the computer.

8-5 Dot-matrix printers form characters as combinations of dots. They have poorer resolution and are less expensive than letter-quality printers.

8-6 Six major categories of microcomputer application and an example of each are:

a Home and hobby: budgeting
b Word processing: correspondence
c Professional: electronic work sheet
d Educational: LOGO
e Small Business: accounting
f Engineering and scientific: physics

8-7 CAI is computer-assisted instruction; CMI is computer-managed instruction; CAD is computer-assisted design; and CAM is computer-assisted manufacturing.

8-8 An electronic work sheet is a display of rows and columns. It can be used for scheduling, cost estimating, planning, and the examination of "what if" situations.

8-9 Small-business applications of personal computers require high performance systems because they handle large volumes of data and complex programs.

8-10 Courseware is software that is used for educational purposes. An example is a program that teaches keyboarding skills.

8-11 The four microcomputer generations are classified in terms of the word size of the MPU. They are the 4-bit, 8-bit, 16-bit, and 32-bit generations.

8-12 A bus is a circuit along which electronic signals travel.

8-13 The Apple IIe is a second-generation microcomputer, and LISA is a hybrid third-and-fourth-generation microcomputer, with a 16-bit external data path and a 32-bit internal word size.

8-14 A supermicro is a microcomputer with a 32-bit word size, a large amount of RAM, and many of the processing capabilities of large computers.

8-15 RAM has increased along with word size because microcomputer processing speed increases with word size, and faster machines are able to process complex programs and large amounts of data.

8-16 Software standardization is occurring because many applications packages are being written for use with popular operating systems.

8-17 User-friendly software appears to be written in the language of the user and not that of the machine. A menu is a technique for enhancing user friendliness; it provides a user with clearly labeled options.

8-18 CP/M stands for control program/microprocessor.

8-19 The three steps in selecting a personal computer are:
   a Define your requirements.
   b Evaluate available software.
   c Select the hardware.

8-20 The definition of system performance includes descriptions of output, input, processing, and internal and external storage requirements.

8-21 The guideline for selecting system software is to limit your choices to popular operating systems.

8-22 Documentation is important because a user cannot be expected to understand how to use a poorly documented program.

8-22 A personal computer selection checklist is a table that can be constructed to assist in the evaluation of computer systems.

FOR REVIEW AND DISCUSSION

1 Explain why you agree or disagree with *Time* magazine's selection of the personal computer as Man of the Year for 1982.

2 What is relationship between RAM, ROM, and mass storage?

3 What are the most common input and output devices used with personal computers?

4 Under what conditions would you select a hard disk drive for a microcomputer system?

5 What impact do you believe that personal computers will have upon education in the next decade? Give some examples.

6 What types of software packages are associated with professional uses of personal computers?

7 What is the relationship between CAI, CMI, and courseware?

8 What are the differences between the second and third generations of microcomputers? What generation is associated with CP/M? With MS-DOS?

9 It is often stated that software selection is the first step in picking a personal computer. Do you agree or disagree with this statement? Explain your answer.

10 What is a personal computer selection checklist? How is it used?

UNIT
THREE

SYSTEMS ANALYSIS

This unit continues the discussion of the life-cycle sequence for the development of effective computer information systems. We introduced the system development life-cycle approach in Chapter 3. In this unit we will take a closer look at the study-, design-, development-, and operation-phase activities that were introduced in Chapter 3. With the knowledge of computer systems and their elements that we acquired in Unit Two as a background, we will see how a particular problem is identified, how a system is selected to solve the problem, how that system is designed and developed, and how the system is maintained throughout its operational life. The example that we will use in this unit is an inventory-management and sales-analysis application. Chapter 9 will deal with the study phase, Chapter 10 will describe the design and development phases, and Chapter 11 will discuss the operation phase.

This unit also establishes the life-cycle background for learning about programming, an important development-phase activity. In Units Four and Five, we will examine this activity in detail and learn how computer programs are prepared.

CHAPTER 9

SYSTEM STUDY PHASE

PREVIEW   The first phase in developing a computer information system is the study phase. In this phase, the problem is identified and analyzed, and a system is selected to solve the problem. The goal of this chapter is to explain the system selection process, with emphasis upon performance definition and feasibility analysis. By working with a sample system, you will become familiar with three important flowcharting techniques and you will learn how to conduct a feasibility analysis for any system that you may encounter, computer-based or otherwise.

In this chapter you will learn:

1. The two steps in a problem identification
2. The three elements of performance definition
3. The four steps in conducting a feasibility analysis
4. The uses of system flowcharts, data flow diagrams, and hierarchy charts
5. How to prepare project plans and cost schedules

KEY TERMS TO WATCH FOR AND REMEMBER

information service request
  (ISR)
initial investigation
performance definition
feasibility analysis
flowchart
system flowchart
data flow diagram
  (DFD)
hierarchy chart

candidate system matrix
candidate evaluation
  matrix
weighted candidate evalu-
  ation matrix
project plan
cost schedule
study-phase report
decision support system (DDS)

SYSTEM SELECTION PROCESS: AN OVERVIEW

In this book, we have stressed the idea of usability. Usability is the worth of a system to its end users, and it is the most important measure of the effectiveness of a computer data processing system. In Chapter 3, we introduced you to the life-cycle process for developing usable computer information systems. The life-cycle road map that we presented in Chapter 3 is repeated here as Figure 9-1. The four life-cycle phases are study, design, development, and operation. You will learn about the study phase in this chapter.

System selection is the goal of the study phase. Figure 9-2 expands the study phase into steps that illustrate the system selection process. As this figure shows, the first step is problem identification. The second step is **performance definition**. This means determining what the usable outputs of the system must be. The third step in selecting a system is to identify possible systems that might solve the problem and to select one of these. We call the possible solutions *alternatives*, and we call the process of selecting the most cost-effective alternative a **feasibility analysis.** We will describe a feasibility analysis step by step in this chapter. At this point, though, you should notice the two feedback loops that appear in Figure 9-2. The inner feedback path indicates that several alternative, or candidate, solutions to a problem may have to be evaluated. The outer feedback path represents a second evaluation process. As we learn more about the system and about possible problem solutions, we may have to alter our original definition of performance in order to produce practical and usable outputs.

After the systems analyst has completed the feasibility analysis, the study phase is concluded with a recommendation. If the recommendation is to proceed with the project, the design of the selected system takes place in the next phase, the design phase. In the remainder of this chapter, we will describe in more detail the flowchart of Figure 9-2. In Chapter 10, you will learn how to design the selected system in a way that guarantees its usability.

PROBLEM IDENTIFICATION

The first step in system selection is problem identification, which starts with the discovery that a problem exists. It concludes with both the person with the business problem (the user) and the person assigned to solve the problem (the

FIGURE 9-1

The life-cycle phases.

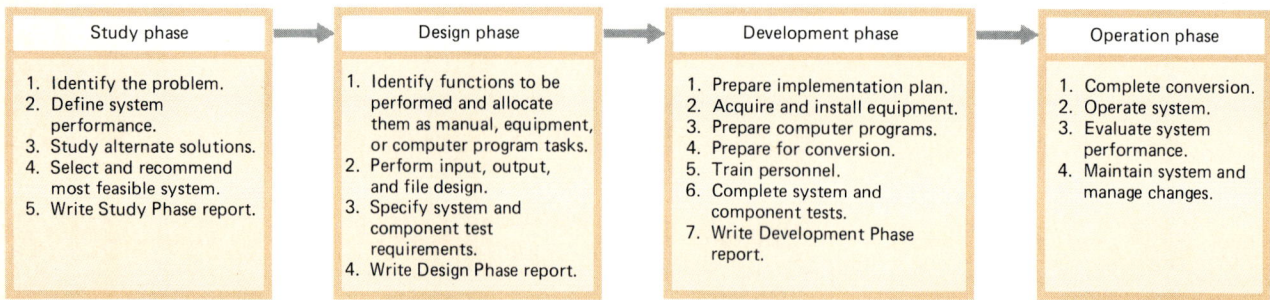

Study phase	Design phase	Development phase	Operation phase
1. Identify the problem. 2. Define system performance. 3. Study alternate solutions. 4. Select and recommend most feasible system. 5. Write Study Phase report.	1. Identify functions to be performed and allocate them as manual, equipment, or computer program tasks. 2. Perform input, output, and file design. 3. Specify system and component test requirements. 4. Write Design Phase report.	1. Prepare implementation plan. 2. Acquire and install equipment. 3. Prepare computer programs. 4. Prepare for conversion. 5. Train personnel. 6. Complete system and component tests. 7. Write Development Phase report.	1. Complete conversion. 2. Operate system. 3. Evaluate system performance. 4. Maintain system and manage changes.

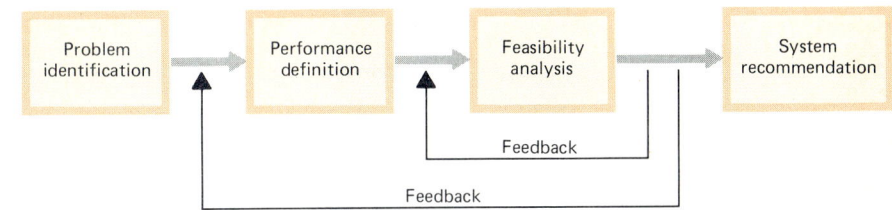

FIGURE 9-2
The system selection process.

systems analyst) in agreement about the exact problem to be solved. In a small business, the user of a system may also be the individual who must work out the detailed solution. In a large business, this is seldom the case. For example, if you were the proprietor of a small clothing store, you might keep a card file of your inventory and use this to reorder merchandise, or you might personally use a microcomputer system for this purpose. If you or your clerk failed to record sales properly or if some cards were mislaid, you would have to fix up the system. On the other hand, if you were the merchandising manager for a large chain of clothing stores and discovered that you were not able to keep local stores stocked with popular items because the sales data which you received were incorrect, you would be responsible for correcting the problem. However, a systems analyst, familiar with both inventory management and data processing, would probably be assigned the responsibility for working out a detailed, technical solution that satisfied you, the user. We will use task titles as though the tasks were performed by different individuals, although we recognize that in some instances, the same person could be the user, the systems analyst, and even the programmer and computer operator. Whatever the case, the system selection procedure follows the steps outlined in this chapter.

Problem identification begins with the identification of a problem and may lead to the need for a new or an improved system. The user may discover the inadequacy of the existing system, or a government regulation—such as the need to report the value of goods in inventory on a certain date—may trigger the need for a new or revised system. A systems analyst may observe problems with the current system and point these out to the principal user. Whatever the means by which a problem is brought to light, its identification and understanding involves two steps: a written problem statement and an initial investigation.

Problem Statement   Effective systems cannot be created without descriptive documentation, which is added to as system design and development proceed. Documentation begins with a clear statement of the problem to be solved. In many companies, the problem statement is included on a form that is used to request services from the organization responsible for developing information systems. This organization, which we will call "information services," often is responsible for systems analysis, programming, and computer operations.

OUTLOOK BRIGHT FOR SYSTEMS ANALYSTS

Nature of the work Many essential business functions and scientific research projects depend on systems analysts to plan efficient methods of processing data and handling the results. Analysts begin an assignment by discussing the data processing problem with managers of specialists in the area concerned to determine the exact nature of the problem and to break it down into its component parts. If a new inventory system is desired, for example, systems analysts must determine what new data needs to be collected, the equipment needed for computation, and the steps to be followed in processing the information.

Analysts use various techniques, such as cost accounting, sampling, and mathematical model building to analyze the problem and devise a new system. Once a system has been developed, they prepare charts and diagrams that describe its operation in terms that managers or customers can understand. They also may prepare a cost-benefit analysis to help the client decide whether the proposed system is satisfactory.

If the system is accepted, systems analysts translate the logical requirements of the system into the capabilities of the computer machinery or "hardware." They also prepare specifications for programmers to follow and work with them to "debug" the system.

The problems systems analysts must solve range from monitoring nuclear fission in a power plant to forecasting sales for an appliance manufacturing firm. Because the work is so varied and complex, analysts specialize in either business or scientific and engineering applications.

Some analysts improve systems already in use by developing better procedures or adapting the system to handle additional types of data. Others do research, called advanced systems design, to devise new methods of systems analysis.

Training, other qualifications, and advancement There is no universally acceptable way of preparing for a job as a systems analyst because employer's preferences depend on the work being done. However, college graduates generally are sought for these jobs; for some of the more complex jobs, persons with graduate degrees are preferred. Employers usually want analysts with a background in accounting, business management, or economics for work in a business environment while a background in the physical sciences, mathematics, or engineering is preferred for work in scientifically oriented organizations. A growing number of employers seek applicants with a degree in computer science, information science, or data processing. Regardless of college major, most employers look for people who are familiar with programming languages. Courses in computer concepts, systems analysis, and data retrieval techniques offer good preparation for a job in this field.

Prior work experience is important. Nearly half of all persons entering this occupation have transferred from other occupations, especially from the role of computer programmer. In some industries, all systems analysts begin as programmers and are promoted to analyst positions after gaining experience.

Systems analysts must be able to think logically and should like working with ideas. The ability to concentrate and pay close attention to details is important. Although most systems analysts work independently, they sometimes work in teams on large projects. They must be able to communicate effectively with technical personnel such as programmers as well as with users who have no computer background.

Employment outlook It's no secret that the outlook for systems analysis is getting brighter all the time. Demand is skyrocketing: the government now believes there will be 400,000 systems analysts in 1990, a 119 percent increase from 1978. In addition to opportunities that will result from growth, some openings will occur as systems analysts advance to managerial positions or enter other occupations. Because many of these workers are relatively young, few positions will result from retirement or death.

The demand for system analysts is expected to rise as computer capabilities are increased and computers are used to solve problems in a larger variety of areas. Sophisticated accounting systems, telecommunications networks, and complex mathematical systems used in scientific research are examples of new approaches in problem solving. Throughout the 1980s we can expect systems analysts to be harnessing the computer's resources to solve problems we may not even have recognized yet.

Source: *Profile of the Systems Professional,* Association for Systems Management Bookshelf Series, Cleveland, 1981.

INFORMATION SERVICE REQUEST			Page 1 of 1	

INFORMATION SERVICE REQUEST Page __1__ of __1__

JOB TITLE: Inventory reorders system	NEW ☒	REQUESTED DATE: 3/1/19xx	REQUIRED DATE: 12/31/19xx
	REV. ☐	AUTHORIZATION	

OBJECTIVE: To provide centralized reordering for ten stores in Region A.	LABOR		OTHER	
	HOURS	AMOUNT	HOURS	AMOUNT
	2500	$50,000	Computer time (To be determined)	

ANTICIPATED BENEFITS: 1. Reduced cost of inventory.
2. Fewer inventory items out-of-stock.

OUTPUT DESCRIPTION	INPUT DESCRIPTION
TITLE: Reorders Summary	TITLE: Sales Transactions
FREQUENCY: QUANTITY:	FREQUENCY: On-line QUANTITY: 1000 per day per store
PAGES: COPIES:	COMMENT: Data on item, quantity, clerk,
COMMENT: Lists quantity on hand,	work station, and department.
quantity on order, and delivery date.	
Type of output to be determined.	
TITLE:	TITLE: Inventory Received
FREQUENCY QUANTITY:	FREQUENCY: On-line QUANTITY: 500 per day
PAGES: COPIES:	COMMENT: Data to update quantity
COMMENT:	on hand.

TO BE FILLED OUT BY REQUESTOR

REQUESTED BY: J. Herrick G. Herrick	DEPARTMENT: Inventory	TITLE: Manager	TELEPHONE: Ext. 509
APPROVED BY: S. Sampson S. Sampson	DEPARTMENT: Sales	TITLE: Vice president	TELEPHONE: Ext. 602

TO BE FILLED OUT BY INFORMATION SERVICES

FILE NO: S7134	ACCEPTED ☒ NOT ACCEPTED ☐		
SIGNATURE: B. Humin B. Humin	DEPARTMENT: Info. Services	TITLE: Manager	TELEPHONE: Ext. 478

REMARKS: S. Simon to perform initial investigation. ISR to be reviewed in two
weeks.

FORM NO. C-6-1	ADDITIONAL INFORMATION: USE REVERSE SIDE OR EXTRA PAGES

FIGURE 9-3
Information service request.

Information Service Request

Figure 9-3 shows a typical **information service request (ISR)** form. It is simplified to emphasize the principles involved. The ISR is for a system to manage inventory reorders for 10 clothing stores from a centralized location. This system could be part of an overall inventory management system. As we can see by inspection of Figure 9-3, this ISR not only provides for the entry of information about the job and its objectives but also furnishes space for statements of anticipated benefits and the description of required outputs and inputs. The statement of anticipated benefits justifies the expenditure of the people and machine resources needed to develop the new or improved system.

Often, the systems analyst and the user work together to complete the ISR. The person who needs the system usually has ideas about the outputs that the system must produce and has considerable knowledge about the input information that is available. Sometimes, all the inputs and outputs cannot be defined, and it is not possible to fill out all sections of the ISR completely. Some gaps are to be expected, because the ISR usually is followed by an initial investigation. The initial investigation may, in fact, introduce significant changes to the original concept.

INITIAL INVESTIGATION

After the ISR is completed, the systems analyst begins the initial investigation. The purpose of the initial investigation is to clarify the problem and to complete the analyst's understanding of all facts and activities related to the problem. The analyst begins the initial investigation with fact-finding activities. These activities include studying the characteristics of the organization affected by the system, analyzing written information, such as manuals and reports helpful to the system being studied, preparing data flow diagrams, and conducting personal interviews.

Data Flow Diagrams

Data flow diagrams, or **DFDs,** are useful tools for analyzing existing systems. A data flow diagram is a network that describes the flows of data and the processes that change, or transform, data throughout a system. Figure 9-4 is an example of a data flow diagram that might describe the existing decentralized inventory reorders system. Four specialized symbols are used to draw DFDs, and these are illustrated in Figure 9-4. The lines with arrows, called *directed lines*, represent the flow of data. The circles represent a process that transforms data. The squares represent data sources or destinations, and the open-ended rectangle represents data storage. Data flow diagrams can be expanded to show successive levels of detail. Sufficient expansion should be performed during the initial investigation to be certain that both the analyst and user personnel share a common understanding of the existing system and its data flow.

Personal Interviews

Personal interviews are among the most fruitful of all methods of obtaining information and ensuring that the new system will work properly. An analyst must remember that many people fear that computers will replace them in their jobs. In fact, most computer-based systems create jobs to replace those they eliminate. Many companies would prefer to retrain loyal employees of proven worth rather than to replace them by unknown persons who may possess

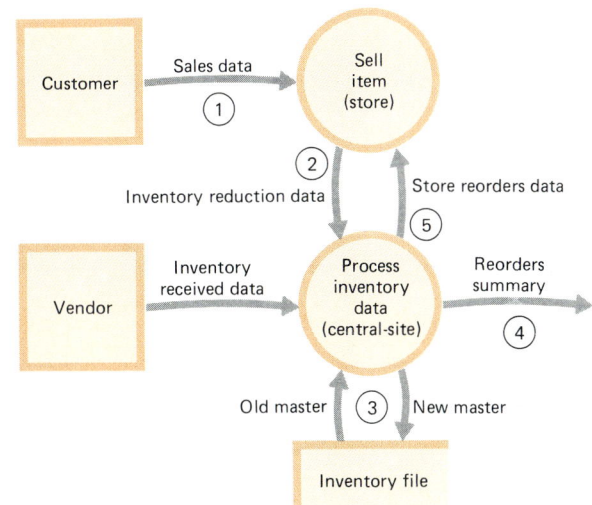

FIGURE 9-4

Data flow diagram for an inventory reorders system. (1) Store sells item. (2) Sales-related inventory data sent to control site. (3) Inventory file updated to reflect reductions and items received. (4) Reorders summary report produced. (5) Reorders data sent to stores.

special skills. The analyst can learn much about problems and about potential solutions if person-to-person communications are honest and, if possible, reassuring to persons whose jobs will be altered by a computer-based system.

Modified Information Service Request

After the systems analyst has completed gathering facts and holding personal interviews, he or she is able to evaluate the initial ISR. At this point, the systems analyst may accept the ISR as written or prepare a modified version of it. The new ISR becomes the basis for a review with the user. The outcome of the review should be a final version of the ISR that contains the changes agreed upon by the analyst and the user.

Figure 9-5 shows a modified version of the ISR for the sample system. As a result of examining the existing inventory system, the analyst recommended that the new system incorporate an additional output—a sales analysis report. This report would use the same data elements needed to identify items that had to be reordered, and it would be of value to the sales department. As a consequence, the name of the system was changed from Inventory Reorders to Reorders–Sales Analysis.

In addition, the analyst suggested a study of the feasibility of providing the stores with online access to current inventory reorders and sales status information and limited capability for local data processing. After some discussion, the systems analyst and the user agreed that the number of reports that had to be printed daily at the central site could be reduced to two: a reorders summary and a composite sales analysis. Note also that an estimate has been made now of the computer time and cost required to develop the system and that a limit has been placed on the expenditures for a one-month study phase.

INFORMATION SERVICE REQUEST			Page __1__ of __1__		
JOB TITLE: Reorders/sales analysis system	NEW ☒ REV. ☐	**REQUESTED DATE:** 3/1/19xx		**REQUIRED DATE:** 12/31/19xx	
OBJECTIVE: To provide centralized reordering and daily sales analysis for 10 stores in Region A.		AUTHORIZATION			
		LABOR		**OTHER**	
		HOURS	AMOUNT	HOURS	AMOUNT
		2500	$50,000	100 (Computer time)	$5000

ANTICIPATED BENEFITS: 1. Reduced cost of inventory.
2. Fewer inventory items out-of-stock.
3. Improved sales analysis.

OUTPUT DESCRIPTION	INPUT DESCRIPTION
TITLE: Reorders Summary	**TITLE:** Sales Transactions
FREQUENCY: Daily **QUANTITY:** 1	**FREQUENCY:** On-line **QUANTITY:** 1000 per day per store
PAGES: 2 **COPIES:** 2	**COMMENT:** Data on item, quantity,
COMMENT: Lists quantity on hand, quantity on order, and delivery date. Local CRT inquiry with hardcopy as needed.	clerk, work station, and department.
TITLE: Composite Sales Analysis	**TITLE:** Inventory Received
FREQUENCY: Daily **QUANTITY:** 1	**FREQUENCY:** On-line **QUANTITY:** 500 per day
PAGES: 5 **COPIES:** 2	**COMMENT:** Data to update quantity
COMMENT: List daily sales by clerk. Local CRT inquiry with hardcopy as needed.	on hand.

TO BE FILLED OUT BY REQUESTOR				
REQUESTED BY: J. Herrick *J. Herrick*	**DEPARTMENT:** Inventory	**TITLE:** Manager		**TELEPHONE:** Ext. 509
APPROVED BY: S. Sampson *S. Sampson*	**DEPARTMENT:** Sales	**TITLE:** Vice president		**TELEPHONE:** Ext. 602

TO BE FILLED OUT BY INFORMATION SERVICES				
FILE NO: S7134	**ACCEPTED** ☒	**NOT ACCEPTED** ☐		
SIGNATURE: B. Humin *B. Humin*	**DEPARTMENT:** Info. Services	**TITLE:** Manager		**TELEPHONE:** Ext. 478

REMARKS: S. Simon assigned as systems analyst and project manager. Study Phase expenditures not to exceed $5000 and Study Phase to be completed in one month.

FORM NO. C-6-1	ADDITIONAL INFORMATION: USE REVERSE SIDE OR EXTRA PAGES

FIGURE 9-5
The final version of the information service request.

After that time, a decision will be made whether or not to continue with the design phase.

The ISR is more than good documentation. It is a contract between the user and the systems analyst. Also, it sets the stage for user involvement throughout the entire life of the project. Armed with this ISR, the analyst works with the user to define more completely the performance required of the system.

FEEDBACK   **9-1** What is the goal of the study phase?
9-2 Who discovers the need for a new system?
9-3 What is an ISR?
9-4 What is the purpose of the initial investigation?
9-5 What is a data flow diagram?

PERFORMANCE DEFINITION   The performance definition process ends with the definition of the outputs of the system in a language that is clear to the user. This process has three steps: (1) recognition of the limits, called *constraints*, on the system, (2) statement of objectives, and (3) a formal definition of the outputs of the system. This process makes use of the information that appears on the final version of the ISR. It could result in changes to the ISR as the system is studied in increasing depth.

General Constraints   There are general constraints that limit all candidate solutions that may be considered. Examples are limitations upon time and funds, availability of personnel and computer resources, federal laws, and management policies. For our example, the clothing-store chain might wish to install an inventory management system for the centralized ordering of articles for all stores within a particular geographic area. In this way, orders could be placed for items for all stores when the total inventory reached a preset reorder point. In addition, items that were surplus at some stores could be transferred to fill orders at other stores. General constraints for this system might include the following:

1. All local sales information will be provided to an existing central computer site within a 24-hour period.
2. An inventory master file will be maintained and updated at a central site.
3. The system will be installed and operational within 11 months.
4. The system will not cost more than $60,000 to design and develop.

Specific Objectives   Specific objectives of the system are taken from the anticipated benefits that appear on the ISR. These objectives should be stated in tangible, or measurable, terms if possible. "Before and after" statements often are effective in making objectives tangible. Thus, for the inventory management system, some tangible objectives might be:

1. To reduce the total dollar volume of goods in inventory from $1,000,000 to $200,000 within three months of system operation and to maintain it at that level.

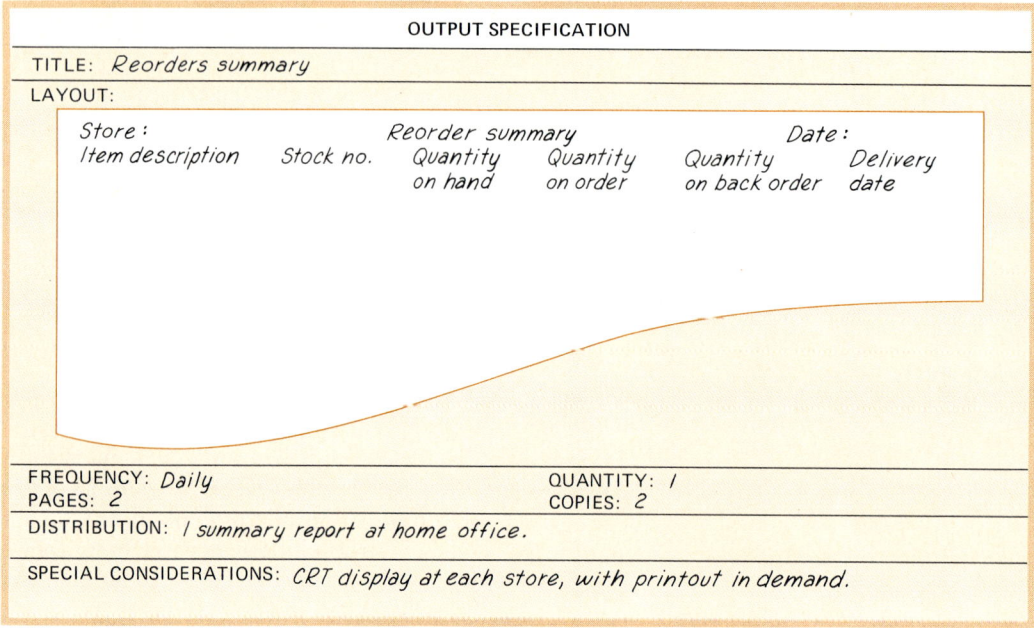

(a)

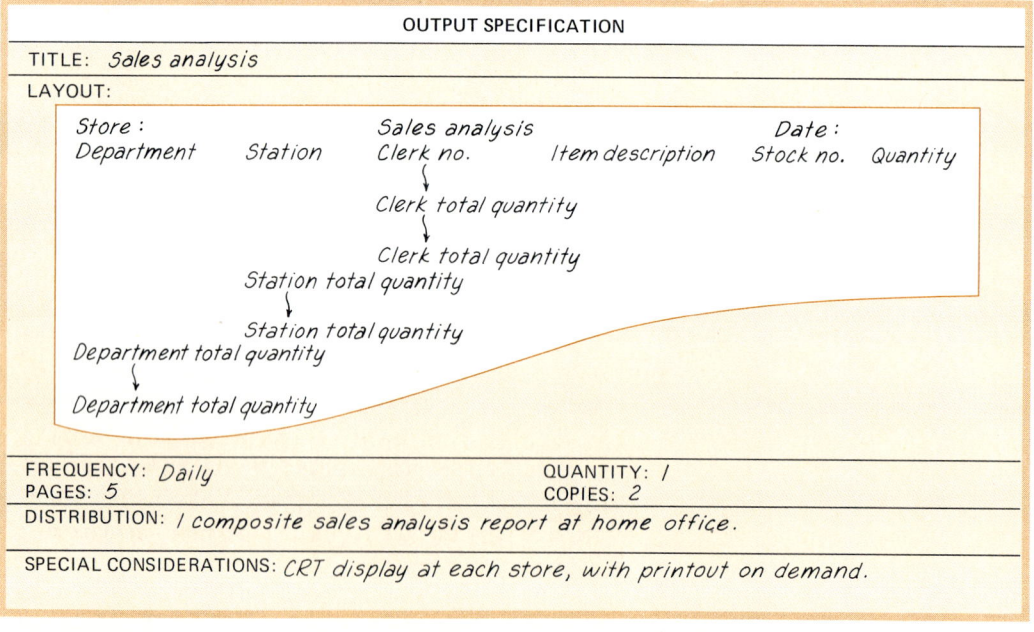

FIGURE 9-6   (b)
Output layouts. (a) Reorders summary.
(b) Sales analysis.

2. To reduce the number of times that an item cannot be found in inventory from 10 percent to 0.1 percent within six months of installation of the new system.

Not all benefits are tangible. Intangible benefits are also important. For example, **decision support systems (DSS),** which provide information about competitive products or aid in policy and planning decisions, often have benefits that can be measured only by the company's long-term profitability. However, most systems that have intangible benefits also have tangible ones, and wherever possible these should be stated in measurable terms. An important reason for stating objectives in a measurable way is to provide a means of evaluating the performance of the system after it has been installed. Performance measurements are a major indicator of the success or failure of the system. After specific objectives have been stated, the system outputs needed to meet these objectives can be described.

Output Descriptions   The user should be provided with descriptions or pictorial representations of the major outputs of the system. At this point, the media for all outputs may not be known. The candidates to be considered during the feasibility analysis that follows performance definition may use different output media. For example, one candidate system may use a computer-printed report, called a *printout*, and another may use a CRT display.

In some instances, it is possible to provide the user with pictures of the outputs because the most likely output media are known. Even if these change during the feasibility analysis, the user has had a chance to visualize the outputs, and there are meaningful points of reference for changes. In other instances, it is best to defer a pictorial representation until the feasibility analysis has been completed. Nevertheless, a data dictionary, based upon descriptions of data elements, can be provided.

Figure 9-6 is an example that shows sketches of the outputs that an inventory management system (like the example in this chapter) might be expected to produce. Figure 9-6a is a sketch, called a *layout*, of the Reorders Summary, and Figure 9-6b is a layout of the Sales Analysis. In Figure 9-6b, three levels of totals are indicated. The lowest level total is by clerk, the intermediate level is by sales station, and the highest is by department. As the remark under "Special Considerations" indicates, there is to be a CRT display at each store, with hard-copy printout on demand.

FEEDBACK   **9-6** What are the three steps in the system performance definition process? Describe each.

9-7 What is the difference between tangible and intangible benefits?

9-8 What is the purpose of an output layout?

TABLE 9-1   **FEASIBILITY ANALYSIS STEPS**

Step 1	Form systems team
	Describe system data flows
Step 2	Prepare general system data flow charts
Step 3	Select candidate systems
	Prepare candidate system matrix
	Limit number of candidates
Step 4	Evaluate candidate systems
	Prepare candidate evaluation matrix
	Prepare weighted candidate evaluation matrix

FEASIBILITY ANALYSIS

The purpose of the feasibility analysis is to select the best solution to the problem. The best solution is the alternative that is the most cost-effective of all the candidate solutions that are considered. Seldom, if ever, will one really know that the best of all possible solutions has been selected. Usually, the number of candidates that can be considered is limited by time, money, and availability of key personnel. The quality of the solution selected depends entirely upon the quality of the systems team and upon the thoroughness with which the team analyzes alternative solutions. The analysis of alternatives, or feasibility analysis, is performed in the sequence of steps listed in Table 9-1. We will describe each of these steps briefly, starting with the formation of the systems team.

Step 1: Form the Systems Team

The management of a business firm will get the best results if it assigns senior, experienced people to work with the systems analyst. In our example, a typical team would be made up of the systems analyst, an inventory supervisor, and a marketing manager. Technical support could be increased by including a specialist from the data processing department. Teams should be no larger than necessary.

Three to ten people with the right combination of skills can handle most small-to-medium business system feasibility analyses. The tasks of this team are to identify the system candidates, to evaluate these candidates, and to select and recommend the best candidate.

Step 2: Describe System Data Flows

The team develops a graphical description of the general system data flows. The candidates to be considered will fit this general description. The flow of data in business systems is complex and difficult to describe in writing. Therefore, special graphical techniques, called flowcharts, have been developed. A **flowchart** is a pictorial representation that uses predefined symbols to describe data flow in a system or the logic of a computer program. Three types of data flowcharts that are useful to the systems analyst in studying and designing business information systems are **data flow diagrams, system flowcharts,** and **hierarchy charts.**

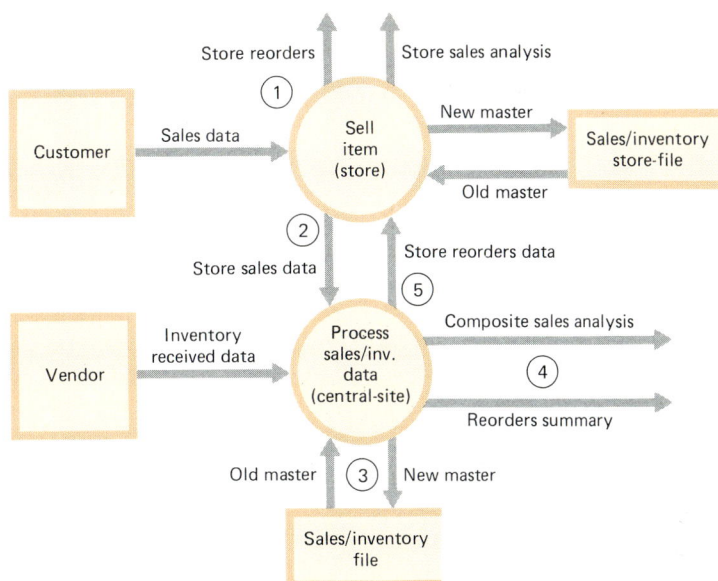

FIGURE 9-7

Data flow diagram for a reorders/sales analysis system. (1) Store sells item and performs local master file update, producing stores sales analysis and reorders data. (2) Sales data sent to central site. (3) Central-site master file updated to reflect inventory reductions and items received. (4) Composite sales analysis and reorders summary reports produced at central site. (5) Reorders data sent to store for use.

Data flow diagrams   As we observed in Figure 9-4, a data flow diagram (DFD) is a powerful tool for describing data flows and transformations in an existing system. Another important use of data flow diagrams is to aid the systems team in identifying potential system solutions. The symbols used to prepare DFDs do not imply any particular physical components. For this reason data flow diagrams are often referred to as *logical abstracts* of physical systems. This feature makes it possible for the systems team to consider a variety of logical solutions to the business information system problem without being influenced by implied physical implementations. Examples are mail versus electronic transmission, local processing versus remote processing, and hard copy versus soft copy. This feature of DFDs is particularly important in instances where output or input media are not known and a pictorial representation would be premature. Figure 9-7 is an example of a data flow diagram for a potential solution to the reorders–sales analysis system problem. In this instance, the DFD displays the logic of a system with both remote and local data processing capabilities.

After logical data flows have been studied, it is necessary to develop physical, real-world descriptions of data flows. System flowcharts, which employ symbols that identify actual data carriers, are useful for this purpose.

System flowcharts   The symbols used for system flowcharts are labeled in Figure 9-8, which is a flowcharting template used by systems analysts and computer programmers. Some of the labeled symbols are used to display both data flow in a system and computer program logic. For this reason, they are called basic symbols. The other labeled symbols are system-related symbols, and many of them resemble the media used—for example, magnetic tape, punched cards, and paper tape. In this chapter, we will learn how basic symbols and system-related symbols are used to draw system flowcharts. The unlabeled symbols are programming-related. They describe the logic of computer programs, and you will learn about them in Chapter 12.

The preparation of system flowcharts proceeds in a top-down manner. This means that the initial flowcharts are broad in scope and limited in level of detail. Successive flowcharts, prepared during the study and design phases, are narrower in scope and present more detail. Figure 9-9 is an example of a top-level flowchart for a possible inventory management system of the type that we have been describing. It uses only the basic symbols to indicate the kinds of operations performed. The inputs to this system are sales transactions and inventory received. The outputs are a summary of reorders and a sales analysis report. All processing is indicated by single symbol labeled Inventory-Sales Processing.

Figure 9-10 is a system flowchart that uses several system-related symbols to provide additional detail about a candidate Reorders–Sales Analysis system. The symbols in this figure show that sales transactions are inputted manually from remote locations and transmitted to a central location for processing. At this location, data on inventory received are entered manually, and an online inventory file is maintained on magnetic disk. The Reorders–Sales Analysis

FIGURE 9-8

System flowchart symbols.

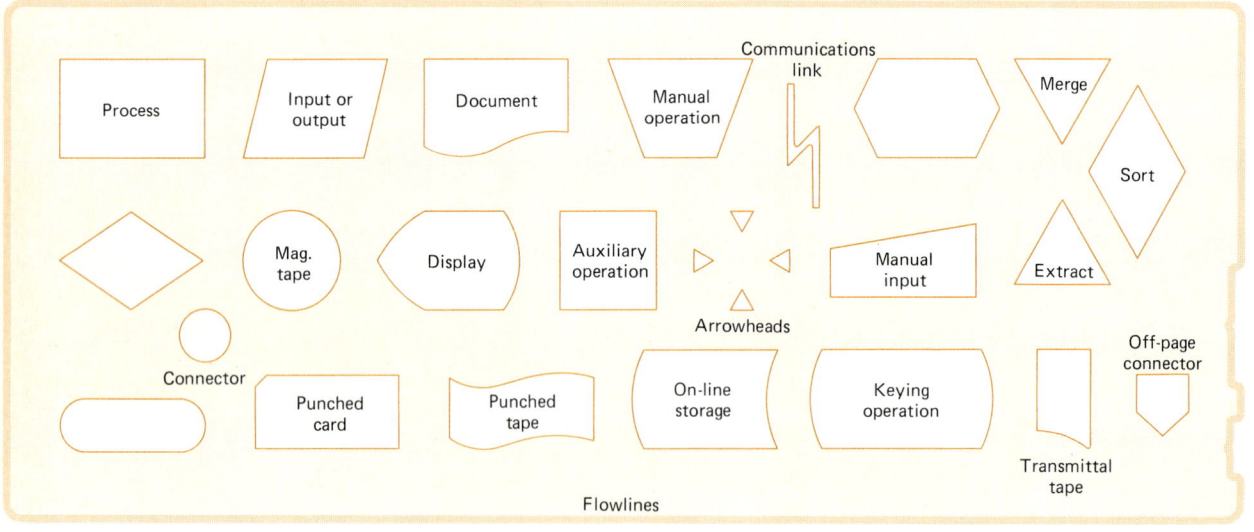

Basic symbols		Systems-related symbols			
Process	Flowlines	Document	Magnetic tape	Manual input	Keying operation
Input or output	Connector	Manual operation	Display	Extract	Transmittal tape
Arrowheads	Off-page connector	Merge	Punched card	Punched tape	Communications
		Sort	Auxiliary operation	On-line storage	link

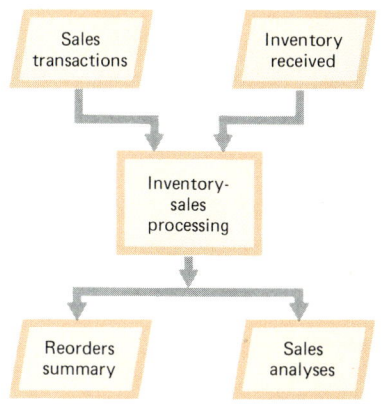

FIGURE 9-9

Basic symbols used to show a top-level flowchart for the reorders/sales analysis system flowchart.

program, as indicated, not only maintains the master file but also produces both hard-copy and soft-copy outputs. Actually, the Reorders–Sales Analysis program is not a single program but is composed of modules called *subprograms*. As the system design proceeds, additional detailed system flowcharts are prepared to display the input to and outputs from each subprogram. Examples of subprogram functions other than file maintenance are correcting and formatting input data from each remote site, performing calculations, and producing each of the system outputs. Each module can be expanded as necessary into additional levels of detail, so that by the end of the design phase, the inputs, storage locations, and outputs for all computer subprograms are clearly visible to the programmers assigned to the project during the development phase.

Hierarchy charts   Hierarchy charts are alternatives to the system flowcharts that we have described. These charts are a graphical presentation of the functions to be performed by a system. They present the functions to be performed in a top-down, hierarchical (that is, most important task first) sequence. Because they resemble a treelike organization chart, hierarchy charts are in a format that is familiar to most users. The use of hierarchy charts improves communication between the analyst and the user because the user can often understand such charts better than system flowcharts. Figure 9-11 is a hierarchy chart drawn for the sample Reorders–Sales Analysis system. Each function on the chart is shown as a box, and the description within each box uses a verb (action) and an object (data affected). An example is the box labeled Update Inventory Master File.

FIGURE 9-10

Systems-related symbols used to show a detailed flowchart in a reorder/sales analysis system.

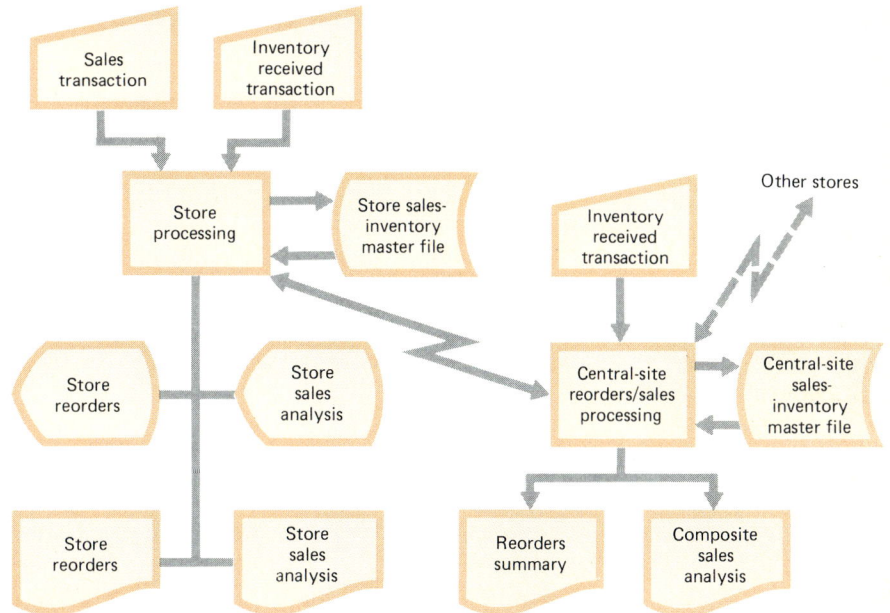

The topmost box is labeled 0.0, and the numbering proceeds, from top to bottom, as 1.0, 2.0, and 3.0, and from there to 1.1, 1.2, and so on. At the lowest level of detail, the subprograms that must be written during the development phase are identified.

Complementary techniques   Data flow diagrams, system flowcharts, and hierarchy charts are complementary flowcharting techniques, and the systems analyst selects the graphical representation that is most appropriate. Data flow diagrams are the newest technique, and their use in analysis and general design is increasing.

The data flowcharts drawn at this time are not necessarily the data flowcharts that will appear at the end of the study phase. They are used to start the process of identifying candidate systems. As candidate systems are identified and evaluated, differences in data flow among them become evident. For example, all data storage might not be at the central site, and the flowcharts would have to be modified to indicate local storage and processing. This is to be expected. Once the flowcharts have been drawn, they can be modified as necessary to represent each candidate system until a final selection has been made.

Step 3: Select Candidate Systems   Contrary to what you might expect, the major problem encountered by the team is usually not a scarcity of candidates but rather an overabundance. Almost always more solutions are suggested than there is time to consider. The reason for this is that there are many functions to be performed and a variety of ways of performing each function. Initially, team members suggest candidates without any attempt at evaluation. This process is called *brainstorming*, and it creates a large number of candidates very quickly. A principal task of the team is to

FIGURE 9-11

Hierarchy for a central-site reorders/ sales analysis system.

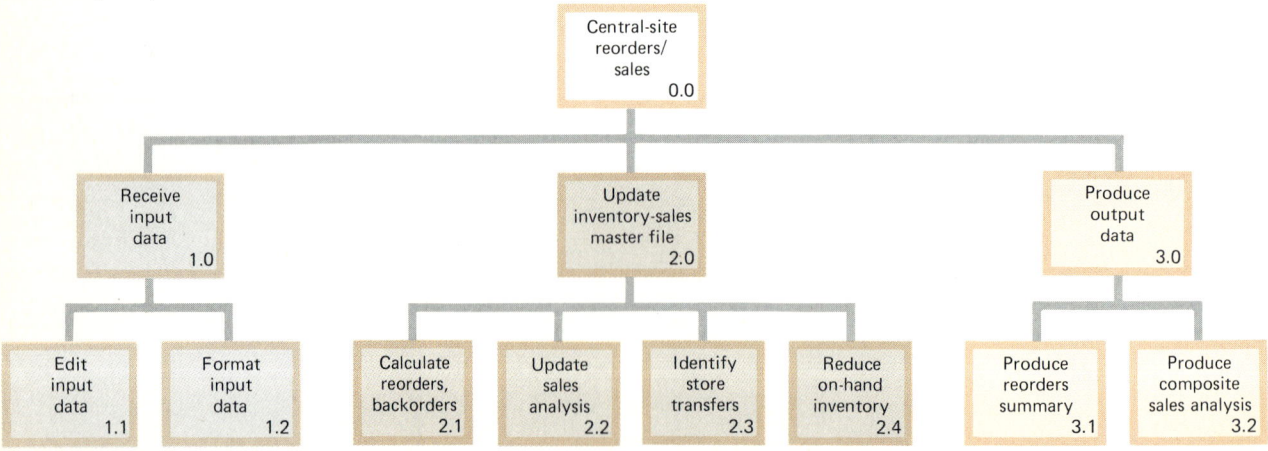

reduce the candidate solutions to a manageable number. This is done by the collective judgment of the team after a limited analysis of each candidate. We will illustrate a technique for generating candidates and for limiting their number by continuing the Reorders–Sales Analysis system example.

A useful technique for summarizing the major characteristics of potential candidates is to prepare a table, called a **candidate system matrix.** Table 9-2 is a candidate system matrix for the Reorders–Sales Analysis system. The entries in the first column of this matrix are the functions that all candidate systems must perform. In this case, these functions are input, communications, storage, processing, and output. The remaining vertical columns of the matrix identify specific candidates by summarizing the manner in which each will perform the required functions. Clearly, a change in the way a single function is performed can generate one or more new candidates. As one example, note that the only difference between candidates C and D is that the latter provides not only a local CRT display of data but also printed reports of the same information. As another, note that System N is the same as System A, except for the substitution of ordinary mail for the electronic communications link. Displaying the candidates in this way assists the team in discussing their relative merits and in making judgments as to which should be evaluated in detail. This selection process emphasizes the importance of assigning experienced and highly qualified persons to the system team.

TABLE 9-2
CANDIDATE SYSTEM MATRIX FOR THE REORDERS–SALES ANALYSIS SYSTEM

Candidate System Functions	A	B	C	D	N
Input	Dumb terminal	Intelligent terminal (all data to central site)	Programmable terminal (summary data to central site)	Programmable terminal (summary data to central site)	Punched paper tape
Communications	Half-duplex	Full-duplex	Simplex	Simplex	Mail
Storage	Central-site magnetic disk (all files)	Central-site magnetic disk (all files)	Local: sales, inventory Central site: total inventory	Local: sales, inventory Central site: total inventory	Central-site magnetic disk (all files)
Processing	Central site	Central site, plus local editing	Local: sales and inventory data Central: inventory management	Local: sales and inventory data Central: inventory management	Central site
Output	Printed reports, mail distribution	Local: CRT Central: printed reports, mail	Local: CRT Central: printed reports, mail	Local: CRT, plus printed reports Central: printed reports, mail	Printed reports, mail

Step 4: Evaluate Candidate Systems

After the candidate systems have been reduced to a number that the team can afford to analyze in detail, the costs and benefits of each must be determined so that a final selection can be made. This is accomplished in two steps. First, solutions selected from the candidate matrix for detailed analysis are entered into a second matrix called a **candidate evaluation matrix.** Next, a modification of this table, called a **weighted candidate evaluation matrix,** is used to arrive at a final selection. We will describe each of these tools in this section.

Candidate evaluation matrix   The team uses a table, called a candidate evaluation matrix, to identify the performance (that is, the effectiveness) and the cost of each candidate. Table 9-3 is an example of a candidate evaluation matrix. This matrix was prepared for the sample Reorders–Sales Analysis system. We have assumed that the systems selected for detailed evaluation are candidates A, B, and D of the candidate system matrix (Table 9-2). These candidates have the following general characteristics:

1. Candidate A transmits all sales transactions to the central-site computer as they occur via a half-duplex line. All data are verified, formatted, and processed at the central site where all files are maintained. Printed reports are mailed to each store for local use.

2. Candidate B uses intelligent terminals at each store to edit and format the input data before transmitting them to the central site. All files are maintained at the central site. A full-duplex line is used for transmission because each store is provided with the capability not only to transmit data to the central site for processing but also to simultaneously access significant processing results for display on a local CRT. Detailed printouts are mailed to the stores.

TABLE 9-3
CANDIDATE EVALUATION MATRIX FOR THE REORDERS–SALES ANALYSIS SYSTEM

Candidate System Criteria	A	B	D
Performance			
Response time	Fair	Very good	Excellent
Error correction	Poor	Very good	Excellent
Flexibility	Good	Very good	Excellent
Growth	Excellent	Very good	Very good
Usability	Fair	Good	Excellent
Cost (10 stores)			
System development	$20,000	$35,000	$50,000
Communications	$ 4,000/mo.	$ 7,000/mo.	$ 1,000/mo.
Local storage	-0-	-0-	$ 2,000/mo.
Local terminal	$ 2,000/mo.	$ 5,000/mo.	$10,000/mo.
Central storage (increment)	$ 1,000/mo.	$ 1,000/mo.	$ 100/mo.
Central processing (increment)	$ 500/mo.	$ 200/mo.	$ 100/mo.

3. Candidate D uses programmable terminals at each store. These terminals are minicomputers that process transactions as they occur and also maintain local files. Both CRT and printed output are available at each store. Only summary information is transmitted to the central site. This information is transmitted at the end of each working day by means of a dial-up simplex line. No record of individual transactions is maintained at the central site.[1]

The first column of the candidate evaluation matrix (Table 9-3) contains the performance and cost features used to compare each candidate. In this example, the performance criteria selected by the team are: response time, error correction, flexibility, growth, and usability. The cost factors are: system development, communications, local storage, local terminal, central storage, and central processing. The entries in columns A, B, and D are the results of the detailed evaluation of each candidate by the team. They are relative results that are expressed in consistent terms across the rows of the matrix for each feature. Within a column, the units vary. Some entries may be qualitative, and others may be quantitative. The qualitative entries (that is, "fair," "good," "excellent") are a team consensus and could have resulted from quantitative considerations. For example, candidate A might have had a data rate of 200 characters per minute for transmission to the central site and might have required 36 hours for return of information by mail—resulting in an overall response time rating of "fair." Similarly, the response time of candidate B could have been rated as "very good" because of its full-duplex communication capability, and that of candidate D as "excellent" because of its independence of central-site processing.

In this particular matrix, all costs are expressed in dollars or dollars per month. System A appears to be the least costly but the poorest in performance; system D appears to be most expensive but best in performance. However, it is difficult to use this matrix to assign quantitative, numeric rankings to each candidate. We can overcome this difficulty by next preparing a different type of matrix, called a **weighted candidate evaluation matrix.**

Weighted candidate evaluation matrix   Because qualitative measures are difficult to compare, the systems team converts the candidate evaluation matrix into a weighted candidate evaluation matrix. Each feature of a candidate system is given a value based upon the importance of that feature. Table 9-4 is a weighted candidate evaluation matrix for our sample system. In this instance, the weighting scale has a range from 1 to 5. Usability, for example was considered by the team to be the most important feature, and it was given a weight of 5.

---

[1] The data flow diagram of Figure 9-7, the system flowchart of Figure 9-10, and the hierarchy chart of Figure 9-11 describe Candidate D. Equivalent flowcharts would be prepared for all of the candidates selected to be evaluated in detail.

TABLE 9-4
WEIGHTED CANDIDATE EVALUATION MATRIX FOR THE REORDERS–SALES ANALYSIS SYSTEM

Candidate system criteria	Weight	A		B		D	
		Rating	Score	Rating	Score	Rating	Score
Performance							
Response time	3	2	6	4	12	6	18
Error correction	4	1	4	5	20	6	24
Flexibility	4	3	12	4	16	5	20
Growth	3	7	21	5	15	5	15
Usability	5	2	10	5	25	7	35
Cost (10 stores)							
System development	3	7	21	4	12	2	6
Communications	4	4	16	2	8	6	24
Local storage	2	7	14	7	14	3	6
Local terminal	2	6	12	4	8	2	4
Central storage	2	3	6	3	6	6	12
Central processing	1	3	3	5	5	6	6
Cost effectiveness score			125		141		170

After the weights are established, each feature of each candidate is assigned a numerical rating, relative to the same feature for all other candidates. Thus, in the example of Table 9-4, the systems team rated candidate A 2 for response time and candidates B and C, 4 and 6, respectively, for the same feature. The rating scale need not be the same as that used to assign weights. In our example, the rating scale is 1 to 7.

The cost-effectiveness score for each candidate is its total score. The systems team calculates this total in two steps. First, all rating entries in the weighted candidate evaluation matrix are multiplied by their weights. Thus, for candidate A, response time received a score of 6, error correction a score of 4, and so on. Next, the scores assigned to each feature are added up to arrive at the total for each candidate. This total is the cost-effectiveness of each candidate, relative to all other candidates. In the example, candidate A has a cost-effectiveness score of 125; B has a score of 141; and D has a score of 170.

SYSTEM RECOMMENDATION

On the basis of the cost-effectiveness scores shown in Table 9-4, the team would recommend candidate D, with a score of 170. An advantage of the use of evaluation matrices is that the user can easily review the decision process. He or she may not agree with the conclusions of the team. Should this occur, the value of the evaluation matrices becomes apparent. Working together, the user and the team can modify any part of the matrices. They can add or delete features and change weights and ratings until they agree upon the most cost-effective candidate.

For our sample Reorders–Sales Analysis system, some of the most significant differences between candidates were in the scoring of response time, error correction, usability, and communications. The user could have made different judgments about these or other entries. Cost might be a more important issue than the team had supposed. For example, Table 9-3 shows that total operating costs (communications, local storage, local terminals, central storage, and central processing) for each of the systems are:

Candidate A: $ 7,500 per month
Candidate B: $13,200 per month
Candidate D: $13,200 per month

The user might decide that candidates B and D were too expensive and assign larger weights to each of the cost components of the weighted candidate evaluation matrix (Table 9-4). Usually, though, the user is involved with the team throughout the feasibility analysis, and the recommendations of the team are accepted.

FEEDBACK

9-9 Identify and describe the four steps of a feasibility analysis.
9-10 Distinguish between:
    a A candidate system matrix
    b A candidate evaluation matrix
    c A weighted candidate evaluation matrix
9-11 What is the purpose of a systems flowchart?
9-12 What is a hierarchy chart?

PROJECT PLAN AND COST SCHEDULE

One important documentation task that the systems selection team must also perform is the preparation of a project plan and a cost schedule. These should be provided to the user along with the results of the feasibility analysis. The **project plan** identifies the major design- and development-phase activities, called *milestones*, and is a method of reporting progress toward completing them. Figure 9-12 is a sample project plan prepared for candidate D.[2] In this figure, the open horizontal bars represent estimates of the times needed to complete the milestone activities. The analyst reports cumulative progress by filling in these bars. As an example of how a project plan chart might look at the end of the second month of the design phase, consider Figure 9-13, which is drawn to show a project that is on schedule. This figure shows that three design-phase activities have been completed and that three additional design activities, including documentation, are partially complete. Notice that the development-phase documentation also is partially complete. This is true be-

---

[2] The milestones listed in Figure 9-12 are explained in Chapter 10, which follows.

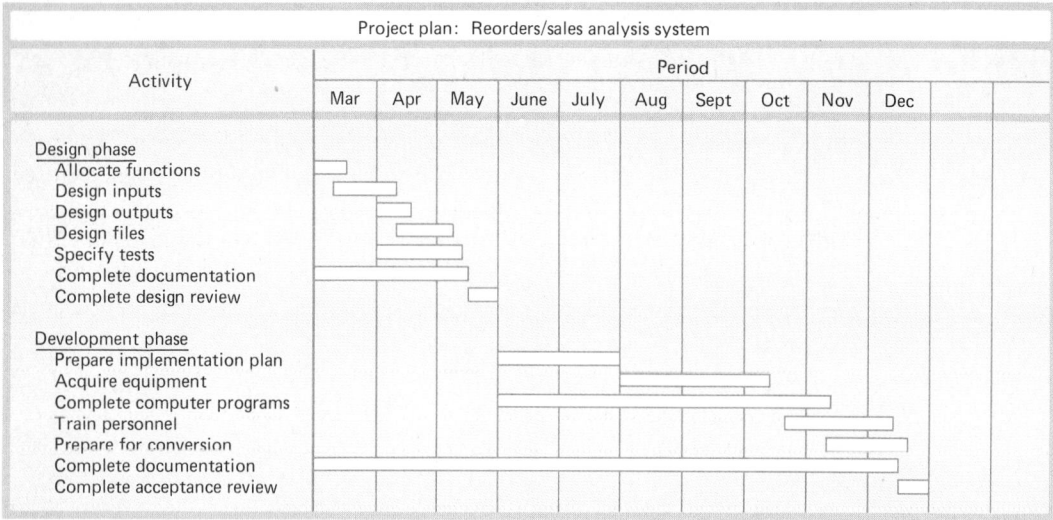

FIGURE 9-12

Project plan.

FIGURE 9-13

The project plan at the end of the second month.

cause documentation is continuous and cumulative. That is, the documentation of earlier phases is incorporated into the documentation of later phases.

The systems analyst also prepares a **cost schedule** to go along with the project plan. In Figure 9-14 estimated cumulative costs are shown by a solid line. Again, looking ahead at a possible design-phase cost report, we observe, in Figure 9-15, that a colored line is added to show actual expenses. In this example, the project exceeded planned cost at the end of the first month and is slightly below planned cost by the end of the second month.

Returning to our study-phase example, we observe that the planned total cost shown in Figure 9-14 corresponds to the total development cost of $50,000 that was presented in the candidate evaluation matrix of Table 9-3.

The results of the study-phase activities, including the project plan and cost schedule, usually are presented to the user as a formal report, called a **study-phase report.** The user reviews this report, and, upon approval by the user, the project moves into the next life-cycle phase, the design phase.

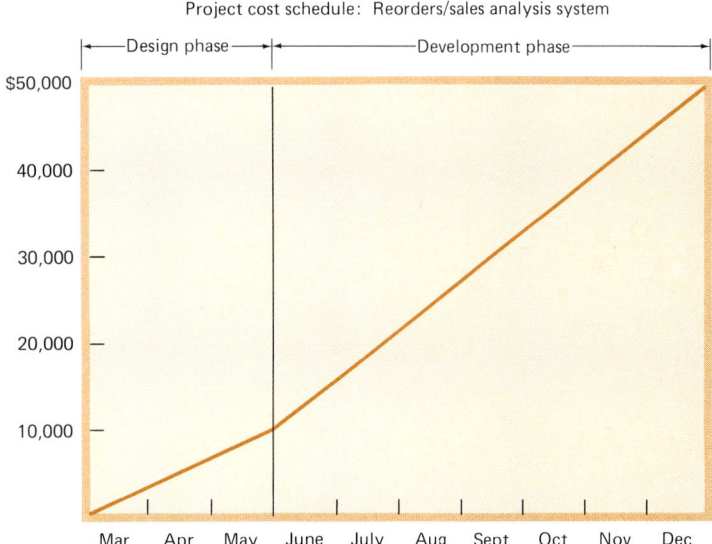

FIGURE 9-14

Project cost schedule.

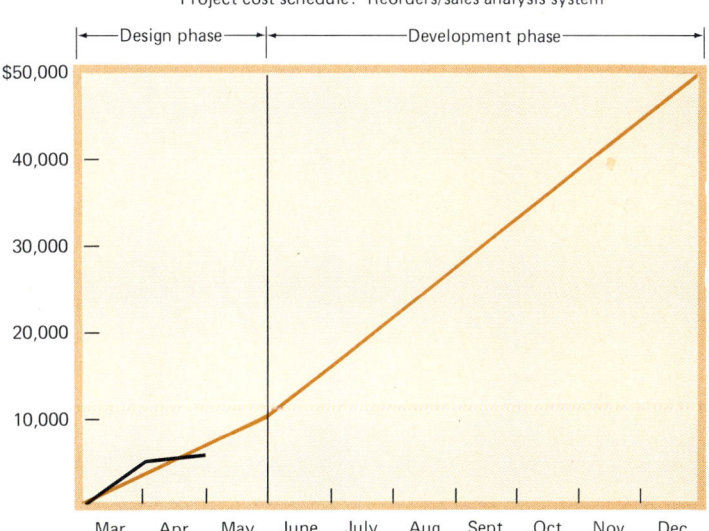

FIGURE 9-15

The project cost schedule at the end of the second month.

FEEDBACK   **9-13** What is a project plan, and how is it used to report progress?
9-14 What is project cost schedule, and how is it used to report costs?
9-15 What is a study-phase report?

SUMMARY   In the computer information system life cycle, the study phase is the phase in which the problem is identified and the best system selected for its solution. Problem identification begins with the recognition of a need for a new or improved system and with the preparation of an initial information service request (ISR). This ISR contains information about the objectives and benefits of the proposed system and about its outputs and inputs. Usually, the systems analyst performs an initial investigation in order to clarify the problem and to acquire background in the problem area. As a result of the initial investigation, the ISR—which may be modified—becomes a contract between the user and the analyst.

Next, the performance expected of the system is defined. This is accomplished by identifying general constraints, specific objectives, and the outputs by which these objectives are to be accomplished. Data flow diagrams are used to describe data flows and transformations in the existing system. They are also useful in studying logical solutions without premature consideration of methods of physical implementation. System flowcharts provide physical detail about the system, and hierarchy charts describe the functions to be performed by the system. Outputs are illustrated by sketches, called layouts, so that the user of the system can visualize the information that the system will provide. Usually, there are a large number of potential, or alternative, systems that can produce the desired outputs. These systems are called candidate systems, and a feasibility analysis must be performed to select the best alternative.

The feasibility analysis begins with the formation of a systems team. The systems-team members have knowledge and experience related to the business problem areas. The team usually suggests many possible alternative systems. These are reduced to a manageable number of candidates by consensus of the systems team, and detailed cost-effectiveness comparisons are made of the remaining candidates.

The cost-effectiveness evaluation makes use of three tables, or matrices:

1. A candidate system matrix, which identifies the functions that all candidate systems must perform and the general manner in which they are to be performed by each

2. A candidate evaluation matrix, which identifies the performance and cost criteria by which alternative systems are to be evaluated and displays their relative evaluations.

3. A weighted candidate evaluation matrix, which modifies the (unweighted) candidate evaluation matrix by applying weighted numeric ratings to score each candidate in a uniform manner.

The candidate with the highest score is recommended to the user as the best system. The recommendation is accompanied by a project plan and a cost schedule for the design and development phases. With the approval of the user, the project enters the design phase of the system development life cycle.

ANSWERS TO FEEDBACK QUESTIONS

9-1 To select a system.

9-2 A user or a systems analyst may discover the need for a system.

9-3 A form, called an information service request, that is used to request services from the information systems organization.

9-4 To clarify a problem and to complete the analyst's understanding of it.

9-5 A data flow diagram is a network that describes data flows and transformations thoughout a system.

9-6 **a** Recognition of limits—establishing the constraints that are the ground rules for all candidate systems.

   b Statement of objectives—statement of the benefits of the system in measurable terms, as far as possible.

   c Description of outputs—sketch or picture of all outputs that the system is to produce.

9-7 Tangible benefits are measurable, often in "before" and "after" terms. Intangible benefits are not immediately evident or directly measurable.

9-8 To provide the user with a picture of a system output for review and comment.

9-9 **a** Form the systems team—assigning experienced persons to work with the systems analyst.

   b Describe system data flow—preparing data flow diagrams, systems flowcharts, and/or hierarchy charts to describe data flow in a system.

   c Select candidate systems—identifying potential solutions and reducing them to a manageable number.

   d Evaluate selected candidate systems—preparing a candidate evaluation matrix and then a weighted candidate evaluation matrix in order to select the most cost-effective system.

9-10 **a** Identifies the functions that all candidates selected for detailed evaluation must perform.

   b Identifies the performance and cost criteria by which candidate systems are to be evaluated.

   c Applies weighted numeric ratings in order to rank the candidates listed in the candidate evaluation matrix.

9-11 To describe the flow of data in a system by means of predefined symbols, many of which resemble actual devices.

9-12 A hierarchy chart is a top-down graphical presentation of the functions to be performed by a system.

9-13 A horizontal bar chart that identifies major milestones. The analyst fills in the bars to report the completion of work stages.

9-14 A chart that is used to compare actual cumulative costs with planned costs.

9-15 A formal report that is prepared at the end of the study phase. It contains the results of the study-phases activities and the recommendations of the project team.

FOR REVIEW AND DISCUSSION

1 Identify and describe briefly the purpose of each of the four major activities in the system selection process.

2 What is the difference between an initial and a final version of an ISR?

3 Why do we define system outputs in the study phase before we define inputs?

4 What are general constraints?

5 Why is it important to state system outputs in a measurable way whenever possible?

6 Why can't we be certain that we have selected the best solution?

7 What types of symbols are used to prepare system flowcharts?

8 Discuss the advantages of hierarchy charts.

9 Explain how a systems analyst would use project plans and project cost schedules to manage a computer-based information system project.

10 What are the two principal functions served by data flow diagrams that are described in this chapter?

CHAPTER 10

SYSTEM DESIGN AND DEVELOPMENT PHASES

PREVIEW   The computer information system selected in the study phase must be designed and developed before it can be operated for its users. The systems team adds the additional personnel needed to perform specialized design and development tasks. The goal of this chapter is to explain the major design-phase tasks and to acquaint you with significant development-phase activities. You will continue to work with the example introduced in Chapter 9. You will study input, output, and file design, and you will become familiar with the development-phase implementation plan.

In this chapter you will learn:

1. The use of expanded system flowcharts and hierarchy charts as general system design tools

2. The rules for effective input design

3. The use of computer print charts and information display system layout sheets in output design

4. What data should be stored on a master file

5. The purpose of and functions performed by data base management systems (DBMS)

6. The major system development activities

KEY TERMS TO WATCH FOR AND REMEMBER

expanded system flowchart
input, process, output (IPO) chart
HIPO chart
computer print chart
information display system layout sheet

data base management system (DBMS)
system tests
computer program tests
implementation
implementation plan
changeover plan

SYSTEM DESIGN   The candidate system selected in the study phase must be designed and then developed. The design-phase activities are an extension, in detail, of the description of the selected system begun in the study phase. In the development phase, the system is "built" to meet the design-phase specification. We will continue to use the Reorders–Sales Analysis system example of the previous chapter to explain the principal design-phase activities and to illustrate the system development process.

System design follows the project plan developed at the end of the study phase (Figure 9-10). The major activities that the systems team undertakes are:

1. General system design
2. Input, output, and file design
3. Design-phase documentation
4. Design-phase review

As necessary, the team adds design specialists. For example, persons skilled in the design of forms for recording input or output data, individuals with in-depth knowledge about a business area—such as inventory—and specialists in data entry devices could be added to the team. They could serve as needed or as full-time team members throughout the design phase. In the next few sections, we will describe the activities that the design team performs.

General System Design

As soon as the design phase begins, the systems design team starts to refine the flowcharts prepared during the study phase of the system development life cycle. Each study-phase flowchart is reviewed for completeness and accuracy. The team then decides upon the best way for the system to perform each of the required data processing functions. All functions will be performed in one of three ways: (1) as a manual task; (2) as an equipment (hardware) task; or (3) as a computer program (software) task. All of the functions should appear on the system flowchart with the method of performance indicated by the appropriate flowchart symbols. Figure 10-1 shows the flowchart for candidate D, which was selected as the system for the Reorders–Sales Analysis system in Chapter 9.

Figure 10-1 is the same as Figure 9-10, prepared for candidate D in the preceding chapter. As you recall, candidate D not only allows for data transmission to the central site for regional inventory management but also provides each store in the region with a distributed data processing capability. As Figure 10-1 shows, each store performs local data processing and file maintenance. Summary information, such as total sales of a particular item, is sent to the central site so that one inventory order can be placed for the region. Each store has available hard-copy sales and inventory data, as indicated by the document symbols, and soft-copy CRT outputs, as shown by the display symbols. Thus, in the distributed data processing system selected, the daily management of inventory and sales is the responsibility of each store. Regional management reviews summary data and performs an inventory reorders service for all stores.

As an example of the need for specialists on the systems design team, consider that a programmable minicomputer will be needed at each store. Because of the very large number of such systems to choose from, the systems team must perform a study of alternatives to select the best system. This activity requires the participation of specialists who are knowledgeable about minicomputers and communications. Note also that the feasibility analysis techniques that we described in Chapter 9 can be applied again. As a matter of fact, there are many opportunities for their use throughout the life-cycle process. As the team becomes more deeply involved in the design process, these analyses decrease in scope and increase in detail. To illustrate, a special point-of-sale terminal might be needed as a component of the selected minicomputer system. Another study of alternatives could be performed in order to select the most appropriate terminal.

An example of a manual task is the entry of inventory data received at the central site. The systems symbol for a manual input identifies this activity on the flowchart of Figure 10-1. The use of equipment to perform all of the actual processing of data is implied by the online storage and the processing symbols used in this figure. The use of computer programs is indicated by entries such as "local sales-inventory program" and "central-site inventory-sales program" inside the process symbols.

All of the system functions that are not performed manually or by equipment are accomplished through the logic of computer programs. Therefore, it is necessary to identify all of the processing steps required before undertaking the development-phase activity of preparing computer programs. In order to do this, the team must examine the system in greater detail. One technique is to expand a high-level system flowchart—such as Figure 10-1 or parts of it—into sufficient detail to identify the inputs, outputs, and files associated with each processing program. Thus, in our example, the major computer programs are the local sales-inventory program and the central-site inventory-sales program. Figure 10-2 is an **expanded system flowchart** for the central-site inventory-sales program.

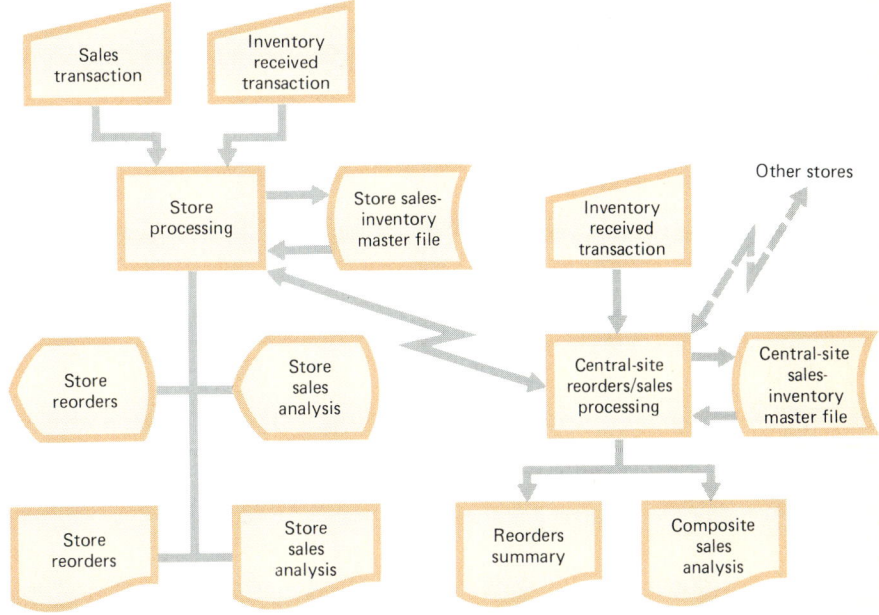

FIGURE 10-1

System flowchart for reorders/sales analysis system (Candidate D).

The programs shown in this figure illustrate four operations that are characteristic of most business data processing systems.

1. Editing input data to ensure its validity
2. Sorting edited data into a sequence for efficient processing
3. Producing meaningful output information
4. Updating a master file (a part of the fundamental business data processing cycle that we described in Chapter 5)

Another technique that is a compatible alternative or supplement to the expanded system flowchart is the expansion of a hierarchy chart into a series of **input, process, output charts,** called **IPO charts**. To continue our example, Figure 10-3 is an IPO chart for the central-site inventory-sales master file update module shown in Figure 10-2.

This IPO chart is also keyed to the hierarchy chart of Figure 9-11, prepared during the feasibility analysis and system selection process described in Chapter 9. Collectively, hierarchy charts and IPO charts are called **HIPO charts,** which means hierarchy plus input, output, processing charts. As this example illustrates, a feature of IPO charts is that they are an effective means of using short, meaningful sentences to describe the processing operations that are required.

After the allocation of functions between manual tasks, equipment tasks, and computer program tasks has been completed, the systems team undertakes the detailed design of inputs, outputs, and files.

Input Design

Input design is the process of converting an external, user-oriented description of the inputs to a system into a machine-oriented format. In most business systems, inputs are generated by devices operated by humans. In these cases, the input design must take into account the human element in order to ensure rapid and accurate data entry from a source document. This will prevent error and speed up data entry. Two important rules to follow in designing source documents for data entry are:

FIGURE 10-2

Expanded system flowchart of the local sales/inventory component for reorders/sales analysis system (Candidate D). The repeated use of the on-line storage symbol does not mean that more than one on-line storage device, such as a magnetic disk, must be used. Input data, intermediate processing results, and results ready to be outputted can be stored at different locations on the same device.

1. Lay out the data elements in a sequence that the data entry operator can follow easily. The normal sequence of data entry is from left to right and from top to bottom of the page.
2. Group the data elements to be entered separately from those that are

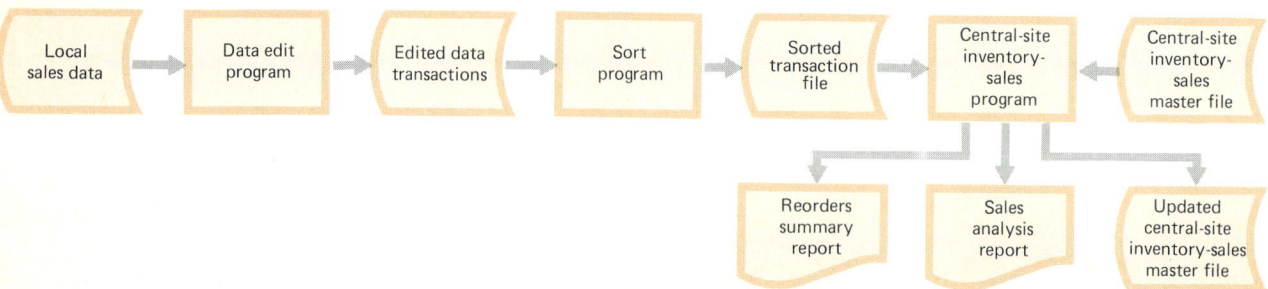

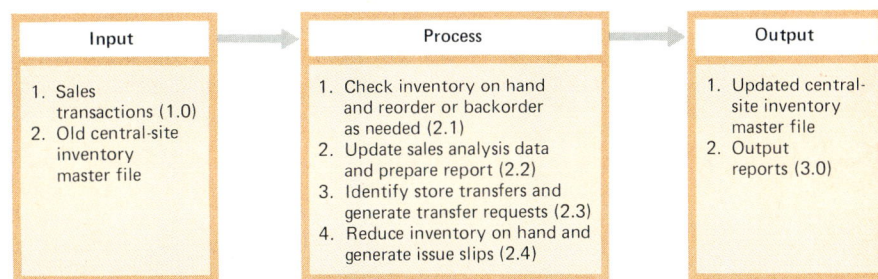

FIGURE 10-3

IPO chart for update central-site inventory master file—Box 2.0 of reorder/sales analysis system (see Figure 9-9).

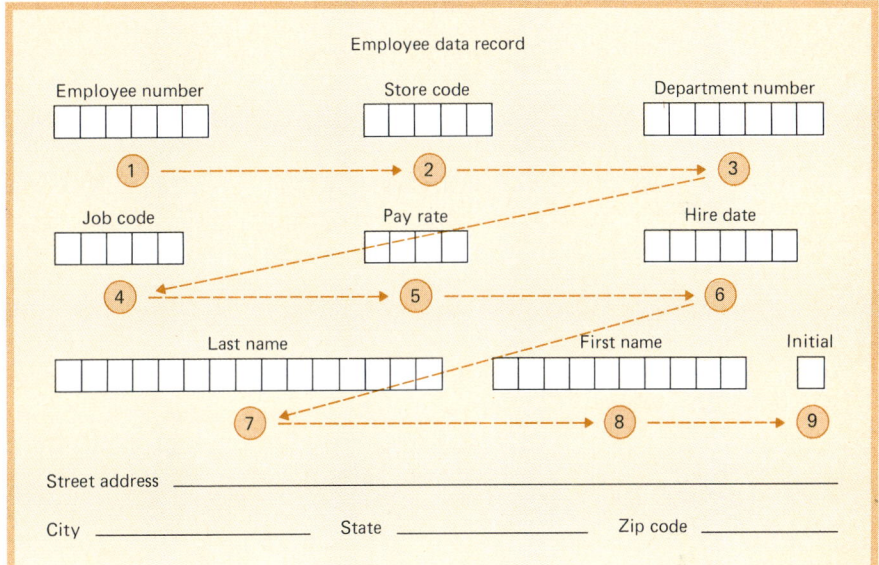

FIGURE 10-4

Example of a well-designed source document for data entry.

not to be entered. This means that the data entry operator does not have to hesitate while skipping over fields that are not to be stored or processed.

Figure 10-4 is an example of good input design. All of the design rules are followed. In addition, "boxes" are provided to identify the data that are to be entered from the source document.

As we have learned, key-to-tape, key-to-disk, and other types of direct data entry devices are used as means of converting data into a machine-readable digital format for subsequent processing.

Often data are entered directly by an operator who is prompted by a CRT display. Figure 10-5a shows a CRT screen display designed to prompt the operator as input entries are made. CRT input design must take into account the dimensions of the screen. Typical dimensions are 24 rows by 80 columns, giving a display potential of 1920 characters. Figure 10-5b is a photograph of an actual screen layout for the sample system.

The principal source of computer output error is not faulty processing.

Rather, it is faulty input. Therefore, it is wise for the designer to indroduce techniques that minimize the need for human operations. As an example, a product code entered by means of a CRT terminal can be used to retrieve a description of the product from computer storage without the need to wait for the operator to key in the description and without the risk of human error. Similarly, sales total and tax computations can be performed automatically. As another example, many stores are using OCR devices to scan customer account number symbols that are embossed on a credit card. This eliminates human transcription of numbers. Laser-beam scanners, such as used in supermarkets, are another means of eliminating human data errors.

FEEDBACK

10-1 Why may additional members be added to the systems team during the design phase?

10-2 What are the three ways in which system functions can be performed? Give an example of each.

10-3 What is the purpose of an expanded system flowchart?

10-4 What is an IPO chart? How does it relate to a HIPO chart?

10-5 What is a subprogram?

Output Design

The design of system outputs starts in the study phase with the information service request (ISR). The ISR leads to the preparation of the report specification layout sketches, such as those shown in Figure 9-6. In the design phase, these layouts become the reference for computer print charts for outputs to be produced by a printer. **Computer print charts** differ from layout sketches in detail. They show the exact location of all of the lines of characters, the spacing between lines, totals and subtotals, and the editing of data fields. Figure 10-6 is an example of a computer print chart for a standard print line of 132 positions.

FIGURE 10-5
CRT input display. (a) CRT input prompting format. (b) Actual CRT input display.

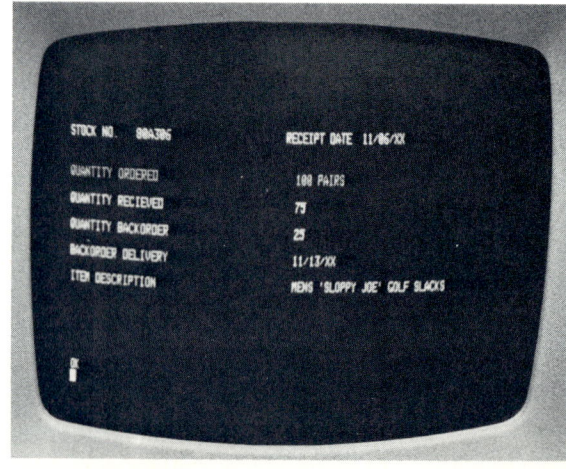

(a)   (b)

FIGURE 10-6

Computer print chart.

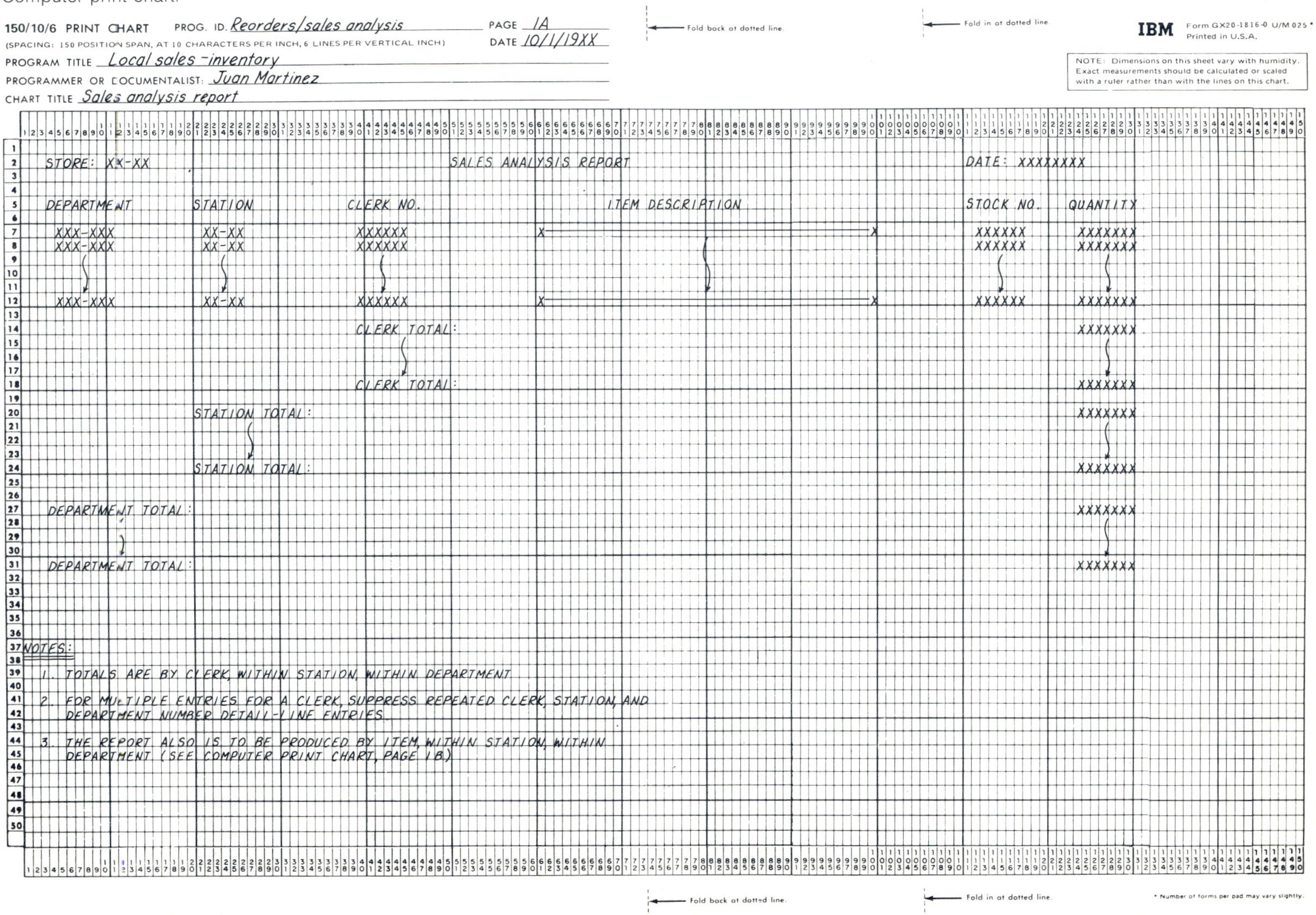

150/10/6 PRINT CHART   PROG. ID. *Reorders/sales analysis*   PAGE *1A*

(SPACING: 150 POSITION SPAN, AT 10 CHARACTERS PER INCH, 6 LINES PER VERTICAL INCH)   DATE *10/11/19XX*

PROGRAM TITLE *Local sales - inventory*

PROGRAMMER OR DOCUMENTALIST: *Juan Martinez*

CHART TITLE *Sales analysis report*

SALES ANALYSIS REPORT

STORE: XX-XX   DATE: XXXXXXXX

DEPARTMENT   STATION   CLERK NO.   ITEM DESCRIPTION   STOCK NO.   QUANTITY

XXX-XXX   XX-XX   XXXXXX   XXXXX   XXXXXXX
XXX-XXX   XX-XX   XXXXXX   XXXXXX   XXXXXXX

XXX-XXX   XX-XX   XXXXXX   XXXXX   XXXXXXX

CLERK TOTAL: XXXXXXX

STATION TOTAL: XXXXXXX

CLERK TOTAL: XXXXXXX

STATION TOTAL: XXXXXXX

DEPARTMENT TOTAL: XXXXXXX

DEPARTMENT TOTAL: XXXXXXX

NOTES:

1. TOTALS ARE BY CLERK WITHIN STATION, WITHIN DEPARTMENT

2. FOR MULTIPLE ENTRIES FOR A CLERK, SUPPRESS REPEATED CLERK STATION, AND DEPARTMENT NUMBER DETAIL-LINE ENTRIES.

3. THE REPORT ALSO IS TO BE PRODUCED BY ITEM WITHIN STATION WITHIN DEPARTMENT (SEE COMPUTER PRINT CHART, PAGE 1B).

IBM   Form GX20-1816-0 U/M 025 *
Printed in U.S.A.

NOTE: Dimensions on this sheet vary with humidity. Exact measurements should be calculated or scaled with a ruler rather than with the lines on this chart.

→ Fold in at dotted line

→ Fold back at dotted line

* Number of forms per pad may vary slightly.

THANK YOU FOR SHOPPING AT m
MAY CO

PLEASE SHOW ANY ADDRESS CHANGE

STREET_____ CITY_____ STATE_____ ZIP_____

MARY SMITH   23 4421 0246 REGULAR
15 MAPLE DRIVE
ANYWHERE, U.S.A.   043365   A

P.O. BOX 30522 TERMINAL ANNEX   AMOUNT PAID $_____
LOS ANGELES, CALIFORNIA 90030   TO INSURE PROPER CREDIT PLEASE RETURN
                                        THIS PORTION WITH YOUR PAYMENT

2344210246100062430000000000006243   **

TO AVOID **FINANCE CHARGE** NEXT MONTH, PAY THE "NEW BALANCE" IN FULL BEFORE YOUR BILLING DATE NEXT MONTH.

PREVIOUS BALANCE	FINANCE CHARGE	PURCHASES	PAYMENTS	CREDITS	BILLING DATE	NEW BALANCE
24.38	.00	62.43	24.38	.00	05-10-84	62.43

DATE	REFERENCE NO.	STORE-DEPT.		DESCRIPTION	AMOUNT
May 06	00060014			PAYMENT-THANK YOU	24.38CR
May 07	24711062	6	831	LINENS-TOWELS-RUGS	15.84
May 07	24711060	6	803	DOMESTICS-BEDDING,	46.59
			845	DOMESTICS - BEDDING	
				**	
				IT'S OUR 55TH ANNIVERSARY SALE WITH THE LOWEST	
				PRICES OF THE YEAR. COURTESY DAYS MAY 17, 18, 19.	

YOUR **FINANCE CHARGE**, IF ANY, IS FIGURED ON THE PREVIOUS BALANCE BEFORE DEDUCTING ANY PAYMENTS OR CREDITS SHOWN ABOVE

WHEN MAKING INQUIRY REFER TO ACCOUNT NO.	PAST DUE AMOUNT	PAYMENT NOW DUE
23 4421 0246 REGULAR		62.43

PERIODIC RATES USED ARE 1½% OF THE ABOVE DETERMINED BALANCE IN AMOUNTS OF **$1,000** OR LESS, AND 1%
OF AMOUNTS IN EXCESS OF **$1,000** WHICH ARE **ANNUAL PERCENTAGE RATES** OF **18%** and **12%** RESPECTIVELY.

G-3101 (REV. 6-77)   NOTICE: SEE REVERSE SIDE FOR IMPORTANT INFORMATION

FIGURE 10-7
Customer charge account statement.

This computer print chart represents the output design for the sample sales analysis report sketched in Figure 9-6*b* of the previous chapter. A print chart such as this becomes a detailed guide for the programmer during the development phase.

When printed outputs are prepared for customers, they often are printed on special forms. Figure 10-7, which is a customer charge account statement, is an example of the layout of a special form of this type.

Not all computer output is printed. We have described other computer output media, such as plotters and CRT displays. Figure 10-8 is an example of an **information display system layout sheet** for the CRT display of comparative store sales summaries for the Reorders–Sales Analysis system. This sheet is useful not only for designing output displays but also for designing input displays, such as shown in Figure 10-5.

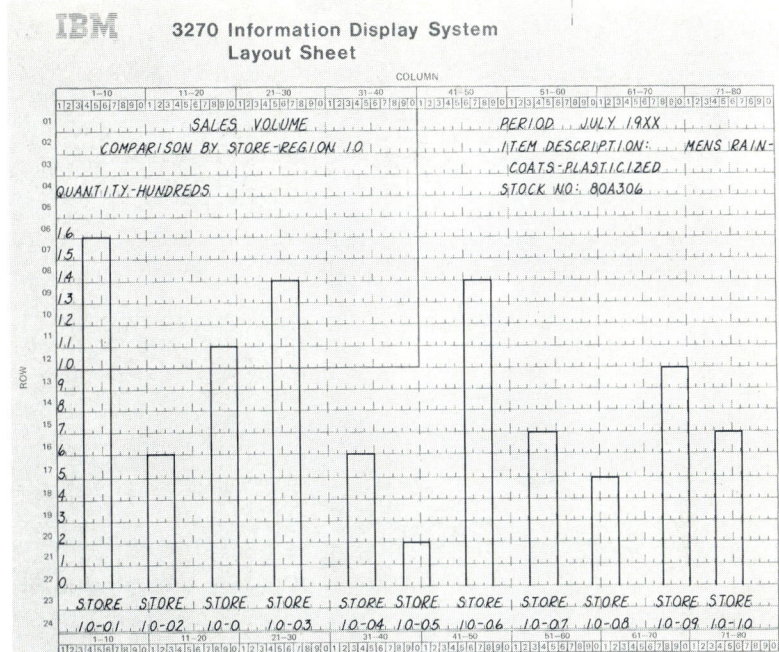

FIGURE 10-8

Information display system layout sheet—comparative store summary sales.

As the flowchart of Figure 10-2 demonstrates, many of the outputs produced by individual computer programs within a system—sometimes called subprograms—are intermediate results. These results are stored on files. Examples are the edited and sorted data transaction files and the current and updated master files. Therefore, file design is an important concern of the systems design team.

File Design

Data files are critical elements of computer information systems because many processing steps require the use of stored data. In order to design effective files, the systems analyst must answer the following questions:

1. What processing steps require the use of files?
2. What data must be stored in files?
3. What storage media should be used?

What processing steps require the use of files?   The processing steps that require the use of files are established as part of the general design of the system. Thus, Figure 10-2 illustrated some typical processing steps requiring the use of files. The files shown were input transactions, edited transactions, sorted transactions, the current master file, and the updated master file. In this section, we will focus upon the most important file, the master file.

TABLE 10-1
MASTER FILE REQUIREMENTS ANALYSIS–SALES ANALYSIS REPORT

	Output report: sales analysis		
Input element	Processing operation	Output field(s)	Master file required?
Stock number	Output fields created from stored data keyed to stock number	Stock number, department, item description	Yes
Station	Input field moved to output	Station	No
Clerk number	Input field moved to output	Clerk number	No
Quantity	Input field moved to output and also stored in main memory to accumulate clerk, station, and department totals. Department totals stored in master file for later transmission of summary data to central site.	Quantity	No
		Clerk, station, and department totals	Yes

What data must be stored in a master file?   The data that must be stored in a master file are determined by examining the sources of the output data elements, or fields. There are three ways to create these fields. First, data can be moved from an input file to an output report area without modification. Second, output data can be created as the result of arithmetic or logical processing operations. Third, output data can be obtained from a master file. In the first way, there is no storage requirement. In the second, a master file may or may not be involved. In the third way, of course, a master file is required. Table 10-1, which shows the master file storage requirement for the Sales Analysis report output of the sample Reorders–Sales Analysis system, illustrates each method of creating output fields. The output fields listed in this table correspond to the output specification prepared in the study phase (Figure 9-6*b*) and to the computer print chart prepared in the design phase (Figure 10-6). As Table 10-1 shows, station and clerk numbers are moved directly to output positions without the use of a master file. Quantity is moved directly to an output area; however, it also must be stored in the master file in order to accumulate clerk, station, and department totals. Department totals are kept in the master file for later transmission to the central site. Stock number is used to retrieve department and item description data previously stored on the master file. This reduces the amount of data that the sales clerk has to enter and eliminates a source of potential error.

The size of the master file can be estimated by adding up the number of characters in the fields that make up one master file record and then multiplying this total by the number of records that must be stored. For example, if the sizes of the fields stored in the master file were:

Stock number: 6 characters
Department: 7 characters

Item description:	40 characters
Clerk total quantity:	6 characters
Station total quantity:	7 characters
Department total quantity:	8 characters

each record would be 74 characters in size. If 5000 transactions had to be processed, the file would have to have sufficient capacity to store 370,000 characters.

What storage media should be used?   The selection of the storage media to be used for a file depends upon the manner in which the file is to be accessed and organized, the amount of data that must be stored, and how rapidly it must be made available to main memory. In Chapter 5 we learned about different types of storage media. These included magnetic tape devices, magnetic disks, and electronic storage devices such as magnetic bubble memory and charge-coupled devices. As you may recall, tape is an effective medium for processing large, active files. However, tape files must be organized and accessed sequentially. If there is a significant requirement to process unsequenced records, then file organizations such as direct or indexed-sequential must be considered, and a medium such as magnetic disk, which permits the random access of data records, should be selected.

Data Base Management Systems (DBMS)

Most business data processing systems require access to a master file. In the past (and in many instances today) programmers set up their own files. If more than one program had to use the same fields of data, these fields often were stored in more than one file. This practice caused a great deal of duplicated data to be stored. In addition, because the files containing duplicate data usually were not updated at the same time, there were frequent discrepancies among reports produced from different files.

Advances in computer hardware and software have produced data storage and management systems that can provide the same data to many programmers. These systems are called **data base management systems** (**DBMS**). As Figure 10-9 shows, the principal components of a data base management system are a

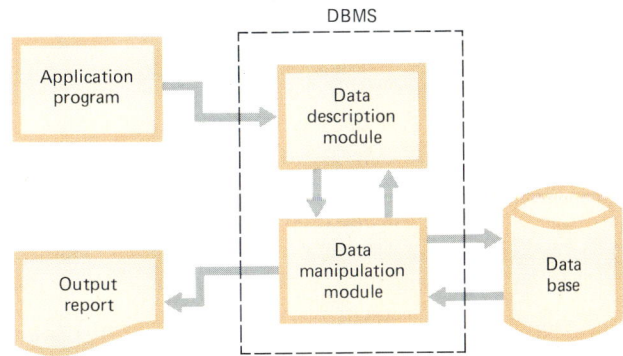

FIGURE 10-9
Data base management system (DBMS) modules.

data description module and a data manipulation module. The data description module of the DBMS analyzes the data requirements of the applications program and transfers control to the data manipulation module, which retrieves the needed data elements from the data base.

Data base management systems free the programmer from the need to worry about the organization and location of data. All of the data needed by an application program can be accessed, regardless of access method, record location, or record content. Programming is speeded up because the programmer can concentrate upon the logic of the application. Most DBMS are designed to interact with the commonly used programming languages such as COBOL and FORTRAN and others that are discussed in subsequent chapters. Many DBMS include special, user-friendly query languages. These languages can be learned readily by nonprogramming users of the system, enabling them to access the data base for information as needed.

FEEDBACK

10-6 What is a computer print chart?

10-7 Where are intermediate processing results stored?

10-8 What is an information display system layout sheet used for?

10-9 What is a DBMS? What are its advantages?

Test Requirements

All computer information systems should be tested thoroughly before they are operated. An important design-phase activity is to specify the tests that must be performed throughout the development phase to demonstrate that the system is functioning properly. There are two major types of tests: **system tests** and **computer program tests.** The system tests are called external tests because they evaluate how well the entire system, of which the computer software is only one component, works. The computer program tests are called internal tests because they are tests of all of the subprograms that make up the overall computer program. The requirements for testing the complete system, including its human and equipment interfaces, are established first, because they determine some of the computer program tests.

Design-Phase Documentation

Before the design of an information system can be considered finished, a complete design-phase report must be prepared and reviewed. Actually, system documentation is an ongoing, cumulative process. The documentation that began in the study phase is added to throughout the design phase. At the end of the design phase, this documentation includes a complete technical specification of the external and internal aspects of the system. The external specification describes the design of the human-oriented system inputs and outputs and the system test requirements. The internal specification relates to the computer program and its components. It includes the data flowcharts, the file design, and the requirements for testing the computer program. The design specification is the "blueprint" from which the system is constructed in the development phase.

Design-Phase Review

After all of the design-phase activities and documentation have been completed, a review of the project is held by the management of the organization that will use the system. The purpose of this review is to decide whether or not to proceed with the development of the system. The design-phase review is a critical review because approval initiates the development-phase activities. The cost of the resources required to develop the actual system usually are much greater than the cost of studying the problem and designing the solution.

The outcome of the design-phase review may vary from approval to proceed to cancellation of the project. Often, the project team is instructed to "cycle" back and redo certain activities (an example of the life cycle at work) before approval is granted. After a favorable design-phase review, the project is ready to enter the development phase.

SYSTEM DEVELOPMENT
Development Phase Activities: An Overview

The major development-phase activities, identified in the previous chapter as project plan milestones (Figure 9-12) are:

1. Prepare implementation plan.
2. Acquire equipment.
3. Complete computer programs.
4. Train personnel.
5. Prepare for conversion.
6. Complete documentation.
7. Complete acceptance review.

Figure 10-10 is an overview of these important development-phase activities. As this figure shows, many of the development activities are performed concurrently. We will describe each of these activities.

FIGURE 10-10
Development-phase activities.

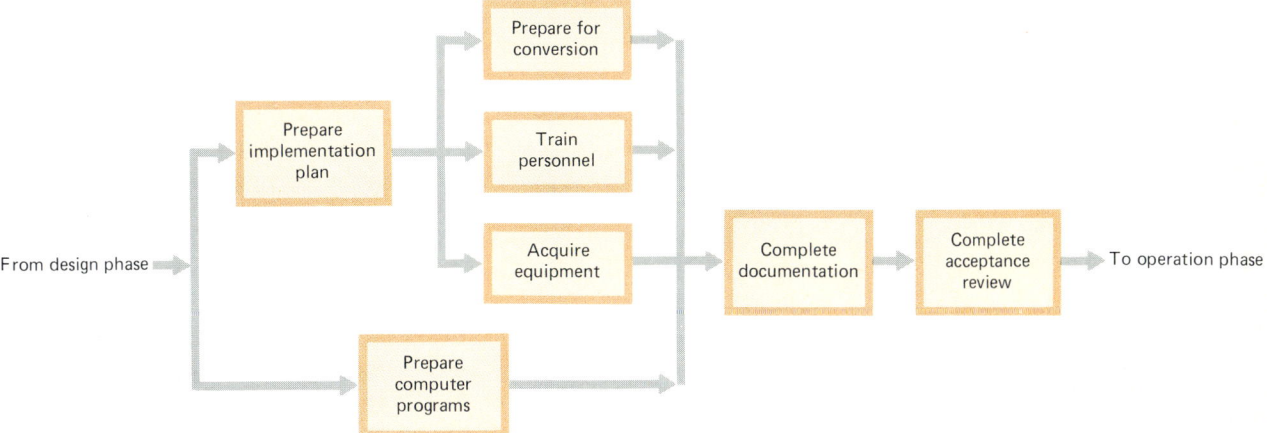

Implementation Plan

Implementation is the process of bringing into operational use a system that has been developed. This process starts at the beginning of the development phase with a plan, called the **implementation plan**. The major parts of the implementation plan are *test plans, training plans, an equipment installation plan,* and a *conversion plan*. The test plan is prepared so that the test requirements established during system design can be met. Both system and computer program tests must be planned in advance, so that all of the elements of the system can be tested before the end of the development phase.

Training plans are necessary to ensure that all personnel who will be associated with the system will have the necessary knowledge and skills. Thus, the manuals that will be needed to train equipment operators, programmers, and users have to be written. Training schedules must be established so that training activities can be coordinated and completed prior to implementation of the system.

If equipment, such as computers or computer-peripheral equipment, is required, it must be available on schedule, in order for the development of the system to proceed and for personnel to be trained. Therefore, a detailed plan for equipment delivery, installation, and checkout must be prepared.

Often, computer applications make use of many of the procedures employed by systems that they are replacing. They may even include computer programs that are part of an existing system. Most importantly, existing files may have to be converted from one medium to another. For example, if inventory records that have been stored in filing cabinets are to be stored on a magnetic disk, the conversion effort could be extensive. Errors and discrepancies that humans can tolerate must be eliminated, in order to prevent incorrect data from entering a computer system.

Equipment Acquisition

When equipment has to be acquired, the design team must allow for extra time because of the possibility of delivery delays. Sometimes, all of the equipment need not be acquired at the same time. This can reduce expenses and allow time to complete the construction of facilities. For example, early delivery could be taken on some sales terminals to check out the equipment and begin training operators.

Computer Program Preparation

The preparation of the computer programs is one of the most important development-phase activities. Working from expanded system flowcharts or IPO charts, programmers develop the logic of computer programs. They write the programs, and they check them out in accordance with test plans. The development of the computer programs, which are an essential part of computer-based business systems, will be discussed in Units Four and Five.

Personnel Training and Preparation for Conversion

The development-phase documentation, which continues the cumulative documentation of the design phase, is the basis for the preparation of training manuals specified in the training plan. All of the forms that are to be used with the system have to be designed, and all of the procedures for their use have to be prepared, so that they can be included in the training manuals.

After all personnel who will interact with the system have been trained, preparations can be made for actually changing over from the old system (if there is one) to the new system. Because many difficulties can occur when a new system is installed, a **changeover plan** should be prepared by the systems team. This plan should minimize problems that might arise from human errors or machine malfunctions. The changeover plan identifies all the activities to be performed during changeover, and assigns responsibilities to individuals.

Development-Phase Documentation and Acceptance Review

The development-phase documentation that has been accumulating is completed prior to an acceptance review. This documentation is the final extension of the documentation begun in the study phase and continued throughout the project. It contains all of the information needed to maintain the system. It includes reports of the results of the system and component tests. At the acceptance review, the principal user decides when to change over to the new system. If the decision is to proceed, the system enters the operational phase, where it becomes part of a larger computer applications environment. Some important characteristics of this environment are described in Unit Six.

FEEDBACK

10-10 Identify the two major types of tests.

10-11 What is the purpose of the design review?

10-12 What is an implementation plan? What are its major parts?

10-13 What is a changeover plan?

SUMMARY

After a computer information system has been selected, it must be designed and developed. The first design activity is general system design. This step is followed by input design, output design, and file design. The general system design ensures that all of the functions that the system must perform are assigned as manual tasks, equipment tasks, or computer program tasks. Expanded system flowcharts and input, processing, output (IPO) charts are used to display all of the system functions. Collectively, hierarchy charts plus IPO charts are called HIPO charts.

Input design is the process of converting a user-oriented description of the inputs to a system into a machine-oriented format. In most cases, data are entered by devices operated by humans, and input design must take into account the human element. Human-operated data entry devices include key-to-tape devices, key-to-disk devices, and CRT terminals. Other devices, such as OCR and laser scanners are means of reducing the need for human data entry.

Systems analysts use computer print charts and information display system layout sheets as output design aids. Computer print charts show the content and location of all lines of characters that are to be printed. Information display system layout sheets are used to design effective visual displays.

File design involves all of the files that a system must use. These files include input transaction files, edited transaction files, sorted transaction files, current master files, and updated master files. The master files are the most important files. The questions that should be asked and answered as part of the master file design process are:

1. What processing steps require the use of files?
2. What data must be stored in files?
3. What storage media should be used?

Data base management systems (DBMS) have been developed. They eliminate the need to maintain separate files which duplicate fields of data that are used by more than one application program.

After the design of a system is approved by the management of the user organization, the system enters the development phase. During the development phase, equipment is acquired, computer programs are prepared, personnel are trained, and preparation is made for changeover from a project environment to an operational environment. Because of the scope and duration of the development activities, this phase is more expensive than the study and design phases. The system development activities include preparation of a plan, called an implementation plan, for bringing the system into operational use. Major components of this plan are test plans, training plans, an equipment installation plan, and a conversion plan.

ANSWERS TO FEEDBACK QUESTIONS

10-1 Members may be added in order to provide special skills.

10-2 **a** As a manual task (example: keyboard entry of data).
     b As a hardware task (actual processing of data).
     c As a software task (a program that provides instructions to the computer).

10-3 To identify all of the processing steps required before programmers start to write the computer programs.

10-4 An input, processing, output chart. IPO charts are expansions of hierarchy charts into successively lower levels of detail.

10-5 A subprogram is a module that is written to perform a specific function within the overall computer program (such as updating a master file).

10-6 A chart that shows all lines of computer output as they are to be produced by a printer.

10-7 They are stored on files.

10-8 It is used to design the output of a CRT device.

10-9 A data base management system. It eliminates duplicate files and speeds up programming.

10-10 System tests and computer program tests.

10-11 To decide whether or not to proceed.

10-12 A plan for bringing a developed system into operation. Its major parts are test plans, training plans, an equipment installation plan, and a conversion plan.

10-13 The process of converting from the old system to the new one. A plan that identifies activities to be performed during changeover and assigns responsibilities to individuals.

FOR REVIEW AND DISCUSSION

1 Identify each of the major system design activities.

2 Why is the development phase usually more expensive than the design phase?

3 Why may studies of alternatives be repeated many times?

4 As the term is used in this chapter, what are subprograms?

5 Compare and discuss the similarities and differences between Figure 10-2, an expanded system flowchart, and Figure 10-3, an IPO chart.

6 Discuss the rules for good practice in source document design.

7 How do computer print charts differ from the layouts of outputs prepared in the study phase.

8 How does a computer print chart aid a programmer?

9 What is the purpose of the design-phase report?

10 Under what conditions might a project not be approved for development after the presentation of the design-phase report?

CHAPTER 11

SYSTEM OPERATION PHASE

PREVIEW After the computer programs have been prepared, and after all of the other system development activities have been completed, the computer information system enters the operation phase. The goal of this chapter is to describe the principal operation-phase activities, which relate to conversion to the new system, performance evaluation, and system modification.

In this chapter you will learn:

1. The two parts of conversion
2. The three methods of changeover
3. How to evaluate system performance
4. How to cope with changes to the system

KEY TERMS TO WATCH FOR AND REMEMBER

conversion	phased replacement
immediate replacement	change control board
parallel operation	baseline document

CONVERTING TO THE NEW SYSTEM In our discussion of system development activities in Chapter 10, we defined implementation as the process of bringing a developed system into operational use. In that chapter, we emphasized that planning for implementation begins early in the developmental process and continues along with the preparation of the computer programs. We also identified a conversion plan as a major element of the overall implementation plan. Now we will examine the actual process of converting from an old system to a new system. We define **conversion** as the performance of all of the activities that result in the turnover of a new system to its user.

Conversion has two parts. These are (1) the physical conversion of procedures, programs, and files and (2) the actual changeover to the new system. The first part must be completed before the end of the development phase, and the second part upon entry into the operation phase.

Conversion of Procedures, Programs, and Files

Often, a new system will retain many of the elements of an old system. Many of the procedures for their use may have to be modified. For example, a manual system might rely upon recording information from sales slips on a register by pen or pencil. By contrast, a computer-related information system may introduce data entry terminals. Clearly, a new computer information system is not always a replacement for a manual system. Often, it is an improvement upon an existing computer data processing system. The new system may retain many of the elements of the old system; however, some of these may have to be modified to work with computer programs or to run on new equipment.

Accurate file conversion is the most important of all the conversion activities. If the information contained in files is not accurate, the entire system is ineffective. Sometimes, data files have to be created for a new system because the system is designed to perform new tasks. In any event, data must be collected from a variety of sources, corrected, and prepared for entry into computer-maintained files. Verifying the validity of data going into new files is an important and time-consuming task. Humans who have been working with the existing data are able to cope with "dirty" records—records that contain minor errors. For example, if a name or identifying number—such as a social security number or a part number—occasionally is in error, a clerk can recognize and compensate for the error. Often, we are able to ignore "garbage"; computers cannot. Many new computer data processing systems fail to work because of the "garbage" that is allowed to enter them. This has given rise to a data processing industry catchword, GIGO, which means "garbage in—garbage out." Clerical personnel who are accustomed to working with file data can be very helpful in cleaning up records.

Changeover to the New System

The way in which changeover to the new system is planned and accomplished can have a major effect upon its performance and acceptance by its users. There are three general methods for changing over to a new system. These are parallel operation, immediate replacement, and phased replacement. They are illustrated in Figure 11-1. No single method is best for all situations. Each has its advantages and disadvantages. The best method depends upon the particular conversion circumstances.

Immediate replacement   As shown in Figure 11-1*a* **immediate replacement** means that all of the old system is discontinued and all of the new system is put into operation on a specified date. This is the most risky changeover method, because problems always occur during changeover and unless there is an alternative or fallback system, the consequences of failure might be catastrophic. For example, one large bank rejected this type of changeover because one day of failure to operate would affect all of its branches, two days would affect all of the banks in the state, and three days would disrupt the commerce of the entire nation.

However, there are some circumstances under which immediate replacement is necessary. If a high percentage of the output is new information, there may be no alternative. If the system is relatively noncritical to business operations so that changeover problems would not trigger a disaster, immediate replacement may be less expensive than other methods. Time and schedule pressures may rule out any other choices. Risk is reduced if a fallback system is available.

Parallel operation   **Parallel operation** means that data are processed at the same time by both the old and the new systems. This type of changeover is illustrated in Figure 11-1b. Advantages of parallel operation are the opportunity to compare the output of both systems and the availability of the old system as a backup. One disadvantage of parallel processing is its cost. Personnel and equipment resources must be provided for the operation of two systems. These resources are not only costly; sometimes they may also not be available. Another disadvantage of parallel operation is the delay in changing over to the new system. People tend to cling to what they are familiar with, and, as a result, the problems that the new system was designed to solve could be prolonged. Also, under some circumstances the new system might be so different from the old system in the functions that it performs, and in its input and output, that parallel operation would not be meaningful.

Phased replacement   As Figure 11-1c illustrates, **phased replacement** is a gradual approach in which complete changeover to the new system takes place incrementally over a period of time. Gradual changeover can be achieved by operating the new system with increasingly larger volumes of data and/or

FIGURE 11-1

System changeover methods.

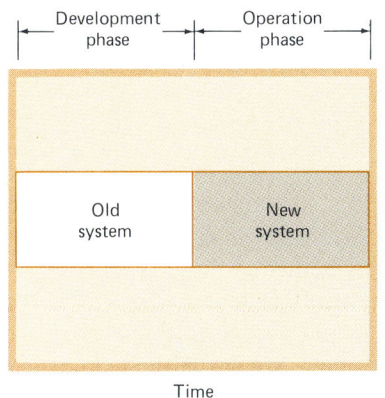

(a) Immediate replacement

(b) Parallel operation

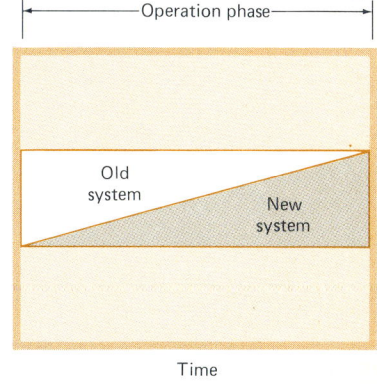

(c) Phased replacement

introducing parts of the new system and replacing the corresponding parts in the old one by them as they are checked out under actual operating conditions. Often, phased replacement is the most effective method of changing over to a new system. It has several advantages. Users can become familiar with the system. Errors need not cause catastrophic failure, and often they can be corrected quickly. Phased replacement is not as expensive as parallel operation and it usually can be handled with existing resources.

Frequently, circumstances limit the usefulness of phased replacement. Examples are lack of time for the gradual replacement of one system by another and many significant differences between the old and the new systems. One danger is the possibility that some errors may creep in and not be detected until the entire system has been in operation for a considerable period of time. However, regardless of the changeover method selected, introduction of a new system into an operational environment is never trouble-free, and recurring crises are to be expected during changeover.

Changeover crisis　No matter how completely conversion has been planned, and no matter how completely the system has been tested, the initial period of operation of a new system is filled with unpredictable crises, because all possible contingencies cannot be foreseen. However, if the system has been well designed and carefully developed, the magnitude and frequency of crises will diminish.

The time that it takes to get through the period of changeover crises depends upon the acceptance of the system by its users. People can increase the effectiveness of a poor system if they support it, but they can make a well-designed system fail if they do not support it. Therefore, before a system goes into operation, it is very important that users be convinced of its merits and be committed to making it work. By educating users about the benefits of a new system, by involving them in its design and development, and by acknowledging their help, the project leader responsible for implementing the new system can do much to ensure its success.

FEEDBACK
11-1 What is conversion, and what are the two parts of conversion?
11-2 What is a dirty record? How can dirty records affect the performance of a computer data processing system?
11-3 Discuss the three ways in which changeover can occur.

EVALUATING
THE SYSTEM
After the changeover crisis period is over, the system is turned over to the data processing department for routine operation. After the system is in operation, it is necessary to evaluate the system to verify whether or not it is meeting its performance objectives. The performance objectives of a system should have been stated clearly during the study phase. It would not have been worthwhile to spend time and money to design and develop a system without knowing what it was supposed to accomplish and how to measure whether or not it was doing it. As we pointed out in Chapter 9, the information service request,

INFORMATION SERVICE REQUEST			Page __1__ of __1__	

JOB TITLE: Reorders/sales analysis system	NEW ☒	REQUESTED DATE: 3/1/19xx	REQUIRED DATE: 12/31/19xx
	REV. ☐		

OBJECTIVE: To provide centralized reordering and daily sales analysis for 10 stores in Region A.	AUTHORIZATION			
	LABOR		OTHER	
	HOURS	AMOUNT	HOURS	AMOUNT
	2500	$50,000	100 (Computer time)	$5000

ANTICIPATED BENEFITS: 1. Reduced cost of inventory.
2. Fewer inventory items out-of-stock.
3. Improved sales analysis.

OUTPUT DESCRIPTION	INPUT DESCRIPTION
TITLE: Reorders Summary	TITLE: Sales Transactions
FREQUENCY: Daily QUANTITY: 1	FREQUENCY: On-line QUANTITY: 1000 per day per store
PAGES: 2 COPIES: 2	COMMENT: Data on item, quantity,
COMMENT: Lists quantity on hand, quantity	clerk, work station, and department.
on order, and delivery date. Local CRT	
inquiry with hardcopy as needed.	
TITLE: Composite Sales Analysis	TITLE: Inventory Received
FREQUENCY: Daily QUANTITY: 1	FREQUENCY: On-line QUANTITY: 500 per day
PAGES: 5 COPIES: 2	COMMENT: Data to update quantity
COMMENT: List daily sales by clerk.	on hand.
Local CRT inquiry with hardcopy as	
needed.	

TO BE FILLED OUT BY REQUESTOR

REQUESTED BY: J. Herrick *J. Herrick*	DEPARTMENT: Inventory	TITLE: Manager	TELEPHONE: Ext. 509
APPROVED BY: S. Sampson *S. Sampson*	DEPARTMENT: Sales	TITLE: Vice president	TELEPHONE: Ext. 602

TO BE FILLED OUT BY INFORMATION SERVICES

FILE NO: S7134	ACCEPTED ☒	NOT ACCEPTED ☐	
SIGNATURE: B. Humin *B. Humin*	DEPARTMENT: Info. Services	TITLE: Manager	TELEPHONE: Ext. 478

REMARKS: S. Simon assigned as systems analyst and project manager. Study Phase expenditures not to exceed $5000 and Study Phase to be completed in one month.

FORM NO. C-6-1	ADDITIONAL INFORMATION: USE REVERSE SIDE OR EXTRA PAGES

FIGURE 11-2

Information service request—final version.

which states the anticipated benefits of the system, becomes the basis for developing specific objectives that are measurable.

Figure 11-2 is the same ISR that was presented in Chapter 9 (Figure 9-5). Some specific objectives that we associated with our sample Reorders–Sales Analysis system at that time were:

1. To reduce total volume of goods in inventory from $1,000,000 to $200,000 within three months of system operation and to maintain it at that level.

2. To reduce the number of times that an item cannot be found in inventory from 10 percent to 0.1 percent within six months of installation of the system.

The advantage of stating these objectives in measurable terms is now evident, because we can devise methods of verifying whether or not they have been accomplished. Thus, we could verify whether or not the first objective had been met by calculating the value of the goods in inventory three months after the system became operational and by calculating it periodically thereafter. Because the inventory is to be maintained by a computer-based system, the needed information should be readily available. A physical check could be made to verify the accuracy of the information supplied by computer. The success with which the second objective was being met could be measured by making a comparison of the number of requests for items and of the number of times items were found to be out of stock.

Of course, benefits are not all tangible and measurable. However, those that are measurable should be expressed numerically. As a general rule, whenever we identify a tangible specific objective, we also should state the measurement that we will make in the operation phase to determine whether or not the system meets the objective.

Mathematical measurements can be made of the cost savings made possible by a computer-based system, and hardware and software operating expenses can be monitored continually. However, people are the final evaluators of information systems. The morale of employees using or affected by a system is a good measure of the success of the project. If the improvements achieved are offset by indicators of poor morale, such as grievances or high absenteeism, then the system is not achieving its objectives.

A very important measure of the effectiveness of a system is its usability, which is its worth, as perceived by its principal users. Users should be polled periodically because the effectiveness of a system can change. Previously undetected problems may emerge, or the circumstances that originally made the system useful may be replaced by other circumstances. Sooner or later, all systems must change in response to changes in their environment. New laws, changes in technology, and changes in the goals and objectives of the business are examples of causes of change. Thus, the ease with which a system can be modified to react to change is also a significant measure of its effectiveness in achieving its objectives.

FEEDBACK   **11-4** When is a system evaluated?

11-5 What is the relationship between the anticipated benefits (stated on the ISR) and system evaluation?

11-6 What is a tangible benefit? An intangible benefit? Give an example of each.

MANAGING CHANGE

One of the greatest benefits of the life-cycle technique for the design and development of computer information systems is its usefulness in managing change. The process for managing and documenting the activities of each life-cycle phase was shown in Chapter 3 (Figure 3-9). It is redrawn here as Figure 11-3 to help demonstrate how change can occur. This figure emphasizes the dynamic nature of the business system environment. As the arrows that lead back toward the beginning of the life cycle indicate, changes can occur at any time. Changes may occur during the study, design, and development phases. Changes always occur during the operational life of a system, and they must be managed. Two important elements of change management are a change control procedure and the use of baseline documents.

Change Control Procedures

It often seems that no sooner is a new system installed than someone wants to change it. Frequent change is disruptive and disturbing. Therefore, some control over changes is required. One method of achieving this control is to have all requests for change evaluated by a **change control board.** This board should be made up of the principal users of the system, a systems analyst, and data processing personnel who are familiar with the system. Normal maintenance operations need not be approved by the change control board, but these operations should be recorded and summarized for periodic reporting to the board. Examples of maintenance activities are modifying the format of a report or rewriting a part of a computer program component to improve its efficiency. Major changes are those that significantly alter the system or require extensive personnel, hardware, or software. An example of a major change would be conversion of the system from batch processing to online terminals. Another

FIGURE 11-3

Computer-based business system life cycle.

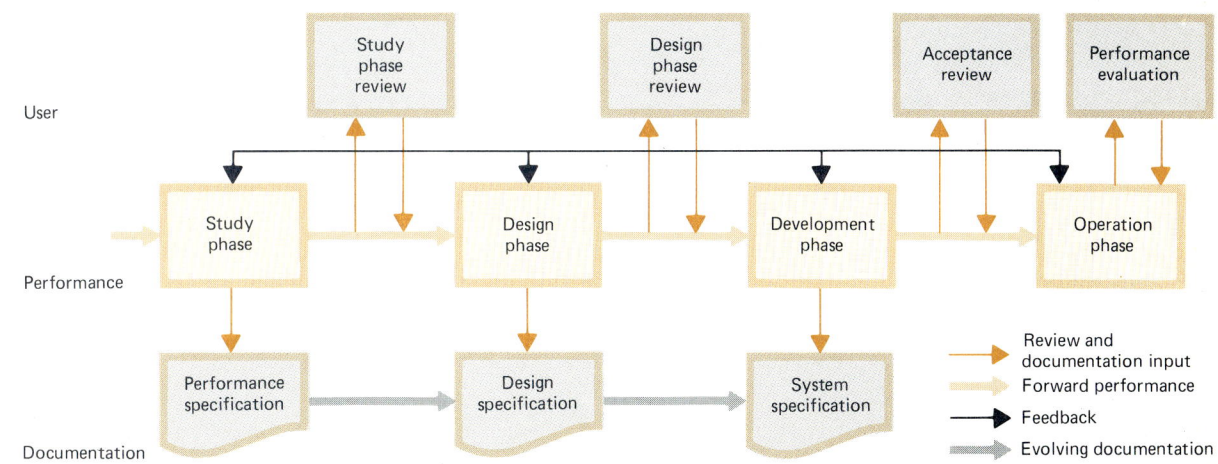

would be expanding a system to meet the special reporting needs of additional users.

Baseline Documents   A significant change requires establishing another systems project and reentering the life cycle at an appropriate point. If the change affects the objectives that the system originally was designed to accomplish, reentry may be as far back as the study phase. At this time, the value of the cost and effort to create good documentation becomes evident. Personnel who formerly worked on the system may no longer be available. Without the existence of documentation, changes would be very difficult and costly to accomplish.

Documentation is the starting point, or baseline, for change. The principal **baseline document** is the system specification, which grew out of the performance and design specifications. The concept of baseline documentation is important because it requires that documentation be created as the system is developed and that it be kept current through the entire life of the system. Figure 11-4 illustrates the baseline documentation concept. The heavy gold arrows in Figure 11-4 identify the performance specification, the design specification, and the system specification as baseline documents. Each of these is a reference for change. The performance specification is created at the end of the study phase, and it is the starting point for the design of the system. For

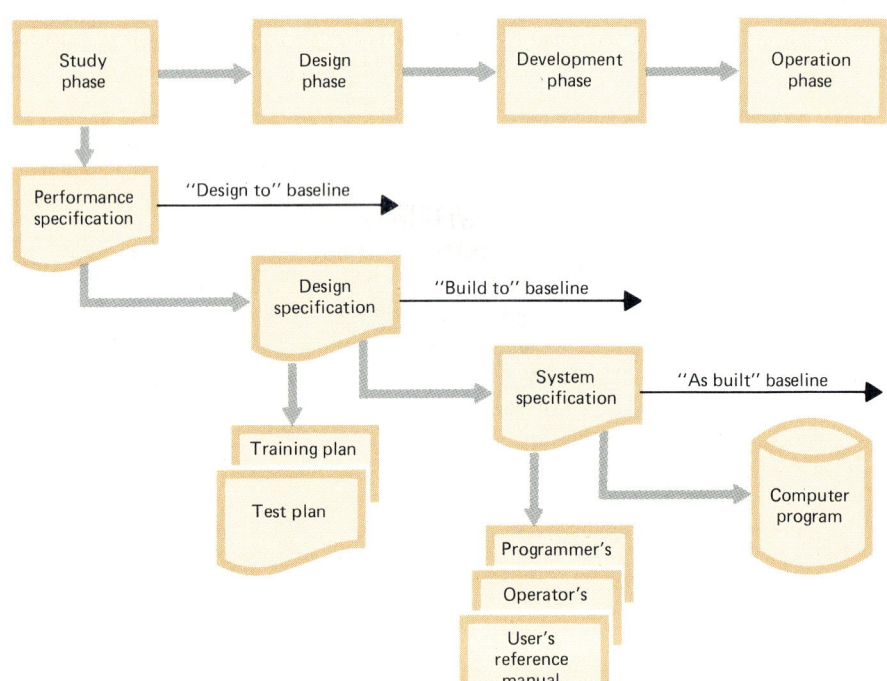

FIGURE 11-4

Baseline documents. The three baseline documents are: (1) the performance specification, which is a "design-to" baseline; (2) the design specification, which is a "build-to" specification; and (3) the system specification, which is an "as-built" specification.

this reason, the performance specification is called the "design to" specification. Major changes in the performance of the system, such as specification of several new outputs, would refer all the way back to this specification, and a new study phase could be required. Design changes, such as changes in the layout of some reports, would only refer back as far as the design specification. This specification is called the "build to" specification because it is the starting point for the development of the system. Finally, changes in the method of developing the system would refer back to the system specification, which describes the manner in which the system was built. An example of a change that would refer back to the "as built" specification is the replacement of a computer subprogram by another that is more efficient. In actuality, since documentation is added to as the system progresses throughout the life-cycle phases, the system specification contains the earlier performance and design specifications. Some changes would begin with those parts of the system specification which corresponded to an earlier document, and the documentation would be changed from that point forward.

In addition to identifying the performance, design, and system specifications as baseline documents, Figure 11-4 identifies other important reference documents, such as test and training plans, and reference manuals. The computer program itself is a reference document, because it records the process by which data are converted into useful information.

These documents are useful not only in managing change but also as sources of information during the day-to-day operation of the system. We have described this operation as "routine." There really is seldom such a thing as routine operation of computer-based information systems. Management of data processing centers and its resources is a responsible job, with daily challenges.

FEEDBACK   **11-7** During what phases of the system life cycle can changes occur?

11-8 What is a baseline document? How many are there, and what is the purpose of each?

11-9 Why does the system specification contain the other two specifications?

SUMMARY   Conversion to a new computer information system has two major components, the physical conversion of procedures and the actual changeover to the new system. Physical conversion of procedures, programs, and files takes place at the end of the development phase. File conversion is the most important conversion activity because inaccurate data make the output of computer data processing systems useless.

Actual changeover to the new system occurs as soon as the system enters the operation phase. The three methods of changeover are:

1. Immediate replacement: discontinuing the old system and putting the new system into operation on a specified date.

2. Parallel operation: processing data by both the old and the new system.

3. Phased replacement: gradual changeover by increasing data volume and/or introducing parts of the new system as they are checked out under actual operating conditions.

Although phased replacement usually is advisable, there are circumstances under which immediate replacement or parallel operation may be required.

Actual changeover is a period of frequent crises because all possible errors cannot be anticipated. The support of system users is important in weathering the problems that will occur during changeover.

At the end of the crisis period the new system becomes operational, and evaluation can take place. This evaluation is based upon verification of the specific objectives developed during the study phase. Finally, evaluation depends upon the acceptance or rejection of a system by its principal users.

The performance of computer data processing systems must be evaluated continually because all systems are subject to influences that cause change. Change must be managed in an orderly manner. Effective change control procedures, such as establishment of a change control board, are necessary. The value of the life-cycle concept, including the creation and maintenance of baseline documentation, is proved when it becomes necessary to cope with change.

ANSWERS TO FEEDBACK QUESTIONS

11-1 The performance of all the activities that result in the turnover of a new system to its user. The two parts are (1) physical conversion of procedures, programs, and files and (2) actual changeover to the new system.

11-2 It contains minor errors. Garbage in (causes) garbage out (GIGO).

11-3 The three ways in which changeover can occur are:

    a Immediate replacement: risky but necessary under certain circumstances, such as many new outputs.

    b Parallel operation: security of a backup but often very expensive.

    c Phased replacement: incremental replacement of a system is advantageous unless new and old systems are very different or unless there is a lack of time.

11-4 After the changeover the crisis period is over.

11-5 The anticipated benefits are the basis for developing specific, measurable objectives. Achievement of these objectives is measured during system evaluation.

11-6 A tangible benefit, such as the reduction of the number of items in inventory, is measurable. An intangible benefit, such as an ultimate increase in profit, is difficult to measure directly.

11-7 During any phase of the life cycle.

11-8 A reference, or starting point, for managing change. There are three baseline documents:
   a Performance specification (the "design to" specification)
   b Design specification (the "build to" specification)
   c System specification (the "as built" specification)

11-9 It contains the performance specification and the design specification because documentation is added to throughout the system life cycle.

FOR REVIEW AND DISCUSSION

1 In what phase (or phases) of the computer information system life cycle does conversion occur?

2 What is the difference between physical conversion and changeover?

3 Give an example of a change to the Reorders–Sales Analysis system (see Chapters 9 and 10) that could affect:
   a The performance specification
   b The design specification
   c The system specification

4 What is the purpose of a change control board?

5 Discuss the value of the life-cycle method of developing computer-based business systems as it relates to change.

6 What are the relative advantages and disadvantages of:
   a Immediate replacement
   b Parallel operation
   c Phased replacement

7 This text describes documentation as a continuous and cumulative activity. Another approach to documentation is to wait and write it after the system has been developed. Discuss the merits of each approach.

UNIT FOUR

COMPUTER PROGRAMMING

In Unit Three, you studied the life-cycle sequence for the development of effective computer information systems—the study, design, development, and operation phases. Programming, a major activity of the development phase, will be studied in detail in this unit. In Chapter 12, you will be introduced to the techniques used to plan the logic of a computer program. Chapter 13 shows how to write instructions to a computer in a programming language. The methods used to communicate and control the computer itself are introduced in Chapter 14. Chapter 15 identifies the two types of computer program errors and introduces methods of finding and correcting them.

CHAPTER 12

PLANNING THE COMPUTER PROGRAM

PREVIEW The key to effective action is planning. To produce an effective computer program, you must first plan the logic. If you attempt to plan the logic approach and write the program at the same time, you will likely become so involved with the required instruction formats that program logic will suffer. The goal of this chapter is to present two common techniques used in the planning of computer program logic.

In this chapter you will learn:

1. The purpose of program planning
2. The nine commonly used flowcharting symbols
3. How to interpret program flowcharts
4. The basic structures of pseudocode
5. How to use pseudocode

KEY TERMS TO WATCH FOR AND REMEMBER

terminal symbol	connector symbol
input-output (I/O) symbol	sequence logic
flowlines	IF . . . THEN
arrowheads	IF . . . THEN . . . ELSE
loop	ENDIF
decision symbol	DOWHILE
process symbol	DOUNTIL
preparation symbol	ENDDO

Computer programs have been described as being the software of the computer system. We are now at the point in the system life cycle where programs are to be written. We must now define the processing steps to be performed by the computer.

THE COMPUTER PROGRAM
The Controlling Function

In Chapter 1, the system functions of inputting, storing, processing, outputting, and controlling were introduced. *Controlling* was defined as the directing of the manner and sequence in which inputting, storing, processing, and outputting are performed. Chapter 5 expanded this concept by introducing the control unit, a piece of hardware that is part of a computer's central processing unit. It was explained that the control unit "controlled" the other hardware elements: input devices, memory, arithmetic logic unit, and output devices. Controlling means that each hardware element performs its function only when it is told to do so by the control unit.

Computer Instructions

How does the control unit know what function is to be performed? It follows instructions that are written by a human (a programmer) and stored in the computer's memory unit. These instructions are called the program. The control unit, and therefore the computer, will do exactly what the instructions say to do.

Programming a Human

Assume that a friend of yours wanted to know how large his payments would be if he borrowed $1200 to buy a stereo record and tape set. The terms are 12 percent annual interest, and the loan must be repaid in three years. Let us further assume that you had taken a business math class and remembered the formula for calculating monthly payments. If you were to write down the required steps to solve the problem, you would be writing a program for your friend to follow. If you write the calculation steps (instructions) correctly *and* in the proper sequence, *and* if your friend followed the instructions carefully, the correct answer for the problem would result.

THE PURPOSES OF PROGRAM PLANNING

If a friend asks you how to calculate monthly payments and you are not familiar with the steps involved, will you be able to explain the required steps? Of course not. The same principle applies to writing computer programs. A programmer cannot write instructions for a computer unless the programmer knows how to solve the problem manually. What will happen if you write instructions for a computer or a human and you leave out some of the steps or write the calculation steps in the wrong sequence? The program will calculate a wrong answer. The instruction sequence—or logic structure—of a computer program can be very complex. To help ensure that the program instructions are appropriate for the problem and are in the correct sequence, programs must be planned. The two major purposes of program planning are to help structure the program logic and to help document the finished program.

Structuring Program Logic

In Chapter 9, the system was planned through system flowcharts, data flow diagrams, and/or HIPO flowcharts. The purpose of these charts was to show what the system does. The systems analyst was responsible for the development of these systems-oriented charts.

By the end of the design phase, the detailed design of the required inputs and outputs is complete. In addition, any required file storage—such as on magnetic tape or disk—has been designed. Program planning is an effort to continue the systems planning to the detail level of computer programs. Program planning attempts to complement system planning by showing how the system does what is required of it. The programmer is responsible for generating the program plan.

Documenting the Completed Program

If the planning done for the programs is retained as a part of the program documentation, it can then be used as a basis for future changes in the program. Once a computer program has been written to solve a particular problem, that program will continue to solve the problem in the same way for as long as it is used. A computer solution will continue to be a good solution until the nature of the problem changes. Unfortunately, the nature of all organizations is to be in a continual state of change. With the passage of time, the computer program will be solving problems that no longer exist—at least not in the same form as when the program was written.

When the time comes for a modification of the computer solution that will match the evolved problem, the original program plans can be used by the programmer to identify those portions of the program that require changes.

FLOWCHARTS

Flowcharting is one technique used in program planning. A *flowchart* is defined as a plan in graphic or pictorial form that uses predefined symbols to illustrate program logic. A flowchart, therefore, is a "picture" of the logic to be included in the computer program. It is the plan to be followed when the program is written.

Flowcharting Standards

An important part of the definition is the reference to predefined symbols. The communication of program logic through flowcharts is made easier through the use of symbols that have standardized meanings. For example, a rectangle always means a process. A national organization called the American National Standards Institute (ANSI) has developed national standards to be used in flowcharting. The International Organization for Standardization (ISO) serves a similar function on an international basis. These bodies have laid out a minimum set of predefined symbols for flowcharting. Some organizations have added symbols beyond those of ANSI and ISO. These symbol shapes were added when additional symbols were needed to aid in the communication of program logic. International Business Machines (IBM) is one organization that has added symbols beneath both the national and international standards. Figure 12-1 illustrates the IBM flowcharting template. A *template* is a plastic or metal guide used to trace the flowcharting symbols. Many of these symbols are used in system flowcharts.

ANSI FLOWCHARTING STANDARDS—TIME FOR A CHANGE?

A review committee of the Association for Computing Machinery (ACM) has urged a careful, independent, comparative examination of documentation alternatives.

The review committee recommended a serious updating and clarification of the existing ANSI flowcharting standard, formally known as X3.5-1970. The committee went on to list 26 areas of the standard which need attention.

Apparently, many programmers do not follow the ANSI standard. It was suggested that many do not follow it because they don't know what it is. The standard is used mainly by those programmers with a college degree in data processing or computer science. Many programmers know the standard but still do not follow it because they feel the standard is too rigid and cumbersome.

There are several alternatives to the ANSI standard. Among these are hardware vendor flowcharting approaches and pseudocode.

The ACM committee suggests that the flowcharting standard would become more familiar to programmers if all publications of the various data processing societies would only use flowcharts conforming fully with the ANSI standard.

Committees of data processing societies, such as ACM, help us to keep our procedures and standards up to date. Many data processing professionals feel that it is time for a change in the flowcharting standard.

The IBM Template The IBM template symbols fall into one of three categories: basic symbols, systems-related symbols, and program-related symbols. Chapter 9 covered basic and systems-related symbols use. This chapter will discuss basic and program-related symbols, which are highlighted in the template example (Figure 12-1).

The Basic Process Loop The **terminal symbol** is used to indicate the beginning, ending, and pauses in the program logic flow. It is the first and last symbol in the program logic. In addition, if the program logic calls for a pause in the program, that also is indicated with a terminal symbol. A pause might be necessary if forms had to be changed in the computer's line printer.

The **input-output (I/O) symbol** is used to indicate all inputting and out-

FIGURE 12-1
IBM flowcharting template.

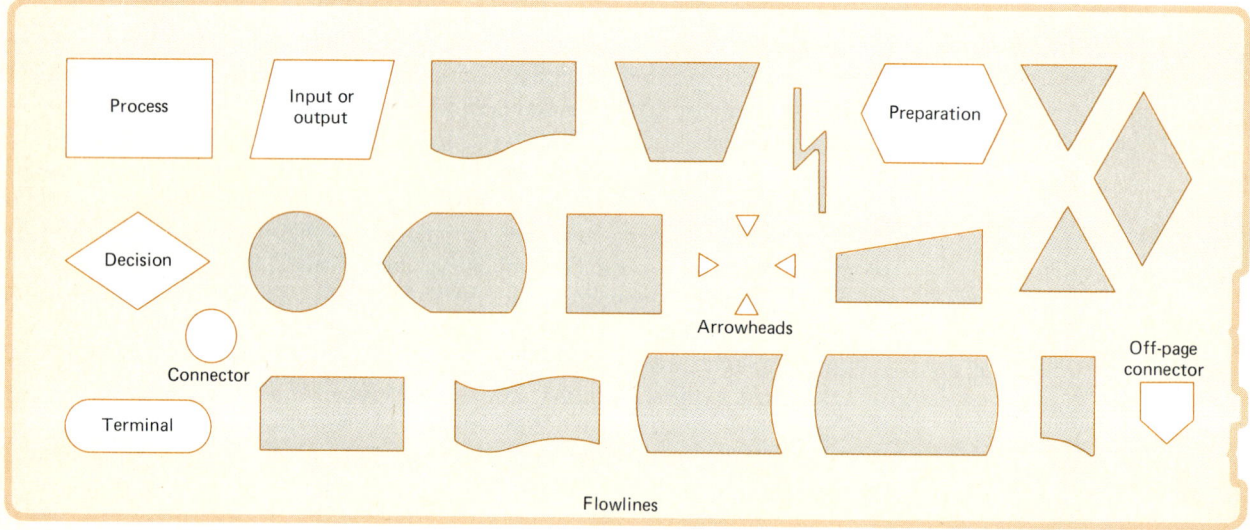

John Adams	456-34-7823	18	Male
George Brown	832-54-3524	21	Male
Jane Carter	457-55-3487	19	Female
Alice Dobbs	486-47-2399	22	Female

FIGURE 12-2
Sample student data output.

putting. Anytime there is a program instruction to input a disk record, a tape record, or a record of any type from an input device, that step will be indicated in the plan with the I/O symbol. Anytime there is a program instruction to output on a printer, magnetic disk, magnetic tape, terminal screen, or any output device, the I/O symbol is used.

The third and fourth symbols are **flowlines** and **arrowheads.** Flowlines connect the flowcharting symbols into a string of symbols to show the sequence-of-logic steps. Arrowheads are used to show the direction of flow. The normal flow of flowcharts is from top to bottom in vertical columns and from leftmost column to rightmost column. Arrowheads are required only when the normal top-to-bottom flow is not to be followed.

FEEDBACK

12-1 What are the two purposes of flowcharts?
12-2 What is a flowcharting template?
12-3 What is the shape of the terminal symbol? What is its purpose?
12-4 What symbol is used to show input or output?
12-5 When should arrowheads be used?

FIGURE 12-3

Initial solution to the student data problem.

Assume that the students in your data processing class had been given an assignment to record some personal data by keying it into a computer through a keyboard (name, social security number, age, sex, and so on). The problem is to create a printed listing of the data shown in Figure 12-2. When the steps required to solve the problem are flowcharted, the flowcharting symbols are used to indicate the general nature of the logical steps. A short description of the specific activity is written within the flowcharting symbol.

We suggest that when you draw any flowchart, proceed as if you were solving the problem manually. Figure 12-3 shows a four-symbol flowchart. Would this flowchart solve the problem of printing a listing of the student data?

The first symbol is a terminal labeled START. It shows that this is the starting point or beginning of our flowchart logic. It does not mean that the computer is to be turned on or that anyone is to press a start button. The second symbol is an I/O symbol that is labeled specifically to show that this step is READ A RECORD—in this example, items that have been keyed into

FIGURE 12-4

A student data problem solution which will list multiple input records.

the computer. That step would input the first record of the student data from the terminal keyboard into the main storage of the computer system. The third symbol is also an I/O symbol and is labeled WRITE A LINE. This logical step indicates that the data previously inputted are to be outputted on the line printer. Note that details such as the names of the fields being inputted or outputted or the specific positions being used are not a part of the logical steps of inputting or outputting. This information already appears in the system design documents and will be included in the computer program as input and output descriptions. The fourth symbol is a terminal labeled STOP. This symbol indicates the conclusion of our logic—that is, the conclusion of the computer program.

The logic depicted in Figure 12-3 therefore, will read only one record, write one line, and then stop. It is not a successful solution to the problem.

Figure 12-4 is a flowchart with a series of read-write pairs to read the first record, write the first line, read the second record, write the second line, and so on, until all the student records have been read.

There are two serious flaws to this solution. First, the number of records in the data must be known prior to writing the program so that the proper number of read-write pairs may be written. Second, if the data were to contain fifty records, the flowchart plan would require a string of a 100 I/O symbols.

In a situation where the same logical steps can be repeated, the flowline can indicate the repetitive nature of the logic by means of a process **loop**. Figure 12-5 illustrates a flowchart with a process loop. Note that in order to prevent confusion, an arrowhead is used on the flowline that goes upward in the flowchart, contrary to the normal downward flow. The process loop of Figure 12-5 solves the problem of an exceedingly long flowchart by reusing the same read-write steps over and over again. It also solves the problem of having to know how many records are in the data, but it also introduces a new problem. The process loop shown does not have a logical ending. It will continue to attempt to read a record and write a line until someone manually cancels the job.

Decisions to be made in a computer program are indicated with a diamond-shaped flowcharting **decision symbol.** All computer decisions consist of comparing two fields within main memory. As a result of this comparison, the computer will know if the two fields contain values that are equal or unequal. If they are unequal, it can tell which of the two fields contains the higher value. In most business problems, decisions can be stated as questions requiring a yes or no answer. Figure 12-6 shows a decision step between the reading of a record and the writing of a line. This decision is a way out of the endless loop of Figure 12-5. If a record with special data to indicate "last record" is entered at the end of the data, a decision can be made as to whether or not the program has read the last record. As an example of this last-record indicator, IBM uses a series of special keys on its terminal keyboards to allow users to request special functions. One of these special functions is to indicate the end of data. The use of this function key inputs data which signals that no more data is to be entered. Other input devices, such as magnetic tape or disk, have a special

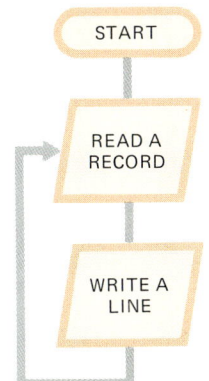

FIGURE 12-5

Student data problem solution with an endless process loop.

record at the end of the data to indicate end-of-file. Different manufacturers and devices may use different methods of signaling the end of input data, but all use some form of end-of-file indicator. If a computer is asked the question, "Last record?" as a decision, the computer is being asked to compare the data just read to the end-of-data signal. The input step and the at-end decision are usually written as a single instruction in the program. Therefore, the at-end decision should almost always be flowcharted immediately after the input symbol.

The process loop in Figure 12-6 will solve the problem of listing the student data on the line printer. It will read a record and determine if it is the last-record indicator. If it is not, it will write a line and loop back to read the next record. The loop will continue until the last record indicator is inputted, at which time the program will stop.

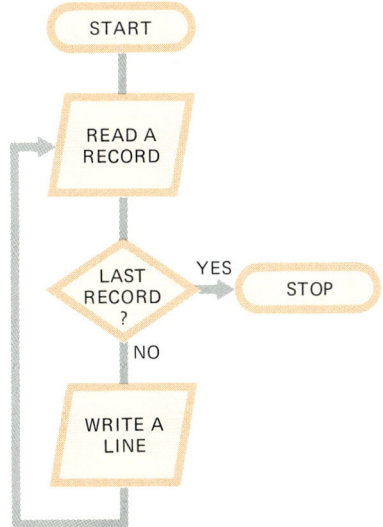

FIGURE 12-6

Final solution of student data problem.

FEEDBACK   **12-6** How can you tell if the input-output symbol is indicating an input or an output?

12-7 What is a process loop?

12-8 What symbol indicates a program decision?

12-9 What kinds of decisions can be made with a computer program?

**Process Loops
with Calculations**

So far, the problem to be solved has been quite simple—reading a record and outputting a line to the printer—with no calculations (processes) involved. In the next example, the problem will be modified. The program now is to produce the same listing, plus a total line containing the number of records read (or lines printed).

The **process symbol** (a rectangle) is used to indicate the arithmetic processes of adding, subtracting, multiplying, and dividing and to show the logical process of moving data from one place in storage to another, for example, to move data from an input area to an output area. The input area is the memory area where data are placed as they are inputted. The output area is the memory area where data must be prior to being outputted. This process of moving data must be considered in some cases. It is covered in Supplement I in detail. It will be ignored in this chapter.

FIGURE 12-7

A process loop which includes a calculation and an end-time total.

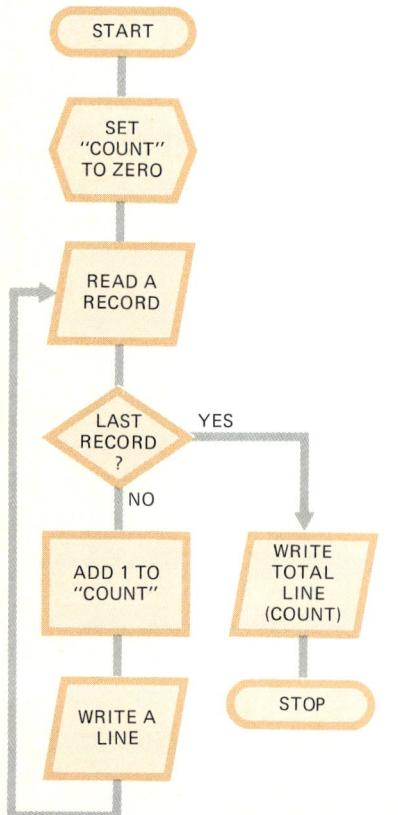

To accumulate the total to be printed in the total line, a process step must be inserted into the read-write loop. To accumulate the total number of records in the data, a new data field—called COUNT in this example—is required. If the count field has a beginning value of 0, and 1 is added to it each time a record is read, the value of the count field is equal to the number of records read when the last-record signal is encountered.

Figure 12-7 illustrates a flowchart that includes the process of adding 1 to the count field each time the loop is repeated. Note that the process could just as easily have been placed after WRITE A LINE as before it. Also note that the last record (the one containing the last-record indicator) does not contain any data to be processed. It will not be counted in the total because the last-record decision takes the program out of the loop before adding 1 to the count field.

With the adding process in the read-write loop accumulating the number of lines being written, when the last-record question is answered yes, the value of the count field will be equal to the total number of data records read and lines printed. All that remains is to actually output the final value.

The second symbol in Figure 12-7 is called the **preparation symbol.** Its function is to assign a value to a field. If a human were told to count the number of records in a file, one would, without specific instructions, begin the count with zero. Most computers will make no such assumption. Anytime a field is used to accumulate totals, the field must be given an initial or beginning value of zero.

If the preparation symbol is not used, the standard process symbol can be used in its place. In the flowchart illustrated in Figure 12-7, the preparation symbol is used to set the count field to a beginning value of zero. Without this logical step, the computer would start counting from whatever value happened to be in memory. The odds of that value's being at zero—so that that the ending count would be accurate—are very small.

FEEDBACK

12-10 What kinds of processes are shown by the process symbol? What is its shape?

12-11 What is the function of the preparation symbol?

12-12 What symbol may be used in place of the preparation symbol?

The Use of Connectors

If a flowchart becomes very long, a problem can arise from the use of flowlines. As the flowchart becomes several columns of symbols, it is likely that flowlines will be criss-crossing and will be confusing to follow. The **connector symbol,** a small circle, can be used as a substitute for flowlines. Figure 12-8 is the same flowchart as Figure 12-7, except that connectors have been used to replace some of the flowlines. The connectors are assumed to link up whenever two or more connectors contain the same character. The connector at the bottom of the first column and the connector to the left of READ A RECORD contain

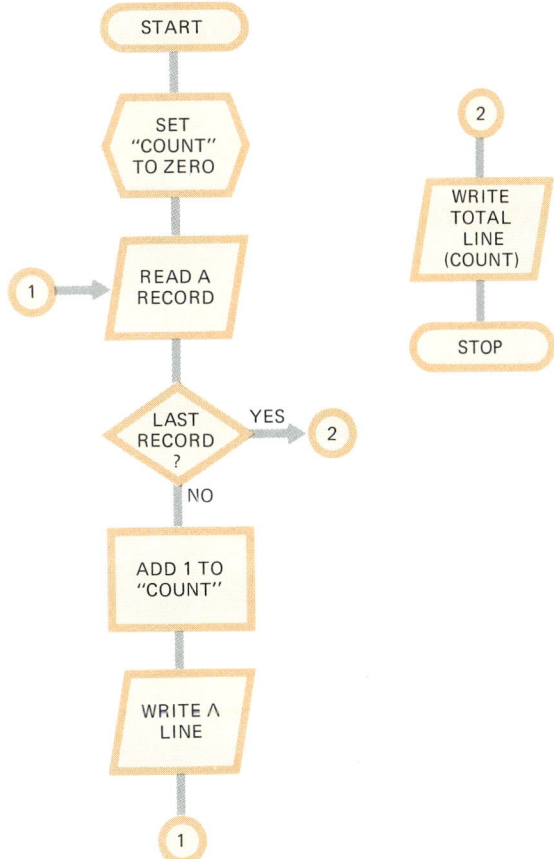

FIGURE 12-8
A process loop using connectors.

the character 1. They are, therefore, assumed to be a common point or to be connected. They provide the same function as a flowline drawn between them without having to cross any other flowlines. Connectors that are leaving the normal flowcharting flow direction, such as the 2 to the right of the LAST RECORD? decision and the bottom of the first column, are called *exit connectors*. Connectors bringing the flow back into the main stream, such as the 1 to the left of the READ A RECORD symbol and the top of the second column, are known as *entry connectors*. Although it is not a rule, it is a common practice in flowcharting to place entry connectors only at the top or to the left of a flowcharting column and to place exit connectors at the bottom or to the right of the flowcharting column. This practice makes it easier to locate the corresponding entry or exit connector.

Although not included in this illustration, there is an additional connector called the *offpage connector*. This symbol is an IBM extension beyond both ANSI and ISO standards. It is used when its corresponding entry or exit connector is found on a separate flowcharting page. Using the offpage connector, rather than the standard connector, can be of great assistance in locating the corresponding connector when the flowchart is many pages long.

Loops with Multiple Exits

Flowcharting logic may require many exit connectors, all tied to one entry connector. Note that a flowchart may contain multiple exit connectors, all containing the same label, without being ambiguous or confusing. However, there may *never* be more than one entry connector containing the same character.

Let's look at an example to illustrate this. Figure 12-9 shows a flowchart with another variation of the student data problem. The problem is to produce a listing and a total, as before, but this time we want to list and total only males in the age range of 18 to 25.

The flowchart in Figure 12-9 is a solution to this problem. Note that there is a series of three decisions, each using an exit connector containing the character 1. The questions are "Is the inputted sex code equal to male?" "Is the inputted age less than 18?" and "Is the inputted age greater than 25?" Each of these connectors takes the logic flow back to the input symbol, bypassing the printer output and total calculation. The flowcharter must be careful not to ask too complex a question in any decision symbol. If the question can be answered with a yes or no and is restricted to a simple statement, it will usually be simple enough to be handled by a computer. In Figure 12-9, the questions "Is the age less than 18?" and "Is the age greater than 25?" are two separate questions or decisions. Remember, when the program asks the question "Is the age less than 18?" it is asking the computer to compare the age field in each input record to a value of 18 and then branch to entry connector 1 if the age field is low. To branch to a connector means to go to the corresponding entry connector. When a series of simple questions like those in Figure 12-9 are combined, computer decisions can appear to be quite sophisticated.

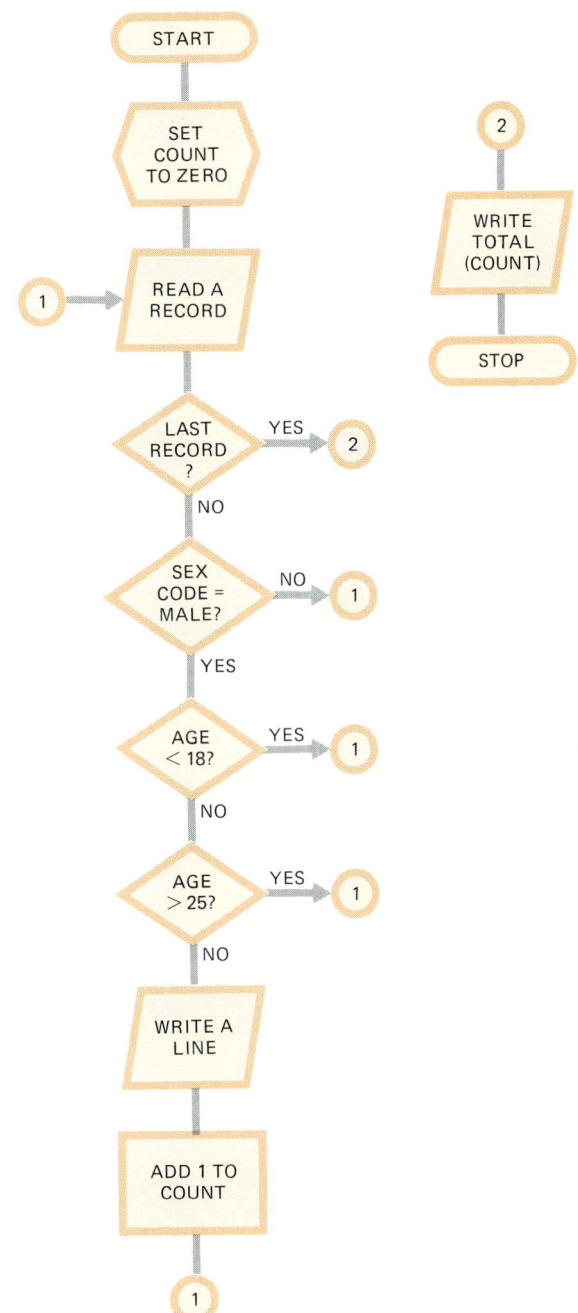

FIGURE 12-9
A process loop with multiple exits. This solution will output student data for males between the ages of 18 and 25. It also prints the total at the end.

12-13 What is the purpose of connector symbols?

12-14 Explain the difference between an entry connector and an exit connector.

12-15 When is the offpage connector used?

End-Time Calculations

Many problems require arithmetic processes to be performed at *end time*, or after the last-record indicator has been read. Using our student data, let's solve the problem of calculating the average age of the class. Only a single line, containing the average, is to be printed. Figure 12-10 depicts that flowcharting solution. Note that the processing loop from READ A RECORD to ADD AGE TO TOTAL AGE does not contain an output symbol. The function of this loop is to accumulate both the total number of students in the class and the total of their ages. The process of dividing the total of the ages by the number of students in the class should not take place until after all records in the file have been read. Therefore, the division process does not take place

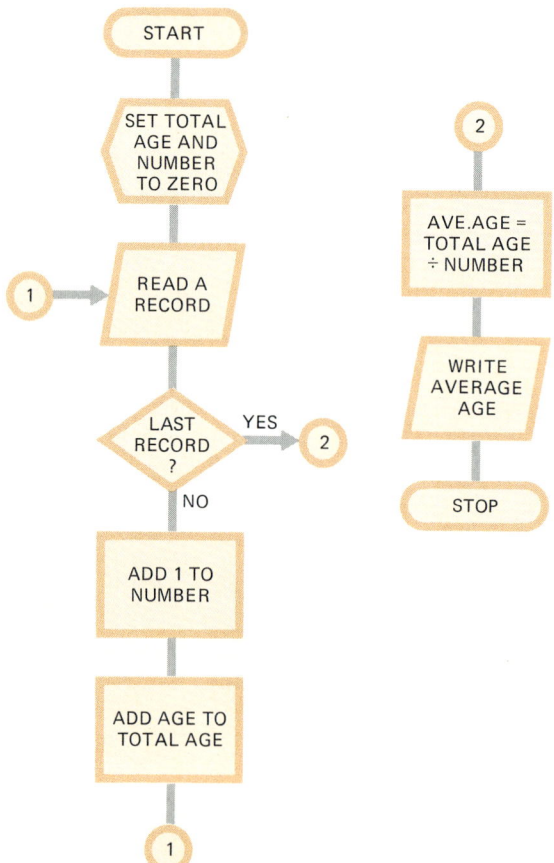

FIGURE 12-10
Process loop with end-time calculations. This solution calculates the average age of the students.

until the last-record decision has an answer of yes and a branch is made to connector 2. After the average has been calculated, it is then ready to be outputted.

Titles and Column Headings

The next problem is to produce a listing from the student data—the same listing that was produced in the first problem discussed in this chapter. A difference will be the addition of a title at the top of each page, column headings, and the limiting of the number of lines to be printed on a page so that a blank area will be left for a margin at the bottom.

Figure 12-11 is an example of the printed output from the problem. While printer paper comes in many lengths (from perforation to perforation), a standard-sized page is 11 inches long. Most computer line printers can print either six or eight lines per vertical inch. The most common setting is six lines per inch, which is the same as most typewriters. Using six lines per inch, a full page consists of 66 possible lines of print. If an inch is allowed for a top margin, and another inch is left for a bottom margin, this leaves 54 (66 minus 12) lines available for printing. Allowing one print line for the title, a second print line for the double space after the title, a third print line for column headings, and two more lines for the triple space to the first detail line, 49 *detail lines* (54 minus 5) are left for the body of each page. The paper in the line printer can be adjusted so that the first printing line of each page, the title, will be 1 inch down from the top. It is the problem of the program logic to determine when enough detail lines have been printed in order to be 1 inch from the bottom perforation. When there is 1 inch left, the program logic must call for a repeating of the title line (which will be printed as the first line of the next page). The easiest way to determine when it is time to repeat the title and column headings is to count the number of detail lines that have been printed.

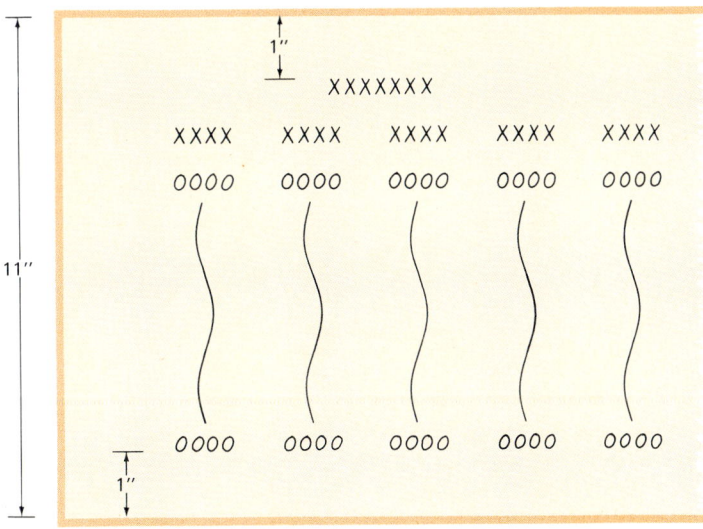

FIGURE 12-11
A sample printer output with vertical dimensions.

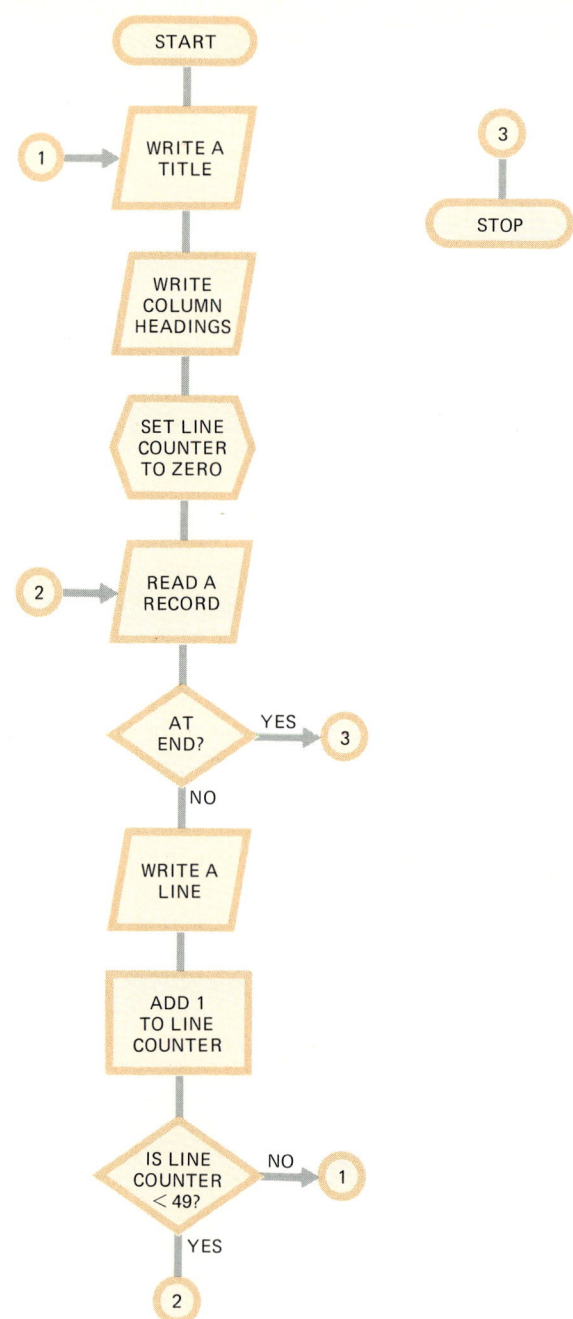

FIGURE 12-12
Process loop with a line counter and
headings.

Figure 12-12 is an example of a flowchart that counts detail lines and repeats the title and column headings each time 49 lines have been printed. Note that *two* loops exist in this illustration. One is the detail process loop from READ A RECORD to the bottom of the column, and the other is a larger loop that includes the output of a title and column headings (the entire left column). Also note that the preparation symbol resetting the line counter field to zero is part of the title line loop. It is necessary to reset the line counter field to zero each time a title is printed so that the number of lines on that one page may be counted.

FEEDBACK

12-16 What is meant by end-time calculations?

12-17 Why would a programmer want to count output lines?

PSEUDOCODE

Pseudocode is another way of planning program logic. The word *code* is a term referring to instructions written in a programming language. Chapter 13 introduces programming languages. You will see the phrase "code the instruction," meaning to write an instruction in the programming language.

Pseudo means imitation or false. *Pseudocode*, therefore, is an imitation of actual computer instructions. Instead of using symbols to describe the programming logic steps, as in flowcharting, pseudocode uses a structure that resembles computer instructions. Pseudocode and flowcharting both accomplish the same thing—a detailed plan for a program.

Why Not Flowchart?

Flowcharting has two major problems. First, flowcharting can be very time-consuming, especially on large, complex programs. Owing to the symbol-string nature of flowcharting, any changes or modifications in the program logic will usually require a completely new flowchart. The required use of the flowcharting template makes flowcharting so tedious that many companies either do not redo them or produce the flowchart by using a computer program to draw it. There are several computer programs available that will read the program's instructions and draw a flowchart of its logic, but these programs are fairly expensive to acquire and use a lot of computer time.

Second, flowcharting does not emphasize the top-down structure of the program. Chapter 4 and Unit Three dealt with structuring the system on a top-down basis. The major areas of the system were identified first, and then each of these major areas was broken down into increasingly detailed steps. To make program design as effective as possible, the programmer should continue the top-down approach into program logic design.

Program Design Language (PDL)

Pseudocode is a program planning technique that emphasizes both the logical steps and a top-down structure for the program. Because it emphasizes the design of the program, pseudocode is also called Program Design Language (PDL).

Pseudocode has two advantages:

1. It structures the program into a sequence that is easy to convert to a programming language.

2. It is easy to write and redo if program modifications are necessary. PDL is easier to write than an actual programming language because it has only a few rules to follow, allowing the programmer to concentrate on the logic of the program.

A disadvantage is that it may be more difficult for a beginner to follow the logic of or write pseudocode, as compared to flowcharting.

FEEDBACK

12-18 Define pseudocode.

12-19 What is the purpose of pseudocode?

12-20 Name the two advantages of pseudocode over flowcharting.

Basic Pseudocode Structures

Pseudocode is made up of three basic logic structures: (1) sequence logic, (2) decision logic, and (3) logic to produce loops.

Sequence logic is used by writing pseudocode instructions in the order, or sequence, in which they are to be performed. The logic flow of pseudocode is from the top to the bottom. Figure 12-13 shows an example of sequence logic structure.

Decision logic is depicted as either an **IF . . . THEN** or an **IF . . . THEN . . . ELSE** structure. Figure 12-14 illustrates these types of decision structures and the comparable flowcharting logic. In this example, IF . . . THEN . . . ELSE says, "If the condition is true, then do process 1, else (if it is not true) do process 2." **ENDIF** indicates the end of the IF . . . THEN . . . ELSE structure. If the decision is not to choose between two processes but simply to decide if a process is to be done or not, the structure will be IF . . . THEN. The example in Figure 12-14 says, "If the condition is true, then do process 1. If it is not true, skip over process 1." In both examples, process 1 and process 2 can actually be one or more processes. The structure is not limited to a single process.

Logic to produce loops uses two structures called the **DOWHILE** and the **DOUNTIL**. They are illustrated in Figure 12-15. Loops in a flowchart are easy to see because of the flowline drawn up to the top of the loop or the connectors at the top and bottom of the loop. Remember, a loop exists anytime an instruction or a group of instructions is repeated. In pseudocode, the loop is from DOUNTIL or DOWHILE (the top of the loop) down to **ENDDO** (the bottom of the loop).

The differences are that in the DOWHILE, the looping will continue as long as the condition is true. The looping stops when the condition is not true.

FIGURE 12-13

Pseudocode sequence structure.

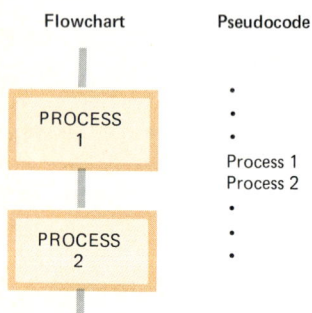

Sequence structure

Flowchart	Pseudocode
PROCESS 1	• • • Process 1 Process 2 • • •
PROCESS 2	

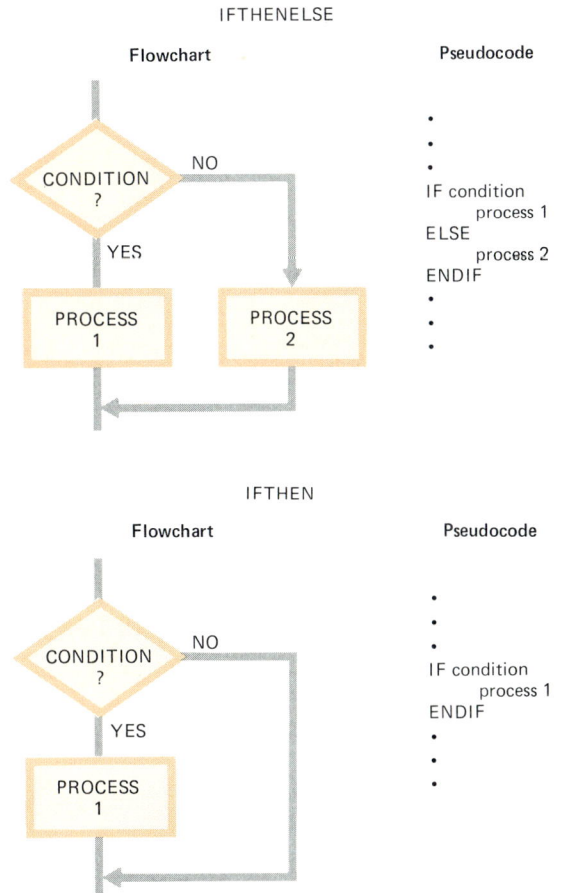

FIGURE 12-14
Pseudocode decision structures—
IFTHEN and IFTHENELSE.

In the DOUNTIL, the looping continues until the condition becomes true. (It loops as long as the condition is not true.) In both the DOUNTIL and the DOWHILE, the loop must contain a statement that will change the condition that controls the loop. If it doesn't, the looping will continue without end. Note that the condition is tested at the top of the loop in the DOWHILE and at the bottom of the loop in the DOUNTIL.

Figure 12-16 is the logic for calculating the average age of the students in a class, assuming that the age of each student is entered through an input device. Figure 12-17 is the pseudocode equivalent to the flowchart shown in Figure 12-10. In the pseudocode example, the first two lines initialize the total-age field and the total-students field to a beginning value of zero. The third line gives a field called "more students" a value of "yes." This field will be used to control the looping. The fourth line will cause the first student data record to be read. The fifth line is the beginning of a loop using the DOWHILE

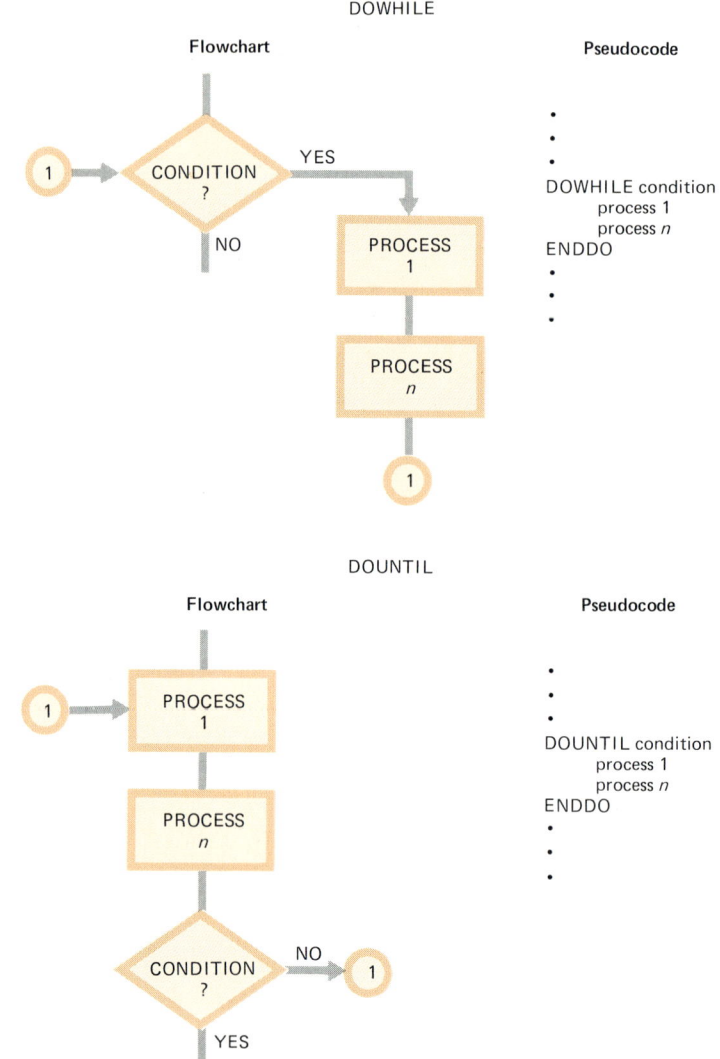

FIGURE 12-15

Pseudocode looping structures—
DOWHILE and DOUNTIL.

structure. It indicates that the loop will continue so long as there are more students—that is, as long as the more-students field has a value of "yes." The loop consists of three instructions: (1) to add 1 to the total-students field, (2) to add the age to the total-age field, and then (3) read the next student data record. If the end-of-file indicator is read, the more-students field is to be given a value of "no." EOF in pseudocode stands for "end of file." This will cause the DOWHILE loop to stop, because the condition (more students) is no longer true. ENDDO simply indicates the end of the DOWHILE loop. When the DOWHILE condition is no longer true, the next logical step will be the

```
total age = 0
total students = 0
more students = yes
read first record
DOWHILE more students
     add 1 to total students
     add age to total age
     read next record
          EOF sets more students = no
ENDDO
calculate average age
print average age
```

FIGURE 12-16
Pseudocode solution to the average age problem.

instruction following the ENDDO. When the DOWHILE loop is completed, all of the student data will have been read, a 1 will have been added to the total-students field for each, and the age in each record will have been added to the total-age field. The next step is to calculate the average age by dividing the total-age field by the total-students field. The last step in the program logic is to print the answer.

One important characteristic of pseudocode is the indenting technique used. Each step within the DOWHILE loop is indented, to show that it is part of the loop. The EOF (end-of-file) statement is indented from the READ NEXT RECORD step to show that it is part of the READ statement.

A second illustration of pseudocode is shown as Figure 12-17. It is the solution to the problem of reading student data, printing the names of male

```
total count = 0
more students = yes
read first record
DOWHILE more students
     IF sex = male
          IF age > 17
               IF age < 26
                    print the name
                    add 1 to total count
               ENDIF
          ENDIF
     ENDIF
     read next record
          EOF sets more students = no
ENDDO
print total count
```

FIGURE 12-17
Pseudocode solution to the student data problem to print males between the ages of 18 and 25. It also prints the total at the end.

students between the ages of 18 and 25, and printing the total number of males on the listing at the bottom of the listing. The problem solution is shown in flowcharting format as Figure 12-9. The first two lines of the pseudocode example assign beginning values to the total-count field and the more-students field. The third line causes the first data record to be read. The fourth line is the beginning of the DOWHILE loop. In this example, a series of decisions and a last-record instruction are included in the loop. The first statement in the DOWHILE loop asks, "Is the sex field equal to male?" If the answer is yes, it asks, "Is the age greater than 17?" If it is, then "Is the age less than 26?" This is a series of three decisions. Each one ends with an ENDIF vertically aligned below the appropriate IF.

Before a student's name will be printed and 1 added to the total-count field, all three conditions (that of being a male, older than 17, and younger than 26) must be true (answered yes). If any of the three conditions is not true, the logic path goes to the READ NEXT RECORD instruction. After the more-students field has been set equal to "no" by the EOF condition, the total-count field will be printed. Note that all the instructions within the DOWHILE loop are indented from the DOWHILE margin. Also note that instructions written within each of the IF . . . THEN structures is indented.

FEEDBACK

12-21 What are the three basic pseudocode structures?

12-22 What is the difference between the IF . . . THEN and the IF . . . THEN . . . ELSE?

12-23 What is the difference between the DOUNTIL and the DOWHILE?

12-24 What is the purpose of the ENDIF and ENDDO?

SUMMARY

The development phase is the phase in which the system's computer programs are written. The programs are lists of instructions that will be followed by the control unit of the central processing unit (CPU). The instructions of the program must be complete and in the appropriate sequence, or else the wrong answers will result. To guard against these errors in logic and to document the program's logical approach, logic plans should be developed.

There are two common techniques for planning the logic of a program. The first technique is flowcharting. A flowchart is a plan in the form of a graphic or pictorial representation that uses predefined symbols to illustrate the program logic. It is, therefore, a "picture" of the logical steps to be performed by the computer. Each of the predefined symbol shapes stands for a general operation. The symbol shape communicates the nature of the general operation, and the specifics are written within the symbol. A plastic or metal guide called a template is used to make drawing the symbols easier.

The second technique for planning program logic is called pseudocode. Pseudocode is an imitation of actual program instructions. It allows a program-like structure without the burden of programming rules to follow. Pseudocode is less time-consuming for the professional programmer than is flowcharting. It also emphasizes a top-down approach to program structure.

Pseudocode has three basic structures: sequence, decision, and looping logic. With these three structures, any required logic can be expressed.

ANSWERS TO FEEDBACK QUESTIONS

12-1 To help structure the program logic and to help document the finished program.

12-2 A plastic or metal guide used to trace the flowcharting symbols.

12-3 The terminal symbol is an oval shape. Its purpose is to indicate the beginning, ending, and pauses in the program logic flow.

12-4 The parallelogram shows input and output.

12-5 Arrowheads should be used anytime the logic flow direction may be confusing.

12-6 By the words written inside the symbol.

12-7 A process loop exists anytime a series of instructions is repeated.

12-8 The decision symbol is diamond-shaped.

12-9 The computer can compare two memory fields and determine if they are equal or unequal. If they are unequal, it can tell which is larger.

12-10 Addition, subtraction, multiplication, division, and logical operations such as data moves. It is a rectangle.

12-11 To assign a value to a field.

12-12 The process symbol.

12-13 To replace flowlines where they would be confusing.

12-14 An exit connector is the point at which the logic flow leaves the normal downward flow. The entry connector is the point at which the logic flow returns to the normal flow.

12-15 The offpage connector is used whenever the connection point is on a different page of the flowchart.

12-16 Calculations that are processed after the end of the input file.

12-17 To logically determine when the bottom of the printed output page was reached.

12-18 A planning technique that is an imitation of actual programming instructions.

12-19 Like flowcharting, to help structure the program logic and to help document the finished program.

12-20 **a** It is easy to convert to a programming language.
   b It is easy to write and to redo if modifications are required at a later time.

12-21 Sequence logic, decision logic, and logic to produce loops.

12-22 In the IF . . . THEN . . . ELSE, statements to be processed if the condition is true and statements to be processed if the condition is false are both included. In the IF . . . THEN, only statements to be processed when the condition is true are included.

12-23 The DOUNTIL loops until a condition becomes true; the DOWHILE loops as long as the condition remains true.

12-24 The ENDIF marks the end of the IF . . . THEN or IF . . . THEN . . . ELSE structure. The ENDDO marks the end of the DOUNTIL or DOWHILE structure.

FOR REVIEW AND DISCUSSION

1   Why should computer programs be planned prior to being written?

2   Can a flowchart be drawn for a task if the person drawing the flowchart cannot perform the task manually?

3   Why are there standards for the symbols used in drawing flowcharts?

4   What is the meaning of the rectangle-shaped symbol?

5   Why should the at-end decision be drawn immediately after the input symbol?

6   Draw a flowchart of the logical steps needed to produce a printed listing of all students over the age of 18 in a class. (The input records contain the students' names and ages.)

7   Draw a flowchart of the logical steps needed to print the name and age of the oldest and youngest student in the class. (The input records contain the students' names and ages.)

8   Describe the three basic pseudocode structures.

9   Write the pseudocode to solve the problem described in question 6.

10 Write the pseudocode to solve the problem described in question 7.

CHAPTER 13
PROGRAMMING LANGUAGES

PREVIEW   This chapter continues the development of computer programs that was begun in Chapter 12. In this chapter, we will see how the logical steps of our program plan will be written as program instructions. The goal of this chapter is to introduce some of the common languages used in writing programs.

In this chapter you will learn:

1. The nature of machine language
2. The nature of symbolic languages
3. The orientation and characteristics of six common programming languages: BASIC, COBOL, FORTRAN IV, PASCAL, PL/I, and RPG II

KEY TERMS TO WATCH FOR AND REMEMBER

coding
coding form
machine code
symbolic code
assembler-level languages

mnemonic
problem-oriented languages
business-oriented languages
mathematically oriented languages

The techniques of flowcharting and pseudocode allow the programmer to plan the steps to be followed by a computer in order to solve a problem. These plans serve as the "blueprints" for the computer program.

WRITING PROGRAM INSTRUCTIONS   Let's assume that we have studied the problem, designed a logical plan (our flowchart or pseudocode), and are now ready to write the program instructions. The process of writing program instructions is called **coding.** The instructions will be written on a form called a **coding form**. The instructions we write will be recorded in a machine-readable form using a keypunch, key-to-tape, or key-to-disk, or entered directly into computer memory through a terminal keyboard. Most computer centers currently enter programs using terminals, but some use punched cards or some other form of offline data recording. Whatever the input medium, the purpose is to enter the program instructions into the computer's memory.

The computer cannot understand instructions written in just any old way. The instructions must be written according to a set of rules. These rules are the foundation of a programming language. There are several programming languages that are commonly used. Six of these languages will be presented in this chapter. Many of the words and symbols used in programming have the same meaning in all of the languages. The major difference between the languages is the structure of the instructions. We will be looking at these structures in this chapter.

THE DEVELOPMENT OF PROGRAMMING LANGUAGES

A programming language must convey the logical steps of the program plan in such a way that the control unit of the CPU can interpret and follow the instructions. Programming languages have improved throughout the years, just as computer hardware has improved. They have progressed from machine-oriented languages that use strings of binary 1s and 0s to problem-oriented languages that use common mathematical and/or English terms.

Machine Code

The first programs were written in **machine code.** Machine code is the fundamental language of the computer. It is written as strings of binary 1s and 0s. Each instruction tells the control unit of the CPU what to do and the length and location of the data fields that are involved in the operation. Typical operations involve reading, adding, subtracting, writing, and so on. The string of 1s and 0s required for an addition, subtraction, or the like is determined by the nature of the computer logic circuitry or the design of the computer. Therefore, each computer design has its own unique machine codes. Figure 13-1 is an example of machine code for an IBM 4300 series computer. The first 8 bits are the operation code. In this case, 11111010 means to add two fields in main storage. The operation code indicates the "action" that is to occur.

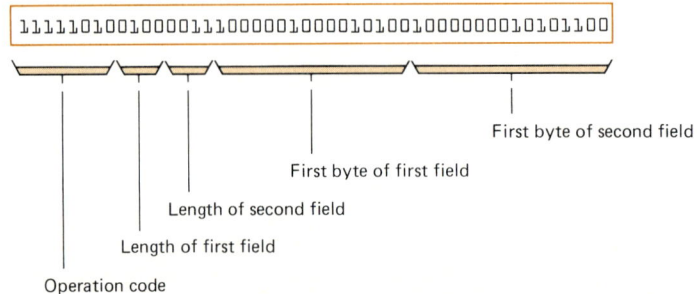

111110100100001110000010000101001000000010101100

First byte of second field

First byte of first field

Length of second field

Length of first field

Operation code

FIGURE 13-1
Machine code to add two fields.

The next 4 bits (0100) tell the control unit that the first field to be added is 5 bytes in length. The next 4 bits (0011) mean that the second field to be added is 4 bytes in length. Remember, a data field in memory is a string of bytes. The length of the string must be defined. When you get to Supplement III, which deals with number systems, you will see that binary 0100 is equal to a decimal value of 4 and that binary 0011 is equal to decimal 3. The length portion of a machine code instruction is written as 1 less than the actual length of the field. The next 16 bits indicate the starting position in memory of the first field (the location of the first byte of the string). The last 16 bits indicate the starting position of the second field.

Writing a program in machine code has several disadvantages:

1. Machine code is difficult to learn. It is necessary for the programmer either to memorize the bit patterns for each operation or to constantly refer to a reference card. The programmer must also keep track of field lengths and field locations in a format that is not easily remembered.

2. It is easy to make errors using machine code. As we can see in the example, it would be easy to transpose 1s and 0s either in coding or in data entry.

3. It is difficult to correct or modify machine-coded programs. Figure 13-1 is an example of a single addition instruction. Imagine what a program consisting of hundreds of instructions would look like. A programmer would be looking at many pages of 1s and 0s. To locate the part of the program that requires modification would be a difficult job at best.

4. Because the machine-code bit patterns depends on the computer design, each computer of a different design has a different machine-code set of instructions. If, after becoming proficient in the machine code for a particular machine, a company should change to another computer, the programmer may be required to learn a new machine-code language and would have to rewrite all of the existing programs.

In summary, writing a program in machine code is so difficult and time-consuming that it is rarely used.

Symbolic Code

Computers were in use for only a short time before it became apparent that writing programs in machine code was terribly inefficient. In an effort to avoid some of the disadvantages of machine code, symbolic programming languages were developed. **Symbolic code** substitutes symbolic names (words) for the binary strings of machine code. The first symbolic languages were called **assembler-level languages.** Figure 13-2 is an example of the IBM's 4300 series assembler instruction to add the field called AMOUNT to the field called TOTAL. It accomplishes the same logical step as the machine-code example in Figure 13-1. Assembler substitutes a mnemonic operation code for the binary operation code. A **mnemonic** technique is any memory aid or memory-aiding technique. A mnemonic code is usually a strict abbreviation of the words it

FIGURE 13-2

Assembler code to add two fields.

```
AP        TOTAL,AMOUNT
```

stands for. The mnemonic operation code AP stands for "add packed." (*Packed* refers to packed decimal—a decimal format that will be discussed in Supplement IV.) In this case, the two fields involved in the addition are TOTAL and AMOUNT. Each of the symbolic field names is equated to the field length and the starting point of the field in main storage. There are two obvious advantages of symbolic code over machine code:

1. It is easier to learn and to use a mnemonic such as AP than to learn and use "11111010" to cause two decimal fields to be added.

2. It is easier to locate, correct, and modify instructions written with mnemonics and symbolic field names.

Two disadvantages of machine code are not solved by using assembler. First, instructions are still being written at the machine-code level—that is, one assembler instruction is substituted for one machine-code instruction. Assembler-level languages are said to be *machine-oriented* because the programmer must be aware of a particular machine's characteristics and requirements as the program is written. If the computer design requires that data be in a particular format, it is the programmer's responsibility to make sure that the data are in the required format or to write instructions to convert those data to the required format.

A second disadvantage is that assembler languages are usually unique to a particular computer series. The only case in which assembler code is compatible with a different computer series is one in which the computer manufacturer has chosen mnemonic operation codes that match those of another manufacturer. This requires similar hardware characteristics, and it is not a common occurrence. A change in a computer CPU still usually requires learning a new language and the converting of all existing programs—a very expensive undertaking.

FEEDBACK
13-1 Define the term *coding*.
13-2 Describe the appearance of machine code.
13-3 What are the major disadvantages of machine code?
13-4 What is a mnemonic code?

Problem-Oriented Languages

Other symbolic languages have been developed to correct the problems of assembler-level languages. These are called **problem-oriented languages.** The common problem-oriented languages are geared toward either business or mathematical problems. All programs have three basic functions. They cause the computer to input data, process it, and output the answers.

A typical business problem is to keep track of the account balances of a store's credit customers. This would be handled by an accounts receivable program. Assuming that the business is doing well, the input volume of charges and payments will be very large. The output volume will also be very large, requiring at least one page (a bill) for each customer that owes the store money each month. The processing activity will consist of an addition for each charge and a subtraction for each payment. You will note that the processing is relatively simple. In fact, the usual business problem consists of high input volume, relatively little processing, and a high output volume. **Business-oriented languages,** therefore, emphasize the ease of data handling rather than calculations.

Mathematical problems tend to be the opposite of business problems. They tend to have a relatively low volume of input, a large volume of calculations (often using higher mathematics), and a relatively small volume of output, such as a single numerical answer. **Mathematically oriented languages** emphasize the ease of performing mathematical calculations, rather than data handling.

The development of problem-oriented programming languages was an attempt to avoid the disadvantages of assembler-level languages. Problem-oriented languages are symbolic languages that use English words and/or mathematical symbols rather than mnemonic codes and are therefore generally easier to write. In addition, the programmer is not required to write a program with particular machine requirements in mind. For example, the data of a field involved in an addition operation may not be in the correct format for the computer being used. A problem-oriented language has the ability to cause the data format to be changed without requiring the programmer to write specific instructions to do so. Problem-oriented languages have many similar automatic features that relieve the programmer of the burden of complying with machine requirements. This automatic feature characteristic of problem-oriented languages also makes them compatible with a wide variety of different computers. This is a very valuable advantage because it means that a company changing computers—even to one from a different manufacturer—will not be required to rewrite all the programs that it is currently using. Some modification of programs is almost always required, but these modifications will be relatively minor.

Two disadvantages of problem-oriented languages are:

1. The programs may be less efficient than programs written in an assembler-level language. That is, the programs take more time to run and require more main storage.

2. Because the automatic features of problem-oriented languages always occur and are not under the control of the programmer, they are less flexible than assembler-level languages. For example, social security numbers are often printed as 123 45 6789 or 123-45-6789. The format with the hyphens is the most commonly used, but most problem-oriented languages do not allow for a simple insertion of hyphens into a number. Assembler languages allow any character to be inserted into a number. This lack of flexibility means that some tasks cannot be done in a problem-oriented language, or can be done only with great difficulty. In most cases, the advantages of problem-oriented languages far outweigh the disadvantages. Most computer installations use a problem-oriented language for most programs and use an assembler-level language for doing special tasks that cannot be easily done otherwise.

FEEDBACK

13-5 What is the typical balance between input-output and processing in business applications? Scientific applications?

13-6 What are the two major advantages of problem-oriented languages over assembler-level languages?

COMMON PROBLEM-ORIENTED LANGUAGES

There are over 200 problem-oriented languages. However, most of these are for very special purposes or are designed to solve problems in a very specific application area. The most common problem-oriented languages are COBOL, FORTRAN, PL/I, RPG, BASIC, and PASCAL.

COBOL

COBOL is the most widely used business-oriented programming language. Its name is an acronym for *co*mmon *b*usiness-*o*riented *l*anguage. COBOL was designed to solve problems that are oriented toward data handling and input-output operations. Of course, COBOL can perform arithmetic operations as well, but its greatest flexibility is in data handling. COBOL also was designed as a self-documenting language. Self-documenting languages are those that do not require a great deal of explanation in order to be understood by someone reading the program instructions. The self-documenting aspect of COBOL is made possible by its sentencelike structure and the very generous maximum symbolic field-name length of 30 characters. With a field-name length of up to 30 characters, the name can clearly identify the field and its purpose.

Figure 13-3 is an example of a COBOL sentence that includes a decision to determine whether or not a telephone area code is equal to 714. If it is not equal to 714, it will add a 1 to a field called TOTAL-OUT-OF-AREA. This decision and arithmetic statement could be used, for example, to determine how many employees have telephone area codes that are different from that of the company. After processing all records, the TOTAL-OUT-OF-AREA field would contain the total of the employees outside of the 714 area code. Notice that this COBOL instruction is very much like an English sentence, even to the point of ending with a period. In COBOL, all field names must be a single word. COBOL uses the space between words and symbols as a delimiter or

FIGURE 13-3
COBOL decision with arithmetic instruction.

```
IF AREA-CODE IS NOT EQUAL TO 714
   ADD 1 TO TOTAL-OUT-OF-AREA.
```

separator. A field name such as AREA-CODE meets the COBOL requirement for a single word name because it has no imbedded spaces, and the hyphen still makes the field name meaningful to humans. The COBOL programmer should make sure that the field names that are used are meaningful, so that the self-documenting feature of the language is not lost. An introduction to the COBOL language is contained in Supplement I.

FORTRAN IV

The FORTRAN IV language is oriented toward solving problems of a mathematical nature. The name FORTRAN comes from the combination of the words *for*mula *tran*slation. As FORTRAN has been improved over the years, a roman numeral has been added to the name to indicate its version. The current version is FORTRAN IV. It has been designed as an algebra-based programming language. Any formula or those mathematical relationships that can be expressed algebraically can easily be expressed as a FORTRAN instruction. FORTRAN is the most commonly used language for scientific applications.

Figure 13-4 is an example of a FORTRAN statement that includes the same decision and arithmetic operation as the COBOL example in Figure 13-3. FORTRAN will appear to use some rather strange field names. This is because of the FORTRAN requirement that the first letter of the field name indicate the format of the data in the field. Field names beginning with the letters I, J, K, L, M, or N mean that the field will contain whole numbers. If any other letter is used, it means that the number value in the field includes fractional values. Since telephone area codes are all whole numbers, the field name must begin with I, J, K, L, M, or N. In this example, IAREA is used as the field name. If the field IAREA is not equal to 714, the current value in the field called NOT714 will be replaced by the current value in NOT714, plus 1. In other words, a 1 will be added to a field called NOT714. Because of FORTRAN's heavy use of mathematical symbols and, for most computers, a maximum field-name length of 6 characters, FORTRAN is not nearly as much like English as COBOL. It should be noted that spaces have no meaning and are ignored in FORTRAN statements. Instead, parentheses, periods, commas, and mathematical symbols are used as word separators. The example in Figure 13-4 could have had a space after IF, before or after .NE., or anywhere else in the statement. Many FORTRAN programmers leave spaces to improve readability.

PL/I

PL/I stands for *p*rogramming *l*anguage I. It was designed as a general-purpose language incorporating features similar to COBOL for data handling instructions and features similar to FORTRAN for mathematical instructions. PL/I

FIGURE 13-4

FORTRAN decision with arithmetic instruction.

```
IF(IAREA.NE.714)NOT714=NOT714+1
```

FIGURE 13-5

PL/1 decision with arithmetic
instruction.

```
IF AREA_CODE ¬ =  714
    THEN OUTSIDE_714  =  OUTSIDE_714 + 1;
```

is much more than a combination of the good features of both COBOL and FORTRAN, as it has many capabilities that are unique. Yet, although PL/I is one of the most versatile and the most powerful of the programming languages, it is not the most commonly used. COBOL and FORTRAN have been available for a longer period of time than PL/I, and many more users work with those languages. Many data processing centers are so firmly established in FORTRAN or COBOL that cost considerations prevent them from switching to PL/I. In addition, not all computer manufacturers provide the PL/I language.

Figure 13-5 is the simple decision instruction, including an ADD instruction that we illustrated in COBOL and FORTRAN. PL/I is more like English than FORTRAN but not quite as much so as COBOL. Note that spaces are used as delimiters or word separators in PL/I. Spaces, therefore, are not allowed to be imbedded in field names. Instead of using a hyphen to fill in spaces in a field name, as COBOL does, PL/I uses the break character, a dash below the space (_). In addition, it uses the relational symbols, instead of English words, in decisions: for example, the equals sign (=) in place of "is equal to." The symbol following the field name AREA–CODE (¬) is a PL/I symbol for "not." The statement reads "if AREA–CODE is not equal to 714, then the current value of OUTSIDE–714 is to be replaced by the current value of OUTSIDE–714, plus 1." A semicolon (;) is used to indicate the end of the PL/I statement. One advantage in documentation over FORTRAN is that the field-name length can be up to 31 characters.

RPG II

RPG II is a business-oriented language. The name stands for *r*eport *p*rogram *g*enerator. RPG is considerably different from other programming languages. RPG is, in effect, a large prewritten program. The programmer simply indicates the options within the master program that are to be used and, through a set of indicators, when they are to be used. RPG was originally referred to as a "quick-and-dirty" programming language. That is, it is quick for the programmer to write and relatively inefficient in its use of main storage and processing speed. The latest version of RPG, called RPG II, greatly improved the language and gave it additional capabilities. Although probably not as efficient as the other programming languages, RPG can duplicate any COBOL program. RPG has an advantage over COBOL in that it requires less training for a programmer to become proficient in it. For this reason, RPG is commonly used on many smaller computers and in small businesses.

Figure 13-6 is the same decision and addition operation as that illustrated in the other languages. In RPG, two instructions are required. The first says that a field called AREAC is to be compared to 714. If it is equal, indicator 03 will be set to an "on" condition. If it is not equal, indicator 03 will be set to an "off" indication. The N03 on the second line indicates that the second instruction is to be executed only if indicator 03 is not on. If this is the case, a 1 will be added to the field called TOTAL, and the result will be placed back in the field called TOTAL. As can be seen from this example, RPG is much less like English than COBOL. Its structure, plus a maximum fieldname length of 6 characters, does not contribute to its being easily understood by human readers of the programs. RPG II is covered in more detail in Supplement II.

BASIC

BASIC is the acronym for *b*eginner's *a*ll-purpose *s*ymbolic *i*nstruction *c*ode. It was developed at Dartmouth College as an easy-to-learn programming language for students and inexperienced programmers. Most BASIC programs are entered and executed through CRT terminals.

FIGURE 13-6
RPG decision with arithmetic instruction.

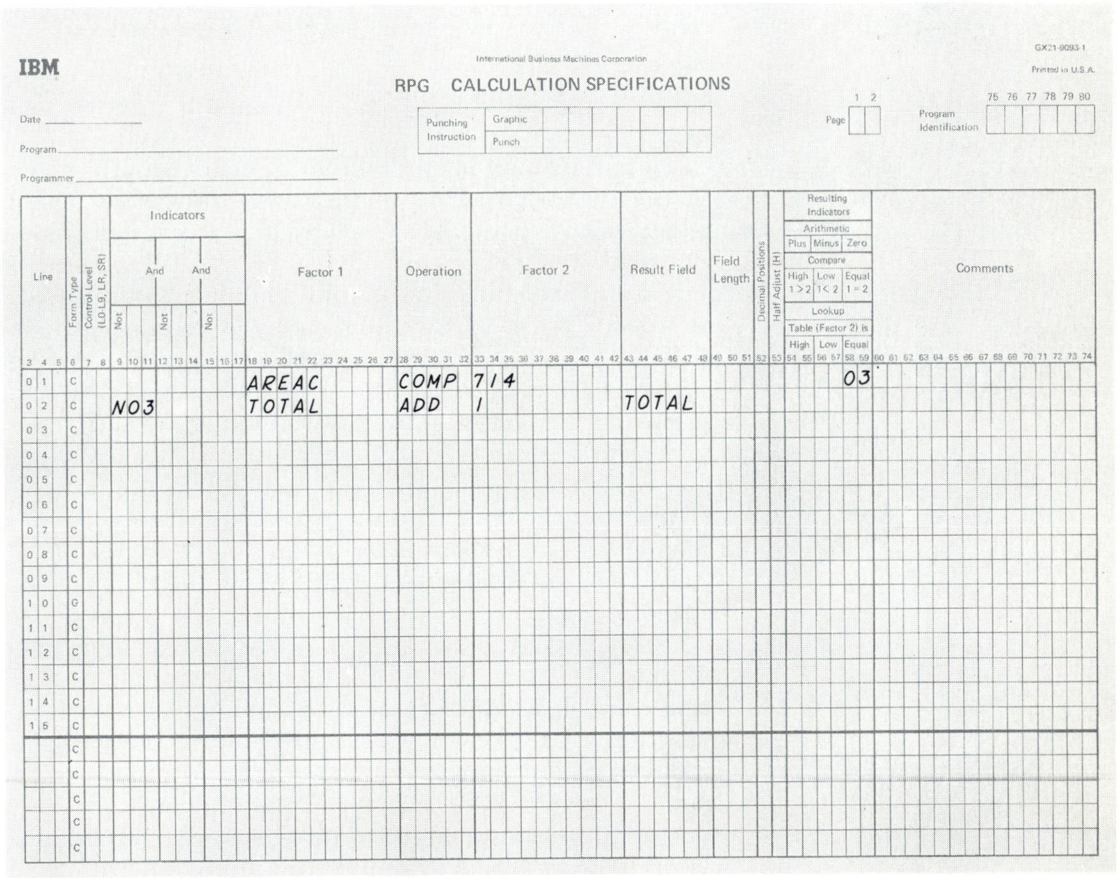
IBM — International Business Machines Corporation
RPG CALCULATION SPECIFICATIONS

Line	Form Type	Control Level	Indicators	Factor 1	Operation	Factor 2	Result Field	Field Length	Decimal Positions	Half Adjust (H)	Resulting Indicators (Plus/High)	(Minus/Low)	(Zero/Equal)	Comments
01	C			AREAC	COMP	714							03	
02	C		N03	TOTAL	ADD	1	TOTAL							

THE NEED FOR STANDARD LANGUAGES

It has been estimated that the total investment in programs in the United States is between $100 billion and $200 billion. Industry is spending enormous sums of money in converting programs to keep its software usable by the latest processors. Conversion is the process by which computer programs are modified to enable their execution on computers other than those for which they were written. Many data processing organizations considering conversion have at least 1000 to 1500 programs to convert.

A General Accounting Office re-port stated that the federal government spends $450 million each year on software conversion. The federal government is planning to establish standards in conversion methodology through the National Bureau of Standards. A recent report by a conversion technology panel stated that the rapid development of hardware (such as minicomputers and new storage devices) is increasing the need for generalized conversion tools.

In addition to the hardware, programming languages are improving. However, software advances will not eliminate the need for conversion.

Programming language standards also will not eliminate the need for conversion but can greatly simplify the conversion process.

Most data processing installations will not consider the use of a programming language that has not been standardized. The conversion costs which would be incurred at a later time are the reason.

The language BASIC has had its first minimal standard published. Many feel that the popularity of BASIC will dramatically increase as BASIC becomes a standard language.

FIGURE 13-7

BASIC decision with arithmetic instruction.

```
30 IF AC <> 714 THEN LET T = T + 1
```

Figure 13-7 is an example of a BASIC statement. The statement reads, "If the field AC is not equal to 714, then let the value of field called T be equal to the field called T plus 1." This is the same area code decision as was previously illustrated. As we can see from this example, BASIC arithmetic statements look a great deal like FORTRAN. BASIC has the same general orientation to mathematics as FORTRAN has. The 30 in the example is the statement's number. All BASIC statements must be numbered. Field names are limited to 2 characters on most computers. The combination of the "less than" and the "greater than" symbols is the equivalent of "not equal." If the field AC is less than or greater than 714, it cannot be equal to 714. BASIC is covered in greater depth in Chapters 16 and 17.

PASCAL

PASCAL was invented in 1970 by Professor Niklaus Wirth of Zurich, Switzerland. It was named after the mathematician Blaise Pascal, who invented one of the earliest practical calculators. PASCAL is a mathematically oriented programming language and, as such, is most commonly used in mathematics, engineering, and computer science departments of colleges and universities. This language is somewhat unusual in that it was designed to be a structured language. This means that the program must be written in logical modules which are in turn called by a main controlling module. Much of PASCAL's popularity is due to work done at the University of California at San Diego, where PASCAL has been implemented on several different computers including microcomputers.

FIGURE 13-8

PASCAL decision with arithmetic instruction.

```
IF AREACODE <> 714, THEN OUTAREA :=OUTAREA+1
```

Figure 13-8 is the same decision and addition operation as that illustrated in the other languages shown in this chapter. This statement reads, "If the field AREACODE is not equal to 714, then the field OUTAREA is to be made equal to the current value of OUTAREA plus 1." As we can see from this example, PASCAL looks a great deal like BASIC and FORTRAN and other math-oriented languages. Note that the "less than" and "greater than" symbols together mean "not equal to," as in BASIC. Also note that PASCAL uses a colon (:) and equal sign (=) in calculation statements. Names of fields in PASCAL may be any length, but characters past the first 8 are ignored. Thus programs written in PASCAL tend to be easier to understand, owing to the longer names.

FEEDBACK

13-7 What is the problem orientation of COBOL? FORTRAN? PL/I? RPG? BASIC? PASCAL?

13-8 What kind of computer activities are emphasized in COBOL? FORTRAN?

13-9 Why are problem-oriented languages more compatible than assembler languages with multiple computers?

THE CONVERSION OF SYMBOLIC LANGUAGES

This chapter has emphasized the advantages of symbolic programming languages over machine code. Most of the symbolic languages are oriented toward the particular application areas of business or science (math). The one problem with all symbolic languages is that none of them can be understood by a computer. The symbolic languages may say AP, ADD, or use a "plus" sign to indicate an addition step, but the only thing that means addition to a computer is its binary machine code. We have symbolic programs that are relatively easy for humans to understand, but they cannot be understood by computers. On the other hand, we have machine code that is understood by the computer, but it is difficult for humans to use. The solution is a translator that translates the symbolic program into machine code. The translator allows the human to work with relatively easy-to-understand symbolic languages and the computer to follow instructions in machine code. The translator is a program itself. It is part of a group of programs, called the operating system, that help us to use the computer. The use of language translators and other operating system programs are discussed in Chapter 14.

SUMMARY

The planning techniques of flowcharting and pseudocode allow the programmer to plan the logical steps to be included in a computer program. The next step is to write or code the logical steps from the plan in a programming language.

TABLE 13-1
CHARACTERISTICS OF COMMON PROGRAMMING LANGUAGES

Language	Language orientation	Instruction format	Compatibility with other computers
Machine code	All areas	Binary digits	Not compatible
Assembler-level	All areas	Mnemonic codes	Usually not compatible
COBOL	Business	English sentences	Compatible
PL/I	All areas	English sentences and math symbols	Compatible
RPG	Business	English words and indicators	Compatible
BASIC	Math	English words and math symbols	Compatible
FORTRAN	Math	English words and math symbols	Compatible
PASCAL	Math	English words and math symbols	Compatible

The first programming language, and the only one a computer's control unit can follow, is called machine code. Machine code consists of a string of binary 1s and 0s. It is difficult to use and is oriented toward specific computer circuitry.

Symbolic languages were developed to make the coding of programs easier. The first of the symbolic languages was called assembler-level language. It uses mnemonic codes in place of the binary strings of machine code. Although assembler languages are easier to use than machine code, they are machine-oriented. They require the programmer to consider the specific requirements of the computer being used when writing the program. Assembler programs are not generally transferable to other computers.

The next development of programming languages was a series of problem-oriented languages. Each of these languages is designed to solve a particular kind of problem—usually, either business or scientific. COBOL and RPG are business-oriented. FORTRAN, PASCAL and BASIC are oriented toward math or science. A language called PL/I is a general-purpose language. Table 13-1 compares the various programming languages in the areas of application, the format of the instructions, and the compatibility of each language with that used by various types of computers.

The only language that a computer can understand is machine code. The symbolic languages were developed strictly for the benefit of the humans involved. The symbolic programs must be translated into machine code before a computer can follow the program's instructions.

ANSWERS TO
FEEDBACK QUESTIONS

13-1 The activity of writing instructions in a programming language.

13-2 Machine code is strings of binary 1s and 0s.

13-3 a It is difficult to learn.

b It is easy to make errors.

c It is difficult to correct or to modify.

d One computer's code is not compatible with codes of other computers.

13-4 A symbolic code that is easy to remember. It is used as a substitute for machine code in assembler-level languages.

13-5 Business applications usually have a large amount of input and output to handle but a relatively small number of calculations. Scientific applications usually have a small amount of input and output and a relatively large number of calculations.

13-6 They are easier to write because they are more like English and they do not require the programmer to write a program with particular machine requirements in mind.

13-7 COBOL and RPG are business-oriented. FORTRAN, PASCAL, and BASIC are math-oriented. PL/I is a general-purpose language.

13-8 a Input-output and data handling activities.
b Arithmetic calculations.

13-9 They do not contain machine-level detail in their instructions. Automatic features of the languages handle particular machine requirements without the programmer's help.

FOR REVIEW AND DISCUSSION

1 What hardware device follows our program's instructions?
2 Which programming languages can be understood by the computer hardware?
3 Why is language compatibility between different types of computers important to a data processing center?
4 Can math-oriented programs be written in COBOL?
5 Can business-oriented programs be written in PASCAL?
6 Describe the appearance of instructions written in COBOL, FORTRAN, PL/I, RPG, BASIC, and PASCAL.
7 What are the general characteristics that distinguish math-oriented and business-oriented programming languages?
8 It is possible to write structured programs in most programming languages. Which programming language was specifically designed for structured programming?
9 The statement ADD AMOUNT TO TOTAL. is an example of what programming language?
10 The statement TOTAL := TOTAL + AMOUNT is an example of what programming language?

CHAPTER 14

RUNNING
THE COMPUTER
PROGRAM

PREVIEW The previous two chapters dealt with the planning of the logical steps to be used in a program and the coding of the program instructions in a symbolic programming language. This chapter illustrates how the programs that we have written are run on a computer. The goal of this chapter is to show how a collection of special programs, called the operating system, is used to make the computer a useful, easy-to-use tool.

In this chapter you will learn:

1. The major functions of an operating system
2. The steps required to run a computer program
3. The nature of job control
4. The function of the language processors
5. The nature of the major service programs

KEY TERMS TO WATCH FOR AND REMEMBER

operating system
control program
memory dump
language processors
low-level languages
assembler
high-level languages
compiler

interpreter
source program
object program
linkage editor
library
librarian
utilities
sort-merge

In Chapter 4 you learned that computer systems are made up of input devices, a control unit, main memory, an arithmetic logic unit, and output devices. You also learned that the function of the control unit is to manage and coordinate the other units in the system. The control unit does this by following instructions that are stored in main memory. When the control unit is following a program's instructions, that program is said to be "running."

Chapters 12 and 13 described the planning and writing of program instructions that are to be followed by the control unit. When the program has been written, the next step is to get it into the main memory of the computer. Remember, main memory is the part of the computer where instructions must be in order for the control unit to follow them.

Near the end of Chapter 13 it was pointed out that all symbolic programs must first be translated to machine code before the control unit can understand them. The translator itself is a program that was probably provided by the computer manufacturer. How do we get our program into main memory? How do we get our symbolic program translated into machine code? How do we tell the computer what program should be run next? The answer to all of these questions is the operating system. The **operating system** is a collection of programs that allow us to schedule the jobs the computer is to perform, to translate symbolic programs into machine code, and to use the computer effectively.

CONTROL
PROGRAMS

A **control program** is an operating system program that controls the computer. It does not calculate answers or print reports. However, it does schedule the activities of the computer and watch over other programs as they run. In order to control the computer, the control program must be a main-memory resident. That is to say, it is always in main memory, along with our program and the data being processed. Let us see what these computer activities are and how our programs are scheduled by the control program.

Control Program Functions

Control programs go by many different names, depending on the manufacturer of the computer. Common names for the control program are supervisor, monitor, executive, or just control program. In this chapter, we shall call the control program the supervisor, the name used by IBM. The operating system used as an example in this chapter is the IBM Disk Operating System (DOS). Its functions are typical of most operating systems. The three main functions performed by the supervisor are to schedule jobs, to schedule input and output, and to monitor other programs as they are running.

Job scheduling   Each program to be run is part of a job for the computer. Of course, humans decide what programs are to be run, but this information must be given to the supervisor, in order to actually run the jobs. The information about the job to be run is communicated to the supervisor through job control statements. These job control statements may be inputted from punched cards,

a secondary storage device, or a terminal. For example, the statement // JOB
PAYROLL tells the supervisor that you have a new job for it and that the job
is called PAYROLL. The slashes at the beginning identify it as a job control
statement.

It takes a series of job control statements to give all the necessary information about a job to the supervisor. Let us look at an example. We have
written a payroll program that will multiply each employee's hours worked by
their hourly pay rates, calculate payroll deductions, calculate the employee's
net pay, and print each employee's paycheck and stub. We shall assume that
the transaction data (employee number and hours worked) are recorded on
magnetic tape. The more permanent data (employee number, employee name,
pay rate, tax exemptions claimed, and so on) are stored in a master file also on
magnetic tape. Remember, instructions being followed and data being processed
must both be in main memory, but main memory is too limited for inactive
data. Secondary storage devices, such as magnetic tape and disk, are used for
storage of data and programs not currently being used. The machine code for
our payroll program has been stored on magnetic disk.

Figure 14-1 shows the job control statements required to run our payroll
program. The first statement tells the supervisor that this is the beginning of
a new job and that the job's name is PAYROLL. The second statement lists
the options that are to be exercised by the supervisor with this program. The
option listed with this program is DUMP. It tells the supervisor program that
if this program should fail because of an operational error, a memory dump is
to be printed. This will be covered in more detail when the program monitoring
function is discussed. The third and fourth statements are called assign statements. They tell the supervisor that the file referred to in the program as file
SYS007 is located on a magnetic tape drive with the address 280 and that file
SYS008 is located on device 281. Note that this identifies the tape drives to be
used and not the reels of tape. Using this system of assigning I/O devices to a
program, any available tape drive can be used without making changes in the
program. The fifth and sixth statements are tape label statements (TLBL).
They provide information to the operating system that will allow the supervisor
to verify that the labels recorded on the magnetic tapes are the correct labels.
This prevents the use of the wrong magnetic tape with the payroll program.
SYS007 is the system number used in the program and was assigned to tape
drive 280. "PAYROLL MASTER" is the file name to be compared to the label

```
//  JOB PAYROLL
//  OPTION DUMP
//  ASSGN SYS007,X'280'
//  ASSGN SYS008,X'281'
//  TLBL SYS007,'PAYROLL MASTER',7,128
//  TLBL SYS008,'PAYROLL DATA',7,146
//  EXEC PAYROLL
/&
```

FIGURE 14-1

Job control statements to execute the
payroll program.

recorded on the tape. The number 7 indicates that the retention period for this tape is seven days. If anyone attempts to record data on top of the file within seven days, a warning message will be outputted on the computer operator's console. The number 128 is the serial number for the reel of tape. The TLBL statement links the program and the master data file. The second TLBL statement identifies the transaction file holding the weekly payroll data called "PAYROLL DATA." It is identified in the program as SYS008, is to be retained for seven days, and is reel number 146. The seventh statement indicates that the program called PAYROLL is to be run. This will cause the supervisor program to load the program called PAYROLL from magnetic disk into main memory and turn control over to it. The /& indicates "end of job." The supervisor would then look for the next // JOB statement.

Input-output scheduling   It takes several instructions in machine code to get the control unit to activate an input or output device. Because the instructions to activate any particular device (a printer, for example) are always the same, it is a waste of time to require each programmer to write the same instructions in every program. A more efficient technique is to make these I/O instructions a part of the operating system and then allow all programs to use them. These standard I/O instructions make up the input-output control system (IOCS). To use these standard instructions, the program signals the supervisor that input from or output to a particular device is required. The supervisor then temporarily takes control of the computer and activates the I/O device. It should be emphasized that the supervisor is a program, so that when we say it "takes control of the computer" we mean that the control unit begins to follow instructions in the supervisor program instead of instructions in our program. After the I/O device is activated, control returns to our program. In effect, whenever our programs require input or output, they ask the supervisor to do it.

Program monitoring   Earlier in this chapter, it was stated that the supervisor is always in main memory. It has to be there to schedule input and output, but it is also there to monitor programs. If an error should cause a program to fail, the supervisor will take control of the computer. What kind of an error will make a program fail? An example is the case of inputting nonnumeric characters (not 0–9) into a numeric field and then attempting an arithmetic operation, such as an addition instruction. The arithmetic logic unit cannot add nonnumeric characters, and execution of the program will stop. The supervisor will then take control of the computer, output an error message to the operator on the console, and cancel our job. If the option statement in our job control says DUMP, the supervisor will cause the contents of memory to be outputted on the line printer.

The output of the contents of memory is called a **memory dump.** It is often useful to see what was in memory in order to determine the cause of the error. Program errors are covered in more detail in Chapter 15. Memory dumps are covered in Supplement IV.

After the job has been cancelled, the supervisor will cause job control statements to be read until it finds the next job statement. The supervisor keeps a stream of jobs going through the computer without allowing program errors to stop the computer for more than a short time.

FEEDBACK

14-1 What is the purpose of a control program?

14-2 What are common names for control programs?

14-3 What are three major functions of the control program?

LANGUAGE PROCESSORS

As we mentioned in Chapter 13 all symbolic programs must be translated to machine code before their instructions can be understood by the control unit. This translation of symbolic instructions to machine code is accomplished through the use of a program called a **language processor.** There are three types of language processors. They are called assemblers, compilers, and interpreters. Each translates symbolic instructions to machine code, but each does it differently.

Symbolic programming languages that are coded at the same level of detail as machine code can be translated in a ratio of one symbolic instruction to one machine code instruction. These languages are referred to as **low-level languages.** Low-level languages are translated to machine code by a program called an **assembler.** Chapter 13 discussed a low-level symbolic programming language called assembler language. Problem-oriented languages such as BASIC, COBOL, FORTRAN, PL/I, and RPG have many functions that occur automatically. These automatic functions take care of specific computer hardware requirements so that the programmer can concentrate on the problem to be solved. Problem-oriented languages, therefore, do not translate from one symbolic instruction to one machine code instruction. It is not unusual for one probelm-oriented language instruction to translate to a dozen machine code instructions. These problem-oriented languages are referred to as **high-level languages.** High-level languages are translated to machine code either by a program called a **compiler** or by a program called an **interpreter.** Both assemblers and compilers translate the entire symbolic program to machine code before the program is run. An interpreter translates each symbolic instruction as the program being translated is running. In other words, it translates one instruction, and the control unit follows the resulting machine code, the next instruction is translated, and the control unit follows the machine code instruction, and so on. The language BASIC usually uses an interpreter. Because interpreters are not commonly used with most languages, the discussion of language processors in the remainder of this chapter will be about assemblers and compilers.

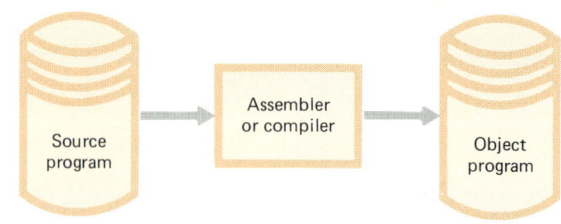

FIGURE 14-2
The conversion of symbolic programs.

Symbolic programs are called **source programs.** The machine code generated by a language processor is called the **object program.** Figure 14-2 shows that source programs are the input to the assembler or compiler. The output of the assembler or compiler is the object program. The object program is typically outputted to a magnetic disk or other high-speed secondary storage device. Figure 14-2 also shows that the object program is treated as output data by the language processor. Remember that the language processors are programs, not hardware.

Figure 14-3 illustrates the job control statements that would be used to compile a COBOL source program into an object program. The first statement indicates that this is a new job and the job's name is COMPILE. The option statement specifies that a list of the source program instructions is to be printed on the line printer and that any errors (COBOL instructions that cannot be successfully translated) are to be listed on the source listing. The third statement causes the COBOL compiler to be loaded from magnetic disk into main memory by the supervisor and control of the computer is to be given to the COBOL compiler. (If the source program had been written in FORTRAN, the card would read "// EXEC FORTRAN." In most cases, the name of the compiler is the name of the programming language.) EXEC is an abbreviation for "execute," which means "run." The next statements are the input to the COBOL compiler—the COBOL source program. The /* indicates "end of data." Remember that the COBOL source statements are input data to the COBOL compiler. The /& indicates "end of job." Our program is now an object program (machine code) stored on a magnetic disk.

```
// JOB COMPILE
// OPTION LIST,ERRS
// EXEC COBOL
   (COBOL source program)
/*
/&
```

FIGURE 14-3
Job control statements to compile the program.

FEEDBACK

14-4 What is the purpose of a language processor?

14-5 What is a source program? Object program?

14-6 Is COBOL a high-level or low-level language? RPG? BASIC?

SERVICE PROGRAMS

Service programs are programs that are commonly used in all data processing centers. Service programs include programs to prepare object programs for execution, to store programs on a magnetic disk, and to sort data recorded on secondary storage devices. They are part of the operating system, so that each installation does not have to duplicate the programming of every other installation.

The Linkage Editor

After a source program has been translated, the resulting object program is not yet ready to be executed. The language processors replace all symbolic names with binary machine code, but before a program can be executed, input-output modules must be added to the object program. These I/O modules provide the linkage to the supervisor when the program asks the supervisor to schedule input or output. This function of preparing the object program for execution is provided by a service program called the **linkage editor.**

Figure 14-4 illustrates the job control that would be used to compile, link-edit, and run a COBOL program. The first statement indicates that it is a new job and gives the job's name. The second statement indicates the options: a source program listing, a listing of compiler errors, and link-editing of the resulting object program. The third statement causes the COBOL compiler to be loaded into main memory and executed. The following statements are the COBOL source program and an end-of-data indicator. At this point, the source program has been translated to machine code. The next statement causes the linkage editor to be loaded into main memory and executed. At the conclusion of the linkage editor's execution, the object program has the required I/O modules added to it. The program is now capable of being executed. The next job control statement says to execute, but does not give a program name. When a program name is not given, it is implied that the program that was just link-edited will be executed. The program's test data and an end-of-data indicator follow. The last statement indicates "end-of-job."

```
// JOB COMPILE AND EXECUTE
// OPTION LIST,ERRS,LINK
// EXEC COBOL
   (COBOL source program)
/*
// EXEC LNKEDT
// EXEC
   (test data)
/*
/&
```

FIGURE 14-4

Job control statements to compile and run a program.

The Librarian

Some of the previous examples of job control statements have indicated that the program to be executed was stored on a magnetic disk. The area on a magnetic disk that is used to hold programs is called a **library.** Any program cataloged (stored) in the library may be executed by naming the program in an // EXEC job control statement. All programs cataloged in the library are listed in a part of the library called the directory. This directory may be outputted on a terminal or on a line printer if anyone wants to see what programs are cataloged. The service program that adds and deletes programs from the library area and maintains the directory is called the **librarian.**

The library will contain programs ready to be loaded into main memory for execution. Programs typically cataloged into the library include the control programs, the language processors, the service programs of the operating system, and any programs regularly used by the data processing installation. The program called PAYROLL in Figure 14-1 would have to be cataloged in the library so that it can be used for each pay period.

Figure 14-5 illustrates the job control statements needed in order to add a program called ACCOUNTS to the library. The first statement states that it is a new job and the job's name. The option statement specifies that a list of the source program and any compiler errors is to be made on the line printer, and that the program is to be cataloged into the library. The third statement provides the name by which the program will be cataloged. IBM calls a program that is cataloged in the library a *phase*. In this example, the phase statement

FIGURE 14-5

Job control statements to catalog a program.

```
// JOB CATALOG ACCOUNTS PROGRAM
// OPTION LIST,ERRS,CATAL
   PHASE ACCOUNTS,*
// EXEC COBOL
   (COBOL source program)
/*
// EXEC LNKEDT
/&
```

indicates that the cataloged program will be called ACCOUNTS. The following statements compile the COBOL program and link-edit the resulting object program. At the conclusion of link-editing, the program is cataloged.

Other librarian functions include deleting entries from the library, renaming entries in the library, reorganizing the library, and outputting the contents of the library directories.

Utility Programs

A third set of service programs is the **utilities.** The utilities provide a means of copying data from any input device to any output device in the system. This provides an easy means of moving data files from one secondary storage device to another for backup. The utilities may also be used to print the contents of a file on the line printer.

The Sort-Merge Program

The **sort-merge** program is the fourth of the major service programs. Sorting and merging files of data stored on secondary storage devices are common functions in almost all data processing centers. If the sequence of data records is to be changed, the sort-merge program must be given the location of the field to be used in sorting and whether the records are to be sorted in ascending or descending sequence. Multiple fields may be used in sorting. For example, records may be sorted by employee number field within a department number field within a store number field. Records can be sorted either alphabetically or numerically. The merge function allows multiple files to be put together in sequence. As an example, a file of new customers could be merged into an existing customer master file that is stored on a magnetic disk.

FEEDBACK

14-7 What are service programs?

14-8 What is the purpose of the linkage editor? The librarian?

14-9 What are utility programs used for?

SUMMARY

The operating system is a collection of programs provided by the computer's manufacturer that allows us to schedule jobs for the computer, to translate source programs into object programs, to sort data stored on secondary storage devices, and to copy data from any input device to any output device. These programs are called control programs, language processors, and utility programs.

The control program (often called the supervisor, monitor, or executive) is a main-storage-resident program. Its functions are to schedule jobs, schedule input and output for our programs, and to monitor the execution of our programs.

The language processors are programs that translate source programs into object programs. There are three types of language processors: assemblers, compilers, and interpreters. Each language has its own language processor.

The service programs are programs that are commonly used in all data processing centers. They have functions that are required by everyone using a computer. Examples of service programs include linkage editors to prepare object programs for execution, a librarian to catalog programs into a library area on magnetic disk, utility programs to transfer data from device to device, and sort-merge programs for sorting data on magnetic tape or disk.

**ANSWERS TO
FEEDBACK QUESTIONS**

14-1 It controls the computer for us.

14-2 Supervisor, monitor, executive, and control program.

14-3 a To schedule jobs on the computer.
b To schedule input and output for our programs.
c To monitor our programs as they run.

14-4 It translates instructions written in a programming language (source programs) to instructions in machine code (object programs).

14-5 a Any program written in a symbolic programming language such as COBOL, FORTRAN, and others.
b The result of translation by a language processor to the binary strings of machine code.

14-6 As problem-oriented languages, COBOL, FORTRAN, and BASIC (and PL/I and RPG) are high-level. Assembler-level languages are low-level.

14-7 Standard programs that all data processing centers need. They are usually provided by the manufacturer of the computer.

14-8 The linkage editor prepares the object program for execution by adding input-output modules to the object program. The librarian maintains an area on magnetic disk for the storage of frequently used programs. It adds programs to and removes programs from the library area and maintains a list (directory) of all programs cataloged in the library.

14-9 They are commonly used to transfer data from one storage device to another.

**FOR REVIEW
AND DISCUSSION**

1 Are the language translators hardware or software?

2 What are the three types of language translators? How are they different from each other?

3 What is an operating system?

4 What are the three main functions performed by the control program?

5 What does the control program do when our programs fail?

6 What is the librarian? What are its functions?

CHAPTER 15

TESTING THE COMPUTER PROGRAM

PREVIEW   In Chapter 14 we noted that computer programs must be tested for accuracy before they can be used with confidence. In addition to planning and writing a program, it is the programmer's responsibility to test the program to see that it will run properly. Any errors found during testing must be corrected before the programmer's job is finished.

The goal of this chapter is to present the two types of program errors and to introduce methods of finding and correcting them.

In this chapter, you will learn:

1. The causes of computer program errors
2. How program errors are identified by the programmer

KEY TERMS TO WATCH FOR AND REMEMBER

bugs	logic errors
testing	syntax errors
debugging	memory dump
coding errors	

So long as computers are programmed by human beings, computer programs will be subject to errors. It is the programmer's responsibility to find the errors and to correct them. The process of finding and correcting errors is called testing and debugging. Program errors are called program **bugs. Testing** is the process of running the computer program and evaluating the program results, in order to determine if any errors exist. **Debugging** is the correction of any errors found during testing. Testing and debugging can be difficult and time-consuming tasks, but the ability to detect and correct programming errors is one of the most important capabilities of a good programmer. A program is not complete until the programmer verifies that it performs as required.

TYPES OF PROGRAM ERRORS

There are two types of bugs to be found in computer programs. They are coding errors and logic errors. In Chapter 14 the concept of writing computer programs in an English-like language and then translating that program into machine language was introduced. The language translators are programs called *language processors*. They input program language statements (source code) and output machine language statements (object code). If the source statements have not been coded exactly as required by the language processor, the language processor will be unable to translate the statements into object code. Instructions that cannot be translated will be labeled as coding errors by the language processor. **Coding errors,** therefore, are translation errors caused by the programmer's writing the instruction incorrectly.

The second type of error, a **logic error,** is an error in planning the program's logic. In this case, the language processor successfully translates the source code into machine code, and the computer follows the instructions. The problem is that the logic being followed does not produce the results that were desired.

In the remainder of this chapter, we will examine some specific examples of coding errors and logic errors to see how they occur and how they can be corrected.

FEEDBACK

15-1 What is a language processor?

15-2 What are two types of program errors?

Coding Errors

Coding errors are errors in statement syntax. Syntax is defined as the pattern or structure of the word order in an instruction. **Syntax errors** in computer programs typically involve incorrect punctuation, incorrect word sequence, undefined terms, or misuse of terms. Coding errors are easy to find, because the language processor points them out to the programmer by printing error messages on the source listing.

Our first example of coding errors is a FORTRAN example. We have not presented any details about FORTRAN, so let's concentrate on the errors and the error messages rather than the language. Figure 15-1 is a FORTRAN program designed to calculate the future value of a bank account. It is to input the beginning dollar amount deposited, the annual interest rate, and the number of years that the money is to be left in the account. There are 20 instructions in this program plus two comment lines at the beginning of the program (C for comment in the first position). They are numbered in the left-hand column of the source program listing. At the bottom of the listing, a message was printed indicating that two coding errors are present in this program. The location of the error is shown by the error messages immediately below the listing of our FORTRAN program.

Errors are listed with an error number, a severity code, a sequence or statement number, and an explanation by this particular FORTRAN compiler.[1]

---

[1] You'll recall from Chapter 14 that a compiler is a language processor used to translate high-level languages like FORTRAN to machine code.

The error number refers to an explanation in the FORTRAN language manual for this compiler. It generally gives more details than the explanation in this error message. Different errors have different levels of severity. A severity of 8 is the most serious and will not allow the program to run.

The first error in this example is in statement number 4. The explanation given for this error is "unbalanced parentheses." FORTRAN syntax requires that parentheses always be in pairs of left and right parentheses. In this example, the closing parenthesis is missing from the statement. It should have been placed immediately after the future value entry. FORTRAN uses the FORMAT statement to describe the layout or format of input and output records. A FORTRAN coding rule states that the FORMAT statement must have an opening parenthesis after the word FORMAT and a closing parenthesis at the end of the statement.

The other error in the program is in line 11. It is also a syntax error. Line 11 contains a DO statement. The error explanation is that there is an "invalid DO value." FORTRAN uses commas to separate instruction entries, but they are never used at the end of a statement. Rekeying this instruction and eliminating the last comma will correct the error.

FIGURE 15-1

FORTRAN example with errors.

```
IBM SYSTEM/34 FORTRAN IV RELEASE 08                             PAGE 001    01/23/84   14:01

           C      PROGRAM TO CALCULATE THE FUTURE VALUE OF A COMPOUND          COMP INT
           C      INTEREST ACCOUNT                                             COMP INT
                                                                              COMP INT
      1    1      WRITE(3,100)                                                COMP INT
      2    100    FORMAT('1',46X,'FUTURE VALUE OF COMPOUND INTEREST ACCOUNT')  COMP INT
      3           WRITE(3,200)                                                COMP INT
      4    200    FORMAT('0',28X,'PRESENT VALUE',10X,'PERIOD INT RATE',10X,    COMP INT
                 1'PERIODS',10X,'FUTURE VALUE'                                COMP INT
      5           WRITE(3,300)                                                COMP INT
      6    300    FORMAT('0')                                                 COMP INT
      7           LINES=0                                                     COMP INT
                                                                              COMP INT
      8    2      READ(2,400,END=4)PRES,RATE,IPER                             COMP INT
      9    400    FORMAT(F6.2,4X,F4.3,5X,I4)                                  COMP INT
     10           FUT=PRES                                                    COMP INT
     11           DO 3 I=1,IPER,                                              COMP INT
     12           FUT=FUT*(1+RATE)                                           COMP INT
     13    3      CONTINUE                                                    COMP INT
     14           WRITE(3,500)PRES,RATE,IPER,FUT                             COMP INT
     15    500    FORMAT(' ',31X,F7.2,16X,F5.3,17X,I4,12X,F10.2)             COMP INT
     16           LINES=LINES+1                                              COMP INT
     17           IF(LINES .EQ. 45)GO TO 1                                   COMP INT
     18           GO TO 2                                                     COMP INT
                                                                              COMP INT
     19    4      STOP                                                        COMP INT
     20           END                                                        COMP INT

                          ERRORS FOR THIS COMPILATION


      ERROR                      STATEMENT
      NUMBER    SEVERITY   ISN   NUMBER    EXPLANATION

      FORT-0070      8     0004            UNBALANCED PARENTHESES
      FORT-0035      8     0011            INVALID DO VALUE

      002 TOTAL ERRORS FOR THIS COMPILATION
      8 WAS THE HIGHEST SEVERITY
```

It should be noted that in high-level languages such as FORTRAN and COBOL a single error often causes multiple error messages to be generated. There are two reasons for multiple error messages. One is that high-level language instructions often require multiple machine steps. The other reason is that symbolic instructions are often dependent upon other instructions. As an example, if the instruction containing an error is one that defines a field name, all instructions in the program using the field name will be listed as errors. The error message will say that a field being used is not a defined name.

In Chapter 14 you learned that there are different kinds of language translators to convert source programs into object programs. If the language processor is an interpreter, rather than a compiler, the translation of the program statements occurs during execution of the program, rather than as a separate translation step prior to executing the program. Most BASIC language translators are interpreters. Figure 15-2 is an example of a BASIC program containing a syntax error. In this example of a BASIC program, the problem was to average two numbers that are to be entered through the terminal keyboard. When the five statements of the program were entered, there was no indication of coding errors, because no attempt had been made to translate the instructions. When the operator entered RUN, the program was translated and executed, one instruction at a time. The INPUT statement outputted a question mark to indicate that it was ready for input. The operator then entered a 4 and a 12. When statement 30 was reached, a coding error was found. The LET statement is the arithmetic instruction in BASIC. It says, "Let C [the average] be equal to A plus B [the two input values] divided by 2." There should be parenthesis around the "A + B," so that the addition step will occur before the step of dividing by 2. In this example, the problem is a missing closing parenthesis, which should be placed between the B and the slash.

COBOL is a high-level language oriented toward business problems. Figure 15-3 is a portion of a COBOL program that contains translation errors. As you can see, it is an English-like language. The COBOL compiler prints line numbers down the left-hand column of the source program listing. The purpose of the program is to output a list of student data that includes the students' names, class standing, and age. COBOL requires the programmer to write

```
10   REM PROGRAM TO AVERAGE TWO NUMBERS
20   INPUT A,B
30   LET C=(A+B/2
40   PRINT C
50   END

RUN
? 4,12
SYNTAX ERROR IN 30
OK
30
```

FIGURE 15-2
BASIC program with syntax error.

instructions to move data from one place in memory to another. There will be an area of memory that will receive data as they are inputted and a separate area to hold data waiting to be outputted. Some high-level languages automatically move the data from the input area to the output area of memory. COBOL

FIGURE 15-3

COBOL program example with errors.

```
IBM SYSTEM/34      A N S I      C O B O L        RELEASE 08 / MOD 00 - PAGE    5  01/23/84   13:41.55

STMC -A...B... C O B O L    S O U R C E    S T A T E M E N T S .........IDENTFCN SEQ/NO S

           /                                                        STUDENTS 0131
    80   21-SET-UP-PRINT-LINE.                                      STUDENTS 0132
    81       MOVE STUDENTS-NAME-IN TO STUDENT-NAME-OUT.             STUDENTS 0133
    82       PERFORM 211-CLASS-STANDING.                            STUDENTS 0134
             MOEV AGE-IN TO AGE-OUT.                                STUDENTS 0135
                                                                   STUDENTS 0136
    83   22-TEST-FOR-HIGH-LOW-AGE.                                  STUDENTS 0137
    84       IF AGE-IN IS GREATER THAN HIGH-AGE                     STUDENTS 0138
    85           MOVE AGE-IN TO HIGH-AGE.                           STUDENTS 0139
    86       IF AGE-IN IS LESS THAN LOW-AGE                         STUDENTS 0140
    87           MOVE AGE-IN TO LOW-AGE.                            STUDENTS 0141
                                                                   STUDENTS 0142
    88   23-WRITE-A-LINE.                                           STUDENTS 0143
    89       IF PRINTED-LINES IS GREATER THAN 49                    STUDENTS 0144
    90           PERFORM 231-TITLE-AND-HEADINGS                     STUDENTS 0145
    91           MOVE 3 TO SPACING                                  STUDENTS 0146
    92           MOVE ZERO TO PRINTED-LINES.                        STUDENTS 0147
    93       WRITE A-LINE FROM DETAIL-LINE                          STUDENTS 0148
                 AFTER ADVANCING SPACING.                           STUDENTS 0149
    94       ADD 1 TO PRINTED-LINES.                                STUDENTS 0150
    95       MOVE 1 TO SPACING.                                     STUDENTS 0151
                                                                   STUDENTS 0152
    96   211-CLASS-STANDING.                                        STUDENTS 0153
    97       IF UNITS-IN IS LESS THAN 30                            STUDENTS 0154
    98           MOVE 'FRESHMAN' TO CLASS-STANDING-OUT.             STUDENTS 0155
    99       IF UNITS-IN IS GREATER THAN 29 AND LESS THAN 60        STUDENTS 0156
   100           MOVE 'SOPHOMORE' TO CLASS-STANDING-OUT.            STUDENTS 0157
   101       IF UNITS-IN IS GREATER THAN 59 AND LESS THAN 90        STUDENTS 0158
   102           MOVE 'JUNIOR' TO CLASS-STANDING-OUT.               STUDENTS 0159
   103       IF UNITS-IN IS NOT LESS THAN 90                        STUDENTS 0160
   104           MOVE 'SENIOR' TO CLASS-STANDING-OUT.               STUDENTS 0161
                                                                   STUDENTS 0162
   105   231-TITLE-AND-HEADINGS.                                    STUDENTS 0163
   106       WRITE A-LINE FROM TITLE-LINE                           STUDENTS 0164
                 AFTER ADVANCING PAGE.                              STUDENTS 0165
   107       WRITE A-LINE FROM COLUMN-HEADINGS                      STUDENTS 0166
                 AFTER ADVANCING 2 LINES.                           STUDENTS 0167


    PROGRAM SIZE = DATA DIVISION + PROCEDURE DIVISION + LITERALS + DTF/BUFFERS

        2482              724              749              80           929

                            DIAGNOSTICS

     ERROR  LVL STMC TYPE  TEXT

    CBL-0326 E     81   P   STUDENTS-NAME-IN IS NOT A DEFINED NAME
    CBL-0441 E     82   P   NEW STATEMENT EXPECTED -- MOEV FOUND -- REST OF STATEMENT IGNORED


       2 E LEVEL MESSAGES      0 C LEVEL MESSAGES      0 W LEVEL MESSAGES

    CBL-1019  C OR E LEVEL DIAGNOSTICS DETECTED
    END OF COMPILATION
```

```
10 INPUT A
20 RPINT A
30 END

RUN
? 34
SYNTAX ERROR IN 20
OK
20
```

FIGURE 15-4

BASIC program with unrecognizable word.

does not. The portion of the COBOL example in Figure 15-3 that contains errors is called 21-SET-UP-PRINT-LINE. Its purpose is to move data from the input area to the output area. The instruction 21-SET-UP-PRINT-LINE is called a paragraph or procedure name. Note that the procedure names are positioned a few spaces to the left of the other statements. Statement 81 contains the first error. The error-message text says "STUDENTS-NAME-IN is not a defined name." From this error message, the programmer knows that the field called STUDENTS-NAME-IN was not previously defined to the COBOL compiler. In COBOL programs, all field names must be defined in a part of the program called the DATA DIVISION. An inspection of the DATA DIVISION will reveal the missing definition. In this example, the field STUDENTS-NAME-IN should have been STUDENT-NAME-IN.

The second translation error is in statement 82. Note that statement 82 is actually two lines. The second line of statement 82 contains the error and was not recognized as a separate instruction. The error is in the first word of the statement. The word MOVE has been misspelled. Instructions must begin with a COBOL verb indicating the action to take place. Examples of COBOL verbs are READ, WRITE, ADD, and MOVE. When the compiler did not recognize MOEV as the COBOL verb MOVE, it assumed that the line was a continuation of the previous line and did not assign it a statement number. The error-message text says, "New statement expected—MOEV found—rest of statement ignored." The period at the end of the PERFORM instruction of statement 82 told the compiler that it was at the end of a statement, but the next word found was not recognized as an appropriate new statement beginning. The remaining portion of the statement does not begin with a COBOL verb, so the compiler skipped over the rest of the statement.

Figure 15-4 is a BASIC language example with an unrecognizable word. The error message indicates a syntax error in statement 20. Statement 20 begins with a misspelling of the word PRINT.

All coding errors must be found and corrected before there is any chance of running the program and getting correct results. The language processors output error messages that indicate the number of the statement with errors and give hints as to the nature of the error. It is a relatively easy task, therefore, to find and correct this type of error.

FEEDBACK

15-3 What are syntax errors?

15-4 How does a programmer find coding errors?

Logic Errors

After all coding errors have been found and corrected, the programmer must test the logic of the program plan. If the planning of the program has been flawless, there will be no logic errors to correct. In order to plan flawless program logic, a programmer must take into consideration all logical situations that may occur. In complex programs, this can be a very difficult task.

In order to determine whether or not a logic error exists, the program must be run, using sample data with known answers. By running the program and comparing the program's answers to the known correct results, the accuracy of the logic plan can be determined. In order to completely test the program logic, the sample data must test each logical function of the program. Logic errors are typically due either to missing logic or to incorrect logic. If the logic is wrong, the answers generated from the sample data will be wrong. These errors are the easiest of the logic errors to find. Errors caused by missing logic result from logical situations that the program was not designed to handle. As an example, suppose that a numeric field is to be used in an arithmetic process and that a data entry operator enters a value for the field that is not numeric. The program logic should determine that the data are not numeric prior to attempting the arithmetic process. If that logic is missing and nonnumeric data are used in an arithmetic operation, the program will fail. This type of bug can be difficult to find. The only way for this error to occur is for nonnumeric data to be entered into a numeric field. It is possible for the program to be used for weeks, months, or years before this happens and the error in program logic shows up.

Figure 15-5 is a BASIC program that averages two numbers. The program was run, and no coding errors were discovered. Examination of the program output, however, shows that the average of 5 and 12 is equal to 5. Because we know that the answer is 8.5, we know that the program contains a logical error. Most logic errors can be found by examining that portion of the program that deals with the wrong answer. Examination of the average calculation in statement 30 shows that it is logically correct—that is, the sum of A and B is divided by 2, and the average is placed in field C. Statement 40 is supposed to print the average. Note that statement 40 prints the value of field A, the first input value, instead of C, the average value. Therefore, the error occurred because the instruction told the computer to output the wrong field's value.

```
10   REM PROGRAM TO AVERAGE TWO NUMBERS
20   INPUT A,B
30   LET C=(A+B)/2
40   PRINT A
50   END

RUN
? 5,12
 5
OK
```

FIGURE 15-5

BASIC program with a logic error.

```
10   REM PROGRAM TO AVERAGE TWO NUMBERS
20   INPUT A,B
30   LET C=A+B/2
40   PRINT C
50   END

RUN
? 4,12
 10
OK
```

FIGURE 15-6

BASIC program with arithmetic-logic error.

Figure 15-6 is the same BASIC program, but it contains a different logical error. The sample run indicates that 4 and 12 average to 10. The answer should be 8. In this example, it is the calculation step that is in error. There is a predetermined sequence for performing arithmetic calculations. The sequence is exponentiation steps first, then multiplication or division, and last addition or subtraction. This predetermined sequence can be altered with the use of parentheses. All arithmetic operations within parentheses are performed before performing arithmetic calculations outside of the parentheses. In this example, field A has a value of 4 and field B has a value of 12. Because division calculations occur before addition calculations, field B is being divided by 2, giving a value of 6. That result is then added to field A, giving our wrong answer of 10. The correct logical steps would be to add field A to field B and then to divide their sum by 2. The correction for this bug, therefore, is to put parentheses around the addition step, in order to force it to be performed first.

The cause of most logic errors can be found by studying the source code producing the incorrect results. However, some errors are difficult to find, and simple inspection of the source program does not reveal the nature of the error. Language processors include tools and techniques to enable the programmer to follow the program's logic. These are known as *debug packages* or *tracing routines*. They assist the programmer in following the logic by printing out intermediate calculation results and field values that are used in making logical decisions in the program. Using these techniques, the programmer can follow the program's execution step by step in order to determine where the logic is in error. In a few cases, the logic error can be so difficult to find, and the number of fields involved so numerous, that the only way to uncover the source of the error is to look at a printout of the contents of memory. This printout is called a **memory dump.** Most programmers of high-level languages resort to the use of memory dumps only when all else fails. The memory dump lists the instructions and data being held in memory in their raw form, that is, their binary or equivalent form.

The memory dump will contain numeric data in a pure binary format and/or data held as character codes. A detailed discussion of binary numbers and shortcut notation for binary is included in Supplement III, Number Systems.

The character codes are explained in detail in Supplement IV, which also includes a sample memory dump.

FEEDBACK

15-5 How does a programmer determine that a logic error exists?

15-6 What causes logic errors?

15-7 What tools are provided through the language processors to find logic errors?

15-8 What is a memory dump?

SUMMARY

There are two kinds of errors or bugs with which programmers must deal. The first type is the coding error. Such errors are syntax errors that prevent the language processor from successfully translating the source program to object program code. The language processor identifies the nature and the location of the error on the source program listing, so these errors are relatively easy to find and correct. The second type of bug is the logic error. The computer program can be successfully translated, but the program does not produce the desired results. These errors are generally much more difficult to find and to correct than are coding errors. Logic errors can be avoided through careful planning of the program logic, but it is the programmer's responsibility to test thoroughly all of the program's functions, in order to verify that the program performs according to specifications.

There are many tools provided to the programmer to help in debugging the program logic. These tools are called debug packages or tracing routines. They assist the programmer in following the logic by printing out calculation results and field values used in making logical decisions in the program. In a few cases, it may be necessary to use a memory dump—a printout of the instructions and data held in the computer's memory—in order to find the cause of logic errors.

15-1 A program used in translating source programs to object programs.

15-2 Coding errors and logic errors.

15-3 Errors involving punctuation, word sequence, undefined terms, or misused terms.

15-4 They are identified by the language processor.

15-5 Incorrect results in program output indicate logic errors.

15-6 Flaws in the logic plan. This typically means that the plan is missing required logic or that the logic is incorrect.

15-7 Debug packages or tracing routines that allow the programmer to trace through the program's logic.

15-8 A printout of the contents of memory that is used in locating logic errors that are difficult to find.

In statements 1 to 5, is the error a coding error or a logic error?

1 The word PRINT is spelled PRNIT in a BASIC instruction.

2 In a calculation, an asterisk (*) is used instead of the slash (/).

3 A field name is spelled AMT in one part of the program and AMOUNT in another part.

4 A period is missing after a procedure name in COBOL.

5 A calculation step is missing from the program.

6 Describe the nature of coding errors. Give examples.

7 Describe the nature of logic errors. Give examples.

8 Which type of error is the more difficult to find? Why?

9 What tools are available to the programmer to help locate logic errors?

10 What is a memory dump? When would it be used with high-level languages?

UNIT
FIVE

PROGAMMING
IN BASIC

In Unit Four you were introduced to the computer program development cycle. The five steps in this development cycle are to define the problem to be solved, plan a solution to the problem, code the solution in a programming language, test and debug the program, and complete the program documentation.

In this unit, you will gain additional background in the computer program development cycle using the BASIC language. In Chapter 16 you will learn enough BASIC to write simple programs. Chapter 17 introduces additional instructions in BASIC and more practice using the instructions in Chapter 16.

CHAPTER 16

GETTING STARTED IN BASIC

PREVIEW Chapter 13 introduced us to programming languages and Chapter 14 presented examples of the steps required to run a program. In this chapter we will see how the logical steps of our program plans can be written as program instructions using the language BASIC.

In this chapter you will learn:

1. The nature of the language BASIC
2. The relationship between planning and coding a program solution
3. How to input and output data in BASIC
4. How to perform calculations in BASIC
5. How to code decisions in BASIC
6. How to write loops in BASIC.

KEY TERMS TO WATCH FOR AND REMEMBER

REM	PRINT
INPUT	constant
IF-THEN	NEW
END	LET
RUN	FOR-NEXT
LIST	variable

In Chapter 13 we described several problem-oriented languages for writing programs. In this chapter, we will concentrate on one of them, BASIC, in order to see how programs are coded from our logic plans. BASIC has become a very popular language in systems where many users share the use of a computer through terminals and it has become a universal language for personal computers. Its most common use is through a visual display terminal. The program and data are commonly entered through the terminal keyboard, with output shown on a screen. Most computing systems have a BASIC interpreter or compiler available. Literally all personal computers can use the language BASIC.

BASIC is an easy programming language to learn and use because of its many default options. Default options are the assumptions that will be made if the programmer says nothing. For example, if the programmer has not yet learned how to describe the horizontal spacing of an output line, BASIC will default to a number of standard output zones. The number of output zones depends upon the width of the output screen. The standard Apple II Plus and Apple IIe each have a 40-character line which is divided into three print zones. The Radio Shack TRS-80 has 64 characters per line and is divided into four zones. Terminals and microcomputers with an 80-character line are divided into five standard print zones. This allows a beginning programmer to write programs very early in learning BASIC by using the default print zones to format output lines. As the programmer becomes more efficient or has a requirement for other than the default print zones, he or she may override the default by writing more detailed BASIC instructions.

The language BASIC is mathematically oriented. That is, its typical use is to solve problems of a mathematical nature. Because BASIC programs are usually executed from a terminal or microcomputer where input is entered through a keyboard and printed output is relatively slow, problems of a business nature requiring large volumes of input-output data are usually not practical.

STANDARD ANSI BASIC

In the years following the introduction of BASIC at Dartmouth College, many different versions of BASIC came into being. Many of these versions added instructions to make the language more powerful in handling tables of data, using data files on disk or diskette, and formatting output data. These modifications made BASIC more useful to a wider variety of users, including businesses. Unfortunately, the various versions of BASIC became so different from each other that they were no longer a single language but many incompatible languages. An effort to define a minimal standard BASIC was begun in 1975 by a committee of the American National Standards Institute (ANSI). All examples in this chapter follow those standards as defined by the ANSI committee X3J2. Many versions of BASIC go beyond the ANSI standard. This chapter will examine the extensions to standard BASIC as implemented in the Apple II Plus, BASIC-80 (commonly available with the CP/M operating systems), the IBM Personal Computer, and the Radio Shack TRS-80 Level 2 BASIC.

Many computer systems require a "log on" routine to identify the user and to get access to the central processing unit through a terminal. Many minicomputer systems require that a user account number be entered before a BASIC program can be run. As there is no standard for "log on" or accounting procedures, this chapter does not include techniques for logging on or signing off any particular computer system. That procedure can best be presented

TABLE 16-1   **COMMON SYSTEM COMMANDS**

Command	Meaning	Example systems
NEW	Clears memory in preparation for a "new" program	Apple, BASIC-80, IBM PC, TRS-80
CLS	Clears the terminal screen; does not clear memory	BASIC-80 (non-Apple), IBM PC, TRS-80
HOME	Clears the terminal screen; does not clear memory	Apple, BASIC-80 (in Apple version)
LIST	Lists the instructions of the program in memory	Apple, BASIC-80, IBM PC, TRS-80
RUN	Causes the instructions of the program in memory to be followed	Apple, BASIC-80, IBM PC, TRS-80

FIGURE 16-1

The flowchart for averaging two numbers.

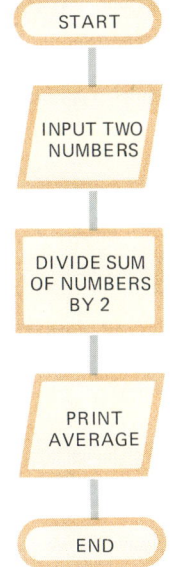

through information from the data center being used. There are, however, a few commands that are useful to all BASIC programmers. Table 16-1 lists five commands, their meaning, and example systems that use the command.

The **NEW** command is used to erase the current contents of memory in preparation for a new program. This command should be used prior to entering a program whenever the contents of the memory are unknown.

The CLS and HOME commands clear the terminal screen. CLS is the form most commonly used. HOME is used on the Apple. It should be noted that these commands clear the screen but have no effect on the program or data in memory.

Programmers often wish to review the instructions which are held in memory. The **LIST** command will display all instructions of the program currently in memory.

To cause the computer to follow the instructions of a program in memory, the **RUN** command is used.

The BASIC instructions in this chapter are presented through a series of simple program examples. These sample programs deal with two forms of data. One form is called a **constant.** Constant data is data that is written into the program and will not change in value during the running of the program. The second type of data is called a **variable.** A variable is a memory location whose value may change or vary. Variables are also called fields.

Averaging Two Numbers

The first problem is to average two numbers inputted through a keyboard. Figure 16-1 is the flowchart for the solution of the problem. The first step is to input the two numbers. The second step is to add the two numbers together and divide by 2 to calculate the average. The third step is to print the answer.

Figure 16-2 is the BASIC program written from the flowchart. The language BASIC is said to be line-oriented. That is, each instruction must be numbered. A common convention is to number the lines counting by tens so that additional instructions may be inserted between existing instructions at a

```
10   REM        PROGRAM TO AVERAGE TWO NUMBERS
20   REM
30   REM        VARIABLES:  A =AVERAGE
40   REM                    N1=FIRST NUMBER TO AVERAGE
50   REM                    N2=SECOND NUMBER
60   REM
70   INPUT N1,N2
80   LET A=(N1+N2)/2
90   PRINT A
100  END
```

FIGURE 16-2
The BASIC program to average two numbers.

later time. The instructions will be listed and executed in line-number sequence.

The REMark statement   The first six lines contain **REM** statements. Figure 16-3 shows the format and an example of the REM statements. A REM statement is a remark being made for the purpose of explaining or documenting a program step. It has no effect on the program logic. The instruction must have a line number, the key word REM, and any remark that the programmer wishes to make. In our example, the remark statements were used to name the program, document the variables (fields) used by the program, and provide appropriate blank lines for readability.

The INPUT statement   The next statement is the **INPUT** statement. Its format is shown in Figure 16-4. The statement must begin with a line number, have the key word INPUT, and a list of variable field names that are to have values inputted from the keyboard. Each INPUT statement may input values for one or more variables.

Each variable used in a program must have a name. The rules for naming variables in standard BASIC are quite simple. If the variable is to contain only numeric values, the variable name consists of a single letter plus an optional single-digit number. Examples of legitimate numeric-variable names include A, B, R, N1, N2, and X0. Numeric-variable names such as AMOUNT, PAY, and TOTAL are not allowed in standard BASIC but are allowed in many other versions of BASIC. Table 16-2 illustrates the rules for numeric-variable names

FIGURE 16-3
REM statement.

```
line   REM   remark . . .
10     REM   PROGRAM TO AVERAGE TWO NUMBERS
```

FIGURE 16-4
The INPUT statement.

```
line   INPUT var1,var2, . . . ,varN
70     INPUT N1,N2
```

TABLE 16-2   **RULES FOR NUMERIC-VARIABLE NAMES**

Computer	Rule	Example
ANSI standard	A single letter or a letter-and-number digit	A, N, N1, N2, B0
Apple	One or two letters or a letter-and-number digit. (Note that the Apple allows longer names to be used but ignores all characters beyond the first two)	A, R, JS, MG, E3
BASIC-80	Up to 40 letters, number digits, and decimal points are allowed as long as the first character is a letter	N, N1, TOTAL, YEAR.TO.DATE.SALES
IBM PC	Up to 40 letters, number digits and decimal points are allowed as long as the first character is a letter	N, N2, TOTAL, YEAR.TO.DATE.SALES
TRS-80	One or two letters or a letter-and-number digit are allowed. (Note that the TRS-80 allows longer names to be used, but ignores all characters beyond the first two)	A, B, N1, TN

for standard BASIC and for common versions found on microcomputers. Almost all versions of BASIC allow for longer variable names than does the ANSI standard. Note that BASIC-80 and IBM PC BASIC each allow variable names up to 40 significant characters. Many versions of BASIC allow longer and more meaningful variable names to be used, but they ignore characters beyond the first few.

Data that are not all number characters in the range of 0 through 9 are referred to as *character strings*. Variables which will hold these character strings are called *string variables*. As an example, a person's name (all alphabetic characters) and a street address (both alphabetic and numeric characters) are character strings. Variables which may hold these data must be string variables. Standard BASIC states the rule for naming string variables as a letter and a dollar sign ($). Variable names of A$, B$, and N$ are valid ANSI BASIC string-variable names. Table 16-3 lists some of the common variations, or extensions, of the standard string-variable name rule. These variations tend to be in the number of characters allowed in the string name. Note that all string-variable names must end with a dollar sign.

In our example program to average two numbers, the input statement variable names are N1 and N2. These are numeric-variable names, which are as meaningful as possible within the standard naming rules.

When an input statement is executed, it causes a question mark and a space (?) to be outputted to the screen as an input prompt. The *input prompt* tells the operator that input is being requested by the program. In Chapter 17 you will see how the input prompt can be expanded into a message for the operator.

TABLE 16-3   **RULES FOR CHARACTER STRING VARIABLE NAMES**

Computer	Rule	Example
ANSI standard	A single letter and a dollar sign	A$, B$, C$, Z$
Apple	One or two letters or a letter-and-number digit followed by a dollar sign. (Note that the Apple will allow longer names but requires that the last character be a dollar sign. All characters beyond the first two and the dollar sign are ignored)	A$, A1$, TN$, NA$, NAME$ (same as NA$)
BASIC-80	Up to 40 letters, number digits, decimal points, and a dollar sign. The first character must be a letter and the last character must be the dollar sign	A$, NAME$, PRODUCT.CODE$, LOCATION.2.$
IBM PC	Up to 40 letters, number digits, decimal points, and a dollar sign. The first character must be a letter and the last character must be the dollar sign	A$, NAME$, STREET.ADDRESS$, ZIP.PLUS.4.$
TRS-80	One or two letters or a letter-and-number digit followed by a dollar sign. (Note that the TRS-80 will allow longer names, but the last character must always be a dollar sign. Only the first two characters and the dollar sign are used as the name)	A$, NA$, N1$, NAME$ (same as NA$)

FEEDBACK   **16-1** What is a default option?

16-2 What type of programs are best suited for BASIC?

16-3 BASIC is line-oriented. What does that mean?

16-4 What is the purpose of the REM statement?

16-5 What is the standard BASIC rule for naming numeric variables? String variables?

16-6 What is an input prompt?

The LET statement   All arithmetic operations are accomplished through the **LET** statement. Figure 16-5 shows examples of the LET statement. It consists of a line number, the key word LET, a variable to serve as the answer field, an equal sign, and an arithmetic expression (formula). The arithmetic expression shows the steps required to calculate the answer. In the example program line 80 reads, "Let the value of the variable called A be equal to the sum of

```
line  LET var=arithmetic expression
80    LET A=(N1+N2)/2
150   LET F=3
160   LET H=J
```

FIGURE 16-5
The LET statement.

TABLE 16-4   **HIERARCHY OF ARITHMETIC OPERATIONS**

Step One	^ Exponentiation (or involution)[1]
Step Two	{ * Multiplication / Division
Step Three	{ + Addition − Subtraction

[1] BASIC uses two arithmetic operation symbols that are not common outside of programming—the circumflex (^) for exponentiation and the asterisk (*) for multiplication. Some versions of BASIC use the up arrow (↑) for exponentiation.

the variables called N1 and N2 divided by 2." Note that the number 2 in the expression never changes as a value. It is, therefore, a numeric constant. The other examples in Figure 16-5 would read, "Let the value of the variable called F be equal to 3″ and "Let the value of the variable called H be equal to the value in variable J." The arithmetic expression may contain many calculation steps. In our program example it is necessary to add variable N1 to variable N2 and then divide the sum by 2. The programmer must be careful not to write the instruction so that N2 is divided by 2 and then that result added to N1.

The sequence of arithmetic operations is controlled by the programmer by using the hierarchy of operations built into the language. Table 16-4 illustrates this hierarchy of operations. The first arithmetic level is exponentiation (raising a number to a power, like 4^3). The second level is multiplication and division, and the third level is addition and subtraction. This means that all exponentiation steps are performed first, all multiplication and division steps are next, and finally, all addition and subtraction steps are carried out. If there are multiple arithmetic operations on the same hierarchical level, the leftmost is performed first, progressing toward the right. That is, if an addition and a subtraction were in the same statement, the one on the left would be performed first. For our example program, this will result in an incorrect answer. The hierarchy rules can be manipulated by the use of parentheses. All arithmetic operations enclosed within parentheses are performed first, and then operations outside of the parentheses can proceed. The instruction 80 LET A = (N1 + N2)/2 will cause variable N1 to be added to variable N2, and then that sum will be divided by 2. If there are multiple operations enclosed within the parentheses, the same hierarchy rules apply within the parentheses. It should be noted that the programmer may have parentheses within parentheses to control the sequence of arithmetic operations.

FEEDBACK   **16-7** What symbols are used in BASIC to indicate addition? Subtraction? Multiplication? Division? Exponentiation?

16-8 In the statement LET E = A + B/C * D ∧ 3, what would be the order of operations?

```
line    PRINT list
90      PRINT A
170     PRINT "NOW IS THE TIME"
180     PRINT "THE ANSWER IS→",A
```

FIGURE 16-6
The PRINT statement.

```
line    END
100     END
```

FIGURE 16-7
The END statement.

```
RUN
? 6,8
7
Ok
```

FIGURE 16-8
Output from the average program.

The PRINT statement   Figure 16-6 depicts the **PRINT** statement. The PRINT statement consists of the line number, the key word PRINT, and a list indicating what is to be outputted. This list may consist of constants, the names of variables, or both. Of course, if the name of a variable is included in the list, it is the value held in the variable which will be outputted. Just as variables are either numeric or string, constants may be either type as well. Numeric constants consist of numeric digits. They will not be mistaken for a variable because all variables begin with a letter. String constants may contain any character. String constants must be enclosed within quotation marks. The quotation marks prevent string constants from being mistaken for variables. Line 90 of our example program calls for the outputting of the value in the numeric variable A (average). The average was calculated in the LET statement on line 80. Notice it is not necessary to indicate the horizontal positioning of the average in the output line. Since A is the first item in the output list, it will be outputted in the first (left) print zone. If multiple items are in the output list and are separated by commas, the fields will be printed in separate print zones.

The END statement   The last statement in the sample program is the **END** statement. Figure 16-7 shows that the format of the END statement is the line number and the key word END. Its function is to stop the operation of the program.

To run our averaging program, we enter the word RUN through the terminal. The RUN command will cause the program that was just entered into memory to execute. Figure 16-8 illustrates the running of our program. In this example, the operator entered the numbers 6 and 8 to be averaged. The OK is a common BASIC prompt indicating that a program is no longer running and the computer is waiting for your next command.

An Improved Solution   In our first solution to the problem of averaging two numbers, the first thing to occur is the outputting of a question mark and a space as an input prompt, asking the operator to input the two numbers. The operator must be familiar with the program to know what is expected as input. Figure 16-9 shows an improved version of the program to average two numbers. The first statements are the same remarks used in the first program. Line 70 is a PRINT statement to output a message to the operator explaining the nature of the data to be entered. Any data to be outputted exactly as they are indicated in the instruction are constants. String constants must be enclosed within quotation marks. Line

```
10  REM        PROGRAM TO AVERAGE TWO NUMBERS
20  REM
30  REM        VARIABLES:  A =AVERAGE
40  REM                    N1=FIRST NUMBER TO AVERAGE
50  REM                    N2=SECOND NUMBER
60  REM
70  PRINT "ENTER TWO NUMBERS TO BE AVERAGED";
80  INPUT N1,N2
90  LET A=(N1+N2)/2
100  PRINT "THE AVERAGE IS",A
110  END
```

FIGURE 16-9
Improved average program.

70 indicates that the message ENTER TWO NUMBERS TO BE AVERAGED is to be outputted. The INPUT statement of line 80 would then output the input prompt and wait for the data to be entered. The PRINT statement in line 100 combines a constant and a variable value to be outputted. The constant identifies the value of the variable A.

FEEDBACK

16-9 What is the purpose of the PRINT statement?
16-10 What is the PRINT statement output description default?
16-11 What is the function of the END statement?
16-12 What is a constant?

Figure 16-10 illustrates the input from the operator (the numbers to be averaged) and the output from the modified simple program (the answer). The operator types in the command RUN to activate the program. The program would then output the constant from line 70. The INPUT statement from line 80 would cause the input prompt to be printed. If the two numbers to be averaged were 6 and 8, the operator would enter those numbers, separated by a comma, through the keyboard. The program would then output the constant and the answer. There will probably be a number of spaces between the constant and the answer printed from line 100 of the example, because the answer (variable A) will be printed in the next available print zone. The comma that separates the constant from the variable A in the PRINT instruction indicates that the next print zone is to be used. If a semicolon had been used instead of a comma, the next output would immediately follow the constant. One way of overriding the print zone default, therefore, is to use a semicolon instead of a comma to separate the items in the output list.

```
RUN
ENTER TWO NUMBERS TO BE AVERAGED
? 6,8
THE AVERAGE IS              7
Ok
```

FIGURE 16-10
Output from the improved average program.

```
Ok
100  PRINT "THE AVERAGE IS";A
RUN
ENTER TWO NUMBERS TO BE AVERAGED
? 6,8
THE AVERAGE IS 7
Ok
```

FIGURE 16-11
Instruction insertion.

Figure 16-11 depicts how the operator can change instructions in an existing program. When the BASIC interpreter is waiting for input on most systems, it outputs OK (some systems use other prompts). To add a new instruction to an existing program, the programmer should select a line number that has not yet been used but reflects the appropriate position within the program. The new instruction is then simply entered. BASIC will insert the new instructions into the program in sequence by their line numbers. The possible insertion of new instructions is the reason that line numbers are typically counted by tens. To delete a statement from a program, simply enter its line number and leave the rest of the line blank. To replace an existing instruction, enter a new instruction with the same line number as the line to be replaced. To produce a listing of the modified program, the operator would enter the command LIST.

Figure 16-11 shows a PRINT statement with a line number of 100. Because the program already has a PRINT statement with a line number of 100, the new line 100 will replace the old line 100. In the new line 100, a semicolon was used instead of a comma to separate the constant and the variable called A. After the operator enters RUN, the program execution causes the ENTER TWO NUMBERS TO BE AVERAGED to be outputted. The next statement causes the input prompt, and the operator enters a 6 and an 8. The output THE AVERAGE IS is now properly spaced, because the value of the variable called A is printed immediately after the constant instead of skipping over to the next default print zone. The space preceding the 7 in the example output is the space reserved for the sign of a numeric value (plus signs are not printed).

FEEDBACK

16-13 How are new instructions added to an existing program?
16-14 How are instructions changed in an existing program?
16-15 How are instructions deleted from a program?

Compound-Interest Problem

The next example problem is one in which the operator may enter a beginning amount of money to be deposited into a bank account and the number of years that the money is to be left in the account. The money is to earn interest at 10 percent, compounded annually. All interest earned is left in the account. The program is to output the final amount that will be accumulated by the end of the specified number of years.

Figure 16-12 is a flowchart for the solution of this problem. The solution includes a message to the operator for both the deposit amount and the number

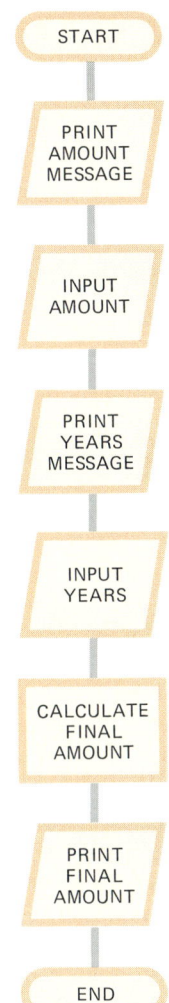

FIGURE 16-12
Compound interest flowchart.

of years to explain the required entry. The final amount is to be calculated by using the formula for compound interest, which is: the ending amount (E) is equal to the deposit amount (D), multiplied by 1 plus the rate of interest for the period taken to the power of the periods. As an equation, it reads

$$E = D (1 + R)^Y$$

In the example, the period is equal to one year because it is to be compounded annually. Therefore, the interest rate for the period is 10 percent, and the number of periods is the number of years. The final amount is then to be outputted.

Figure 16-13 is the coded BASIC solution that follows the flowchart in Figure 16-12. This example shows that the program has just been entered and

```
10  REM       PROGRAM TO COMPOUND INTEREST AT 10%
20  REM
30  REM       VARIABLES:  D=DEPOSIT AMOUNT
40  REM                   E=ENDING AMOUNT
50  REM                   Y=YEARS DEPOSIT IS IN ACCOUNT
60  REM
70  PRINT "DEPOSIT AMOUNT";
80  INPUT D
90  PRINT "NUMBER OF YEARS";
100  INPUT Y
110  LET E=D * (1+.1) ^ Y
120  PRINT "THE ENDING AMOUNT IS";E
130  END

Ok
RUN
DEPOSIT AMOUNT? 100
NUMBER OF YEARS? 3
THE ENDING AMOUNT IS 133.1
Ok
```

FIGURE 16-13
Compound interest program.

is now being executed. Note that the PRINT statement in line 70 ends with a semicolon. The semicolon will cause the next output to be printed immediately after the constant DEPOSIT AMOUNT. The next statement is line 80, which is an INPUT. Because of the ending semicolon on line 70, the input prompt from line 80 will be printed immediately after the constant output of line 70. Note the use of parentheses in the LET statement of line 110. The parentheses will cause the 1 to be added to the .1 before it is raised to the power of Y. If the parentheses were not included, the 1 would be added as the last arithmetic step rather than the first, giving an incorrect answer. The last part of Figure 16-13 shows the result of running the BASIC program. After the operator keys in RUN, the program will output the prompt message DEPOSIT AMOUNT, with the input prompt printed immediately after the message. After the final amount is printed, the END statement terminates the BASIC program and the system prints out OK to indicate that it is ready to accept a new command.

FEEDBACK
16-16 What is the use of the semicolon in PRINT statements?
16-17 What is a prompt message?

A Compound-Interest Solution for Multiple Problems

The compound-interest problem solution that has been presented solves only one problem before program execution is stopped. If more compound-interest problems are to be solved, RUN must be reentered in order to run the program again. A more common solution for this type of problem would be for the program to loop back to the beginning of the program until there is some indication that there are no more problems to be solved.

Figure 16-14 illustrates a flowcharted solution that will continue requesting

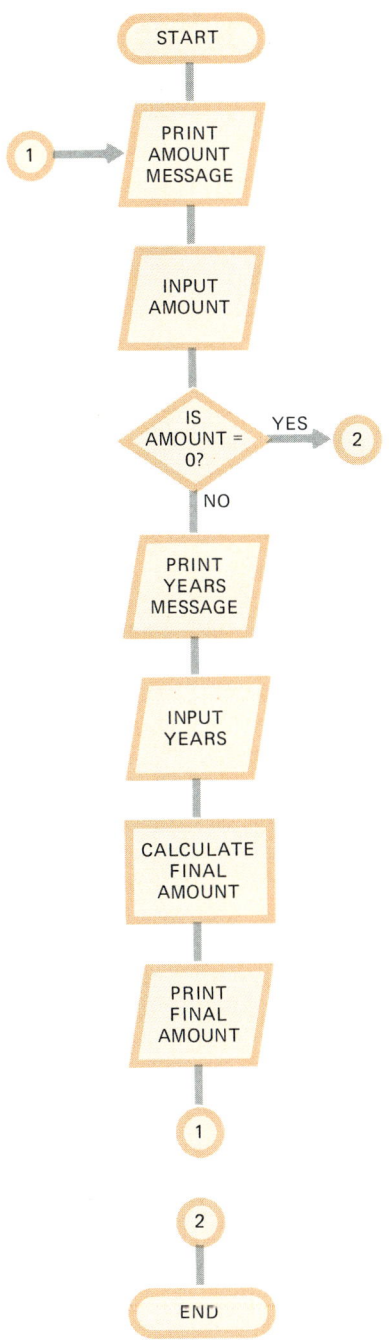

FIGURE 16-14
Compound interest
flowchart with loop.

new amounts and years for new problems until the operator enters a deposit amount of zero. There are two changes in this solution from the previous solution. A decision symbol (diamond) has been inserted immediately following the input of the deposit amount value to determine if the program is to be stopped, and a connector has been placed following the outputting of the final amount, directing the logic flow back up to the beginning of the program.

The GOTO and IF-THEN statements   Whenever the logic flow leaves the normal downward flow, it is called a logic branch. There are two types of branches—conditional and unconditional. A conditional branch is one in which the logic flow leaves the main stream only when a particular condition exists. The decision "Is the amount equal to zero?" in the decision symbol is an example of a conditional branch. An unconditional branch is one in which the branch is always made, without considering any conditions. The connector below the final amount output symbol directs the logic flow back up to the top of the program under all conditions. It is, therefore, an unconditional branch.

Figure 16-15 illustrates both the unconditional and conditional branch statements. The unconditional branch is called a **GOTO**, and the conditional branch is called the **IF-THEN**. The unconditonal branch has a line number, the key word GOTO, and a statement number. The statement number is the line number of any other statement in the program. It will cause the statement on that line to be executed next. In the example, line 140 indicates that the logic flow is to go to statement 70. The instruction on line 70 will be executed next. The conditional branch contains a line number, the key word IF, a condition, the key word THEN, and the number of the statement to be executed if the condition is true.

The "condition" being tested is usually the relationship between two variables or between a variable and a constant. The relationship is how the first variable (or constant) compares (high, equal, or low) to the second variable (or constant). In the example, on line 90, if the variable D is equal to zero, the program will go to statement 150. If the condition is not true, execution proceeds with the following line number. It should be noted that in many versions of BASIC, the statement following the key word THEN can be any BASIC statement and does not have to be a branch. Table 16-5 is a list of the acceptable relational symbols that may be used in the IF-THEN statement condition.

FIGURE 16-15
Unconditional and conditional branches.

```
line   GOTO  line
140    GOTO  70

line   IF condition THEN line
90     IF D=0 THEN 150
150    IF L<50 THEN 200
160    IF N>150 THEN 210
```

TABLE 16-5 **IF-THEN RELATIONAL SYMBOLS**

Symbol	Meaning
=	Is equal to
<	Is less than
>	Is greater than
= <	Is equal to or less than (not greater than)
= >	Is equal to or greater than (not less than)
< >	Is less than or greather than (not equal to)

FEEDBACK

16-18 What is an unconditional branch?

16-19 What instruction causes an unconditional branch?

16-20 What is a conditional branch?

16-21 What instruction is used for conditional branching?

Figure 16-16 is the coded BASIC solution for the compound-interest problem, including a GOTO and an IF-THEN statement. The program will continue requesting new amounts until the operator enters a 0 for the amount deposited. When a 0 is entered, a branch will be made to the END statement.

Calculation Loops

The example problem for calculating an ending balance that is compounded annually has been solved by using the formula for compound interest. If the programmer did not know the compound-interest formula, the problem could be solved by using a calculation loop. This can be accomplished by calculating the simple interest for each period. The flowchart in Figure 16-17 is a solution for the compound-interest problem that uses a calculation loop instead of the compound-interest formula. Note that the flowchart is the same as the previous example through the inputting of the number of years. The next three steps make up the calculation loop. The first of these steps is the process of multiplying the amount by 1.1 $(1 + .1)$. When the amount is multiplied by the interest rate plus 1, the resulting answer is equal to the simple interest for that

```
10   REM      PROGRAM TO COMPOUND INTEREST AT 10%
20   REM
30   REM      VARIABLES: D=DEPOSIT AMOUNT
40   REM                 E=ENDING AMOUNT
50   REM                 Y=YEARS DEPOSIT IS IN ACCOUNT
60   REM
70   PRINT "DEPOSIT AMOUNT";
80   INPUT D
90   IF D=0 THEN 150
100  PRINT "NUMBER OF YEARS";
110  INPUT Y
120  LET E=D * (1+.1) ^ Y
130  PRINT "THE ENDING AMOUNT IS";E
140  GOTO 70
150  END
```

FIGURE 16-16

Compound interest program with loop.

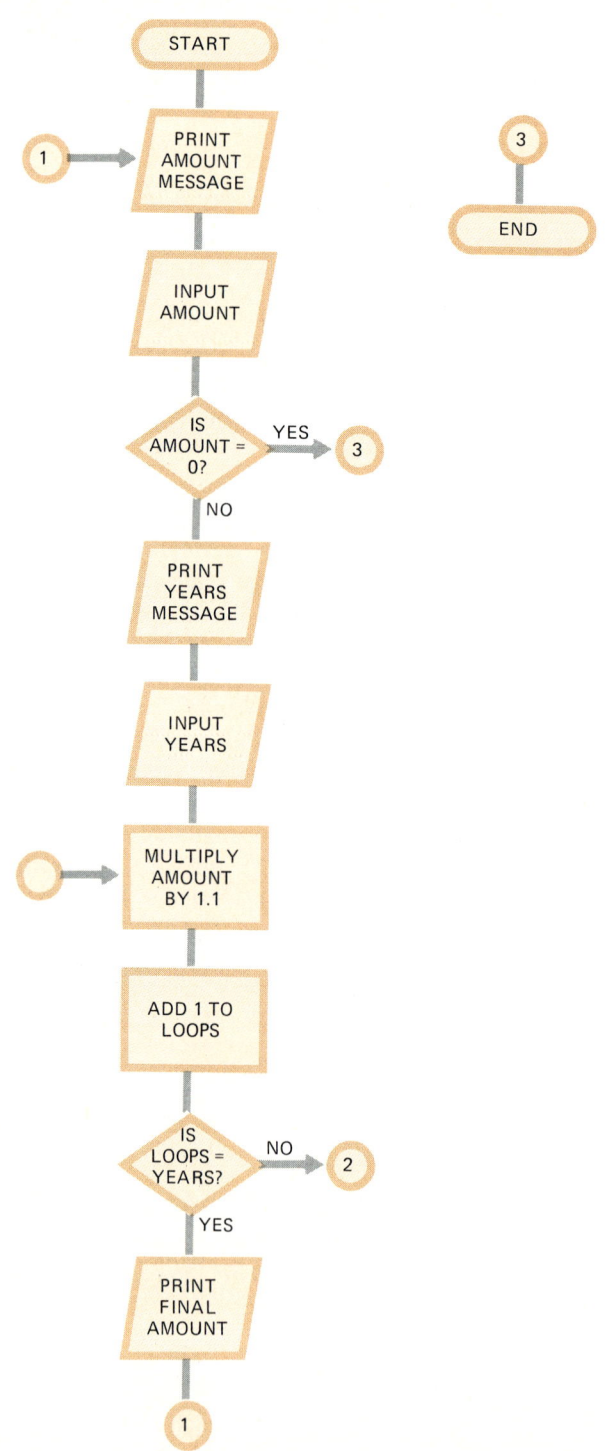

FIGURE 16-17
Compound interest flowchart with
calculation loop.

period, plus the original amount. This step will calculate the interest in the problem for one year. The process must be repeated once for each year that the interest is to be compounded. The second process is to add 1 to a variable called "L" (loops). The variable L will be used to count the number of times that the amount has been multiplied by 1.1. The last step in the loop is a decision to determine if the calculation loop has been repeated a number of times equal to the number of years. If the number of times through the loop is not equal to the number of years, the logic will branch back to repeat the loop. When the number of times through the loop is equal to the number of years, the ending amount will have been calculated and is ready to be printed. Figure 16-18 is the coded solution following this flowchart.

The FOR-NEXT statements In the above example, the programmer is writing the instructions to control the looping. The BASIC language has two instructions that are designed to control looping automatically. They are called the **FOR** and the **NEXT** statements. Figure 16-19 illustrates the FOR and the NEXT statements. The FOR consists of a line number, the key word FOR, a

FIGURE 16-18

Compound interest program with calculation loop.

```
 10  REM              PROGRAM TO COMPOUND INTEREST AT 10%
 20  REM
 30  REM              VARIABLES:  D=DEPOSIT AMOUNT
 40  REM                          L=LOOPS IN CALCULATION
 50  REM                          Y=YEARS DEPOSIT IS IN ACCOUNT
 60  REM
 70  PRINT "DEPOSIT AMOUNT";
 80  INPUT D
 90  IF D=0 THEN 170
100  PRINT "NUMBER OF YEARS";
110  INPUT Y
120  LET D=D * 1.1
130  LET L=L+1
140  IF L<Y THEN 120
150  PRINT "THE ENDING AMOUNT IS";D
160  GOTO 70
170  END
```

Calculation loop → { 120, 130, 140 }

```
line  FOR var=first value TO last value STEP increment
line  NEXT var
120   FOR L=1 TO Y
        .
        .
        .
140   NEXT 1
200   FOR C=1 TO 12 STEP 2
        .
        .
        .
240   NEXT C
```

FIGURE 16-19

FOR and NEXT statements.

variable to be used for controlling the looping, an equals sign, the controlling variable's beginning value, the key word TO, the controlling variable's maximum allowable value, the key word STEP, and the value to be added to the controlling variable each time through the loop. The key word STEP and the increment value are optional. If they are left out, the increment value is assumed to be 1. The NEXT statement consists of a line number, the key word NEXT, and the name of the controlling variable. This variable name must be the same name used in the FOR statement. The FOR statement is always the first statement in the loop, and the NEXT is always the last statement in the loop. It should be noted that in the FOR statement, the beginning value, the ending value, and the increment value may be numeric-constant values or they may be the names of numeric variables that contain the values.

In the example, line 120, the FOR statement indicates that the variable L is to be begun with a value of 1. Because the STEP value has been omitted, each time the loop is repeated an increment value of 1 will be added to the variable L. The variable L will be allowed to increment up to and including the value of the variable Y. It is the NEXT statement at the bottom of the loop that causes the incrementing of variable L. In this example, the statements placed between the FOR and the NEXT statements will be executed a number of times equal to the value in the variable called Y. Figure 16-20 is a BASIC program for compound interest that uses the FOR and NEXT statements. In this example, the LET statement of line 130 will be executed a number of times equal to the number of years inputted in line 110.

BASIC LIBRARY FUNCTIONS

The main emphasis of BASIC is to be an easy language that even the inexperienced programmer can use. BASIC is also a mathematically oriented program language. Being consistent with the above points, the language BASIC has a series of arithmetic functions that are preprogrammed for the use of the BASIC

FIGURE 16-20

Compound interest program using FOR and NEXT statements.

```
10   REM       PROGRAM TO COMPOUND INTEREST AT 10%
20   REM
30   REM       VARIABLES:  D=DEPOSIT AMOUNT
40   REM                   L=LOOPS IN CALCULATION
50   REM                   Y=YEARS DEPOSIT IS IN ACCOUNT
60   REM
70   PRINT "DEPOSIT AMOUNT";
80   INPUT D
90   IF D=0 THEN 170
100  PRINT "NUMBER OF YEARS";
110  INPUT Y
120  FOR L=1 TO Y
130      LET D=D * 1.1
140  NEXT L
150  PRINT "THE ENDING AMOUNT IS";D
160  GOTO 70
170  END
```

Calculation loop { 120, 130, 140 }

TABLE 16-6   **ARITHMETIC FUNCTIONS**

Function	Description
abs(X)	Absolute value of X
atn(X)	Arctangent of X (answer in radians)*
cos(X)	Cosine of X (X in radians)
exp(X)	Exponential of X
int(X)	Largest integer not larger than X
log(X)	Natural log of X
rnd	Generates a random number between 0 and 1 inclusive
sgn(X)	Algebraic sign of X: -1 if X is negative, 0 if X is zero, and $+1$ if X is positive
sin(X)	Sine of X (X in radians)
sqr(X)	Square root of X (positive)
tan(X)	Tangent of X (X in radians)

* There are 57.29578° per radian.

programmer. These routines include most of the arithmetic functions that would be used to solve mathematical problems. They include routines that would be difficult for many programmers to write themselves. These standard functions are listed in Table 16-6. Some BASIC compilers and interpreters have functions beyond those listed here.

Figure 16-21 is an example using the square-root function. The problem is to calculate the hypotenuse (C) of a right triangle, given the other two sides $(A$ and $B)$. The relationship between the hypotenuse and the other two sides

FIGURE 16-21

Calculating hypotenuse using square root function.

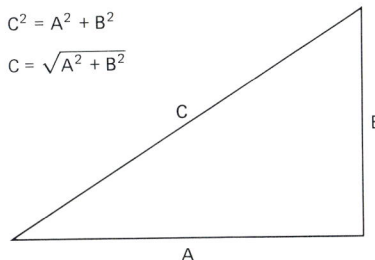

$$C^2 = A^2 + B^2$$

$$C = \sqrt{A^2 + B^2}$$

```
10   REM          PROGRAM TO CALCULATE THE HYPOTENUSE OF A RIGHT TRIANGI
20   REM
30   REM          VARIABLES:  A=SIDE A
40   REM                      B=SIDE B
50   REM                      C=SIDE C (HYPOTENUSE)
60   REM
70   PRINT "SIDES A AND B";
80   INPUT A,B
90   LET C=SQR (A ˆ 2+B ˆ 2)
100  PRINT "THE HYPOTENUSE=";C
110  END
```

is: the hypotenuse squared is equal to the sum of the squares of the remaining sides ($C^2 = A^2 + B^2$). The hypotenuse (C) is equal to the square root of the sum of the squares for sides A and B ($C = \sqrt{A^2 + B^2}$). Finding a square root manually can be a time-consuming operation. Line 90 of the example code shows how easily the square-root function can be used.

FEEDBACK

16-22 What instructions are provided in BASIC to control loops?

16-23 What are library functions?

16-24 How are library functions used?

SUMMARY

After the problem solution has been planned through flowcharting, pseudocode, or other planning techniques, the solution is coded in a programming language by following the logic plan. One of the easiest programming languages to learn is BASIC.

The language BASIC was developed specifically for the beginning programmer. Its key design goal was simplicity. This was accomplished in part by establishing defaults for many functions in order to reduce the required programming detail.

The REM statement allows the programmer to place remarks into the program to help document the program. We learned how to input data into main memory and how to output data from main memory to an output device with the INPUT and PRINT statements. After data have been inputted, we can perform arithmetic operations on them with the LET statement. We can perform difficult arithmetic operations using prewritten library functions, as well as the simple steps of exponentiation, multiplication, division, addition, and subtraction. Instructions to cause unconditional branches with the GOTO statement and conditional branches with the IF-THEN statement were introduced. In addition, we presented the FOR and NEXT statements, which control looping in our programs. The END statement is used to stop the program's execution.

ANSWERS TO
FEEDBACK QUESTIONS

16-1 The assumption that will be made in BASIC if the programmer does not code instruction details.

16-2 BASIC is mathematically oriented and does not provide for large volumes of either input or output data.

16-3 It means that every line must be numbered and that the instructions are referred to by the line number.

16-4 To allow remarks to appear in the program listing for documentation.

16-5 Numeric-variable names are a single letter, plus an optional number digit. String-variable names are a letter and a dollar sign.

16-6 A question mark and a space, which tells the operator that the computer is waiting for input.

16-7 The arithmetic symbols used by BASIC are + for addition, − for subtraction, * for multiplication, / for division, and ∧ for exponentiation.

16-8 The steps would be:

a D raised to the power of 3

b B divided by C

c The answer from step **a** multiplied by the answer from step **b**

d A added to the answer from step **c**

16-9 It is used to output variable values or constants.

16-10 The output line description defaults to a series of print areas called zones. The number of print zones depends upon the screen width.

16-11 It stops the running of the program.

16-12 A value to be used as it is written in the instruction.

16-13 By using an unusued line number on the instruction to be added. The new instruction will be placed in proper sequence by line number.

16-14 By using the line number of the statement to be changed with the new statement.

16-15 By entering the line number and leaving the rest of the line blank.

16-16 It causes the next output to be immediately after the previous value.

16-17 A message to be outputted to the operator to explain the nature of the required input.

16-18 One that is always taken.

16-19 GOTO.

16-20 A conditional branch causes or doesn't cause a branch, depending on a stated condition.

16-21 The IF-THEN statement.

16-22 FOR and NEXT statements.

16-23 Preprogrammed arithmetic functions that can be used in your BASIC program.

16-24 They are used within the LET statement.

FOR REVIEW AND DISCUSSION

1 Code the BASIC instructions to modify the program in Figure 16-9. Change the program to average three numbers instead of two.

2 Modify the BASIC program shown in Figure 16-13 so that it will input the annual interest rate instead of always using 10 percent.

3 Modify the BASIC program shown in Figure 16-20 to compound the interest four times a year instead of once a year.

CHAPTER 17

CONTINUING WITH BASIC

PREVIEW   Chapter 16 introduced us to the programming language BASIC. In that chapter, instructions were presented to allow the student to code simple programs. In this chapter we will present additional BASIC instructions, operating system commands, and the concepts of structured programs.

In this chapter you will learn:

1. The use of the magentic diskette to store programs
2. The structured programming constructs and how to implement them in BASIC
3. How to format numeric output data
4. How to direct program output to a printer

KEY TERMS TO WATCH FOR
AND REMEMBER

LLIST	READ-DATA
SAVE	CLS
LOAD	HOME
RUN	TAB
FILES	IF-THEN-ELSE
CATALOG	PRINT USING
KILL	WHILE-WEND
DELETE	LPRINT
GOSUB-RETURN	LPRINT USING

As noted in Chapter 16, there is a standard for the language BASIC. It is, however, a minimal standard covering only the most common BASIC instruction. In this chapter, we shall use more instructions that go beyond the minimal standard. The specific versions of BASIC covered here are Applesoft (Apple II and the Apple IIe), BASIC-80 (common to many microcomputers using the CP/M operating system), extended IBM PC BASIC, and BASIC as implemented on the Radio Shack TRS-80 Models I and III. The BASIC in this chapter also applies in those cases where there is a "look-alike" of another manufacturer. As an example, the Franklin Ace is a software look-alike of the Apple II and Apple IIe.

PRINTED LISTINGS AND THE DISK OPERATING SYSTEM (DOS)

In Chapter 16 you learned how to use the commands NEW, LIST, and RUN. These commands are part of the operating system which allows us to control the computer. The above commands are always a part of the operating system on microcomputers when we use BASIC. These commands, however, are only a few of the operating system commands available to us.

Printed Listings

The LIST command causes the instructions of the program in memory to be "listed" on the screen of the terminal. This display of instructions is very useful, but many times you will want a printed copy of the program instructions. Many versions of BASIC include the command **LLIST** to cause program listings to be printed rather than displayed. The BASIC-80, IBM PC, and TRS-80 versions all have the LLIST command; the Apple does not.

The Apple can direct output to a printer by sending the output data to a specified plug or "slot" inside the Apple. The most common slot used to hold the printer interface card is slot number 1. The Apple command to redirect output is PR# plus the appropriate slot number. If the printer interface card is in slot 1, the command would be PR#1. Slot O in the Apple is used for memory extension cards. The command PR#O will direct the output back to the screen. The Apple, therefore, requires three commands to print a program listing:

PR#1 (to direct output to the printer)
LIST (to produce the listing)
PR#O (to redirect the output back to the screen)

Disk Commands

Many, if not most, microcomputers have diskette drives attached to them for the purpose of storing programs and data. Those microcomputers that do not have diskette drives are often attached to a magnetic disk. This attachment may be direct or through a local area network. In either case, the disk is used in the same way as the diskette. To utilize the diskette drive, additional system commands are required. The operating system which contains the disk-oriented commands is typically called the *disk operating system* (DOS). Table 17-1 summarizes the LLIST and disk commands.

SAVE command   If you are writing useful programs, you certainly do not want to reenter the program through the keyboard each time you want to run it.

The most practical place to store programs is on magnetic diskettes. Each diskette has an area on it called the directory or catalog. It contains the name and location of each program and data file stored on the diskette. To store or save a program on a diskette, we must enter a **SAVE** command and the name we wish to use for the program. The format of the SAVE command is

SAVE "program name"

For example, if we wish to call our program PAYROLL, the command would be

SAVE "PAYROLL"

Note that the quotation marks (") are not used with the Apple microcomputer. The maximum length of the program name varies with the operating system used but is typically eight characters.

If you SAVE a program using a name that has already been used, the program on the diskette will be erased and the name will be assigned to the new program being saved. That means that you can save a new version of an old program by using the same program name. It is recommended that you protect yourself from disasters as you enter and work on your program by saving it every 15 minutes or so. That way if there is a power failure, the computer gets turned off, or you just foul up the program, you have a copy of the program stored on diskette. The most you will lose is the changes you have made since the last SAVE.

TABLE 17-1   **COMMON SYSTEM COMMANDS**

Command	Meaning	Example systems
LLIST	Lists the instructions of the program in memory on the printer	BASIC-80, IBM PC, TRS-80
SAVE "program"	Saves the program in memory on a diskette	*Apple, BASIC-80 IBM PC, TRS-80
LOAD "program"	Loads "program" from the diskette into memory	*Apple, BASIC-80 IBM PC, TRS-80
RUN "program"	Causes the program on diskettes called "program" to be loaded into memory and its instructions followed	*Apple, BASIC-80, IBM PC, TRS-80
CATALOG	Lists the diskette table of contents on the screen	Apple
FILES	Lists the diskette table of contents on the screen	BASIC-80, IBM PC, TRS-80
DELETE program	Erases the program from the diskette	Apple
KILL "program"	Erases the program from the diskette	BASIC-80, IBM PC, TRS-80

*The quotation marks (") are not used with the program name on the Apple.

LOAD command   Now that the program is stored on the diskette, we can cause a copy of the program to be loaded from the diskette into memory. Remember that inputting from magnetic diskette (or any other input device) does not erase it. The program is still recorded on the diskette after the load operation. The command to load the program into memory is

>   LOAD "program name"

If we wanted to load the "payroll" program we saved earlier, the command would be

>   LOAD "PAYROLL"

Again, note that the Apple DOS does not use the quotation marks around the program name. The program in memory can now be LISTed and changed in any way we wish. The LOAD command is a convenient way of getting a copy of the program back into memory if you are not finished entering or debugging it yet.

RUN command   As we learned in Chapter 16, we can cause the instructions of any BASIC program in memory to be followed by keying in the **RUN** command. To run a program stored on a diskette, we could LOAD the program and then RUN it. There is an easier way, however, using the DOS version of the RUN command. The format of the DOS RUN command is

>   RUN "program name"

To run the program named "payroll," the command would be

>   RUN "PAYROLL"

Remember, there are no quotation marks around the program name when using the Apple. This form of the RUN command accomplishes both the load and run functions.

FILES (CATALOG) command   It is often necessary to find out what programs and data files are stored on a diskette. The command to display the directory or catalog of the diskette varies with the operating system being used. On the most recently developed systems (BASIC-80 and IBM PC), the command is **FILES**. The Apple DOS uses the command **CATALOG**. The TRS-80 Models I and III use the command **CMD "D:drive"** (where "drive" is equal to the number of the diskette drive being used). The first drive on a TRS-80 is referred to as drive O. Thus, the command to display the contents of drive O would be

CMD "D:O"

Note that these commands are the form to use from within BASIC. If you are in the "system mode," a different command may be required. For example, the command DIR will display the DIRectory of the diskette in the system mode with BASIC-80 (CP/M), IBM PC, and the TRS-80 (Models I and III). The Apple DOS uses the CATALOG command in both BASIC and the system mode.

KILL (DELETE) command   We now know how to save, load, and run programs. In addition, we can display the table of contents of the diskette to see what we have stored there. The last disk operating function to be discussed here is the removing or erasing of programs from the diskette. The most common commands used to erase a stored program are the **KILL** and **DELETE** commands. The BASIC-80, IBM PC, and TRS-80 systems use the KILL command. The format is KILL "program name." For example,

KILL "PAYROLL"

will erase the program "payroll" from the diskette. On the Apple system, the DELETE command is used. Its format is

DELETE program name

Therefore, to erase the payroll program on an Apple, the command would be DELETE PAYROLL.

FEEDBACK   **17-1** What is the command to cause a printed program listing? Is the command available in all versions of BASIC?
17-2 What is the command to output a program currently in memory to a diskette?
17-3 What is the command to run a program that is stored on a diskette but is not currently in primary memory?

STRUCTURED PROGRAMS IN BASIC   Structured programming techniques have one overall objective. That objective is to clarify the program logic so that it is easy to code, debug, and, if necessary, modify. This objective is accomplished by making the logic modular in its structure. That is, each major logical function will be planned and coded separately. Then the execution of these logical modules will be controlled by a main module, which reflects the logic of the overall solution.

Figure 17-1 is a flowchart representing the solution to the problem of calculating average sales. It should be noted that there are several alternative methods of planning program logic, such as psuedocode. The problem state-

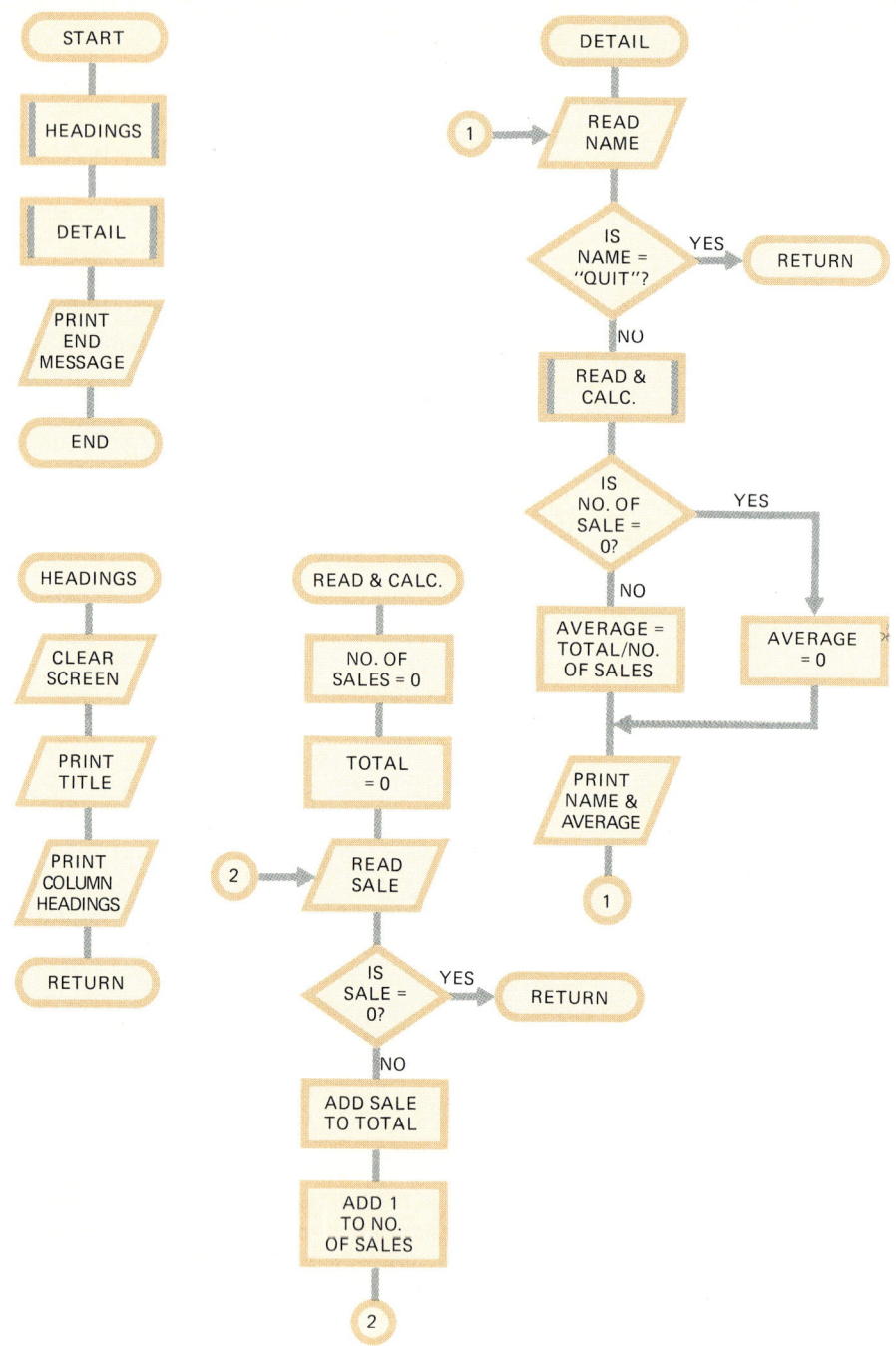

FIGURE 17-1

Flowchart for problem of calculating average sales.

ment specifies that the input data will be the salesperson's name and the dollar amount of each sale made by that person. The last record in the input data file will have "quit" as the salesperson's name. There is no data to be processed in this last record. The program is to output the salesperson's name and the average sale amount. In addition, the output is to have a title line, column headings, and a message at the end of the report.

At first glance, Figure 17-1 appears to be four separate flowcharts. This is because each of the major logical functions has been planned separately. The main logic module begins with a terminal symbol labeled START and ends with a terminal symbol labeled END. This module describes the overview logic of our solution—we will output the report headings, process all the detailed records, print the ending message, and end the program. You will recall from Chapter 12 that the rectangle with the two vertical lines is called the predefined process. A predefined process is one that is defined or described elsewhere. In this case the predefined processes "headings" and "detail" are also flowcharted in Figure 17-1.

The first predefined process to be executed is called HEADINGS. Its flowcharted logic begins with a terminal symbol labeled HEADINGS. The flowchart shows that we plan to clear the screen, output a title, and output column headings. The last symbol is another terminal symbol labeled RETURN. The RETURN indicates that the logical control is to "return" to the main logic module following its predefined process. In this example the predefined process HEADINGS would transfer control to the module of the same name. At the end of that module, the "return" transfers logical control back to the symbol following the HEADINGS predefined process (DETAIL).

The next logical function in our program solution is the predefined process called DETAIL. The DETAIL process begins with a terminal symbol labeled DETAIL. The first steps in the DETAIL module are to input the name of a salesperson and to compare that name with "quit." If the name is "quit," the logic will return to the main module, output the ending message, and end the program. If the name is not equal to "quit," the program will read sale amounts for that salesperson and calculate the appropriate totals required to compute the average sales. The execution of these steps is indicated in the predefined process labeled READ AND CALC. The number of sales for any one salesperson is unknown and must be counted as the data is processed. The last sale amount for each person is recorded as a zero. The zero is not to be counted as a sale, but it is used as a signal to indicate the end of the sales data for that person. After all sales for a particular salesperson have been totaled and counted, we may calculate the average sale. The logic of the DETAIL flowchart tests the number of sales prior to calculating the average. This step is to avoid the possibility of dividing by zero. If the number of sales is zero, then the average is zero. If the number of sales is not zero, then we will calculate the average by dividing the total by the number of sales. After the average is calculated, it is printed along with the salesperson's name. The logic then loops back to the beginning of the module to input the next name.

The GOSUB and RETURN Instructions

To implement the module structure shown with the predefined process symbols, BASIC uses the **GOSUB** instruction. The format of the GOSUB instruction is

    linenumber GOSUB linenumber

For example, if the first instruction in the HEADINGS module was coded on line number 300, the main module predefined process HEADINGS would be coded as

    100 GOSUB 300

Each time a GOSUB instruction is encountered, the system keeps track of the location of the instruction following the GOSUB. The logic will branch to this stored instruction address when the system encounters a **RETURN** instruction. The RETURN instruction has no other information required. It will always "return" to the instruction following the last GOSUB executed.

The READ and DATA Instructions

It is not unusual to accumulate input data for a period of time prior to processing that data. In our example problem the sales data could represent sales over a period of time. We may wish to average the sales for the first week of the month, the first two weeks, the first three weeks, and the entire month. If this is the case, we will not want to reenter the sales for the first week when we run the program at the end of the second week. In short, we want to be able to accumulate and save the data entered for each week. If the data to be accumulated is a large volume, we will want to save it on a diskette or magnetic disk. The creation of disk and diskette files is beyond the coverage of this text. There is, however, a way of building reasonable quantities of data into the program itself. This is accomplished with the **DATA** statement. The format of the DATA statement is

    linenumber DATA constant1,constant2, . . .,constantN

The constants in the DATA statement may be numeric and/or string constants, for example,

    230 DATA "JEFF SMITH", 34.56, 44, 12.98, 24.95, 0

The number of constants in a single data statement is limited only by the maximum instruction length of your computer. Typically, this is about 255 characters. DATA statements are not executable statements; that is, they do not cause anything to happen during the running of the program. They are used to hold constant data. DATA statements may be placed anywhere in the program. When a program is running, all DATA statements are treated as though they make up one large data statement called the *data block*.

The instruction to "input" or "access" the data in the data block is the

READ instruction. The format of the READ instruction is

linenumber READ list

The "list" in the READ statement is one or more variable names. These variables may be numeric or string names. If there is more than one name in a list, each variable name must be separated with a comma. Examples include

430 READ N$
550 READ S
800 READ A$,C,B$,H,J

When a READ instruction is executed, the next available constant from the data block is moved to the variable in the READ list. If the READ statement has a list of five variables such as the example above on line 800, the next five constants from the data block will be moved to the five variables. As READ statements are executed, the data block is "used up." If we attempt to READ data after we have reached the end of the data block, the execution of our program will end and an error message will be displayed. For that reason we have included a "dummy" salesperson's name of "quit" to logically indicate the end of the data block. Care must be taken to not attempt to READ a string constant from the data block into a numeric variable. If this happens, an error situation called a "data type mismatch" will occur, and the program will be terminated. In our example the data block will be made up of several groups of data. Each group will contain a name and a series of sale amounts. The last sale amount in each series is a value of zero. Knowing the pattern of data in the data block will allow us to logically know when it is appropriate to read a string constant (a name) and when to read a numeric constant (a sale amount).

The CLS or HOME Statement

It is not unusual to want to clear the display screen prior to outputting it. In the example problem discussed earlier in this chapter, an average sales report is to be outputted to the screen. The report is to include a title and column headings. This is certainly a case where you would want to clear system commands and miscellaneous "junk" off of the screen before you print the title. The instruction to accomplish this is the **CLS** (on most microcomputer systems) or the **HOME** (on the Apple). The CLS (HOME) instruction is both a command and an instruction. If you key in CLS (HOME) on the keyboard and press the enter (return) key, the screen will clear and the cursor will be moved to the upper-left corner of the screen. If you want to use it as an instruction within a program, the only difference is the addition of a line number. If you use the instruction

330 CLS
330 HOME

the screen will clear each time the instruction is executed.

The TAB Function

In the previous chapter we learned about default options and how they made BASIC simpler to learn and use. One of these defaults is the print zones used by the PRINT statement—each comma in the print line moves the cursor forward to the next print zone. The 40-column Apple screen has three print zones. The 64-column TRS-80 screen has four print zones, and the 80-column screens have five print zones. The print zones can be convenient and easy to use; but if it doesn't fit the requirements of the problem being solved, there are other choices. One of the most common ways of controlling the horizontal spacing in a PRINT statement is the **TAB** function. The TAB function is coded as part of a PRINT statement list. It moves the cursor to any output position desired, not just to the beginning of the next print zone. The format of the TAB function is TAB(position), where "position" is the horizontal position on the line to place the cursor. If we wanted to output a name (N$) beginning in position 12 and an average (A) in position 57, the print statement would look like this:

470 PRINT TAB(12);N$;TAB(57);A

The semicolon (;) is used as the "separator" in the list to prevent the cursor from moving on to the next print zone.

The IF-THEN-ELSE Instruction

A conditional branch instruction, the IF-THEN, was introduced in Chapter 16. The format was given as

linenumber IF condition THEN linenumber

If the "condition" was true (it existed), then a branch to the last line number occurred. If the condition was false, the program execution continued with the next instruction. This is the IF statement as described by the BASIC Minimal Standard. It is, however, far more restrictive than is allowed in almost all versions of BASIC in use. All the versions described in this text allow the programmer to specify the "truth statement" in a form other than just a statement number (implying a GOTO to that statement). The more popular format for the IF statement is

linenumber IF condition THEN statement

The "statement" can be any statement (instruction) you wish to conditionally execute. Examples of this format are

440 IF N$ = "QUIT" THEN RETURN
800 IF A <> B THEN LET A = B

Almost all versions of BASIC allow the programmer to code multiple statements on a single line. That is, each instruction does not have to be on its own line with a line number. If you code multiple statements with a single line number, each of the statements has to be separated by a colon (:). The following example illustrates this format:

900 LET A = B / C : LET B = O

Both LET statements are on line 900; they will be executed in sequence. It is also common to place REM statement on the same line as another statement to help explain the function of the first statement, for example,

900 GOSUB 300 : REM PRINT THE REPORT HEADINGS

This line uses the REM to explain the reason for doing the GOSUB. Make sure that the REM statement is the last statement on the line or the remaining statements will be considered part of the remark and not recognized as statements. If an IF statement condition is false, execution proceeds with the next *line number*. If you combine multiple statements on a line and the first one is an IF statement, *all* the remaining statements on that line will be executed if the condition is true, and *all* the remaining statements will be skipped if the condition is false. For example, let us assume that we want to compare variable A to variable B; if A is less than B, we want to add A to B and add 1 to variable C. The instruction can be coded as

750 IF A < B THEN LET B = A + B : LET C = C + 1

Either *both* LET statements will be executed or *neither* of them will be executed, depending on the values in A and B.

The IF statement, as we have described it, is called the IF-THEN and is the coded equivalent to the flowchart segment in Figure 17-2a. It assumes that we want program execution to continue with nothing special happening if the

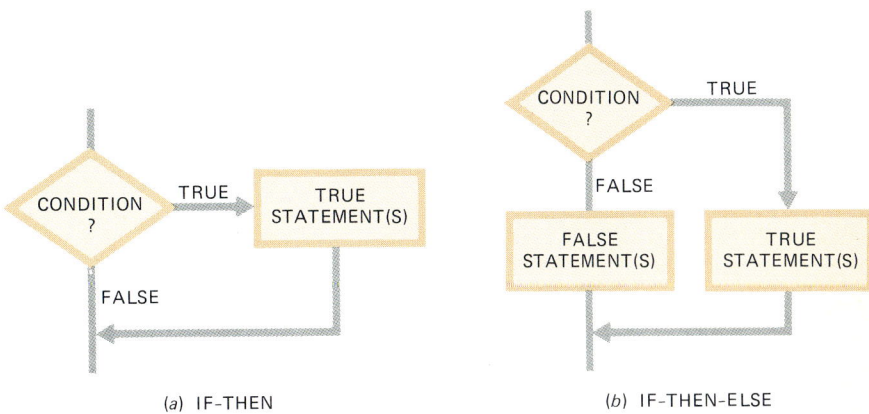

FIGURE 17-2

Flowchart segments—the IF statement.

(a) IF-THEN

(b) IF-THEN-ELSE

tested condition is false. Figure 17-2b is a flowchart segment that illustrates a situation where there are two choices. One choice is to be executed only if the condition is true, and one choice is to be executed only if the condition is false. This logic construct is called the **IF-THEN-ELSE.**

Let's assume that we want to compare variables A and B. If A is less than B, we will add B to A; else (if A is not less than B) we will subtract B from A. The IF-THEN-ELSE logic can be constructed as the following statements:

```
600 IF A < B THEN LET A = A + B : GOTO 620
610 LET A = A − B
620 . . .
```

If A is less than B, we will perform the add *and* GOTO line 620 (skipping line 610). If A is not less than B, we will skip to the next line number (line 610) and perform the subtraction.

Some of the newer versions of BASIC (BASIC-80 and IBM PC) have an IF-THEN-ELSE statement. Its format is

```
line IF condition THEN true statement(s) ELSE false statement(s)
```

The example shown above with lines 600 and 610 could be coded as

```
600 IF A < B THEN LET A = A + B ELSE LET A = A − B
```

On ASCII terminals and microcomputers, the control J (hold down the control key while pressing the J key) causes the cursor to drop down a line without terminating the statement. Programmers often use this to make statements more readable. The above statement could be written as

```
600 IF A < B

    THEN LET A = A + B

    ELSE LET A = A − B
```

This format does not change the logic of the statement, but it does separate the condition, truth statement, and false statement to make it easier to understand.

A Program to Calculate Average Sales

Earlier in this chapter we described the requirements for a program to calculate the average sales for each salesperson in our organization. The data for each person will consist of the salesperson's name and the dollar amount of each sale he or she made. The number of sales made by any one salesperson is

```
10 REM          PROGRAM TO CALCULATE AVERAGE SALES
20 REM
30 REM          VARIABLES:    A  = AVERAGE OF SALES
40 REM                        N  = NUMBER OF SALES
50 REM                        N$ = SALESPERSON'S NAME
60 REM                        S  = SALE AMOUNT
70 REM                        T  = TOTAL OF SALES
80 REM
100 GOSUB 300 : REM PRINT REPORT HEADINGS
110 GOSUB 400 : REM DETAIL PROCESSING
120 PRINT:PRINT "END OF REPORT"
130 END
200 REM
210 REM          DATA TO BE PROCESSED
220 REM
230 DATA "JEFF SMITH",34.56,44,12.98,24.95,0
240 DATA "ROD AMBOY",120,34,23.45,14.5,0
250 DATA "RICHARD WHITE",35.67,0
260 DATA "MARY BOBCOY",0
270 DATA "DIANE FOX",12.34,14.15,0
280 DATA "QUIT"
300 REM
310 REM          CLEAR THE SCREEN AND PRINT TITLES
320 REM
330 HOME
340 PRINT TAB(29);"S A L E S   R E P O R T"
350 PRINT
360 PRINT TAB(12);"SALESPERSON";TAB(55);"AVERAGE SALE"
370 PRINT:PRINT
380 RETURN
400 REM
410 REM          DETAIL PROCESSING
420 REM
430 READ N$
440 IF N$ = "QUIT" THEN RETURN
450 GOSUB 500 : REM READ AND TOTAL SALES AMOUNTS
460 IF N = 0
        THEN LET A = 0
        ELSE LET A = T / N
470 PRINT TAB(12);N$;TAB(57);A
480 GOTO 430
500 REM
510 REM          READ AND TOTAL SALES AMOUNTS
520 REM
530 LET N = 0
540 LET T = 0
550 READ S
560 IF S = 0 THEN RETURN
570 LET T - T + S
580 LET N = N + 1
590 GOTO 550
```

FIGURE 17-3

BASIC program to calculate average sales.

```
                S A L E S   R E P O R T

       SALESPERSON            AVERAGE SALE

       JEFF SMITH             29.1225
       ROD AMBOY              47.9875
       RICHARD WHITE          35.67
       MARY BOBCOY            0
       DIANE FOX              13.245
```

FIGURE 17-4
Sample output—average sales.

unknown, but the last sale amount given for each person will be a value of zero. This zero value will be used as a sign that there are no more sales for this person. The sales data will be coded in DATA statements. The last record in the data block will have a salesperson name of "quit" to indicate that there are no more records to process. The logic for an approach to the solution of this problem was shown in the flowchart of Figure 17-1. Figure 17-3 is the BASIC program coded from the flowchart. This coded solution was coded using the Apple version of BASIC-80. The HOME instruction (only found on the Apple version of BASIC-80) is used to clear the screen, and the IF-THEN-ELSE instruction (not found in Apple BASIC) is illustrated. In this example, the data block is formed by the DATA statements on lines 230 through 280. These DATA statements could have been placed anywhere in the program. Note the use of the REM statement to document the program and to identify the program modules. Figure 17-4 is the output generated by the program in Figure 17-3.

FEEDBACK

17-4 Describe the functions of the GOSUB and RETURN instructions.

17-5 What is the "data block" and how is it formed?

17-6 What is the instruction to clear the screen?

17-7 What is the difference between the IF-THEN and the IF-THEN-ELSE instructions?

FORMATTING NUMERIC OUTPUT

If you examine the output shown in Figure 17-4, you will see that there are a few undesirable characteristics in the format of the "normal" numeric output. The average sale amounts are not rounded off to the nearest cent, the decimal points are not aligned, and no decimal positions print if the average is a whole number. BASIC normally suppresses all nonsignificant zeros to the left of whole numbers and to the right of fractional values.

Instruction Format:

```
linenumber PRINT USING "edit string";list
```

Examples:

Instruction	Result
480 PRINT USING "####.##";A	1234.50
970 PRINT USING "$$###.##";A	$1234.50
980 print using "$$###,.##";A	$1,234.50

FIGURE 17-5
PRINT USING format and examples.

The PRINT USING Instruction

There are many situations where it is desirable to edit numeric values. The process of "editing" a number includes specifying the number of digits to be printed, rounding off to a specified number of positions, the insertion of commas, the insertion of a dollar sign, and the printing of a specific number of decimal positions. Numeric data can be edited using the **PRINT USING** instruction. Figure 17-5 illustrates the PRINT USING instruction format and some examples of its use.

The "edit string" is a string constant containing characters to control the editing process. The number sign (#) symbol is used to indicate the number of number digits to print. The positioning of the decimal point in the string specifies the number of decimal positions to print and where to round off. A floating dollar sign is indicated by the double dollar sign in the edit string. A "floating" dollar sign is when the dollar sign always prints immediately to the left of the first whole number digit. If a comma is included in the edit string, commas will be printed to separate the thousands from the hundreds, the millions from the thousands, and so on.

An Improved Solution to Calculate Average Sales

Figure 17-6 is the coding for an improved version of the program to calculate average sales. The PRINT statement used in the original coding shown in Figure 17-3 has been replaced with lines 470 and 480. Line 470 is used to print the name of the salesperson. Line 480 prints the average sale. Note the semi-colon (;) at the end of the PRINT statement in line 470 to cause the average sale to be printed on the same line as the salesperson's name. Figure 17-7 shows the output from the improved solution code. The average sale is now rounded off to the nearest cent, the decimal points are aligned, and two decimal digits print for each average.

```
10 REM           PROGRAM TO CALCULATE AVERAGE SALES
20 REM
30 REM           VARIABLES:    A  = AVERAGE OF SALES
40 REM                         N  = NUMBER OF SALES
50 REM                         N$ = SALESPERSON'S NAME
60 REM                         S  = SALE AMOUNT
70 REM                         T  = TOTAL OF SALES
80 REM
100 GOSUB 300 : REM PRINT REPORT HEADINGS
110 GOSUB 400 : REM DETAIL PROCESSING
120 PRINT:PRINT "END OF REPORT"
130 END
200 REM
210 REM           DATA TO BE PROCESSED
220 REM
230 DATA "JEFF SMITH",34.56,44,12.98,24.95,0
240 DATA "ROD AMBOY",120,34,23.45,14.5,0
250 DATA "RICHARD WHITE",35.67,0
260 DATA "MARY BOBCOY",0
270 DATA "DIANE FOX",12.34,14.15,0
280 DATA "QUIT"
300 REM
310 REM           CLEAR THE SCREEN AND PRINT TITLES
320 REM
330 HOME
340 PRINT TAB(29);"S A L E S   R E P O R T"
350 PRINT
360 PRINT TAB(12);"SALESPERSON";TAB(55);"AVERAGE SALE"
370 PRINT:PRINT
380 RETURN
400 REM
410 REM           DETAIL PROCESSING
420 REM
430 READ N$
440 IF N$ = "QUIT" THEN RETURN
450 GOSUB 500 : REM READ AND TOTAL SALES AMOUNTS
460 IF N = 0
        THEN LET A = 0
        ELSE LET A = T / N
470 PRINT TAB(12);N$;TAB(57);
480 PRINT USING "####.##",A
490 GOTO 430
500 REM
510 REM           READ AND TOTAL SALES AMOUNTS
520 REM
530 LET N = 0
540 LET T = 0
550 READ S
560 IF S = 0 THEN RETURN
570 LET T = T + S
580 LET N = N + 1
590 GOTO 550
```

FIGURE 17-6

Improved BASIC program to calculate average sales with the PRINT USING instruction.

```
                    S A L E S   R E P O R T

          SALESPERSON              AVERAGE SALE

          JEFF SMITH                   29.12
          ROD AMBOY                    47.99
          RICHARD WHITE                35.67
          MARY BOBCOY                   0.00
          DIANE FOX                    13.25
```

FIGURE 17-7
Sample output with the PRINT USING.

```
          END OF REPORT
```

FEEDBACK

17-8 What does the PRINT USING statement do beyond the PRINT statement?

17-9 Do all versions of BASIC have a PRINT USING instruction?

17-10 What is meant by the term "editing" when applied to numeric data?

THE DO-WHILE CONSTRUCT

Programs are made up of three basic types of logical structures—sequence, selection, and loops. The sequence structure is simply the execution of instructions in sequence. This structure is coded by writing instructions in the order you wish them to be executed. The selection structure allows the selection of the next instruction(s) to be executed through the use of a conditional branch, such as the IF-THEN and the IF-THEN-ELSE. Loops may be constructed in a variety of ways. The examples in Chapter 16 and the previous examples in this chapter formed the loop with a GOTO instruction as the last instruction in the loop. We made a way out of the loop by placing a decision within the loop.

An alternative way of showing the logic of the loop is illustrated in Figure 17-8. This construct is known as the DO-WHILE. The loop always begins with a decision to test the controlling condition. That is, it begins with a decision to see if it is necessary to go through the loop again. The instructions within the loop are executed as long as (while) the controlling condition is true. The bottom of the loop always directs execution back to the decision at the top

FIGURE 17-8
Flowchart segment—the DO-WHILE construct.

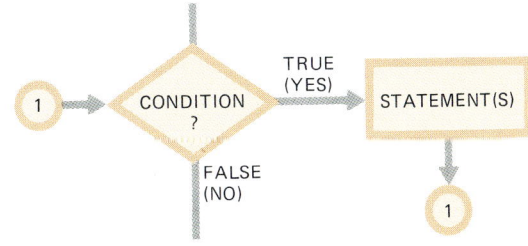

of the loop. If the condition tested in the decision becomes false, execution proceeds with the instruction following the DO-WHILE construct.

The WHILE and WEND Instructions

The later versions of BASIC (BASIC-80 and IBM PC) contain instructions designed to make it easy to code the DO-WHILE construct. The DO-WHILE instructions are the **WHILE** and the **WEND.** The first instruction in the loop is the WHILE statement. The last statement in the loop is always the WEND (*While END*). The instruction(s) to be executed within the loop are coded between the WHILE and the WEND statements. The format of the WHILE is

linenumber WHILE condition

The condition in the WHILE statement may be any condition that can be used in an IF statement. This condition controls the looping. As long as this condition is true, the instructions in the loop will be executed. The format of the WEND statement is

linenumber WEND

The flowchart in Figure 17-9 reflects the logic of the problem to calculate average sales described earlier. The logic has been modified from that shown in Figure 17-1 to take advantage of the DO-WHILE construct. There are two loops in the flowchart—one in the main logic module and one in the module called READ & CALC. The main module DO-WHILE begins with a test to see if the name just read is not equal to "quit." If the condition is true (the name is not equal to quit), the instructions within the module called DETAIL will be executed. The looping will continue "while" the name is not equal to "quit." When the answer to the question within the decision symbol is no (a false condition), looping will stop. The second DO-WHILE construct compares the value of the sale amount to zero. While the sale amount value is greater than zero, a sales total will be accumulated, the number of sales counted, and the next sale amount will be read. When the condition becomes false, the logic will "return" to the DETAIL module to calculate the average sale.

It should be noted that whenever the condition that controls the loop is based upon input data (a common situation), two input steps are required— one just prior to the DO-WHILE and one at the bottom of the loop. The first read is required to get the data necessary to make the decision that first time the condition is tested. This first read statement is often called the "priming read." The read at the end of the loop provides the data for all comparisons after the first one. Logically, the read at the end of the loop is just ahead of the decision while instructions within the loop are being executed.

Figure 17-10 illustrates the BASIC code to implement the logic shown in the flowchart of Figure 17-9. The DO-WHILE construct in the main logic

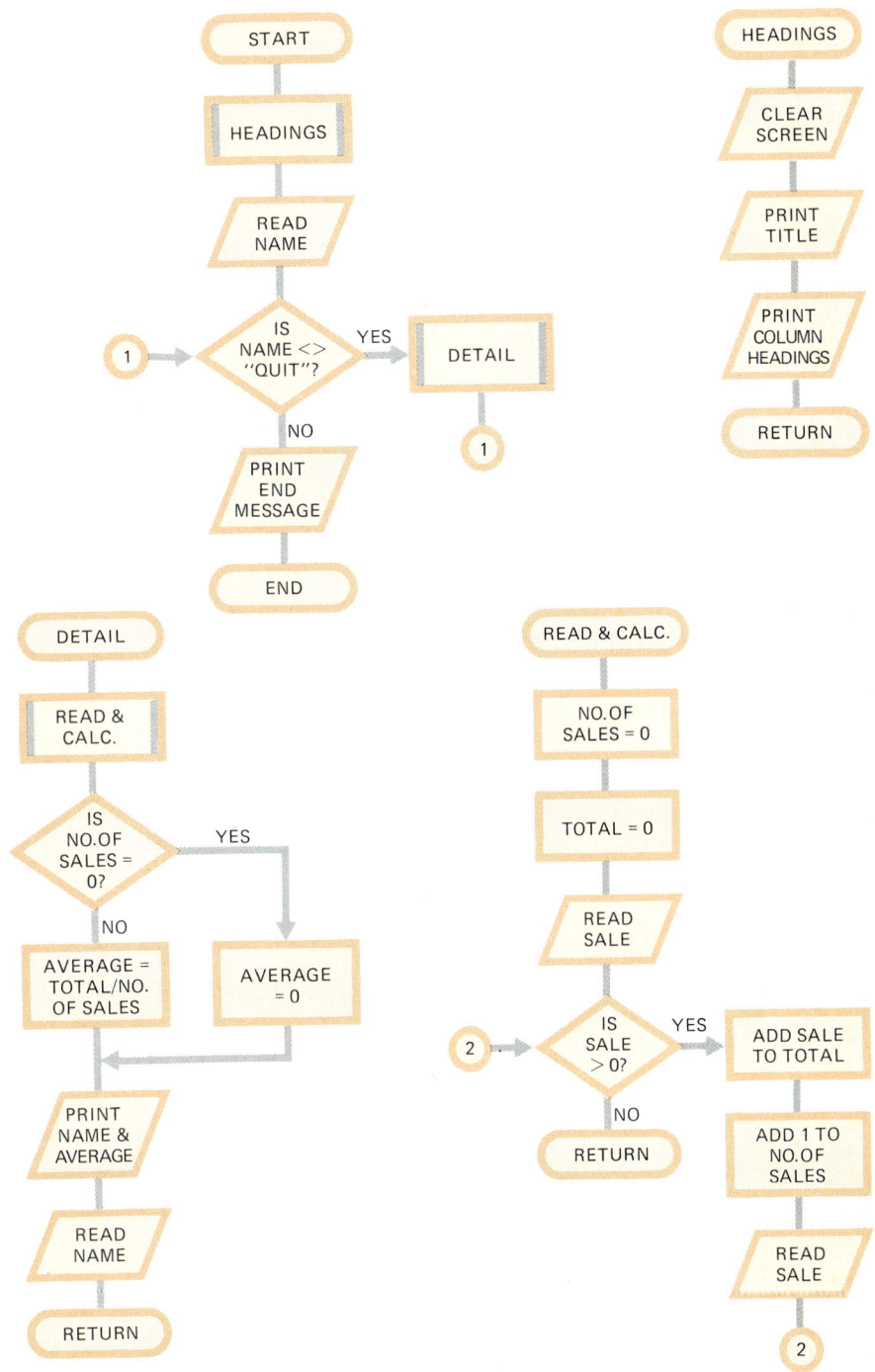

FIGURE 17-9

Flowchart of the problem to calculate average sales using the DO-WHILE construct.

```
10 REM          PROGRAM TO CALCULATE AVERAGE SALES

20 REM          VARIABLES:    A  = AVERAGE OF SALES
30 REM                        N  = NUMBER OF SALES
40 REM                        N$ = SALESPERSON'S NAME
50 REM                        S  = SALE AMOUNT
60 REM                        T  = TOTAL OF SALES

100 REM         *** MAINLINE LOGIC ***

110 GOSUB 300 : REM PRINT REPORT HEADINGS
120 READ N$
130 WHILE N$ <> "QUIT"
140    GOSUB 400 : REM DETAIL PROCESSING
150 WEND
160 PRINT:PRINT "END OF REPORT"
170 END

200 REM         *** DATA TO BE PROCESSED ***

210 DATA "JEFF SMITH",34.56,44,12.98,24.95,0
220 DATA "ROD AMBOY",120,34,23.45,14.5,0
230 DATA "RICHARD WHITE",35.67,0
240 DATA "MARY BOBCOY",0
250 DATA "DIANE FOX",12.34,14.15,0
260 DATA "QUIT"

300 REM         *** CLEAR THE SCREEN AND PRINT TITLES ***

310 HOME
320 PRINT TAB(29);"S A L E S   R E P O R T"
330 PRINT
340 PRINT TAB(12);"SALESPERSON";TAB(55);"AVERAGE SALE"
350 PRINT:PRINT
360 RETURN

400 REM         *** DETAIL PROCESSING ***

410 GOSUB 500 : REM READ AND TOTAL SALES AMOUNTS
420 IF N = 0
        THEN LET A = 0
        ELSE LET A = T / N
430 PRINT TAB(12);N$;TAB(57);
440 PRINT USING "####.##";A
450 READ N$
460 RETURN

500 REM         *** READ AND TOTAL SALES AMOUNTS ***

510 LET N = 0
520 LET T = 0
530 READ S
540 WHILE S > 0
550    LET T = T + S
560    LET N = N + 1
570    READ S
580 WEND
590 RETURN
```

FIGURE 17-10

BASIC program with the WHILE and WEND statements.

module is in lines 130 through 150. The second DO-WHILE is in the module called READ AND TOTAL SALES AMOUNTS on line 540 through line 580.

FEEDBACK **17-11** What are the three basic types of logical structures?
17-12 What are the two instructions necessary to form a DO-WHILE loop?
17-13 What is a "priming read"?

PRINTER OUTPUT The BASIC language is truly a personal programming language. It was designed to input data from the terminal and output the answers back to the terminal. There are, however, times when a "hard copy" or printed copy of the program output is required.

The LPRINT Instruction All versions of BASIC provide for printed program output. The later versions of BASIC (BASIC-80, IBM PC, and the TRS-80) have a specific output instruction to send data to a printer. This instruction is the **LPRINT** statement. The "L" in LPRINT stands for *L*ine printer. The use of the term "line printer" is misleading. Microcomputers use character printers, not line printers. In the literature of microcomputers, however, the term "line printers" refers to any printer. They output lines rather than display data. The format and options of the LPRINT instruction are exactly the same as the PRINT instruction. Both PRINT and LPRINT instructions may be mixed within the same program if output is to be sent to both the display and the printer. The LPRINT instruction is not available in the Apple version of BASIC.

Early in this chapter, printed program listings were discussed. The Apple BASIC technique for printing a listing was through the use of the commands PR#1 and PR#0. PR#1 causes all output to be sent to the device connected to slot #1. PR#0 causes the output to be redirected back to the display. These commands may also be used as instructions within an Apple BASIC program by giving them a line number. To cause all program output to be sent to the printer (assumed in slot 1), execute the instruction

    linenumber PR#1

From that point in the program, all output is directed to slot 1 (the printer). To redirect output back to the display, execute the instruction

    linenumber PR#0

The LPRINT USING Instruction The **LPRINT USING** instruction is the printer output version of the PRINT USING statement. The format is identical in both instructions. The Apple version of BASIC does not include either the PRINT USING or the LPRINT

```
10 REM          PROGRAM TO CALCULATE AVERAGE SALES

20 REM          VARIABLES:   A  = AVERAGE OF SALES
30 REM                       N  = NUMBER OF SALES
40 REM                       N$ = SALESPERSON'S NAME
50 REM                       S  = SALE AMOUNT
60 REM                       T  = TOTAL OF SALES

100 REM          *** MAINLINE LOGIC ***

110 GOSUB 300 : REM PRINT REPORT HEADINGS
120 READ N$
130 WHILE N$ <> "QUIT"
140    GOSUB 400 : REM DETAIL PROCESSING
150 WEND
160 LPRINT:LPRINT "END OF REPORT"
170 END

200 REM          *** DATA TO BE PROCESSED ***

210 DATA "JEFF SMITH",34.56,44,12.98,24.95,0
220 DATA "ROD AMBOY",120,34,23.45,14.5,0
230 DATA "RICHARD WHITE",35.67,0
240 DATA "MARY BOBCOY",0
250 DATA "DIANE FOX",12.34,14.15,0
260 DATA "QUIT"

300 REM          *** CLEAR THE SCREEN AND PRINT TITLES ***

310 HOME
320 LPRINT TAB(29);"S A L E S   R E P O R T"
330 LPRINT
340 LPRINT TAB(12);"SALESPERSON";TAB(55);"AVERAGE SALE"
350 LPRINT:LPRINT
360 RETURN

400 REM          *** DETAIL PROCESSING ***

410 GOSUB 500 : REM READ AND TOTAL SALES AMOUNTS
420 IF N = 0
        THEN LET A = 0
        ELSE LET A = T / N
430 LPRINT TAB(12);N$;TAB(57);
440 LPRINT USING "####.##";A
450 READ N$
460 RETURN

500 REM          *** READ AND TOTAL SALES AMOUNTS ***

510 LET N = 0
520 LET T = 0
530 READ S
540 WHILE S > 0
550    LET T = T + S
560    LET N = N + 1
570    READ S
580 WEND
590 RETURN
```

FIGURE 17-11

BASIC program with the LPRINT and
LPRINT USING statements.

USING instructions. Figure 17-11 is a modified version of the calculate average sales program that will output to a printer rather than to the display. The changes are the use of the LPRINT and LPRINT USING instructions on lines 160, 320, 330, 340, 350, 430, and 440.

FEEDBACK

17-14 What is the difference between the PRINT and the LPRINT instructions?

17-15 Can numeric data be edited if they are to be printed rather than displayed?

INTERACTIVE PROGRAMS

Interactive programs are those that allow the user to enter data through the keyboard while the program is running and to get immediate answers. The earlier programs in this chapter using the READ and DATA statements were not interactive because the input data was "built into" the program. Each time the program is run, the same report will be outputted unless we change the program (DATA statements). Let us assume that we are to write an interactive program. The program is to allow the user to enter a series of numeric values (number of entries is unknown). The program is to calculate and output the average of the series of entered numbers. The user is to signal the program that he or she is finished entering the series of numbers by entering a final value of -99. This last value is not to be included in the calculated average. Figure 17-12 presents a flowchart with a possible solution to the problem. The logic includes the outputting of a message telling the user how to end the series of inputted values (enter -99). A DO-WHILE loop will be executed to count the number of values entered, to accumulate the total of the values entered, and to input the next value while the number inputted is not equal to -99.

The INPUT Instruction

One of the problems to be aware of when writing interactive programs is that users have to be "prompted," or told, what type of data is to be entered and when they are to enter it. In Chapter 16, a PRINT statement was used to prompt the user just ahead of the INPUT statement. Almost all versions of BASIC go beyond the minimal standard discussed in Chapter 16. Most BASIC versions allow for an optional outputting of a prompt from within the INPUT instruction. The format of this INPUT statement is

linenumber INPUT "prompt string"; list

The prompt string will first be outputted to the display. The computer will then wait for the user to key in the data to be inputted and press the enter (return) key.

The BASIC code to implement the logic of Figure 17-12 is shown in Figure 17-13.

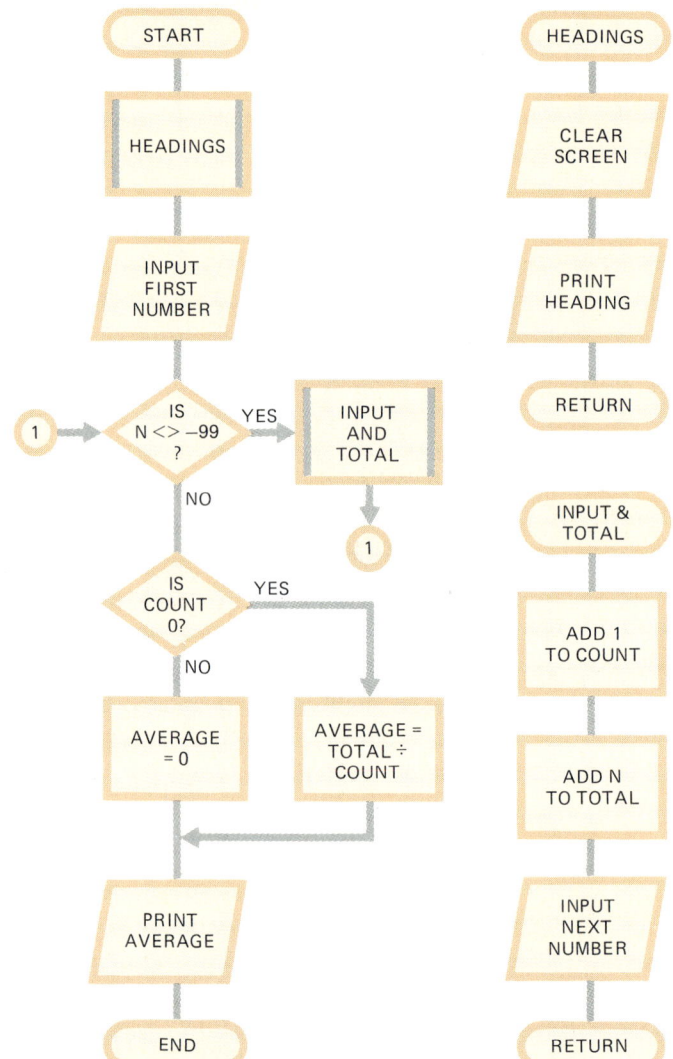

FIGURE 17-12

The Last Record Test   Interactive programs must have some way of telling when all of the data has been entered. In our example, we told the user to enter an amount of −99 to signal that he or she is ready to terminate the program (at least the data entry portion). Each time data are entered, the program logic must check to see if we have entered data to be processed or the signal that we are finished. This checking of the data is called the *last record test*.

Program to Average a Series of Numbers   Figure 17-14 is the BASIC code to implement the flowchart logic shown in Figure 17-13. Note that the input prompts and the user's responses remain on the screen. It is important to make the interactive program as "friendly" as possible. A friendly program is one that helps the user with appropriate

```
10 REM          PROGRAM TO AVERAGE A SERIES OF NUMBERS

20 REM          VARIABLES:   A = AVERAGE
30 REM                       C = COUNT OF NUMBERS
40 REM                       N = NUMBER
50 REM                       T = TOTAL OF NUMBERS

100 REM          *** MAINLINE OF LOGIC ***

110 GOSUB 210 : REM CLEAR SCREEN AND PRINT HEADING MESSAGE
120 INPUT "FIRST NUMBER";N
130 WHILE N <> -99
140     GOSUB 300 : REM INPUT AND TOTAL NUMBERS
150 WEND
160 IF C <> 0
        THEN LET A = T / C
        ELSE LET A = 0
170 PRINT:PRINT "THE AVERAGE IS -->";
180 PRINT USING "#####.##";A
190 END

200 REM          *** CLEAR SCREEN AND PRINT HEADING MESSAGE ***

210 HOME
220 PRINT TAB(24);"ENTER -99 TO INDICATE END OF DATA":PRINT
230 RETURN

300 REM          *** INPUT AND TOTAL NUMBERS ***

310 LET C = C + 1
320 LET T = T + N
330 INPUT "NEXT NUMBER ";N
340 RETURN
```

FIGURE 17-13

BASIC interactive program to average a series of numbers.

```
                    ENTER -99 TO INDICATE END OF DATA

          FIRST NUMBER? 123
          NEXT NUMBER ? 14
          NEXT NUMBER ? 351
          NEXT NUMBER ? 782
          NEXT NUMBER ? 438
          NEXT NUMBER ? -99

          THE AVERAGE IS -->      341.60
          Ok
```

FIGURE 17-14

Sample output from an interactive BASIC program.

prompts. It is very important that the user understands what he or she is to enter as the last record signal to the program.

FEEDBACK   **17-16** What is an interactive program?

17-17 What is the purpose of an input prompt?

SUMMARY

The LIST command causes the instructions of a program to be "listed" on the terminal screen. Many versions of BASIC include the LLIST command to output the program listing on a printer.

Many, if not most, microcomputers have diskette drives attached to them to store programs and data. There are a series of commands designed to allow access to those diskette drives. The common disk operating system (DOS) commands are SAVE, LOAD, RUN, FILES (or CATALOG), and KILL (or DELETE).

Structured programs are coded in logical modules. These modules are executed using the GOSUB and RETURN instructions.

If a relatively small amount of data is to be stored, it can be made a part of the program itself. The instruction to store data is called the DATA statement. All the DATA statements in a program together make up the data block. Data in the data block can be accessed by using the READ statement.

The CLS command (HOME on an Apple) causes the screen to clear and positions the cursor in the upper-left corner. This command can also be used as an instruction in a program by coding it with a line number.

The TAB function is used as part of a PRINT statement list to horizontally position the output data on the line. It is used when the print zone default is not appropriate for the program requirements.

The two formats of the conditional branch statement in BASIC are the IF-THEN and the IF-THEN-ELSE. The IF-THEN format is used when there is one or more instructions to be executed if the condition being tested is true, but no specific instruction(s) to execute if the condition is false. If there are instructions to be executed when the condition is true and other instructions to be executed only when the condition is false, the IF-THEN-ELSE format is used.

All output is normally left-justified in BASIC. The PRINT USING statement can be used where numeric output data is to be edited. Common edit functions are specifying the number of digits to print, rounding off, inserting commas and/or dollar signs, and the alignment of decimal positions.

The DO-WHILE is one of the common structured programming constructs. It is implemented in BASIC with the WHILE and WEND instructions. The WHILE statement is always the first instruction in the loop, and the WEND is always the last statement.

If printed program output is required, most versions of BASIC include the LPRINT and LPRINT USING instructions. These instructions function identically to the PRINT and PRINT USING with the exception that they output to the printer rather than the terminal display.

Interactive programs are those that "interact" with the terminal operator. That is, the program gets its input data from the terminal keyboard while the program is running. The input data are immediately processed and the answers are outputed to the terminal or printer.

ANSWERS TO FEEDBACK QUESTIONS

17-1 The command to cause a printed program listing is the LLIST. The command is available in BASIC-80, IBM PC, and the TRS-80.

17-2 The SAVE command is used to output the program currently in primary memory to the diskette drive.

17-3 The command to run a program stored on a diskette is RUN "program name."

17-4 The GOSUB instruction saves the address of the following instruction and then does an unconditional branch to the given line number. The RETURN instruction uses the stored address to "return" to the instruction following the last executed GOSUB.

17-5 The data block is formed with DATA statements. It contains all the constant data from all DATA statements in the program.

17-6 The CLS instruction is used to clear the terminal screen. The HOME instruction is used on the Apple microcomputer.

17-7 The difference between the IF-THEN and the IF-THEN-ELSE instructions is that the IF-THEN-ELSE format has one or more instructions to be executed only when the IF condition is false. The IF-THEN format does not have any specific instructions to be executed with a false condition.

17-8 The PRINT USING statement allows output data to be edited.

17-9 BASIC-80, IBM PC BASIC, and TRS-80 BASIC include the PRINT USING statement. The Apple version of BASIC does not.

17-10 Editing numeric data means that the output data can be rounded off, commas and/or dollar signs inserted, a specified number of decimal positions printed, and decimal points aligned.

17-11 The three basic types of logical structures are sequential, selection, and loops.

17-12 The formation of a DO-WHILE requires the WHILE and WEND instructions.

17-13 "Priming read" refers to the input statement used to "prime" a DO-WHILE loop by reading the first data used in the WHILE condition.

17-14 The PRINT statement outputs to the terminal display. The LPRINT statement outputs to a line printer.

17-15 Data can be edited as it is being outputted to a printer by using the LPRINT USING instruction.

17-16 An interactive program is one where the user keystrokes the input data through the keyboard while the program is running. The data are processed and the answers are almost immediately outputted.

17-17 The purpose of the input prompt is to let the computer user know what type of data are to be entered and when they are to be entered.

FOR REVIEW AND DISCUSSION

1 Are all versions of BASIC the same? If not, why not?

2 Modify the program shown in Figure 17-10 so that the data is entered interactively instead of from DATA statements.

3 Modify the program shown in Figure 17-13 so that the data is inputted from DATA statements rather than from the keyboard. Continue to use a data value of -99 to mark the end of the number series.

System **UNIT SIX**

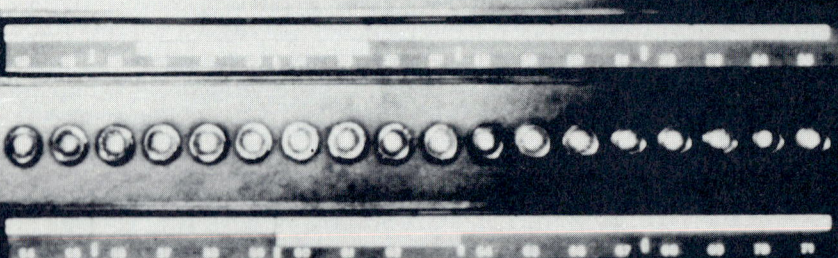

COMPUTERS AND SOCIETY

The previous units of this text familiarized you with computer information systems, with elements and applications of those systems, with the system development life-cycle process, and with the fundamentals of computer programming. In most instances the focus was upon the present and the near future. In this unit we will focus upon the people who develop information systems and will make some projections and forecasts about the future of the information society.

Chapter 18, "People in Information Systems," describes trends in the location of the information services organization in a business firm and describes career opportunities in the computer information systems field. Chapter 19, "Tomorrow and Beyond," includes forecasts about the knowledge industries and their socioeconomic impact. It concludes with some speculations about robots and artificial intelligence.

CHAPTER 18

PEOPLE IN INFORMATION SYSTEMS

PREVIEW   Computer data processing systems are developed, operated, and maintained by people. These people belong to a group, or department, that often is called information services. The goal of this chapter is to describe the organization of an information services group, to acquaint you with career opportunities in information services, and to emphasize the importance of a good relationship between information services and its users.

In this chapter, you will learn:

1. Where information services fits into the corporate organization chart
2. The major management jobs in information services
3. The principal job opportunities in corporate systems and in data processing operations

KEY TERMS TO WATCH FOR AND REMEMBER

programmer-analyst	data base administrator
applications programmer	systems programmer
data control clerk	response time
data entry operator	turnaround time
librarian	throughput time
microcomputer resource center	systems analyst
computer operator	

THE LOCATION OF INFORMATION SERVICES   Information service is made up of machines and people, all with assigned tasks to perform. The people in information services must meet production standards and schedules in order to provide satisfactory service to many different departments in the business firm. The users, or customers, of information services

355

may come from many locations and management levels within the company. Therefore, the placement of information services on the organization chart is important to its success.

In the 1950s and 1960s, information services usually reported to a financial officer of the company, often the controller. As information needs outside of finance developed, they usually did not receive very high priorities from the financial executive responsible for information services. The traditional financial functions of payroll, accounts payable, accounts receivable, and general accounting always tended to take precedence over equally important requirements in other areas, such as production planning and scheduling, sales forecasting, corporate management, and personnel services. During the 1970s, a trend to locate the people in information services elsewhere than in finance developed. This trend is illustrated in Figure 18-1.

As this figure shows, as an interim development information services often became the responsibility of an executive—typically the vice president of administration—who was responsible for general administrative support. However, this administrator was able to devote only a fraction of his or her time to information services and computer technology. For this reason, in the 1980s and beyond information services will be the single responsibility of a high-level executive. This executive will understand computers and how they can be used to solve many types of business problems. As the islands of technology—data processing, office automation, and communications—continue to merge, this individual will assume responsibility for all of the information resources of a corporation. He or she will be responsible for all jobs related to the design, development, and maintenance of business systems and for the operation of data processing equipment. Our discussions here will be oriented toward the information service center in a corporation of moderate size. However, except for the number of people involved, the tasks performed in a small company or a large one are the same, and job titles and descriptions are similar.

FIGURE 18-1

Trend in the location of information services.

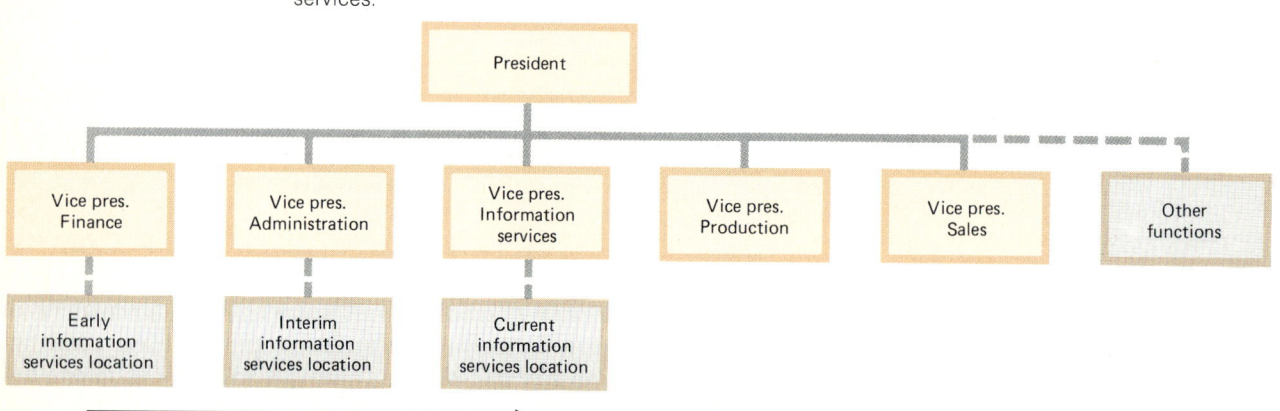

CAREERS IN INFORMATION SERVICES

Job opportunities in information services have increased in number and will continue to do so in the future. These jobs will be not only in data processing but also in other occupations that will feel the impact of computers. For example, people who operate transaction terminals in banks, markets, and department stores or who work in automated word processing centers have computer-related jobs. Here we discuss only job opportunities for persons who wish to pursue careers in an information services department (or center).

The two primary functions performed by information services people are developing, maintaining, and supporting corporate information systems and providing the computer operations and systems programming support needed to ensure the successful operation of these systems. These functions are shown in the organization chart of Figure 18-2, where they are grouped under corporate systems or under data processing operations. We will explain these boxes by describing the jobs of the people who occupy them.

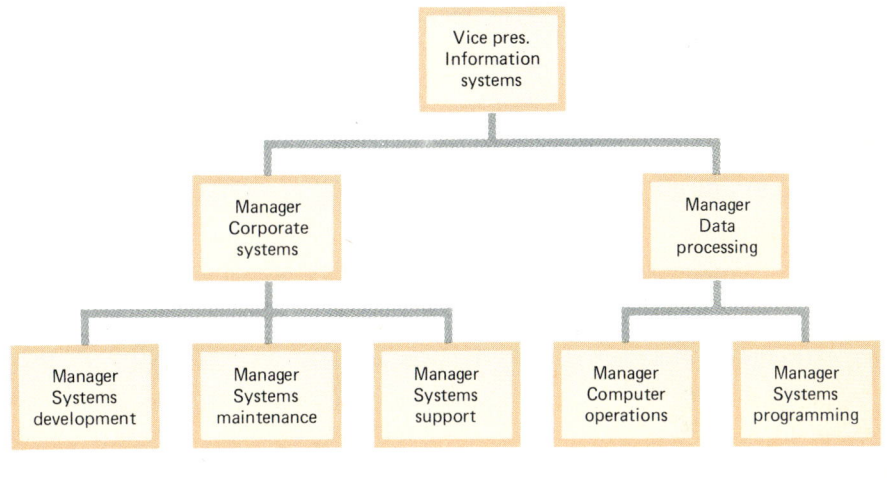

FIGURE 18-2
Information services organization.

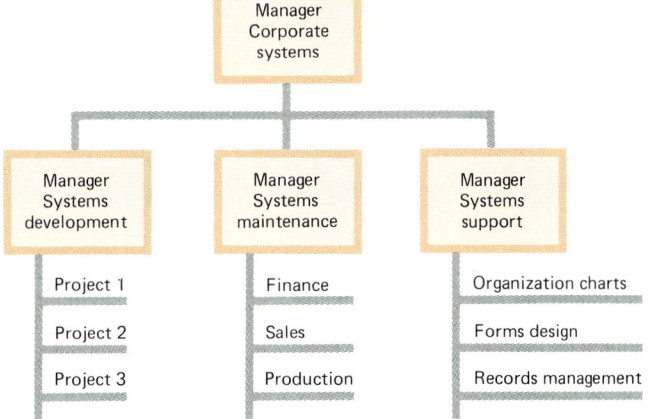

FIGURE 18-3
Corporate systems organization.

Jobs in Corporate Systems   Figure 18-3 on page 357, which is an expansion of the left branch of Figure 18-2, gives us a closer look at the jobs in corporate systems.

Manager of corporate systems   The manager of corporate systems supervises all systems analysis and programming tasks. This person also manages the systems development, systems maintenance, and systems support groups. The manager of corporate systems is responsible for all of the life-cycle activities associated with the study, design, and development of all computer-based information systems. This person shares with the manager of data processing the responsibility for maintaining the systems that have entered the operation phase and reports directly to the vice president responsible for information services. The managers of systems development, systems maintenance, and systems support report to the manager of corporate systems.

Manager of systems development   The manager of systems development is responsible for new information systems throughout the study, design, and development phases of the life cycle. In the organization that we have shown in Figure 18-3, each new systems development task is set up as a project team. The leaders of the project teams report to the manager of systems development. For example, the systems analyst in charge of the team that developed the Reorders–Sales Analysis system that we studied earlier was a project leader. The manager of systems development was responsible for reviewing the progress of that project. After a project is completed, it becomes the responsibility of the manager of systems maintenance.

Manager of systems maintenance   The manager of systems maintenance is responsible for monitoring the performance of, and making minor changes to, information systems that have been developed and have completed changeover. Usually, members of the systems maintenance staff are assigned responsibility for specific applications areas, such as finance, sales, and production. When significant system modifications are required, the application may be reassigned as a systems development project. As an example, systems maintenance personnel might change the format of output reports. However, they would not add new reports that would change the original objectives of the system.

Manager of systems support   The manager of systems support directs activities that provide general support for all systems analysis functions. Examples are preparing and updating organization charts, designing forms, managing records, and preparing and distributing corporate policies and procedures.

Thus far, we have described the senior management positions in corporate systems. Systems analysts, programmer-analysts, and applications programmers report to these managers. Some of the principal activities of these professionals are described in the next three sections.

Systems analyst **Systems analysts** work with information system users to study problems. They identify possible solutions to these problems, analyze the feasibility of these solutions, and recommend the most cost-effective one. They are active in all phases of the life cycle of an information system. They are responsible for the design and development of the information system that they recommend in the study phase. They participate in maintaining operational systems and may provide specialized services as members of the systems support staff.

Programmer-analyst **Programmer-analysts** work with systems analysts and with applications programmers. They may participate in the design of information systems as analysts. Often they prepare the technical specifications, such as system and computer program logic flowcharts, used by programmers during the development phase. They also may write some of the computer applications programs or supervise the activities of applications programmers.

Applications programmer In the development phase, **applications programmers** prepare computer program logic flowcharts. They also write, debug, and test computer programs. They are responsible for fully documenting their work. Figure 18-4 shows an applications programmer at work at his desk.

Some programmers work in the information processing center. Typically, programmers share an office with another programmer or they are assigned private cubicles, such as the one shown in Figure 18-4. Other programmers may be stationed at locations remote from the computer center. Programmers use terminals to enter and debug their programs.

FIGURE 18-4
Applications programmer. This applications programmer, shown at his desk, is consulting a reference manual before writing on the coding sheet in front of him. (Courtesy Mount San Antonio College)

FEEDBACK   **18-1** Why do most information service groups no longer report to finance?
18-2 Describe the following jobs in corporate systems:
    a Manager of corporate systems
    b Manager of systems development
    c Manager of systems maintenance
    d Manager of systems support
    e Systems analyst
    f Programmer-analyst
    g Applications programmer

Jobs in Data Processing Operations

Manager of data processing   The manager of data processing supervises the operation of all computer equipment and is responsible for the systems programming support of the computer operating system. Figure 18-5, which is an expansion of the right side of Figure 18-2, lists the major tasks performed in data processing operations. Typical jobs in data processing operations are described in the sections that follow.

Manager of computer operations   The manager of computer operations establishes schedules for the use of equipment. This manager instructs and assigns personnel and maintains records of equipment usage and operating efficiency. The manager of computer operations reports to the manager of data processing. Figure 18-6 shows a manager of computer operations in her office. This office usually is located next to the machine room and often has a window so that the manager can remain constantly aware of ongoing activity. Some important jobs in computer operations are described next.

Data control supervisor   The data control supervisor prepares schedules for all data that enter and leave the computing center. This person maintains appropriate records and supervises data control clerks. Entry-level positions

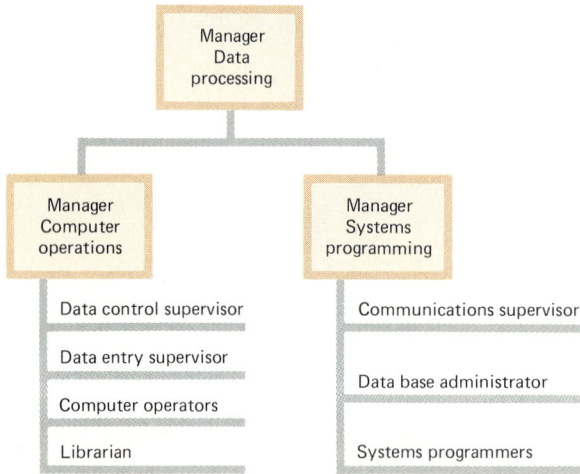

FIGURE 18-5
Data processing operations organization.

FIGURE 18-6

Manager of computer operations. The manager of computer operations is responsible for seeing that all work gets out on schedule. When there are scheduling problems, this manager must listen to user complaints. (Courtesy Mount San Antonio College)

are **data control clerk** or data control trainee. Figure 18-7 shows a data control supervisor seated at her desk. All of the tasks scheduled for the day flow through her section. All must be checked in and checked out. Appropriate control balances, such as the number of checks to be processed, are prepared, and these balances are checked before work is released to the user.

Data entry supervisor The data entry supervisor is responsible for all personnel operating data entry devices such as key-to-disk devices and video terminals. **Data entry operator** or trainee are entry-level positions. Often, data entry operators are stationed at locations remote from the computer. Usually, data entry operators use a keyboard. Therefore, they should be able to type. The timeliness and usability of data processing output often depends upon the

FIGURE 18 7

Data control supervisor. On a busy day, work sometimes can pile up at data control. (Courtesy Mount San Antonio College)

FIGURE 18-8
Senior computer operator. (Eli Heller/
Picture Group)

speed and accuracy of the data entry operator. Some specialized training is required. This training usually is provided by the manufacturer of the data entry machine or by the employer.

Computer operator   **Computer operators** use equipment of varying degrees of complexity. A lead operator is the supervisor of a shift. Senior operators usually operate the console of the central processor. A senior operator is shown in Figure 18-8. Another operator is shown at a keyboard in Figure 18-9.

FIGURE 18-9
Computer operator. (Courtesy Four-
Phase Systems)

Computer operators work in the computer center and are given specialized training for the equipment that they are to operate. Operators should have an aptitude for, and should enjoy working with, machines. Operators have a great deal of responsibility for the efficient use of machines and for the validity of their output.

Librarian The **librarian** maintains a library of magnetic tapes. This person inspects tapes for wear and replaces those that are worn-out. The librarian erases tapes with data that are no longer required and makes new tapes or data tapes available for processing as they are needed. Figure 18-10 shows a tape librarian working in the vault in which magnetic tapes are stored. Often, hundreds—and sometimes thousands—of different tapes have to be stored and located quickly in order for data processing operations to proceed on schedule. The tape librarian has a very responsible task because wrong data or lost data can cause delays in producing useful output.

Manager of systems programming The manager of systems programming develops plans for acquisition of computer hardware and software, prepares standards for operating system software, and trains personnel in the use of this software. This person directs the technical-support activities related to communications networks, automated office equipment, data base management systems, and special-purpose software packages. Systems programming jobs are not entry-level positions. Often, these jobs provide career growth paths for applications programmers who possess strong technical aptitudes. Some typical jobs in systems programming are described next.

Communications supervisor The communications supervisor is responsible for all technical activities related to data communications. The continuing growth in the use of distributed data processing systems makes this position one of importance. This supervisor directs the activities of technical persons who are knowledgeable about communications devices, languages, and applications.

Data base administrator The **data base administrator** is responsible for the definition, organization, and use of data bases. Because the integrity of all of the programs that share a data base depends upon the accuracy of the data base, only a very experienced and well-trained person should be given this job. This person not only protects the data base but also trains and assists applications programmers in the use of data base languages and data access methods.

Systems programmer **Systems programmers** provide technical operating system software support. This support ranges from complex software programming to maintaining utility programs, subroutines, and job control language. Often, systems programmers must work with manufacturers of software prod-

FIGURE 18-10

Tape librarian. This tape librarian is replacing one reel of tape and selecting another from the tape vault. Some vaults may hold hundreds of reels of tape. (Courtesy Mount San Antonio College)

ucts. They must evaluate these products for the data processing center and must maintain them if they are used. Systems programmers are valuable project team members who can make major contributions to feasibility and design studies.

FEEDBACK

18-3 To whom does the manager of data processing report?

18-4 Describe the following jobs in data processing operations:
   a Manager of data processing
   b Manager of computer operations
   c Data control supervisor
   d Data entry supervisor
   e Computer operator
   f Manager of systems programming
   g Communications supervisor
   h Data base administrator
   i Systems programmer

Salaries in Information Services

Thus far, we have described the structure of the information services organization and some of the jobs performed by the people in the organization. Positions such as we have described exist at several levels of skill, education, and experience. One way that we can distinguish between jobs within a classification (for example, systems analyst, programmer, operator) is to establish levels of responsibility and work performance ranging from manager to trainee. Table 18-1 is a useful grouping of levels that can be applied to most information services jobs. We shall refer to these levels as we relate salaries to jobs.

The salaries of information services personnel vary with installation size and geographic location. Larger installations pay more for senior personnel than do smaller ones. Similarly, salaries tend to be higher than average in large cities than in small ones. Figure 18-11 plots relative weekly salaries for selected information services positions. Job levels are indicated for each position shown. Systems analysts and systems programmers receive higher top salaries than do applications programmers. All three earn more than do computer operators, data control clerks, and data entry operators. Senior managers, such as the managers of corporate systems and data processing operations, enjoy substantially higher salaries than the managers who report to them.

In general, the most highly paid professionals are those with the greatest responsibility or with the greatest analytic and creative talents. Salaries for many jobs can be correlated with the point at which individuals begin to apply their skills in the life-cycle sequence. As Figure 18-12 indicates the earlier the entry into the life cycle, the higher the salary earned. This figure explains why systems analysis is a career objective for many persons in information services

TABLE 18-1   **JOB LEVELS IN INFORMATION SERVICES**

Job title	Job description
Manager (or Supervisor)	In full charge of a section or department; may personally supervise operations or may direct them through a subordinate
Lead	Considered the assistant manager where an assistant manager title does not appear; may perform technical tasks in addition to supervising others
Senior	Works at the highest technical level of an activity; usually works independently but may direct persons of lower classifications
A	Works under general supervision; may work independently on most tasks; requires only general supervision for other tasks
B	Works under direct supervision; works on some tasks with only general supervision; needs instruction and guidance for other tasks
C	Works under immediate supervision; work is checked carefully and limited to specific tasks
Trainee	Usually a probationary employee with no previous experience

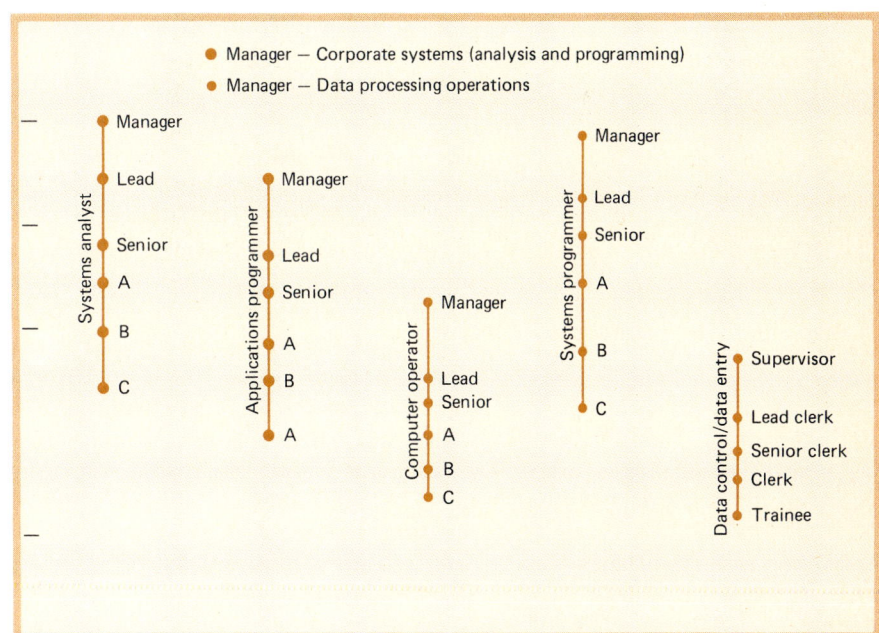

FIGURE 18-11

Relative weekly salaries in information services. Actual salaries vary greatly throughout the country, and data processing salaries tend to keep up with inflation. The chart shows relative salaries for the job levels described in Table 18-1.

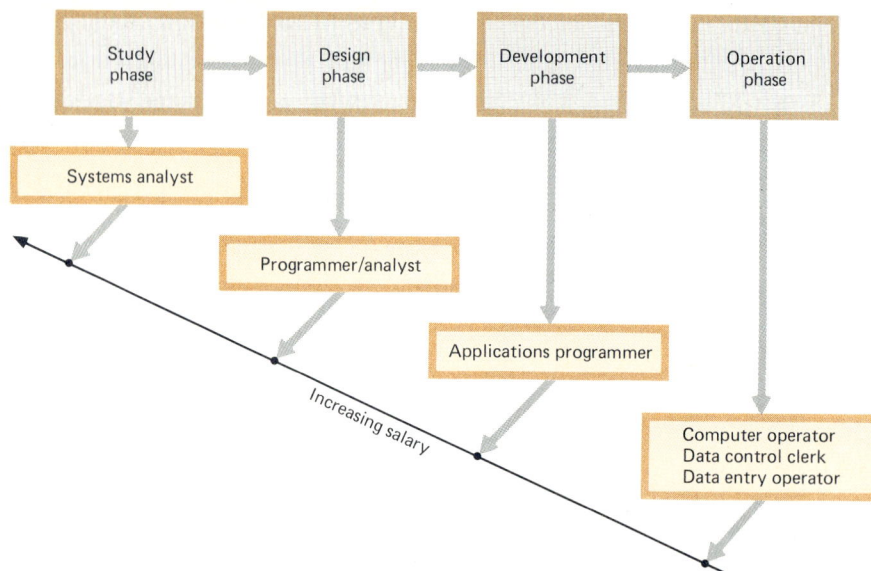

FIGURE 18-12

Salaries and the computer-based system life cycle. The lines leading from the life-cycle phases to the position boxes indicate the point at which persons on those positions enter the life-cycle sequence. The lines from the position boxes to the "increasing salary" line show the relative salaries of the positions.

organizations. The jobs shown also illustrate an upward career path that is followed by many individuals who enter the data processing field as clerks, operators, or programmer trainees. Many employers prefer to fill vacancies by promoting people from within their companies.

INFORMATION SERVICES AND THE USER

In the previous chapter we described the changeover crisis and stated that after this crisis was passed, the system was turned over to the data processing organization for routine operation. In reality, "routine" operations in a data processing center are very nonroutine. They are performed in an environment that is filled with day-to-day problems. Typically, hundreds of jobs, scheduled and unscheduled, must be processed daily, and the results must be made available to users at a specified time. Changes in priorities, equipment problems, operations difficulties, and the complexities of scheduling all contribute to the challenge of the job of the data processing operations manager. For these reasons, the user's perceptions of the information service organization and the relationships between users and information services personnel are critical factors. They affect the working environment of the information processing center, and ultimately determine its success or failure.

The User's View of Information Services

After a computer system goes into operation, the user of the system expects to receive punctual and correct information. The user's evaluation of the timeliness of service provided usually is based upon a "door-to-door" concept of response time and does not take into account components of response time that

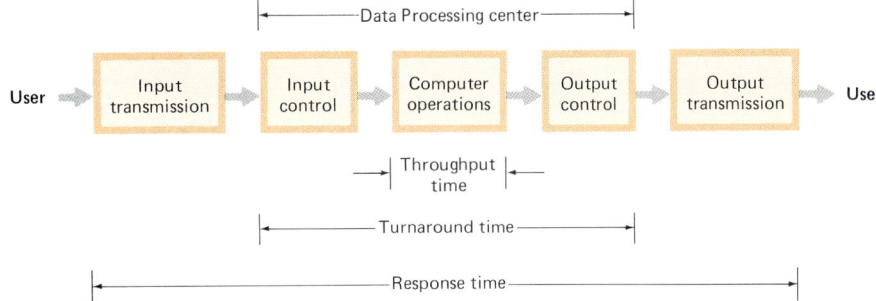

FIGURE 18-13

Response time and its components.

information services may not be able to control, such as delays in delivery of input data to the computer center. Figure 18-13 shows the components of the overall response time perceived by the user.

The **response time** is the total time that elapses between submission of input data by a user and its return as computer output. **Turnaround time** is the elapsed time between the arrival of data at the data processing center and the availability of output information for delivery or transmission to the user. **Throughput time** is the time required for work to be processed by personnel and equipment in computer operations. A manager of data processing can do a great deal to control throughput time and turnaround time. Schedules for processing work and for assigning personnel should be established and continually reviewed for their effectiveness. A task often assigned to the systems programming staff is the development of methods for measuring computer efficiency. Also, standards of performance should be set for all data processing tasks. Standards manuals should be created and maintained for systems analysis, for programming, and for operations. Good documentation pays off when problems arise and troubleshooting begins.

Delays in input and output transmission often are difficult for the data processing manager to cope with. This is particularly true if data are physically delivered to the computer center for processing in batches and the results similarly delivered to the user. Distributed data processing techniques often can provide a solution to the data transmission problems. If the cost is justified, providing a user with a terminal or some other type of I/O device can greatly improve the user's perception of response time. In addition, some of the overall response-time responsibility is shared by the user. Under many circumstances, as we noted in our discussion of communications and distributed data processing in Chapter 7, service and usability of information can be improved greatly by providing users with moderate-to-extensive stand-alone processing capabilities—with the computer center processing only data that have been edited and that may be in summary form. Often users can be provided with personal computers and trained to supply some of their own information needs. Many corporations have established **microcomputer resource centers** for this purpose.

THE MICROCOMPUTER RESOURCE CENTER

Microcomputers, particularly personal computers, are becoming increasingly visible on the corporate scene. The advantages of distributed data processing are evident for many business information system applications. Two important advantages are enhanced usability through user involvement and the ability to process only summary data at a centralized location. A disadvantage is allowing the user community to develop information systems and data bases that duplicate, often inaccurately, systems that should be maintained for corporatewide access and use.

An approach that some corporations have found successful is to establish a **microcomputer resource center** within the information services organization to assist users in evaluating their software and hardware needs for microcomputers. The responsibility of the manager of the information center is to work with users who feel that they can increase their productivity through the use of microcomputers. Where it is necessary to preserve and to provide access to current corporate data, users are required to become part of the corporate information network, using com-

munications terminals to meet their information needs. However, users are encouraged to acquire the literacy required to operate a microcomputer as a personal computer whenever it appears that there is no need to access corporate data bases and that the individual can make cost-effective use of one. Information center personnel will train the user and assist him or her in selecting the microcomputer system most appropriate for personal use. An increasing number of managers will use microcomputers both as communications terminals and as personal computers.

Customer Relations

In this chapter, we selected "information services" as the name for the data processing organization because that name helps us to remember that this organization performs a service for its customers. Users should always be treated as valued customers because occasions will always arise when the good will of a user has to be drawn upon. As we noted at the beginning of this section, many things can happen to upset the routine of data processing operations. Schedules will slip because of human and machine error. It is seldom cost-effective to acquire a computer system with the capacity to handle all peak loads. There will be times, such as at the end of the month or year, when mistakes will occur and some reports will be delayed. Therefore, the questions and complaints of all users should be responded to promptly and courteously at all times in order to maintain good public relations. Good public relations will pay off in the user's support and understanding during periods of difficulty. This support will greatly improve the morale and the general operating environment in the data processing center.

FEEDBACK

18-5 What is a microcomputer resource center?
18-6 What is response time?
18-7 Distinguish between turnaround time and throughput time.

SUMMARY

The information services organization is responsible not only for developing computer information systems but also for operating and maintaining them. This organization is made up of the machines and people required to meet the information needs of a corporation. Initially, when business systems were primarily financial, the information services organization reported to a financial officer. However, as the importance of information needs in areas other than finance was recognized, this organization began to report to a nonfinancial officer, such as the vice president of administration. Today, there is a strong trend to assign this responsibility to an executive who is concerned only with information services. Typically, this person has a title such as vice president of information services.

The two primary functions performed by information services are the development and maintenance of corporate systems and the performance of data processing operations. Each function requires the services of persons with special job skills. Typical jobs in corporate systems are systems analyst, programmer-analyst, and applications programmer. Jobs in data processing operations include computer operator, data control clerk, data entry operator, computer operator, and tape librarian. Within each job classification, positions exist at several skill levels. These levels range from trainee to manager. Salaries are commensurate with education, experience, and responsibility. There are many entry-level positions in information services, and there are opportunities for career growth.

Users of information services usually evaluate the services that they receive in terms of the "door-to-door" response time. This response time is the total elapsed time between submission of data by a user and its return as computer output. A component of response time, which is difficult for the data processing manager to control, is the time required to transmit data to and from the computer center. Distributed data processing techniques often can increase the usability of the system and can allow the user to share some of the responsibility for response time with the data processing center. Microcomputer resource centers can assist users in selecting personal computers to meet their special information needs.

Problems will always occur in data processing operations because of the large volume of work that must be processed. Therefore, good user relationships are essential if support and understanding are to be had during periods of difficulty.

ANSWERS TO FEEDBACK QUESTIONS

18-1 Because many information needs have developed outside of the financial area.

18-2 **a** Manager of corporate systems supervises all systems analysis and programming tasks.

b Manager of systems development manages development of new systems throughout the study, design, and development phases of the life cycle.

c Manager of systems maintenance is responsible for monitoring performance of and maintaining operational systems.

d Manager of systems support directs all systems analysis support activities.

  e Systems analyst identifies, studies, and solves information systems problems.

  f Programmer-analyst works with systems analysts and applications programmers to design and develop information systems.

  g Applications pogrammer prepares flowcharts and writes, debugs, and tests computer programs.

18-3 To the executive in charge of information systems.

18-4 a Manager of data processing operations is responsible for operation of all data processing equipment and for systems programming.

  b Manager of computer operations schedules and assigns personnel to operate data processing equipment.

  c Data control supervisor schedules and monitors the flow of data into and out of the computer center.

  d Data entry supervisor supervises personnel who operate data entry devices.

  e Computer operator operates data processing equipment.

  f Manager of systems programming directs activities related to the procurement and maintenance of system software.

  g Communications supervisor is responsible for data communications activities, such as remote data entry.

  h Data base administrator is responsible for the definition, organization, and use of data bases.

  i Systems programmer provides technical operating system software support.

18-5 A microcomputer resource center is a corporate service operated to assist users in selecting a personal computer when it is appropriate to do so.

18-6 The total elapsed time between submission of input data by a user and its return as useful computer output.

18-7 Turnaround time is the elapsed time between the arrival of data at the data processing center and the availability of output information for delivery or transmission to the user. Throughput time is the time required for work to be processed by the personnel and equipment in computer operations.

FOR REVIEW AND DISCUSSION

1 What are the advantages and disadvantages of the following organizational locations for information services?

 a Reporting to a financial executive

 b Reporting to the vice president of administration

 c Reporting to the vice president of information services

2 Discuss career opportunities in information services.

3 Distinguish between throughput time, response time, and turnaround time.

4 Relate salaries in information services to the life-cycle sequence for the development of computer-based business systems.

5 What is the meaning of the following statement: "Users can make a bad system perform well; they can also make a good system perform poorly"?

6 Under what conditions would it be desirable to provide users with personal computers? Under what conditions would it not be desirable to do so?

CHAPTER 19

TOMORROW AND BEYOND

PREVIEW Smart machines are machines that contain microprocessors or microcomputers, and they will affect us profoundly throughout the remainder of this century. The industries that produce information processing products and services will become dominant. The goal of this chapter is to forecast some major socioeconomic changes resulting from smart machines and to speculate about some of their effects on the future.

In this chapter you will learn:

1. About smart machines and the dominance of the knowledge industries.
2. Significant technical and socioeconomic trends and their impact on the ways in which we will live and work.
3. Future developments in computer system architecture and in managing the information system life-cycle development process.
4. Some speculations about artificial intelligence and a future shared by humans and high-performance robots.

KEY TERMS TO WATCH FOR AND REMEMBER

smart machine	cybernetics
projection	superconductivity
forecast	robot
knowledge industries	servomechanisms
expert program	artificial intelligence

THE CHALLENGE OF CHANGE

In earlier chapters of this text, we emphasized our nation's transition from an industrial society to a postindustrial, or information, society. This transition has but barely begun, and it will continue at an accelerated rate throughout our lifetimes. As John Naisbitt, a prominent socioeconomic forecaster, has pointed out, we are living in the "time of the parenthesis," the time between eras. However, as contrasted with the shift from an agricultural to an industrial society, which took 100 years, the shift from an industrial society to an information society is taking place at a much faster rate. This means that changes are occurring so rapidly that there is little, if any, time for humans to react to them; instead, we must learn to anticipate the future. This chapter is designed to focus upon that future, to describe existing trends, and to speculate about probable extrapolations of those trends.

To a significant extent, all of the trends that we will discuss are due to past and pending developments in **smart machines.** Smart machines are machines that have imbedded microprocessors or microcomputers. Not all of these machines will be computers as we know them today. Most will be parts of other devices that we will encounter daily, serving us in the home, assisting us in the office, improving our productivity in the factory, acting as intermediaries in our contacts with government, and challenging us in our leisure time. Some of these smart machines will be natural extensions of machines that we are familiar with today, such as telephones, automobiles, and television sets. Others will be devices of which we cannot yet conceive.

In speculating about the future, it is important to distinguish between **projections** and **forecasts.** A projection is an extension of past events into the future. As contrasted with a projection, a forecast is an effort to anticipate future events that have a reasonable probability of occurring. Speculation about the future of computers and about their potential impact, for better or worse, upon our civilization is a topic that intrigues many social and physical scientists. We have included selected references for the topics discussed at the end of this chapter. However, the responsibility for the specific projections and forecasts is ours.

TEN SOCIOECONOMIC TRENDS

Much has been written about the increasing role that computers and information processing will have upon our society, affecting almost every aspect of human endeavor. Although there are many alternate forecasts, certain central trends appear to have emerged. Assuming that there are no major wars or political revolutions, no devastating economic or social changes in the major developed nations, and no totally unexpected scientific developments, ten important trends appear to be:

1. Economic activities will continue to become increasingly service-oriented, as contrasted with product-oriented.

2. The **knowledge industries**—the industries that provide information processing products and services—will become the dominant industries in the United States.

3. Computers of all sizes will increase in number and uses, with continuing improvements in performance and reductions in size and cost and with the number of microcomputers and supermicrocomputers far exceeding all others.

4. The requirements for increased productivity will cause **cybernetics**—the use of computers coupled with automatic machinery to control and carry out complex operations—to become widespread.

5. Enormous numbers of smart machines will become components of cybernetic systems and consumer products.

6. The need to educate people about computers coupled with the use of computers in the educational process will combine to change the methods of teaching and the contents of most courses of study in schools and colleges.

7. The diffusion of microcomputers and the widespread increase in communications systems will enable many people to live and work at locations remote from a place of employment.

8. Competition for interesting and creative jobs will increase. People will stay in school longer to acquire specialized skills. They will also return to school more often in order to update these skills or to acquire new ones.

9. Advances in communications will cause the classical vertical, or hierarchical, flow of information in industries to be replaced by concurrent information flows in all directions, changing the way in which computer information systems are developed and in which work is managed and performed.

10. People and organizations will accept high-technology innovations more readily than in the past; leisure time will expand; and there will be a need to balance the coldness of technology with the warmth of our home environments and with increased contact between humans.

These forecasts accent both the challenge of change and the possibilities and opportunities that the future holds. They provide the background for the speculations that follow.

THE KNOWLEDGE INDUSTRIES

The industries that provide information products or services will become known as the **knowledge industries.** Throughout the remainder of this century, expansions in worldwide revenues for the information-related industries will continue at the current rate of increase, which is a doubling in amount every five years. Figure 19-1 shows the anticipated worldwide revenues for U.S. firms engaged in information processing activities. Revenues show an increase from $18 billion in 1971 to $64 billion in 1981. By 1991 they will have increased to $256 billion. Figure 19-2 shows the details of this market increase by type of equipment between 1975 and 1995. The principal information products are automated office equipment and systems, computer data processing systems, and voice, data, video, and other communications systems.

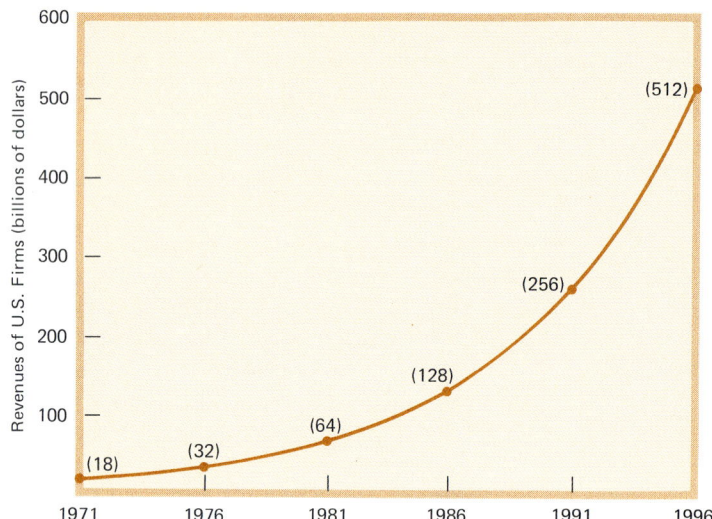

FIGURE 19-1

Worldwide information processing
revenues for U.S. firms are expected to
double approximately every five years.
At this rate revenues will exceed $500
billion by 1996.

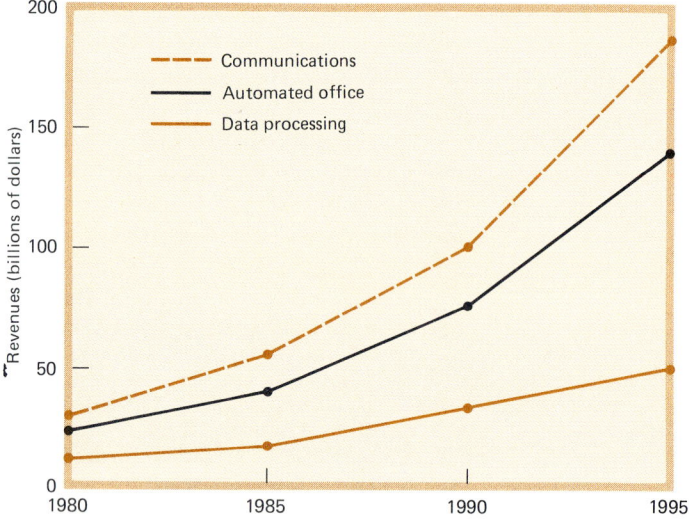

FIGURE 19-2

The major segments of market growth
in information processing are in
automated office equipment and
systems, computer data processing
systems, and communications systems
of all types, including voice, video,
and data. The market size for each
segment is steadily increasing, with
the greatest rate of increase in
communications.

Figure 19-3 is a forecast of user spending for information processing as a
percentage of gross national product (GNP) and as a per capita expense. The
graph is based upon the cost of equipment and services obtained from the
knowledge industries and upon estimates of internal overhead costs for personnel and facilities. User spending, which was 2.1 percent of the GNP in 1970,
will increase from 8.3 percent in 1985 to 21 percent by 1995. Similarly, per
capita expense, which was $101 in 1970, will increase from $670 in 1985 to
$2400 by 1995.

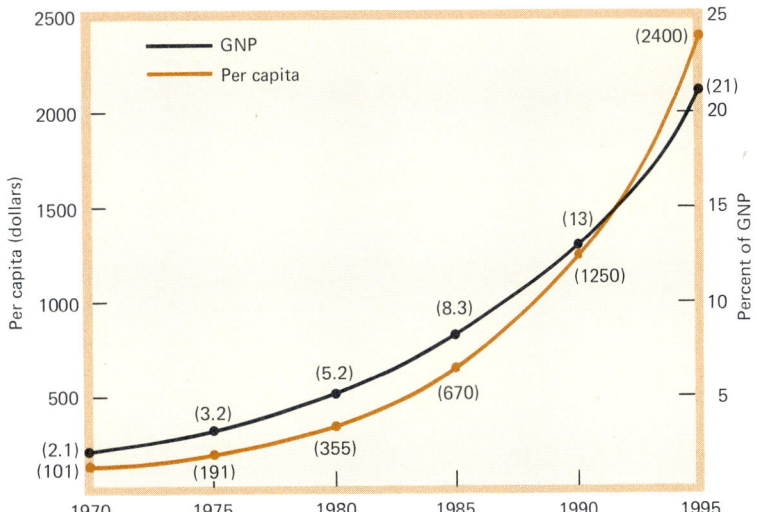

FIGURE 19-3
User spending for information processing equipment and services will increase to 21 percent of the gross national product (GNP) by 1995. This will be equivalent to $2400 per person.

COMPUTER INFORMATION SYSTEMS

Computer System Architecture

The computer system architectures of the future will be extensions of the hardware, software, and firmware discussed in Chapter 4. The circuits used in the central processing units and memories of computers will continue to be produced in ever-increasing quantities.

In a colloquium about the growth of the semiconductor industry, Gordon Moore, president of Intel Corporation, a major semiconductor manufacturer, stated that by 1986 the semiconductor industry could be producing about 10^{14} circuit functions per year. A circuit function is a logic (on-off) gate or a memory bit, and 10^{14} functions is 100 trillion functions. Even though a single "smart" product might use many thousands of circuit functions, the projected impact upon the capabilities of common products such as watches and automobiles is difficult to imagine. Gordon Moore projected an increase in total circuit-function usage from approximately 310 billion in 1976 to approximately 10 trillion in 1986. Pocket calculators will become very powerful computers, and many additional capabilities will be added to watches, video games, and automobiles. For example, automobiles will be able to protect the lives of passengers in many ways. They will be able to detect approaching vehicles and will alert the driver. They will be able to monitor the driver's physical condition and take over, if necessary, in order to avoid a collision. Spare parts and self-repairable features will add to the realiability of automobiles. Automatic traffic control and navigation systems for automobiles also will come into being.

With a production capacity of 10^{14} circuit functions, the semiconductor industry will be able to meet 10 times the anticipated demand by 1986. Therefore, there will be adequate capacity for countless additional applications. Another tenfold increase in production capacity by the end of the 1980s will provide about a quarter of a million circuit functions per year for every person on earth.

The circuits and components used in computer mainframes (CPU plus main memory) will continue to become smaller, faster, and cheaper. Also, although more complex, they will be more reliable because of design improvements. Performance will increase more than a thousandfold by the end of the century, and the cost for individual data processing operations will decrease accordingly.

The speed of the central processing unit will be measured in millions of instructions per second (MIPS). Supercomputers capable of performing more than 10,000 MIPS will be developed. They will achieve their performance by harnessing the potential of many powerful microcomputers working in parallel.

The speeds and densities of memories will also increase vastly, with great reductions in cost per bit stored. By 1990 storage densities of a million bits or more per chip will be achieved. These densities will be achieved by the electronic storage devices, such as magnetic bubble memories (MBMs) and charge-coupled devices (CCDs) that we learned about in Chapter 5. In the 1990s rotating electromechanical memories such as magnetic tape and magnetic disk could be completely phased out. By the end of the same decade, new storage technologies will find broad usage. An example is the Josephson junction, which we mentioned briefly in Chapter 5. This junction relies upon a physical phenomenon that, when temperatures are close to absolute zero ($-459.69°$ Farenheit), permits the electrons making up an electric current to penetrate barriers that ordinarily would restrain them. This phenomenon is called **superconductivity** and has led to laboratory demonstrations of high-speed switching circuits. Josephson junctions will permit circuits that represent 1s and 0s to operate at speeds that are a hundred times faster than those achievable with integrated circuits today. When it becomes possible to store data in molecules such as those that make up simple one-celled organisms (like the ameba), computer system power will no longer be measured by size. A person will be able to conceal in one hand a processing power greater than that of the largest of today's computers. The processing power of a complete computer mainframe will be reduced to a size that can be contained on a one-quarter-square-inch chip of silicon by the extension of large-scale integration (LSI) of circuits to very-large-scale integration (VLSI). Many VSLI components already have been demonstrated. The next step is $VLSI^2$, which stands for very-large scale-integration-indeed!

As a matter of fact, the United States government already has taken this step in a program called VHSIC, which stands for very-high-speed integrated circuits. The VHSIC program, considered by many to be the most important federally sponsored scientific activity since the space exploration program, involves research both in integrated-circuit techniques and in management methods for reducing the time span between design and implementation. The market for VLSI and VLSI circuits is estimated to approach $100 billion by 1990.

**Software
and Firmware**

The use of firmware, which is software substituted for hardware and stored in read-only memory, was described in Chapter 4. Because of the need to design systems to meet an incalculable number of computer data processing needs, firmware will become the most significant tool of computer architects. Firmware will make possible the cost-effective production of smart machines of all types.

Software operating systems with enhanced capabilities will be developed. However, software advances will lag behind hardware developments. By the mid-1990s, users will no longer have to be concerned about computer operating systems. The functions performed by these systems will be automatic. They will not involve the user and therefore will be "invisible" to the user. As an example, comprehensive data base management systems will exist, and a person using a simple query language will be able to extract from the data base information formatted to meet an individualized reporting need.

Job opportunities will continue to increase for applications programmers. However, in many instances, circuits deposited on silicon chips will be available for complete applications, such as payroll, accounts receivable, and inventory control. Such chips already are in use. It is possible to buy a programmable calculator into which chips can be inserted to perform specific functions. Examples are real estate calculations, statistical analyses, and aircraft navigation. Extensions of the "program-on-a-chip" technique to smart machines are limitless.

**Input, Output,
and Communications**

Because they often have to interact with our physical, nonelectronic world, most input and output units and systems will not be reduced in size or in cost to the same degree as computer mainframes. However, one of the predominant characteristics of future computer data processing systems will be the reliance upon terminals and communications links. Terminals of all types will abound. Distributed data processing systems will dominate the applications marketplace. Satellite communications systems will provide low-cost and high-volume data transmission services for users all over the earth.

These systems will provide almost instantaneous communication between offices, individuals, and special facilities. They will increase the time value of information by making it available whenever and wherever it is needed for operational or managerial decision making. The software required to control communications between the elements of large computer-communications networks is very complex. However, such networks should be developed and in operation in the 1990s.

**Computer Information
System Development**

Just as software will lag behind hardware, the development and widespread use of the structured analysis and design techniques required to manage effectively the life cycles of complex computer information systems will lag behind software developments. However, the greatly increased computer literacy of populations that have been exposed since birth to computers—at home, in

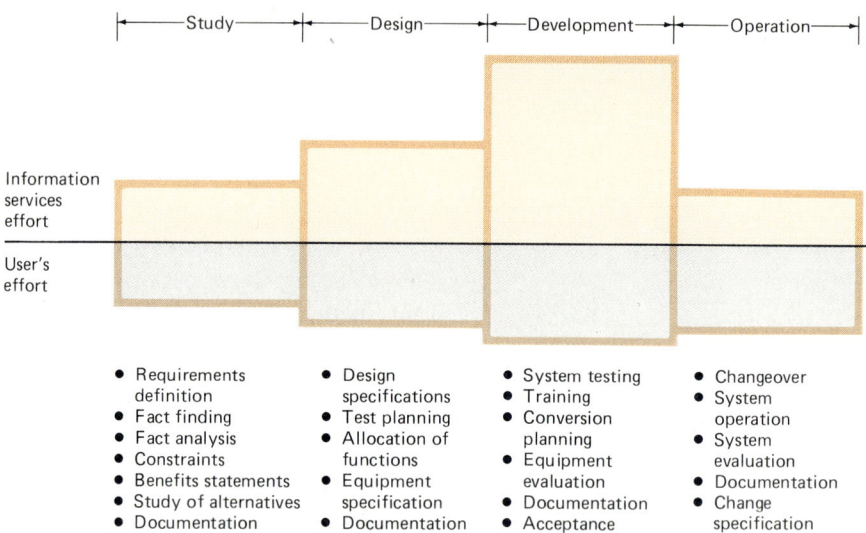

Study	Design	Development	Operation

Information
services
effort

User's
effort

FIGURE 19-4

In the future the efforts of users will increase in the development of computer information systems throughout all the life-cycle phases. This figure lists many of the significant activities to which users will be able to make significant contributions. The result will be an improvement in the usability of these systems.

- Requirements definition
- Fact finding
- Fact analysis
- Constraints
- Benefits statements
- Study of alternatives
- Documentation
- Study phase review

- Design specifications
- Test planning
- Allocation of functions
- Equipment specification
- Documentation
- Design review

- System testing
- Training
- Conversion planning
- Equipment evaluation
- Documentation
- Acceptance review

- Changeover
- System operation
- System evaluation
- Documentation
- Change specification

schools, and in business—will overcome many of the communications problems that have existed between users and computer professionals.

Users will become more involved in the development of computer information systems, both centralized and decentralized. They will play a more active role throughout all phases of the system development life cycle. Figure 19-4 shows how user participation, as contrasted with that of information services professionals, will increase throughout the system development life cycle. Nevertheless, management of all of the life-cycle activities will remain a challenge well into the twenty-first century.

FEEDBACK

19-1 What is a projection? A forecast?

19-2 What is a smart machine?

19-3 How will computer central processing units and memories be affected by future technical developments?

19-4 What impact will advances in communications have upon where and how people work?

19-5 What are the knowledge industries? What growth is forecast for them?

THE HIGH-TECH HOME

The combined capabilities of computers and communications systems will revolutionize the home and our daily living habits. Telephones, thermostats, and television sets will be replaced by greatly enhanced communication and control systems. Ways in which smart machines will relieve us of boredom and enrich our leisure time will include:

1. Utilizing data entry stations, communications networks, and large, shared data bases, many individuals will be able to perform most of their occupational tasks at home. Electronic mail and electronic conferences will eliminate much of the need for business travel.

2. Two-way information services, such as Videotex, will be widely used. Shopping will be done from the home. Catalog items, from furniture to produce, will be displayed on a TV screen, and purchases will be made by the push of a button.

3. Meal planning and preparation will be electronic. The home computer will keep track of the inventory of foods in the cupboard and freezer. Tasty menus will be prepared that use items before they exceed a maximum storage time. Food inventories will be replenished automatically.

4. Homes will be paperless. The home computer will be able to generate a softcopy (CRT display) equivalent of newspapers, books, and periodicals at individualized knowledge stations. The same machine will prepare and maintain budgets, pay bills, and prepare income tax returns.

5. Many of the educational services provided by schools will be available in the home. Computer-assisted instruction, based upon the presentation of materials and monitoring of student progress by computer, will be used to teach courses from first grade through graduate school.

6. Society will be checkless. All payments for services in the home and outside will be handled automatically by electronic funds transfer (EFT).

7. Many of the computer-aided medical services available in hospitals will be extended to the home. By allowing a remote computer to measure temperature, pulse, and blood pressure and by answering progressively more probing sets of questions, persons will be able to avail themselves of medical or psychiatric screening services. Since voice-activated data entry stations will be commonplace, patients will be able to talk to their electronic doctors.

8. Most household chores will be fully automated. Robot vacuum cleaners, garbage disposal units, washing machines, and gardeners will keep the home and its environment at an optimum state of livability. Should a household device fail, repairs will be made automatically after consultation with a computerized technician.

9. Personal computing and video computer games will provide endless hours of leisure time activity. Personal computing will become so cheap that it will be able to be used abundantly, even wasted. Personal computers will be as inexpensive as portable radios are today, and we will build them as hobbies. Electronic chips will provide an array of capabilities for personal computers. Similar chips will provide for video games of increasing variety and sophistication. Some of these home entertainment centers will be connected to a master home computer and TV display system. Others will be self-contained. All will be smart machines that will teach us how to play games, keep score for us, or play against us when human competition is not available.

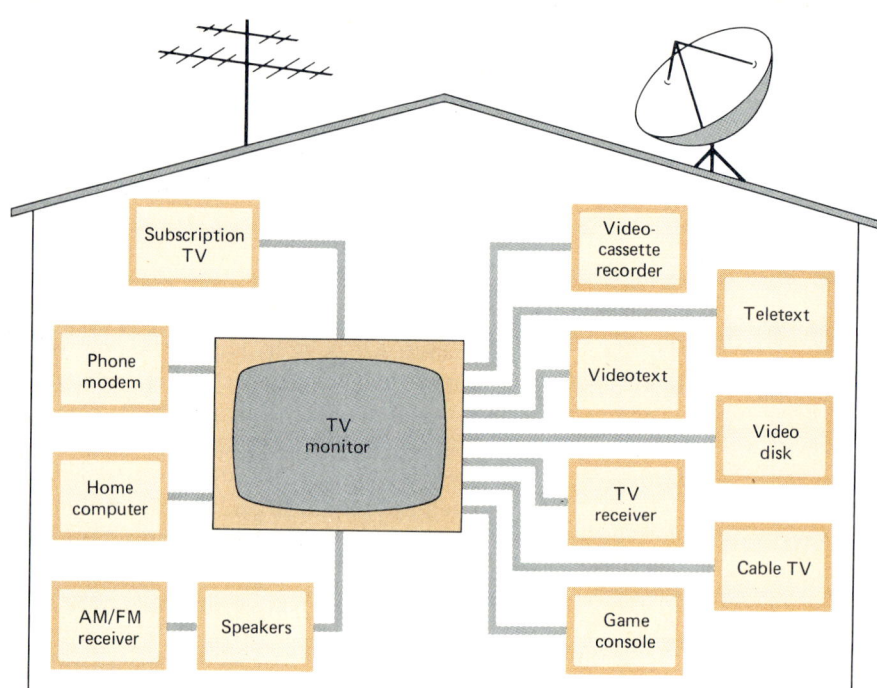

FIGURE 19-5

The high-tech home will provide consumers with an array of options in supplying their television monitors and speaker systems with services and entertainment. In home entertainment centers of the future, many of the components shown separately will be combined into single console.

As video, audio, and computer-game technologies continue to merge, consumers will move ever closer to the electronic household. Figure 19-5 illustrates the array of options that persons will have in bringing programs and information to their home television screens. With options like these, most members of the information society will enjoy a standard of living and many resources formerly available only to upper-middle-class people in the United States.

SUPERCOMPUTERS

We usually think of supercomputers as machines that are remote from the consumer. We see them as hidden away in government, university, and research laboratories and as having little impact on our daily lives. This will not always be the case in the future. Computers that are much more powerful than the largest machines that are available at present will be built to solve such problems as weather prediction and control, to design aircraft, and to support information utilities. It is interesting that the problem of accurate weather prediction was one that caused von Neumann, whom we mentioned in Chapter 2, to become interested in computers. At present, we can assemble all of the data needed to forecast tomorrow's weather, but, unfortunately, we cannot complete our computations until next week. Certainly, timely weather prediction and, perhaps, control will affect us each day.

Similarly, scientists are continuing to design better aircraft for us to fly in.

However, even with the aid of the most powerful modern computers, aerodynamicists must plan for many months—often years—of testing new designs under simulated flight conditions in research facilities called wind tunnels. For example, the U.S. space shuttle required 45,000 hours of wind-tunnel testing. The reason that so much testing time is required is that present-day computers do not have sufficient capacity to handle anything but *approximations* of equations that describe the motion of aircraft or spacecraft under all flight conditions.

Since we will, in many instances, be linking our home computers and data bases to larger systems in order to draw upon their resources, and since these systems will have to provide services to millions of other users, many information utilities will be created. There may be an educational utility, an entertainment utility, a communications utility—or some combination of these. Certainly, the government's use of computers will increase. The Congress and government agencies, such as the Internal Revenue Service, are continuing to extend their data bases and computational resources. This has raised concerns about invasion of the privacy to which individuals are entitled. Faced with a future in which large computers will be able to communicate and to share data, citizens will have to remain alert to the possibility of undesirable inroads upon personal privacy.

How big will the supercomputers of the future be? Well, in in terms of size, the central processing unit and internal memory for a computer as powerful as the most powerful machine that we know today should fit easily on a wafer by the mid-1990s. Hundreds of thousands of such wafers connected in parallel would be awe-inspiring in power. The possibility that in the future a machine or machines with more than human intelligence will wrest control of our plan away from us is of real concern to some forecasters.

CYBERNETICS: ROBOTS AND ARTIFICIAL INTELLIGENCE

Robots

We have defined cybernetics as the use of computers coupled with automatic machinery to control and carry out complex operations. Robots are cybernetic systems. The Robotics Institute of America defines a **robot** as a reprogrammable, multifunction manipulator designed to move material, parts, tools, or specialized devices through various programmed motions for the performance of a variety of tasks. The key words in this definition are "reprogrammable" and "variety." Robots can be programmed to perform a number of different functions; they are different from automated machines, which are designed only to perform a single function. Thus, a robot can make a series of spot welds during the assembly of a particular model of a car and can change welding patterns for other models. Also, when no longer needed for welding, the robot can be reprogrammed to perform another task, such as material handling.

The following nine attributes are required for a robot to be useful:

1. A hand to grip a piece of work
2. An arm to move the hand in three planes

Karel Čapek, an imaginative Czech dramatist of the 1920s, may have had an inspired and frightening vision of the future. In Čapek's well-known play, *R.U.R.*, a firm called Rossum's Universal Robots mass-produces synthetic "men" and "women." Capek coined the word "robot" from the Czech word "robit," which means work. Capek's robots become so efficient at work and so intelligent that they revolt, taking over industrialized society and eliminating the human race. They even study their own blueprints and learn how to replace themselves as they wear out.

Today, part of Capek's prophesy is coming true. Although modern robots are far from taking over the world, their use is more widespread than many of us may suspect. By 1981 approximately 300 U.S. and foreign corporations were producing over 400 different robot models. Although these robots may not exactly resemble humans, they are performing many of the monotonous tasks performed by factory production workers. These mechanical creatures are computer-programmed to function by themselves and usually have one or more hydraulically powered arms and hands. With these hands they can hold their tools and grip assembly-line items, sorting them and performing other routine tasks. Unlike their human counterparts, the robots do not become bored. They can work day and night without becoming tired and without complaining. They do not belong to unions; they receive no paid vacations; and they are not late to work on Monday mornings.

The use of robots was accepted more enthusiastically abroad than in the United Sates because of the labor shortage in many industrialized countries. Automobile manufacturers are the largest single industrial users of robots. Volvo, Renault, Toyota, and Fiat are among the foreign automobile manufacturers who are using robots. Productivity has increased and humans have been freed to perform jobs they like better. For example, Fiat installed 18 robots in a body shop, assigning 20 workers to other jobs. Production increased from 250 auto frames per day to 500, and absenteeism of reassigned human workers decreased by a factor of three.

Following foreign examples, U.S. firms now are increasing their use of robots. As is the case overseas, the principal users of robots are automobile manufacturers. Other areas offer great potential for applied robotics. The multibillion-dollar food industry can use robots to perform many tasks, from food processing to preparation and service. The energy industries can also use robot workers—for example, in dangerous deep-pit work or in offshore drilling operations. Certainly robots could become radiation-immune workers and be used in atomic energy facilities.

While self-thinking mechanical workers, such as Čapek's robots, may not be on the immediate horizon, robots are providing an answer to the demands of an increasingly competitive, service-oriented economy. The cost of robots has grown only 40 percent since the first mechanical worker was employed. In the same period salaries of human workers increased 200 percent—and, after all, the cost of robots can be amortized in five years.

3. A wrist with two or three articulations
4. Sufficient power to move the piece of work
5. Manual controls so that an operator can control limb motions
6. A memory to store a sequence of instructions
7. A means of executing the sequence of instructions stored in memory
8. The ability to function at speeds equal to or greater than a person
9. Reliability in performing directed tasks

Robots can be classified according to the level of technology employed in their design. Three classification levels are: low-technology, medium-technology, and high-technology. Low-technology robots are open-loop systems, which means that no feedback is provided for correction. The programs that control them have a limited number of steps, and the robots are able to perform tasks with good repeatability.

Medium-technology robots are closed-loop systems, called **servomechanisms,** that use feedback for accurate control of position and velocity. The basic control elements for these robots are microcomputers, which can easily be reprogrammed. Most of the robots manufactured at present are medium-technology systems. Figure 19-6 shows medium-technology robots at work. General Motors has predicted that by the end of the 1980s 90 percent of all new machinery will be under computer control, operated by mechanisms that we have classified as medium-technology robots.

High-technology robots have all of the attributes of medium-technology robots with one important addition. They are equipped with external sensors that provide information about the external environment, considerably enhancing their capabilities. Video cameras, proximity sensors, and tactile sensors are examples of external sensors that might be provided for high-technology robots. The robot servant that cleans house and serves cocktails is an example of a high-technology robot.

The pace of development activities underway in universities and in the plants of the more than 300 firms that are making robots is such that we can anticipate a large increase in the number of robots of all types in the next decade. Even though robot workers are an acknowledged necessity and contribute greatly toward increased productivity, many people have voiced at least

FIGURE 19-6

These medium-technology robots are busy at work on an automobile assembly line. The automobile industry makes extensive use of robots. They contribute to improvements in both productivity and overall product quality.

two principal concerns about cybernetic systems. One concern is the displacement of human workers, and the other is dominance of the planet by a silicon-
based intellect capable of displacing the human race. With respect to the first
concern, an optimistic viewpoint is that many new smart industries and computer-related job opportunities will be created and that we will be able to make
profitable use of shorter working hours and more leisure time. The second
concern represents a pessimistic outlook toward developments in artificial intelligence.

**Artificial
Intelligence**

Artificial intelligence, like real intelligence, is elusive and difficult to define. In
very general terms, a machine with reasoning, learning, and thinking capabilities that resemble those of humans could be said to possess **artificial intelligence**
(AI). More specifically, the ability to produce original ideas is considered to be
a necessary attribute of artificial intelligence. As contrasted with the computer
programs that you have studied in this book, AI programs deal with knowledge
and not with numbers. Although there still is little agreement among researchers about what it means to say that a machine "thinks," there is general
agreement that problem solving by computers requires large data banks. A
machine with an artificial-intelligence program could apply knowledge acquired
in one area to solve a problem in a different area.

Among the early applications of artificial intelligence are the so-called
expert programs. These are programs that enable a computer to act as a
consultant in a specialized area of knowledge. An example is a program that
assists the designers of computer systems to select the components that best
meet specific customer needs. Another is a program that is given data about a
sick patient and is able to develop a tentative diagnosis. This program follows
sets of rules for searching its data banks and for adding to data supplied by
the patient.

With the continuing trend toward high-capacity memories and inexpensive computer power, scientistswill develop many commercially useful AI systems. At present the United States is the leading nation in artificial-intelligence
research and development. However, interest is increasing in other countries.

In keeping with our definition of artificial intelligence, R2D2 and C3PO,
the heros of *Star Wars* and its sequels, could be considered to be high-technology
robots possessed of artificial intelligence. However, there is no reason to assume
that in the future intelligent machines will resemble humans or necessarily
think in the same ways that humans think. It seems to be a certainty that by
early in the next century we will develop computers with memories equal in
storage capacity to those of humans and of a size comparable to the human
brain. It is not very probable that by that time computers will be able to think
like humans. After all, the human brain as it is today is much more complex
than any computer. Although computers can perform repetitive operations
faster than humans and can process and remember huge quantities of data
without overloading the way a human brain might, computer memory still is

a set of separate storage locations that have no thinking capacity. Control and logic are performed elsewhere. By contrast, the human brain is made up of cells that appear to communicate directly with countless other cells at a subconscious level. Humans display their intelligence by innovative responses to changing conditons. Machines do not do this, except to the limited degree that they have been programmed for branching to alternative sequences of actions. As a result of sophisticated programs, computers have been taught to be excellent competitors in games such as chess.

However, the rate of change in computer memory technology is such that computers are beginning to match and to exceed humans in many ways. As Robert Jastrow pointed out in an essay in *Time* magazine, raw human intelligence has changed but little in the last 100,000 years, and computer power is continuing to increase dramatically. A forecast based upon Jastrow's essay is:

1. Humans will remain in control and superior in intelligence to computers until the 1990s, when memories built of devices such as magnetic bubbles and Josephson junctions will begin to match the reasoning power of the human brain.

2. Humans and computers will have a mutually advantageous, or symbiotic, interdependence. Humans will bring intuition to this relationship, and machines will provide brute reasoning power. Humans will provide for the computer's needs for maintenance, repair, and reproduction. The computer, in turn, will minister to the social and economic needs of humans.

3. After a period of time (perhaps a few centuries), the thinking power of machines will far outmatch that of humans. Even after that, the symbiotic relationship between human and machine may continue, or, perhaps, the dominant intelligence on this planet will be silicon.

Of course, the above is but one of many possible future scenarios. We should remember that smart machines, as we understand them today, do not have minds of their own or wills that are analogous to those of humans. Conclusions reached by machines are only the logical results of a program written by a human for the purpose of converting input data into usable results. Of course, we are developing sophisticated programs that do enhance the logical capabilities (reasoning power?) of machines. These programs will enable machines to modify their own behavior on the basis of experience (learning?) and to construct other machines with enhanced abilities (reproduction?). How far the reasoning, learning, and reproducing capabilities of machines will progress, and what type of artificial intelligence machines will possess in future centuries, will be determined by humankind's actions in managing or delegating to machines the needs of society Whether or not artificial intelligence surpasses human intelligence and whether or not we stay in control of our future, our lives and those of generations to come will be vastly affected by computers and other smart machines.

FEEDBACK   **19-6** How will smart machines affect the home?

19-7 What types of problems can supercomputers help to solve?

19-8 What is cybernetics?

19-9 What are the three types of robots?

19-10 What are the attributes of artificial intelligence?

19-11 How might humans and machines have a mutualy advantages relationship?

SUMMARY   The shift from an industrial to an information society is taking place at so fast a rate that it is difficult for humans to adapt to the frequency of change. It is necessary to anticipate the future. Our projections and forecasts about the future are linked by the concept of a smart machine, a machine that has imbedded microprocessors or microcomputers. The components of our speculations are:

1. The trend toward a service-oriented society served by advanced computer communications systems will continue, with the knowledge industries as the dominant industries and with countless uses of smart machines as components of cybernetic systems and consumer products.

2. Order-of-magnitude improvements will continue to be made in computer hardware through the further miniaturization of central processing units and storage, with the use of communications networks becoming widespread.

3. Systems and applications software will also improve, as will techniques for managing the design and development of large computer information systems. The keys to the latter will be user education and user involvement in all phases of the system development life cycle.

4. The need to educate people about computers and the use of computers in the classroom will combine to change the methods of teaching and courses of study in schools and colleges.

5. Consumers will make ever-increasing use of the products and services provided by the knowledge industries as leisure time increases.

6. Supercomputers that are much more powerful than those of today will be built, and they will be challenged by as yet unsolved problems.

7. Advanced cybernetic systems will be designed and developed. Robots will become commonplace, and advances will be made in artificial intelligence. The relationship between humans and machines may become a symbiotic one, with humans providing intuition and machines providing reasoning power. The future of this relationship will depend upon what humanity decides to manage or elects to delegate to intelligent machines.

ANSWERS TO   **19-1** A projection is an extension of past trends into the future. A forecast
FEEDBACK QUESTIONS   is an effort to describe some future events that have a reasonable probability of occurring.

19-2 A smart machine is a machine with an imbedded microprocessor or microcomputer.

19-3 Central processing units and memories will become more compact and less expensive per unit component, making possible more powerful and reliable computers of all sizes.

19-4 Advances in communications will enable people to live and to work at remote locations; they will alter the classical vertical information hierarchy, providing prompt information to workers at all levels.

19-5 The knowledge industries are the industries that provide information processing products and services. They will grow and become the dominant industries.

19-6 Smart machines will be found in great abundance everywhere in the home, altering the ways in which we shop, spend our leisure time, and handle our business affairs.

19-7 Supercomputers can help to solve problems such as weather forecasting, aerodynamics, and space flight and can make possible information utilities of many kinds.

19-8 Cybernetics is the use of computers coupled with automatic machinery to control and carry out complex operations.

19-9 The three types of robots are low-technology, medium-technology, and high-technology.

19-10 Some attributes of artificial intelligence are originality, access to large data banks, and the ability to apply knowledge acquired in one area to solve a problem in a different area.

19-11 Some foresee a symbiotic relationship between humans and machines where humans provide intuition and machines provide brute reasoning power.

FOR REVIEW AND DISCUSSION

1 Some patterns of life are forecast for the United States in the future. How will these relate to computer applications?

2 Why will firmware be used extensively in the future?

3 Discuss the relative advances forecast for hardware, software, and applications management.

4 Describe and discuss the forecast that the knowledge industries will become dominant in the United States.

5 What is an information utility? Describe some possible future information utilities.

6 Comment on the future scenario presented for the possible relationship between humans and machines.

7 What impact will changes in the dissemination of information have upon the role of middle managers in industry?

8 Discuss the attributes of artificial intelligence described in the text. Do you agree or disagree that these might adequately describe a "thinking" machine? Explain your answer.

9 In his book *Megatrends* John Naisbett stated that high-tech should be accompanied by high-touch. Do you feel that this is important or unimportant? Explain.

10 What effect do you think that computers will have upon educational needs and classroom processes?

FURTHER READING

J. S. Albus, "Robots in the Workplace: The Key to a Prosperous Future," *The Futurist,* February 1983, pp. 22–27.

————, "Artificial Intelligence: The Second Computer Age Begins," *Business Week,* March 8, 1982, pp. 66–75.

J. M. Callahan, "The State of Industrial Robotics" *BYTE,* October 1982 pp. 128–142.

H. Cleveland, "Information as a Resource," *The Futurist,* December 1982, pp. 34–39.

V. T. Coates, "The Potential Impact of Robotics," *The Futurist,* February 1983, pp. 28–32.

M. L. Dertouzous, and J. Moses, *The Computer Age: A Twenty-Year View,* MIT Press, Cambridge, Mass., 1980.

T. A. Dolotta, et al., *Data Processing in 1980–1985: A Study of Limitations to Progress,* Wiley, New York, 1976, Chapter 2.

F. Hopsgood, "Inside a Robotics Lab: Avoiding Obstacles," *Technology Illustrated,* May 1983, pp. 33–35.

T. Henkel, "Chip Technology," *Computerworld,* Nov. 17, 1982, pp. 37–38.

————, "Japanese Seek the Key to Artificial Intelligence," *Los Angeles Times,* December 20, 1982.

Robert Jastrow, "Toward an Intelligence Beyond Man's" *Time,* Feb. 20, 1978.

R. A. Karmann, and T. L. Johnson, "The Main-Frame Computer: A Glimpse into the Future," *Journal of Systems Management,* February 1983, pp. 6–9.

M. Kornbluth, "The Electronic Office: How It Will Change the Way You Work," *The Futurist,* June 1982, pp. 37–41.

————, *Information Processing in the United States: A Quantitative Summary,* AFIPS Press, New Jersey, 1977.

J. Mathias, "Data Communications Management: Future Developments," *Journal of Systems Management,* November 1982, pp. 8–13.

Pender M. McCarter, "Where is the Industry Going?" *Datamation,* February 1978, pp. 99–105.

J. Naisbitt, *Megatrends,* Warner Books, New York, 1982.

L. W. Samney, "VHSIC: A Status Report," *IEEE Spectrum,* December 1982, pp. 34–39.

————, "Technology '83," *IEEE Spectrum,* January 1983.

C. Truxal, "The Very High-Tech Home," *IEEE Spectrum,* January 1983, pp. 64–67.

N. Weiner, *Cybernetics,* Wiley, New York, 1948.

SUPPLEMENTS

SPECIAL TOPICS

This section of the book contains supplementary material to expand on the coverage of programming languages and to discuss number systems and character codes. The programming language BASIC was introduced in Chapter 16. Other programming languages are covered in Supplement I (COBOL) and Supplement II (RPG II). Number systems used in computer memories are discussed in Supplement III, including binary, octal, and hexadecimal number systems. Other formats used in computer memory are discussed in Supplement IV, including BCDIC, EBCDIC, and ASCII.

SUPPLEMENT I
COBOL

PREVIEW Chapter 13 introduced us to programming languages, and Chapter 14 presented examples of the steps required to run a program. In this supplement, we will see how the logical steps of our program plan can be written as program instructions using the COBOL language. The goal of this supplement is to acquaint you with the process of coding a program solution by using COBOL.

In this supplement you will learn:

1. The nature of COBOL
2. The relationship between planning and coding a program solution
3. How to input and output data in COBOL
4. How to perform calculations in COBOL
5. How to write decisions in COBOL
6. How to write process loops in COBOL

KEY TERMS TO WATCH FOR AND REMEMBER

coding form
Area A
Area B
identification division
environment division
data division
procedure division
sections

paragraphs
sentences
picture clause
group item
elementary item
value clause
literal

In Chapter 13 we described several problem-oriented languages for writing programs. In this supplement, we will concentrate on one of them—in order to see how programs are coded from our logic plans.

COBOL is the most commonly used business-oriented programming language. Its name comes from *co*mmon *b*usiness-*o*riented *l*anguage. Problems of a business nature typically involve large volumes of input and output data but do not require complex mathematical calculations. Therefore, the instructions in COBOL are oriented toward data handling, rather than mathematical calculations.

THE COBOL CODING FORM

As is the case with all programming languages, COBOL has a specific format for its instructions. The COBOL **coding form** shown in Figure I-1 is an example of the form used to record COBOL instructions by the programmer. Each line of the coding form was originally intended to be recorded on a punched card. Thus, the coding form is laid out with 80 columns, which represent the 80 card columns of a standard card. Even though most COBOL programs are now keyed on a terminal keyboard, we still refer to the recording of characters in columns.

FIGURE I-1

The COBOL coding form.

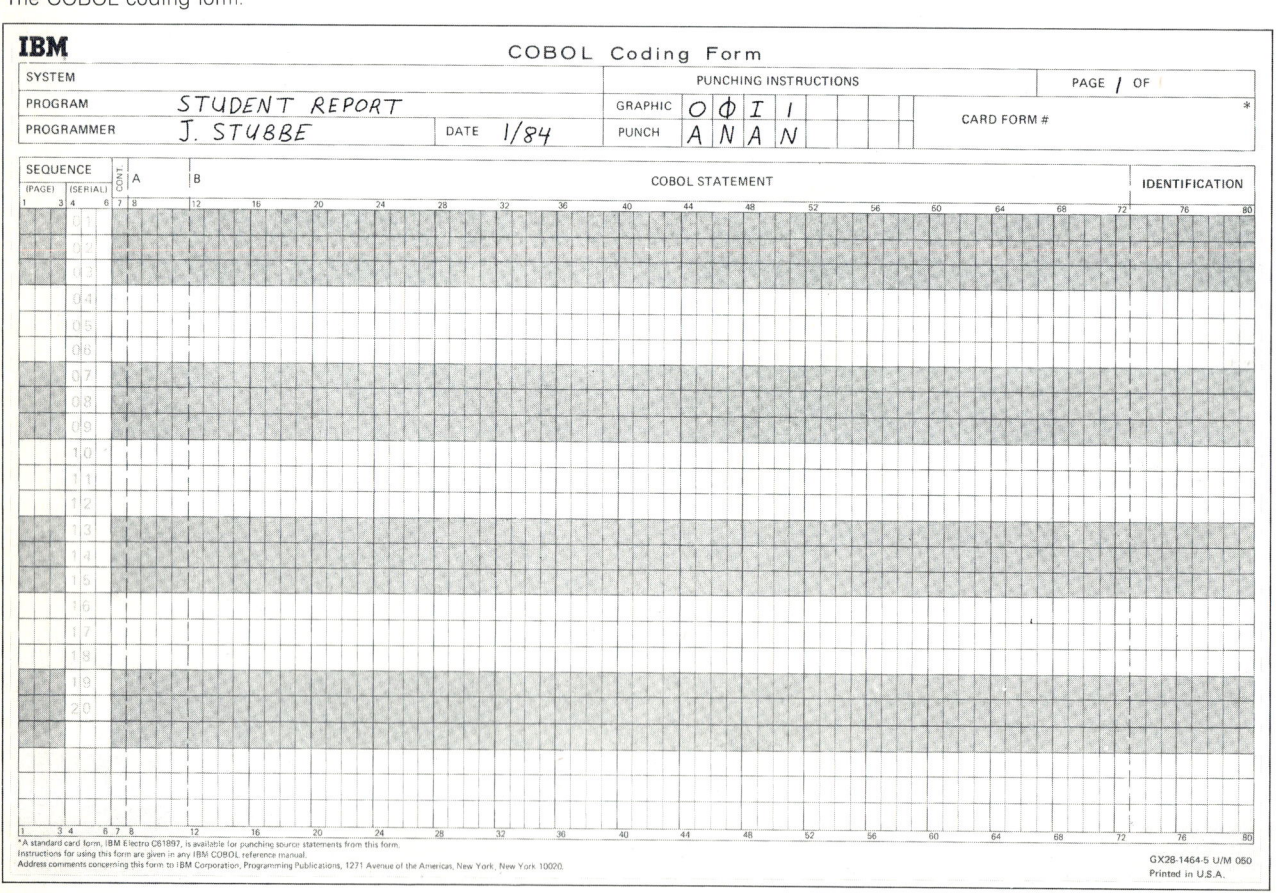

Punching Instructions

The top portion of the COBOL coding form contains information about the system, the program, and the programmer. In addition, punching instructions are given. Many computing centers provide programmers with terminals for entering their COBOL source programs or changing existing programs. Some computing centers assist programmers by providing data entry services. These services include the original entry of COBOL instructions from the coding forms by a professional data entry operator. In some cases the data entry operators may also key in corrections or modifications to existing programs.

The punching instructions are intended to help the programmer communicate with the data entry operator. The area of communication involves characters written on coding sheets that may be confused with other characters. As an example the letter O and the number 0 look alike when written but are two different characters on the keyboard. It is important for the data entry operator to know which is which. To tell the operator which character is intended, something must be done to alter the appearance of one character or the other.

In the example in Figure I-1 the punching instructions show that 0s are written with a slash through them (∅), but the letter O does not have a slash. This is communicated by writing the character as it will be used in the graphic area of the punching instructions. Then in the punch area the programmer indicates which symbol is the alphabetic character (A) and which is the numeric character (N). Other symbols that are often confused because of their similar appearance are the letter I and the number 1, as well as the letter Z and the number 2. Any character that might be confused with another character should be illustrated in the punching instructions area.

COBOL Instructions

There are four specific fields that make up each COBOL instruction. They are the sequence, continuation, COBOL statement, and identification fields. Each of these fields uses specific columns. Each line on the coding form is divided up into 80 small squares. Each of these squares represents one column. Just above the first coding line is a series of small printed numbers that run from 1 through 80, representing the 80 columns of the COBOL instruction.

Sequence field   The sequence field occupies the first six columns of the COBOL instruction. The sequence field data is optional—that is, the COBOL compiler does not require that the sequence field be used. The purpose of the sequence field is to allow the COBOL instruction lines to be numbered so that the sequence of instructions can be checked. The sequence field numbers are very helpful if the instructions are punched into cards which may get out of order or if an editor is used to make corrections on a terminal. Many editors refer to lines by their sequence number. Even though the coding form shows the sequence field subdivided into three positions for a page number and three positions for a line number, sequence numbers may be less than six digits and may appear anywhere in positions 1 through 6.

Continuation field   Column 7 is the continuation field. It is used in two different ways. First, it may be used to indicate the continuation of a nonnumeric **literal** by placing a hyphen (-) in column 7 of the continuation line. Second, the continuation field may be used to indicate that whatever follows is a remark by the programmer. An asterisk (★) makes the line a remark line. A slash (/) may also be used to indicate a remark line, except that it will cause the paper to advance before the remark is printed. This is a convenient way of controlling the format of the printed listing of the source program.

COBOL statement field   The COBOL statement field is the heart of the COBOL instruction. It is the portion of the instruction that really tells the computer what you want it to know or do. The COBOL statement is divided into two areas. They are called **Area A** and **Area B.** As you can see in Figure I-1, Area A consists of columns 8, 9, 10, and 11. Area B is from column 12 through column 72. There are COBOL rules that dictate the kinds of entries that must begin in Area A and those that must begin in Area B. These rules will be discussed later in this supplement.

Identification field   The identification field is another optional field. Its purpose is to provide an identification of the program, and it may be up to 8 characters in length. The same name is entered into every line of the program.

COBOL PROGRAM STRUCTURE

Every programming language has its own unique structure. The structure of a COBOL program tends to be more like English than most other computer languages. This characteristic often results in longer programs than the other languages, but the programs are relatively easy to understand and modify. COBOL programs are divided into units called divisions, sections, paragraphs, and sentences.

Divisions

Every COBOL program is divided into four divisions. They are called the identification, environment, data, and procedure divisions. Each of these divisions has different purposes in the program. Table I-1 summarizes these purposes.

The **identification division** is always the first division in a COBOL program. Its purpose is to identify the name of the program and any other information about the program that would be useful for identification purposes. Such useful information includes the programmer's name, the name of the data processing center, the date that the program was written, the date that the program was compiled, security requirements, and remarks explaining the function of the program. The identification division does not contain any program logic. Its major function is to document the program.

The second division is called the **environment division.** Its function is to describe the environment of the program. Our environment is made up of our

TABLE I-1   **THE COBOL DIVISIONS**

Division	Purpose
Identification	a. Always identifies the program by name
	b. May also identify the author (programmer), installation name, date written, date compiled, security, and remarks
Environment	a. Names the computer systems to be used with the source and object programs
	b. Associates each file used by the program with an input or output device
Data	a. Describes, names, and allocates main memory space to all files, records, and fields used by the program
Procedure	a. Describes all of the logical steps to be performed by the computer

surroundings and the things we live with. The environment of the COBOL program is the computer hardware. This division identifies the computing system to be used with the program and all input and output devices that will be required by the program. If a COBOL program is to be run on a different type of computer, most of the required program changes will be in this division.

The **data division** is the third division of a COBOL program. The purpose of the data division is to assign names and to allocate space within main memory for all files, records, and fields to be used by the program.

The last division is called the **procedure division**. The procedure division contains all of the instructions that the computer is to follow in solving our problem. It contains all of the program logic and is the division that must be planned.

Sections   Sections are subdivisions of divisions. The only division that does not allow sections is the identification division. The environment and data divisions always have sections. The procedure division may have sections, but they are not required.

Paragraphs   Paragraphs are a further breakdown of sections. If there are no sections, paragraphs are a breakdown of the division.

Sentences   The smallest structural unit of a COBOL program is the sentence. The sentence contains the detailed descriptions and procedures of the program.

In summary, sentences are found within paragraphs, paragraphs are found within sections, and sections are found within divisions.

FEEDBACK   **I-1** What is the purpose of the coding form punching instructions?

I-2 What are the fields that make up a COBOL instruction?

I-3 Name the four COBOL divisions in the order in which they appear in a program.

A COBOL EXAMPLE PROGRAM

Because of the English-like wording and the emphasis upon readability of COBOL programs, there seems to be a minimum size for COBOL programs that is much longer than programs written in other languages. Many programmers of other languages joke about the "writer's cramp" that you get from COBOL. However, COBOL is one of the easiest languages to understand and to modify. This chapter will present a COBOL example that contains most of the basic COBOL instructions.

The Problem Statement

The problem that we will solve is as follows. We are to input student data that has been recorded on magnetic disk. This data consists of each student's name, the number of units (or credits) that the student has earned to date, and the student's age. The program is to output a student report that lists the student's name, class standing (first-year student, sophomore, junior, or senior), and age. In addition, the program is to print a final line at the bottom of the report that will indicate the age of the oldest and the youngest student in the file. The report is to include an appropriate title and column headings at the top of each page. It should include data on no more than 50 students on each page of the report.

For this example program, a first-year student is defined as a student who has completed less than 30 units. A sophomore is a student who has completed from 30 to 59 units. A junior has completed from 60 to 89 units, and any student who has completed 90 units or more is classified as a senior. Figure I-2 is an example of this report.

There are many logical approaches to this problem that will produce the required report. The following example is only one way to approach the problem.

COBOL Names

Before we begin a discussion of our COBOL solution to the problem, let's go over one important rule. We will be making up names for the files, records, and fields used by our program. There are some specific rules concerning the makeup of these names. These rules are shown in Table I-2. First, any data name we use must not exceed 30 characters in length. That is a rather generous length that should allow the programmer to make up names that are meaningful

FIGURE I-2
Student report sample output.

```
              STUDENT LISTING (WITH HIGHEST AND LOWEST AGE)

          STUDENT NAME              CLASS STANDING          AGE

          HENRY CRUTCH              SENIOR                  47
          GEORGE HOODSPITH          SOPHOMORE               20
          JOHN JONES                SENIOR                  25
          MARY SMITH                FRESHMAN                18
          MARY ELLEN WINKS          SOPHOMORE               36

    THE OLDEST STUDENT IN THE FILE IS 47.   THE YOUNGEST STUDENT IN THE FILE IS 18.
```

TABLE I-2	**RULES FOR COBOL DATA NAMES**
1	COBOL data names may contain from 1 to 30 characters.
2	Acceptable characters include the alphabetic characters (A-Z), numeric characters (0-9), and the hyphen (-).
3	The name must contain at least one alphabetic character.
4	The name must not contain any embedded blanks (that is, all names must appear to be a single word).

relative to the data. Second, the characters allowed in names are letters (A–Z), numbers (0–9), and the hyphen (-). Third, the name must contain at least one letter. Fourth, all names must be a single word with no blanks between letters or numbers.

The COBOL compiler identifies the end of a word by finding a space. If you want to call a field GROSS PAY (because that is what the data refers to), you are violating the fourth rule—all names must be a single word. GROSSPAY is an acceptable name, but that is difficult for humans to read. The COBOL solution is to call the field GROSS-PAY. Because there are no spaces, it looks like one word to the compiler. Using the hyphen allows programmers to assign names that are easy to understand.

FEEDBACK   **I-4** What is the maximum length of a COBOL data name?
I-5 What are the allowable characters in a data name?

The Identification Division

The first division of a COBOL program is the identification division. As we stated earlier, its purpose is to identify the program and to supply useful information about the program. Figure I-3 is a COBOL coding form containing the identification division for our example program. The identification division must begin with the division heading (IDENTIFICATION DIVISION.). Two things should be noted about this first entry. First, all division names begin in Area A of the COBOL statement—that is, column 8. Second, all division names end with a period. The COBOL compiler uses the period to identify the end of a COBOL sentence.

The identification division has a series of paragraphs that may be used. Each of these paragraph names must also begin in Area A and end with a period. The sentences in each of the paragraphs must be written in Area B of the COBOL statement. Each of the paragraph names has a predefined meaning for the compiler. The programmer may not make up different paragraph names.

Program-ID   The only paragraph that is required by the COBOL compiler is the PROGRAM-ID paragraph. The sentence in this paragraph is the name of the program. The name is made up by the programmer. In this example, the name of the program is STUDENTS. Note that the sentence ends with a period.

Author   The remaining paragraphs of the identification division are optional according to the rules of COBOL. They are commonly used, however, because they provide valuable documentation for the program. The AUTHOR paragraph contains the name of the programmer or programmers who wrote and/ or modified the program. It is often useful to know who wrote the program, so that when changes in the program become necessary, the original programmer—if available—can make them.

Remarks   One of the most important entries in the identification division is not a paragraph but REMARK lines. These lines are used to record the purpose or functions of the program. REMARK lines have an asterisk (*) in column 7.

Other paragraphs   In addition to the paragraphs used in our example program, paragraphs called INSTALLATION, DATE-WRITTEN, DATE-COMPILED, and SECURITY may be used. Many COBOL compilers allow the programmer to use the DATE-COMPILED paragraph name and omit any

FIGURE I-3

Example identification division.

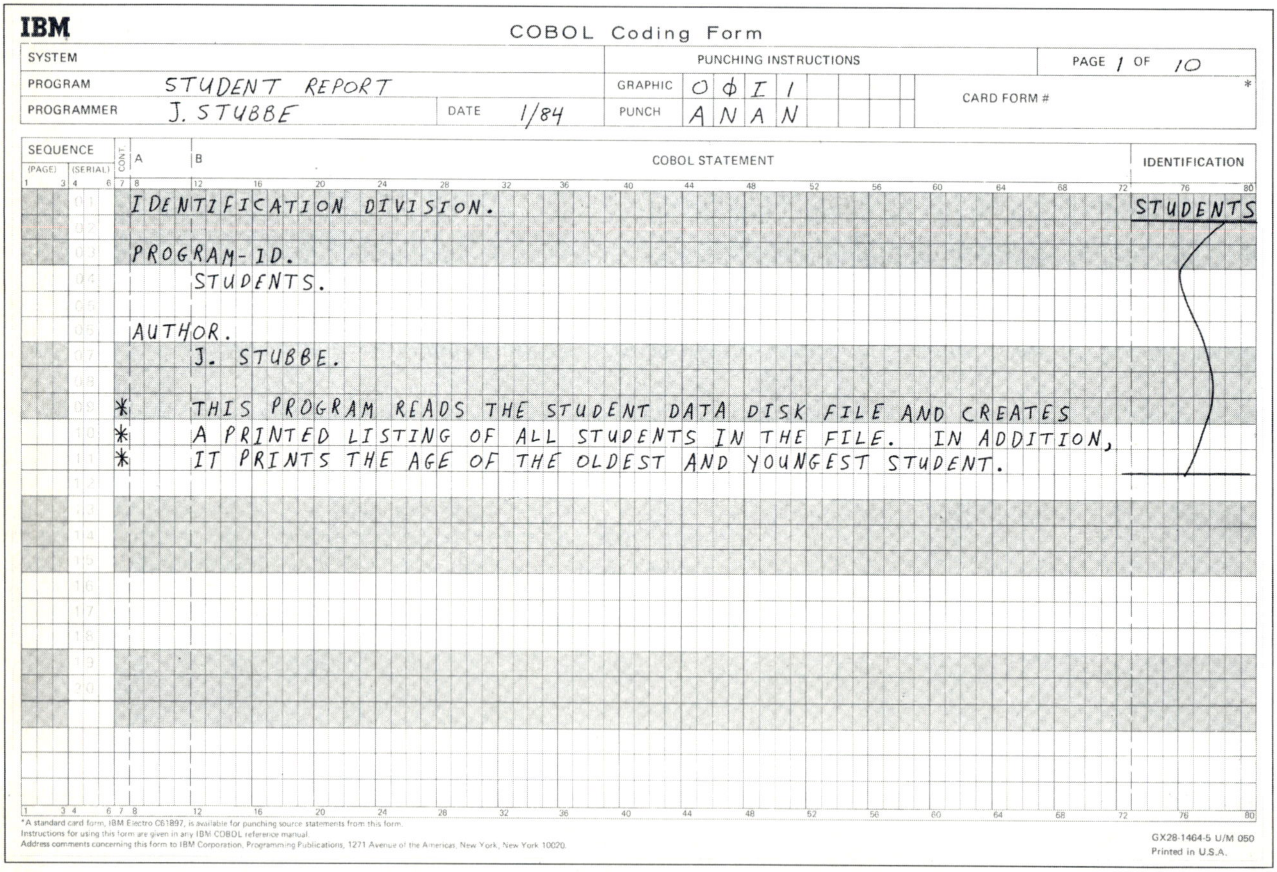

```
IBM                          COBOL  Coding  Form
SYSTEM                                    PUNCHING INSTRUCTIONS           PAGE 1 OF 10
PROGRAM   STUDENT  REPORT          GRAPHIC  O Ø I I        CARD FORM #
PROGRAMMER  J. STUBBE       DATE  1/84  PUNCH  A N A N

SEQUENCE  A  B              COBOL STATEMENT                     IDENTIFICATION

     IDENTIFICATION  DIVISION.                                  STUDENTS

     PROGRAM-ID.
         STUDENTS.

     AUTHOR.
         J. STUBBE.

   * THIS PROGRAM READS THE STUDENT DATA DISK FILE AND CREATES
   * A PRINTED LISTING OF ALL STUDENTS IN THE FILE.  IN ADDITION,
   * IT PRINTS THE AGE OF THE OLDEST AND YOUNGEST STUDENT.
```

*A standard card form, IBM Electro C61897, is available for punching source statements from this form.
Instructions for using this form are given in any IBM COBOL reference manual.
Address comments concerning this form to IBM Corporation, Programming Publications, 1271 Avenue of the Americas, New York, New York 10020.

GX28-1464-5 U/M 050
Printed in U.S.A.

entry within the paragraph. The compiler will insert the appropriate date when the program is compiled. This ensures an appropriate date in this paragraph.

The Environment Division

The environment division deals with the hardware to be used by the program. Our sample program uses two sections within this division—the configuration section and the input-output section. Figure I-4 illustrates the environment division entries for our program.

The configuration section The configuration section consists of two paragraphs—SOURCE-COMPUTER and OBJECT-COMPUTER. The purpose of this section is to name the computer system that will be used with the source program and the computer system that will be used with the object or machine-language program after compilation. In our example program, the computer system being used is an IBM System 34 computer. It will be both the source computer and the object computer.

FIGURE I-4

Example environment division.

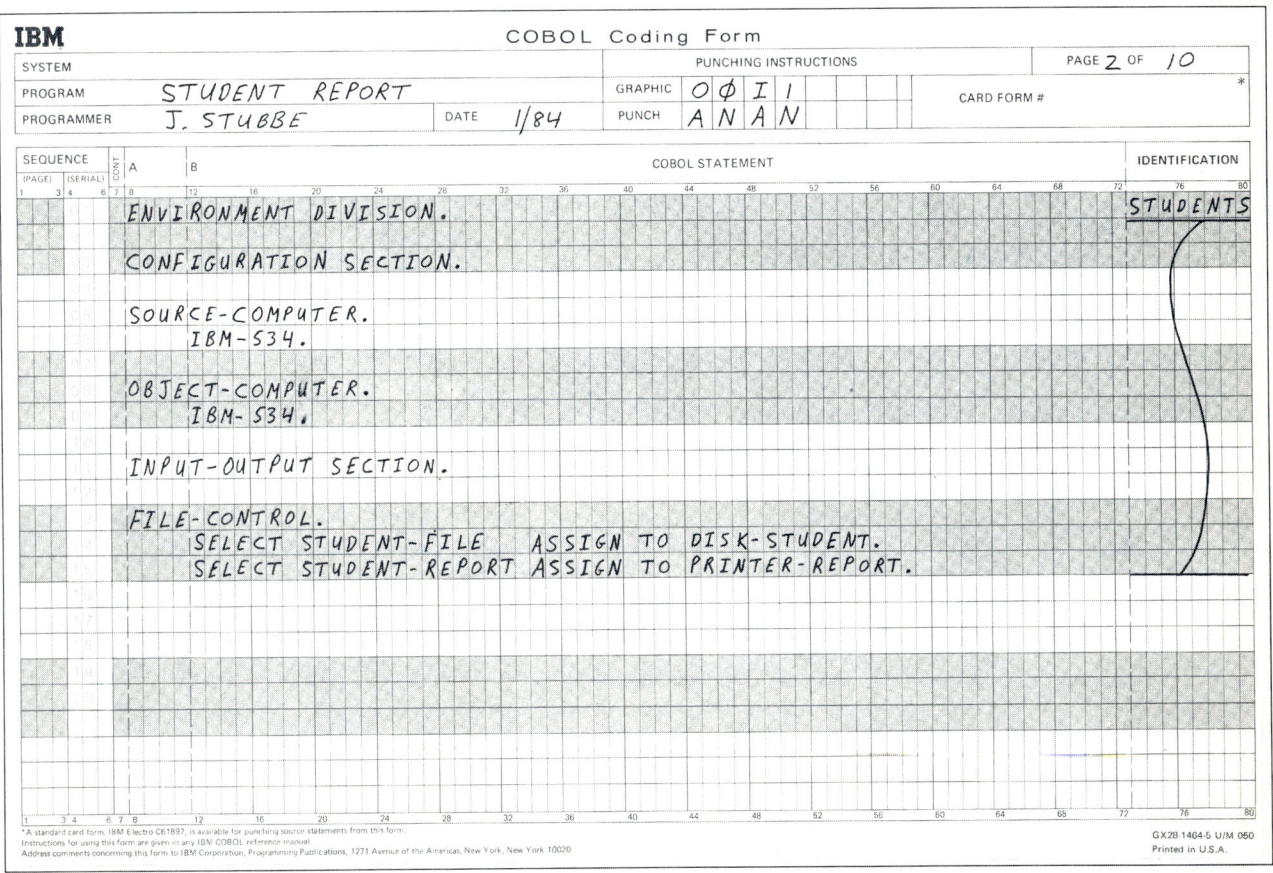

The input-output section   The second section is the input-output section. The FILE-CONTROL paragraph used in this section has the purpose of associating file names to particular input or output devices. In our example program, we have two data files—an input file of data on magnetic disk, which we are calling STUDENT-FILE, and an output file called STUDENT-REPORT, which is to be outputted on the computer's line printer. In the example FILE-CON-TROL paragraph, files are assigned to the magnetic disk and the line printer. In the procedure division of our program, when we say to input a STUDENT-FILE record, the computer will know that it should input from the magnetic disk because of these FILE-CONTROL entries.

The Data Division

The purpose of the data division is to allocate space for and assign names to all files, records, and fields that are to be used by the program. Remember, all names that we assign must be no longer than 30 characters and may contain only letters, numbers, and hyphens. Our example program uses two data division sections—the file section and the working-storage section.

File section   The file section is used to define all of the files, records within those files, and fields within those records. Therefore, all file, record, and field names directly associated with input or output operations are defined in this section.

Figure I-5 illustrates the file section for our example program. The first entry in the section is the section name. Note that it begins in Area A and ends with a period. Each file is defined with an FD (file description) entry. The letters FD must begin in Area A. All other entries in the FD must be in Area B. The purpose of the FD entry is to name the file and to describe characteristics of the file. In our example program, the first file is named STUDENT-FILE. The characteristics of the file are that each record within the file is 40 characters in length, there is a record at the beginning of the file to act as a label for the file, and the records that make up the file are called STUDENT-RECORD. Files that are recorded on magnetic tape or magnetic disk may have a special record at the beginning of the file to identify the file. This record is called the label record. If the label record is present, the programmer will code LABEL RECORD IS STANDARD in the FD for the file. This entry indicates that the label record is there and that its layout is standard for that computer. If there is no label record present, the entry LABEL RECORD IS OMITTED is used. The last entry is a description of the record identified as the data record. The data record description follows an outline format. The first level is the 01 (or record) level. It is the highest category in our outline format. The 01 must be in Area A. Levels 02–49 are increasingly detailed breakdowns of the record. That is, 02s are subdivisions of 01, 03s are subdivisions of 02, and so on. As you can see in Figure I-5 the input record called STUDENT-RECORD is broken down into five fields. After each level indicator of 02, we have coded the name of the field. Two of the fields are named FILLER. This is a special COBOL word that is assigned to record areas that will not be referred to again in the program. FILLER is used to account for all fields that are not named (because it is not necessary to refer to them in the program).

In addition to naming the record and its fields, we must communicate to the compiler the field size and how the data in the field is to be treated. This data description is made with a **picture clause.** Any record or field that is broken down into smaller units is called a **group item.** In our example, STUDENT-RECORD is broken down into five smaller units. STUDENT-RECORD, therefore, is a group item. Any record or field that is not further broken down is called an **elementary item.** STUDENT-NAME-IN, UNITS-IN, AGE-IN, and the FILLERs are all examples of elementary items. All elementary items must have a picture clause. Group items must not have a picture clause.

There are two commonly used picture-clause entries—X and 9. A picture of 9 indicates that the field is to be handled numerically. That is, decimal positions may have to be accounted for, plus and minus signs may be generated,

FIGURE I-5

Example data division file section.

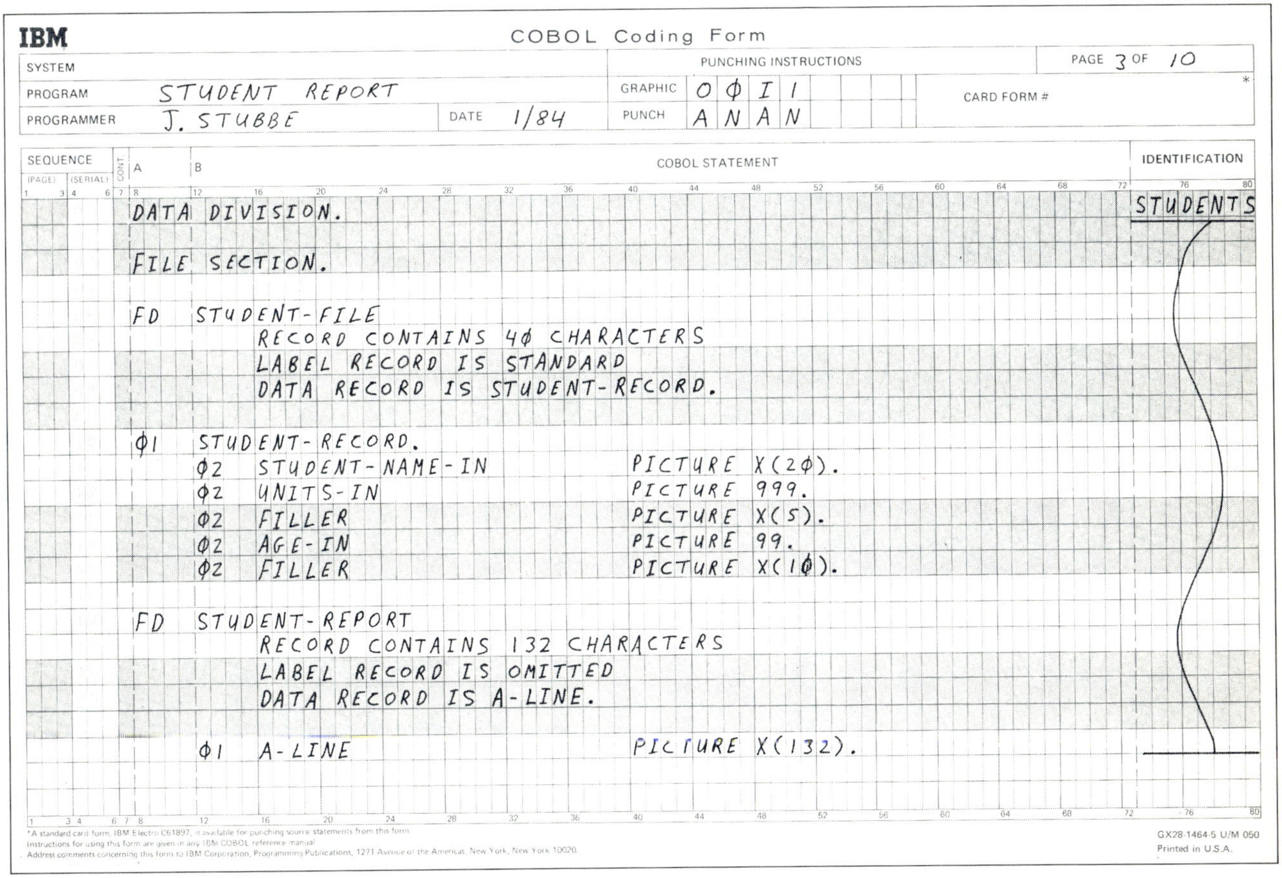
IBM COBOL Coding Form

SYSTEM | PUNCHING INSTRUCTIONS | PAGE 3 OF 10

PROGRAM STUDENT REPORT | GRAPHIC O Ø I 1 | CARD FORM #

PROGRAMMER J. STUBBE | DATE 1/84 | PUNCH A N A N

SEQUENCE (PAGE) (SERIAL) | CONT. | A | B | COBOL STATEMENT | IDENTIFICATION STUDENTS

```
DATA DIVISION.

FILE SECTION.

FD  STUDENT-FILE
        RECORD CONTAINS 4Ø CHARACTERS
        LABEL RECORD IS STANDARD
        DATA RECORD IS STUDENT-RECORD.

Ø1  STUDENT-RECORD.
    Ø2  STUDENT-NAME-IN             PICTURE X(2Ø).
    Ø2  UNITS-IN                    PICTURE 999.
    Ø2  FILLER                      PICTURE X(5).
    Ø2  AGE-IN                      PICTURE 99.
    Ø2  FILLER                      PICTURE X(1Ø).

FD  STUDENT-REPORT
        RECORD CONTAINS 132 CHARACTERS
        LABEL RECORD IS OMITTED
        DATA RECORD IS A-LINE.

    Ø1  A-LINE                      PICTURE X(132).
```

*A standard card form, IBM Electro C61897, is available for punching source statements from this form.
Instructions for using this form are given in any IBM COBOL reference manual.
Address comments concerning this form to IBM Corporation, Programming Publications, 1271 Avenue of the Americas, New York, New York 10020.

GX28-1464-5 U/M 050
Printed in U.S.A.

and data which are shorter in length than their fields are to be aligned at the right-hand end of the field. Fields with a picture of X are alphanumeric items or fields. These fields will not have signs or decimal points. Data that are shorter than their fields are to be aligned at the left-hand end of the field. Each 9 or X indicates one position. Therefore, PICTURE 999 indicates a numeric field of three positions or digits. In our example program, UNITS-IN is a numeric field of three digits and requires three positions in the input record. PICTURE X(20) is the same as writing a string of 20 X's. Picture X(20), therefore, indicates an alphanumeric field using 20 positions in the input record. The record is always described from left to right. Because the field STUDENT-NAME-IN is the first field mentioned, the 20 positions used for the field will be positions 1–20. The field UNITS-IN is three digits long and is described immediately after STUDENT-NAME-IN. Therefore, UNITS-IN is in positions 21–23. The third field is a FILLER that is five positions long. The next five positions would be 24–28. The remaining positions are defined in the same way. The total of all of the picture clauses must equal the record size stated in the FD entry.

The output file in our example program is called STUDENT-REPORT. This file was associated with the line printer in the environment division. The entire printed report is the file. Each line of the report is a record. In this example, the record is 132 print positions long. The name given to the line or record is A-LINE. In this example, the output record is not broken down into smaller units. It is, therefore, an elementary item with a picture clause. It should be noted that modern COBOL compilers allow the programmer to abbreviate PICTURE as PIC.

The working-storage section   The working-storage section is used to describe records and fields that are not directly associated with files. These fields and records fall into two categories—independent fields and record descriptions. Independent fields are single fields that stand alone and are not associated with any other field. As an example our program will be using a field called ALL-FINISHED to control the number of times we process input records. It is not used in conjunction with any other field. Record descriptions of output lines (such as title lines, detail lines, total lines, etc.) are commonly included in working storage. One advantage of defining fields within the working-storage section is that elementary fields may have a **value clause.** The value clause assigns a beginning value to the field. This value, of course, may be changed during the running of the program.

Five independent fields are used in our example program (see Figure I-6). Two (ALL-FINISHED and SPACING) are used for logic control. The other three (HIGH-AGE, LOW-AGE, and PRINTED-LINES) are result fields. To identify these functions, group levels of CONTROL-FIELDS and RESULT-FIELDS have been assigned. Using a group name to identify common functions of independent fields makes debugging and program modification easier. Note that ALL-FINISHED has been given a beginning value of "no," HIGH-AGE a value of "O," and LOW-AGE a beginning value of "99," using value clauses. We will discuss these fields in the section on procedures division.

The value given as the beginning value of a field must be consistent with the field's picture clause. That is, if the PICTURE is 9, the value must be numeric characters (0–9); if the PICTURE is X, any character except the apostrophe may be used. These values are called **literals.** Alphanumeric literals (PICTURE X) must be enclosed by apostrophes. Because alphanumeric literals have their beginnings and endings identified by apostrophes, the apostrophe itself cannot be part of the literal.

The working-storage section also contains group items that describe the output lines. Figures I-7 and I-8 show four group items that will be used in our example program. Each of these four groups has PICTUREs that total 132, the same as the length of one printed line. The groups in this example

FIGURE I-6
Working storage fields.

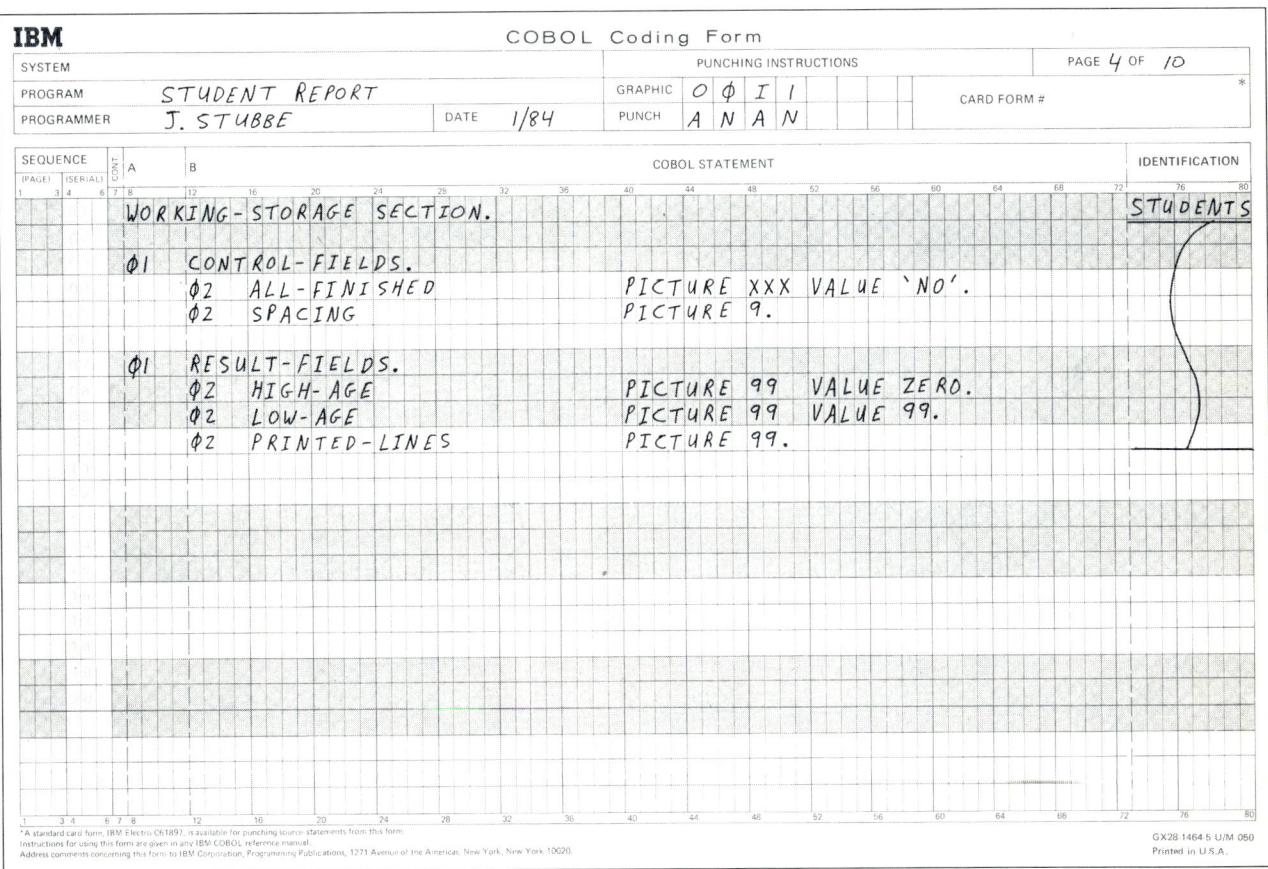

are called TITLE-LINE, COLUMN-HEADINGS, DETAIL-LINE, and AGE-LINE. If you look back to Figure I-2, which showed an example output for our program, you can see that each of these groups represents a different type of output line.

The first group, TITLE-LINE, has three elementary fields. All three have the name of FILLER, because these individual fields will not be referenced in the procedure of the program. Remember that records are defined from left to right. So the field's FILLER of 44 positions with a value of spaces will make up the left margin of the title line. The second FILLER, with a length of 45, has a value that will be used as the report title. The last FILLER in the group represents 43 positions with a value of spaces to be used as the right margin. The first and last FILLER, being nearly equal, will center the title value on the page.

The second group, COLUMN-HEADINGS, has seven elementary fields. As in the title line, all are named FILLER. This line begins with 42 positions for a left margin, a value of "student name" as the first column heading, 14

FIGURE I-7
Working-storage title-line and column-headings.

IBM COBOL Coding Form

SYSTEM | PUNCHING INSTRUCTIONS | PAGE 5 OF 10
PROGRAM STUDENT REPORT | GRAPHIC O Ø I 1 | CARD FORM # *
PROGRAMMER J. STUBBE | DATE 1/84 | PUNCH A N A N

SEQUENCE (PAGE) (SERIAL) | CONT. | A | B | COBOL STATEMENT | IDENTIFICATION

```
       Ø1  TITLE-LINE.                                                  STUDENTS
           Ø2  FILLER                      PICTURE X(44) VALUE SPACES.
           Ø2  FILLER                      PICTURE X(45)
               VALUE 'STUDENT LISTING (WITH HIGHEST AND LOWEST AGE)'.
           Ø2  FILLER                      PICTURE X(43) VALUE SPACES.

       Ø1  COLUMN-HEADINGS.
           Ø2  FILLER                      PICTURE X(42) VALUE SPACES.
           Ø2  FILLER                      PICTURE X(12)
               VALUE 'STUDENT NAME'.
           Ø2  FILLER                      PICTURE X(14) VALUE SPACES.
           Ø2  FILLER                      PICTURE X(14)
               VALUE 'CLASS STANDING'.
           Ø2  FILLER                      PICTURE X(1Ø) VALUE SPACES.
           Ø2  FILLER                      PICTURE XXX VALUE 'AGE'.
           Ø2  FILLER                      PICTURE X(37) VALUE SPACES.
```

*A standard card form, IBM Electro C61897, is available for punching source statements from this form.
Instructions for using this form are given in any IBM COBOL reference manual.
Address comments concerning this form to IBM Corporation, Programming Publications, 1271 Avenue of the Americas, New York, New York 10020.

GX28-1464-5 U/M 050
Printed in U.S.A.

spaces to separate the columns, the next column heading, and so on, until both margins, the actual column headings, and the spaces between the column headings have all been defined.

The third group, DETAIL-LINE, describes the line that will contain a student's name, class standing, and age. The first filler is 38 spaces to be used as left margin. The second field is a 20-position field called STUDENT-NAME-OUT. This field is the same size and picture as the STUDENT-NAME-IN in the input record. The third field represents spaces between columns. The fourth field (CLASS-STANDING-OUT) is 9 positions in length and holds the name of the class for the student. The field is 9 positions long in order to allow for the longest class name—sophomore. The fifth field represents 13 more spaces between the columns. The sixth field (AGE-OUT) is a field of 2 spaces for the student's age. The last field represents the right margin.

The last group, AGE-LINE, describes the last line to be printed on the report. It will consist of 27 spaces of left margin and the value "the oldest student in the file is." Then we have a field (HIGH-AGE-OUT) holding the

FIGURE I-8

Working-storage detail-line and age-line.

```
01  DETAIL-LINE.
    02  FILLER                   PICTURE X(38) VALUE SPACES.
    02  STUDENT-NAME-OUT         PICTURE X(20).
    02  FILLER                   PICTURE X(13) VALUE SPACES.
    02  CLASS-STANDING-OUT       PICTURE X(9).
    02  FILLER                   PICTURE X(13) VALUE SPACES.
    02  AGE-OUT                  PICTURE 99.
    02  FILLER                   PICTURE X(37) VALUE SPACES.

01  AGE-LINE
    02  FILLER                   PICTURE X(27) VALUE SPACES.
    02  FILLER                   PICTURE X(34)
        VALUE 'THE OLDEST STUDENT IN THE FILES IS '.
    02  HIGH-AGE-OUT             PICTURE 99.
    02  FILLER                   PICTURE X(39)
        VALUE '.  THE YOUNGEST STUDENT IN THE FILE IS '.
    02  LOW-AGE-OUT              PICTURE 99.
    02  FILLER                   PICTURE X(28) VALUE '.'.
```

COBOL Coding Form

SYSTEM

PROGRAM STUDENT REPORT

PROGRAMMER J. STUBBE   DATE 1/84

PUNCHING INSTRUCTIONS

GRAPHIC O Ø I I

PUNCH A N A N

PAGE 6 OF 10

CARD FORM #

IDENTIFICATION: STUDENTS

highest age we found in the file. The second half of the line consists of spaces between columns, a literal value for the youngest student, the lowest age, and a right margin. Each of these four groups has picture clauses that, when added together, total 132 positions.

FEEDBACK

I-6 What is the purpose of the picture clause? What do X and 9 represent?

I-7 Explain the difference between an elementary item and a group data item.

I-8 What is the purpose of the value clause? Where may it be used?

The Procedure Division

So far, in our example program, we have identified the program, assigned hardware to the files, and described all the files, records, and fields to be used by the program. The last division is called the procedure division. It contains the logical procedures that we have planned for our problem solution.

In our example program, our procedure division does not use any sections. All paragraph names begin in Area A, and all sentences within the paragraph are in Area B of the COBOL statement. The procedure division for this example has been written in what is called a structured format. The general idea of a structured format is to group logical activities so that the program is easy to follow and easy to modify.

A program is structured by breaking it up into logical groups of instructions, with each group performing one function in the program. These groups of instructions are called modules. The first module in the program contains the main logic. The instructions in this first module often "call in" other, more detailed modules. The COBOL instruction that is used to call in another module is called the PERFORM statement. If we have coded PERFORM 3-WRITE-OLDEST-AND-YOUNGEST, the computer will perform (execute) the instructions found in the paragraph called 3-WRITE-OLDEST-AND-YOUNGEST and then return to the instruction following the PERFORM.

Another form of the PERFORM statement is called the PERFORM-UNTIL. It will cause the named paragraph to be performed over and over again until a specific condition exists. An example is PERFORM 2-PROCESS-ING UNTIL ALL-FINISHED = 'YES'. This instruction will cause the instructions in 2-PROCESSING to be performed over and over until the field called ALL-FINISHED has a value of "yes." COBOL PERFORMs are flow-charted as predefined processes.

Our example COBOL program's main logic paragraph is called 0-MAIN-LINE. Figure I-9 is a flowchart describing this main paragraph. COBOL requires that an instruction called the OPEN must be executed before any file can be used. Its purpose is to declare the file as an input or an output file, to handle file labels (if the data division FD entries indicate the presence of a label record), and to make the file available for processing. As you will see, when we are finished with a file, we must execute a statement called a CLOSE. This flowchart does not give much information about the details, but it does

FIGURE I-9

Flowchart for student report program's main logic.

START

INITIAL-IZATION

TITLE AND HEADINGS

PROCESS RECORDS UNTIL FINISHED

PRINT OLDEST AND YOUNGEST

CLOSE FILES

STOP

give an overview of the program logic. The two symbols that indicate procedures must be defined in more detail later.

Figure I-10 illustrates the coding for this main logic paragraph. The first entry in the procedure division must be the name of the division. The second entry is the name of our main paragraph. We have called it 0-MAINLINE. The first instruction in this paragraph is a PERFORM instruction to execute a paragraph 1-INITIALIZATION. A PERFORM instruction causes the instructions within the named paragraph to be executed and then returns to the instruction following the PERFORM instruction. The paragraph 1-INITIALIZATION is used to accomplish any function that must be done early in our program logic and done only once. One such function is to open the file called STUDENT-FILE as an input file and the file called STUDENT-REPORT as an output file. The second instruction causes a title line and column headings to be printed on the first page. The third instruction indicates that at this point in the program, we are to perform the instructions in a paragraph called 2-PROCESSING. It also states that we will repeatedly perform the paragraph

FIGURE I-10

Coding for student report program's main logic.

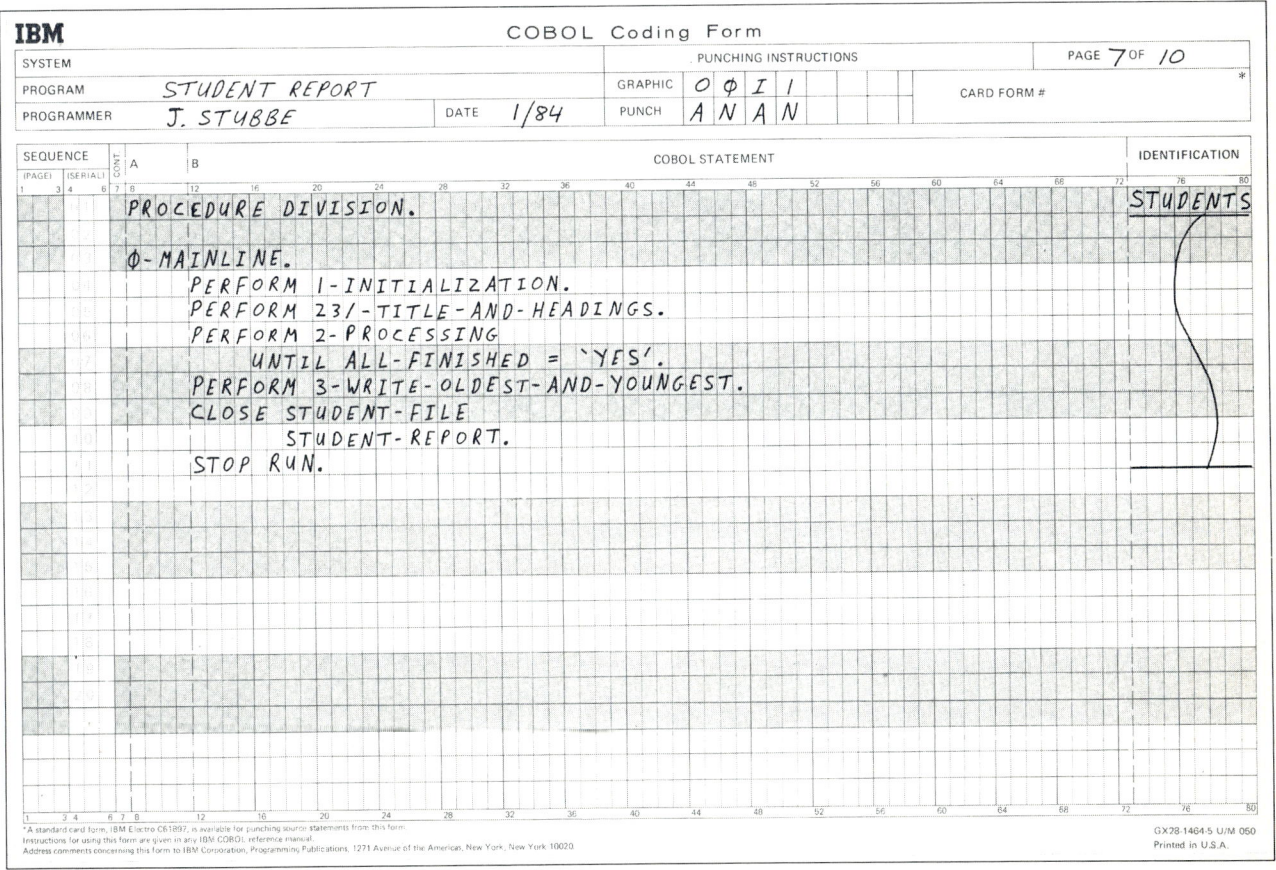

until a field called ALL-FINISHED has a value equal to "yes." As you will recall, ALL-FINISHED is a field that we defined in the working-storage section of our data division. It was assigned a beginning value of "no." We will look at the details within the paragraph 2-PROCESSING shortly.

The last PERFORM indicates that we will perform a paragraph called 3-WRITE-OLDEST-AND-YOUNGEST. This procedure will set up and output the last line of our report. The details of this paragraph will also be discussed later. Next, the two files are closed, and the running of the program is stopped. The programming technique used in this program calls for each paragraph to begin with a number. This makes it easier for us to find the paragraph names if we must use the source program listing at a later time. In addition, the mainline is numbered 0. All paragraphs referred to within the mainline have a single-digit number—in this example, 1, 2, and 3. As you will see, all paragraphs referred to in paragraphs 1, 2, and 3 will have a two-digit number. That is, all paragraphs performed from paragraph 1 will be numbered 11-, 12-, and so on. All paragraphs performed from paragraph 2 will be numbered 21-, 22-, and so on. All paragraphs performed by two-digit paragraphs will have three digits, and so on. Using this programming technique, anyone studying the procedure division will know that a single-digit paragraph name is being performed from the 0-MAINLINE, all two-digit paragraphs are performed from a single-digit paragraph, and so on.

The paragraph 0-MAINLINE contains an exception to this standard. The second PERFORM instruction refers to a paragraph called 231-TITLE-AND-HEADINGS. The 231- would indicate that the PERFORM statement was in paragraph 23 rather than the mainline. The reason for this exception is that the paragraph 231-TITLE-AND-HEADINGS is also performed in paragraph 23-WRITE-A-LINE. Since the title and column headings will be printed only once from the mainline and may be printed several times from the lower-level paragraph, we gave the paragraph a heading of 231- rather than a single digit.

Figure I-11 is the flowchart for the three procedures referred to in the 0-MAINLINE paragraph. The first flowchart describes the opening of the files and the reading of the first record of the input file. It is common in structured programming to read the first record in an initialization paragraph and to read the second record on with a read statement at the end of the detail processing paragraph. The second flowchart in Figure I-11 describes the logic of 2-PROCESSING. In this paragraph three additional routines will be performed. The first will be to move the appropriate fields to the detail line. The second procedure will determine if the age of the student in the record being processed is a new high age or a new low age. The third procedure will output the detail line. The last step will be to read the next record. If a last-record indicator was inputted, "yes" will be moved to a field called ALL-FINISHED. Remember, this procedure was to be repeated until the field ALL-FINISHED has a value of "yes." We now see that ALL-FINISHED will have a value of "yes" only after the last record has been read.

The RETURN will return control to the mainline PERFORM, where

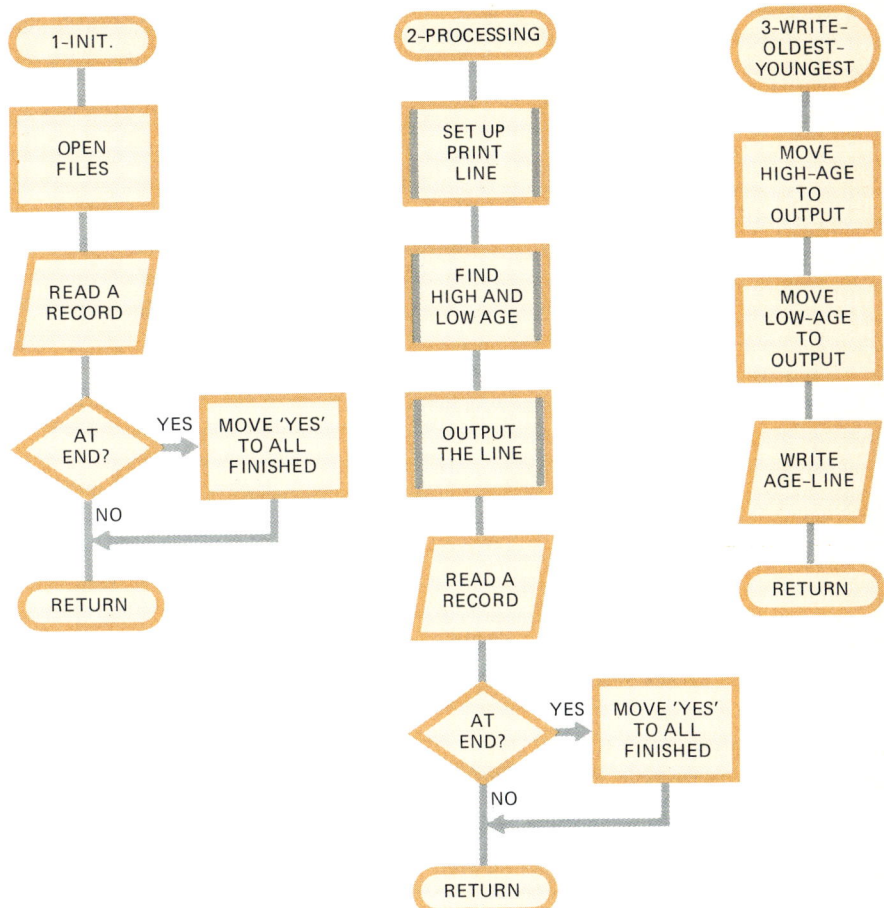

FIGURE I-11

Flowcharts for student report program's processing and oldest-youngest output routines.

ALL-FINISHED will be checked for a value of "yes." If ALL-FINISHED does *not* have a value of "yes," this procedure will be repeated. The third flowchart in Figure I-11 are the details of the third procedure of the mainline. The first step is to move the value in the HIGH-AGE field to the appropriate AGE-LINE field. The second step is to move the LOW-AGE field value to the appropriate AGE-LINE field. The last step is to output the AGE-LINE and return to the mainline.

Figure I-12 is the coding for these three procedures. The first three instructions are PERFORMs, which will each execute another paragraph. Note that all three paragraphs being performed in paragraph 2 begin with a 2-. This relates the paragraph being performed to the paragraph that does the PERFORM. The last instruction is a READ statement. As you can see, the READ statement includes the logic of both the inputting of a record and the at-end decision. If the end-of-file record is inputted, the value "yes" will be moved to the field called ALL-FINISHED. Since this is the last instruction in the paragraph, control will return to the PERFORM-UNTIL in the mainline where the value in ALL-FINISHED will be compared to the value "yes." If they are not equal, the paragraph 2-PROCESSING will be performed again.

Paragraph 3-WRITE-OLDEST-AND-YOUNGEST is the third routine to be performed from the mainline. The first step in this paragraph is to move the value of the field HIGH-AGE (result field) to HIGH-AGE-OUT (in the line AGE-LINE). The second instruction does the same thing, but for the lowest age. The last instruction causes the line AGE-LINE to be outputted. The format of this instruction is always to write the name of the record associated with the output file in the file section—in this example, A-LINE. FROM AGE-LINE causes the data in the AGE-LINE group to be moved to the output record A-LINE prior to printing the line. The last part of the instruction indicates that the line will be written after the paper in the printer has been advanced two lines. That will provide the double space between the last detail line and the AGE-LINE on the report.

FIGURE I-12
Coding for student report program's processing and oldest-youngest output routines.

IBM COBOL Coding Form

SYSTEM
PROGRAM STUDENT REPORT
PROGRAMMER J. STUBBE DATE 1/84
PUNCHING INSTRUCTIONS: GRAPHIC / PUNCH
PAGE 8 OF 10
CARD FORM #

```
       1-INITIALIZATION.                                               STUDENTS
           OPEN INPUT  STUDENT-FILE
                OUTPUT STUDENT-REPORT.
           READ STUDENT-FILE RECORD
               AT END
                   MOVE 'YES' TO ALL-FINISHED.

       2-PROCESSING.
           PERFORM 21-SET-UP-PRINT-LINE.
           PERFORM 22-TEST-FOR-HIGH-LOW-AGE.
           PERFORM 23-WRITE-A-LINE.
           READ STUDENT-FILE RECORD
               AT END
                   MOVE 'YES' TO ALL-FINISHED.

       3-WRITE-OLDEST-AND-YOUNGEST.
           MOVE HIGH-AGE TO HIGH-AGE-OUT.
           MOVE LOW-AGE TO LOW-AGE-OUT.
           WRITE A-LINE FROM AGE-LINE
               AFTER ADVANCING 2 LINES.
```

*A standard card form, IBM Electro C61897, is available for punching source statements from this form.
Instructions for using this form are given in any IBM COBOL reference manual.
Address comments concerning this form to IBM Corporation, Programming Publications, 1271 Avenue of the Americas, New York, New York 10020.
GX28-1464-5 U/M 050
Printed in U.S.A.

2-Processing details   In the paragraph called 2-PROCESSING, three procedures are to be performed—to set up the print line, to test for a new high or low age, and to output the detail line.

Figure I-13 is the flowchart for these three procedures. The first of these procedures is to set up the print line. The first step in that procedure is to

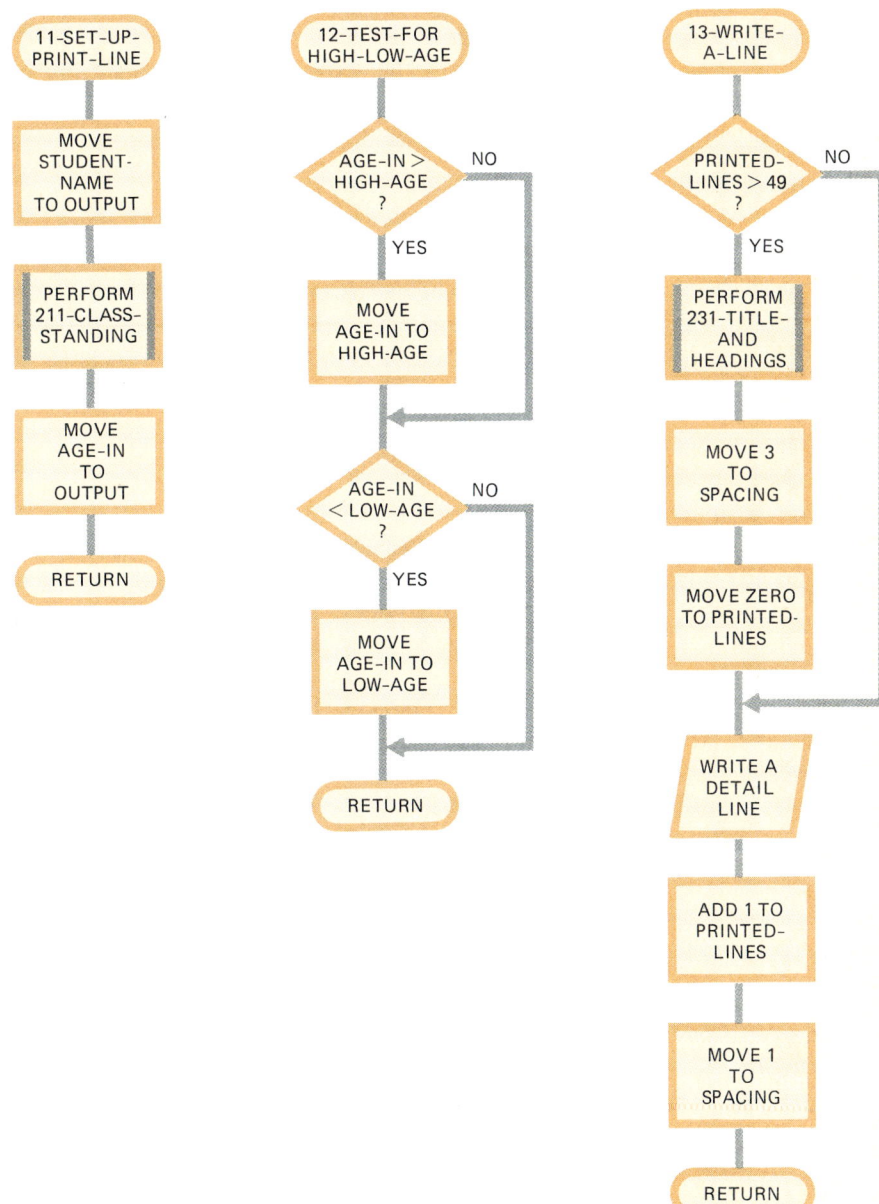

FIGURE I-13

Flowcharts for set-up, test for high-low age, and write a line routines.

move the student's name from the input record to the detail-line output record. The second step is to determine the class standing of the student. Remember, the input record data includes the number of units that the student has completed. The program logic must determine the class standing on the basis of the units completed. This determination is a procedure to be performed called 211-CLASS-STANDING. The third step is to move the student's age from the input record to the output record. This completes the setting up of the print line, and the logic now returns to 2-PROCESSING.

The second procedure is to find out whether or not the record being processed contains an age that is higher than the highest age processed so far or is lower than the lowest age processed so far. The first step in this procedure is to compare the age in the input record to the working-storage field called HIGH-AGE. HIGH-AGE is the field that will eventually be printed out as the highest age. Remember that HIGH-AGE was given a beginning value of 0 in the data division. If the input age is greater than HIGH-AGE, the input age is to be moved to the HIGH-AGE field. If it is not greater than HIGH-AGE, we go directly to the next decision. The second decision is to find out whether or not the age in the input record is lower than the LOW-AGE field. If it is, the input age is moved to the LOW-AGE field. If it is not less than LOW-AGE, we go to the end of the routine which returns us to 2-PROCESSING.

The third routine is to output the detail line. It also checks to see if title and column heading lines are required and causes them to be printed when necessary. The first step is to determine if we need a title and column headings. The first PRINTED-LINES is used to count the number of detail lines printed on a page. We have decided that we want a maximum of 50 lines on each page. If PRINTED-LINES has a value greater than 49, we have printed 50 lines and the title and column heading routine is to be performed. A value of 3 is to be moved to the spacing field (to cause a triple space on the next detail line), and the PRINTED-LINES field is set back to 0, in order to count the lines on the next page. If the PRINTED-LINES field is not greater than 49, these three steps will be skipped.

The next steps are to output the detail line, add 1 to the PRINTED-LINES field, and move 1 to SPACING (to give single spacing on the next detail line). The logic then returns to the 2-PROCESSING routine.

The COBOL code for this logic is shown in Figure I-14. In the routine to test for a new high or low age, we have two decisions written as IF statements. Each of these instructions is written with the word IF, and then a condition is stated. If the condition does exist (if the condition statement is true), the statement following the condition is executed. If you wish, you may have more than one statement to be executed if the condition is true. In our example, if the condition AGE-IN IS GREATER THAN HIGH-AGE is true, AGE-IN will be moved to the HIGH-AGE field. If the condition in the IF statement is not true, the computer will skip to the next sentence. In routine 23- we have an IF statement that requires three statements be executed if the condition is true. These statements are indented for readability.

The second sentence in routine 23- is to output the detail line. The last portion of the sentence, AFTER ADVANCING SPACING, controls the vertical spacing of our output. It will space the paper a number of lines equal to the value in the field SPACING. That is, if SPACING has a value of 1, it will advance a single space; a value of 2 will cause a double space; and so on.

The last two instructions add 1 to the number of printed lines and set up single spacing for the next time we output a detail line.

Third-level routines Paragraphs 21- and 23- contain PERFORM instructions for more detailed procedures. The first one is paragraph 211-, which determines the student's class standing, and the second is paragraph 231-, which executes the printing of title and column-heading lines.

Figure I-15 contains the flowcharts for these two procedures. The determination of class standing requires a series of decisions. The first decision is to determine whether or not the number of units completed by the student is fewer than 30. If this is true (the student has completed fewer than 30 units),

FIGURE I-14

Coding for set-up, test for high-low age, and write a line routines.

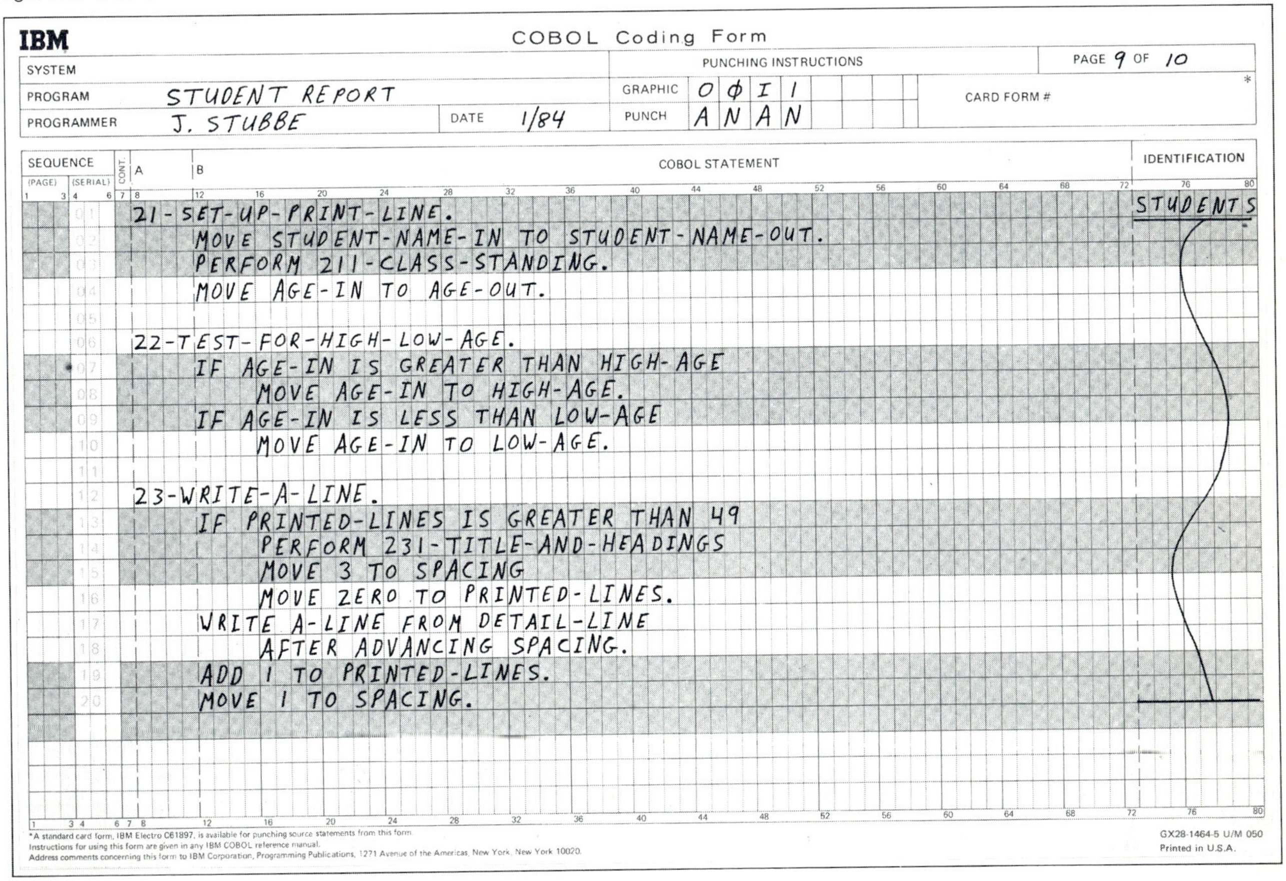

```
IBM                              COBOL Coding Form                    PAGE 9 OF 10

SYSTEM                                    PUNCHING INSTRUCTIONS
PROGRAM      STUDENT REPORT        GRAPHIC  O  Ø  I  I        CARD FORM #
PROGRAMMER   J. STUBBE    DATE 1/84  PUNCH  A  N  A  N

SEQUENCE  CONT                COBOL STATEMENT                      IDENTIFICATION

01  21-SET-UP-PRINT-LINE.                                          STUDENTS
02      MOVE STUDENT-NAME-IN TO STUDENT-NAME-OUT.
03      PERFORM 211-CLASS-STANDING.
04      MOVE AGE-IN TO AGE-OUT.
05
06  22-TEST-FOR-HIGH-LOW-AGE.
07      IF AGE-IN IS GREATER THAN HIGH-AGE
08          MOVE AGE-IN TO HIGH-AGE.
09      IF AGE-IN IS LESS THAN LOW-AGE
10          MOVE AGE-IN TO LOW-AGE.
11
12  23-WRITE-A-LINE.
13      IF PRINTED-LINES IS GREATER THAN 49
14          PERFORM 231-TITLE-AND-HEADINGS
15          MOVE 3 TO SPACING
16          MOVE ZERO TO PRINTED-LINES.
17      WRITE A-LINE FROM DETAIL-LINE
18          AFTER ADVANCING SPACING.
19      ADD 1 TO PRINTED-LINES.
20      MOVE 1 TO SPACING.
```

*A standard card form, IBM Electro C61897, is available for punching source statements from this form.
Instructions for using this form are given in any IBM COBOL reference manual.
Address comments concerning this form to IBM Corporation, Programming Publications, 1271 Avenue of the Americas, New York, New York 10020.

GX28-1464-5 U/M 050
Printed in U.S.A.

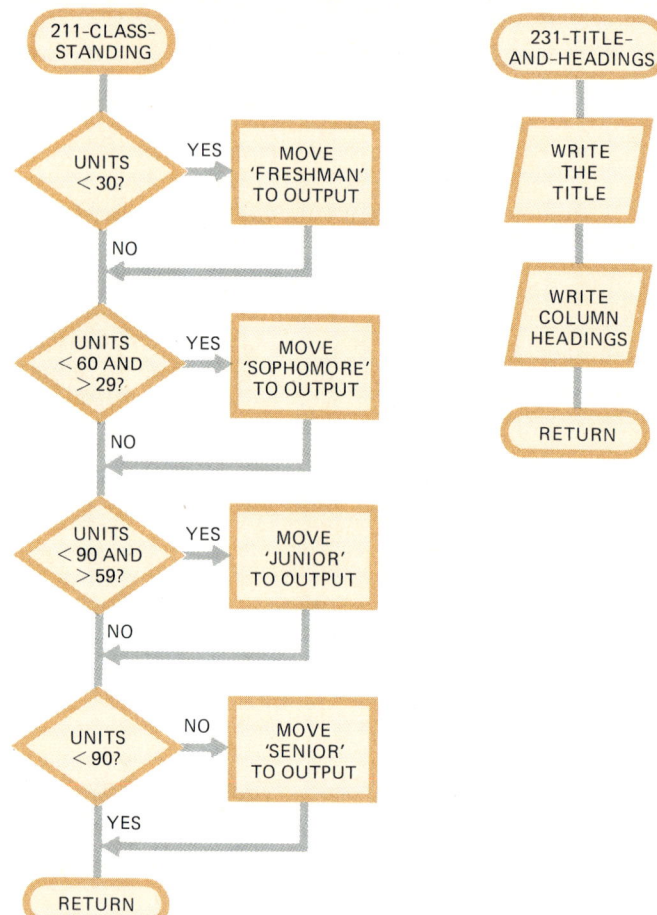

FIGURE I-15

Flowcharts for class standing and title/headings routines.

we will move the word FRESHMAN to the output detail line before going on to the next decision. If the condition is false, we will go on to the next decision. The second decision is to determine whether the number of units is between 30 and 59. If the number of units is between 30 and 59, we will move SOPHOMORE to the detail line. We will then determine whether the number units is between 60 and 89. If this condition is true, we will move JUNIOR to the detail line. The last decision is to see if the number of units is less than 90. If it is not less, we will move SENIOR to the detail line. The last step is to return to paragraph 21-. The second procedure is to print a title and the column heading line.

Figure I-16 is the COBOL code for our last two routines. The instructions in paragraph 211- are the same as the IF instructions we have seen before,

```
IBM                              COBOL Coding Form

SYSTEM                                      PUNCHING INSTRUCTIONS          PAGE 10 OF 10
PROGRAM      STUDENT REPORT          GRAPHIC  O Ø I I    CARD FORM #              *
PROGRAMMER   J. STUBBE      DATE  1/84   PUNCH  A N A N

SEQUENCE  C  A  B            COBOL STATEMENT                      IDENTIFICATION
(PAGE)(SERIAL)                                                    STUDENTS

211-CLASS-STANDING.
    IF UNITS-IN IS LESS THAN 3Ø
        MOVE 'FRESHMAN' TO CLASS-STANDING-OUT.
    IF UNITS-IN IS GREATER THAN 29 AND LESS THAN 6Ø
        MOVE 'SOPHOMORE' TO CLASS-STANDING-OUT.
    IF UNITS-IN IS GREATER THAN 59 AND LESS THAN 9Ø
        MOVE 'JUNIOR' TO CLASS-STANDING-OUT.
    IF UNITS-IN IS NOT LESS THAN 9Ø
        MOVE 'SENIOR' TO CLASS-STANDING-OUT.

231-TITLE-AND-HEADINGS.
    WRITE A-LINE FROM TITLE-LINE
        AFTER ADVANCING PAGE.
    WRITE A-LINE FROM COLUMN-HEADINGS
        AFTER ADVANCING 2 LINES.
```

FIGURE I-16

Coding for class standing and title/headings routines.

with the exception of the second and third IF statements. In these two IFs the condition to be checked is actually two conditions. As an example, in the second IF the number of units will be compared to both 29 and 60. This double condition allows us to establish a range of acceptable values. The last IF statement in the paragraph illustrates the use of a negative condition; that is, the condition we are looking for exists when the number of units is *not* less than 90. This is equivalent to stating the condition as equal to or greater than 90.

Paragraph 231- contains two WRITE statements. The first one outputs the title line. Normally, we would want the title to be printed on the line printer at the beginning of the next page. AFTER ADVANCING PAGE causes the paper in the line printer to advance to the beginning of the next page before the line is printed. The second WRITE instruction will print the column headings two spaces below the title.

FEEDBACK **I-9** How does the PERFORM statement function?

I-10 When are label records on magnetic disk or tape files processed?

I-11 How does the COBOL compiler identify the end of an instruction?

I-12 Several instructions in our example program are written on two or more lines. Why are the continuing lines indented?

Figure I-17 is the source listing of our example program as it was outputted by the COBOL compiler. This listing will be used as a reference for making any changes to our program. Note that this particular compiler prints the sequence numbers (columns 1–6) on the far right side of the listing and puts its own statement numbers at the left. The coding forms are of no value after the program has been entered into the computer system and compiled.

FIGURE I-17

The student program source listing.

```
IBM SYSTEM/34      A N S I    C O B O L      RELEASE 08 / MOD 00 - PAGE    1  01/16/84  11:58.23

STMC -A...B... C O B O L    S O U R C E    S T A T E M E N T S .........IDENTFCN SEQ/NO S


    1   IDENTIFICATION DIVISION.                                          STUDENTS 0001
                                                                          STUDENTS 0002
    2   PROGRAM-ID.                                                       STUDENTS 0003
            STUDENTS.                                                     STUDENTS 0004
                                                                          STUDENTS 0005
    3   AUTHOR.                                                           STUDENTS 0006
            J. STUBBE.                                                    STUDENTS 0007
                                                                          STUDENTS 0008
    *       THIS PROGRAM READS THE STUDENT DATA DISK FILE AND CREATES     STUDENTS 0009
    *       A PRINTED LISTING OF ALL STUDENTS IN THE FILE.  IN ADDITION   STUDENTS 0010
    *       IT PRINTS THE AGE OF THE OLDEST AND YOUNGEST STUDENT.         STUDENTS 0011
                                                                          STUDENTS 0012
    4   ENVIRONMENT DIVISION.                                            STUDENTS 0013
                                                                          STUDENTS 0014
    5   CONFIGURATION SECTION.                                           STUDENTS 0015
                                                                          STUDENTS 0016
    6   SOURCE-COMPUTER.                                                 STUDENTS 0017
            IBM-S34.                                                     STUDENTS 0018
                                                                          STUDENTS 0019
    7   OBJECT-COMPUTER.                                                 STUDENTS 0020
            IBM-S34.                                                     STUDENTS 0021
                                                                          STUDENTS 0022
    8   INPUT-OUTPUT SECTION.                                            STUDENTS 0023
                                                                          STUDENTS 0024
    9   FILE-CONTROL.                                                    STUDENTS 0025
   10       SELECT STUDENT-FILE    ASSIGN TO DISK-STUDENT.               STUDENTS 0026
   11       SELECT STUDENT-REPORT ASSIGN TO PRINTER-REPORT.             STUDENTS 0027
                                                                          STUDENTS 0028
   12   DATA DIVISION.                                                   STUDENTS 0029
                                                                          STUDENTS 0030
   13   FILE SECTION.                                                    STUDENTS 0031
                                                                          STUDENTS 0032
   14   FD  STUDENT-FILE                                                 STUDENTS 0033
            RECORD CONTAINS 40 CHARACTERS                               STUDENTS 0034
            LABEL RECORD IS STANDARD                                     STUDENTS 0035
            DATA RECORD IS STUDENT-RECORD.                               STUDENTS 0036
                                                                          STUDENTS 0037
   15   01  STUDENT-RECORD.                                              STUDENTS 0038
   16       02  STUDENT-NAME-IN      PICTURE X(20).                      STUDENTS 0039
   17       02  UNITS-IN             PICTURE 999.                        STUDENTS 0040
   18       02  FILLER               PICTURE X(5).                       STUDENTS 0041
```

```
19      02  AGE-IN                    PICTURE 99.                 STUDENTS 0042
20      02  FILLER                    PICTURE X(10).              STUDENTS 0043
                                                                  STUDENTS 0044
21  FD  STUDENT-REPORT                                            STUDENTS 0045
            RECORD CONTAINS 132 CHARACTERS                        STUDENTS 0046
            LABEL RECORD IS OMITTED                               STUDENTS 0047
            DATA RECORD IS A-LINE.                                STUDENTS 0048
                                                                  STUDENTS 0049
22  01  A-LINE                        PICTURE X(132).             STUDENTS 0050
    /                                                             STUDENTS 0051
23  WORKING-STORAGE SECTION.                                      STUDENTS 0052
                                                                  STUDENTS 0053
24  01  CONTROL-FIELDS.                                           STUDENTS 0054
25      02  ALL-FINISHED              PICTURE XXX VALUE 'NO'.     STUDENTS 0055
26      02  SPACING                   PICTURE 9.                  STUDENTS 0056
                                                                  STUDENTS 0057
27  01  RESULT-FIELDS.                                            STUDENTS 0058
28      02  HIGH-AGE                  PICTURE 99   VALUE ZERO.    STUDENTS 0059
29      02  LOW-AGE                   PICTURE 99   VALUE 99.      STUDENTS 0060
30      02  PRINTED-LINES             PICTURE 99.                 STUDENTS 0061
                                                                  STUDENTS 0062
31  01  TITLE-LINE.                                               STUDENTS 0063
32      02  FILLER                    PICTURE X(44) VALUE SPACES. STUDENTS 0064
33      02  FILLER                    PICTURE X(45)               STUDENTS 0065
            VALUE 'STUDENT LISTING (WITH HIGHEST AND LOWEST AGE)'. STUDENTS 0066
34      02  FILLER                    PICTURE X(43) VALUE SPACES. STUDENTS 0067
                                                                  STUDENTS 0068
35  01  COLUMN-HEADINGS.                                          STUDENTS 0069
36      02  FILLER                    PICTURE X(42) VALUE SPACES. STUDENTS 0070
37      02  FILLER                    PICTURE X(12)               STUDENTS 0071
            VALUE 'STUDENT NAME'.                                 STUDENTS 0072
38      02  FILLER                    PICTURE X(14) VALUE SPACES. STUDENTS 0073
39      02  FILLER                    PICTURE X(14)               STUDENTS 0074
            VALUE 'CLASS STANDING'.                               STUDENTS 0075
40      02  FILLER                    PICTURE X(10) VALUE SPACES. STUDENTS 0076
41      02  FILLER                    PICTURE XXX VALUE 'AGE'.    STUDENTS 0077
42      02  FILLER                    PICTURE X(37) VALUE SPACES. STUDENTS 0078
                                                                  STUDENTS 0079
43  01  DETAIL-LINE.                                              STUDENTS 0080
44      02  FILLER                    PICTURE X(38) VALUE SPACES. STUDENTS 0081
45      02  STUDENT-NAME-OUT          PICTURE X(20).              STUDENTS 0082
46      02  FILLER                    PICTURE X(13) VALUE SPACES. STUDENTS 0083
47      02  CLASS-STANDING-OUT        PICTURE X(9).               STUDENTS 0084
48      02  FILLER                    PICTURE X(13) VALUE SPACES. STUDENTS 0085
49      02  AGE-OUT                   PICTURE 99.                 STUDENTS 0086
50      02  FILLER                    PICTURE X(37) VALUE SPACES. STUDENTS 0087
                                                                  STUDENTS 0088
51  01  AGE-LINE.                                                 STUDENTS 0089
52      02  FILLER                    PICTURE X(27) VALUE SPACES. STUDENTS 0090
53      02  FILLER                    PICTURE X(34)               STUDENTS 0091
            VALUE 'THE OLDEST STUDENT IN THE FILE IS '.           STUDENTS 0092
54      02  HIGH-AGE-OUT              PICTURE 99.                 STUDENTS 0093
55      02  FILLER                    PICTURE X(39)               STUDENTS 0094
            VALUE '.  THE YOUNGEST STUDENT IN THE FILE IS '.      STUDENTS 0095
56      02  LOW-AGE-OUT               PICTURE 99.                 STUDENTS 0096
57      02  FILLER                    PICTURE X(28) VALUE '.'.    STUDENTS 0097
                                                                  STUDENTS 0098
58  PROCEDURE DIVISION.                                           STUDENTS 0099
                                                                  STUDENTS 0100
59  0-MAINLINE.                                                   STUDENTS 0101
60      PERFORM 1-INITIALIZATION.                                 STUDENTS 0102
61      PERFORM 231-TITLE-AND-HEADINGS.                           STUDENTS 0103
62      PERFORM 2-PROCESSING                                      STUDENTS 0104
            UNTIL ALL-FINISHED = 'YES'.                           STUDENTS 0105
63      PERFORM 3-WRITE-OLDEST-AND-YOUNGEST.                      STUDENTS 0106
64      CLOSE STUDENT-FILE                                        STUDENTS 0107
            STUDENT-REPORT.                                       STUDENTS 0108
65      STOP RUN.                                                 STUDENTS 0109
```

```
 66    1-INITIALIZATION.                                              STUDENTS 0110
 67        OPEN INPUT   STUDENT-FILE                                   STUDENTS 0111
                OUTPUT STUDENT-REPORT.                                 STUDENTS 0112
 68        READ STUDENT-FILE RECORD                                    STUDENTS 0113
               AT END                                                  STUDENTS 0114
 69                MOVE 'YES' TO ALL-FINISHED.                         STUDENTS 0115
                                                                       STUDENTS 0116
 70    2-PROCESSING.                                                   STUDENTS 0117
 71        PERFORM 21-SET-UP-PRINT-LINE.                               STUDENTS 0118
 72        PERFORM 22-TEST-FOR-HIGH-LOW-AGE.                           STUDENTS 0119
 73        PERFORM 23-WRITE-A-LINE.                                    STUDENTS 0120
 74        READ STUDENT-FILE RECORD                                    STUDENTS 0121
               AT END                                                  STUDENTS 0122
 75                MOVE 'YES' TO ALL-FINISHED.                         STUDENTS 0123
                                                                       STUDENTS 0124
                                                                       STUDENTS 0125
 76    3-WRITE-OLDEST-AND-YOUNGEST.                                    STUDENTS 0126
 77        MOVE HIGH-AGE TO HIGH-AGE-OUT.                              STUDENTS 0127
 78        MOVE LOW-AGE TO LOW-AGE-OUT.                                STUDENTS 0128
 79        WRITE A-LINE FROM AGE-LINE                                  STUDENTS 0129
               AFTER ADVANCING 2 LINES.                                STUDENTS 0130
                                                                       STUDENTS 0131
 80    21-SET-UP-PRINT-LINE.                                           STUDENTS 0132
 81        MOVE STUDENT-NAME-IN TO STUDENT-NAME-OUT.                   STUDENTS 0133
 82        PERFORM 211-CLASS-STANDING.                                 STUDENTS 0134
 83        MOVE AGE-IN TO AGE-OUT.                                     STUDENTS 0135
                                                                       STUDENTS 0136
 84    22-TEST-FOR-HIGH-LOW-AGE.                                       STUDENTS 0137
 85        IF AGE-IN IS GREATER THAN HIGH-AGE                          STUDENTS 0138
 86            MOVE AGE-IN TO HIGH-AGE.                                STUDENTS 0139
 87        IF AGE-IN IS LESS THAN LOW-AGE                              STUDENTS 0140
 88            MOVE AGE-IN TO LOW-AGE.                                 STUDENTS 0141
                                                                       STUDENTS 0142
 89    23-WRITE-A-LINE.                                                STUDENTS 0143
 90        IF PRINTED-LINES IS GREATER THAN 49                         STUDENTS 0144
 91            PERFORM 231-TITLE-AND-HEADINGS                          STUDENTS 0145
 92            MOVE 3 TO SPACING                                       STUDENTS 0146
 93            MOVE ZERO TO PRINTED-LINES.                             STUDENTS 0147
 94        WRITE A-LINE FROM DETAIL-LINE                               STUDENTS 0148
               AFTER ADVANCING SPACING.                                STUDENTS 0149
 95        ADD 1 TO PRINTED-LINES.                                     STUDENTS 0150
 96        MOVE 1 TO SPACING.                                          STUDENTS 0151
                                                                       STUDENTS 0152
 97    211-CLASS-STANDING.                                             STUDENTS 0153
 98        IF UNITS-IN IS LESS THAN 30                                 STUDENTS 0154
 99            MOVE 'FRESHMAN' TO CLASS-STANDING-OUT.                  STUDENTS 0155
100        IF UNITS-IN IS GREATER THAN 29 AND LESS THAN 60            STUDENTS 0156
101            MOVE 'SOPHOMORE' TO CLASS-STANDING-OUT.                 STUDENTS 0157
102        IF UNITS-IN IS GREATER THAN 59 AND LESS THAN 90            STUDENTS 0158
103            MOVE 'JUNIOR' TO CLASS-STANDING-OUT.                    STUDENTS 0159
104        IF UNITS-IN IS NOT LESS THAN 90                            STUDENTS 0160
105            MOVE 'SENIOR' TO CLASS-STANDING-OUT.                    STUDENTS 0161
                                                                       STUDENTS 0162
106    231-TITLE-AND-HEADINGS.                                        STUDENTS 0163
107        WRITE A-LINE FROM TITLE-LINE                                STUDENTS 0164
               AFTER ADVANCING PAGE.                                   STUDENTS 0165
108        WRITE A-LINE FROM COLUMN-HEADINGS                           STUDENTS 0166
               AFTER ADVANCING 2 LINES.                                STUDENTS 0167


PROGRAM SIZE = DATA DIVISION + PROCEDURE DIVISION + LITERALS + DTF/BUFFERS

    2498              724              765            80         929


NO ERRORS DETECTED FOR THIS COMPILATION

END OF COMPILATION
```

SUMMARY

After the problem solution has been planned, the program is ready to be coded. The most common business-oriented language is COBOL. COBOL is a high-level, English-like language designed to handle the data manipulation required in most business programs. The data manipulation capability gives the programmer a great deal of flexibility in handling input and output.

Like most languages, COBOL has a unique coding form that is to be used when you write COBOL instructions. These instructions are written as sentences that look like English sentences. This appearance makes the COBOL procedure easy to read and understand. One disadvantage of this English-like coding is its length. The programmer must write longer instructions in COBOL than in many other languages.

All COBOL programs consist of four major parts, called divisions. These divisions are called the identification division, environment division, data division, and procedure division. The identification division identifies the program by name. It may also identify the programmer, the date that the program was written and/or compiled, and remarks about the program. All hardware descriptions are written in the environment division. This division names the computer system to be used and the input and output devices that will be required by the program. This division will require a change if the program is to be run on a different type of computer than was originally intended. All data—files, records, and fields—are named and described in the data division. The data names that we assign should be meaningful relative to the data. The names may consist of up to 30 characters and contain letters, numbers, and hyphens. All names must appear to be a single word. That is, no spaces may appear within a data name. The last division, the procedure division, contains all of the logic steps in the solution of our problem. This is the division that we planned through flowcharting or pseudocode.

ANSWERS TO FEEDBACK QUESTIONS

I-1 They show the data entry operator how the programmer is writing the numeral 0 and the letter O, the numeral 1 and the letter I, and any other characters that may be confused.

I-2 Sequence, continuation, COBOL statement, and identification.

I-3 Identification, environment, data, and procedure.

I-4 The maximum is 30 characters.

I-5 Letters (A–Z), numbers (0–9), and the hyphen (-).

I-6 It indicates the length of the field and the type of data that the field is to hold. A PICTURE of X means alphanumeric data. A PICTURE of 9 means numeric data.

I-7 A group item is a data item that is broken down into smaller items. An elementary item is not broken down any further.

I-8 To assign a beginning value to a field. It may be used only in the working-storage section of the data division.

I-9 It causes the execution of instructions in the paragraph named in the PERFORM statement. When the instructions in the paragraph have

been executed, control returns to the statement following the PER-
FORM statement.

I-10 During execution of the OPEN statement.

I-11 By findng a period.

I-12 It is helpful to indent all instruction lines after the first line. This makes it easier for people who read the program to see where the instruction ends.

FOR REVIEW AND EXERCISE

1 Statistics show that the typical programmer spends 80 percent of his or her time in making changes to existing programs and 20 percent in coding new programs. How does COBOL make program modification easier for the programmer?

2 What is the general purpose for writing programs using a structured approach?

3 What is the purpose of the punching instructions on a COBOL coding form?

4 Describe the value of the sequence field on the COBOL instruction.

5 Name the four divisions of a COBOL program. Briefly state the purpose of each division. Are all four divisions required in every COBOL program?

6 Name the four rules for forming COBOL data names.

7 What is the purpose of the picture clause? What do X and 9 represent?

8 What is the purpose of the value clause? Where may it be used?

9 How does the PERFORM statement function?

10 Explain the purpose of indenting continuing lines when an instruction requires more than one line.

SUPPLEMENT II
RPG II

PREVIEW   Chapter 13 introduced us to programming languages, and Chapter 14 presented
examples of the steps required to run the program. In this supplement, we will
see how the logical steps of a program can be written in the language Report
Program Generator (RPG). The goal of this supplement is to acquaint you with
the process of coding a program by using RPG II.

In this supplement you will learn:

1. The nature of the language RPG II
2. How input and output files are described
3. How input is specified
4. How calculations are specified
5. How to write output specifications

KEY TERMS TO WATCH FOR AND REMEMBER

control card specifications   calculation specifications
file description specifications output-format specifications
input specifications   indicators

RPG is a high-level, problem-oriented language. The name RPG stands for
report program generator. The type of problems RPG was designed to solve
requires the generation of reports. RPG is therefore a business-oriented language. As we will see, RPG source code is very symbolic. That is, it does not
use an English sentence structure. RPG II, the current version of the language,
is an updated, more powerful version of RPG. It is a very common programming language among small businesses that use minicomputers. Although some
larger computer installations use RPG also, its greatest popularity is with
smaller data processing centers.

RPG CODING FORMS   Most program languages have their own unique coding forms. RPG has several coding forms. In this supplement, we will be using four of the RPG coding forms: the control card and file description specifications, input specifications, calculation specifications, and output specifications.

Figure II-1 illustrates these four forms. All of the RPG coding forms have

FIGURE II-1
RPG coding forms.

a few common characteristics. On each form, the first two positions are used

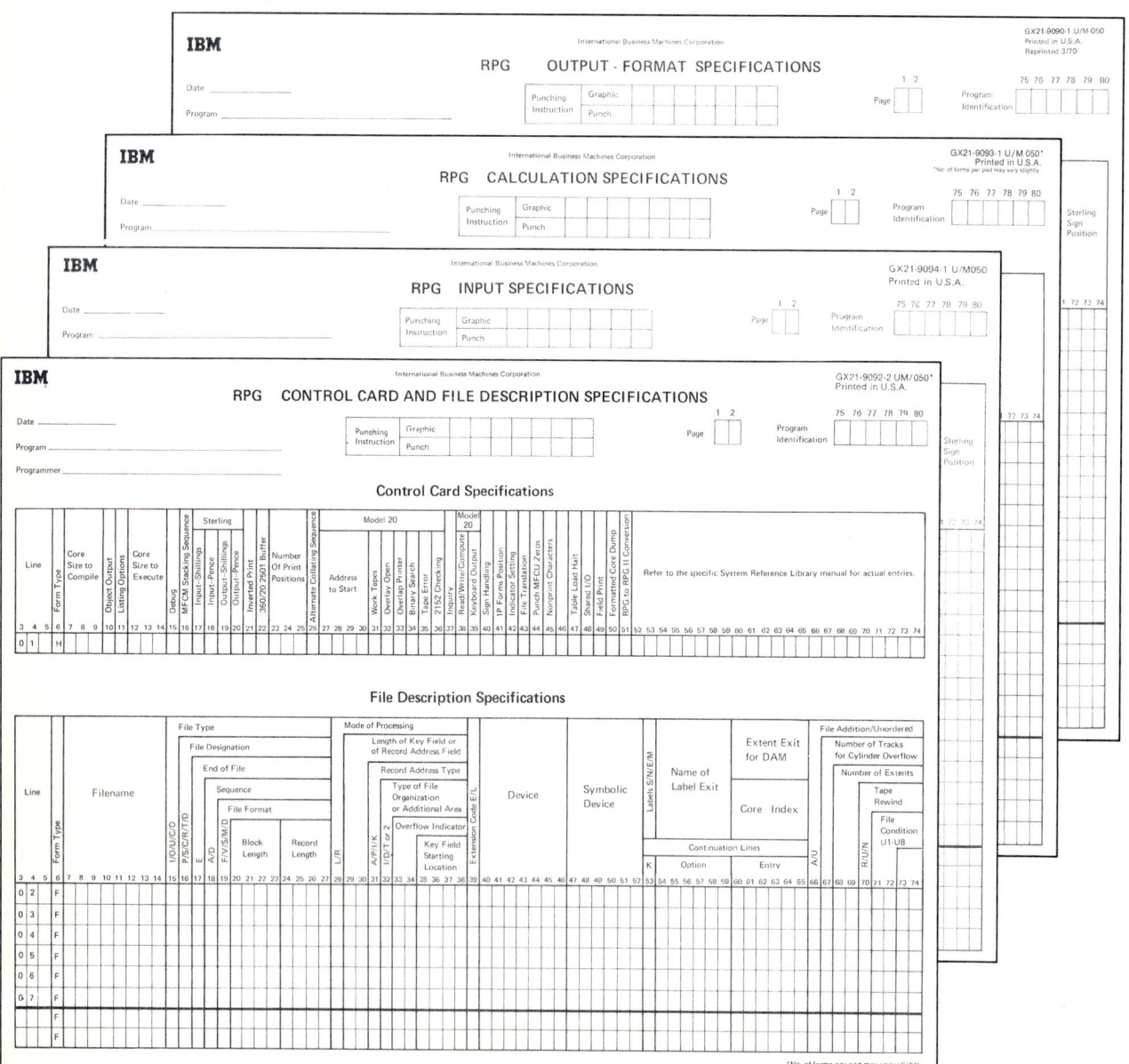

to indicate the coding form page number. The page number is shown near the upper right-hand corner on each page. The page number will be entered into the first two columns of each coding form line. Positions 3, 4, and 5 contain the line number of the coding form page. Column 6 contains a letter to designate the type of coding form. The information recorded in positions 7–74 differs for each coding form. Columns 75–80 contain the program identification. The program identification information is shown in the upper right-hand corner of each coding form. Each line of the source program will have the same identification.

THE RPG CYCLE

RPG is an unusual programming language, compared to most other languages. Much of the detailed control of the program logic is not available to the programmer. As an example, there are no READ or WRITE instructions in RPG. Instead, RPG follows the data processing cycle of inputting the data, processing the data, and outputting the results. This input-processing-output cycle is repeated until all of the data has been processed. The processing cycle cannot be controlled by the programmer. However, the programmer does describe the input, processing steps, and output.

AN RPG EXAMPLE PROGRAM

The RPG program that we will discuss inputs student data that includes the student's name, age, and the number of units of college work completed. The purpose of the program is to produce a student report that lists all students in the input file. Each detail line will include the student's name, college class standing, and age. A first-year student is considered to be one who has completed fewer than 30 units. If the number of units is from 30 to 59, the student is considered to be a sophomore. If between 60 and 89 units have been completed, the student is a junior; and if the student has completed 90 units or more, the standing is that of senior. At the end of the student report, we are to output the age of the youngest and oldest students in the input file.

Figure II-2 illustrates the first coding form in our RPG problem solution. As you can see, the first page has a page number of 1 and a program identification of STUDEN in the upper right-hand corner. It should be noted that the line numbers and form type have been preprinted on the coding form.

Control Card Specifications

The first line on the first coding form is the **control card specifications.** Information in the control card specification tells the compiler which options you wish to use for the program. As an example, the programmer can specify where the object program from the compiler is to be outputted or may indicate that a source listing is not required. Even if none of the special options is required, most RPG compilers require that the control card specification be the first record in the source program. In our example, we would enter the page number in columns 1 and 2, the line number in columns 3–5, an H (heading) for the form type in column 6, the amount of memory available to us in columns 12–14, and the program identification in columns 75–80. None of the other options is required for our example program.

File Description Specifications

The lower half of the first coding form is used for **file description specifications**—to describe the input and output files to be used by our program.

In our example, the two files used are called STUDENTS and REPORT. The next coding form field is the file type. The file called STUDENTS is an input (I) file, and REPORT is the output (O) file. The file designation of P for the input file indicates that it is the primary file. The next entry is in the file format field. Both of our files have records that are fixed (F) in length. That is, every record we read is 40 characters in length, and every line we write will be 132 characters in length. The last field we will use is the device field. Its purpose is to specify the devices that the computer will be inputting from and

FIGURE II-2

Example RPG control card and file description specifications.

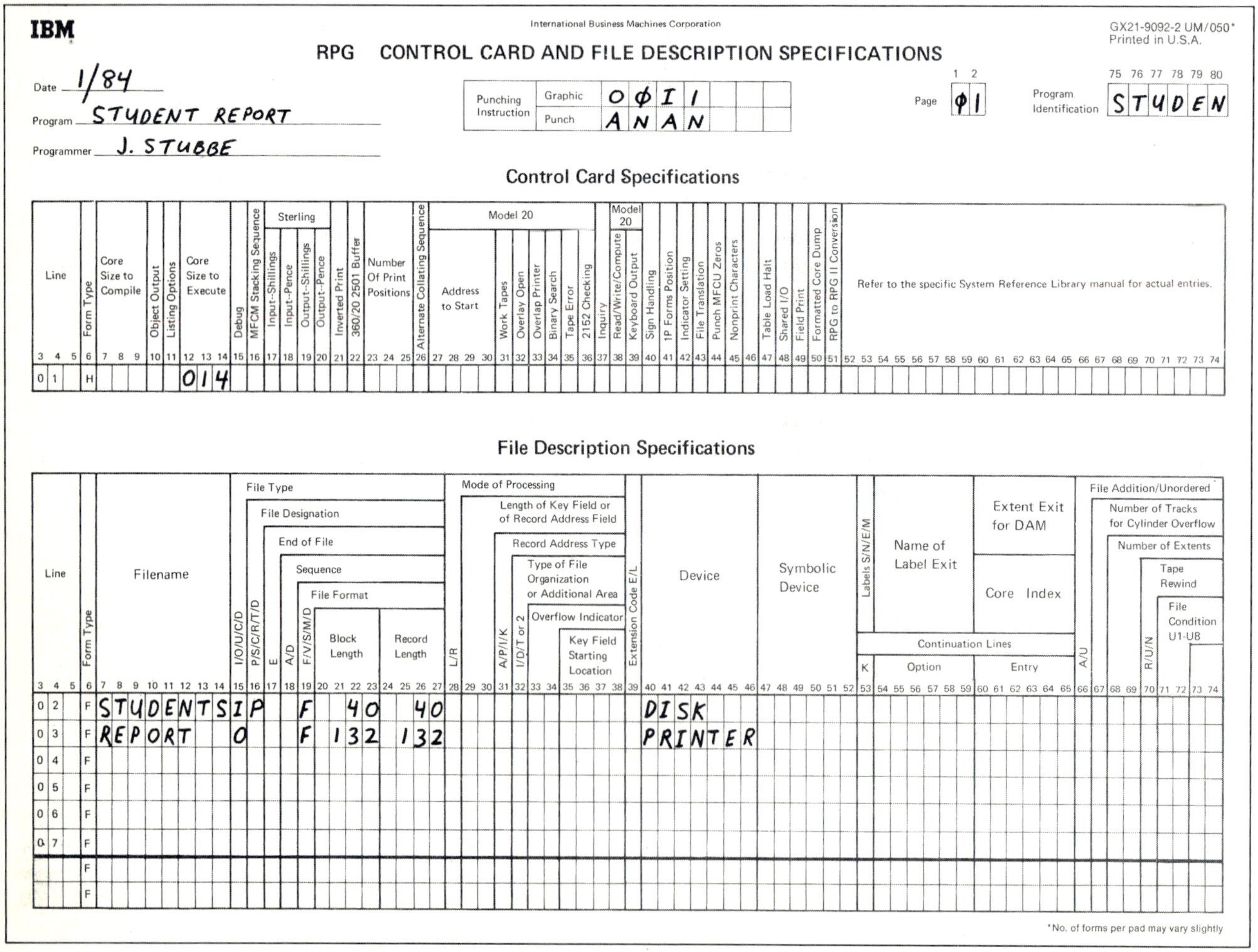

outputting to. Here the input device is the magnetic disk and the output device is the line printer.

Input Specifications

Input specifications are illustrated in Figure II-3. The first entry is the input file name—in our example, STUDENTS. This file name must match the name that was specified for the input file on the first coding form page. The next field is the sequence field. Entry NS indicates that the input data is not in any particular sequence. The next entry is the record-identifying indicator. RPG uses a series of **indicators.** The programmer controls the indicators that are numbered 01–99. By specifying 01 in the record-identifying indicator field, we are telling RPG to turn on indicator number 1 whenever it inputs a record. The next three lines identify the location and name of the input record fields. The first field is in columns 1–20 and is the student's name. The units field is

FIGURE II-3
Example RPG input specifications.

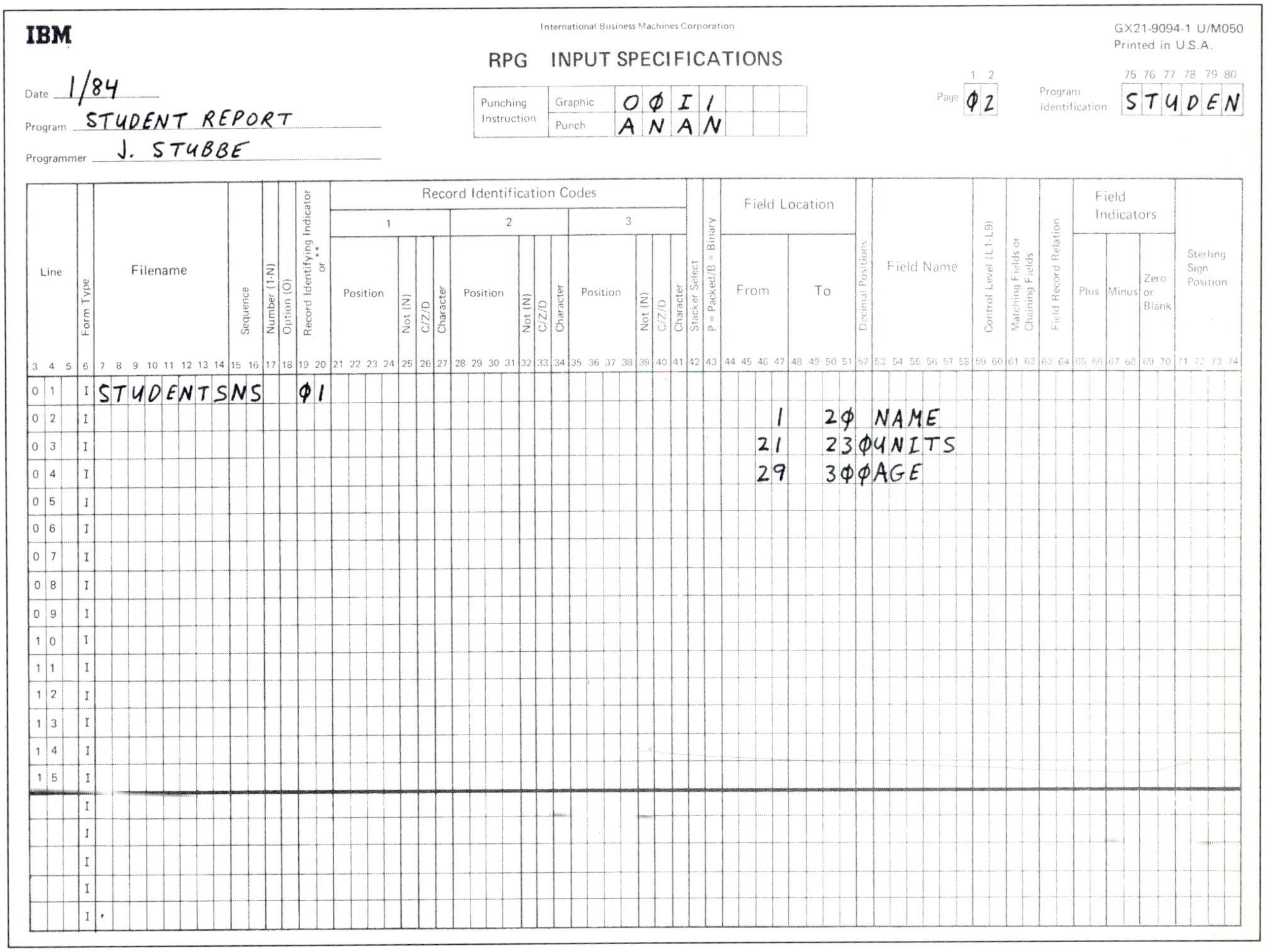
IBM International Business Machines Corporation GX21-9094-1 U/M050 Printed in U.S.A.

RPG INPUT SPECIFICATIONS

Date 1/84
Program STUDENT REPORT
Programmer J. STUBBE

Punching Instruction: Graphic 0 Ø I / ; Punch A N A N
Page Ø2
Program Identification STUDEN

Line	Form Type	Filename	Sequence	Record Identifying Indicator	Field Location From	Field Location To	Decimal Positions	Field Name
01	I	STUDENTS	NS	Ø1				
02	I				1	2Ø		NAME
03	I				21	23	Ø	UNITS
04	I				29	3Ø	Ø	AGE

in columns 21–23. Note that the decimal positions field contains a 0. If the decimal positions field is left blank, it implies that the field is not numeric. If a number appears in the decimal positions field, it implies that the field is numeric. In our example, the 0 indicates that the field contains whole numbers with no decimal positions. The third field is the student's age and is in columns 29 and 30.

Calculation Specifications

Figure II-4 shows the **calculation specifications** for our sample RPG program. The first logical task in our sample program is to determine the class standing of each student, based upon the number of units of credit earned by the student. The objective of the first three lines is to turn on indicator 10 if the class standing is freshman, 20 if the class standing is sophomore, 30 if the class standing is junior, and 40 if the class standing is senior.

FIGURE II-4

Example RPG calculation specifications.

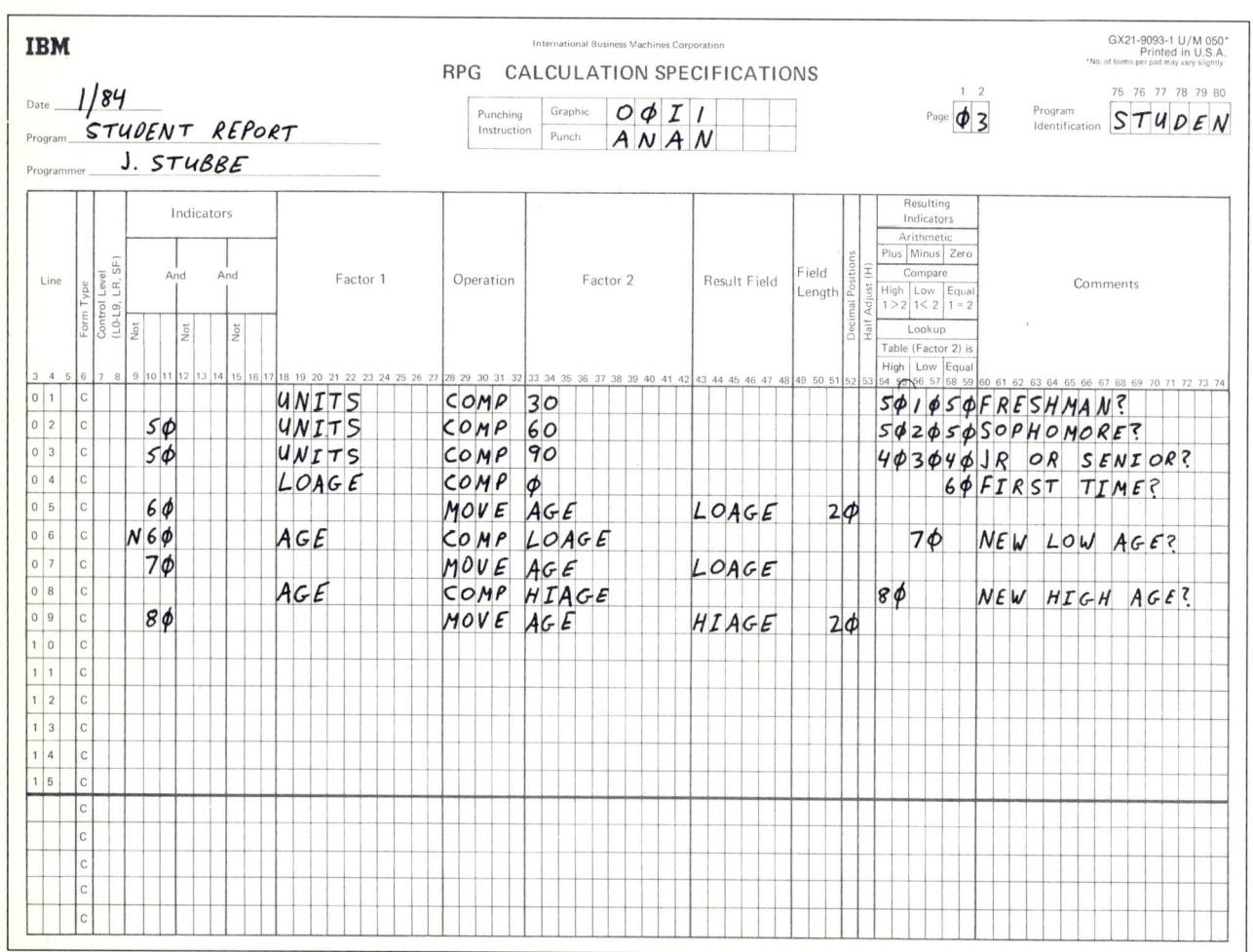

The first line compares the input units to a value of 30. If you look at the column headings associated with the COMPARE, you will see that the indicator specified in columns 54 and 55 is turned on if the first factor is greater than the second. The indicator specified in columns 56 and 57 will turn on if the first factor is less than the second, and the indicator specified in columns 58 and 59 is turned on if the first factor is equal to the second factor.

The first line of code, therefore, will turn on indicator 10 if the units field is less than 30 and turn on indicator 50 if the units field is equal to or greater than 30. At this point, either indicator 10 or indicator 50 has been turned on.

The second line has a 50 in columns 10 and 11. This means that the line will be executed only if indicator 50 is turned on. In our example, this line would be executed only if the student were not a freshman. The second line compares the units field to 60. If the number of units is less than 60 (a sophomore), indicator 20 will be turned on. Otherwise, indicator 50 will remain on. The third line also is to be executed only if indicator 50 is on. In our example, it would mean that the student is neither a freshman nor a sophomore. The third line compares the units field with 90. If the units field is less than 90, the student is a junior, and indicator 30 is turned on. If the units field is equal to or greater than 90, the student is a senior and indicator 40 will be turned on. At this point, indicator 10, 20, 30, or 40 will be turned on, indicating the appropriate class standing.

When execution of an RPG program begins, all numeric fields have a beginning value of 0. The fourth line compares the low-age field (LOAGE) to a value of 0. LOAGE is the field that will hold the lowest student age encountered so far in the input file. If LOAGE is equal to 0, we must be processing the first record in the field. The instruction on line 4 will turn on indicator 60 if we are processing the first student's record. The fifth line will be executed only if indicator 60 is on. It will move the age of the first student to the LOAGE field. Because LOAGE was not part of the input specifications, it has not yet been defined. Columns 51 and 52 on line 5 define LOAGE as a two-digit numeric field with no decimal positions. Line 6 indicates that if indicator 60 is not on, the age field is to be compared to LOAGE. If the age is less than the LOAGE value, indicator 70 will be turned on, indicating that we have found a new low age. Line 7 will be executed only if indicator 70 is on. It will cause the age field value, our new low age, to be moved to LOAGE. Line 8 compares age to HIAGE (high age). HIAGE is the name of the field that will hold the highest age in the file. If the input age field is greater than HIAGE, indicator 80 will be turned on, indicating that we have found a new high age. Line 9 will be executed only if indicator 80 is turned on. It will cause the age field, our new high, to be moved to HIAGE. Line 8 also defines HIAGE as a two-digit numeric field with no decimal positions.

Output-Format Specifications

Figure II-5 illustrates the **output-format specifications.** It holds the descriptions of the title line, column heading line, and detail line. The first line indicates that the file's name is REPORT and that the type of output is a heading (H). It also indicates that the printer paper is to be skipped to channel 01 (the top of the page) before printing. The output indicator tells RPG to print the line only when indicator 1P is on. Indicator 1P stands for first page and is on at the beginning of the RPG program execution. Lines 2 and 3 describe the title to be printed. Note that even though two lines were required to code the title, the title will be printed as a single line. Line 4 describes another heading (H) type line. This line represents the column headings. The line printer is to space two lines before printing and three lines after printing the column headings. The column headings will print only when the 1P indicator is on. The three values to be used as column headings and their ending print positions are coded on lines 5, 6, and 7. Line 8 describes the detail line (D). The line printer is to space one line after printing and will print only

FIGURE II-5

Example RPG output-format specifications.

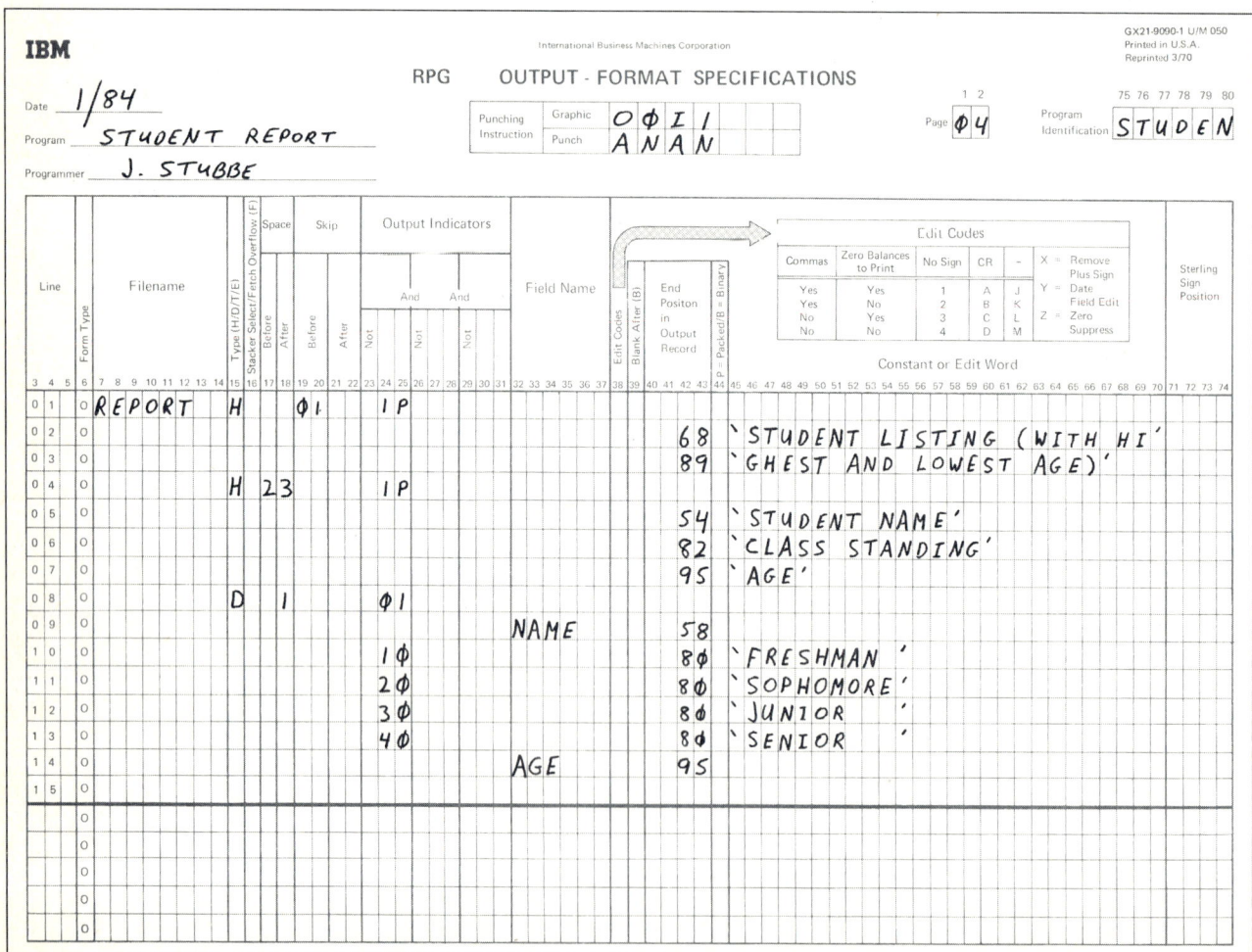

when indicator 01 is on. As you will recall, indicator 01 is the indicator we specified as the input-record identifying indicator. Therefore, a detail line will be printed for each input record. Lines 9 through 14 describe the output line. The first field is the student's name (ending in print position 58). The last field is the student's age (ending in position 95).

The middle field will be "freshman," "sophomore," "junior," or "senior" depending upon the indicator turned on during our calculation specification compares. If indicator 10 is on, the word "freshman" will be printed. If indicator 20 is on, the word "sophomore" will be printed, and so on.

Figure II-6 continues the output-format specifications. The last output line to describe is the line for the total (T), indicating the oldest and youngest students in the file. Line 1 indicates that the line printer is to space one line

FIGURE II-6

Example RPG output-format specifications, continued.

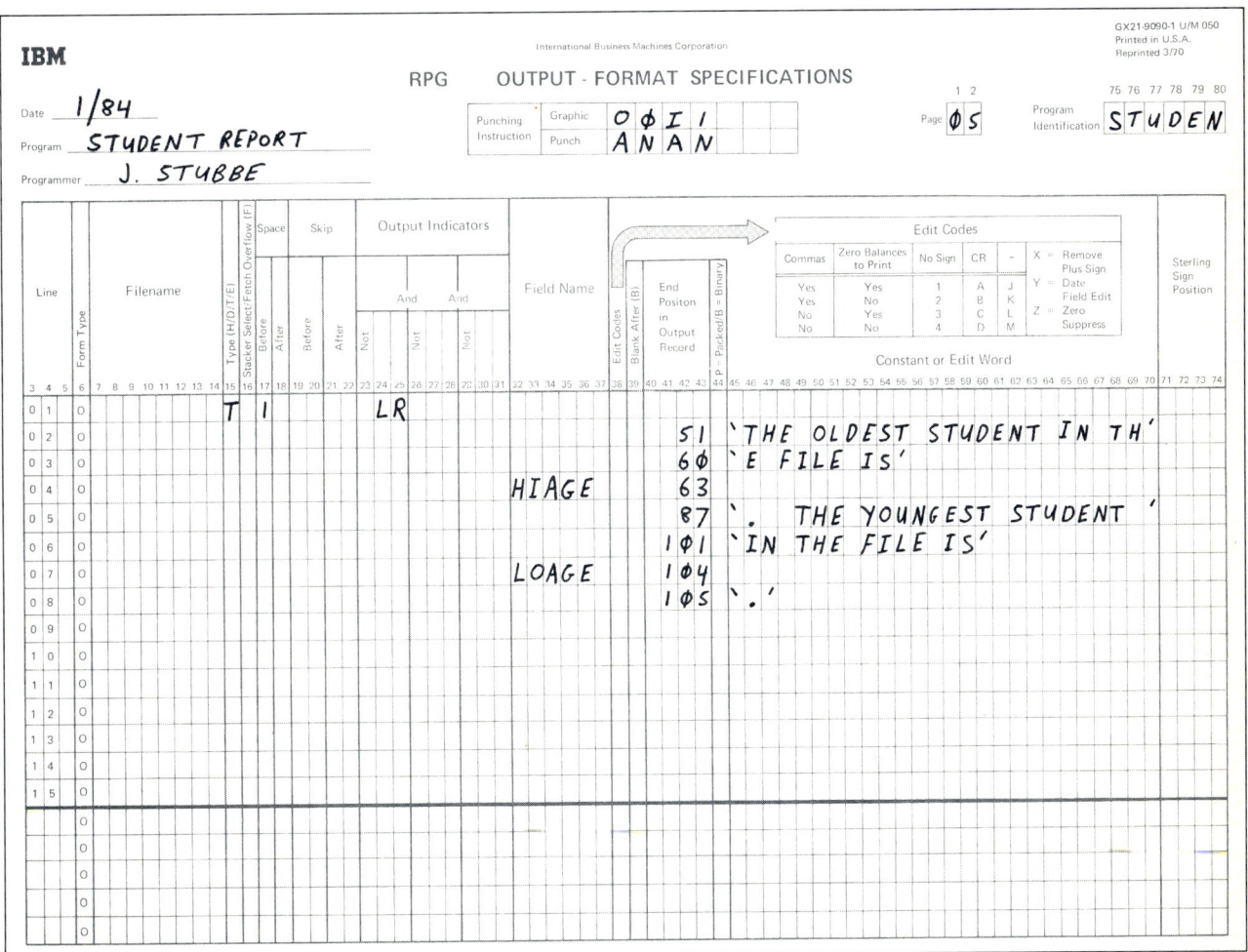

```
                 STUDENT LISTING (WITH HIGHEST AND LOWEST AGE)

          STUDENT NAME                  CLASS STANDING          AGE

     HENRY CRUTCH                         SENIOR                 47
     GEORGE HOODSPITH                     SOPHOMORE              20
     JOHN JONES                           SENIOR                 25
     MARY SMITH                           FRESHMAN               18
     MARY ELLEN WINKS                     SOPHOMORE              36

THE OLDEST STUDENT IN THE FILE IS 47.  THE YOUNGEST STUDENT IN THE FILE IS 18.
```

FIGURE II-7
Example RPG program output.

FIGURE II-8
RPG arithmetic calculations.

IBM International Business Machines Corporation — GX21-9093-1 U/M 050* Printed in U.S.A. *No. of forms per pad may vary slightly

RPG CALCULATION SPECIFICATIONS

Date ______ Program ______ Programmer ______

Punching Instruction: Graphic / Punch — Page 1 2 — Program Identification 75 76 77 78 79 80

Line	Form Type	Control Level (L0-L9, LR, SR)	Indicators (Not, And, Not, And, Not)	Factor 1	Operation	Factor 2	Result Field	Field Length	Decimal Positions	Half Adjust (H)	Resulting Indicators: Arithmetic Plus / Compare High 1>2 / Lookup Table (Factor 2) is High	Minus / Low 1<2 / Low	Zero / Equal 1=2 / Equal	Comments
01	C			HOURS	MULT	RATE	GPAY	6	2	H				
02	C													
03	C			COUNT	ADD	1	COUNT							
04	C													
05	C			GPAY	SUB	DEDUCT	NETPAY	6	2					
06	C													
07	C			TOTAL	DIV	COUNT	AVE	6	2	H				
08	C													
09	C													
10	C													
11	C													
12	C													
13	C													
14	C													
15	C													
	C													
	C													
	C													
	C													
	C													

before printing the total line. The total line will print only when the last-record (LR) indicator is on. This indicator is turned on by inputting the last data record. Lines 2 through 8 describe the fields that make up the total line.

The Output   Figure II-7 is a sample report produced by our RPG program.

Arithmetic Calculations   In our example program, the calculation specifications illustrated were COMPARE and MOVE operations. It is also possible to add, subtract, multiply, and divide in RPG. Figure II-8 shows four arithmetic calculations. On line 1, a field called HOURS is multiplied by a field called RATE. The answer field is called GPAY. GPAY has a field length of six digits—two of which are decimal positions. The H in column 53 indicates that the answer field is to be rounded off (half adjusted). Line 3 illustrates an addition operation. The field COUNT is added to a 1. The answer is to be placed in the field called COUNT. Because COUNT has been defined earlier, a field length is not required. The instruction on line 5 subtracts the field DEDUCT from GPAY and places the answer in a field called NETPAY. Line 7 illustrates a division operation. The field TOTAL is divided by the field COUNT and the answer is placed in a field called AVE, which will be rounded off (half adjusted) to two decimal places.

FEEDBACK   **II-1** What does the indicator 1P stand for? When does it go on?
II-2 When does the LR indicator go on?
II-3 What are the programmer-specified indicators called?

SUMMARY   RPG II is a high-level, problem-oriented language. RPG stands for *r*eport *p*rogram *g*enerator. It is oriented towards the production of reports in a business environment.

RPG is a symbolic language that uses short (6-character) field names and indicators. It is most common among the smaller data processing centers.

There are several coding forms used in RPG. Four different coding forms were introduced in this chapter. Each coding form contains descriptions of the input, the calculations, and the output. RPG uses these descriptions as it follows the cycle of input-process-output.

ANSWERS TO FEEDBACK QUESTIONS   **II-1** 1P stands for "first page." It is on at the beginning of program execution.
II-2 The LR (last-record) indicator goes on when the last data record has been processed.
II-3 The programmer specified indicators are 01–99.

FOR REVIEW AND DISCUSSION

1 What does RPG stand for?

2 What is the RPG cycle?

3 Judging from the sample RPG program in this chapter, rate RPG in its ease of coding.

4 Judging from the sample RPG program in this chapter, rate the ease of modifying an existing RPG program.

5 RPG II is sometimes called a "nonprocedural" language. Why?

6 What is the purpose of each of the RPG coding forms used in this supplement?

7 What is the range of numbers used to identify RPG indicators? What are the two special system indicators used in this supplement? What are their purposes?

8 How long can field names be in RPG? How could this length limit be a disadvantage to programmers?

9 How are numeric fields rounded off in RPG?

10 RPG is most popular in small data processing installations. Why would RPG be more popular than COBOL or other business-oriented languages?

SUPPLEMENT III

NUMBER SYSTEMS

PREVIEW   The writing of error-free programs is the major task of programmers. In the process of debugging computer programs, a programmer may have to use memory dumps—a printout of memory contents. The goal of this supplement is to introduce the number systems used in computer memories and in memory dumps.

In this supplement you will learn:

1. The basic characteristics of the binary, octal, and hexadecimal number systems

2. The procedure for converting binary, octal, or hexadecimal numbers to decimal numbers

3. The procedure for converting decimal numbers to binary, octal, or hexadecimal numbers

4. How octal and hexadecimal numbers may be used as shortcut notation for binary numbers

5. How to add and subtract binary, octal, and hexadecimal numbers

KEY TERMS TO WATCH FOR AND REMEMBER

number system	hexadecimal
base	fixed-point numbers
decimal	fixed-length fields
binary	word
octal	character code

The basis of all our calculating is counting. Early humans counted on fingers. When 10 fingers were not adequate for the required calculation, stones, pebbles, or notches in sticks were used to indicate values.

When a formal **number system** was developed, almost all societies developed a number system based on 10 fingers. This number system is known as base 10 or decimal. It incorporates the concepts of place value and of having a symbol to represent a value of 0. Place value is the concept of digit positions having a particular value, such as a 1s column, 10s column, and so on.

The development of a number system based on 10 has not been developed by all societies in history. A few primitive societies have developed number systems based on 2. There is some evidence to show that some of the pharaohs of ancient Egypt used a number system based on 49. This number system was very complex and difficult to learn. The purpose of its use was probably to make calculations and numerical records obscure for the masses. By far, the most common numbering system is based on 10.

Number systems other than base 10 are encountered by programmers. In early computers, an engineering decision was made to design computer circuitry to use base 2, or the **binary** numbering system. It was simpler to design circuitry for memory and arithmetic logic units that showed two states, "off" and "on" (0 and 1). These two states can most easily be represented with binary numbers. Modern computers continue to be based on binary.

If program errors occur, programmers can usually debug the programs by using the language processor's error messages and debugging routines provided in most languages. As mentioned in Chapter 15, there are a few occasions when the error cannot be determined without looking at the raw data contained in a computer's memory. A common way of looking at the contents of a computer's memory is to print out the memory contents on the line printer. This printout is called a memory dump. If memory dumps were to be printed using binary numbers, the programmer would be confronted with many pages of 1s and 0s. All program instructions and data are held in memory in binary number form.

Because of the quantity of printout that would be required in a memory dump of binary digits and the lack of digit variety (0s and 1s), a shortcut notation for the binary digits is desirable. Two number systems, base 8 and base 16, are commonly used as a shortcut notation for binary. The shortcut techniques and the relationships between bases 2 and 8 and bases 2 and 16 will be explained later in this supplement. A computer programmer, therefore, will have occasion to deal with binary (base 2), **octal** (base 8), and **hexadecimal** (base 16) numbers, as well as decimal (base 10) numbers. The relationships between different number systems are not difficult to see. Most number-system characteristics are the same as decimal number characteristics. In the sections that follow, we will learn how to convert values from one number system to another. We will also learn how to add and subtract in different number systems.

BASICS OF NUMBER SYSTEMS

There are two characteristics of all number systems that are suggested by the value of the base. In all numbering systems, the value of a base determines the number of different digit characters available in the numbering system. The first of these choices is always zero. The second characteristic is that the maximum value of a single digit is always equal to one less than the value of

Base 10
Ten digit choices (equal to the base)
0 1 2 3 4 5 6 7 8 9
Largest single digit is 9 (1 less than the base)

Base 2
Two digit choices (equal to the base)
0 1
Largest single digit is 1 (1 less than the base)

Base 8
Eight digit choices (equal to the base)
0 1 2 3 4 5 6 7
Largest single digit is 7 (1 less than the base)

Base 16
Sixteen digit choices (equal to the base)
0 1 2 3 4 5 6 7 8 9 A B C D E F
Largest single digit is F or 15 (1 less than the base)

FIGURE III-1

Characteristics of base 10 (decimal),
base 2 (binary), base 8 (octal), and
base 16 (hexadecimal).

the base. Figure III-1 illustrates these characteristics, using bases 10, 2, 8, and 16.

Decimal Characteristics

Both number-system characteristics can be illustrated easily in our common decimal number system. Figure III-1 shows that base 10 has number digit choices that range from 0 through 9, or 10 digit choices. The largest single digit is equal to 9, which is one less than the base.

Binary Characteristics

The general number-system characteristics are also easily applied to binary numbers. The number of digit choices is 2 (0 and 1). The largest single digit is equal to 1, which is one less than the value of the base. Any value greater than 1 must be represented by more than one digit, just as in decimal, any value over 9 requires more than one digit. Figure III-1 shows the characteristics of base 2.

Octal Characteristics

The octal number system, or base 8, is also consistent with the general number-system characteristics. As shown in Figure III-1, a base of 8 indicates that there are eight digit choices in the number system. The eight digits are 0 through 7. The largest single digit in base 8 is equal to 7, or one less than the base.

Hexadecimal Characteristics

Base 16, or hexadecimal numbers, will be the least familiar. The base of 16 suggests choices of 16 single-character digits. The first 10 digit choices are 0 through 9. An additional six digit symbols are required for hexadecimal numbers. To be conveniently used, the additional six symbols had to be available on computer printers and have a commonly known sequence. The letters A through F fulfilled these requirements. In the hexadecimal number system, therefore, the letters A through F are number digits. The number A has a decimal-equivalent value of 10 and the hexadecimal F has a decimal-equivalent value of 15. The largest single digit in base 16 is F (which is equal to decimal 15), one less than the value of the base. Thus, base 16 fits our two number-system characteristics. Figure III-1 illustrates the characteristics of base 16.

CONVERTING FROM ONE NUMBER SYSTEM TO ANOTHER

Any whole-number value in one number system can be represented in any other number system. Because of the predominant use of decimal numbers, numbers expressed in decimal are much more meaningful to us than are values expressed in other number systems.

When visiting foreign countries, most travelers must convert the prices of goods and services from the foreign currency to their own currency before they can judge the cost of the goods or services. The same situation exists for programmers. Because the input and final output values will be in decimal, numbers in other number systems often must be converted to decimal. There are also conditions that make it convenient to convert from a decimal system to some other number system. There are many methods or techniques that can be used to convert numbers from one base to another. This chapter will illustrate one technique used in converting to base 10 from any other base and a second technique to be used in converting from base 10 to any other base.

Converting to Base 10

In order to convert numbers to decimal values, it is necessary to determine column values or place values. Figure III-2 illustrates the general rule for determining column values and the specifics for base 10, base 2, base 8, and base 16. The general rule for determining column values is that the first (or right-hand) whole-number column value is equal to the value of the base to the zero power.[1] Any number to the zero power is equal to 1. Therefore, all

---

[1] Note that superscript numbers show powers. For example, $10^4 = 10 \times 10 \times 10 \times 10 = 10,000$. Subscript numbers show the base. The number 6_{10} is the number 6 in base 10.

General $BASE^4$	$BASE^3$	$BASE^2$	$BASE^1$	$BASE^0$
Base 10				
10^4	10^3	10^2	10^1	10^0
10,000	1000	100	10	1
Base 2				
2^4	2^3	2^2	2^1	2^0
16	8	4	2	1
Base 8				
8^4	8^3	8^2	8^1	8^0
4096	512	64	8	1
Base 16				
16^4	16^3	16^2	16^1	16^0
65,536	4096	256	16	1

FIGURE III-2
Determining column values for bases 10, 2, 8, and 16. The equivalent decimal value is shown in color for each column.

WHAT NUMBER SYSTEM DOES YOUR CALCULATOR USE?

With the tremendous success and popularity of hand calculators, we see hand calculators designed for specific kinds of calculations.

For the programmer who just does not want to add or subtract hexadecimal numbers, a hexadecimal calculator is available. The keyboard allows entry of all hexadecimal digits from 0 through F. The calculator is used in the same way as a standard calculator except that the values entered and the answer are in hexadecimal.

A recent advertisement in an aviation supply catalog described a sexagesimal calculator. It is a calculator which effectively uses base 60. Its primary purpose is to perform addition, subtraction, multiplication, and division with the data expressed in hours and minutes. When adding minutes, for example, the calculator carries 1 to the hours position whenever it gets a total of 60 or more seconds. Since navigation problems often involve time problems, this calculator may be useful to the pilot who would rather spend $37 than the extra time that would be involved in conversion.

bases have a column value of 1 for the first column. The second column is equal to the value of the base to the first power. The value of any number to the first power is equal to that same number. Therefore, the second-column value in all number systems is equal to the value of the base. The third-column value is equal to the base to the second power, or the base value times itself. The value of the columns from right to left continue to increase in value by one more power for each column. For example, the fourth-column value is the base to the third power, the fifth-column value is the base to the fourth power, and so on.

This general rule for determining the column values can be illustrated with the familiar base of 10. In decimal, the first-column value would be equal to 10 to the zero power, or 1; the second-column value would be 10 to the first power, or 10. The third-column value is equal to 10 to the second power, or 100 (10×10). The fourth-column value is 10 to the third power, or 1,000 ($10 \times 10 \times 10$). The fifth-column value is equal to 10 to the fourth power, or 10,000 ($10 \times 10 \times 10 \times 10$). This same process can be used for determining the column values of a number in base 2, base 8, base 16, or any other base.

Two things should be noted about determining these column values. First, the resulting column values are in equivalent decimal, not in the original base. Second, a shortcut method of determining the column values is that the first, or right-hand, column is always the 1s column. The second-column value is equal to the value of the first column times the base. The third-column value is equal to the second-column value times the base. In all number systems, the value of a column can be determined by multiplying the value of the base times the value of the column to its right.

Table III-1 lists the three steps used to convert to a base 10 value from any other number system. Step 1 is to determine the column value of each digit in the number to be converted to decimal. The second step is to multiply the column value times the digit in the column. This multiplication step is repeated for each digit of the number to be converted. The third step is to sum the products calculated in Step 2. The total is the equivalent value in decimal. In the next three sections, we'll apply these steps to see how they work.

$10110_2 = ?_{10}$

Step 1 Determine column values

16s	8s	4s	2s	1s
1	0	1	1	0_2

Step 2 Multiply column values times column digits

16s	8s	4s	2s	1s
$\times 1$	$\times 0$	$\times 1$	$\times 1$	$\times 0$
16	0	4	2	0

Step 3 Sum the products

```
  16
   0
   4
   2
 + 0
 ───
  22
```

$10110_2 = 22_{10}$

FIGURE III-3
Converting binary to decimal.

TABLE III-1   **CONVERTING TO DECIMAL FROM ANOTHER BASE**

Converting to base 10

Step 1	Determine the column value of each digit (in decimal).
Step 2	Multiply the column value by the digit in the column. Repeat this step for each digit of the number to be converted.
Step 3	Sum the products calculated in Step 2. The total is the equivalent value in decimal.

Binary to decimal   Figure III-3 shows the three steps used to convert the binary number 10110 to its equivalent decimal. The first step is to determine the column values. The first-column value is always 1. Two times the first-column value (1) is equal to the value of the second column (2). Two times the second-column value (2) is equal to the third-column value (4). Two times the third-column value (4) is equal to the fourth-column value (8). Two times the fourth-column value (8) is equal to the fifth-column value (16). The column values double because the base is 2.

The second step in our conversion procedure (Table III-1) is to multiply the column values times the column digits. The third step is to add the products from step 2. Since the total in this example is equal to 22, binary 10110 is equal to decimal 22.

Octal to decimal conversion   Figure III-4 illustrates the steps required to convert octal 257 to its equivalent decimal value. The first step is to determine the column values. The first column of any numbering system is equal to 1. The base (8) times the first column (1) is equal to the value of the second column (8). The base times the second column (8 × 8) is equal to the third column, and so on. The second step is to multiply each column value times its

$257_8 = ?_{10}$

Step 1 Determine column values

64s	8s	1s
2	5	7_8

=

Step 2 Multiply column values times column digits

64s	8s	1s
$\times 2$	$\times 5$	$\times 7$
128	40	7

Step 3 Sum the products

128
40
 7
___
175

$257_8 = 175_{10}$

FIGURE III-4
Converting octal to decimal.

column digit. The third step is to add the products from step 2. The total in this example is equal to 175. Therefore, 257 in octal is equal to 175 in decimal.

Hexadecimal to decimal conversion   Figure III-5 shows the steps required to convert hexadecimal 2B3C to its equivalent decimal value. The first step is to determine column values. Remember that the first column (rightmost) is always 1 and that each column is worth the value of the column to its right, times the base (16). In hexadecimal, the first column value is 1, the second column equals 16 (16×1), the third column equals 256 (16×16), and the fourth column equals 4096 (16×256). The second step is to multiply the column values determined in step 1 by the digit in the column. Note that hexadecimal digits

$2B3C_{16} = ?_{10}$

Step 1 Determine column values

4096s	256s	16s	1s
2	B	3	C_{16}

=

Step 2 Multiply column values times column digits

4096s	256s	16s	1s
$\times 2$	$\times 11$	$\times 3$	$\times 12$
8192	2816	48	12

Note: Remember $B_{16} = 11_{10}$ and $C_{16} = 12_{10}$.

Step 3 Sum the products

8,192
2,816
   48
   12
_____
11,068

$2B3C_{16} = 11,068_{10}$

FIGURE III-5
Converting hexadecimal to decimal.

of A through F must be converted to their equivalent decimal value of 10 through 15 before multiplying. In this case, B becomes 11 and C becomes 12. The third step is to add the products from step 2. The sum of the products in this example is 11,068. Therefore, 11,068 is the decimal equivalent of hexadecimal 2B3C.

FEEDBACK   **III-1** Convert 10110011_2 to decimal.

III-2 Convert 246_8 to decimal.

III-3 Convert $2AE_{16}$ to decimal.

Converting from Base 10   At times, the programmer will need to convert a decimal number to binary, octal, or hexadecimal. The following technique will convert any decimal value to any other base. It is usually called the *division-remainder technique*.

Table III-2 lists the steps in using the division-remainder technique. The first step is to divide the decimal number to be converted by the value of the new base. Therefore, if the conversion is to binary, divide by 2; if the conversion is to octal, divide by 8; and if the new base is 16, divide by 16. Step 2 is to record the remainder from step 1 as the rightmost digit of the new base number. The first remainder becomes the digit in the first (rightmost) column. Note that when dividing by 2 to convert to binary, the remainder must be a 0 or a 1; when dividing by 8 for octal conversion, the possible remainders will be 0 through 7; and when dividing by 16 for hexadecimal conversion, the possible remainders will be from 0 through 15 (F). In each case, the possible remainders are equivalent to the possible digits in the new number system. Step 3 is to divide the answer of the previous division by the new base. Step 4 is to record the remainder from step 3 as the next digit (to the left) of the new base number. Steps 3 and 4 must be repeated, recording remainders from right to left, until getting an answer of 0 in step 3. Do not forget to record the remainder when the division answer is equal to 0. Using this technique, the conversion requires a division operation for each digit of the new base number.

Decimal to binary conversion   Figure III-6 illustrates the steps for converting the decimal number 26 to its binary equivalent. The first step is to divide the decimal value (26) by the new base (2). The second step is to record the remainder (0) as the 1s column digit in the binary number. The third step is

TABLE III-2   **CONVERTING FROM BASE 10 TO A NEW BASE USING THE DIVISION-REMAINDER TECHNIQUE**

Converting from base 10

Step 1	Divide the decimal number to be converted by the value of the new base.
Step 2	Record the remainder from step 1 as the rightmost digit of the new base number.
Step 3	Divide the *answer* of the previous divide by the new base.
Step 4	Record the *remainder* from step 3 as the next digit (to the left) of the new base number. Repeat steps 3 and 4, recording remainders from right to left, until after getting an answer of 0 in step 3.

$26_{10} - ?_2$

Step 1   Divide by the new base

$$\frac{13}{2\overline{)26}}$$
$$\frac{26}{0}$$

Step 2   Record the remainder as rightmost digit
$26_{10} = 0_2$

Step 3   Divide answer of previous division by the new base

$$\frac{6}{2\overline{)13}}$$
$$\frac{12}{1}$$

Step 4   Record the remainder as the next digit; if answer to division was zero, stop; otherwise repeat Steps 3 and 4
$26_{10} = 10^2$

Step 3   Divide answer of previous division by the new base

$$\frac{3}{2\overline{)6}}$$
$$\frac{6}{0}$$

Step 4   Record the remainder as the next digit; if answer to division was zero, stop; otherwise repeat Steps 3 and 4
$26_{10} = 010_2$

Step 3   Divide answer of previous division by the new base

$$\frac{1}{2\overline{)3}}$$
$$\frac{2}{1}$$

Step 4   Record the remainder as the next digit; if answer to division was zero, stop; otherwise repeat Steps 3 and 4
$26_{10} = 1010_2$

Step 3   Divide answer of previous division by the new base

$$\frac{0}{2\overline{)1}}$$
$$\frac{0}{1}$$

Step 4   Record the remainder as the next digit; if answer to division was zero, stop; otherwise repeat Steps 3 and 4
$26_{10} = 11010_2$

FIGURE III-6
Converting decimal to binary.

to divide the answer of the previous divide (13) by the new base. The fourth step is to record the remainder (1) as the next digit. If the answer to the division in step 3 had been equal to 0, the conversion would be completed. If the answer to the division in step 3 was greater than 0, steps 3 and 4 must be repeated. Note that in this example, a total of five division steps were required. When the last division resulted in an answer of 0 and the remainder was recorded, decimal 26 had been converted to binary 11010.

Decimal to octal conversion   Figure III-7 depicts the steps required to convert decimal 416 to its octal equivalent. Using the division-remainder technique of converting from a decimal value to a new base, the example conversion requires a series of three divide operations by the new base (8). The remainder from each division is recorded as a digit of the equivalent octal number. Note that the remainders are recorded from right to left. The sequence of dividing and recording the remainder continues until after an answer of 0 was generated from a division operation. After recording the last remainder, the decimal

---

$$416_{10} = ?_8$$

Step 1   Divide by the new base

$$\begin{array}{r} 52 \\ 8\overline{)416} \\ 40 \\ \hline 16 \\ 16 \\ \hline 0 \end{array}$$

Step 2   Record the remainder as rightmost digit
$$416_{10} = 0_8$$

Step 3   Divide answer of previous division by the new base

$$\begin{array}{r} 6 \\ 8\overline{)52} \\ 48 \\ \hline 4 \end{array}$$

Step 4   Record the remainder as the next digit; if answer to division was zero, stop; otherwise repeat Steps 3 and 4
$$416_{10} = 40_8$$

Step 3   Divide answer of previous division by the new base

$$\begin{array}{r} 0 \\ 8\overline{)6} \\ 0 \\ \hline 6 \end{array}$$

Step 4   Record the remainder as the next digit; if answer to division was zero, stop; otherwise repeat Steps 3 and 4
$$416_{10} = 640_8$$

FIGURE III-7
Converting from decimal to octal.

Decimal	Hexadecimal
0	0
1	1
2	2
3	3
4	4
5	5
6	6
7	7
8	8
9	9
10	A
11	B
12	C
13	D
14	E
15	F

FIGURE III-8

Decimal-hexadecimal equivalents.

number conversion is complete. In this example, decimal 416 is equal to octal 640.

Decimal to hexadecimal conversion   Using the division-remainder technique, the decimal number is divided by the new base, and the resulting remainder becomes a digit in the new number system. It must be remembered that the remainder is always a single digit in the new number system. Therefore, if a remainder of 10 through 15 results when converting to hexadecimal, the remainder must be converted to a hexadecimal digit of A through F. Figure III-8 illustrates decimal and hexadecimal equivalent values. Figure III-9 shows the steps required to convert decimal 941 to its equivalent hexadecimal value. In the first step, dividing by 16 results in a remainder of 13. This decimal value must be converted to its hexadecimal digit equivalent of D. In the second division, the remainder is a decimal 10, which must be converted to hexadecimal A. The third division results in an answer of 0. After recording the last remainder (3), the decimal number has been converted. Decimal 941 is equivalent to hexadecimal 3AD.

$$941_{10} = ?_{16}$$

Step 1   Divide by the new base

$$
\begin{array}{r}
58 \\
16\overline{)941} \\
80 \\
\overline{141} \\
128 \\
\overline{13} = D
\end{array}
$$

Step 2   Record the remainder as rightmost digit

$$941_{10} = D_{16}$$

Step 3   Divide answer of previous division by the new base

$$
\begin{array}{r}
3 \\
16\overline{)58} \\
48 \\
\overline{10} = A
\end{array}
$$

Step 4   Record the remainder as the next digit; if answer to division was zero, stop; otherwise repeat Steps 3 and 4

$$941_{10} = AD_{16}$$

Step 3   Divide answer of previous division by the new base

$$
\begin{array}{r}
0 \\
16\overline{)3} \\
0 \\
\overline{3}
\end{array}
$$

FIGURE III-9

Converting from decimal to hexadecimal.

Step 4   Record the remainder as the next digit; if answer to division was zero, stop; otherwise repeat Steps 3 and 4

$$941_{10} = 3AD_{16}$$

FEEDBACK   **III-4** Convert 430_{10} to hexadecimal.
III-5 Convert 163_{10} to octal.
III-6 Convert 26_{10} to binary.

SHORTCUT NOTATIONS   As indicated early in this supplement, it is very useful to have a shortcut notation for binary numbers when printing out the contents of memory. If the contents of memory were printed in binary, several pages of 0s and 1s would be required. The length of the output and the narrow choice of characters makes this form very difficult to use for a memory dump. To reduce the volume and print time of the memory dump and to show memory content with a greater variety of symbols, either the octal or hexadecimal number system is used as a shortcut notation. All computers use either octal or hexadecimal as their shortcut notation, depending upon the memory organization of the machine. If the basic unit of storage (such as a byte) is a multiple of 3 bits, octal is used as the shortcut. If the basic unit of storage is a multiple of 4 bits, hexadecimal is used as the shortcut notation. Because the selection of the shortcut notation is determined by the memory organization of the machine, any particular computer will always use either octal or hexadecimal, but not both. Therefore, programmers are not required to convert between octal and hexadecimal.

Table III-3 shows the relationship of octal and hexadecimal to binary. First, note that the maximum value for a single digit of octal (7) is equal to the maximum value of three digits of binary. The value range of one digit of octal duplicates the value range of three digits of binary. If octal digits are

TABLE III-3   **RELATIONSHIP OF OCTAL AND HEXADECIMAL TO BINARY**

Octal	Binary	Hexadecimal	Decimal
0	0	0	0
1	1	1	1
2	10	2	2
3	11	3	3
4	100	4	4
5	101	5	5
6	110	6	6
7 ⟶	111	7	7
10	1000	8	8
	1001	9	9
	1010	A	10
	1011	B	11
	1100	C	12
	1101	D	13
	1110	E	14
	1111 ⟵⟶	F	15
	10000	10	16

substituted for binary digits, the substitution is on a one-to-three basis. Computers using octal as the shortcut notation can represent the binary contents of memory in one-third of the space and time required when using binary.

Second, note that the maximum value of one digit in hexadecimal is equal to the maximum value of four digits in binary. Thus, the value range of one digit of hexadecimal is equivalent to the value range of four digits of binary. Therefore, hexadecimal shortcut notation is a one-to-four reduction in the volume of a memory dump.

Programmers may be required to reduce binary digits to a shortcut notation or to expand a shortcut notation to its binary equivalent.

Octal Notation

Table III-4 illustrates the steps to convert from binary to octal and from octal to binary. In converting from binary to octal, the first step is to divide the binary digits into groups of three, starting from the rightmost end. If the number of binary digits is not equal to a multiple of 3, zeros may be added on the left-hand side. The second step is to convert each group of three binary digits into one octal digit. Each group is converted as if it were a separate entity. The rightmost bit of the group has a column value of 1, the second column a value of 2, and the third column a value of 4. As Table III-3 shows, octal numbers up through 7 are equal to decimal digits. Therefore, the binary-to-decimal conversion discussed earlier may be used.

In converting from octal to binary, the first step is to convert each octal digit to a three-digit binary number. Again, since decimal and octal digits are equal up through 7, the octal digits may be treated as though they were decimal digits for this conversion. Step 2 is to run together the resulting binary groups into a single binary number. Figure III-10 illustrates the conversion of binary 110011 to octal. The first step is to divide the binary digits into two groups of three. The second step is to convert each group into one digit of octal. In this example, binary 110 converts to an octal 6, and 011 converts to an octal 3. Binary 110011, therefore, is equal to octal 63.

TABLE III-4   OCTAL SHORTCUT NOTATION

Binary to octal		Octal to binary	
Step 1	Divide the binary digits into groups of three (starting from the right).	**Step 1**	Convert each octal digit to a three-digit binary number. (You may treat the octal digits as decimal for this conversion.)
Step 2	Convert each group of three binary digits into one octal digit. (Use the binary-to-decimal conversion discussed earlier. Decimal digits 0–7 are equal to octal digits 0–7.)	**Step 2**	Run all of the resulting binary groups into a single binary number.

$110011_2 = ?_8$

Step 1 Divide the binary digits into groups of 3
110 011

Step 2 Convert each group into 1 digit of octal
$110 = 6 \quad 011 = 3$
$110011_2 = 63_8$

FIGURE III-10
Binary to octal.

$246_8 = ?_2$

Step 1 Convert each octal digit to 3 binary digits
$2 = 010$
$4 = 100$
$6 = 110$

Step 2 Run the binary groups together
2   4   6

$246_8 = 010100110_2$

FIGURE III-11
Octal to binary.

Figure III-11 depicts the expansion of octal to three binary digits. It may be necessary to add zeros to the left of the number, in order to make groups of three binary digits. The first step results in three groups of binary. Step 2 is to run the binary groups together as a single binary number.

FEEDBACK   **III-7** Show binary 101110 in octal notation.
III-8 What is the binary equivalent of octal 2614.

Hexadecimal Notation   Table III-5 lists the steps for the reduction of binary to hexadecimal and the expansion of hexadecimal to binary. In reducing binary to hexadecimal, the first step is to divide the binary digits into groups of four. Count off the binary groups, starting from the rightmost digit. The second step is to convert each group of four binary digits to one hexadecimal digit. The binary column values from right to left will be 1, 2, 4, and 8. It is convenient to use the binary-to-decimal technique discussed earlier in this chapter, but remember that resulting decimal values 10–15 should be written as hexadecimal digits A–F. In expanding hexadecimal to binary, the first step is to convert the decimal equivalent of each hexadecimal digit to four binary digits. Remember, hexadecimal digits 0–9 are equal to decimal digits 0–9, and hexadecimal digits A–F are equal to decimal 10–15. Step 2 is to run all of the binary groups into a single binary number.

TABLE III-5   **HEXADECIMAL SHORTCUT NOTATION**

Binary to hexadecimal		Hexadecimal to binary	
Step 1	Divide the binary digits into groups of four (starting from the right).	**Step 1**	Convert the decimal equivalent of each hexadecimal digit* four binary digits.
Step 2	Convert each group of four binary digits to one hexadecimal digit.* (Use the binary-to-decimal conversion in Table III-1, but represent the decimal values 10–15 as hexadecimal A–F).	**Step 2**	Run all of the binary groups into one binary number.

* Hexadecimal digits 0–9 equal decimal digits 0–9, and hexadecimal digits A–F are equal to decimal 10–15.

Figure III-12 illustrates the reduction of binary 11010111 to its hexadecimal equivalent. The first step divides the binary number into two groups of four digits. Step 2 converts each group of four binary digits to one hexadecimal digit. In this example, the binary reduces to hexadecimal D7.

Figure III-13 depicts the expansion of hexadecimal to its equivalent binary. The first step to convert hexadecimal A9 to binary is to convert the decimal equivalent of each hexadecimal digit to four binary digits. The second step is to run the resulting groups of four binary digits into a single string of binary.

$11010111_2 = ?_{16}$

Step 1   Divide the binary digits into groups of 4
1101 0111

Step 2   Convert each group of 4 binary digits to 1 hexadecimal digit
$1101_2 = 13_{10} = D_{16}$
$0111_2 = 7_{10} = 7_{16}$
$11010111_2 = D7_{16}$

FIGURE III-12

Binary to hexadecimal.

$2A9_{16} = ?_2$

Step 1   Convert the decimal equivalent of each hexadecimal digit to 4 binary digits
$2_{16} = 2_{10} = 0010_2$
$A_{16} = 10_{10} = 1010_2$
$9_{16} = 9_{10} = 1001_2$

Step 2   Run all the binary groups into one binary number

2   A   9

FIGURE III-13

Hexadecimal to binary.

$2A9_{16} = 001010101001_2$

FEEDBACK   **III-9** Show binary 11000101 in hexadecimal notation.
III-10 Expand hexadecimal 2AC to its binary equivalent.

ARITHMETIC   When working with memory dumps to locate errors, a programmer will be required to perform simple addition and subtraction of address values. These addresses will be either in octal or hexadecimal, depending upon the computer's memory organization. In some cases, the programmer may also add or subtract binary values to verify arithmetic results. The next portion of this chapter presents the steps needed to add and subtract in binary, octal, and hexadecimal.

Addition   The steps required to add two numbers are the same in all number systems. Therefore, the addition steps that we all use for decimal numbers can also be applied to adding binary, octal, and hexadecimal values. The easiest approach to adding values of a number system other than decimal is to add the column digits as if they were decimal. Because all binary and octal digit symbols are also decimal symbols, adding them as decimal digits is easy. Hexadecimal digits, however, use some symbols that are not included as decimal digits. These added symbols, A through F, should be converted to their equivalent decimal values of 10 through 15 before the addition is attempted.

The general steps of addition are described in Table III-6. Addition always begins by adding the rightmost column. If the column total is equal to or greater than the value of the base, a "carry" will occur. Whenever a 1 is carried to the next column, the value being carried is equal to the value of the base. As an example, if two decimal numbers were being added and the first column total was equal to 12, a 1 would be placed in the next column which would be a carry of 10 (the value of the base). Remember, a 1 in the 10s column is equal to 10 in the 1s column. After carrying a 1 to the next column, the remaining value is entered for the first column. These steps are repeated for each column until the entire number has been added. Let's look at some applications of these steps.

Adding in decimal   The general addition steps can be demonstrated in decimal. Figure III-14 illustrates the addition of 479 and 463. The first step is to add the 1s column of 9 and 3, for a total of 12. Because 12 is greater than a single digit in decimal, a 1 must be carried to the next column. Because the value of the base is always carried, a 2 is placed below the 1s column (12 minus 10).

TABLE III-6   **STEPS IN ADDITION**

Step 1   Add the first column (rightmost).

Step 2   If the column total from step 1 is equal to or greater than the base, subtract the value of the base from the column total and carry a 1 to the next column. (If the column total is still equal to or greater than the base, repeat step 2.)

Step 3   If there are additional columns or carry occurred in step 2, add the next column and repeat step 2.

$$479_{10}$$
$$+463_{10}$$

Step 1   Add the first column (rightmost)

$$9$$
$$+3$$
$$\overline{12}$$

Step 2   If the column total from Step 1 is equal to or greater than the base, subtract the value of the base from the column total and carry a 1 to the next column

$$1$$
$$479$$
$$+463$$
$$\overline{2}$$

Step 3   If there are additional columns or a carry occurred in Step 2, add the next column and repeat Step 2

$$1$$
$$7$$
$$+6$$
$$\overline{14}$$

Step 2   If the column total from Step 1 is equal to or greater than the base, subtract the value of the base from the column total and carry a 1 to the next column

$$11$$
$$479$$
$$+463$$
$$\overline{42}$$

Step 3   If there are additional columns or a carry occurred in Step 2, add the next column and repeat Step 2

$$1$$
$$4$$
$$+4$$
$$\overline{9}$$

Step 2   If the column total from Step 1 is equal to or greater than the base, subtract the value of the base from the column total and carry a 1 to the next column

$$11$$
$$479$$
$$+463$$
$$\overline{942}$$

FIGURE III-14
Adding in decimal.

$$10111_2$$
$$+01110_2$$

Step 1 Add the first column (rightmost)

$$1$$
$$+0$$
$$\overline{1}$$

Step 2 If the column total from Step 1 is equal to or greater than the base, subtract the value of the base from the column total and carry a 1 to the next column

$$10111$$
$$+01110$$
$$\overline{1}$$

Step 3 If there are additional columns or a carry occurred in Step 2, add the next column and repeat Step 2

$$1$$
$$1$$
$$\overline{2}$$

Step 2 If the column total from Step 1 is equal to or greater than the base, subtract the value of the base from the column total and carry a 1 to the next column

$$1$$
$$10111$$
$$+01110$$
$$\overline{01}$$

Step 3 If there are additional columns or a carry occurred in Step 2, add the next column and repeat Step 2

$$1$$
$$1$$
$$+1$$
$$\overline{3}$$

Step 2 If the column total from Step 1 is equal to or greater than the base, subtract the value of the base from the column total and carry a 1 to the next column

$$1\,1$$
$$1\,0\,1\,1\,1$$
$$+0\,1\,1\,1\,0$$
$$\overline{1\,0\,1}$$

Step 3 If there are additional columns or a carry occurred in Step 2, add the next column and repeat Step 2

$$1$$
$$0$$
$$+1$$
$$\overline{2}$$

FIGURE III-15
Adding in binary.

Step 2   If the column total from Step 1 is equal to or greater than the base, subtract the value of the base from the column total and carry a 1 to the next column

```
  1 1 1
  1 0 1 1 1
+ 0 1 1 1 0
    0 1 0 1
```

Step 3   If there are additional columns or a carry occurred in Step 2, add the next column and repeat Step 2

```
   1
   1
 + 0
   2
```

Step 2   If the column total from Step 1 is equal to or greater than the base, subtract the value of the base from the column total and carry a 1 to the next column

```
1 1 1 1
  1 0 1 1 1
+ 0 1 1 1 0
  0 0 1 0 1
```

Step 3   If there are additional columns or a carry occurred in Step 2, add the next column and repeat Step 2

```
   1
 + 0
   1
```

Step 2   If the column total from Step 1 is equal to or greater than the base, subtract the value of the base from the column total and carry a 1 to the next column

```
1 1 1 1
  1 0 1 1 1
+ 0 1 1 1 0
1 0 0 1 0 1
```

FIGURE III-15 (Continued)

The next step is to add the 10s column of 1, 7, and 6, for a total of 14. Again, a 1 must be carried to the next column. The column total of 14 minus 10 (the base) leaves a value of 4 in the 10s column. The last column of 1, 4, and 4 totals 9. Because this value is indicated as a single digit, no carry occurs and the total is equal to 942.

Adding in binary   The same addition steps used in adding decimal numbers can be applied to binary. Figure III-15 describes the steps necessary to add binary 10111 to binary 01110. The first step is to add the 1s column of 1 and 0. The column total is 1 and is a single binary digit; therefore, no carry occurs.

$$265_8$$
$$+434_8$$

Step 1 Add the first column (rightmost)

$$5$$
$$+4$$
$$\overline{9}$$

Step 2 If the column total from Step 1 is equal to or greater than the base, subtract the value of the base from the column total and carry a 1 to the next column

$$1$$
$$265$$
$$+434$$
$$\overline{1}$$

Step 3 If there are additional columns or a carry occurred in Step 2, add the next column and repeat Step 2

$$1$$
$$6$$
$$+3$$
$$\overline{10}$$

Step 2 If the column total from Step 1 is equal to or greater than the base, subtract the value of the base from the column total and carry a 1 to the next column

$$11$$
$$265$$
$$+434$$
$$\overline{21}$$

Step 3 If there are additional columns or a carry occurred in Step 2, add the next column and repeat Step 2

$$1$$
$$2$$
$$+4$$
$$\overline{7}$$

Step 2 If the column total from Step 1 is equal to or greater than the base, subtract the value of the base from the column total and carry a 1 to the next column

$$11$$
$$265$$
$$+434$$
$$\overline{721}$$

FIGURE III-16
Adding in octal.

The next step is to add the next column of 1 and 1, which equals 2. Because a decimal value of 2 cannot be indicated as a single digit in binary, a carry will occur. To carry, a 1 is placed above the column to the left. This carry is equal to the value of the base (2 in binary). A 1 in the 2s column is equal to a 2 in the 1s column. Because a value of 2 out of a column total of 2 is being carried, the remaining column value is 0. The third column values of 1, 1, and 1 totals to a decimal 3. Again, carry will result. A 1 in the fourth column carried 2 of the 3 leaving a 1 below the third column. The addition continues in the same manner for each column, as illustrated in Figure III-15.

Adding in octal   Figure III-16 depicts the steps for adding octal 265 to octal 434. The first step is to add the 1s column of 5 and 4, which totals decimal 9. Because the maximum decimal value for a single digit in octal is 7, carry must occur. A 1 is carried to the top of the next column which carries a value equal to the base (8). A 1 in the 8s column is equal to 8 in the 1s column. Since 8 of the column total of 9 have been carried, the difference of 1 is recorded below the first column. The second column of 1, 6, and 3 totals a decimal 10. A carry of 1 to the third column carries a value of the base. Since 8 of the 10 in the second column have been carried, the difference of 2 is recorded below the second column. The last column of 1, 2, and 4 totals to a decimal 7. Since decimal 7 is equal to octal 7, no carry occurs and the 7 is recorded below the third column.

Adding in hexadecimal   The last addition example is Figure III-17, which depicts adding hexadecimal 5A9 to hexadecimal A86. The first step of adding 9 and 6 results in a total of decimal 15. Decimal 15 can be represented as the single hexadecimal digit F and is recorded below the first column. The second column adds A and 8. Hexadecimal A is equal to decimal 10. Therefore, the column total is equal to decimal 18. Because 18 is greater than a single hexadecimal digit, a 1 is carried to the third column. This carries 16 (the base) of the total 18, and the remaining 2 is recorded below the second column. The third column of 1, 5, and A (decimal 10) equals a total of 16. Again, the column total exceeds the maximum size of one hexadecimal digit, so a carry must occur. In carrying the value of the base (16), the entire column value of 16 is being carried, so a 0 is recorded for the third column. The last step is to simply record the 1 from the last carry as the fourth column.

FEEDBACK   **III-11** Add the following *binary* values:

$$\begin{array}{r} 10110 \\ + \ 11011 \\ \hline \end{array}$$

III-12 Add the following *octal* values:

$$\begin{array}{r} 465 \\ +277 \\ \hline \end{array}$$

$$5A9_{16}$$
$$+A86_{16}$$

Step 1   Add the first column (rightmost)

$$9$$
$$+6$$
$$\overline{15} = F$$

Step 2   If the column total from Step 1 is equal to or greater than the base, subtract the value of the base from the column total and carry a 1 to the next column

$$5A9$$
$$+A86$$
$$\overline{F}$$

Step 3   If there are additional columns or a carry occurred in Step 2, add the next column and repeat Step 2

$$A \quad \text{\textit{Note:} } A = 10$$
$$+8$$
$$\overline{18}$$

Step 2   If the column total from Step 1 is equal to or greater than the base, subtract the value of the base from the column total and carry a 1 to the next column

$$1$$
$$5A9$$
$$+A86$$
$$\overline{2F}$$

Step 3   If there are additional columns or a carry occurred in Step 2, add the next column and repeat Step 2

$$1$$
$$5$$
$$+A$$
$$\overline{16}$$

Step 2   If the column total from Step 1 is equal to or greater than the base, subtract the value of the base from the column total and carry a 1 to the next column

$$11$$
$$5A9$$
$$+A86$$
$$\overline{02F}$$

Step 3   If there are additional columns or a carry occurred in Step 2, add the next column and repeat Step 2

$$1$$
$$+0$$
$$\overline{1}$$

Step 2   If the column total from Step 1 is equal to or greater than the base, subtract the value of the base from the column total and carry a 1 to the next column

$$11$$
$$5A9$$
$$+A86$$
$$\overline{102F}$$

FIGURE III-17
Adding in hexadecimal.

III-13 Add the following *hexadecimal* values:

$$\begin{array}{r} 3AC \\ +\ 2B9 \\ \hline \end{array}$$

Subtraction

The principles of subtraction using decimal numbers can be applied to subtraction of other bases as well. Table III-7 lists the general steps of subtraction. It consists of two steps, which are repeated for each column of the numbers. The first step is to determine if it is necessary to borrow. If the subtrahend (the lower digit) is larger than the minuend (the top digit), it is necessary to borrow from the column to the left. The value borrowed depends upon the base of the number. The value borrowed is always the decimal equivalent of the base. Thus, in binary, 2 is borrowed; in octal, 8 is borrowed; in hexadecimal, 16 is borrowed. The second step is simply to subtract the lower value from the top value.

Subtracting in decimal The general subtraction steps can be demonstrated with decimal values. Figure III-18 shows the steps for subtracting decimal 183 from decimal 346. The first operation is to determine if borrowing is necessary. Since 3 is less than 6, no borrowing is required. The 3 is subtracted from 6,

TABLE III-7 **STEPS IN SUBTRACTION**

Step 1	If the subtrahend digit of the column is larger than the minuend digit, borrow from the column to the left. (Note: The value borrowed is always equal in decimal to the value of the base.)
Step 2	Subtract the lower value from the top value.

$$\begin{array}{r} 346_{10} \\ -183_{10} \\ \hline \end{array}$$

1st operation (Steps 1 and 2 from Table III-7)

$$\begin{array}{r} 346 \\ -183 \\ \hline 3 \end{array}$$

2d operation

$$\begin{array}{r} 2\ 14 \\ \not{3}\not{4}6 \\ -183 \\ \hline 63 \end{array}$$

3d operation

$$\begin{array}{r} 2\ 14 \\ \not{3}\not{4}6 \\ -183 \\ \hline 163 \end{array}$$

FIGURE III-18
Subtracting in decimal.

and the remainder of 3 is recorded. The second column is subtracting 8 from 4; therefore, borrowing is required. A 1 is borrowed from the column to the left (leaving 2). Since the base is 10, 10 is the value being borrowed. The 4 in the second column and the 10 borrowed make 14. Taking 8 from 14 leaves 6. The third operation is to subtract 1 from the remaining 2 of the third column. These general steps can be applied to any number system.

$$10101_2$$
$$-01110_2$$

1st operation (Steps 1 and 2 from Table III-7)

$$10101$$
$$-01110$$
$$\overline{1}$$

2d operation

$$02$$
$$101\!\!\not{0}1$$
$$-01110$$
$$\overline{11}$$

3d operation

$$0202$$
$$1\!\!\not{0}1\!\!\not{0}1$$
$$-01110$$
$$\overline{11}$$

4th operation

$$12$$
$$0\!\!\not{2}02$$
$$1\!\!\not{0}1\!\!\not{0}1$$
$$-01110$$
$$\overline{111}$$

5th operation

$$12$$
$$0\!\!\not{2}02$$
$$1\!\!\not{0}1\!\!\not{0}1$$
$$-01110$$
$$\overline{0111}$$

6th operation

$$12$$
$$0\!\!\not{2}02$$
$$1\!\!\not{0}1\!\!\not{0}1$$
$$-01110$$
$$\overline{00111}$$

FIGURE III-19
Subtracting in binary.

Subtracting in binary   Figure III-19 illustrates the steps of subtracting binary 01110 from binary 10101. The first column does not require borrowing, and the 0 is subtracted from the 1. In the second column we are subtracting 1 from 0, so borrowing must occur. A 1 is borrowed from the column to the left. The 1 borrowed from the third column becomes 2 in the second column (because the base is 2). A 1 in the 4s column is equal to 2 in the 2s column. Subtraction can then proceed by subtracting 1 from 2 in the second column. The third column is also subtracting 1 from 0, and borrowing is again required. The fourth column contains a 0 and thus has nothing to borrow. Therefore, the borrowing must be from the fifth column. Borrowing 1 from the fifth column gives 2 in the fourth column. A 1 in the 16s column equals 2 in the 8s column. Now the fourth column has something to borrow. When 1 of the 2 in the fourth column is borrowed, it becomes 2 in the third column. The subtraction of 1 from 2 gives a difference of 1. Subtraction of the fourth column is now 1 from 1, giving 0. The fifth column subtraction is 0 from 0, giving 0.

Subtracting in octal   If borrowing is required in octal, the decimal equivalent of 8 is borrowed. Figure III-20 shows the subtraction of octal 275 from octal 734. In the first column, we are subtracting 5 from 4, so borrowing is necessary. Remember, 1 in the 8s column is equal to 8 in the 1s column. When 1 is borrowed from the second column, 8 is added to the first column, giving a total of 12 (in decimal). Taking 5 from 12 results in a 7 for the first column.

$$7\ 3\ 4_8$$
$$-2\ 7\ 5_8$$

1st operation (Steps 1 and 2 from Table III-7)

$$7\ 2\ 12$$
$$7\ 3\ 4$$
$$-2\ 7\ 5$$
$$\overline{7}$$

2d operation

$$10$$
$$6\ 2\ 12$$
$$7\ 3\ 4$$
$$-2\ 7\ 5$$
$$\overline{3\ 7}$$

3d operation

$$10$$
$$6\ 2\ 12$$
$$7\ 3\ 4$$
$$-2\ 7\ 5$$
$$\overline{4\ 3\ 7}$$

FIGURE III-20
Subtracting in octal.

In the second column, we are to subtract 7 from 2, and borrowing is again required. Borrowing 1 from the third column adds 8 to the second column, for a total of 10. Subtracting 7 from 10 results in a difference of 3. In the third column 2 is taken from 6, leaving 4.

Subtracting in hexadecimal   Subtracting in "foreign" number systems is most easily done using decimal equivalent values. When subtracting in hexadecimal, it is necessary that hexadecimal digits of A through F be converted to their decimal equivalents before subtracting. Figure III-21 illustrates the subtraction of hexadecimal 48F from hexadecimal A7B. The first column is the subtraction of F from B (or, in decimal, subtraction of 15 from 11). Borrowing is required. Borrowing 1 from the second column adds 16 to the first column. In the first column, we now subtract 15 from 27, resulting in 12. Because this subtraction result is in decimal, the 12 must be converted to a hexadecimal C. In the second column, we subtract 8 from 6, and again borrow. Borrowing 1 from the third column adds 16 to the second column, for a total of 22. Taking 8 from 22 is equal to decimal 14, or hexadecimal E. The last column subtracts 4 from 9, leaving 5.

$$
\begin{array}{r}
A\,7\,B_{16} \\
-4\,8\,F_{16}
\end{array}
$$

1st operation (Steps 1 and 2 from Table III-7)

$$
\begin{array}{r}
{\scriptstyle 6\ 27} \\
A\ 7\ \not{B} \\
-4\ 8\ F \\
\hline
C
\end{array}
\qquad
\begin{array}{r}
11 \\
+16 \\
\hline
27
\end{array}
\qquad
\begin{array}{r}
27 \\
-F = 15 \\
\hline
12 = C
\end{array}
$$

2d operation

$$
\begin{array}{r}
{\scriptstyle 22} \\
{\scriptstyle 9\ 6\ 27} \\
\not{A}\ 7\ \not{B} \\
-4\ 8\ F \\
\hline
E\ C
\end{array}
\qquad
\begin{array}{r}
6 \\
+16 \\
\hline
22
\end{array}
\qquad
\begin{array}{r}
22 \\
-8 \\
\hline
14 = E
\end{array}
$$

3d operation

$$
\begin{array}{r}
{\scriptstyle 22} \\
{\scriptstyle 9\ 6\ 27} \\
\not{A}\ 7\ \not{B} \\
-4\ 8\ F \\
\hline
5\ E\ C
\end{array}
$$

FIGURE III-21
Subtracting in hexadecimal.

FEEDBACK   **III-14** Subtract the following *binary* values:

$$
\begin{array}{r}
10101 \\
-\ 01110 \\
\hline
\end{array}
$$

III-15 Subtract the following *octal* values:

$$
\begin{array}{r}
243 \\
-\ 164 \\
\hline
\end{array}
$$

III-16 Subtract the following *hexadecimal* values:

$$
\begin{array}{r}
A36 \\
-\ 29C \\
\hline
\end{array}
$$

FIXED-LENGTH FIELDS   The binary values discussed in this chapter are used to express numeric data in a format known as fixed-point numbers. **Fixed-point numbers** are defined as whole, signed binary numbers. A signed number has either a plus sign or minus sign associated with it. Fields that contain values in this binary format are called **fixed-length fields.** The length of a fixed-length field is a unit called a **word.** The definition of a word varies with the size and the manufacturer of a computer. As a typical example, the IBM 4300 and 30XX series computers use a word that is 32 bits long. Small computers use a word with a length of 8 or 16 bits. Some machines have a word size greater than 32 bits.

Arithmetic operations are fastest when the data are in a binary format in fixed-length fields. This is most important in mathematically oriented programs. FORTRAN, a scientific programming language, handles numeric data fields as fixed-length binary data.

A second choice of format for storing data in the computer is to use **character codes.** Each character is a letter, symbol, or single digit represented in binary as a zone-and-digit combination. Fields containing data in a character-code format are not fixed in length but vary in length on a character-by-character basis. The business-oriented languages, such as COBOL and RPG, use character codes for most data. Character codes will be discussed in detail in Supplement IV.

SUMMARY   Programmers can usually debug their programs by using language processor error messages and debugging routines provided in most languages. On occasion, bugs in the program will cause errors in the program output that the programmer cannot trace without using a memory dump. When a memory dump is required, the programmer will be dealing with number systems other than decimal. A programmer should be familiar with binary, octal, and hexadecimal numbers and should be able to convert between decimal and any of these other bases. In order to find instructions and data in the memory dump, the programmer will be required to perform simple addition and/or subtraction of binary, octal, and hexadecimal values.

Numeric values held in memory in the binary format discussed in this chapter are called fixed-point numbers. They are held in memory as fixed-length fields. Numeric data held in this format are used for high-speed arithmetic processing. A second data format, called character codes, is covered in detail in the next chapter.

ANSWERS TO FEEDBACK QUESTIONS

III-1 $10110011_2 = 179_{10}$

III-2 $246_8 = 166_{10}$

III-3 $2AE_{16} = 686_{10}$

III-4 $430_{10} = 1AE_{16}$

III-5 $163_{10} = 243_8$

III-6 $26_{10} = 11010_2$

III-7 $101110_2 = 56_8$

III-8 $2614_8 = 010110001100_2$

III-9 $11000101_2 = C5_{16}$

III-10 $2AC_{16} = 001010101100_2$

III-11 110001_2

III-12 764_8

III-13 665_{16}

III-14 00111_2

III-15 057_8

III-16 $79A_{16}$

FOR REVIEW AND DISCUSSION

1 Why should programmers be familiar with binary, octal, and hexadecimal number systems?

2 Why are octal and/or hexadecimal number systems used as shortcut notation?

3 Why must a programmer convert between the decimal system and some other number system?

4 When would a programmer have to add or subtract in octal or hexadecimal?

5 Convert 1435_{10} to hexadecimal. Convert $35AC_{16}$ to decimal.

6 Convert 8612_{10} to octal. Convert 3173_8 to decimal.

7 Convert 135_{10} to binary. Convert 11001110_2 to decimal.

8 Add $34CA_{16}$ to $99CF_{16}$. Subtract 957_{16} from $F123_{16}$.

9 Add 537_8 to 476_8. Subtract 467_8 from 1473_8.

10 Add 11011101_2 to 01110101_2. Subtract 101010_2 from 1010101_2.

SUPPLEMENT IV
CHARACTER CODES

PREVIEW Supplement III introduced the number systems that are used in computer memory and in memory dumps. This supplement continues the presentation of formats used in computer memory to record data. The goal of this supplement is to present the most commonly used computer character codes.

In this supplement you will learn:

1. The binary-coded decimal interchange code (BCDIC)
2. The extended binary-coded decimal interchange code (EBCDIC)
3. The packed decimal number format
4. The American Standard Code for Information Interchange (ASCII)

KEY TERMS TO WATCH FOR AND REMEMBER

Hollerith card code
zone rows
digit rows
binary-coded decimal
    interchange code (BCDIC)
extended binary-coded
    decimal interchange
    code (EBCDIC)

zoned decimal
packed decimal
American Standard Code
    for Information Inter-
    change (ASCII)
American Standard Code
    for Information Inter-
    change-8 (ASCII-8)

All computers use coding systems to hold data in memory. In Supplement III we learned about binary numbers. The binary-number format introduced, called fixed-point format, is a numeric format. We must also have codes for alphabetic characters and special symbols. As you shall see, there are also two other numeric formats. A character code, called EBCDIC, was introduced in Chapter 5.

HOLLERITH CODE   Figure IV-1 shows a punched card only slightly different from the original punched card designed by Herman Hollerith for the 1890 U.S. Census. This **Hollerith card code** is made up of 12 horizontal punching areas called rows. The lower 10 rows in this example have the name of the row printed on the card face. These rows are known as the 0 row, 1 row, 2 row, etc. The top of the card has two rows with no printing on the card face. The top is the 12 row. The next row is called the 11 row. The card also has 80 vertical columns that cut across all 12 rows. The small numbers printed between the 0 and 1 rows and at the bottom edge of the card identify the 80 columns. One character may be stored in each column. If you understand the Hollerith code, the memory codes are easy to learn. In the Hollerith card code, each character (letter, number digit, or special symbol) is punched in a card column. The card column cuts across the 12 rows of the Hollerith card. The top three rows (12, 11, and 0) are the **zone rows,** and rows 0–9 are the **digit rows.** In this code, the 0 row is sometimes used as a zone and sometimes as a digit row. If the character is a number digit, the 0 row is used as a digit row. If the character is a letter or a special symbol, the 0 row is used as a zone.

FIGURE IV-1

Hollerith card. The standard 80-column punched card uses the coding scheme invented by Hollerith and differs from his card only slightly in size. It is called the Hollerith card.

Table IV-1 illustrates the alphabetic and numeric characters in the Hollerith card code. Note that the alphabetic characters are divided into three character groups. The first nine characters (A through I) use the 12 zone, the

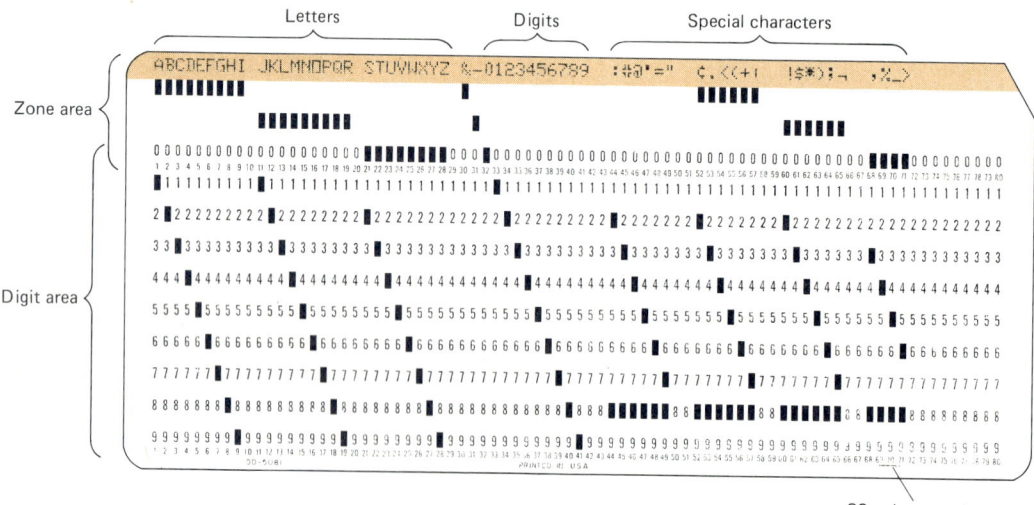

second nine characters (J through R) use the 11 zone, and the last eight characters (S through Z) use the 0 zone. The numeric characters 0–9 do not use a zone.

As shown in Table IV-1, numeric characters each require one row punch (a digit) and each of the alphabetic characters require two punches (a zone and a digit).

In Chapter 5, we described computer memory as a series of electronic switches. These switches are collected into groups (commonly called bytes) to record a character of data. Each switch is either "on" or "off." These switch conditions can be recorded as binary digits. The "off" condition is recorded as a 0, and the "on" condition is recorded as a 1. If the Hollerith code were to be used as a memory code, it would require a group of 12 switches to represent the equivalent of a card column. Each switch would indicate a punched or not-punched condition for each row within the card column.

Table IV-2 illustrates the Hollerith card code as a binary code. Note that the character A requires a 12-row punch and 1-row punch in a card. The binary code equivalent is 100100000000. The 1s are equivalent to a hole in a card.

The Hollerith card code is not used as an internal coding system because it requires 12 bits, or binary digits, to record each character of data. There are other, more efficient coding systems that require smaller bit groups to indicate a character. However, many of these other coding systems are based upon the Hollerith card code.

TABLE IV-1   THE ALPHABETIC AND NUMERIC CHARACTERS IN THE HOLLERITH CARD CODE

Character	Zone	Digit	Character	Zone	Digit
A	12	1			
B	12	2	S	0	2
C	12	3	T	0	3
D	12	4	U	0	4
E	12	5	V	0	5
F	12	6	W	0	6
G	12	7	X	0	7
H	12	8	Y	0	8
I	12	9	Z	0	9
			0	None	0
			1	None	1
J	11	1	2	None	2
K	11	2	3	None	3
L	11	3	4	None	4
M	11	4	5	None	5
N	11	5	6	None	6
O	11	6	7	None	7
P	11	7	8	None	8
Q	11	8	9	None	9
R	11	9			

TABLE IV-2   **THE HOLLERITH CARD CODE USED AS AN INTERNAL CODE**

	Bit Number										
Character	12	11	0	1	2	3	4	5	6	7	8	9
A	1	0	0	1	0	0	0	0	0	0	0	0
C	1	0	0	0	0	1	0	0	0	0	0	0
E	1	0	0	0	0	0	0	1	0	0	0	0
G	1	0	0	0	0	0	0	0	0	1	0	0
I	1	0	0	0	0	0	0	0	0	0	0	1
J	0	1	0	1	0	0	0	0	0	0	0	0
L	0	1	0	0	0	1	0	0	0	0	0	0
N	0	1	0	0	0	0	0	1	0	0	0	0
P	0	1	0	0	0	0	0	0	0	1	0	0
R	0	1	0	0	0	0	0	0	0	0	0	1
S	0	0	1	0	1	0	0	0	0	0	0	0
U	0	0	1	0	0	0	1	0	0	0	0	0
W	0	0	1	0	0	0	0	0	1	0	0	0
Y	0	0	1	0	0	0	0	0	0	0	1	0
Z	0	0	1	0	0	0	0	0	0	0	0	1
1	0	0	0	1	0	0	0	0	0	0	0	0
3	0	0	0	0	0	1	0	0	0	0	0	0
5	0	0	0	0	0	0	0	1	0	0	0	0
7	0	0	0	0	0	0	0	0	0	1	0	0
9	0	0	0	0	0	0	0	0	0	0	0	1

TABLE IV-3   **A SUMMARY OF THE HOLLERITH CARD CODE PLAN**

Character group	Zone row	Digit row
A–I	12	1–9 (The digit is equal to the character's position within the character group.)
J–R	11	1–9 (The digit is equal to the character's position within the character group.)
S–Z	0	2–9 (The digit is equal to the character's position within the character group, plus 1.)
0–9	None	0–9 (The digit is equal to the numeric character.)

Table IV-3 is a summary of the Hollerith code that shows the logic plan of the code. This logic plan also applies to some of the memory codes.

FEEDBACK   **IV-1** What character is recorded in Hollerith code with row punches of 12 and 6?

IV-2 What punches would be required to record the word COMPUTER?

IV-3 How many card columns will be required to hold the word COMPUTER in the card?

BINARY-CODED DECIMAL INTERCHANGE CODE (BCDIC)

One of the early memory codes that was based upon the Hollerith code is the **binary-coded decimal interchange code (BCDIC)**. The BCDIC is a 6-bit code—that is, it requires memory groups of 6 binary digits. The first 2 bits represent the equivalent of the Hollerith code zones. The last 4 bits represent the equivalent of the Hollerith code digits. The Hollerith code has four possible zones (12, 11, 0, and no zone). These four zone possibilities are indicated in BCDIC as the binary equivalent of the values 3, 2, 1, and 0 (11, 10, 01, and 00). The 4 digit bits are the basis for the BCDIC name. The Hollerith digits for alphabetic and numeric characters have a value range from 0 through 9. In BCDIC, these decimal values are coded as binary digits. Thus, binary digits are used to code the decimal digit value. This is the reason that the code is called a binary-coded decimal. Most people call BCDIC the binary-coded decimal code or just BCD.

Table IV-4 illustrates the alphabetic and numeric characters in BCDIC. Note that the character 0 has a digit value equal to 10, rather than 0. The BCDIC is consistent with the Hollerith card code in its division of the alphabetic characters into three groups. The digit value of each BCDIC character is equal to the digit value used in the Hollerith code (with the exception of the 0).

Supplement III presented the use of the octal and hexadecimal number systems as shortcut notation for binary. Because BCDIC is a 6-bit code, it divides evenly into two 3-bit halves. Each of these 3-bit halves can be repre-

TABLE IV-4   **THE ALPHABETIC AND NUMERIC CHARACTERS IN BINARY CODED DECIMAL INTERCHANGE CODE (BCDIC)**

Character	Binary Zone	Binary Digit	Octal	Character	Binary Zone	Binary Digit	Octal
A	11	0001	61	S	01	0010	22
B	11	0010	62	T	01	0011	23
C	11	0011	63	U	01	0100	24
D	11	0100	64	V	01	0101	25
E	11	0101	65	W	01	0110	26
F	11	0110	66	X	01	0111	27
G	11	0111	67	Y	01	1000	30
H	11	1000	70	Z	01	1001	31
I	11	1001	71				
J	10	0001	41	1	00	0001	01
K	10	0010	42	2	00	0010	02
L	10	0011	43	3	00	0011	03
M	10	0100	44	4	00	0100	04
N	10	0101	45	5	00	0101	05
O	10	0110	46	6	00	0110	06
P	10	0111	47	7	00	0111	07
Q	10	1000	50	8	00	1000	10
R	10	1001	51	9	00	1001	11
				0	00	1010	12

Character	Binary	Octal
A	110 001	61
B	110 010	62
J	100 001	41
K	100 010	42
S	010 010	22
T	010 011	23
1	000 001	01
2	000 010	02

FIGURE IV-2

BCDIC character codes in binary and octal.

sented by 1 octal digit. Thus, a three-to-one digit reduction results from using octal as shortcut notation of BCDIC. Figure IV-2 shows examples of BCDIC characters in both binary and octal.

FEEDBACK

IV-4 What binary digits are required to represent the character L in BCDIC?
IV-5 What octal digits are used for the character L in BCDIC?
IV-6 Show the binary digits to record the word CAT in BCDIC.

EXTENDED BINARY-CODED DECIMAL INTERCHANGE CODE (EBCDIC)

One of the major problems with the BCDIC code is that it has only 64 unique bit combinations, or 64 different character possibilities. Modern data processing often requires a symbol variety greater than 64 characters. It is not uncommon to require lower-case alphabetic characters and a fairly large selection of special symbols in addition to upper-case and numeric characters.

The solution was to extend the BCDIC code from a 6-bit code to an 8-bit code. The added 2 bits are used as additional zone bits, expanding the zone to 4 bits. The resulting code is called the **extended binary-coded decimal interchange code.** The name is too long to use conveniently; therefore, most people pronounce its abbreviation—EBCDIC—"ebb-see-dick." EBCDIC extends the number of possible characters from 64 to 256. This allows a large variety of printable characters and several nonprintable control characters. The control characters are used to control such activities as printer vertical spacing. All of the 256 bit combinations have not yet been assigned characters, so the code can still grow as new requirements develop.

Table IV-5 illustrates the alphabetic and numeric characters in EBCDIC. Note the similarity of EBCDIC to the Hollerith card code. The alphabetic characters are divided up into the same three character groups, and the digit values are consistent with the digit values in the Hollerith code. The zone values are equal to the decimal values of 12, 13, and 14 (1100, 1101, and 1110). The numeric characters of 0 through 9 all have a zone of binary 1111 (a decimal value of 15). One important difference between the BCDIC code and EBCDIC

TABLE IV-5   **THE ALPHABETIC AND NUMERIC CHARACTERS IN THE EXTENDED BINARY-CODED DECIMAL INTERCHANGE CODE (EBCDIC)**

Character	Binary Zone	Binary Digit	Hexadecimal	Character	Binary Zone	Binary Digit	Hexadecimal
A	1100	0001	C1				
B	1100	0010	C2	S	1110	0010	E2
C	1100	0011	C3	T	1110	0011	E3
D	1100	0100	C4	U	1110	0100	E4
E	1100	0101	C5	V	1110	0101	E5
F	1100	0110	C6	W	1110	0110	E6
G	1100	0111	C7	X	1110	0111	E7
H	1100	1000	C8	Y	1110	1000	E8
I	1100	1001	C9	Z	1110	1001	E9
				0	1111	0000	F0
J	1101	0001	D1	1	1111	0001	F1
K	1101	0010	D2	2	1111	0010	F2
L	1101	0011	D3	3	1111	0011	F3
M	1101	0100	D4	4	1111	0100	F4
N	1101	0101	D5	5	1111	0101	F5
O	1101	0110	D6	6	1111	0110	F6
P	1101	0111	D7	7	1111	0111	F7
Q	1101	1000	D8	8	1111	1000	F8
R	1101	1001	D9	9	1111	1001	F9

is that the zone values of the characters A through 9 decrease in BCDIC from the equivalent of decimal 3 down to 0, while in EBCDIC, the zone values increase from the equivalent of 12 through 15. This means that sorting data in memory that is coded in BCDIC will result in the numbers being sorted in front of letters. Sorting EBCDIC characters results in numbers appearing after letters.

Table IV-6 shows the zone indications of the Hollerith-related coding systems. It illustrates the Hollerith zone, the BCDIC zone, and the equivalent EBCDIC zone. The digit values are the same in all three codes, with the exception of the character 0 in the BCDIC code. Because EBCDIC is an 8-bit grouping, it divides evenly into two 4-bit groups. Each of these 4-bit groups can be represented by 1 hexadecimal digit. Hexadecimal, therefore, is a four-

TABLE IV-6   **ZONE INDICATIONS OF THE HOLLERITH-RELATED CODING SYSTEMS**

Character group	Hollerith card zone	BCDIC zone	EBCDIC zone
A–I	12 row	11	1100
J–R	11 row	10	1101
S–Z	0 row	01	1110
0–9	None	00	1111

Character	Binary	Hexadecimal
A	1100 0001	C1
B	1100 0010	C2
J	1101 0001	D1
K	1101 0010	D2
S	1110 0010	E2
T	1110 0011	E3
1	1111 0001	F1
2	1111 0010	F2

FIGURE IV-3

EBCDIC characters in binary and hexadecimal.

to-one shortcut notation for the binary of EBCDIC. Figure IV-3 shows examples of EBCDIC characters in both binary and hexadecimal.

Numeric EBCDIC Characters

We have said that numeric characters for 0 through 9 have a zone of binary 1111 (decimal 15 or hexadecimal F). The digit values are the same as the numeric characters—that is, 0 through 9 (0000–1001). However, there are some special considerations that apply to numeric values. One important one is the sign of the number. We must have a way of indicating whether or not the number is signed. If it is, we must know if it is a positive value or a negative one. Figure IV-4 contains examples of signed and unsigned EBCDIC numbers. As you can see, the zone position of the right-hand digit is the sign indicator. A sign indicator of hexadecimal C is a plus sign, hexadecimal D is a minus sign, and a hexadecimal F means the number is unsigned. Unsigned numbers, of course, are treated as positive values. Note that the only zone affected by the sign is the zone of the rightmost digit. All other zones remain Fs.

Numeric value	EBCDIC code
	sign indicator
123	F1F2F3
	sign indicator
+123	F1F2C3
	sign indicator
−123	F1F2D3

Sign	Zone (sign indicator)
plus	C
minus	D
unsigned	F

FIGURE IV-4

EBCDIC numbers with signs (hexadecimal notation).

| | | | ZD ZD SD | zoned decimal |
| | | | DD DS | packed decimal |

Z = the zone
D = the digit
S = the sign

Field value	Zoned decimal	Packed decimal
123	F1F2F3	123F
+123	F1F2C3	123C
−123	F1F2D3	123D
1234	F1F2F3F4	01234F

FIGURE IV-5
Zoned and packed decimal.

Zoned decimal   The decimal value of 123, coded in EBCDIC, is F1F2F3. If you ignore the F zones, you can see the decimal digits 123. Because each decimal digit has a zone with it, numbers coded in EBCDIC are called **zoned-decimal** numbers. Numeric data input into the computer are usually zoned decimal numbers. Printers can print only those number characters that are in a zoned-decimal format. Most arithmetic logic units, however, cannot perform arithmetic operations on zoned-decimal data. Before arithmetic operations can take place, the data must be converted to another format.

Packed decimal   One acceptable format is binary (discussed in Supplement III). A character code format is also acceptable. It is a modified form of zoned decimal called **packed decimal.**

Figure IV-5 compares zoned decimal data and packed decimal data formats. Remember that the sign of the number is held in the zone portion of the rightmost byte. The sign must be preserved as we change the data from zoned decimal to packed decimal. The conversion begins with the rightmost byte. The zone half and the digit half of the byte are reversed. This moves the sign to the far right. The second step is to drop out all remaining zones. The digits are placed two to a byte. Note that the conversion process "packs" the numeric data into fewer bytes than required for zoned-decimal data. There are 2 digits in each byte. If the packing process does not completely fill a byte, it will be filled with a zero. As an example, F1F2F3F4 will convert to packed decimal 01234F.

FEEDBACK

IV-7 Using hexadecimal notation, write the EBCDIC coding for the word CAT.

IV-8 Write the EBCDIC coding for the value +576 (use hexadecimal).

IV-9 Write +576 as a packed-decimal number (use hexadecimal).

Although the BCDIC and EBCDIC codes are popular memory codes, they are not the only codes being used. Another popular code is the American Standard Code for Information Interchange (ASCII) ASCII is pronounced "ask-ee." It was designed to be a national standard code. ASCII is also accepted as an international code by the International Organization for Standardization (ISO) under the name of International Standard 646. ASCII is used throughout the world. Several American computer manufacturers have adopted it as their computers' internal code. In fact, it is used by most microcomputer manufacturers. ASCII is a 7-bit code. Microcomputers using 8-bit groups use the 7-bit ASCII code by leaving the first bit (leftmost) of each group as a zero. The first 3 bits indicate the zone, and the last 4 bits indicate the digit. In a 7-bit code, there are 128 unique bit combinations, or 128 possible characters.

ASCII is not related to the Hollerith card code. Table IV-7 illustrates the numeric and alphabetic characters in ASCII. The alphabetic characters are divided into two groups in ASCII, rather than into the three groups used in the BCD codes. The first group of alphabetic characters is from A through O. The digit values for these characters run from 1 (binary 0001) through 15 (binary 1111). The last 11 characters (P through Z) have a digit value that runs from 0 (binary 0000) through 10 (binary 1010). The number characters of 0 through 9 have a digit value that also runs from zero (0000) through nine (1001). The zone indication for the numeric characters is equal to a decimal 3

TABLE IV-7   **NUMERIC AND ALPHABETIC CHARACTERS IN THE AMERICAN STANDARD CODE FOR INFORMATION INTERCHANGE (ASCII)**

Character	Binary Zone	Binary Digit	Hex	Decimal	Character	Binary Zone	Binary Digit	Hex	Decimal
0	011	0000	30	48	J	100	1010	4A	74
1	011	0001	31	49	K	100	1011	4B	75
2	011	0010	32	50	L	100	1100	4C	76
3	011	0011	33	51	M	100	1101	4D	77
4	011	0100	34	52	N	100	1110	4E	78
5	011	0101	35	53	O	100	1111	4F	79
6	011	0110	36	54	P	101	0000	50	80
7	011	0111	37	55	Q	101	0001	51	81
8	011	1000	38	56	R	101	0010	52	82
9	011	1001	39	57	S	101	0011	53	83
A	100	0001	41	65	T	101	0100	54	84
B	100	0010	42	66	U	101	0101	55	85
C	100	0011	43	67	V	101	0110	56	86
D	100	0100	44	68	W	101	0111	57	87
E	100	0101	45	69	X	101	1000	58	88
F	100	0110	46	70	Y	101	1001	59	89
G	100	0111	47	71	Z	101	1010	5A	90
H	100	1000	48	72					
I	100	1001	49	73					

(011). The zone indications for the two alphabetic groups are equivalent to decimal 4 and 5 (100 and 101), respectively. Note that the number characters have a zone value that is less than the zone for letters. Therefore, numbers will be placed ahead of letters during a sort. ASCII characters are usually indicated by using hexadecimal as the shortcut notation. Because the zone is only three bits, the zone values in hexadecimal run from 0 (0000) through 7 (0111).

FEEDBACK

IV-10 What is the binary coding for the character M in ASCII?
IV-11 What is the hexadecimal coding for the character 3 in ASCII?
IV-12 Write the hexadecimal coding for the word DOG in ASCII.

AMERICAN STANDARD CODE FOR INFORMATION INTERCHANGE-8 (ASCII-8)

A newer version of the ASCII code, called ASCII-8, is illustrated in Table IV-8. It is an extended version of ASCII in that it uses an 8-bit group, rather than a group of 7. The code capacity is extended to 256 character choices. The additional bit is added to the zone bits. The character groups and the digit values within the character groups are identical for ASCII and ASCII-8. The zone values, however, are different. The zone for the numeric characters is equal to 5 (0101). The zone value for the two alphabetic groups are 10 and 11 (1010 and 1011), respectively. Other than the zone-value differences, ASCII

TABLE IV-8   **NUMERIC AND ALPHABETIC CHARACTERS IN AMERICAN STANDARD CODE FOR INFORMATION INTERCHANGE-8 (ASCII-8)**

Character	Binary Zone	Binary Digit	Hexadecimal	Character	Binary Zone	Binary Digit	Hexadecimal
0	0101	0000	50	J	1010	1010	AA
1	0101	0001	51	K	1010	1011	AB
2	0101	0010	52	L	1010	1100	AC
3	0101	0011	53	M	1010	1101	AD
4	0101	0100	54	N	1010	1110	AE
5	0101	0101	55	O	1010	1111	AF
6	0101	0110	56	P	1011	0000	B0
7	0101	0111	57	Q	1011	0001	B1
8	0101	1000	58	R	1011	0010	B2
9	0101	1001	59	S	1011	0011	B3
A	1010	0001	A1	T	1011	0100	B4
B	1010	0010	A2	U	1011	0101	B5
C	1010	0011	A3	V	1011	0110	B6
D	1010	0100	A4	W	1011	0111	B7
E	1010	0101	A5	X	1011	1000	B8
F	1010	0110	A6	Y	1011	1001	B9
G	1010	0111	A7	Z	1011	1010	BA
H	1010	1000	A8				
I	1010	1001	A9				

and ASCII-8 are identical. ASCII-8 also uses hexadecimal as its four-to-one shortcut notation.

IV-13 What is the binary coding for the character P in ASCII-8?

IV-14 What is the hexadecimal coding for the character 8 in ASCII-8?

IV-15 Write the hexadecimal coding for the word FROG in ASCII-8.

MEMORY DUMPS

Chapter 15 defined a memory dump as a printout of the contents of computer memory that uses a shortcut notation of either octal or hexadecimal. If memory has been designed to use BCDIC as its internal code, it will have 6-bit groupings. Therefore, the shortcut notation used in its memory dump will be octal, representing each 6-bit group as 2 octal digits. If memory has been designed to use EBCDIC, ASCII, or ASCII-8 as its internal code, hexadecimal will be used as its shortcut notation in memory dumps. Memory may contain data as character codes or as binary numbers. These data formats may both be found in memory. Because there is not a program in control to indicate how the internal binary should be interpreted for printing, the memory dump prints out the data as binary values or zone-digit combinations in its raw form, using a shortcut notation of octal or hexadecimal. The interpretation of the data is left to the programmer.

Figure IV-6 shows some examples of decimal values as zoned-decimal and packed-decimal codes as well as binary numbers. For these examples, a word of binary is assumed to be 4 bytes (32 bits). In the first example, the value +123 is used. By ignoring the zones in zoned decimal, you can see the decimal value 123. It's even easier to see the decimal value in packed decimal. To determine the decimal value of binary (hexadecimal notation) 7B, you will have to convert it to decimal by means of the techniques presented in Supplement III. In the second example, the value +4668 is shown. Note that the binary equivalent (shown in hexadecimal) is 123C, the same as decimal +123 in a packed-decimal format. If a programmer sees 123C in a memory dump, is it decimal +123 as a packed-decimal number or decimal +4668 in a binary format? You cannot tell by looking at the memory dump. The programmer will have to check, in order to see what data format is being used in the program. FORTRAN uses binary formats, and COBOL and RPG usually use decimal codes.

Value	Zoned decimal	Packed decimal	Binary (hexadecimal)
+123	F1F2C3	123C	0000007B
+4668	F4F6F6C8	04668C	0000123C
+41,083	F4F1F0F8C3	41083C	0000A07B

FIGURE IV-6
Decimal, packed decimal, and binary.

Figure IV-7 is an example of a page of a memory dump. The particular computer used for this memory dump uses EBCDIC as its internal code. Therefore, the shortcut notation illustrated is hexadecimal. Each grouping (byte) in memory is assigned a number, called its storage address. This storage address is a binary value. The leftmost column in the memory dump example is the address column. The remaining columns represent the memory data. The address in the memory column refers to the first byte of data shown on that line. Each line of data consists of 64 hexadecimal digits, or 32 bytes of data. Note that the values down the address column increase by hexadecimal 20 (decimal 32). As an example, the contents of byte 1C02C0 are found just to the right of the address column entry 1C02C0. The content of that byte is hexadecimal C8, which is equivalent in EBCDIC to the letter H. If byte 1C02C0 is the first byte of data in the line, byte 1C02C1 must be the next byte of data in the line. The content of byte 1C02C1 is hexadecimal C5, or the letter E. The content of byte number 1C02BF is found at the right-hand end of the line addressed as 1C02A0. Count each byte of data on the line in hexadecimal. The last byte in the line will be 1C02BF. The content of that byte is E3 or the letter

FIGURE IV-7

An example of a memory dump from a computer using the EBCDIC (hexadecimal notation).

1C0080	001C009E	001C00A0	001C0330	02B10202	001C0194	00000000	021C0194	20000050
1C00A0	47000000	47000000	00000000	00000000	00008000	0C000003	001C00D8	001C00E0
1C00C0	001C03AC	089CC909	001C01E5	000000C0	07004700	00000000	091C01E5	20000050
1C00E0	05A00700	4110A22E	4500A012	001C0078	001C00B0	0A02024F	A103A153	5810A23E
1C0100	58F10010	45EFC00C	5810A242	58F10010	45EF0008	9240A103	D24EA104	A103D204
1C0120	A104A0B2	D213A116	A0B7D203	A134A0CB	D204A146	A0D4581C	A23E58F1	001045EF
1C0140	000CF224	A0D6A0D4	FA32A1D7	A0D6FA10	A1D8A246	47F0A026	C24FA103	A1DDF321
1C0160	A124A10B	96F0A126	F363A144	A1C796F0	A14A5810	A23E58F1	001045EF	000C0700
1C0180	4110A236	4500A0AE	001C0078	001C00B0	0A020A0E	F5F4F3F2	F1C2C1C4	40D5C5E6
1C01A0	E240E2E3	E4C6C640	40404040	40F1F2F3	F4404040	40404040	00000440	40404040
1C01C0	40404040	--SAME--						
1C01E0	40404040	4540F5F4	F3F2F140	40404040	40404040	40404040	C2C1C440	05C5E6E2
1C0200	40E2E3E4	C6C64040	40404040	40404040	40404040	4040F1F2	F3F44040	40404040
1C0220	40404040	40404040	40404040	40404040	40404040	40C9E3C5	D440D5D6	4B404040
1C0240	40404040	40404040	40404040	40C4C5E2	C3D9C9D7	E3C9D6D5	40404040	40404040
1C0260	404040D8	E4C105E3	C9E3E840	40404040	40404040	404040C1	D4D6E4D5	E3404040
1C0280	40404040	--SAME--						
1C02A0	40404040	40404040	40404040	40404040	40404040	40404040	40000123	4C001CE3
1C02C0	C8C540D5	E404C2C5	D940D6C6	40C9E3C5	D4E24D07	D9D6C3C5	E2E2C5C4	40C9E240
1C02E0	40404040	40404040	40E3C8C5	40E3D6E3	C1D340C1	D4D6E4D5	E340C9E2	40404040
1C0300	4040404C	40404040	40404040	40404040	5B5BC2D6	D7C5D54C	5B5BC2C3	D3D6E2C5
1C0320	001C00B0	001C0078	1CC1D3E8	E2C9E240	0A320000	0A320000	47F0F01A	0A320000
1C0340	C9D1C3C6	E9C9E9F0	33000A00	91801002	4710F026	0A0750EC	F06858E0	10209101
1C0360	10044780	F04C9140	10024710	F04658E0	F06847F0	F01A58E0	101C07FE	D501F060
1C0380	E0004770	F05A47F0	F04658E0	F06807FE	615C0C00	10220000	A01C0114	40404D5
1C03A0	0A320000	0A320000	0A320000	47F0F01A	C9D1C4C6	E9E9E9E9	34010A00	91801002
1C03C0	4710F026	0A07C7FE	00000000	00000000	00000000	0000000C	C000000	00000000
1C03E0	00000000	--SAME--						
1FFFE0	0000000C	0000C000	00C00000	00000000	00000000	00000000	C000000	00000000

T. It should be noted that hexadecimal 40 is the EBCDIC character for a blank. In the computer used for this memory dump example, fixed-point binary values are held in a memory unit called a word. It is equal to 32 bits or 4 bytes. The address of the word always refers to the byte at the left end of the word. As an example, the word at location 1C0140 contains the hexadecimal digits 000CF224. This is a binary value represented in hexadecimal. To determine the equivalent decimal value, the hexadecimal value must be converted to decimal, using the hexadecimal-to-decimal techniques discussed in Supplement III. In this example 000CF224 is equivalent to a decimal value of 848,420.

Zoned-decimal and packed-decimal data can also be found in this example memory dump. The value 1234 is in a 4-byte field beginning at address location 1C0216. The decimal value $+0001234$ is in a 4-byte packed-decimal field beginning at address location 1C02B9.

FEEDBACK   **IV-16** What is a memory dump?
IV-17 What is a storage address?
IV-18 When is hexadecimal used as the shortcut notation? Octal?

SUMMARY There are several character codes commonly used as internal computer codes. An early code called the binary-coded decimal interchange code (BCDIC) and its modern replacement, called extended binary-coded decimal interchange code (EBCDIC), have common characteristics with the Hollerith card code. The BCDIC is a 64-character code that uses 6-bit groups. Octal is its shortcut notation. EBCDIC has 256 character possibilities. As an 8-bit group code, it uses hexadecimal as its shortcut notation. Number characters in EBCDIC are called zoned-decimal numbers. A second decimal format, called packed-decimal, is usually required to perform arithmetic operations on decimal fields. Two codes that are not based on the Hollerith card code are the American Standard Code for Information Interchange (ASCII) and the American Standard Code for Information Interchange-8 (ASCII-8). These two codes were developed by a committee of the American National Standards Institute. ASCII is a 7-bit code with 128 character possibilities. ASCII-8 is an 8-bit code with 256 character possibilities. Both ASCII and ASCII-8 use hexadecimal as their shortcut notation. Using memory dumps will require the interpretation of either octal or hexadecimal, depending upon the shortcut notation used by the computer. Addresses, as well as data, are indicated in the memory dump. Data may be in either a binary format or a character code format. When the use of a memory dump is required in order to track down program logic errors, it is necessary to be familiar with character codes and number systems other than decimal.

**ANSWERS
TO FEEDBACK
QUESTIONS**

IV-1 The character F.

IV-2 12-3, 11-6, 11-4, 11-7, 0-4, 0-3, 12-5, and 11-9.

IV-3 Eight.

IV-4 100011.

IV-5 43.

IV-6 C = 110011; A = 110001; T = 010011.

IV-7 C3C1E3.

IV-8 F5F7C6.

IV-9 576C.

IV-10 1001101.

IV-11 33 (hexadecimal).

IV-12 D = 44; O = 4F; G = 47.

IV-13 10110000.

IV-14 58 (hexadecimal).

IV-15 F = A6; R = B2; O = AF; G = A7.

IV-16 A printout of the contents of memory.

IV-17 Each group of binary positions in memory (byte or word) is numbered. This number is known as its storage address.

IV-18 Hexadecimal notation is used when the memory character groupings are 7 or eight bits, such as in EBCDIC, ASCII, and ASCII-8. Octal notation is used for the 6-bit code BCDIC.

**FOR REVIEW
AND DISCUSSION**

1 Why is the Hollerith card code not used as a memory code?

2 How many possible characters are allowed for in the BCDIC code? EBCDIC? ASCII? ASCII-8?

3 Why do we have a packed decimal format?

4 Why can't the memory dump be printed in characters, instead of in octal or hexadecimal notation?

5 How does the programmer know what type of character codes are being shown in the memory dump?

6 Using octal notation, show the BCDIC coding for the word "computer."

7 Using hexadecimal notation, show the EBCDIC coding for the word "program."

8 Using hexadecimal notation, show the EBCDIC zoned-decimal coding for +324. Show the same value as packed-decimal code.

9 Using hexadecimal notation, show the ASCII coding for the word "microcomputer."

10 Using hexadecimal notation, show the ASCII-8 coding for the word "terminal."

GLOSSARY

Access gap The gap in cost per bit stored and access time between the magnetic core and semiconductor memories and the rotating, electromechanical memories. See also gap-filler.

Access time The time required for a computer to locate and transfer data to or from a storage medium.

Accumulator A local storage area, called a register, that holds the results of computer processing operations.

Active file A file for which there are transactions for most of the stored records during each processing cycle.

Address A numerical location within memory, typically referring to a byte number or a word number.

Address register A local storage register which contains the address of the next instruction to be executed. See also local storage.

American National Standards Institute (ANSI) A national organization with the purpose of establishing uniform standards within the United States.

American Standard Code for Information Interchange (ASCII) A commonly used 7-bit internal code. ASCII is also accepted as an international code by the International Organization for Standardization (ISO) under the name of International Standard 646.

American Standard Code for Information Interchange-8 (ASCII-8) An extended 8-bit version of the American Standard Code for Information Interchange.

Analog computer A computer that simulates real-time, physical systems, using an electrical analogy to the process being studied. Analog computers measure signals that vary continuously with time. Compare with digital computer.

ANSI See American National Standards Institute.

Applications Programmer See programmer.

Architecture See computer architecture.

Artificial intelligence Pertains to machines that possess reasoning, learning, and thinking capabilities that resemble those of humans.

ASCII See American Standard Code for Information Interchange.

ASCII-8 See American Standard Code for Information Interchange-8.

Assembler The language process used to convert low-level languages from source code to object code.

Assembler-level languages Low-level languages which translate to object code on a one-to-one basis from source code.

Automatic Teller Machine (ATM) A machine that allows bank customers to deposit and withdraw funds electronically and to transfer funds between accounts.

Auxiliary storage The same as secondary storage or secondary memory. See memory.

Bandwidth The range of frequencies available for data transmission. The broader the bandwidth, the greater the volume of data transmission possible.

Base 2 See binary.

Base 8 See octal.

Base 10 See decimal.

Base 16 See hexadecimal.

Baseline document A document that is a reference, or baseline, for changes to a computer data processing system. The principal baseline documents are the performance specification, the design specification, and the system specification.

BASIC A programming language, originated at Dartmouth College, for the purpose of providing an easy-to-learn programming tool for the beginning programmer. The acronym stands for Beginner's All-purpose Symbolic Instruction Code.

BCD Code See Binary Coded Decimal Interchange Code.

BCDIC See Binary Coded Decimal Interchange Code.

Binary The numbering system using base 2. It has two digit choices—0 and 1. It is the numbering system used internally to record both numeric and alphabetic characters.

Binary Coded Decimal Interchange Code (BCDIC) A six-bit internal code that has 64 character choices.

Block See physical record.

Blocking factor The number of logical records in a physical record.

Broadband Pertains to a data communications system that handles high volumes of data, typically up to a million bits/second or more.

Bug An error in a computer program.

Bus A group of circuits that provides the communications paths between the elements of a digital computer system.

Business A combination of personnel, facilities, materials, and equipment to accomplish specific objectives and to achieve defined goals. A business is a system that is made up of smaller systems called subsystems. It is a system of systems.

Business-oriented languages Any programming language which is specifically designed to handle business problems. They emphasize ease of data handling rather than calculations. Common examples are COBOL and RPGII.

Byte A fixed number of adjacent bits that represent a meaningful written language symbol (character). The most common byte size is eight bits.

Calculation loop

Candidate evaluation matrix A table that

identifies the performance and cost criteria by which alternative systems are to be evaluated and their relative evaluations.

Candidate system matrix A table that identifies the functions that all candidate, or alternative, systems must perform and the general manner in which these functions are to be performed by each system.

Card bed The card path area on a keypunch or data recorder from the right of the punch station to the left of the read stations.

Card punch An output device that converts data from a binary format in main storage to coded hole patterns in a punched card. Also see keypunch.

Card reader An input device that converts data coded onto punched cards into a binary format for entry into main storage.

Carriage control device The device on a line printer that controls the vertical spacing of the paper.

Central Processing Unit (CPU) The combination of the control unit and the arithmetic-logic unit.

Chain printer A printer that uses a rotating print chain.

Change control board A method of achieving control over changes to computer data processing systems during the operation phase.

Changeover Actual changeover from an old system to a new system. It is the part of conversion that occurs when a system enters the operation phase. See conversion.

Changeover crisis The period of difficulty that is encountered when a new system is first put into operation.

Channel Name given to small internal computers used to speed up input and output operations. Also a horizontal strip running the full length of a magnetic tape and used for recording data.

Character Any of the written language symbols: letters, numbers, and special symbols.

Character code The representation of a character as a zone-and-digit combination. Common character codes include the Hollerith card code, EBCDIC, and ASCII.

Character printer A printer with a print mechanism that prints one character at a time.

Charge-coupled Device (CCD) An electronic

storage device that uses the properties of electrons within certain semiconductors to represent binary 1s and 0s.

COBOL A common business-oriented programming language. The acronym stands for COmmon Business Oriented Language.

Coding The process of writing computer instructions in a programming language.

Coding form The form on which program instructions are written. Each programming language has its own unique coding forms.

COM See Computer Output Microfilm.

Combined moving-head and fixed-head magnetic disk A magnetic disk system that combines the use of an access mechanism and the distribution of read/write heads over some of the disk surfaces. See moving-head magnetic disk and fixed-head magnetic disk.

Comment An entry in a computer program for the purpose of documentation or explanation; designed to assist anyone reading the source program listing. Comments do not contain program logic and are not translated by the language processor.

Common carrier A communications company, such as AT&T, which provides voice and data transmission services.

Communications Satellite Corporation (COMSAT) A privately owned company, chartered by the U.S. Congress for voice and television signal communication by satellite.

Compiler A language processor for high-level languages.

Computer architecture The purposeful combination of hardware and software into an effective, user-oriented computer system.

Computer network A distributed data processing system in which multiple computers are linked together. The two types of computer networks are the star network and the ring network.

Computer Output Microfilm (COM) An output device that uses combined electronic, photo-optical, and electromechanical techniques to convert digital computer output to records that can be stored as rolls of microfilm or as frames of microfilm stored on cards called microfiche.

Computer print chart A chart that shows all the detail to be produced for a report by a computer system printer.

Computer printout See printout.

Computer system architect A person who performs computer system architecture. See computer architecture.

COMSAT See Communications Satellite Corporation.

Conductor A substance that permits electricity to pass through it easily.

Constant A value written into a program instruction. The value does not change during the execution of the program.

Constraint A condition, such as time or money, that limits the solutions to the problem that may be considered.

Control program An operating system program with the purpose of controlling the computer. The control program's major functions are job scheduling, input/output scheduling, and program monitoring.

Control storage Read-only memory (ROM) that contains firmware programs, called microprograms, which aid the control unit in directing all the operations of a computer system.

Controlling Directing the manner and sequence in which the basic data processing operations of inputting, storing, processing, and outputting are performed.

Conversion The process of changing from an old system to a new one. The two parts of conversion are (1) physical conversion of procedures, programs, and files and (2) actual changeover to the new system.

Core plane Magnetic cores strung (wired) together in a plane in a pattern that enables combinations of cores to represent binary-coded characters.

Cost-effective Pertains to the efficiency of a computer system. It means that both performance and the cost of that performance should be evaluated for any system before it is selected to solve a problem.

CRT See video display.

Cybernation The use of computers coupled with automatic machinery to carry out complex operations.

Data A collection of facts, unorganized but able

to be organized. These facts are unrefined, or raw, information.

Data adapter A device that adapts the characteristics of input and output devices to the internal requirements of computers for storing data.

Data base A set of related files.

Data base management system A software system that stores data and manages their organization and access for all applications programmers using that data base. Its two components are a data description module and a data manipulation module.

Data Communications System An electronic system that transfers data from one point to another.

Data element A meaningful collection of related characters. Also called a field or data item.

Data entry system A distributed data processing system that uses terminals to communicate with a central-site computer. See also dumb terminal, intelligent terminal, and programmable terminal.

Data item See data element.

Data module A protective package that contains a number of rotating, magnetic disks as well as their associated access mechanisms.

Data processing A series of actions or operations that convert raw information (data) into useful information.

Data processing system A system that accomplishes data processing. It includes the necessary resources, which are people, materials, facilities, and equipment.

Data rate See data transfer rate.

Data recorder A keyboard device for punching data into cards. It incorporates a memory unit to hold data until a full card's data have been keyed. After the memory is filled, the card is punched. See also keypunch.

Data transfer rate Pertains to the rate at which data can be transferred from main memory to another medium on which data are recorded. For magnetic tape the data transfer rate is equal to the product of the tape speed and the recording density.

DBMS See data base management system.

DDP See distributed data processing.

Debug packages A collection of programming routines designed to assist the programmer in finding program logic errors.

Debugging The process of finding and correcting program errors (bugs).

Decimal The numbering system based on 10.

Default The assumption that will be made by a program if a contradicting statement is not made by the programmer. An example is the source program listing provided by language processors. The listing is provided unless the programmer specifies otherwise.

Design phase The life-cycle phase during which the detailed design of the system selected in the study phase occurs.

Design specification A document completed during the design phase that describes how to develop the system in the language of programmers and other technical personnel.

Detail file See transaction file.

Detail lines A line in the body of a printed output, not including heading or total lines.

Development phase The life-cycle phase during which a system is constructed to meet the requirements specified in the design phase.

Digit area The rows 0–9 on the Hollerith card that are used to represent numbers or, in combination with zone area punches, letters and some special symbols. Digit areas also are used on other punched card codes and with internal computer codes.

Digital computer A computer that works with discrete quantities. Digital computers count and use numbers to simulate real-time processes. Compare with analog computer.

A low-speed digital output device that can produce complex graphs and drawings.

Digitizer A low-speed input device that converts graphic and pictorial data into binary, numeric inputs for a digital computer.

Disk See magnetic disk.

Disk cartridge A single magnetic disk in a protective package.

Disk pack A number of magnetic disks connected by a central shaft and enclosed in a protective package.

Diskette See floppy disk.

Distributed Data Processing (DDP) Any arrangement of computers and/or communications systems that, as an alternative to wholly central-site data processing, places data processing capabilities at the location of the end-user.

Document Reader An optical input device that is able to read documents printed in a special type font. The document content is, roughly, equal to a line on a punched card. See also page reader.

Drum printer A line printer that uses a solid, rotating, cylindrical drum.

Dumb terminal A data entry system, used in distributed data processing, that has no local processing capability.

E-time Pertaining to the time required for the arithmetic-logic unit to carry out instructions moved to the control unit during I-time. See also I-time.

EBCDIC See Extended Binary Coded Decimal Interchange Code.

Electrostatic printer A high-speed printer that uses charged pins to form character matrices on chemically treated paper.

Electrothermal printer A high-speed printer that uses heated elements to create characters as matrices of small dots on heat-sensitive paper.

Electron-Beam Addressed Memory (EBAM) An electronic storage device that uses electrical circuits to control a beam that reads from or writes on a metal oxide semiconductor surface.

Electronic Funds Transfer (EFT) An electronic system that facilitates the exchange of money.

Elementary Item In COBOL a data element which is not broken down into smaller units.

End user See user.

Era Refers to the four computer eras: Early Era: 1940–1955; Growing Era: 1955–1964; Refining Era: 1964–1979; Maturing Era: 1979–2000.

Expanded system flowchart A system flowchart, developed in the design phase, to show the inputs, files, and outputs associated with each processing program.

Exponentiation The process of raising a number to a power, such as 3^2.

Extended Binary Coded Decimal Interchange Code (EBCDIC) An eight-bit code that uses zone-and-digit areas to represent characters.

Feasibility analysis An evaluation of alternative problem solutions in order to select the most cost-effective (best) system, taking into account constraints that limit the solutions that may be considered.

Field Meaningful groups of consecutive columns on a punched card, or consecutive memory positions in primary and secondary storage.

File A collection of related records.

Firmware A sequence of instructions (software) that is substituted for hardware. This sequence of instructions is stored in (hardware) read-only memory (ROM). See also read-only memory.

Fixed-head magnetic disk A magnetic disk system that eliminates the use of an access mechanism by distributing all the read/write heads over the disk surfaces.

Fixed-length fields Standard length fields holding binary data. The standard lengths are called halfwords, fullwords, and doublewords. The number of bits per word varies between computer models and manufacturers.

Fixed-point numbers Whole, signed binary numbers. See also floating-point numbers.

Flatbed digitizer See rectangular-coordinate digitizer.

Flippy disk A floppy disk that records data on both sides.

Floating-point numbers Signed binary numbers held in a fraction-exponent format. As an example, 1234 would be recorded as the equivalent of $.1234 \times 10_4$.

Floppy disk A soft, flexible magnetic disk used on small computer systems.

Flowchart A pictorial representation that uses predefined symbols to describe either data flow in a system or the logic of a computer program.

Forecast An effort to describe some future events that have a reasonable probability of occurrence.

FORTRAN IV A high-level, mathematically oriented programming language. The name comes from FORmula TRANslation.

Frame A vertical strip on magnetic or paper tape on which a single character, or byte, can be stored.

Full-duplex system A communications system that can transmit data in both directions at the same time.

Function switches (keypunch) The switches just above the keyboard on a keypunch or data recorder. They are used to turn on or off the major punching functions.

Gap-filler Pertains to the electronic memory technologies, such as magnetic bubble memory (MBM) and the charge-coupled device (CCD), that fill the access gap between the magnetic core and semiconductor memories and the rotating, electromechanical memories.

Generation Refers to the three computer generations: vacuum tube, transistor, and integrated circuit.

GIGO Garbage in—garbage out. Pertains to the fact that most computer errors are not machine errors; they are data errors, caused by incorrect input data or incorrect data in files.

Goal A broadly stated purpose of a business.

Graphic digitizer See digitizer.

Group item In COBOL, data items that are broken down into smaller units. As an example, if a date field is broken down into month, day, and year fields, the date field is a group item.

Half-duplex system A communications system that can transmit data in both directions, but only in one direction at a time.

Hardware The physical components of a computer data processing system.

Hexadecimal A numbering system using a base of 16. Its digits range from 0 to F. It is commonly used as a shortcut notation for groups of four binary digits.

Hierarchy A multilevel grouping; for example, a data storage hierarchy of characters, fields, records, and files or hierarchy plus input, process, and output (HIPO) charts.

Hierarchy plus Input, Process, and Output (HIPO) chart A graphical representation of the software functions to be performed by a system. HIPO charts present the functions to be performed in a top-down hierarchial sequence.

High-level languages Those programming languages in which instructions translate from one source instruction to several object instructions. Examples are COBOL, FORTRAN, RPG, AND PL/I.

HIPO See hierarchy plus input, process, and output chart.

Hollerith card A punched card with 80 vertical columns, designed by Dr. Herman Hollerith.

Hollerith code A 12-bit code that uses zone and/or digit area punches to represent characters (letters, numbers, and special symbols). See also Hollerith card, zone area, and digit area.

Holography A potentially high-capacity data memory system that is based upon techniques for recording images on film without the use of a lens.

Hybrid computer A computer that combines measuring capability of an analog computer and the counting capability of a digital computer.

I-time Pertains to the time required to move an instruction from main storage to the control unit. See also E-time.

Image-scan digitizer A graphic digitizer that uses optical scanning techniques to reproduce entire drawings.

Immediate replacement A changeover method whereby the old system is discontinued and the new system is put into operation at a specified time.

Impact printer Printers, such as line printers and character printers, that use electromechanical mechanisms that cause hammers to strike against the printed paper.

Implementation plan A plan for bringing a system that has been developed into operational use. Its major parts are a test plan, a training plan, an equipment-installation plan, and a conversion plan.

Inactive file A file for which transactions do not involve most of the stored records during each processing cycle.

Independent item In COBOL, elementary item fields which are not associated with any group item or record.

Information Raw information is a collection of unorganized facts called data. Useful information is the result of data processing. The term "information" usually refers to useful information.

Information display system layout sheet A

sheet that shows all the detail for a CRT display.

Information flow The creation and movement of documents that support product flow and meet the other information needs of a company. Compare with product flow.

Information Service Request (ISR) A form used to request service from the information services department. See next entry.

Information services Pertains to the group, or department, in an organization that is responsible for developing information systems.

Initial investigation An investigation performed by a systems analyst to clarify the business problem and to strengthen the analyst's background in the problem area.

Input Processing Output (IPO) chart An expansion of a HIPO chart into additional levels of detail.

Input prompt An output on a computer terminal that tells the terminal operator that the computer is waiting for input.

Inputting The process of entering data, which are facts that have been gathered and recorded, into a data processing system.

Integer number Any whole number, i.e., any number without a decimal point.

Integrated circuit Refers to a microminiaturization technology that forms thousands of transistors and other electronic components on thin wafers of silicon by using photographic etching and chemical processes. The levels of integrated circuit technology, as measured by component density, are: small-scale integration (SSI), medium-scale integration (MSI), large-scale integration (LSI), very-large-scale integration (VLSI), and very-large-scale integration indeed (VLSI^2)!

Intelligent machines See smart machines.

Intelligent terminal A data entry system used in distributed data processing that has a limited local data processing capability.

Interpreter A language processor for high-level programming languages that translates the source code as the program is executed. It is the most common language processor for BASIC.

Interrecord gap The space between records on magnetic tape.

Josephson-junction A potential high-capacity data memory system based upon the properties of super-cold circuits.

Justification Refers to the order in which data is punched into a field on a punched card. Left justification (for alphabetic and alphanumeric data) means starting with the leftmost column. Right justification (for numeric data) means starting with the rightmost column.

K A symbol for expressing storage capacity. K is equal to 2^{10}, or 1024. Units of K usually are bytes or words.

Key field A special field that distinguishes one record from another.

Key-to-disk devices Input data recording devices that convert operator keystrokes into coded data that are stored magnetically on disks or diskettes.

Key-to-tape devices Input data recording devices that convert operator keystrokes into coded data that are stored magnetically on tape reels, cassettes, or cartridges.

Keypunch A keyboard device for punching data into cards. The holes which represent the character to be recorded are punched into the card as the key is stroked. See also data recorder.

Keypunch instruction sheet A sheet that communicates the layout of a punched card to the person who punches the card.

Knowledge industries The industries that perform data processing and provide information products and services.

Label record A machine-readable record that is used to identify a data file. The label record is the first record of the file.

Language processor A program that is used to translate source program instructions to object or machine language instructions. See assembler, compiler, and interpretor.

Laser-beam printer A high-speed printer that uses a combination of laser-beam and electrophotographic techniques to create printed output at speeds in excess of 13,000 lines per minute.

Laser-beam scanner See universal product code.

Layout The result of locating and positioning the fields that are to be punched into a card. Also a sketch of a system output.

Life-cycle concept A time-sequenced, structured approach to the development of complex systems. The life cycle of computer data processing systems has four phases: study, design, development, and operation.

Line printer A printer with a mechanism that appears to print an entire line at one time.

Literal Any data to be outputted or used exactly as it is contained in an instruction of a program.

Local storage Storage areas, called registers, used by the central processing unit to interpret instructions and perform arithmetic and logical operations. See also storage register and address register.

Logical operators In FORTRAN, symbols used to show a logical relationship between two data items. Examples are .EQ. for equal and .LT. for less than.

Logical record Data record on which a computer performs arithmetic and logical operations. See record.

Loop Any group of program instructions that is executed in a repetitive manner.

Low-level languages Those programming languages that translate from one source instruction to one object instruction. See also assembler-level.

Machine code Computer instructions that may be executed by the central processor control unit. These instructions are in a binary format and are also called object code.

Magnetic Bubble Memory (MBM) An electronic storage device that uses the properties of certain materials, under applied magnetic fields, to represent binary 1s and 0s.

Magnetic core Tiny rings made of iron that have magnetic properties that can be polarized to represent a binary 1 or 0.

Magnetic disk A rotating, electromechanical secondary storage device that uses a thin circular disk coated with a magnetic material as a recording medium.

Magnetic-ink character recognition (MICR) Pertaining to input devices that can read cards and paper documents imprinted with a magnetic ink.

Magnetic tape A rotating, electromechanical secondary storage device that uses a long plastic strip coated with a magnetic material as a recording medium.

Master file A file that contains records that are to be preserved.

Mathematically oriented languages Problem-oriented languages that emphasize the ease of performing mathematical calculations rather than data handling. The most common mathematically oriented language is FORTRAN IV.

Maxicomputer A large computer in the general cost range of $400,000 to $10 million or more.

Memory The area inside the computer mainframe (primary memory) where data and instructions are stored. Also the area in an auxiliary storage device (secondary memory) where data and instructions are stored.

Memory dump A printout of the contents of memory.

MICR See magnetic-ink character recognition.

Microcomputer A microprocessor plus main memory (and input and output circuitry). Also a small computer in the general cost range of $400 or less to $10,000.

Microfiche See computer output microfilm.

Microfilm See computer output microfilm.

Microprocessor A microminiaturized central processing unit (control unit plus arithmetic-logic unit) on a silicon wafer known as a chip.

Microprogram See control storage.

Microsecond One one-millionth of a second.

Midicomputer A large computer in the general cost range of $40,000 to $1 million.

Millisecond One one-thousandth of a second.

Minicomputer A small computer in the cost range of $4000 to $100,000.

Mnemonic A technique used as a memory aid or memory-aiding device. A mnemonic typically is a strict abbreviation. As an example, the mnemonic AP stands for add packed.

Moving-head magnetic disk A magnetic disk system that uses a single access mechanism to position all the read/write heads.

Multiple processor Pertains to computer systems that share processing operations among more than one processor. Multiprocessing is one example of the use of multiple processors.

Multiprocessing Pertains to computer systems

that use more than one central processing unit.

Multiprogramming Concurrent execution of segments of two or more programs by a computer.

Nanosecond One one-billionth of a second.

Narrowband Pertains to a data communications system that handles low volumes of data, typically from 45 to 300 bits/second.

Network See computer network, star network, or ring network.

96-column card A punched card with 96 columns for recording data in a binary-coded decimal (BCD) code.

Nonconductor A substance through which electricity cannot pass.

Nonimpact printer High-speed page printers that use chemical, thermal, laser-beam, or xerographic techniques instead of electromechanical print mechanisms.

Object program The machine language program which results from the translation of a source program by a language processor.

Objective A short-term, specific accomplishment necessary to the achievement of a goal. See goal.

OCR See optical character-reader.

Octal The numbering system using base 8. Octal digits have a value range from 0 to 7. It is commonly used as a shortcut notation for groups of three binary digits.

Office of the future Pertains to future office systems in which functions such as document preparation, storage, retrieval, reproduction, and distribution will be altered by advances in computer-communications systems.

Operating system A collection of programs provided by the computer's manufacturer that allow us to schedule the jobs the computer is to perform, to translate symbolic programs into machine code, and to use the computer effectively.

Operation phase The life-cycle phase during which the system constructed in the development phase is used.

Optical bar-code reader An optical input device that is able to interpret combinations of marks (bars) that represent data.

Optical Character Reader (OCR) An optical

input device that is able to detect symbols in special type fonts by use of a scanning mechanism.

Optical Mark Reader(OMR) An optical input device that is able to interpret pencil marks on paper media.

Outputting The process of producing a useful information output.

Packed decimal A modified form of zoned decimal that places two decimal digits into each byte of the field with the exception of the rightmost byte, which contains one digit and the sign of the field. See also zoned decimal.

Page printer A printer with a mechanism that appears to print an entire page at one time.

Page reader A high-capacity optical input device that is able to scan and interpret an entire page that is typed in a special font. See also document reader.

Paper tape punch An output device that converts data from a binary format in main storage to coded hole patterns punched into paper tape.

Paper tape reader An input device that converts data punched into paper tape into a binary format for entry into main storage.

Parallel operation A changeover method whereby data is processed by both the old and the new system until performance of the new system is verified.

Parity Bit An extra bit (in a byte) that enables the computer to check for internal errors.

Performance definition The process of defining the performance of a system by identifying constraints, establishing objectives, and describing outputs.

Performance specification A document completed during the study phase that describes what a system is to do in the language of the user.

Personal computing The use of a computer (usually a microcomputer) by individuals for applications such as entertainment, home management, and hobbies.

Phased replacement A changeover method whereby changeover to the new system takes place gradually.

Physical record Data transferred to and from

main storage as a unit, called a block. On magnetic tape the physical record is the area between gaps. The block-size of a physical record is one or more logical records. See logical record and blocking factor.

Picosecond One one-trillionth of a second.

PL/I A high-level programming language oriented toward both business and mathematical programs. PL/I stands for Programming Language I.

Place value The value of a symbol that corresponds to its position in a number.

Primary memory See memory.

Primary storage The same as primary memory. See memory.

Principal user The person who in practice will accept or reject the computer-based business system.

Printer An output device that is able to print data stored in main memory in a format that is readable by humans.

Printout A form of computer system output. It is printed on a page by an output device called a printer.

Problem-oriented languages Programming languages that are oriented toward solving a particular type of problem. Problem-oriented languages have automatic features which relieve the programmer of the burden of writing machine-oriented instructions.

Process loop See loop.

Processing Performing arithmetic operations and/or logically manipulating input data in order to convert them into a desired output.

Product flow The flow of raw materials into finished goods. Compare with information flow.

Program A sequence of instructions that direct the operations of a digital computer.

Program Design Language (PDL) See pseudocode.

Program drum A device on the keypunch used to program automatic functions. Basic functions that may be programmed include field definition, automatic skipping, automatic duplication, and alphabetic shift.

Programmable terminal A data entry system, used in distributed data processing, that has extensive local data processing capabil-

ity. A programmable terminal may be used as a stand-alone data processing system.

Programmer The person who prepares a set of computer instructions. An applications programmer prepares computer instructions in order to solve a particular problem. A systems programmer prepares computer programs, called an operating system, designed to simplify the use of the computer.

Project cost schedule A schedule of costs, which accompanies a project plan. It is used to report actual costs and to compare them with estimated costs.

Project plan A horizontal bar chart that identifies major milestones and reports progress in achieving them.

Projection An extension of past trends into the future.

Pseudocode An imitation of actual computer instructions used in program logic planning.

Random access A method of accessing records that permits them to be written or read directly without regard to their sequence.

Read-Only Memory (ROM) An area of memory that can only be read (copied electronically) and not written on (modified electronically) by a computer system user. ROM is used to store firmware. See also firmware.

Real number In FORTRAN, any number that contains a decimal point. The most common format of real numbers is called floating-point.

Record A collection of related data elements. Also a recorded transaction.

Rectangular-coordinate digitizer A graphic digitizer that produces binary, numeric inputs related to the x and y coordinates of a drawing.

Register See local storage.

Response time The total elapsed time between submission of data by a user and its return as computer output.

Ring network A computer network in which there is no host (star) and in which all stations are equal. See also star network.

Robot An automatic machine that performs routine, seemingly human tasks.

RPG II A high-level, business-oriented programming language. RPG stands for Report Program Generator.

Satellite Business Systems (SBS) An all-digital satellite communications network owned jointly by IBM, Aetna, and COMSAT.

SBS See Satellite Business Systems.

Secondary memory See memory.

Secondary storage The same as auxiliary storage or secondary memory. See memory.

Self-punch reader An input data recording device that is able to read data imprinted from embossed credit cards and to convert the data into patterns of holes punched into the same card.

Semiconductor A substance that can be made to conduct or not conduct, thus representing a binary 1 or 0. See also conductor and nonconductor.

Sequential access A method of accessing records that requires that they be written or read in sequence, one after the other.

Service programs Programs that are commonly used in all data processing centers. Service programs include programs to prepare object programs for execution, to store programs on a magnetic disk, and to sort data recorded on secondary storage devices. They are part of the operating system.

Shared-logic word processing system A word processing system in which two or more work stations share the processing and storage capabilities of a small business computer.

Simplex system A communication system that can transmit data only in one direction.

Smart machines Machines with embedded microprocessors or microcomputers.

Software The set of computer programs, procedures, and associated documentation related to the effective operation of a data processing system.

Source document A document on which data that are to be recorded in machine-readable code originates, that is, the original handwritten or typewritten document.

Source program Any program in a symbolic programming language. The source program must be translated to object program format before it may be executed.

Specialized common carrier A communications company that sells broadband, point-to-point communications services in selected high-density areas.

Specific objective A measurable (if possible) benefit of a system, usually stated in "before" and "after" terms.

Stand-alone In the context of distributed data processing or word processing, stand-alone pertains to a computer system that has an independent (from a central-site computer) processing and storage capability.

Star network A computer network in which there is a host (star) computer that communicates with and controls satellite systems.

Storage See memory.

Storage address See address.

Storage register A local storage area. All data and instructions enter and leave the computer through the storage register. See also local storage.

Storing Filing data or information so that they can be made available for data processing.

Study phase The life-cycle phase during which a problem is identified, alternative solutions are studied, and the most feasible solution recommended.

Subsystem A system that is part of a larger system, See business.

Supercomputer Pertains to the largest computer systems available. Applications for future supercomputers include weather forecasting, spacecraft simulation, and information utilities.

Symbolic code Written program instructions using English words and/or mathematical symbols as substitutes for binary machine language. Symbolic code is also called source code or source programs.

Symbolic language Pertains to the use of human-understandable symbols to represent combinations of binary digits.

Syntax The pattern or structure of word order. In computer instructions syntax refers to the required word order and punctuation of the instruction.

System A combination of personnel, material, facilities, and equipment working together to convert inputs into outputs. A system includes its methods and procedures. A system may be made up of subsystems. It may refer to a major element of a business.

System flowchart A flowchart that uses predefined symbols to describe data flow in a system.

System life cycle See life-cycle concept.

System specification A document completed during the development phase which contains all the critical system documentation and which is the basis for all manuals, procedures, and changes to the system.

Systems analysis A general term for problem-solving techniques that conform to the life-cycle concept. See life-cycle concept.

Systems analyst The individual who performs systems analysis activities throughout the life cycle of a computer data processing system. The systems analyst bridges the communications gap between the user and the computer programmer.

Systems approach See life cycle concept.

Systems programmer See programmer.

Tape See magnetic tape.

Tape cartridge Relatively low data rate storage medium used on small computer systems.

Tape cassette Relatively low data rate storage medium used on small computer systems.

Tape drive See tape transport.

Tape reader An input device that detects special symbols on cash register and adding machine tapes.

Tape reel Relatively high data rate storage medium used on larger computer systems (as contrasted with tape cassettes or cartridges, which are used on smaller systems).

Tape transport A mechanism for writing (recording) on magnetic tape and for reading (inputting) from magnetic tape.

Teleprocessing Transmission of data to a computer from a remote terminal for processing at a central site.

Teletypewriter An inexpensive input and output device that uses paper tape and is often a component of a small computer system.

Template A plastic or metal guide used to trace flowcharting symbols.

Terminal A device that communicates with a computer to enter data or receive information. See data entry system.

Testing The process of running the computer program and evaluating the program results in order to determine whether any errors exist.

Throughput time The time required for work to be processed in computer operations.

Time-shared service The use of the resources of a remote central computer and the sharing of these resources with other users. Some word processing systems use time-shared services.

Tracing routines Routines to aid the programmer in following the logic of a program during execution of the program. See debug packages.

Track A horizontal strip, or channel, running the full length of a magnetic tape and used for recording data. Also one of many circular concentric rings on magnetic disk used for storing data.

Transaction An event that creates a fact that can be recorded as input to a data processing system.

Transaction file A file in which current data are stored for subsequent processing. Also called a detail file.

Turnaround time The elapsed time between the arrival of data at a data processing center and the availability of output information for delivery to the user.

Unit record machine An electromechanical machine used to process data punched into cards. Each card containing data is called a unit record.

Universal Product Code (UPC) An optical bar code that appears on almost all retail packages and which is read by a laser beam scanner. See also optical bar-code reader.

Usability The worth of a system as evaluated by the persons who must use it. Usability is an important measure of the cost-effectiveness of a system. See cost-effectiveness.

User Any individual who in the course of performing a job must provide input data to, or use information generated by, a computer-based system.

Utilities Programs which provide a means of copying data from any input device to any output device in the system. They provide an easy means of moving data files from one secondary storage device to another.

Value-added carrier A communications company that leases networks from a common carrier and combines messages from customers into packets for point-to-point transmission.

Variable Field Length (VFL) fields Fields holding character code data that may be of any length (whatever is determined necessary by the programmer). The fields vary as a whole number of bytes. See fixed-length fields.

Variable name In FORTRAN, the name assigned to a data field.

Video display A cathode ray tube (CRT) unit that can present data stored in memory to a user in a suitable alphanumeric format. Video displays are used for graphic design, as low-speed and low-cost input and output terminals, and as management information stations.

Voice recognition unit An input device that is able to convert spoken words into binary data suitable for input to a digital computer.

Voice response unit An output device that uses words or messages that have been recorded on a magnetic medium.

Voiceband Pertains to a data communications system that handles moderate volumes of data, typically from 300 to 9600 bits/second.

Weighted candidate evaluation matrix A table that modifies the candidate evaluation matrix by applying weighted numeric ratings in order to score each candidate in a uniform manner.

Word Fixed-size storage areas which store binary equivalents to decimal numbers. Instructions also are stored in words. See fixed-length fields.

Word-processing system Office system that performs operations on words for the efficient transfer of ideas from one person to another.

Xerographic printer A high-speed printer that uses xerographic techniques to produce printed outputs at speeds in excess of 9000 lines per minute. It can reduce computer output to regular page size and can produce multiple copies.

Zone area The 0, 11, and 12 rows on the Hollerith card that are used in combination with digit area punches to indicate letters and some special symbols. Zone areas also are used on other punched-card codes and with internal computer codes.

Zoned decimal Any numeric character coded in the Extended Binary Coded Decimal Interchange Code (EBCDIC). Each decimal digit occupies one byte of storage.

INDEX

Access gap, 97
Access time, 82–83
Accumulator, 68
ACM (Association for Computing Machinery), 246
Acronyms in primary storage, 85
Active files, 88
Addresses, 61, 477–478
AI (artificial intelligence), 386–387
Aiken, Howard, 20
Alphanumeric data, 115–116
ALU (arithmetic logic unit), 21, 68–69, 473
American National Standards Institute (ANSI), 245, 246, 304
American Standard Code for Information Interchange (ASCII), 474–475
American Standard Code for Information Interchange-8 (ASCII-8), 475–476
Analog computers, 56
Androbot, Inc., 57
ANSI (American National Standards Institute), 245, 246, 304
Apple Computer, Inc.:
    Apple I, 163, 170
    Apple II, 157, 170
    Apple IIe, 170, 171, 304
    Apple II Plus, 304
    LISA, 157, 170, 171, 174
Applications programmers:
    job description of, 359

Applications programmers (*Cont.*):
    job opportunities for, 379
Applications software, 21–22, 58–59
    microcomputer, 164–166, 171–174, 176
    programmers of, 359, 379
Archival storage, 95
Area A, COBOL statement field, 398
Area B, COBOL statement field, 398
Arithmetic logic unit (ALU), 21, 68–69, 473
Arrowheads, 247
Artificial intelligence (AI), 386–387
ASCII (American Standard Code for Information Interchange), 474–475
ASCII-8 (American Standard Code for Information Interchange-8), 475–476
Assembler-level languages, 267, 283
    problem-oriented languages compared with, 269–270
Assemblers, 283
Association for Computing Machinery (ACM), 246
Atanasoff, John, 20
Atanasoff-Berry computer, 20
Automated office, 144–149
    data communications in, 145
    data processing in, 144
    electronic mail in, 148
    problems in, 148–149
    voice store-and-forward systems in, 148

Automated office (*Cont.*):
    word processing in, 145–148
    (*See also* Electronic office)
Auxiliary memory (*see* Secondary storage)
Averaging numbers in BASIC:
    calculating average sales, 329–331, 336–339
    series of numbers, 348–349
    two numbers, 305–312

Babbage, Charles, 18–19
Bandwidth, 135
Bar-code readers (scanners), 121–122
    in Magic Wand Speaking Reader, 7
Base, 438
    (*See also* Number systems)
Base 2 number system (*see* Binary number system)
Base 8 number system (*see* Octal number system)
Base 10 number system (*see* Decimal number system)
Base 16 number system (*see* Hexadecimal number system)
Baseline documents (specifications), 49, 236–237
BASIC (Beginner's All-purpose Symbolic Instruction Code), 273–274, 301–350
    averaging a series of numbers in, 348–349
    averaging two numbers in, 305–312

493

BASIC (*Cont.*):
 calculating average sales in, 329–331, 336–339
 calculation loops in, 317–320
 CATALOG command in, 328–329
 changing instructions in, 312
 CLS command in, 305
 CMD "D:drive" command in, 328–329
 coding errors in, 292
 compound interest problem in, 312–320
 default options of, 304, 334
 DELETE command in, 329
 DIR command in, 329
 DO-WHILE command in, 341–342
 END statement in, 310
 FILES command in, 328–329
 FOR-NEXT statement in, 319–320
 GOSUB-RETURN instruction in, 332
 GOTO statement in, 316
 hierarchy of operations in, 309
 HOME command in, 305
 HOME statement in, 333
 IF-THEN statement in, 316–317
 IF-THEN-ELSE statement in, 334–336
 INPUT command in, 347
 INPUT statement in, 306–307
 interactive programs in, 347–349
 interpreter for, 283
 KILL command in, 329
 LET statement in, 308–309
 library functions of, 320–322
 LIST command in, 305
 LLIST command in, 326
 LOAD command in, 328
 LPRINT command in, 345
 LPRINT USING command in, 345–347
 NEW command in, 305
 output zones in, 304
 PRINT statement in, 310, 334
 PRINT USING instruction in, 339
 printer instructions in, 345–349
 quotation marks in, 310, 328
 READ-DATA instruction in, 332–333

BASIC (*Cont.*):
 REM (remark) statement in, 306
 RUN command in, 305, 310, 328
 SAVE command in, 326–327
 semicolon in, 314
 string-variable names in, 307
 TAB function in, 334
 WHILE-WEND command in, 342, 344
Batch processing, 81
Baud, 135
BCDIC (binary-coded decimal interchange code), 469–470
Beam-addressed metal oxide semiconductor (BEAMOS), 98–99
Berry, Clifford, 20
Binary-coded decimal interchange code (BCDIC), 469–470
Binary codes, 19, 469–470
 bytes and, 61–63
 words and, 63
 (*See also* Binary number system)
Binary (base 2) number system, 61, 438
 adding in, 455–458
 characteristics of, 439
 converting from decimal number system in, 444–446
 converting to decimal number system from, 442
 fixed-length fields in, 463
 shortcut notations for hexadecimal number system and, 450–451
 shortcut notations for octal number system and, 449–450
 subtracting in, 461
 (*See also* Binary codes)
Bits, 61
Boot strapping, 158
BPI (bytes per inch), 86
Brainstorming, 200–201
Branches, 67
Broadband transmission mode, 135
Buffers, 115
Bugs, 289
 (*See also* Debugging; Programming, errors in)
Buses, 71, 168
Business-oriented languages, 269
 COBOL (*see* COBOL)

Business-oriented languages (*Cont.*):
 RPG II (*see* RPG II)
Business systems, 38–51
 business levels and information uses in, 43–44
 computer-based, 8, 44–46
 (*See also* Computer data processing systems)
 goals and objectives of, 38–39
 information generators in, 42–43
 product flow and information flow in, 40–42
 as system of systems, 39–40
Bytes, 61–63
Bytes per inch (BPI), 86

Cache memory, 100
CAD (computer-aided design), 117, 167
CAI (computer-assisted instruction), 165, 166, 381
Calculation loops, 317–320
Calculation specifications in RPG II, 430–431
CAM (computer-aided manufacturing), 167–168
Candidate evaluation matrix, 202–203
 weighted, 203–204
Candidate system matrix, 201
Čapek, Karel, 384
Card readers, 124
Careers:
 in electronic office, 149–150
 in information services (*see* Information services, careers in)
CATALOG command, 328–329
Cathode ray tubes (CRTs), 115–117
CCDs (charge-coupled devices), 98, 378
Central processing units (CPUs):
 arithmetic logic unit in, 21, 68–69, 473
 batch processing by, 81
 control unit in, 19, 66–69
 future trends in, 378
 microprocessor units (MPUs) as, 100, 156–158, 170–171
 multiple (*see* Multiprocessing)
Chain printers, 113–114
Change control board, 235–236
Channels, 70

Character codes, 463, 465–478
American Standard Code for Information Interchange (ASCII), 474–475
American Standard Code for Information Interchange-8 (ASCII-8), 475–476
binary-coded decimal interchange code (BCDIC), 469–470
extended binary-coded decimal interchange code (EBCDIC), 62, 85–86, 470–473
Hollerith card code, 466–468
for memory dumps, 476–478
Character printers:
dot-matrix, 112, 160
ink-jet, 112
letter-quality, 111–112, 160
Character strings, 307
Characters, 10
Characters per inch (CPI), 86
Charge-coupled devices (CCDs), 98, 378
Chips, silicon (*see* Integrated-circuit technology)
CLOSE statement, 410
CLS command, 305
CLS statement, 333
CMD "D:drive" command, 328–329
CMI (computer-managed instruction), 165, 166
COBOL (Common Business Oriented Language), 270–271, 395–423
CLOSE statement in, 410
coding errors in, 292–294
coding form for, 396–398
COBOL instructions on, 397–398
punching instructions on, 397
compiling of, 284
data division in, 399, 404–410
environment division in, 398–399, 403–404
FD (file description) entry in, 404–406
FILLER field in, 404–405
identification division in, 398, 401–403
IF statement in, 416, 418–419
names in, 400–401
OPEN instruction in, 410

COBOL (*Cont.*):
PERFORM statement in, 410, 411
PERFORM-UNTIL statement in, 410
problem statement for, 400
procedure division in, 399, 410–419
program structure of, 398–399
READ statement in, 413
sample programs in, 400–420
Coding:
binary, 19, 469–470
bytes and, 61–63
words and, 63
(*See also* Binary number system)
errors in, 290–294
forms for, 265
COBOL, 396–398
RPG, 426–427
(*See also* Programming languages)
COM (computer output microfilm), 124–125
Commodore International, PET computer, 170
Common carriers, 135–136
specialized, 135
value-added, 136
Communications, 132–133
satellite, 136–139, 379
(*See also* Data communications)
Communications Satellite Corporation (COMSAT), 136
Compilers, 283
Compound interest, calculation of, in BASIC, 312–320
Computer-aided design (CAD), 117, 167
Computer-aided manufacturing (CAM), 167–168
Computer-assisted instruction (CAI), 165, 166, 381
Computer data processing systems, 18–23, 44–46
advantages of, 22–23
computer information systems compared to, 46
cycle of, 79–81
origins of, 20
principles of, 18–22

Computer graphics:
in animation, 13
input-output devices for: digital plotters, 126
digitizers, 125
visual display terminals (VDTs), 115–117
Computer information systems:
definition of, 45–46
development of, 379–380
future trends in, 377–380
life-cycle method of developing (*see* Life-cycle method)
problems of early, 44–45
Computer literacy, 6–7
Computer-managed instruction (CMI), 165, 166
Computer operators, 362–363
Computer output microfilm (COM), 124–125
Computer print charts, 216–218
Computer program tests, 222
Computer system architects, 56
Computer system architecture, 56–73
defined, 58
functional units of, 58, 60–72
central processing unit in (*see* Central processing units)
input-output units as (*see* Input-output units)
storage units as (*see* Storage units)
future trends in, 377–380
microcomputer, 168–174, 381
generations in, 168–172
software evolution in, 172–174
types of computers and, 56–58
Connector symbols, 251–252
Constant data, 305
Control card specifications in RPG II, 427–428
Control programs, 280–283
input-output scheduling by, 282
job scheduling by, 280–282
microprocessor (CP/M), 173
program monitoring by, 282–283
Control storage, 65
Control units, 19, 66–69

Controlling, 9, 244
Conversion:
    changeover to new system in, 230–232
    operation phase of, 229–232
    preparation for, 224–225
    of procedures, programs, and files, 230
    software, 274
Cost-effective system, 23
Cost schedules, 206–207
Courseware, 166
CP/M (control program/microprocessor), 173
CPUs (see Central processing units)
CRTs (cathode ray tubes), 115–117
Cursors, 115, 158
Cybernetics, 375, 383–387
    artificial intelligence (AI) in, 386–387
    robots in, 57, 383–386

Daisy wheels, 111
Data, 7
Data banks, 11
    microcomputers and, 161–162
Data base administrator, 363
Data base management systems (DBMS), 221–222
Data bases, 10, 22
    information utilities and, 136, 137
Data blocks, 332–333
Data carriers, 40
Data communications, 133–139
    in the automated office, 145
    electronic funds transfer (EFT) in, 381
    electronic mail and, 148
    microcomputers and, 161–162
    networks in, 22, 142–143, 161–162
    services for, 134–135
    transmission in, 134
    trends in, 135–139
        information utility as, 136, 137
        satellites as, 136–139, 379
Data control clerks, 361
Data division in COBOL, 399, 404–410
Data elements, 10
Data entry operators, 361–362
Data entry systems, 140–141
Data flow diagrams (DFDs), 190, 197

Data modules, 91, 92
Data processing, 7–12
    advantages of computer, 22–23
        (See also Computer data processing systems)
    in the automated office, 144
    basic operations of, 9–12
    cycle of, 79–81
    distributed (see Distributed data processing)
    principles of computer, 18–22
    resources for, 8
    word processing and (see Electronic office)
Data processing systems, 8
Data recorders, 110
Data storage, 61–63
    of bytes, 61–63
    as coded characters (see Character codes)
    in storage units (see Storage units)
    of words, 63
Data transfer rate, 86
DBMS (data base management systems), 221–222
DDP (see Distributed data processing)
Debug packages, 296
Debugging, 289
    character codes in (see Character codes)
    memory dumps in, 282–283, 296
    number systems in (see Number systems)
Decimal (base 10) number system, 438
    adding in, 452–455
    characteristics of, 439
    converting from, 444–447
        to binary number system, 444–446
        to hexadecimal number system, 447
        to octal number system, 446–447
    converting to, 440–444
        from binary number system, 442
        from hexadecimal number system, 443–444
        from octal number system, 442–443
    subtracting in, 459–460
Decision support systems (DSS), 44, 195
Decision symbols, 248–249

Default options, 304, 334
DELETE command, 329
Design phase of life-cycle method (see Life-cycle method, design phase of)
Design specification, 49
Detail lines, 255–257
Development phase of life-cycle method (see Life-cycle method, development phase of)
DFDs (data flow diagrams), 190, 197
Digit rows, 466
Digital computers, 56
Digital plotters, 126
Digital Research Corporation, 173
Digitizers, 125
Diodes, 26
DIR command, 329
Direct files, 90
Disk cartridges, 90
Disk operating systems (DOS), 158, 173, 326–329
Disk packs, 90, 91
Diskettes (see Floppy disks)
Distributed data processing (DDP), 28, 139 144, 379
    computer networks in, 22, 142–143, 161–162
    concept of, 139
    data entry systems, 140–141
    definition of, 139
    management considerations in, 143–144
    shared-logic word processing systems and, 146–148
    stand-alone systems in, 141
Division-remainder technique, 444
Documentation:
    of completed computer program, 245
    of computer information system, 49, 236–237
    managing change and, 236–237
    in system design phase, 222
    in system development phase, 224–225
Doping, 26
DOS (disk operating system), 158, 173, 326–329
Dot-matrix printers, 112, 160
DOUNTIL instruction, 258–259

DO-WHILE construct:
in BASIC, 341–342
in pseudocode, 258–262
Drum printers, 113
DSS (decision support systems), 44, 195
Dumb terminals, 140–141

E-time, 68
EBAM (electron-beam-addressed memory), 98–99
EBCDIC (extended binary-coded decimal interchange code), 62, 470–473
magnetic tape for, 85–86
Eckert, J. Presper, 20
EDVAC computer, 19, 20
Electron-beam-addressed memory (EBAM), 98–99
Electronic Discrete Variable Computer (EDVAC), 19, 20
Electronic funds transfer (EFT), 381
Electronic mail, 148
Electronic office, 149–150
administrative structure of, 150
careers in, 149–150
office functions in, 149
(See also Automated office)
Electronic worksheet, 164–165
Electrophotographic techniques, 114
Elementary items, 405
End of file (EOF), 260–262
END statement, 310
End time, 254
ENDDO, 260–261
ENDIF, 258, 262
ENIAC computer, 20
Entry connectors, 252
Environment division in COBOL, 398–399, 403–404
Environmental software, 174
EOF (end of file), 260–262
Exit connectors, 252
Expanded system flowcharts, 213–214
Expert programs, 386
Extended binary-coded decimal interchange code (EBCDIC), 62, 470–473
magnetic tape for, 85–86

FD (file description) entry, 404–406
Feasibility analysis in life-cycle method, 186, 196–204
describing system data flows in, 196–200
evaluating candidate systems in, 202–204
forming systems team in, 196
selecting candidate systems in, 200–201
Federal Communications Commission, 135
Ferris, David L., 157
Fields, 62–63
definition of, in COBOL, 404–406
fixed-length, in binary number system, 463
Files, 10
active, 88
conversion of, 230
definition of, in COBOL, 404–406
design of, 219–221
data in master file and, 220–221
processing steps in, 219
storage media and, 221
direct, 90
end of, in pseudocode, 260–262
inactive, 88
indexed-sequential, 90
master, 80, 219–221
specifications for, in RPG II, 428–429
transaction (detail), 80
FILES command, 328–329
FILLER field, 404–405
Firmware, 59
future trends in, 379
Fixed-length fields, 463
Fixed-point numbers, 463
Fixed-word-length computers, 63
Floppy disks:
as input-output devices, 109–110
as storage units, 93, 161
Flowcharts, 48–49, 196–200, 245–257
basic process loops in, 246–247, 250–251
data flow diagrams (DFDs) in developing, 190, 197
defined, 245
end-time calculations in, 254–255

Flowcharts (Cont.):
expanded system, 213–214
hierarchy charts, 199–200
HIPO (hierarchy plus input, processing, output) charts, 214
IBM template in, 245–246
IPO (input, processing, output) charts, 214
loops with multiple exits in, 252
problems of, 257
process loops with calculations in, 250–251
standards for preparing, 245–246
student data problem on, 247–249
system, 197–199, 213–214
titles and common headings in, 255–257
use of connectors in, 251–252
Flowlines, 247
FOR-NEXT statement, 319–320
Forecasts, 374
FORTRAN IV, 271
coding errors in, 290–292
Full-duplex transmission, 135

General-purpose computers, 63
Genus I (robot), 57
Geostar satellite system, 138
Goals, 39
GOSUB-RETURN instruction, 332
GOTO statement, 316
Graphics, computer:
in animation, 13
input-output devices for: digital plotters, 126
digitizers, 125
visual display terminals (VDTs), 115–117
Group items, 405

Half-duplex transmission, 135
Hard copy, 40
Hard disks, microcomputer, 161
Hardware, 21
binary number system and, 61
in environment division of COBOL, 398–399, 403–404
microcomputer: described, 157–162
selection of, 176–177

Heath Company, Hero 1, 57
Hexadecimal (base 16) number system, 438
 adding in, 458
 characteristics of, 439–440
 converting from decimal number system to, 447
 converting to decimal number system from, 443–444
 shortcut notations for, 450–451
 subtracting in, 462
Hierarchy:
 memory, 10, 100
 of operations in BASIC, 309
Hierarchy charts, 199–200, 214
High-level languages, 283
 (*See also* Programming languages)
HIPO (hierarchy plus input, processing, output) charts, 214
Hoff, Marcian E. ("Ted"), Jr., 170
Hollerith Herman, 11–12, 466
Hollerith card code, 466–468
Holography, 99
HOME command, 305
Home computers (*see* Personal computers)
HOME statement, 333
Hybrid computers, 56–57

I-time, 68
IBM Corporation, 12, 20
 floppy disk introduction by, 93
 flowcharting template of, 245–246
 Magnetic Tape Selectric Typewriter (MT/ST) of, 146
 Personal Computer (PC) of, 170, 171, 173, 304
 System/360 series of, 25
 3850 Mass Storage Facility of, 95
 650 computer of, 20
Identification division in COBOL, 398, 401–403
IF statements in COBOL, 416, 418–419
IF-THEN statement:
 in BASIC, 316–317
 in pseudocode, 258, 262
IF-THEN-ELSE statement:
 in BASIC, 334–336
 in pseudocode, 258

Immediate replacement in conversions, 230–231
Implementation, 224
Inactive files, 88
Indexed-sequential files, 90
Indicators, 429
Information display system layout sheet, 218–219
Information flow, 40
Information resource management, 31–34
 defined, 32
 management challenge and, 32–34
 merging technologies and, 31–32
Information service request (ISR), 189–190
 modified, 191–193
Information services, 355–369
careers in, 357–366
 corporate systems and, 358–359
 data processing operations and, 360–364
 employment opportunities for programmers and microcomputer software market, 30–31, 379
 salaries in, 364–366
 location of, in organization, 355–356
 users and, 366–368
Information utility, 136, 137
Ink-jet printers, 112
Input, processing, output (IPO) charts, 214
INPUT command, 347
Input-output control system (IOCS), 282
Input-output (I/O) symbol, 246–247
Input-output (I/O) units, 107–130
 card readers as, 124
 in COBOL, 404
 computer output microfilm (COM) as, 124–125
 description of, in system study phase, 195
 design of, in system development, 216–219
 digital plotters as, 126
 digitizers as, 125
 environment of, 70
 future trends in, 379
 I/O interfaces and, 70, 108

Input-output (I/O) units (*Cont.*):
 keyboard devices (terminals) as, 6, 115–119, 379
 in distributed data processing (*see* Distributed data processing)
 point-of-sale devices, 22, 119, 121–122
 teleprinter terminals, 117
 teleprocessing, 132
 visual display terminals (VDTs), 115–117
 magnetic media devices as, 109–110, 161
 magnetic data recorders, 110
 magnetic disks, diskettes, and tapes, 109–110
 microcomputer, 93, 158–160
 plotters as, 126
 printers as, 111–115, 117, 255–257, 345–347
 character printers, 111–112, 160
 line printers, 112–114
 page printers, 114–115
 scanners as, 119–123
 magnetic ink character recognition (MICR), 122
 optical scanners, 7, 119–122
 speed of, 108
 using, 108
 voice recognition and response devices as, 127
Input prompts, 307
Input specifications in RPG II, 429–430
INPUT statement, 306–307
Inputting, 9
Instruction storage, 64
Integrated-circuit (IC) technology, 25–26, 84–85, 100–103
 component density in, 100–102
 future trends in, 377–378
 large-scale integrated (LSI) circuits in, 25, 102, 378
 medium-scale integrated (MSI) circuits in, 102
 small-scale integrated (SSI) circuits in, 25, 102
 solid-state circuits in, 81
 very-high-speed integrated (VHSIC) circuits in, 378

Integrated-circuit (IC) technology
    (*Cont.*):
    very-large-scale integrated (VLSI)
        circuits in, 25, 102, 103, 157, 378
Intel Corporation, 170, 377
Intelligent memory, 100
Intelligent terminals, 141, 147–148
Interactive programs in BASIC,
    347–349
Interfaces, I/O, 70, 108
Internal storage (*see* Primary storage)
International Organization for
    Standardization (ISO), 245, 474
International Telecommunications
    Satellite Consortium
    (INTELSTAT), 136
Interpreters, 283
Interrecord gap, 86, 88
I/O interfaces, 70, 108
IPO (input, processing, output) charts,
    214
ISR (information service request),
    189–190
    modified, 191–193

Jastrow, Robert, 387
Job control statements, 280–282
Jobs:
    in electronic office, 149–150
    in information services (*see*
        Information services, careers in)
Josephson junctions, 99, 378
Joystick, 158–159

K (storage size), 64
Key field, 80–81
Keyboard devices (*see* Terminals)
KILL command, 329
Knowledge industries, 23–24, 374–376

LAN (local area networks), 143
Language processors, 283–284
    coding errors and, 290–294
Languages (*see* Programming languages)
Large-scale integrated (LSI) circuits,
    25, 102, 378
Laser-beam printers, 114
Laserfile, 97
Last record test, 348

LET statement, 308–309
Letter-quality printers, 111–112, 160
Librarian:
    information services, 363
    program, 285–286
Library, 285
    BASIC, 320–322
Life-cycle method, 34, 47–50
    design phase of, 48, 211–223
        data base management systems
            (DBMS) in, 221–222
        design-phase documentation in, 222
        design-phase review in, 223
        file design in, 219–221
        flowcharts in, 48–49, 196–200
        general system design in, 212–214
        input design in, 214–216
        output design in, 216–218
        test requirements in, 222
    development phase of, 48, 223–225
        documentation and acceptance
            review in, 225
        equipment acquisition in, 224
        implementation plan in, 224
        overview of, 223
        programming in (*see* Programming;
            Programming languages)
        training personnel and preparing
            for conversion in, 224–225
    for microcomputer selection, 174–177
    operation phase of, 48, 229–238
        conversion to new system in,
            229–232
        evaluating system in, 232–234
        system modification in, 235–237
    study phase of, 47, 185–209
        feasibility analysis in, 186,
            196–204
        initial investigation in, 190–193
        overview of, 186
        performance definition in, 186,
            193–195
        problem identification in, 186–190
        project plan and cost schedule in,
            205–207
        system recommendation in,
            204–205
    system analysis and the systems
        analyst in, 50

Light pens, 116–117
Line printers, 112–114
    chain, 113–114
    drum, 113
Linkage editor, 285
LIST command, 305
Literals, 398, 407
LLIST command, 326
LOAD command, 328
Local-area networks (LAN), 143
Local storage, 65–66
Logic branches, 316
Logic errors, 290, 294–297
Logical records, 86
Loops, 248
    in BASIC, 317–320
    basic process, in flowcharts, 246–247,
        250–251
    multiple exit, 252
Low-level languages, 283
LPRINT command, 345
LPRINT USING command, 345–347
LSI (large-scale integrated) circuits, 25,
    102, 378

Machine code, 266–267
    conversion of symbolic language to,
        275, 283–284
Magic Wand Speaking Reader, 7
Magnetic bubble memory (MBM), 97,
    378
Magnetic-core storage, 83
Magnetic data recorders, 110
Magnetic diskettes:
    as input-output units, 109–110
    as storage units, 93, 161
Magnetic disks:
    disk operating system (DOS) and,
        158, 173, 326–329
    floppy: as input-output devices,
        109–110
        as storage units, 93, 161
    as input-output devices, 109–110
    microcomputer, 93, 109–110, 161
    as storage, 89–93, 161
        combined moving- and fixed-head,
            91
        data recording on, 89–90
        fixed-head, 90–91

Magnetic disks, as storage (*Cont.*):
    magnetic tape compared with, 93,
      221
    moving-head, 90
Magnetic drums, 93
Magnetic ink character recognition
    (MICR), 122
Magnetic tapes:
    as input-output devices, 109–110
    as storage, 85–88
      blocking factor in, 86–88
      cassettes and cartridges for, 86
      data recording on, 85–86
      data transfer rate with, 86
      file access and organization of, 88
      magnetic disk compared with, 93,
        221
      reels for, 85
Main memory (*see* Primary storage)
Mainframes, 378
Management:
    of corporate systems, 358
    of data processing operations,
      360–362
Management information system (MIS),
    44
Management levels, 43–44
    information requirements and, 45–46
Mark I computer, 20
Mass storage, 95, 156
Master files, 80
    design of, 219–221
Mathematically oriented languages, 269
    BASIC (*see* BASIC)
    FORTRAN IV, 271, 290–292
    PASCAL, 274–275
    PL/I, 271–272
Matsushita Electric Industrial
    Company, 96
Mauchly, John, 20
Maxicomputers, 28
Medium-scale integrated (MSI) circuits,
    102
Memory, 60
    (*See also* Primary storage; Secondary
      storage; Storage units)
Memory dumps, 282–283, 296
    character codes for (*see* Character
      codes)

Memory dumps (*Cont.*):
    number systems in (*see* Number
      systems)
Memory hierarchies, 10, 100
Menus, 173–174
Metal-oxide semiconductors (MOS), 84
    beam-addressed (BEAMOS), 98–99
    charge-coupled devices (CCDs) and,
      98, 378
MICR (magnetic ink character
    recognition), 122
Microcode (microprograms), 65
Microcomputer resource centers, 367,
    368
Microcomputers, 26, 28
    applications software for, 164–166,
      171–174, 176
    data banks for, 161–162
    floppy disks for: as input-output
      devices, 109–110
      as storage units, 93, 161
    hardware for, 157–162, 176–177
    hybrid computers and, 57–58
    processing units (MPUs) of, 100,
      156–158, 170–171
    storage units for, 93, 157–158,
      160–161
    word processing with, 164
    (*See also* Personal computers; *specific
      brands of microcomputers*)
Microelectronics, 25–26
    binary number system and, 61
    (*See also* Integrated-circuit
      technology)
Microfiche, 124–125
Microfilm, computer output (COM),
    124–125
Microfloppies, 161
Microprocessor units (MPUs), 100,
    156–158, 170–171
Microprograms (microcode), 65
Microseconds, 25
Microwave Communications, Inc.
    (MCI), 135–136
Midicomputers, 28
Milliseconds, 24
Minicomputers, 26, 28
MIS (management information system),
    44

Mnemonics, 267–268
Modems, 134
    microcomputer, 161–162
Monitors, microcomputer, 159
Moore, Gordon, 377
MOS (*see* Metal-oxide semiconductors)
MPUs (microprocessor units), 100,
    156–158, 170–171
MSI (medium-scale integrated) circuits,
    102
Multiple exit loops, 252
Multiprocessing, 70–72, 103

N-zone, 26
Naisbitt, John, 374
Nanoseconds, 25
Narrowband transmission mode, 135
National Semiconductor, 170
NEC Advanced Personal Computer,
    170, 171
Networks, 22, 142–143
    local-area (LAN), 143
    microcomputers and, 161–162
    ring, 143
    star, 142
NEW command, 305
Nippon Electric Co., PC-8200, 157
Number systems, 437–464
    arithmetic of, 452–462
    basics of, 438–440
    binary (*see* Binary number system)
    converting from one to another,
      440–447
    decimal (*see* Decimal number system)
    fixed-length fields in, 463
    hexadecimal (*see* Hexadecimal
      number system)
    octal (*see* Octal number system)
    shortcut notations in, 448–451

Object programs, 284
Objectives, 39
OCR (optical character readers),
    119–120
Octal (base 8) number system, 438
    adding in, 458
    characteristics of, 439
    converting from decimal number
      system to, 446–447

Octal (base 8) number system (*Cont.*):
  converting to decimal number system
    from, 442–443
  shortcut notations for, 449–450
  subtracting in, 461–462
Off-line storage, 93
Office automation (*see* Automated
    office; Electronic office)
Offpage connectors, 252
OMR (optical mark readers), 120–121
On-line storage, 93
OPEN instruction, 410
Operands, 64
Operating systems, 280–287
  control programs in, 173, 280–283
  disk (DOS), 158, 173, 326–329
  language processors in, 283–284,
    290–294
  service programs in, 284–286
Operation phase of life-cycle method
    (*see* Life-cycle method, operation
    phase of)
Operators:
  computer, 362–363
  data entry, 361–362
Optical character readers (OCR),
    119–120
Optical-disk storage systems, 95–97
  erasable, 96
Optical mark readers (OMR), 120–121
Osborne, Adam, 157
Osborne Computer Corp., 157
Output (*see* Input-output units)
Output-format specifications in RPG II,
    431–435
Output zones in BASIC, 304
Outputting, 9

P-zone, 26
Packed decimals, 473
Page printers, 114–115
Paragraphs in COBOL, 399
Parallel arithmetic, 63
Parallel operation in conversions, 231
PASCAL, 274–275
Pascal, Blaise, 274
PDL (program design language),
    257–258
PERFORM statement, 410, 411

PERFORM-UNTIL statement, 410
Performance definition in life-cycle
    method, 186, 193–195
  general constraints in, 193
  output descriptions in, 195
  specific objectives in, 193–195
Performance specifications, 49
Peripheral devices, 158
Personal computers, 155–179
  BASIC language and (*see* BASIC)
  functional units of, 157–162
  future uses of, 12–15, 380–382
  selection of, 174–178
    checklist for, 177–178
    steps in, 174–177
  trends in architecture of, 168–174,
    381
    microcomputer generations,
      168–172
    software evolution, 172–174
  uses for, 163–168
    educational, 165–166
    engineering and scientific, 167–168
    home and hobby, 163
    professional, 164–165
    small business, 166–167
    word processing, 164
Phased replacement in conversions,
    231–232
Photoresist, 26
Physical records, 88
Picture clauses, 405–406
PL/I, 271–272
Plotters, 126
Point-of-sale (POS) devices, 22, 119
  bar-code readers and, 121–122
Postindustrial society, 23–31
  classification of computers in, 26–28
  computer generations in, 24–26
  employment opportunities in, 30–31
  knowledge industries in, 23–24,
    374–376
  measures of change in, 28–30
Preparation symbols, 250–251
Primary (main) storage, 21, 60–61,
    83–85
  acronyms in, 85
  input-output (I/O) devices and (*see*
    Input-output units)

Primary (main) storage (*Cont.*):
  magnetic-core, 83
  random access memory (RAM), 84,
    157, 170–171, 178
  read-only memory (ROM), 59, 158
  semiconductor, 84–85
Principal users, 50
  development of information systems
    and, 380
  information services and, 366–368
  system effectiveness and, 234
Print chains, 113–114
PRINT statement, 310, 334
PRINT USING instruction, 339
Printers, 111–115
  BASIC instructions for, 345–349
  chain, 113–114
  dot-matrix, 112, 160
  drum, 113
  ink-jet, 112
  laser-beam, 114
  letter-quality, 111–112, 160
  microcomputer, 160
  page, 114–115
  program logic and, 255–257
  teleprinter terminals as, 117
Problem-oriented languages, 268–275
  advantages and disadvantages of,
    269–270
  business, 269
    COBOL as (*see* COBOL)
    RPG II as (*see* RPG II)
  development of, 269
  mathematical, 269
    BASIC as (*see* BASIC)
    FORTRAN IV as, 271,
      291–292
    PASCAL as, 274–275
    PL/I as, 271–272
Procedure division in COBOL, 399,
    410–419
Process symbols, 250
Processing units, 100–103
  central (*see* Central processing units)
  input-output devices and (*see* Input-
    output units)
  microprocessor (MPUs), 100,
    156–158, 170–171
Product flow, 40

Program Design Language (PDL), 257–258
Program planning, 243–263
  computer programs in, 244
  flowcharts in (*see* Flowcharts)
  pseudocode in, 257–262
  purposes of, 244–245
Programmer-analysts, job descriptions of, 359
Programmers:
  applications, 359, 379
  employment opportunities for, 30–31, 379
  systems, 22, 59
    job descriptions of, 363–364
Programming, 224
  errors in, 289–297
    coding, 290–294
    logic, 290, 294–297
    (*See also* Debugging)
  languages used in (*see* Programming languages)
  operating systems and (*see* Operating systems)
  planning phase in (*see* Program planning)
  tests in, 222
  (*See also* Software)
Programming languages, 265–276
  assembler-level, 267, 269–270, 283
  BASIC (*see* BASIC)
  character codes and (*see* Character codes)
  COBOL (*see* COBOL)
  conversion of symbolic, 275, 283–284
  development of, 266–270
    machine code in, 266–267, 275, 283–284
    problem-oriented, 268–270
    symbolic code in, 267–268
  FORTRAN IV, 271, 290–292
  language processors for, 283–284, 290–294
  PASCAL, 274–275
  PL/I, 271–272
  RPG II (*see* RPG II)
  writing program instructions for, 265–266
Programs, 6, 22
  branching in, 67–68

Programs (*Cont.*):
  conversion of, 230
  languages used in (*see* Programming languages; *specific languages*)
  of operating system, 280–287
    control programs, 173, 280–283
    language processors, 283–284, 290–294
    service programs, 284–286
Project plans, 205–206
Projections, 374
Pseudocode, 257–262
  basic structures of, 258–262
  flowchart problems and, 257
  program design language (PDL) and, 257–258
Punched cards, 11–12, 19
  card readers for, 124
  character code for, 466–468

Quotation marks in BASIC, 310, 328

Radio Shack, TRS 80, 171, 304
Random access, 88
Random access memory (RAM), 84, 157, 170–171, 178
READ-DATA instruction, 332–333
Read-only memory (ROM), 59, 158, 170–171
READ statement, 413
Records, 10
  definition of, in COBOL, 404–406
  logical, 86
  physical, 88
Registers, 64
REM (remark) statement, 306
Reprographics, 31
Response time, 367
Ring networks, 143
Robotics International, 57
Robots, 383–386
  personal, 57
ROM (read-only memory), 59, 158, 170–171
Rotational delay, 90
RPG II (Report Program Generator II), 272–273, 425–435
  arithmetic calculations in, 435
  calculation specifications in, 430–431
  coding forms for, 426–427

RPG II (Report Program Generator II) (*Cont.*):
  control card specifications in, 427–428
  cycle of, 427
  file description specifications in, 428–429
  input specifications in, 429–430
  output-format specifications in, 431–435
  sample program in, 427–435
RUN command, 305, 310, 328

Satellite communications, 136–139, 379
SAVE command, 326–327
Scanners, 119–122
  bar-code readers, 7, 121–122
  optical character readers (OCR), 119–120
  optical mark readers (OMR), 120–121
Secondary (auxiliary) storage, 21, 64–65, 85–99
  electromechanical, 85–97
    described, 82–83
    magnetic disks in, 89–93, 161
    magnetic drums in, 93
    magnetic tape in, 85–88
    mass storage in, 95, 156, 160–161
    optical-disk systems in, 95–97
  electronic, 97–99
    advanced memory systems, 99
    charge-coupled devices (CCDs) in, 98, 378
    described, 82–83
    electron-beam-addressed memory (EBAM), 98–99
    magnetic bubble, 97, 378
  as input-output units (*see* Input-output units)
  in memory hierarchy, 10, 100
Sections in COBOL, 399
Seek time, 90
Semicolons in BASIC, 314
Semiconductor memory, 84–85
Semiconductors, 84–85
  future trends in, 377–378
  metal-oxide, 84, 98–99
  silicon as, 26
  (*See also* Integrated-circuit technology)

Sentences in COBOL, 399
Sequence logic, 258
Sequential access, 88
Service programs, 284–286
  librarian, 285–286
  linkage editor, 285
  sort-merge program, 286
  utility programs, 286
Servomechanisms, 385
Shared-logic word processing systems, 146–148
Shoup, Richard, 13
Silicon, 26
Silicon chips (*see* Integrated-circuit technology)
Simplex transmission, 134
Small-scale integrated (SSI) circuits, 25, 102
Smart machines, 374
Soft copy, 40, 381
Software:
  applications, 21–22, 58–59
    microcomputer, 164–166, 171–174, 176
    programmers of, 359, 379
  conversion of, 274
  employment opportunities and, 30–31, 379
  future trends in, 379
  languages for (*see* Programming languages)
  microcomputer, 164–166, 171–174
    evaluation of, 176
    evolution of, 172–174
  systems, 21–22, 58
Solid-state circuits, 81
Sort-merge programs, 286
Source programs, 284
Source Telecomputing Corporation, 136, 137
Speech synthesis, 7, 127
Stand-alone systems, 141
  for word processing, 146
Star network, 142
Storage units, 60–66, 81–100
  components and criteria for, 81–83
    cost, capacity, and access time in, 82–83
    solid-state circuits and, 81
  control and local, 65–66

Storage units (*Cont.*):
  data storage and, 61–63
    (*See also* Character codes)
  future trends in, 378
  instruction, 64
  magnetic data recorders as, 110
  magnetic diskettes as, 93, 161
  magnetic disks as (*see* Magnetic disks)
  magnetic drums as, 93
  magnetic tapes as, 85–88
  memory hierarchies in, 100
  microcomputer, 93, 157–158, 160–161
  primary storage and (*see* Primary storage)
  secondary storage and (*see* Secondary storage)
  selection of, 221
  storage size (K), 64
Storing, 9, 22
String constants, 310
String variables, 307
Strings, character, 307
Study phase of life-cycle method (*see* Life-cycle method, study phase of)
Study-phase report, 207
Subprograms, 199, 219
Subsystems, 39
Supercomputers, 382–383
Superconductivity, 378
Supermicros, 171
Symbolic code, 267–268
  (*See also* Programming languages)
Syntax errors, 290
System development life cycle (*see* Life-cycle method)
System flowcharts, 197–199, 213–214
System selection (*see* Life-cycle method)
System specifications, 49
System tests, 222
System/360, 25
Systems analysis, 50
  (*See also* Life-cycle method)
Systems analysts, 34, 50
  career outlook for, 188
  job descriptions of, 359
Systems programmers, 22, 59
  job description of, 363–364
Systems software, 21–22, 58

TAB function, 334
Tandy Corporation, TRS 80, 171, 304
Tape drives (transports), 86
Tape label statements (TLBL), 281–282
Teleconferencing, 150
Telenet, 136, 137
Teleprinter terminals, 117
Teleprocessing, 132
Templates, 245–246
Terminal symbols, 246
Terminals (keyboard devices), 6, 115–119, 379
  in distributed data processing:
    computer networks, 22, 142–143, 161–162
    data entry systems, 140–141
    management considerations and, 143–144
    stand-alone systems, 141
  dumb, 140–141
  intelligent, 141
    portable, 147–148
  microcomputer, 158
  point-of-sale, 22, 119, 121–122
  programmable, 141
  teleprinter, 117
  teleprocessing, 132
  visual display (VDTs), 115–117
Testing:
  of computer programs, 289
  in system design phase, 222
  in system development phase, 224
Texas Instruments:
  Magic Wand Speaking Reader, 7
  Portable Memory Terminal, 147–148
Throughput time, 367
Time-shared word processing systems, 148
TLBL (tape label statements), 281–282
Topo (robot), 57
Tracing routines, 296
Transaction-driven processing, 81
Transaction (detail) files, 80
Transactions, 10
Transistors, 24–25
Turnaround time, 367
Tymeshare, 136, 137

Unit record machines, 12
UNIVAC I computer, 20

Universal product code (UPC), 121–122
Usability, 33, 132, 186
User-friendly software, 173
Users, 50
  development of information systems
    and, 380
  information services and, 366–368
  system effectiveness and, 234
Utilities, 286
  information, 136, 137

Vacuum tubes, 24
Value clauses, 406
Variable data, 305
Variable field length, 63
Variable word-length storage, 63
Very-large-scale integrated (VLSI)
  circuits, 25, 102, 103, 157, 378
VHSIC (very-high-speed integrated
  circuits), 378

VisiCalc, 164–165
Visual display terminals (VDTs),
  115–117
  alphanumeric data on, 115–116
  graphic displays on, 116
  light pens and, 116–117
VLSI (very-large-scale integrated)
  circuits, 25, 102, 103, 157, 378
Voice mail, 148
Voice prints, 127
Voice recognition and response devices,
  127
Voice store-and-forward systems,
  148
Voiceband transmission mode, 135
von Neumann, John, 19, 20, 24,
  382

Western Union Telegraph Company,
  135–137

WHILE-WEND command, 342,
  344
Wirth, Nicklaus, 274
Word processing systems, 14
  in the automated office, 145–148
  data processing and (*see* Electronic
    office)
  growth of, 146
  with microcomputers, 164
  optical character readers (OCR) and,
    120
  types of systems for, 146–148
Words, 63
  length of, 463
Wozniak, Steve, 163

Zenith Radio Corporation, 57
Zone rows, 466
Zoned decimals, 473